Martin Luther as Comforter

Studies in the History of Christian Traditions

Founded by

Heiko A. Oberman†

Edited by

Robert J. Bast

Knoxville, Tennessee

In cooperation with

Henry Chadwick, Cambridge
Scott H. Hendrix, Princeton, New Jersey
Paul C.H. Lim, Nashville, Tennessee
Eric Saak, Indianapolis, Indiana
Brian Tierney, Ithaca, New York
Arjo Vanderjagt, Groningen
John Van Engen, Notre Dame, Indiana

VOLUME 133

Martin Luther as Comforter

Writings on Death

By

Neil R. Leroux

BRILL

LEIDEN • BOSTON
2007

ISSN   1573-5664
ISBN   978 90 04 15880 1

For Joyce, Shelly, and Amanda
In memory of Brian

CONTENTS

PREFACE

Much of the analysis in Chapters One through Six involves close reading of Luther's texts. When I quote Luther, I provide my own translation from the *Weimarer Ausgabe* (*WA*), providing volume, page, and line numbers. A colon (:) separates volume and page; a period (.) separates page and line numbers. When I quote or cite from English editions of Luther's texts, I cite only volume and page. In quotations, I sometimes offer a more syntactically literal translation than English grammar usually prescribes. When this occurs, my intention is to follow Luther's syntax, in German or in Latin, in order to permit his parallel structures to emerge. It is hoped that such a translation will allow the reader to appreciate better Luther's rhetorical style, which contributes substantially to his arguments' becoming clearer and/or more compelling. In addition, where warranted, I have documented and commented on other English translations of a given phrase or clause (*LW*, PE, or Tappert), in order to call attention to how they have not—for whatever reason—chosen to mirror Luther's syntax in their translation.

In the analysis that provides ubiquitous paraphrases and quotations of Luther's language, I have frequently included the original words, phrases, clauses, or even sentences in square brackets—when furnishing a direct quote, or in parentheses—when I paraphrase. In order to make reading easier, in the main text of the analysis I have placed these original terms in italics, and I have capitalized the German nouns. In the footnotes, however, where I normally quote entire sentences or paragraphs (in German or Latin), I have not used italics for these quotes. In other words, italics distinguish foreign words in the main text, and in the footnotes such distinction is usually unnecessary and would sometimes lead to confusion with original titles of works in Latin or German. In all cases I have retained the original spelling of *WA*.

In the analysis I frequently identify a particular rhetorical or grammatical strategy (or figure) by employing its technical name in Latin or transliterated Greek. I have not placed these terms in italics, and I have often (though, by no means, always) provided a short explanation of the term when I use it. For a complete definition of each term, see the Appendix: Glossary of Rhetorical Terms. Latin terms that signify parts of an oration or letter are in italics in my analysis.

Finally, unless otherwise specified, when I quote Scripture in my own arguments and analysis, I use the Revised Standard Version, copyright 1971, by the Division of Christian Education of the National Council of the Churches of Christ of the United States of America.

ACKNOWLEDGEMENTS

While I take full responsibility for any errors in this book, I must also thank so many individuals and institutions for generous assistance and encouragement. Robert Bast graciously accepted my work for inclusion in his series, Studies in the History of Christian Traditions, and I am grateful for the constructive criticisms offered by his anonymous reader. Boris Van Gool at Brill Academic Publishers always offered timely assistance, as did his production staff. My own fine institution, The University of Minnesota, Morris (UMM), provided salary supplement during my sabbatical year, as well as funds for travel through In-State and Out-of-State travel grants. The Graduate School of The University of Minnesota, Twin Cities (UMTC), provided a Faculty Summer Research Fellowship, which was matched by the McKnight Foundation's Summer Fellowship program. Additional travel funds came from UMTC's Office of International Programs.

I owe great thanks to Sandy Kill of the Rodney A. Briggs Library (UMM) for tireless work in obtaining materials through Inter-Library Loan and the MINTEX system. Matt Conner and Peter Bremer (both of Briggs Library, UMM) also rendered timely and cordial help with research tasks. Amanda Jacobson, Christine Schaerf, Cindy Norberg, and Matt Kauffmann were my work-study students the past few years and were able assistants. UMM colleagues Roger Wareham, Pieranna Garavaso, Janet Erickson, Ken Hodgson, Dwight Purdy, and Jennifred Nellis were splendid advisors and encouragers—ready at all times with the right blend of prodding and affirmation.

Colleagues from far beyond Minnesota proved to be welcome friends along the book's pilgrimage to completion. Thus, I am indebted to Randall Zachmann, David Whitford, Brad Gregory, Timothy Maschke, Kenneth Hagen, Robert Kolb, Austra Reinis, and Franz Posset, Peter Mack, Craig Kallendorf, Bruce Shields, James Tallmon, Peter Matheson, Ulrich Bubenheimer, Corey Liknes, Jaconelle Schuffel, Tom Conley, Claudia Carlos, Beth Manolescu, and Jameela Lares.

I am grateful, as well, to other associations that have helped me grow, particularly through opportunities to present my work for discussion: North American Luther Forum, Sixteenth Century Studies Conference, International Society for the History of Rhetoric, UMM Thursday

Afternoon Faculty Seminar, the Glacial Ridge Area Lutheran Pastors (ELCA), St. Johns and Konsvinger Lutheran churches (ELCA) of Donnelly, MN, and the Evangelical Free Church of Morris, MN.

Finally, I owe an enormous debt to friends who have counseled, supported, and withstood me, not only for the seven recent years of book preparation but also the through some sixteen years prior to that, as I drew strength from the Lord while He ministered through the listening ears of others. Some folks I met through Compassionate Friends or other grief support meetings, some through BeFriender Ministry; others simply found the time to be of help. In particular, I thank Bruce Parmenter, Paul Boatman, Jim and Pat Bland, and Mike Sager. Thanks, most of all, to my family.

LIST OF ABBREVIATIONS

Where possible, abbreviations follow *The SBL Handbook of Style for Ancient Near Eastern, Biblical, and Early Christian Studies*, edited by Patrick H. Alexander et al. (Peabody, Mass., 1999) and Siegfried Schwertner, ed., *Internationales Abkürzungsverzeichnis für Theologie und Grenzgebiete* (Berlin, 1974).

ARG	*Archiv für Reformationsgeschichte*
BHM	*Bulletin of the History of Medicine*
BSac	*Bibliotheca Sacra*
CW	*Call to Worship*
ChrCent	*Christian Century*
CTM	*Concordia Theological Monthly*
CTQ	*Concordia Theological Quarterly*
DS	*Death Studies*
GNT	*Novum Testamentum Graece* (Nestle-Aland, 27th ed. [Münster, 1993])
HTR	*Harvard Theological Review*
JBL	*Journal of Biblical Literature*
JETS	*Journal of the Evangelical Theological Society*
JPC	*Journal of Pastoral Care*
LB	*Luther Bible* (1534 facsimile, ed. S. Füssel [Cologne, 2003])
LuthFor	*Lutheran Forum*
LuJ	*Lutherjahrbuch*
LQ	*Lutheran Quarterly*
LTSB	*Lutheran Theological Seminary Bulletin*
LW	*Luther's Works: American Edition*, 55 vols. (ed. J. Pelikan and H. T. Lehman [St. Louis and Philadelphia, 1955–1986])
LXX	Septuagint (ed. C. L. Brenton [Grand Rapids, 1978])
MQR	*Mennonite Quarterly Review*
NEJM	*New England Journal of Medicine*
NT	New Testament
OER	*Oxford Encyclopedia of the Reformation*
OT	Old Testament
PE	*Luther's Works*, 6 vols. (ed. A. J. Holman [Philadelphia, 1916–1943])

RSQ	*Rhetoric Society Quarterly*
RSV	Revised Standard Version
SCES	Sixteenth Century Essays and Studies
SCJ	*Sixteenth Century Journal*
SeptBib	*Luther's "September Bible"* (facsimile, ed. K. A. Strand [Ann Arbor, 1972])
SHCT	Studies in the History of Christian Traditions
SMRT	Studies in Medieval and Reformation Traditions
SSM	*Social Science and Medicine*
Tappert	*Luther: Letters of Spiritual Counsel*, ed. T. G. Tappert (Philadelphia, 1955)
ThTo	*Theology Today*
TRE	*Theologische Realenzykopädie*, 17 vols. (Berlin, 1979–2000)
Vulgate	*Biblia Sacra Iuxta Vulgatam*, 3rd ed., ed. R. Weber (Stuttgart, 1983)
WA	*D. Martin Luthers Werke. Kritische Gesamtausgabe*, 67 vols. (Weimar, 1883–1997)
WABr	*D. Martin Luthers Werke. Kritische Gesamtausgabe, Briefwechsel*, 15 vols. (Weimar, 1930–1978)
WATr	*D. Martin Luthers Werke. Kritische Gesamtausgabe, Tischreden*, 6 vols. (Weimar, 1912–1921)
WW	*Word & World*
ZVGS	*Zeitschrift des Vereins für Geschichte Schlesiens*

INTRODUCTION

Confusion over death today abounds. In one sense we are fascinated by it, and in another we avoid all talk of it.[1] We watch movies about it, especially in its fictitious and violent forms,[2] and we are inundated by reports and images of actual deaths (famine, war, plague, natural disasters, terrorism, etc.) on the news—which, on cable stations, is now broadcast around the clock.[3] In the twentieth century child mortality

---

[1] "When individuals who are dying or bereaved complain that 'death is a taboo subject,' this does not mean that there are no publicly available languages for talking about death but that these languages do not make sense of the experiences and feelings of the individual and his or her friends, family and neighbours. They therefore do not know what to say or how to say it"; Tony Walter, *The Revival of Death* (London, 1994), 23f. On p. 2 Walter says, "What we find today is not a taboo but a babel of voices proclaiming various good deaths. As one clergyman put it to me, 'There is no such thing as postmodern death. Just a million and one individual deaths'"; see also Allan Kellehear, "Are We A 'Death-Denying' Society? A Sociological Review," *SSM* 18 (1984): 713–723, now updated in chapter 5 of his *Experiences Near Death* (New York, 1996); Tony Walter, "Modern Death: Taboo or Not Taboo?" *Sociology* 25 (1991): 293–310. See also Geoffrey Gorer, "The Pornography of Death," *Encounter* 5 (October 1955): 49–52, reprinted in his *Death, Grief, and Mourning* (Garden City, N.Y., 1965), 192–199; James J. Farrell, *Inventing the American Way of Death, 1830–1920* (Philadelphia, 1980); Philip A. Mellor and Chris Shilling, "Modernity, Self-Identity and the Sequestration of Death," *Sociology* 27 (1993): 411–431. Joseph Bayly's book, *The View from A Hearse* (Elgin, Ill., 1969), was published in paperback in 1992 under the telling title, *The Last Thing We Talk About* (Colorado Springs, Col.). Bayly was a bereaved parent, having buried three sons, each on separate occasions: the first at 18 days, after surgery; the second at 5 years, of leukemia; the third at 18 years, following a sledding accident complicated by mild hemophilia (p. 66).

[2] Ned W. Schultz and Lisa M. Huet, "Sensational! Violent! Popular!: Death in American Movies," *Omega* 42 (2000–2001): 137–149. Bayly, *The Last Thing We Talk About*, 23, notes that, "The ready availability of the gun that insulates a killer against personal contact with those he kills—feeling their flesh—provides a coward's advantage." Additionally, observing carnage from the comfort of one's living room magnifies the insulation. All that is heightened with violent video games is the feeling of control over, not accountability for, the killing.

[3] "While our first-hand learning about dying and grieving may be nonexistent, our second-hand learning is almost too much, too various and often unrelated to our own lives. We watch thousands of movie deaths in various stylized forms; we watch the consequences of even more deaths on the news and see people grieving from Northern Ireland to South Africa to wherever the latest bomb or earthquake has struck.... We know far too much for our own good about how people die and grieve the world over, and far too little about how they do so in our own family and our own culture. If ever there were a state of anomie, or normlessness, this is it"; Tony Walter, *The Revival of Death*, 122; Tony Walter, Jane Littlewood, and Michael Pickering, "Death in

dropped significantly in most industrialized nations of the world[4]—as did maternal death from childbirth[5]—and parents now agree that the greatest tragedy they can imagine for themselves is the death of a child, what Joseph Bayly calls a "period placed before the end of the sentence."[6] Writing about the British Isles but including the USA and Australasia, Tony Walter reasons that we moderns find death 'more galling' than our predecessors because our technologies permit vast control over our existence:

---

the News: The Public Invigilation of Private Emotion," *Sociology* 29 (1995): 579–596; Tony Walter, "Disaster, Modernity, and the Media," in *Death and Religion in a Changing World*, ed. Kathleen Garces-Foley (London, 2006), 265–282.

[4] Charles A. Corr, Clyde M. Nabe, and Donna M. Corr, *Death and Dying, Life and Living*, 4th ed. (Belmont, Calif., 2003), 20–25. Of the USA, they say: "Overall death rates for infants—newborns and children under 1 year of age—were nearly 23 times higher in 1900 than in 1999: 162.4 versus 7.1 infant deaths per 1,000 live births" (25). Mortality data is available from the Statistical Abstract of the United States online at: <http://www.census.gov/prod/2004pubs/04statab/vitstat.pdf> and from the World Health Organization online at: http://www.who.int/healthinfo/statistics/whostat2005_mortality_en.pdf. WHO data for 2003, the most recent data, show neonatal mortality rates for the Region of the Americas and the European Region as nearly identical. See also Arthur E. Imhof, "From the Old Mortality Pattern to the New: Implications of A Radical Change From the Sixteenth to the Twentieth Century," *Bulletin of the History of Medicine* 59 (1985): 1–29.

[5] According to Corr, Nabe, and Corr (25), "Maternal death rates of 608 per 100,000 live births in 1915 had been reduced to 7.1 by 1995 (*U.S. Bureau of the Census*, 1998) but rebounded to 9.9 in 1999 (D. L. Hoyert, et al., "Deaths: Final Data for 1999," *National Vital Statistics Reports*, 49(8) [Hyattsville, Md., 2001]).

[6] Joseph Bayly, *The Last Thing We Talk About*, 65. Corr, Nabe, and Corr (25): "[P]arents in 1900 were far more likely to be confronted by the death of one of their children than were parents in the latter half of the century." As references, they cite Paul C. Rosenblatt, *Bitter, Bitter Tears: Nineteenth-Century Diarists and Twentieth-Century Grief Theories* (Minneapolis, 1983) and P. Uhlenberg, "Death and the Family," *Journal of Family History* 5 (1980): 313–320. As a bereaved parent of a deceased teenager, I have been told by dozens of parents, over more than 20 years, that they cannot imagine how they would 'handle' such a loss. In the mid-1980s a director of a chain of several small community funeral homes told me that the most tragic death situation he deals with is the death of an adolescent. Tony Walter argues that another measure of such 'premature' deaths is the number of people—all of whom "assume a stable and predictable future"—affected by such a death: "[C]hildren assume their teacher will be there throughout the school year, our massive investment in education assumes that children will live to adulthood, parents assume their children will outlive them, sports clubs assume their sport will make them healthier and live longer, the military suppress thoughts of death and encourage hopes of seeing the world and learning a trade to set the soldier up once military service is over"; *The Revival of Death*, 62; Bill Young and Danai Papadatou, "Childhood Death and Bereavement across Cultures," in *Death and Bereavement Across Cultures*, ed. Colin Murray Parkes, Pittu Laungani and Bill Young (London, 1997), 191–205.

> Whatever else it is, death is the final triumph of nature, the triumph of inevitable physical decay over our will to stay young and healthy.... For those who can at the flick of a switch turn night into day, winter into summer, it is puzzling to understand how the light can eventually go out for good. For people who think every problem has a technological solution it is disturbing to discover that for some illnesses there is no cure. For people who are used to taking the car into the garage for service, knowing they can buy a new model if the news is bad, it is disturbing to find themselves frightened as they enter the hospital for a checkup.[7]

Indeed, much evidence for Walter's thesis can be garnered from my own culture, particularly when one considers what we spend on health care, much of which is devoted to extending life.[8] Although the search of Juan Ponce de León (1460–1521) for the fountain of youth was unsuccessful, the work of Cambridge computer scientist Aubrey de Grey has drawn the serious, yet skeptical, attention of Yale surgeon and bioethicist Sherwin Nuland, author of *How We Die*, winner of the National Book Award in 1994.[9] According to Nuland, de Grey has "mapped out his proposed course in such detail that he believes it may be possible for his objective [the theoretical means by which human beings might live thousands of years] to be achieved within as short a period as 25 years."[10] Despite the fact that our average life expectancy at birth has gained more than 50 percent in the last century, the gains have been due primarily to a decrease in the number of deaths during

---

[7] Tony Walter, *Funerals And How to Improve Them* (London, 1990), 41.

[8] On the development of modern medicine and of the contemporary medical establishment's commitment to prolonging life, see Darrel W. Amundsen, "The Physician's Obligation to Prolong Life: A Medical Duty without Classical Roots," *The Hastings Center Report* 8 (August 1978): 23–30; "Medicine and Faith in Early Christianity," *BHM* 56 (1982): 326–350; Gary B. Ferngren, "Early Christianity as A Religion of Healing," *BHM* 66 (1992): 1–15; Joel Shuman, "Desperately Seeking Perfection: Christian Discipleship and Medical Genetics," *Christian Bioethics* 5 (1999): 139–153; Daniel Callahan, "Death and the Research Imperative," *NEJM* 432 (2 March 2000): 546–556; David M. Cutler, Allison B. Rosen, and Sandeep Vijan, "The Value of Medical Spending in the United States, 1960–2000," *NEJM* 355 (2006): 920–927.

[9] Sherwin B. Nuland, *How We Die: Reflections on Life's Final Chapter* (New York, 1994).

[10] Sherwin Nuland, "Do You Want to Live Forever?" *Technology Review* 108 (February 2005): 36–45, here at 37. For a criticism of life-extending research involving cloning and embryonic stem cells, see William P. Cheshire, Jr., "In Search of the Philosopher's Clone: Immortality through Replication," in *Aging, Death, and the Quest for Immortality*, ed. C. Ben Mitchell, Robert D. Orr, and Susan A. Salladay (Grand Rapids, 2004), 175–192.

the early years of life.[11] Accordingly, our perception tends to be that dying is becoming increasingly associated with the elderly.[12] One observer said that today's youth-centered perspective continues to see age as "something to be fought, denied, ignored, and avoided at all costs."[13]

However, galling though they be, death and dying have provoked intense research in several fields in ways other than towards death avoidance—research that has in turn affected the practice of care for the sick as well as the dying.[14] Since the 1970s students in the USA

---

[11] In 1900 life expectancy at birth for the average American male was only 48.3 years; for the average female, 51.1. By the middle of the century these figures had increased to 66 for males and 71.7 for females. At the end of the century the figures were 75.7 and 82.7, respectively; C. Ben Mitchell, "The Quest for Immortality," in Mitchell, Orr, and Salladay, eds., *Aging, Death, and the Quest for Immortality*, 153–62, here at 155.

[12] Corr, Nabe, and Corr, 28. Compared to previous generations, our dying can now be a more drawn-out affair: "In only a decade or two we have shifted from a society in which many members refused to contemplate their mortality or were denied the opportunity to do so, to one in which a very substantial proportion of the middle-aged and elderly know that they or close kin have a life-threatening disease which may not kill them for years but in whose shadow they must in the meantime live. Even those who do live long healthy lives are likely to know family members who are living with cancer, heart disease or HIV"; Tony Walter, *The Revival of Death*, 50. Two recent works on end-of-life issues are Margaret Pabst Battin, *Ending Life: Ethics and the Way We Die* (Oxford, 2005) and Robert H. Blank and Janna C. Merrick, ed., *End-of-Life Decision Making: A Cross-National Study* (Cambridge, Mass., 2005).

[13] Gregory Waybright, "Local Church Ministry to and through Older Adults," in *Aging, Death, and the Quest for Immortality*, 107–20, here at 108. Waybright concludes that Americans need to be better prepared for death and can do so by recognizing that "the act of growing old is often more difficult than dying" (119).

[14] Paul Ramsey, "The Indignity of 'Death with Dignity,'" *Hastings Center Studies* 2 (May 1974): 50–62; Robert Jay Lifton, "On Death and the Continuity of Life: A 'New' Paradigm," *History of Childhood Quarterly* 1 (1974): 681–696; Alasdair MacIntyre, "Patients as Agents," in *Philosophical Medical Ethics: Its Nature and Significance*, ed. S. F. Spicker and H. T. Engelhardt (Dordrecht, 1977), 197–212; "Medicine Aimed at the Care of Persons Rather Than What…?" in *Changing Values in Medicine*, ed. Eric J. Cassell and Mark Siegler (Frederick, Md., 1979), 83–96; Robert L. Sevensky, "Religion and Illness: An Outline of Their Relationship," *Southern Medical Journal* 74 (1981): 745–750; "The Religious Foundations of Health Care: A Conceptual Approach," *Journal of Medical Ethics* 9 (1983): 165–169; David Royse, "The Near-Death Experience: A Survey of Clergy's Attitudes and Knowledge," *JPC* 39 (March 1985): 331–342; Stanley Hauerwas, "Reflections on Suffering, Death, and Medicine," in *Suffering Presence* (Notre Dame, Ind., 1986), 23–38; M. Powell Lawton, Miriam Moss, and Allen Glicksman, "The Quality of the Last Year of Life of Older Persons," *The Milbank Quarterly* 68 (1990): 1–28; Gilbert Meilaender, "Mortality: The Measure of Our Days," *First Things* (February 1991): 14–21; idem, "'Love's Casuistry': Paul Ramsey on Caring For the Terminally Ill," *Journal of Religious Ethics* 12 (fall 1991): 133–156; Lindsay Prior and Mick Bloor, "Why People Die: Social Representations of Death and Its Causes," *Science as Culture* 3 (1992): 346–374; Peter Kreeft, *Love Is Stronger Than Death* (San Francisco, 1992); Charles Taylor, "Philosophical

have studied 'death and dying' in the classroom,[15] yet few teenagers have experienced a personal encounter with death in their own family or among close friends.[16] Consequently, since death at a young age is

---

Reflections on Caring Practices," in *The Crisis of Care: Affirming and Restoring Caring Practices in the Helping Professions*, ed. Susan S. Phillips and Patricia Benner (Washington, D.C., 1994), 174–187; Jeffrey S. Levin, "Religion and Health: Is There an Association, Is It Valid, and Is It Causal?" *SSM* 38 (1994): 1475–1482; Mina Mills, Huw T. O. Davies, and William A. Macrae, "Care of Dying Patients in Hospital," *British Medical Journal* 309 (3 September 1994): 583–586; Wendell Berry, "Health Is Membership," in *Another Turn of the Crank* (Washington, D.C., 1995), 86–109; Jack D. McCue, "The Naturalness of Dying," *JAMA* 273 (April 5, 1995): 1039–1043; Alan C. Mermann, "Learning to Care for the Dying," *Facing Death: Where Culture, Religion, and Medicine Meet*, ed. Howard M. Spiro, Mary G. McCrea Curnen, and Lee Palmer Wandel (New Haven, 1996), 52–59; William J. Bouwsma, "Conclusion: Retrospect and Prospect," in *Facing Death*, 189–198; Jeffrey S. Levin, "How Religion Influences Morbidity and Health: Reflections on Natural History, Salutogenesis and Host Resistance," *SSM* 43 (1996): 849–864; Gary Laderman, *The Sacred Remains: American Attitudes Toward Death, 1799–1883* (New Haven, 1996); Anne L. Simmonds, "Pastoral Perspectives in Intensive Care: Experiences of Doctors and Nurses with Dying Patients," *JPC* 51 (1997): 271–281; Christopher G. Ellison and Jeffrey S. Levin, "The Religion-Health Connection: Evidence, Theory, and Future Directions," *Health Education & Behavior* 25 (1998): 700–720; Harold G. Koenig and David B. Larson, "Use of Hospital Services, Religious Attendance, and Religious Affiliation," *Southern Medical Journal* 91 (1998): 925–932; Marion Davis et al., "Incorporating Palliative Care into Critical Care Education: Principles, Challenges, and Opportunities," *Critical Care Medicine* 27 (1999): 2005–2013; Keith G. Meador and Shaun C. Henson, "Growing Old in A Therapeutic Culture," *Theology Today* 57 (2000): 185–202; Ingolf U. Dalferth, "'I Determine What God Is!': Theology in the Age of 'Cafeteria Religion," *Theology Today* 57 (2000): 5–23; Robert H. Albers, "The Faith Factor in Wholistic Care: A Multidisciplinary Conversation," *WW* 21 (2001): 51–60; Robert C. Roberts, "Psychotherapy and Christian Ministry," *WW* 21 (2001): 42–50; Mark J. Hanson, "Defining Health and Health-Related Concepts: Conceptual and Theological Considerations," *WW* 21 (2001): 23–31; Archie Smith, Jr., "'Look and See If There Is Any Sorrow Like My Sorrow?': Systemic Metaphors for Pastoral Theology and Care," *WW* 21 (2001): 5–15; Harold G. Koenig, Michael E. McCullough, and David B. Larson, *Handbook of Religion and Health* (Oxford, 2001); Peter Marshall, *Beliefs and the Dead in Reformation England* (Oxford, 2002); Michael A. Milton, "'So What are You Doing Here?': The Role of the Minister of the Gospel in Hospital Visitation, or A Theological Cure for the Crisis in Evangelical Pastoral Care," *JETS* 46 (2003): 449–463; Joel James Shuman and Keith G. Meador, *Heal Thyself: Spirituality, Medicine, and the Distortion of Christianity* (Oxford, 2003).

[15] Elisabeth Kübler-Ross, *On Death and Dying* (New York, 1969); Peter J. Donaldson, "Denying Death: A Note Regarding Some Ambiguities in the Current Discussion," *Omega* 3 (1972): 285–290; Robert Jay Lifton and Eric Olson, *Living and Dying* (New York, 1974); Joseph A. Durlak and Lee Ann Riesenberg, "The Impact of Death Education," *DS* 15 (1991): 39–58; Thomas Attig, *How We Grieve: Relearning the World* (New York, 1996); David W. Moller, *Confronting Death: Values, Institutions, and Human Mortality* (New York, 1996); Corr, Nabe, and Corr, *Death and Dying, Life and Living* (2003); Clifton D. Bryant, ed., *Handbook of Death and Dying*, 2 vols. (Thousand Oaks, Calif., 2003).

[16] A seminary classmate (in the late 1970s) once told me he had never attended a funeral until he was called upon to preside at one. In the mid-1990s a former dean of students at my university told me that a significant traumatic experience that many

such a rarity, an "illusion of invulnerability pretty well defines [the] resting state" for many young students. Thus, "[o]ne of life's crueler ironies is that we're most vulnerable at those very moments when we feel in least danger."[17]

In addition, more experienced adults who have reckoned with human mortality—such as family members of terminally ill patients—have increasingly expressed frustration with what they find to be insensitive doctors.[18] The modern hospice movement is one instrument to which people who are unfamiliar with death and inexperienced at caring for the dying turn to try to restore a sense of 'dignity' to one's dying, through seeking humane care and a social network to the dying experience.[19] However, providing personal companionship or accompani-

---

college students face is the death of a grandparent—the first such death of a close relative in their lifetime.

[17] Mary A. Fischer, "Thrills That Kill," *Reader's Digest*, February 2006, 116–122; Robert Levine, *Persuasion: How We're Bought and Sold* (Hoboken, N.J., 2003), 8. Levine (9) argues that in America today, "Most people are convinced they have a better chance of living past eighty than the next person. In one study, college students (the maestros of perceived invulnerability—take it from a professor), after being informed the average age of death in the United States is seventy-five, went on to estimate their own age of death at, on average, eighty-four years." The study cited is C. R. Snyder, "Unique Invulnerability: A Classroom Demonstration in Estimating Personal Mortality," *Teaching of Psychology* 24 (1997): 197–199. Snyder conducted the same study in two consecutive years. In the second study he told students in advance that they were predicted to overestimate their age of death. He reports that many students stayed after class to inform him, some of them vehemently, as to why in their case they would live longer than statistical averages. Of course, some of them will be correct, for 'average' describes no one in particular. What would be interesting to learn—and what Snyder did not report in the study—is how many students predict an early death for themselves.

[18] The vast improvements in health that resulted in most deaths occurring in hospital have had their trade-offs, according to Tony Walter: "As physical and financial beings people welcomed this, but as meaning-creating and self-determining individuals many felt lost. Medical discourse and bureaucratic practices failed to articulate private grief"; *The Revival of Death*, 26; Jane E. Brody, "Facing Up to the Inevitable: In Search of a Good Death," *New York Times*, 30 December 2003, F5; idem, "Doctors Should Keep Bonds to Dying Patients," *Minneapolis Star-Tribune*, 12 August 2004, E10. According to Walter, *The Revival of Death* (31), there has been a significant change in recent decades regarding doctors' willingness to tell patients they have an incurable disease. In 1961 only 12% of American doctors would tell the patient; in 1979 the figure was 98%. For a study on the reverse situation, see John Hinton, "Whom Do Dying Patients Tell?" *British Medical Journal* 281 (1980): 1328–1330.

[19] Dignity goes hand in hand with control. Tony Walter quotes a hospice doctor: "There's a lot of talk of dignity in the wards these days. But there's no dignity in dying: you can't have your bottom wiped with dignity. You can't either enter or exit this life in a dignified way, or not at least in a society like ours that doesn't allow dependence. Only patients themselves can allow dignity to be conferred and they have to work at

ment in dying may not be the entire answer to the fear and attempted avoidance of death in modern and postmodern society.[20] Moreover, the tendency to ignore or flee death is by no means recent. What resources are there then for 'preparation' for death?

Responding to one observer[21] of New York City's plans to commemorate the tragedy of '9–11,' Gerhard Sauter argues that "confusing Christian freedom with careless and reckless self-determination" was recognized as a danger long ago by Martin Luther.[22] Sauter suggests that hospice may provide assistance in dying but not necessarily preparation for death. He avers that Luther sought to help people prepare for death long before they become 'terminally ill.' Luther opened his Invocavit Sermons of 1522 thus:

> The summons of death comes to us all, and no one can die for another. Everyone must fight his own battle with death by himself, alone. We

---

it: by humour, by patience, by silence"; *The Revival of Death*, 140. The hospice movement began in Britain in the 1960s, started by Cicely Saunders, who was driven by a deep Christian commitment, according to Tony Walter; cf. Cicely Saunders, "The Last Stages of Life," *American Journal of Nursing* 65 (March 1965): 70–75. On hospice, see L. Paradis and S. Cummings, "The Evolution of Hospice in America Toward Organisational Homogeneity," *Journal of Health and Social Behaviour* 27 (1986): 370–386; Clive F. Seale, "What Happens in Hospices: A Review of Research Evidence," *SSM* 28 (1989): 551–559; Sandol Stoddard, "Hospice in the United States: An Overview," *Journal of Palliative Care* 5, no. 3 (1989): 10–19; Nicky James and David Field, "The Routinization of Hospice: Charisma and Bureaucratization," *SSM* 34 (1992): 1363–1375; Corr, Nabe, and Corr 184–187, 195–199. Scholars considering a Christian perspective on death and dying have noted the nonreligious orientation that hospice and similar programs have taken in recent years, particularly in the United States; cf. Tony Walter, "Death in the New Age," *Religion* 23 (1993): 127–145; idem, *The Revival of Death*, 29, 163; Lucy Bregman, *Beyond Silence and Denial: Death and Dying Reconsidered* (Louisville, Ky., 1999); idem, *Death and Dying, Spirituality and Religions: A Study of the Death Awareness Movement*. American University Studies in Theology and Religion 228 (New York, 2003); Tony Walter, "Hospices and Rituals after Death: A Survey of British Hospice Chaplains," *International Journal of Palliative Nursing* 9, no. 2 (2003): 80–85. For a positive characterization of hospice and, particularly, a strong argument for the holistic concept of palliative care, see Jackie Cameron, "Palliative Care: Suffering and Healing at the End of Life," in Mitchell, Orr, and Salladay, eds., *Aging, Death, and the Quest for Immortality*, 134–149; cf. Tony Walter, "Developments in Spiritual Care of the Dying," *Religion* 26 (1996): 353–363; idem, "The Ideology and Organization of Spiritual Care: Three Approaches," *Palliative Medicine* 11 (1997): 1–10; idem, "Spirituality in Palliative Care: Opportunity or Burden?" *Palliative Medicine* 16 (2002): 133–139.

[20] Gerhard Sauter, "How Do 'I' Encounter My Own Death?" *Theology Today* 60 (2004): 497–507, here at 498; Richard G. Dumont and Dennis C. Foss, *The American View of Death: Acceptance or Denial?* (Cambridge, Mass., 1972).

[21] Jack Hitt, "The American Way of Death Becomes America's Way of Life," *New York Times*, 18 August 2002, Week in Review, 1, 6.

[22] Gerhard Sauter, "My Own Death," 501.

can shout into another's ears, but everyone must himself be prepared for death, for I will not be with you then, nor you with me. Therefore everyone must himself know and be armed with the chief things which concern a Christian (LW 51:70).[23]

Immersed in Luther's theology of death, Sauter's own project strives to strengthen our *'theological perception of death.'*[24] He argues that Luther challenged his listeners to think about *"what it means for a Christian to be a person;"*[25] that one's solitude of complete dedication of one's 'self' to God is not the loneliness of sheer autonomy that ends in desperate self-isolation.[26] Luther, Sauter maintains, shows that baptism overturns the sequence of our natural way of thinking about death—that it is the conclusion of life—offering instead another sequence: *Life follows death.*[27] Even though we die alone, we are not deserted but have the *communio* of all that is available in Christ.[28]

Sauter finds Luther's theology of death not only in the Invocavit Sermons, which he preached from 9–16 March 1522, upon his return (against the Elector's orders and at great personal risk) to Wittenberg from Wartburg castle. In this same article Sauter also quotes from Luther's "Sermon on Preparing to Die" (1519), where he insists: "Christ's life overcame my death in his death, that his obedience blotted out my sin in his suffering, that his love destroyed my hell in his forsakenness."[29] Furthermore, in an article originally published four years earlier,[30] Sauter explores Luther's theology of death by examining his preaching on the resurrection (1 Cor. 15), which he had done on 17 different Sunday afternoons (11 August 1532 to 27 April 1533).[31] As it happens, after delivering the first sermon in that series, Luther preached two messages for the funeral of Elector John the Steadfast:

---

[23] Ibid., 501. For an analysis of the Invocavit Sermons, see Neil R. Leroux, *Luther's Rhetoric: Strategies and Style in the Invocavit Sermons* (St. Louis, 2002).

[24] Sauter, "My Own Death," 497, emphasis Sauter's.

[25] Ibid., 501, emphasis Sauter's.

[26] Ibid.

[27] Ibid., 504.

[28] Ibid., 506.

[29] *LW* 42:109, quoted by Sauter, "My Own Death," 507.

[30] Gerhard Sauter, "Luther on the Resurrection: The Proclamation of the Risen One as the Promise of Our Everlasting Life with God," *LQ* 15 (2001): 195–216; originally published as "Die Verkündigung des Auferstandenen als Zusage des Lebens bei Gott" in *Relationen-Studien zum Übergang vom Spätmittelalter zur Reformation: Festschrift zu Ehren von Prof. Dr. Karl-Heinz zu Mühlen*, ed. Athina Lexutt and Wolfgang Matz (Münster, 2000), 383–398.

[31] *WA* 36:478–696.

18 and 22 August, both of which were grounded in 1 Thess. 4:13–18, and of which I shall say more later.[32]

Thus Luther had much to say about death, and I have now suggested two different genres of discourse—preaching and consolation literature—that he explored to bring comfort to those facing issues pertaining to death. Since industrialized societies today regard 'death and taxes' as two certainties amongst a universe of relativism and uncertainty, contemporary readers should find what sixteenth-century readers (who were subject to these same certainties) discovered: that Luther's remarks about death are worth hearing. But why are they so?

We fear and try to avoid death—differently than our predecessors only in degree—because we take it to be what Lloyd Bitzer calls a nonrhetorical exigence—a necessary imperfection that cannot be modified by discourse.[33] However, Mark Twain observed that we talk constantly about the weather, yet 'do' nothing about it. Both he and Bitzer note correctly that for both death and the weather we can 'modify' neither through discourse alone. Still, we use discourse aplenty to enable us to cope with these exigences.[34] As with one of Bitzer's own examples of a rhetorical situation (the situation generated by the John F. Kennedy assassination in 1963),[35] death itself provides several topics embedded within it that present rhetors and audiences with exigences needing discourse to address them. Moreover, the resources available to a rhetor—the material facts of the situation and the linguistic strategies and style—not only are those the rhetor uses to make the most persuasive discourse possible; they are also available to us as reader-critics, enabling us to perceive the appeal (logic and power) the discourse has.

So, by examining Luther's writings on death and suffering, this book helps us to consider several important aspects of death.[36] And by looking closely at *how* Luther argues, we can learn the power his discourse has to convince readers what *can* be done about death: it cannot be avoided, but we can face it victoriously. Moreover, scholars have begun

---

[32] *LW* 51:231–255; *WA* 36:237–270.

[33] Lloyd F. Bitzer, "The Rhetorical Situation," *Philosophy and Rhetoric* 1 (1968): 1–14, here at 6.

[34] Bitzer (6f.) lists "death, winter, and some natural disasters, for instance" as exigences that are not rhetorical. Further, he argues that exigences that cannot be modified, or can be "modified only by means other than discourse," are not rhetorical exigences.

[35] Ibid., 9.

[36] Ronald Rittgers, "The Reformation of Suffering," *Crux* 38 (December 2002): 15–21; John C. Clark, "Luther's View of Cross-Bearing," *BSac* 163 (2006): 335–347.

to discover Luther's role as a *Seelsorger*, a healer of souls;[37] consequently, his writings on death are the very discourse for encountering Luther's efforts to comfort. This is particularly important if one finds the orientation, scope, and depth of contemporary pastoral care to have drifted from its historic, biblical moorings.[38]

---

[37] August Nebe, *Luther as Spiritual Adviser*, trans. Charles A. Hay and Charles E. Hay (Philadelphia, 1894); Helmut Appel, *Anfechtung und Trost im Spätmittelalter und bei Luther* (Leipzig, 1938); Johann Simon Schöffel, "Luther als Seelsorger," *Luther* 23 (1941): 1–10; Gerhard Krause, "Luthers Stellung zum Selbstmord: Ein Kapitel seiner Lehre und Praxis der Seelsorge," *Luther* 36 (1965): 50–71; Philip J. Secker, "Martin Luther's Views on the State of the Dead," *CTM* 38 (1967): 422–435; Arthur E. Becker, "Luther as Seelsorger," in *Interpreting Luther's Legacy: Essays in Honor of Edward C. Fendt*, ed. Fred W. Meuser and Stanley D. Schneider (Minneapolis, 1969), 136–150; Roland H. Bainton, "Luther: Pastor, Consoler, Preacher," in *Encounters with Luther*, Vol. 1, *Lectures, Discussions and Sermons at the Martin Luther Colloquia 1970–74*, ed. Eric W. Gritsch (Gettysburg, 1980), 167–180; Yoshiro Ishida, "Luther the Pastor," in *Piety, Politics, and Ethics: Reformation Studies in Honor of George Wolfgang Forell*, ed. Carter Lindberg. SCES 3 (Kirksville, Mo., 1984), 27–37; Martin Treu, "Trost bei Luther: Ein Anstoß für heutige Seelsorge," *Pastoraltheologie* 73 (March 1984): 91–106; Hans-Martin Barth, "'Pecca fortiter, sed fortius fide…': Martin Luther als Seelsorger," *Evangelische Theologie* 44 (1984): 12–25; George Kraus, "Luther the *Seelsorger*," *CTM* 48 (1984): 153–163; Klaus-Peter Jörns, "Luther als Seelsorger," *Wege zum Menschen* 37 (1985): 489–498; Martin Treu, "Die Bedeutung der consolatio für Luthers Seelsorge bis 1525," *LuJ* 53 (1986): 7–25; Gerald Krispin, "The Consolation of the Resurrection in Luther," *Lutheran Theological Review* 2 (fall-winter, 1989–1990): 38–51; Gerhard Ebeling, "Der theologische Grundzug der Seelsorge Luthers," in *Luther als Seelsorger*, ed. Joachim Heubach. Veröffentlichungen der Luther-Akademie e. V. Ratzeburg 18 (Erlangen, 1991), 21–48; Christian Möller, "Luthers Seelsorge und die neueren Seelsorgekonzepte," in *Luther als Seelsorger*, 109–128; Christian Möller, "Martin Luther," in *Geschichte der Seelsorge in Einzelporträts*, vol. 2, ed. Christian Möller (Göttingen, 1992), 25–44; Gerhard Ebeling, "Luthers Gebrauch der Wortfamilie 'Seelsorge,'" *LuJ* 61 (1994): 7–44; Ute Mennecke-Haustein, "Luther als Seelsorger," in *Martin Luther ungewohnt*, ed. Evangelische Akademie Baden (Karlsruhe, 1996), 55–78; Maurice E. Schild, "Luther as Comforter," in *Perspectives on Martin Luther: Papers from the Luther Symposium held at Luther Seminary Adelaide, South Australia, 22–23 March, 1996, Commemorating the 450th Anniversary of the Reformer's Death*, ed. M. W. Worthing (North Adelaide, So. Australia, 1996), 9–20; Rudolf Keller, "Luther als Seelsorger," *Lutherische Kirche in der Welt* 44 (1997): 101–118; Gerhard Ebeling, *Luthers Seelsorge: Theologie in der Vielfalt der Lebenssituationen an seinen Briefen dargestellt* (Tübingen, 1997); Richard G. Ballard, "The Pastoral Care of the Sick and Dying and of the Bereaved," *LuthFor* 34 (spring 2000): 37–41; Franz Posset, "Lehrer der Seelsorge: Das ökumenische Potential der Seelsorge-Konzeption des alten Luther," *Luther* 72 (2001): 3–17; Herbert Anderson, "Whatever Happened to *Seelsorge*?" *WW* 21 (2001): 32–41; Timothy J. Wengert, "'Peace, Peace…Cross, Cross': Reflections on How Martin Luther Relates the Theology of the Cross to Suffering," *Theology Today* 59 (2002): 190–205; Reinhard Slenczka, "Luther's Care of Souls for Our Times," *CTQ* (2003): 33–63.

[38] John T. McNeill, *A History of the Cure of Souls* (New York, 1951); E. Brooks Holifield, *A History of Pastoral Care in America: From Salvation to Self-Realization* (Nashville, 1983); Eberhard Winkler, "Luther als Seelsorger und Prediger, *Leben und Werk Martin Luthers von 1526 bis 1546: Festgabe seinem 500. Geburtstag*, ed. Helmar Junghans, Vol. 1 (Göttingen,

We have already discussed how one considers one's own forthcoming death. Chapters One and Two will explore in depth how Luther addressed this matter. Chapters Three through Six take us deeper into how the deaths of others bring loss; each chapter addresses matters and occasions of loss and threat—grieving a loss, expressing grief[39] through mourning, using funerals to make meaning out of loss, offering comfort to the bereaved, aiding the suffering and dying, and honoring and burying the dead. As we begin exploring these questions, we shall analyze some of Luther's writings, revealing the context and style, thus accounting for how he used discourse to bring meaning, comfort, and hope. First, we recall that Luther had occasion in 1519 to write two different works whose focus is the imminent prospect of a Christian dying.

Chapter One examines Luther's "Fourteen Consolations," which is help in finding comfort for those who may be dying. His counsel to be

---

1983), 225–240; Thomas C. Oden, *Care of Souls in the Classic Tradition* (Philadelphia, 1984); Herbert W. Stroup, Jr., "Pastoral Theology: Reformation or Regression?" *LTSB* 67 (winter 1987): 39–53; Martin Treu, "Zwischen Psychotherapie und Dämonenaustreibung: Beobachtungen und Überlegungen zu Luthers Seelsorge für die Gegenwart," *Luther* 58 (1987): 32–45; Rudolf Keller, "Luther als Seelsorger und theologischer Berater der zerstreuten Gemeinden," *Kirche in der Schule Luthers: Festschrift für D. Joachim Heubach*, ed. Bengt Hägglund and Gerhard Müller (Erlangen, 1995), 58–78; David Cornick, "The Reformation Crisis in Pastoral Care," in *A History of Pastoral Care*, ed. G. R. Evans (London, 2000), 223–234; Susan R. Boettcher, "The Rhetoric of 'Seelsorge' for Miners in the Sermons of Cyriakus Spangenberg," in *Frömmigkeit—Theologie—Frömmigkeitstheologie: Contributions to European Church History. Festschrift für Berndt Hamm zum 60. Geburtstag*, ed. Gudrun Litz, Heidrun Munzert, and Roland Liebenberg. SHCT 124 (Leiden, 2005), 453–466.

[39] The scholarly literature on grief in English-speaking countries alone is immense. Recent studies that trace grief historically as an emotion are Peter N. Stearns, *American Cool: Constructing a Twentieth-Century Emotional Style* (New York, 1994) and Peter N. Stearns and Mark Knapp, "Historical Perspectives on Grief," in *The Emotions: Social, Cultural and Biological Dimensions*, ed. Rom Harré and W. Gerrod Parrott (London, 1996), 134–148; Donald P. Irish, "Diversity in Universality: Dying, Death and Grief," in *The Unknown Country: Death in Australia, Britain and the USA*, ed. Kathy Charmaz, Glennys Howarth, and Allan Kellehear (Houndmills, 1997), 242–256. Yet much research has been done elsewhere: see Tony Walter, "Letting Go and Keeping Hold: A Reply to Stroebe," *Mortality* 2 (1997): 263–266; Margaret Stroebe and Henk Schut, "Culture and Grief," *Bereavement Care* 17 (1998): 7–10; Steven E. Bailley, Michael J. Kral, and Katherine Dunham, "Survivors of Suicide Do Grieve Differently: Empirical Support for a Common Sense Proposition," *Suicide and Life-Threatening Behavior* 29 (1999): 256–271; Margaret Stroebe and Henk Schut, "The Dual Process Model of Coping with Bereavement: Rationale and Description," *DS* 23 (1999): 197–224; Tony Walter, *On Bereavement: The Culture of Grief* (Buckingham, 1999); idem, "Emotional Reserve and the English Way of Grief," *The Unknown Country*, 127–140; idem, "Grief Narratives: The Role of Medicine in the Policing of Grief," *Anthropology and Medicine* 7 (2000): 97–114.

prepared can be considered by today's readers who may try instead to escape.[40] Luther wrote this work specifically for Saxon Elector Frederick the Wise, who was gravely ill and thought to be dying. Early modern German people often turned to the saints as the 'primary link' between this world and the next,[41] and especially to the 'helper saints,' praying to them for assistance.[42] To have such helpers ready to aid implies that

---

[40] *LW* 42:121–166; *WA* 6:104–134.

[41] Carol Piper Heming, *Protestants and the Cult of the Saints in German-Speaking Europe, 1517–21*. SCES (Kirksville, Mo., 2003), 39.

[42] On the fourteen saints, see Georg Schreiber, *Die Vierzehn Nothelfer in Volksfrömmigkeit und Sakralkultur: Symbolkraft und Herrschaftsbereich der Wallfahrtskapelle, vorab in Franken und Tirol*. Schlern-Schriften Veröffentlichungen zur Landeskunde von Südtirol 168 (Innsbruck, 1959); David Hugh Farmer, ed., *Oxford Dictionary of Saints*, 4th ed., (Oxford, 1997), s.v. "Fourteen Holy Helpers"; *New Catholic Encyclopedia*, 2nd ed., s.v. "Fourteen Holy Helpers," by J. Dünninger. On the saints and popular religion, see Max Lackmann, "Thesaurus Sanctorum: Ein vergessener Beitrag Luthers zur Hagiologie," in *Festgabe Joseph Lortz*, ed. Erwin Iserloh and Peter Manns, Vol. 1, *Reformation, Shicksal und Auftrag* (Baden-Baden, 1958), 135–171; Max Lackmann, *Verehrung der Heiligen: Versuch einer lutherischen Lehre von den Heiligen* (Stuttgart, 1958); Père H. Delehaye, *The Legends of the Saints: An Introduction to Hagiography*, trans. V. M. Crawford (Notre Dame, 1961); Bernd Moeller, "Piety in Germany Around 1500," in *The Reformation in Medieval Perspective*, ed. Steven E. Ozment (Chicago, 1971), 50–75; Natalie Zemon Davis, "Some Tasks and Themes in the Study of Popular Religion," in *The Pursuit of Holiness in Late Medieval and Renaissance Religion: Papers From the University of Michigan Conference on Late Medieval and Renaissance Religion*, ed. Charles Trinkaus and Heiko A. Oberman. SMRT 10 (Leiden, 1974), 307–336; John M. McCulloh, "The Cult of Relics in the Letters and 'Dialogues' of Pope Gregory the Great: A Lexicographical Study," *Traditio* 32 (1976): 145–184; Diana Webb, "Eloquence and Education: A Humanist Approach to Hagiography," *Journal of Ecclesiastical History* 31 (1980): 19–39; Peter Brown, *The Cult of the Saints: Its Rise and Function in Latin Christianity*. Haskell Lectures on the History of Religions 2 (Chicago, 1981); R. W. Scribner, "Ritual and Popular Religion in Catholic Germany at the Time of the Reformation," *Journal of Ecclesiastical History* 35 (1984): 47–77; Patrick J. Geary, "The Saint and the Shrine: The Pilgrims' Goal in the Middle Ages," in *Walfahrt kennt keine Grenzen*, ed. Lenz Kriss-Rettenbeck and Gerda Möhler (Munich, 1984), 265–274; James Michael Weiss, "Hagiography by German Humanists, 1483–1516," *Journal of Medieval and Renaissance Studies* 15 (1985): 299–316; Carlos M. N. Eire, *War Against the Idols: The Reformation of Worship from Erasmus to Calvin* (Cambridge, 1986), 8–26; H. George Anderson, J. Francis Stafford, and Joseph A. Burgess, ed., *The One Mediator, The Saints, and Mary*. Lutherans and Catholics in Dialogue 8 (Minneapolis, 1992); Michael Downey, ed., *The New Dictionary of Catholic Spirituality* (Collegeville, Minn., 1993), s.v., "Saints, Communion of"; Patrick J. Geary, *Living With the Dead in the Middle Ages* (Ithaca, N.Y., 1994); Paul Antony Hayward, "Demystifying the Role of Sanctity in Western Christendom," in *The Cult of Saints in Late Antiquity and the Middle Ages: Essays on the Contribution of Peter Brown*, ed. James Howard-Johnston and Paul Antony Hayward (Oxford, 1999), 115–142; Peter Marshall, *Beliefs and the Dead*. On particular saints, see O. Clemen, "Zum St. Annenkultus im ausgehenden Mittelalter," *Archiv für Reformationsgeschichte* 21 (1924): 251–253; Gabrielle M. Spiegel, "The Cult of St. Denis and Capetian Kingship," in *Saints and their Cults: Studies in Religious Sociology, Folklore and History*, ed. Stephen Wilson (Cambridge, 1983), 141–168; Heiko A. Oberman, "The Virgin Mary in Evangelical Perspective," *Journal of Ecumenical Studies* 1 (1964):

one may avoid life-threatening perils or be protected from their harmful effects. That such helpers were depicted in works of art suggests that one can implore them 'on demand.' Countering this, Luther argues that one can at any time assess the strength and comfort available to him through the resources of Christ. In this work Luther not only proposes a Christological—rather than hagiographic—approach to consolation; he also organizes this work (composed originally in Latin, then soon translated into German) spatially and temporally, as was common in medieval sermons, meditations, and works of art.[43] In so doing, he implies that his fourteen consolations—consisting in seven 'evils' and seven 'blessings'—completely replace the fourteen helper saints as a fixture for contemplation.[44] Moreover, Luther's 'how much more' rhetorical strategy demonstrates the priority—and superiority—of Christ over the saints as source of comfort.

Chapter Two analyzes "A Sermon on Preparing to Die,"[45] also written in 1519 but seemingly intended to displace the ubiquitous *ars moriendi*, the 'art of dying (well).' These books, usually amply illustrated, circulated widely in the late middle ages and were designed as instructional guides to help comfort the person having 'taken to bed' and facing imminent death.[46] Although people have probably always wanted—if, after all,

---

271–298; Arthur Carl Piepkorn, "Mary's Place Within the People of God According to Non-Roman-Catholics," *Marian Studies* 18 (1967): 46–83; David F. Wright, "Mary in the Reformers," in *Chosen By God: Mary in Evangelical Perspective*, ed. David F. Wright (London, 1989), 161–183; Virginia Nixon, *Mary's Mother: Saint Anne in Late Medieval Europe* (University Park, Pa., 2004); Charles R. Hogg, Jr., "The Ever-Virgin Mary: Athanasius to Gerhard," *LuthFor* (winter 2004): 18–23; "The Ever-Virgin Mary: Gerhard to the Present," *LuthFor* (spring 2005): 36–39. On Luther's views on the saints, see Lennart Pinomaa, "Die Heiligen in Luthers Frühtheologie," *Studia Theologica* 13 (1959): 1–50; Peter Newman Brooks, "A Lily Ungilded?: Martin Luther, the Virgin Mary and the Saints," *Journal of Religious History* 13 (1984): 136–149; Beth Kreitzer, "Luther Regarding the Virgin Mary," *LQ* 17 (2003): 249–266; Angelika Dörfler-Dierken, "Luther und die heilige Anna," *LuJ* 64 (1997): 19–46; Gerhard Ludwig Müller, "Communio Sanctorum: Das Kirchenverständnis Martin Luthers," *Edith-Stein-Jahrbuch* 4 (1998): 215–223.

[43] George Tavard, "Luther's Teaching on Prayer," *LTBS 67* (winter 1987): 3–22, here at 7f.

[44] That Luther wrote this work lends some support to Carol Piper Heming's thesis that the cult of the saints did not die easily in the sixteenth century, even among regions that accepted the reformation teachings; see her *Protestants and the Cult of the Saints*; cf. Peter Brown, *The Cult of the Saints*.

[45] *LW* 42:99–115; *WA* 2:685–697.

[46] Rainer Rudolf, *Ars Moriendi: Von der Kunst des Heilsamen Lebens und Sterbens*. Forschung zur Volkskunde 39 (Cologne, 1957); Nancy Lee Beaty, T*he Craft of Dying: A Study in the Literary Tradition of the Ars Moriendi in England* (New Haven, 1970), 1–53; Rainer Rudolf, "Ars Moriendi I: Mittelalter," in *TRE* 4:143–149; Rudolf Mohr, "Ars Moriendi

they really must—to die well, one medieval preoccupation was decidedly different from our own. We moderns wish to have it over with quickly and painlessly,[47] but our predecessors wanted more than mere 'dignity' in death; rather, they desired to maintain their rational faculties and will so they might resist the devil right to the end.[48] Moreover, they hungered for assistance in carrying this out.[49] Like "Fourteen Consolations," Luther's book was every bit as successful in sales: 17 editions within two years. Further, in helping the dying person know what to think about and do in his last hours, Luther discusses not one subject but three: sin, death, and hell.[50] Unlike our own time, which has for-

---

II: 16.–18. Jahrhundert," *TRE* 4:149–154; Robert Kastenbaum, "Ars Moriendi," in *Encyclopedia of Death*, ed, Robert and Beatrice Kastenbaum (Phoenix, Ariz., 1989), 17–19; Markus Wriedt, "Johann von Staupitz," in *Geschichte der Seelsorge in Einzelporträts*, vol. 2, ed. Christian Möller (Göttingen, 1992), 45–64; Jacques Laager, ed., *Ars Moriendi: die Kunst, gut zu leben und gut zu sterben: Texte von Cicero bis Luther* (Zürich, 1996); Arthur E. Imhof, "An *Ars Moriendi* for Our Time: To Live a Fulfilled Life; to Die a Peaceful Death," in Spiro, Curnen, and Wandel, eds., *Facing Death*, 114–120; E. van der Veer, "Ars Moriendi bij Luther," *Gereformeerd theologisch tijdschrift* 96 (1996): 20–30; Hilmar M. Pabel, "Humanism and Early Modern Catholicism: Erasmus of Rotterdam's *Ars Moriendi*," in *Early Modern Catholicism: Essays in Honour of John W. O'Malley, S.J.*, ed. Kathleen M. Comerford and Hilmar M. Pabel (Toronto, 2001), 26–45.

[47] Tony Walter, *The Revival of Death*, 31f.; 59f. "He never knew what hit him" was a popular line from the mid-twentieth century, as when Frank McCloud (Humphrey Bogart) in *Key Largo* (John Huston, 1948) described—probably fictitiously—the combat death of her husband George to Nora Templeton (Lauren Bacall). However, the statement represents only one aspect of a modern preference for the 'good death.' According to Tony Walter, a second aspect has now emerged, whereby the postmodern preference for a death with a longer trajectory is that one be fully aware of one's condition, mentally alert yet pain-free, surrounded by loving family and friends, and have no 'unfinished business.' Freedom from pain is doubtless a trans-cultural and trans-historical desire; cf. Gen. 3:16 ("To the woman he said, 'I will greatly multiply your pain in childbearing; in pain you shall bring forth children'"); Rev. 21:4 ("He will wipe away every tear from their eyes, and death shall be no more, neither shall there be mourning nor crying nor pain any more, for the former things have passed away").

[48] For a glimpse of medieval popular beliefs about dying and burial custom, see Erasmus's dialogue (first printed in Basel, 1526), "The Funeral," in *The Colloquies of Erasmus*, trans. Craig R. Thompson (Chicago, 1965), 359–373; Harold Wagner, "Catholic Theology's Main Thoughts on Death," in Spiro, Curnen, and Wandel, eds., *Facing Death*, 137–141; Madeline Gray, *The Protestant Reformation: Belief, Practice and Tradition* (Brighton, 2003), 165–189. On resisting the devil, see Heiko A. Oberman, "Luther and the Devil," *LTSB* 69 (1989): 4–15.

[49] Albrecht Endriß, "Nachfolgung des willigen Sterbens Christi," in *Kontinuität und Umbruch: Theologie und Frömmigkeit in Flugschriften und Kleinliteratur an der Wende vom 15. Zum 16. Jahrhundert*. Beiträge zum Tübinger Kolloquium des Sonder-forschungbereichs 8, ed. Josef Nolte, Hella Tompert, and Christof Windhorst (Stuttgart, 1978), 93–141.

[50] Reiner Preul, "Der Tod des ganzen Menschen: Luthers Sermon von der Bereitung zum Sterben," in *Der 'ganze Mensch': Perspektiven lebengeschichtlicher Individualität. Festschrift*

gotten sin[51] and banished hell,[52] early modern Christians had no such delusions.[53] In both Chapter One and Chapter Two we find Luther advocating—as optional sources of comfort—the use of the Sacrament of the Altar (Eucharist). In Chapter Two he argues the same for both Eucharist and Extreme Unction.[54]

Another issue embedded within the topic of death presents, for many, the opposite of self-preservation—indeed, the patently absurd and surely abhorrent. I speak of martyrdom—dying for one's faith, while providing exemplary testimony to it during one's trial and execution.[55] While not uncommon in the early centuries A.D., Christian martyrdom waned in the middle ages, until it revived again in the Reformation.[56] Today

---

für Dietrich Rössler zum siebzigsten Geburtstag, ed. Volker Drehsen, et al. Arbeiten zur Praktischen Theologie 10 (Berlin, 1997), 111–130.

[51] Karl A. Menninger, *Whatever Became of Sin?* (New York, 1973).

[52] Tony Walter opines that, "Paradoxically it was the First World War, hell on earth, that finally killed off hell below—no field chaplain could even so much as hint that the brave lad he was burying might be going to the wrong place, and thereafter hell disappeared off the agenda in all but the most conservative of churches. And without hell, death lost any spiritual risk, and became a medical and psychological affair"; *The Revival of Death*, 14; cf. Tony Walter, *The Eclipse of Eternity: A Sociology of the Afterlife* (Houndmills, 1996), 1f., 20f. As one born at the end of World War II, I can attest to having heard preaching about hell as a young boy, but it has virtually disappeared in my own circles since 1960. Knowing whether the steady decline in belief in hell has changed will require additional study. A recent survey by *Newsweek* and Beliefnet of 1,004 Americans 18 and older found that 67% responded to the question, "What happens when we die?" by answering, "The soul goes to heaven or hell"; see Jerry Adler, "In Search of the Spiritual," *Newsweek*, 5 September 2005, 48–64, here at 49.

[53] Many moderns would no doubt consider their predecessors as the deluded ones; cf. Jean Delumeau, *Sin and Fear: The Emergence of a Western Guilt Culture, 13th–18th Centuries*, trans. Eric Nicholson (New York, 1990). Walter (*Eclipse*, 2) quotes the Bishop of Durham in 1993: "There can be no Hell for eternity—our God could not be so cruel." In that same year D. A. Carson, "On Distorting the Love of God," *BSac* 156 (1993): 3–12, says "the love of God in our culture has been purged of anything the culture finds uncomfortable. The love of God has been sanitized, democratized, and above all sentimentalized" (5). On p. 6 he quotes Marsha Witten, *All Is Forgiven: The Secular Message in American Protestantism* (Princeton, N.J., 1993), 53: "The transcendent, majestic, awesome God of Luther and Calvin—whose image informed early Protestant visions of the relationship between human beings and the divine—has undergone a softening of demeanor through the American experience of Protestantism, with only minor exceptions." See also the International Theological Commission, "Some Current Questions in Eschatology," *Irish Theological Quarterly* 48 (1992): 209–243.

[54] Friedrich Gerke, "Anfechtung und Sakrament in Martin Luthers Sermon von Sterben," *Theologische Blätter* 13 (1934): 193–204.

[55] Rona M. Fields, *Martyrdom: The Psychology, Theology, and Politics of Self-Sacrifice* (Westport, Conn., 2004).

[56] Gerald C. Studer, "A History of the *Martyrs' Mirror*," *MQR* 22 (1948): 163–179; A. Orley Swartzentruber, "The Piety and Theology of the Anabaptist Martyrs in Van

we recoil at every instance of a suicide bomb and are repulsed by such a notion as dying in a violent action whose primary 'goals' are to kill others, spread fear, and ignite chaos. Yet for one who has come to terms with her own mortality—and understands how, as a Christian: (1) she has already died, and her life is "hid with Christ in God" (Col. 3:3); (2) she has 'died with Christ' and will also 'live with him' (Rom. 6:8); and (3) she must "suffer with him in order that [sh]e may also be glorified with him" (Rom. 8:17)—dying for a benevolent cause, particularly for one's Christian faith, is not necessarily illogical or strange.[57]

Consequently, Chapter Three explores Luther's martyrological literature, written between 1522 and 1527 and consisting in two forms: (1) pamphlets that Luther wrote to congregations and other readers who had been closely touched by the deaths of persecuted believers; (2) his correspondence to those awaiting execution for their faith. In the latter documents Luther discusses the actions of the saints to provide comfort and encouragement to people facing death—especially execution for their faith—while eschewing the notion that saints should be intermediaries. Indeed, the Protestant martyrologies became very popular by the late sixteenth century. However, in the third decade of the century, Luther's early pamphlets had no precise generic pattern to follow. Moreover, in addressing the folks who had been closely touched by the deaths of persecuted believers, he faced countervailing concerns as he identified and promoted the martyrs' stories. The principle of *sola scriptura* reaffirmed the esteem for patience, preparation for death, and devotion to Christ's passion. Readers knew of the deaths of John the Baptist, Stephen, and Jesus himself. Yet the saints' traditional intercessory role had to be repudiated, for it was now seen as problematic.[58]

Braght's *Martyrs' Mirror* I," *MQR* 28 (1954): 5–26; A. Orley Swartzentruber, "The Piety and Theology of the Anabaptist Martyrs in Van Braght's *Martyrs' Mirror* II: The Earliest Testimonies—1539–46," *MQR* 28 (1954): 128–142; Herbert Musurillo, ed. and trans., *The Acts of the Christian Martyrs* (Oxford, 1972); Robert Kolb, *For All The Saints: Changing Perceptions of Martyrdom and Sainthood in the Lutheran Reformation* (Macon, Ga., 1987); Ellen Macek, "The Emergence of a Feminine Spirituality in *The Book of Martyrs*," *SCJ* 19 (1988): 63–80; Brad S. Gregory, "Prescribing and Describing Martyrdom: Menno's *Troestelijke Vermaninge* and *Het Offer des Heeren*," *MQR* 71 (1997): 603–613; David F. Wright, "The Testimony of Blood: The Charisma of Martyrdom," *BSac* 160 (2003): 387–397; Brad S. Gregory, "Martyrs and Saints," *A Companion to the Reformation World*, ed. R. Po-chia Hsia (Malden, Me., 2004), 455–470.

[57] Karl Rahner, "Dimensions of Martyrdom: A Plea for the Broadening of a Classical Concept," *Concilium* 163, no. 3 (1983): 9–11; Lacey Baldwin Smith, *Fools, Martyrs, Traitors: The Story of Martyrdom in the Western World* (New York, 1997), 3–20.

[58] Carol Piper Heming, *Protestants and the Cult of the Saints*, 26.

And certainly there were multiple audiences addressed—not only the community closest to the martyrs, but also a much wider readership, for which the propagandistic value of martyrs' stories was paramount.

As the first of the century's martyrologists, Luther also began his career as hymn writer with his first song (1523), a ballad of the story of the Reformation's first two martyrs,[59] which accompanied an open letter to Christians in the Netherlands.[60] Luther eventually wrote more than 36 hymns and was the greatest advocate of music among the major reformers of the sixteenth century.[61] Thus, this chapter explores

---

[59] Otto Brodde, "'Ein neues Lied wir heben an'! Martin Luther als 'Phonascus,'" *Luther* 34 (1963): 72–82; Martin Brecht, "Zum Verständnis von Luthers Lied, 'Ein feste Burg,'" *ARG* 70 (1979): 106–121; Markus Jenny, "Der Märtyrertod zweier Gesinnungsgenossen in Brüssel ließ Luther zum Lied als dem besten Medium der Propaganda für den neuen Glauben greifen," *Martin Luther und die Reformation in Deutschland* (Frankfurt, 1983), 296f.; Markus Jenny, *Luthers Geistliche Lieder und Kirchengesänge: Vollständige Neuedition in Ergänzung zu Band 35 der Weimarer Ausgabe* (Cologne, 1985), s. v., "Ein neues Lied wir heben an," 75–76; Paul F. Casey, "'Start Spreading the News': Martin Luther's First Published Song," in *In Laudem Caroli: Renaissance and Reformation Studies for Charles G. Nauert*, ed. James V. Mehl. SCES 49 (Kirksville, Mo., 1998), 75–94.

[60] Otto Clemen, "Die ersten Märtyrer des evangelischen Glaubens," *Beiträge zur Reformationsgeschichte aus Büchern und Handschriften der zwickauer Ratsschulbibliothek* 1 (1900–1903): 40–52.

[61] Henry Ward Beecher, "Relations of Music to Worship," *Yale Lectures on Preaching* 2 (Boston, 1902), 114–145; Walter E. Buszin, "Theology and Church Music as Bearers and Interpreters of the *Verbum Dei*," *CTM* 32 (1961): 15–27; Kurt Ihlenfeld, "Die himmlische Kunst Musica: Ein Blick in Luthers Briefe," *Luther* 34 (1963): 83–90; Oskar Söhngen, "Fundamental Considerations for a Theology of Music," in *The Musical Heritage of the Church*, ed. Theodore Hoelty-Nickel (St. Louis, 1963), 6:7–16; Jan M. Rahmelow, "Das Volkslied als publizistisches Medium und historische Quelle," *Jahrbuch für Volksliedforschung* 14 (1969): 11–26; Joe E. Tarry, "Music in the Educational Philosophy of Martin Luther," *Journal of Research in Music Education* 21 (1973): 355–365; Walter Blankenburg, "Luther und die Musik," in *Kirche und Musik: Gesammelte Aufsätze zur Geschichte der Gottesdienstlichen Musik*, ed. Walter Blankenburg (Göttingen, 1979), 17–30; Gerhard Hahn, "Zur Dimension des Neuen an Luthers Kirchenliedern," *Jahrbuch für Liturgik und Hymnologie* 26 (1982): 96–103; Oskar Söhngen, "Music and Theology: A Systematic Approach," *Journal of the American Academy of Religion Thematic Studies* 50, no. 1 (1983): 1–19; Joyce Irwin, "Shifting Alliances: The Struggle for a Lutheran Theology of Music," *JAAR Thematic Studies* 50, no. 1 (1983): 55–69; Inge Mager, "Lied und Reformation: Beobachtungen zur reformatorischen Singbewegung in norddeutschen Städten," in *Das Protestantische Kirchenlied im 16. und 17. Jahrhundert*, ed. Alfred Dürr and Walther Killy. Wolfenbütteler Forschungen 31 (Wiesbaden, 1986), 25–38; Edward Foley, "Martin Luther: A Model Pastoral Musician," *Currents in Theology & Mission* 14 (1987): 405–418; Helen Pietsch, "On Luther's Understanding of Music," *Lutheran Theological Journal* 26 (1992): 160–168; David W. Music, *Hymnology: A Collection of Source Readings.* Studies in Liturgical Musicology 4 (Lanham, Md., 1996), 35–50; Gregory E. Asimakoupoulos, "The Contribution of Martin Luther to Congregational Singing," *Covenant Quarterly* 56 (1998): 23–33; Dennis Marzolf, "Luther in the Pew: Song and Worship," *Reformation & Revival* 8 (1999): 105–120; 123–133; Daniel Zager, "Popular Music and

martyrological discourse in several genres, including dimensions of how music makes meaning, promotes feeling,[62] and contributed to the success of the Reformation.[63]

Chapter Four investigates the issues of grief, bereavement, mourning, and funerals—topics of great interest today, not only through the academic and popular renaissance of 'death and dying' literature but also theologically and socially.[64] For the role and function of the funeral rite has become a research interest, as it attempts to account for rapid and monumental shifts in contemporary funereal practice—in English-speaking countries—in the rites themselves, including the sermon or eulogy, and in the disposal of the body.[65] The funeral sermon has a

---

Music for the Church," *LuthFor* 36 (fall 2002): 20–27; Gordon A. Beck, "Questions About Current Lutheran Music Practices," *LuthFor* 37 (spring 2003): 52–55; Robert F. Hull, Jr., "The Myth of Luther's Barroom Music and A Plea for a Theology of Church Music," *Christian Standard* 128 (4 May 2003): 4–5; Joseph Herl, *Worship Wars in Early Lutheranism: Choir, Congregation, and Three Centuries of Conflict* (Oxford, 2005).

[62] Heinz Kohut, "Observations on the Psychological Functions of Music," *Journal of the American Psychoanalytic Association* 5 (1957): 389–407; Frank Howes, "A Critique of Folk, Popular and 'Art' Music," *British Journal of Aesthetics* 2 (1962): 239–248; Peter Stadlen, "The Aesthetics of Popular Music," *British Journal of Aesthetics* 2 (1962): 351–361; Pinchas Noy, "The Psychodynamic Meaning of Music, Part I: A Critical Review of the Psychoanalytic and Related Literature," *Journal of Music Therapy* 3 (1966): 126–134; , "The Psychodynamic Meaning of Music, Parts II–V," *Journal of Music Therapy* 4 (1967): 7–23, 45–51, 81–94, 128–131; Raymond Durgnat, "Rock, Rhythm and Dance," *British Journal of Aesthetics* 11 (1971): 28–47; John Broeck, "Music of the Fears," *Film Comment* 12 (1976): 56–60; Simon Frith, *Performing Rites: On the Value of Popular Music* (Cambridge, Mass., 1996), 5–82; Charles P. St-Onge, "Music, Worship, and Martin Luther," *Logia* 13, no. 2 (2004): 37–42; Raymond Warren, "Music and Spirituality: A Musician's Viewpoint," *Theology* 109 (2006): 83–92.

[63] Christopher Boyd Brown, *Singing the Gospel: Lutheran Hymns and the Success of the Reformation* (Cambridge, Mass., 2005), 1–25; Claude V. Palisca, *Music and Ideas in the Sixteenth and Seventeenth Centuries.* Studies in the History of Music Theory and Literature 1 (Urbana, 2006), especially chapter 11, "Music and Rhetoric."

[64] Francine Du Plessix Gray, "At Large and At Small: The Work of Mourning," *The American Scholar* 69 (summer 2000): 7–13.

[65] Alfred C. Rush, *Death and Burial in Christian Antiquity* (Washington, D.C., 1941); V. Gordon Childe, "Directional Changes in Funerary Practices During 50,000 Years," *Man* 45 (January–February 1945): 13–19; Robert L. Fulton, "The Clergyman and the Funeral Director: A Study in Role Conflict," *Social Forces* 39 (1961): 317–323; Jessica Mitford, *The American Way of Death* (New York, 1963); Eberhard Jüngel, *Death: The Riddle and the Mystery*, trans. Iain and Ute Nicol (Philadelphia, 1975); Geoffrey Rowell, *The Liturgy of Christian Burial: An Introductory Survey of the Historical Development of Christian Burial Rites* (London, 1977); Robert G. Hughes, *A Trumpet in Darkness: Preaching to Mourners* (Philadelphia, 1985); Eamon Duffy, "An Apology for Grief, Fear and Anger," *Priests & People* 5 (1991): 397–401; H. P. V. Renner, "A Christian Rite of Burial: An Instrument of Pastoral Care," *Lutheran Theological Journal* 26 (1992): 72–77; Tony Walter, "Dust Not Ashes: The American Preference for Burial," *Landscape* 32, no. 1 (1993): 42–48; H. Richard Rutherford, "Luther's 'Honest Funeral' Today: An Ecumenical Compari-

long history, with roots as a classical genre,[66] yet for Luther we have only four funeral messages he preached. Moreover, these messages come from just two occasions: the 'state funerals' of Saxon Elector Frederick the Wise (1525)[67] and of his brother and successor, John the Steadfast (1532).[68] In all four sermons, Luther preached from Paul's eschatological passage in 1 Thess. 4:13–18, and Chapter Four analyzes Luther's arguments in the 1532 sermons.[69] Given the few extant texts from that period and the concomitant abundance of texts from a later emergent genre of the Lutheran funeral sermon,[70] what shape did the

---

son," *Dialog* 32 (summer 1993): 178–184; Jessica Mitford, *The American Way of Death Revisited* (New York, 1998); Bryan D. Spinks, "Adiaphora: Marriage and Funeral Liturgies," *CTQ* 62 (1998): 7–23; Paul P. J. Sheppy, *Death Liturgy and Ritual*, Vol. 2, *A Pastoral and Liturgical Theology* (Aldershot, 2003); Thomas Lynch, "HBO's 'Six Feet Under': Grave Affairs," *ChrCent*, 2 November 2004, 18–23; Edward Schiappa, Peter B. Gregg, and Dean E. Hewes, "Can A Television Series Change Attitudes About Death? A Study of College Students and *Six Feet Under*," *DS* 28 (2004): 459–474; Thomas G. Long, "The Unbearable Lightness of Memorial Services," ibid., 3–8; Thomas E. Dipko, "The Paradox of the Funeral Order," ibid., 15–20; Jesse Garfield Truvillion, "Faith and Integrity At Graveside," ibid., 21–27; Scott Miller, "Reclaiming the Role of Lament in the Funeral Rite," ibid., 34–48.

[66] O. C. Crawford, "Laudatio Funebris," *Classical Journal* 37 (1941): 17–27; Sister Mary Edmond Fern, *The Latin Consolatio as A Literary Type* (St. Meinrad, Ind., 1941); Martin R. P. McGuire, "The Christian Funeral Oration," in *Funeral Orations by Saint Gregory Nazianzen and Saint Ambrose*, trans. Leo P. McCauley et al., with an Introduction by Martin R. P. McGuire. Fathers of the Church 22 (New York, 1953), vii–xxiii; Martin Elze, "Spätmittelalterliche Predigt im Angesicht des Todes," in *Leben angesichts des Todes: Beiträge zum theologischen Problem des Todes: Helmut Thielicke zum 60. Geburtstag*, ed. Bernhard Lohse and H. P. Schmidt (Tübingen, 1968), 89–99; John M. McManamon, "The Ideal Renaissance Pope: Funeral Oratory from the Papal Court," *Archivum Historiae Pontificiae* 14 (1976): 9–70; Susan Powell and Alan J. Fletcher, " 'In die sepulture seu trigintali': The Late Medieval Funeral and Memorial Sermon," *Leeds Studies in English* 12 (1981): 195–228; John M. McManamon, *Funeral Oratory and the Cultural Ideals of Italian Humanism* (Chapel Hill, 1989); David d'Avray, "The Comparative Study of Memorial Preaching," *Transactions of the Royal Historical Society* 40 (1990): 25–42; F. M. Eybl, "Leichenpredigt und Leichenrede," in *Historisches Wörterbuch der Rhetorik*, ed. Gert Ueding (Tübingen, 2001), 5:124–151.

[67] *WA* 17¹:196–227. Frederick died on 5 May 1525, and the funeral sermons were preached on 10 and 11 May.

[68] *LW* 51:231–255; *WA* 36:236–270. John died on 15 August 1532, and the funeral sermons were preached on 18 and 22 August.

[69] Gerhard Ebeling, "Des Todes Tod: Luthers Theologie der Konfrontation mit dem Tode," *Zeitschrift für Theologie und Kirche* 84 (1987): 162–194. At 165, note 18, Ebeling discusses Luther's preaching schedule and the textual history of the sermons. At 189–194 Ebeling provides fresh transcription of the text of the sermon from 22 December 1532 (1 Cor. 15:36f.).

[70] Hugo Grün, "Die Leichenrede im Rahmen der kirchlichen Beerdigung im 16. Jahrhundert," *Theologische Studien und Kritiken: Beiträge für Theologie und Religionswissenschaft* 95/96 (1929): 289–312; Verdun L. Saulnier, "L'Oraison Funèbre au XVIᵉ

funeral sermon take in the early years of the Luther movement? This chapter analyzes how Luther uses the funeral sermon to comfort an audience. These two state funeral messages give us a glimpse of how he offered support for survivors and helped make meaningful sense, in a public ritual, of a Christian's death. Our investigation will bring new perspectives upon such troubling questions facing us today as: (1) What is a funeral? (2) Whose funeral is it? (3) What meaning does grief have for the life of a Christian? and (4) What comfort is there for grief, and from whence does it come?

Chapter Five extends the exploration of bereavement, grief, and mourning. Grief is defined today as reaction—usually emotional response—to loss, particularly the loss of a loved one to death.[71] Bereavement is

---

Siècle," *Bibliothèque d'humanisme et Renaissance* 10 (1948): 124–157; Eberhard Winkler, *Die Leichenpredigt im deutschen Luthertum bis Spener*. Forschungen zur Geschichte und Lehre des Protestantismus 34 (Munich, 1967); Frederic B. Tromly, "'Accordinge to sounde religion': The Elizabethan Controversy Over the Funeral Sermon," *Journal of Medieval and Renaissance Studies* 13 (1983): 293–312; Rudolf Lenz, "Zur Funktion des Lebenslaufes in Leichenpredigten," in *Wer schreibt meine Lebensgeschichte? Biographie, Autobiographie, Hagiographie und ihre Entstehungszusammenhänge*, ed. Walter Sparn (Gütersloh, 1990), 93–104; Cornelia Niekus Moore, "Das erzählte Leben in der lutherischen Leichenpredigt: Anfang und Entwicklung im 16. Jahrhundert," *Wolfenbütteler Barocknachrichten* 29 (2002): 3–22.

[71] Corr, Nabe, and Corr, 210; Margaret S. Stroebe, Wolfgang Stroebe, and Robert O. Hansson, eds., *Handbook of Bereavement: Theory, Research, and Intervention* (Cambridge, 1993), 5; cf. Lyn H. Lofland, "The Social Shaping of Emotion: The Case of Grief," *Symbolic Interaction* 8 (1985): 171–190. Rosenblatt defines grief as "the blended emotional and cognitive reactions to a loss (in agreement with the Balinese studied by Wikan [U. Wikan, *Managing Turbulent Hearts* (Chicago, 1990)], that feelings and thoughts are not separable, at least when it comes to reactions to loss). The reactions to a loss that are most frequently part of grief in the United States include sorrow, anger, depression, anxiety, fear, unpleasant feelings of confusion, disorientation, and other 'down' emotions. But they may also include virtually any 'up' emotion, with the obvious ones being relief that a long and difficult illness has ended and joy at someone's entry to heaven. Grief can be seen as typically an amalgam of differing feeling/thought blends, with the amalgam changing from time to time for any specific person bereaved for a specific loss"; Paul C. Rosenblatt, "Grief That Does Not End," in *Continuing Bonds: New Understandings of Grief*, ed. Dennis Klass, Phyllis R. Silverman, and Steven L. Nickman (Washington, D.C., 1996), 45–58, here at 45. In another essay in that volume, Dennis Klass offers a succinct and technical definition of grief as "the processes by which the bereaved move from the equilibria in their inner and social worlds before a death to new equilibria after a death"; Dennis Klass, "The Deceased Child in the Psychic and Social Worlds of Bereaved Parents During the Resolution of Grief," in ibid., 199–215, here at 200; see also Robert E. Goss and Dennis Klass, *Dead but Not Lost: Grief Narratives in Religious Traditions* (Walnut Creek, Calif., 2005). For an earlier review of the literature on grief, see Beth L. Rodgers and Kathleen V. Cowles, "The Concept of Grief: An Analysis of Classical and Contemporary Thought," *DS* 15 (1991): 443–458.

the objective situation of having lost someone significant.[72] When we ask how may Christians (or anyone) express their grief, we are speaking of mourning,[73] and we open ourselves fully to matters of how our

---

[72] Stroebe, Stroebe, and Hansson, *Handbook*, 5; cf. Corr, Nabe, and Corr, 5.

[73] Stroebe, Stroebe, and Hansson, *Handbook*, 5; Corr, Nabe, and Corr (217) defines mourning as "the processes of coping with loss and grief, and thus the attempt to manage those experiences or learn to live with them by incorporating them into ongoing living." For an historical introduction to bereavement research, see Margaret S. Stroebe, Wolfgang Stroebe, and Robert O. Hansson, "Bereavement Research: An Historical Introduction," *Journal of Social Issues* 44, no. 3 (1988): 1–18. Important foundational studies began with Sigmund Freud, "On Mourning and Melancholia," *The Standard Edition of the Complete Psychological Works of Sigmund Freud* (London, 1959; originally published 1917), 14:237–258. The psychoanalytic tradition continues, however. See, for example, Therese Benedek, "Parenthood as A Developmental Phase: A Contribution to the Libido Theory," *Journal of the American Psychoanalytic Association* 7 (1959): 389–419; George Hagman, "Death of a Selfobject: Toward a Self Psychology of the Mourning Process," *Progress in Self-Psychology* 11 (1995): 189–205; idem, "Mourning: A Review and Reconsideration," *International Journal of Psycho-Analysis* 76 (1995): 909–925; idem, "Bereavement and Neurosis," *Journal of the American Academy of Psychoanalysis* 23 (1995): 635–653; idem, "The Role of the Other in Mourning," *Psychoanalytic Quarterly* 65 (1996): 327–352; Ester R. Shapiro, "Grief in Freud's Life: Reconceptualizing Bereavement in Psychoanalytic Theory," *Psychoanalytic Psychology* 13 (1996): 547–566; Robert Gaines, "Detachment and Continuity: The Two Tasks of Mourning," *Contemporary Psychoanalysis* 33 (1997): 549–571; George Hagman, "Beyond Decathexis: Toward A New Psychoanalytic Understanding and Treatment of Mourning," in *Meaning Reconstruction and the Experience of Loss*, ed. Robert A. Neimeyer (Washington, D.C., 2001), 13–31; and Jerry Adler, "Freud in Our Midst," *Newsweek*, 27 March 2006, 43–49. Other groundbreaking work on grief: Eric Lindemann, "Symptomatology and Management of Acute Grief," *American Journal of Psychiatry* 101 (1944): 141–148; John Bowlby, "Processes of Mourning," *International Journal of Psycho-Analysis* 42 (1961): 317–340; Robert S. Weiss, "Loss and Recovery," *Journal of Social Issues* 44, no. 3 (1988): 37–52; Colin Murray Parkes, "Bereavement as a Psychosocial Transition: Processes of Adaptation to Change," *Journal of Social Issues* 44, no. 3 (1988): 53–65 [reprinted in Stroebe, Stroebe, and Hansson, *Handbook*, 91–101]. Much bereavement, grief, and mourning research presents a model of stages, phases, or tasks, involving a process of adjustment to loss through 'grief work.' For a different view, see Margaret Stroebe and Wolfgang Stroebe, "Does 'Grief Work' Work?" *Journal of Consulting and Clinical Psychology* 59 (1991): 479–482; Margaret Stroebe, "Coping With Bereavement: A Review of the Grief Work Hypothesis," *Omega* 26 (1992–1993): 19–42; Tony Walter, "A New Model of Grief: Bereavement and Biography," *Mortality* 1 (1996): 7–25. Efforts to put these issues into social, cultural, and historical contexts can be found in George R. Krupp and Bernard Kligfeld, "The Bereavement Reaction: A Cross-Cultural Evaluation," *Journal of Religion and Health* 1 (1962): 222–246; Gerard J. Gruman, "Ethics of Death and Dying: Historical Perspective," *Omega* 9 (1978–1979): 203–237; Julie Ann Wambach, "The Grief Process as A Social Construct," *Omega* 16 (1985–1986): 201–211; Margaret Stroebe, et al, "Broken Hearts or Broken Bonds: Love and Death in Historical Perspective," *American Psychologist* 47 (October 1992): 1205–1212; Paul C. Rosenblatt, "Grief: The Social Context of Private Feelings," in Stroebe, Stroebe, and Hansson, *Handbook*, 102–111. Studies of death from a theological, sociological, or anthropological view are Virginia Moore, *Ho for Heaven! Man's Changing Attitude Toward Dying* (New York, 1946); Robert Blauner, "Death and Social Structure," *Psychiatry* 29 (1966): 378–394; Philippe

suffering and loss relate to the bonds we feel toward loved ones—of family, community, and church. Here is where death's impact comes to us as loss of valued persons. People have always tried to console and comfort the grieving, and their attempts come through social exchange and through discursive practices. Moreover, efforts to comfort are shaped in part by—and come to be appreciated for: (1) the losses comforters themselves have had from death and suffering; (2) the relationship of the comforter to the bereaved, and to the deceased.

The genre of the consolatory letter has a long classical and Christian tradition.[74] What can be learned from Luther's consolatory letters? A sampling of his consolatory correspondence, written over two decades (1524–1545) to grieving spouses and parents, informs us not only as to how he used Christian *topoi*; we also learn how Luther drew from his own life experiences in the composition of these letters. We recall that in 1524 he was a celibate friar whose parents were still living, yet even by then three or four of his own siblings had already died.[75] Within a year he married, and in the next six years this family man and his wife had three children. He had also endured plagues, temptations, the deaths of close friends, and several episodes of chronic illnesses; further, he had

---

Aries, *Western Attitudes Toward Death: From the Middle Ages to the Present*, trans. Patricia M. Ranum (Baltimore, 1974); Gary S. Gerson, "The Psychology of Grief and Mourning in Judaism," *Journal of Religion and Health* 16 (1977): 260–274; Bartholomew J. Collopy, "Theology and the Darkness of Death," *Theological Studies* 39 (1978): 22–54; Richard Huntington and Peter Metcalf, *Celebrations of Death: The Anthropology of Mortuary Ritual* (Cambridge, 1979); Philippe Aries, *The Hour of Our Death*, trans. Helen Weaver (New York, 1981); Philip Gill, "Death in The Christian Community: Theology, Funeral Ritual and Pastoral Care From the Perspective of Victor Turner's Ritual Process Model," *Modern Believing* 35, no. 2 (1994): 17–24; Tony Walter, "Natural Death and the Noble Savage," *Omega* 30 (1994–1995): 237–248; James P. Gubbins, "Grief's Lesson in Moral Epistemology: A Phenomenological Investigation," *The Annual of the Society of Christian Ethics* 17 (1997): 145–165; Catherine Bell, "Ritual Tensions: Tribal and Catholic," *Studia Liturgica* 32 (2002): 15–28.

[74] Jane F. Mitchell, "Consolatory Letters in Basil and Gregory Nazianzen," *Hermes* 96 (1968): 299–318; H. G. Haile, "Luther as Renaissance Writer," in *The Renaissance and Reformation Germany: An Introduction*, ed. Gerhart Hoffmeister (New York, 1977), 141–156; Ute Menneck-Haustein, *Luthers Trostbriefe*. Quellen und Forschungen zur Reformationsgeschichte 56 (Gütersloh, 1989); Warren Boutcher, "Literature, Thought or Fact? Past and Present Directions in the Study of the Early Modern Letter," in *Self-Presentation and Social Identification: The Rhetoric and Pragmatics of Letter Writing in Early Modern Times*, ed. Toon Van Houdt, et al. Supplementa Humanistica Lovaniensia 18 (Leuven, 2002), 137–163; Judith Rice Henderson, "Humanist Letter Writing: Private Conversation or Public Forum?" *Self-Presentation and Social Identification*, 17–38.

[75] Martin Brecht, *Martin Luther*, 1:7, says that one sister and two or three brothers died. Two of the brothers died from plague in 1505, the year Martin entered the Augustinian monastery at Erfurt; ibid., 9; cf. Lewis W. Spitz, "Psychohistory and History: The Case of Young Man Luther," *Soundings* 56 (1973): 182–209, here at 194.

also buried an infant (Elizabeth, d. 1528) and both of his parents.[76] In the decade that followed, however, came the most shattering personal death, when in 1542 the Luthers buried their daughter Magdalena (at age 13). Several letters contain personal references to Luther's own losses, and he wrote most of them upon request.[77] Such invitations came because he was a close friend of the bereaved, was professor (and thus was *in loco parentis*) to a now-deceased university student, or because his reputation as compassionate theologian was thought appropriate to address the difficult circumstances facing the bereaved.[78] To us, portions of Luther's letters may seem harsh, for he advised people

[76] Ernst Kroker, *Katharina von Bora, Martin Luthers Frau: Ein Lebens- und Charakterbild.* Biographien bedeutender Frauen 6 (Leipzig, 1906); Ian D. K. Siggins, "Luther's Mother Margarete," *HTR* 71 (1978): 125–150; Lyndal Roper, "Luther: Sex, Marriage and Motherhood," *History Today* 33 (December 1983): 33–38; Steven Ozment, "Luther and the Family," *Harvard Library Bulletin* 32 (1984): 36–55.

[77] A sizable body of modern research exists on studying particular grief situations, especially—grief of spouses (which I am omitting), of parents (in great depth) and, to some extent, siblings: Howard Becker, "The Sorrow of Bereavement," *Journal of Abnormal and Social Psychology* 27 (1933): 391–410; Paul C. Rosenblatt, Douglas A. Jackson, and Rose P. Walsh, "Coping with Anger and Aggression in Mourning," *Omega* 3 (1972): 271–284; *Grief and Mourning in Cross-Cultural Perspective* (n.c., 1976); Catherine M. Sanders, "A Comparison of Adult Bereavement in the Death of A Spouse, Child, and Parent," *Omega* 10 (1979–1980): 303–322; Lynn Videka-Sherman, "Coping with the Death of A Child: A Study Over Time," *American Journal of Orthopsychiatry* 52 (1982): 688–698; Dennis Klass, "Self-help Groups for the Bereaved: Theory, Theology, and Practice," *Journal of Religion and Health* 21 (1982): 307–324; Atle Dyregrov and Stig Berge Matthiesen, "Similarities and Differences in Mothers' and Fathers' Grief Following the Death of an Infant," *Scandinavian Journal of Psychology* 28 (1987): 1–15; John W. James and Frank Cherry, *The Grief Recovery Handbook* (New York, 1988); C. Martel Bryant, "Commentary: Fathers Grieve, Too," *Journal of Perinatology* 9 (1989): 437–441; David E. Balk, "The Self-Concepts of Bereaved Adolescents: Sibling Death and Its Aftermath," *Journal of Adolescent Research* 5 (January 1990): 112–132; "Sibling Death, Adolescent Bereavement, and Religion," *DS* 15 (1991): 1–20; Charles W. Brice, "Paradoxes of Maternal Mourning," *Psychiatry* 54 (February 1991): 1–12; Jane L. Littlewood, et al, "Gender Differences in Parental Coping Following Their Child's Death," *British Journal of Guidance & Counselling* 19 (1991): 139–147; Reiko Schwab, "Effects of A Child's Death on the Marital Relationship: A Preliminary Study," *DS* 16 (1992): 141–154; Simon Shimshon Rubin, "The Death of A Child is Forever: The Life Course Impact of Child Loss," in Stroebe, Stroebe, and Hansson, *Handbook*, 285–299; Jeffrey Kauffman, "Dissociative Functions in the Normal Mourning Process," *Omega* 28 (1993–94): 31–38; Gordon Riches and Pamela Dawson, "'An Intimate Loneliness': Evaluating the Impact of A Child's Death on Parental Self-Identity and Marital Relationships," *Journal of Family Therapy* 16 (1996): 1–22; idem, "Communities of Feeling: The Culture of Bereaved Parents," *Mortality* 1 (1996): 143–161; Dennis Klass, *The Spiritual Lives of Bereaved Parents* (Philadelphia, 1999).

[78] Steven Ozment, *Flesh and Spirit: Private Life in Early Modern Germany* (New York, 1999), 262–265; Lewis Spitz, "Luther's Social Concern for Students," in *The Social History of the Reformation*, ed. Lawrence P. Buck and Jonathon W. Zophy (Columbus, 1972), 249–270.

to moderate their grief. However, empathy also emerges as a tool of comfort, yet this empathy is grounded in the gospel and barely resembles the approach of Western contemporary grief therapies.[79] So we must account for the social and theological context of the sixteenth century and compare it with (and contrast it to) our own. Understanding the cultural background and the theology Luther held enables us to put these strategies of harshness and empathy into perspective.

Chapter Six explores another genre of discourse that challenges our modern child-centered families and our health-conscious and fitness-preoccupied culture.[80] It holds particular promise for people who have a sobering awareness of the prospect of infectious disease or biological agents that might be used in international terrorism, in this post-11 September 2001 world.[81] This chapter analyzes Luther's open letter written to offer advice requested on what to do in the face of mortal danger from infectious disease that threatened German cities ("On Whether One May Flee From A Deadly Plague" [1527]).[82] In this document Luther tackles the ethical and theological dilemmas that

---

[79] Considerable research effort has gone into the question of whether grief is normal or diseased (pathological): Edmund H. Volkart, "Bereavement and Mental Health," in *Explorations in Social Psychiatry*, ed. Alexander H. Leighton, John A. Clausen, and Robert N. Wilson (New York, 1957), 281–307; George L. Engel, "Is Grief a Disease?" *Psychosomatic Medicine* 23 (1961): 19–22; E. K. Rynearson, "Psychotherapy of Pathologic Grief: Revisions and Limitations," *Psychiatric Clinics of North America* 10 (1987): 487–499; Loretta M. Kopelman, "Normal Grief: Good or Bad? Health or Disease?" *Philosophy, Psychiatry, & Psychology* 1 (1994): 209–220; Stephen Wilkinson, "Is 'Normal Grief' A Mental Disorder?" *Philosophical Quarterly* 50 (2000): 289–304.

[80] Linda A. Pollock, *Forgotten Children: Parent-Child Relations from 1500–1900* (Cambridge, 1983), 1. Dennis Klass observes: "In the contemporary developed world, as civic discourse has transformed into opinion polls and as work has moved into bureaucracies, home and children have become the basis of personal identity and the constellation of meanings by which important decisions can be made"; "The Deceased Child," in Klass, Silverman, and Nickman, eds., *Continuing Bonds*, 200, note 1; Klass cites R. F. Baumeister, *Meanings of Life* (New York, 1991) and S. Coontz, *The Way We Never Were: American Families and the Nostalgia Trap* (New York, 1992).

[81] Wolfgang Böhmer, "Martin Luther und das Wittenberger Medizinalwesen zu seiner Zeit," *Die Zeichen der Zeit* 37 (1983): 107–116; Arthur E. Imhof, "From the Old Mortality Pattern to the New" (1985); Heinrich Dornmeier, "Religiös motiviertes Verhalten von Laien und Klerikern in Grenz- und Krisensituationen: die Pest als 'Testfall wahrer Frömmigkeit,'" in *Laienfrömmigkeit im späten Mittelalter: Formen, Funktionen, politisch-soziale Zusammenhänge*, ed. Klaus Schreiner. Schriften des Historischen Kollegs, Kolloquien 20 (Munich, 1992), 331–397; Jürgen Helm, "Wittenberger Medizin im 16. Jahrhundert," *Martin Luther und seiner Universität: Vorträge analßlich des 450. Todestages des Reformators, in Auftrag der Stiftung Leucorea an der Martin-Luther-Universität-Halle-Wittenberg* (Cologne, 1998), 95–115.

[82] *LW* 43:119–138; *WA* 23:339–379.

persons—especially parents and community leaders—face when wide-spread serious illness and death are likely to strike, something startlingly relevant today. Analysis of this work reveals Luther's reasoning and argu-mentation as he helps readers sort through their responsibilities to self, to loved ones, and to persons in their charge. He grapples with notions of God's providence and human responsibility, and how these realms dictate care for the sick and dying. Luther also offers instruction and advice about the burial of the dead, for not unlike today, his generation debated the issues surrounding extramural burial.[83] Moreover, Luther shared strongly held views on respect for the dead and the awareness of one's own finitude before God. In this chapter we see that Luther anticipated the burial debates of some German cities by a decade or more, attempting to balance the dignity with which humans ought to be buried[84] with the need to abstain from what reformers considered a misguided preoccupation with the bodies of the dead.[85] Thus, this

---

[83] Craig M. Koslofsky, *The Reformation of the Dead: Death and Ritual in Early Modern Germany, 1450–1700* (London, 2000), 41–46. See also his "Death and Ritual in Refor-mation Germany" (Unpublished Ph.D. dissertation, U. of Michigan, 1994), 56–132, and Susan C. Karant-Nunn, *The Reformation of Ritual: An Interpretation of Early Modern Germany* (London, 1997), 178–186. See also Hugo Grün, "Das kirchliche Begräbniswe-sen im ausgehenden Mittelalter," *Theologische Studien und Kritiken* 102 (1930): 341–381; Herbert Derwein, *Geschichte des Christlichen Friedhofs in Deutschland* (Frankfurt, 1931); Fritz Schnelbögl, "Friedhofverlegungen im 16. Jahrhundert," *Jahrbuch für fränkische Landesforschung* 34/35 (1974–75): 109–120; Elisabeth Blum, "Tod und Begräbnis in evangelischen Kirchenliedern aus dem 16. Jahrhundert," in *Studien zur Thematik des Todes im 16. Jahrhundert*. Wolfenbütteler Forschungen 22, ed. Paul Richard Blum (Wolfenbüttel, 1983), 97–110; Craig Koslofsky, "Die Trennung der Lebenden von den Toten: Friedhofverlegungen und die Reformation in Leipzig, 1536," in *Memoria als Kultur*. Veröffentlichungen des Max-Planck-Instituts für Geschichte 121, ed. Otto Gerhard Oexle (Göttingen, 1995), 335–385; idem, "Controlling the Body of the Suicide in Saxony," in *From Sin to Insanity: Suicide in Early Modern Europe*, ed. Jeffrey R. Watt (Ithaca, 2004), 48–63; Philip Bachelor, *Sorrow & Solace: The Social World of the Cemetery* (Amityville, N.Y., 2004). Bachelor's work is comprehensive and unique in that it includes not only discussion of grief and bereavement literature but also presents both qualitative and quantitative studies of visitors to cemeteries in Australia—who they are, why they come, how they feel, what they do, etc. Besides a treasure trove of the most recent data (and statements from mourners) on practically every aspect of death, grief, and burial, he includes a glossary of approximately 350 terms associated with death, funerals, beliefs, cemeteries, and mourning.

[84] Susan C. Karant-Nunn, "'Not Like the Unreasoning Beasts': Rhetorical Efforts to Separate Humans and Animals in Early Modern Germany," in *Cultures of Communication from Reformation to Enlightenment: Constructing Publics in the Early Modern German Lands*, ed. James Van Horn Melton (Aldershot, 2002), 225–238, here at 234.

[85] Frederick S. Paxton, *Christianizing Death: The Creation of a Ritual Process in Early Medieval Europe* (Ithaca, 1990); Joachim Whaley, "Symbolism for the Survivors: The Disposal of the Dead in Hamburg in the Late Seventeenth and Eighteenth Centuries,"

chapter brings together one's regard for death and how personal safety and personal duty to the living and dead interact, showing us: (1) how similar or dissimilar are the dangers we worry about, in comparison to those of our predecessors; and (2) how our resources—of technology, wisdom, and divine assistance—compare to those to which Luther turns.

To be sure, when it comes to life experiences that threaten to challenge one's faith—that God alone is to be worshiped and that Christ's atoning death and resurrection are sufficient—nothing in comparison rivals death, grief, and all that goes with them. The death of loved ones is "one of the most frequent and painful of afflictions attendant upon the divinely ordained ordering of human life in community and family."[86] Our confusion about death makes it "difficult to empathize with the terminally ill person and, after his death, with his survivors."[87] Death and grief can give rise to feelings of futility or the desire to venerate the memory of deceased loved ones in idolatrous ways. So the chapters in this book analyze many important works of Luther on death and suffering, works that should prove interesting and relevant to contemporary readers, particularly Christians.

The works analyzed here will show how untenable is the thesis of Richard Marius, *Martin Luther: The Christian between God and Death* (1999).[88]

---

in *Mirrors of Mortality: Studies in the Social History of Death*, ed. Joachim Whaley (New York, 1981), 80–105; Vanessa Harding, "Burial Choice and Burial Location in Later Medieval London," in *Death in Towns: Urban Responses to the Dying and the Dead, 100–1600*, ed. Steven Bassett (London, 1992), 119–135; Eric T. Myers, "The Burial Rites of John Calvin?" *CW* 38, no. 3 (2004–2005): 28–33. On burial in Judaism and Early Christianity see Elizabeth M. Bloch-Smith, "The Cult of the Dead in Judah: Interpreting the Material Remains," *JBL* 111 (1992): 213–224; Jodi Magness, "Ossuaries and the Burials of Jesus and James," *JBL* 124 (2005): 121–154.

[86] Jane E. Strohl, "Luther and the Word of Consolation," *LTSB* 67 (winter 1987): 23–34, here at 27.

[87] Joseph Bayly, *The Last Thing We Talk About*, 20.

[88] For published reviews, see Heiko A. Oberman, "Varieties of Protest," *New Republic*, 16 August 1999, 40–45; idem, "Review of Marius, *Martin Luther: The Christian between God and Death*," *The Historian* 62 (2000): 926–927; Russell C. Kleckley, in *Journal of Religion* 81 (2001): 643–644; Mark U. Edwards, in *ChrCent*, 17 November 1999; Eamon Duffy in *Commonweal*, 10 September 1999; Scott H. Hendrix in *Theology Today* 56 (October 1999); Robert Benne, in *Review of Politics* 62 (2000): 188–191; James D. Tracy, in *Catholic Historical Review* 86 (2000): 324–326; Graham Tomlin, in *Journal of Ecclesiastical History* 51 (2000): 409; Martin Brecht, in *Church History* 69 (2000): 143–147 (with Rejoinder by Marius, 147–149); D. Lyle Dabney, in *Theological Studies* 61 (2000): 156–158; Tom Scott, in *English Historical Review* 114 (1999): 1301–1302; Gerald Strauss, in *History* 28 (1999): 27–28; Carter Lindberg in *LQ* 13 (1999): 359–362. Marius's examination of Luther's writings essentially ends at 1526. Of the writings I have analyzed here in this

Marius set out to show that Luther's fundamental questions were, "Can I believe that God has the power to raise us from the dead?" and "How does the Christian deal with the terror that death evokes while reaching for a faith that the triumph over death is possible?" Moreover, Marius's book holds that Luther's theology arose from those two elemental queries and that his 'furious defense' of his own doctrines stemming from those questions is evidence that they are essentially tenuous dogmas, on shaky biblical grounds. However, as several of my chapters will show, Luther's "greatest terror, ...the fear of death—death in itself" is dwarfed by the superlative confidence the Christian can have in Christ and his resurrection.[89]

Finally, by employing a method of rhetorical analysis that, of course, takes seriously these writings' content and context, but which also scrutinizes carefully the style of the writings—the *way* Luther argues—we will see the power of language to do its most profound tasks. For Luther puts words to work in order to invite a reader's attention—so as to explore the most profound (the Scriptures), speak about the unspeakable (death), evoke the deepest feelings (grief), praise the most lofty (Christ), confound the worst fears (of sin and the devil), refute the enemy's greatest temptations (doubt and unbelief), and promote the most important actions (preparation for eternity).

---

book, Marius comments only briefly on the "Sermon On Preparing to Die," the "Letter to the Christians in the Netherlands," and a few of the consoling letters. However, he does offer a few pages of substantive comment on the 1525 funeral sermons for Frederick the Wise.

[89] Richard Marius, *Martin Luther: The Christian between God and Death* (Cambridge, Mass., 1999), xiiif.

CHAPTER ONE

"THINK ABOUT THESE THINGS":
LUTHER'S "FOURTEEN CONSOLATIONS" (1519)

Self-help books of various sorts—on diets, herbal remedies, exercise, meditation, 'life strategies,' etc.—claim to provide today's afflicted Christian abundant prospects for health and recovery.[1] In early modern Europe people often turned to the saints for assistance and comfort. Luther's "Fourteen Consolations" requires instead that readers turn to Christ.

I. *Orientation to Luther's Document*

This is the longest of Luther's writings that we are examining. Moreover, it puts death into a larger context of suffering and its place in the providence and provision of God. In order to approach Luther's book properly, one needs to be informed about its reception and intention. Consequently, I consider here the production aspects of the book and then take note of its preliminary parts (Preface, Letter of Dedication, and Introduction). Only the last item was included in the original printings; Luther added the first two items in 1536.

Originally written to comfort a gravely ill Frederick the Wise (1463, 1486–1525), Luther's "Fourteen Consolations" was eagerly received by readers of Latin and German. He finished the document in August 1519, and it was first printed in 1520 in Wittenberg.[2] In addition, that same year four more Latin editions were published in Leipzig, Augsburg,

---

[1] "The good choice is no longer the choice that is right according to external authority, but simply the choice that I have made: it is authenticated simply by me, the chooser....Discovering needs thus becomes the project of the individual, ensuing in a never-ending quest for the self, with seekers devouring therapies and self-help psychology books and meditative techniques without end. If once the priest told me how to live, now the therapist helps me to find my own way"; Tony Walter, *The Revival of Death*, 27.

[2] Wittenberg: Johann Rhau-Grunenberg; Josef Benzing, *Lutherbibliographie: Verzeichnis der Gedruckten Schriften Martin Luthers bis zu dessen Tod*. Bibliotheca Bibliographica Aureliana 10 (Baden-Baden, 1965), Nr. 591, designated 'A' in *WA* 6:101.

Cologne, and Zwolle.[3] In 1521 a Latin edition from Basel was released.[4] Also in 1520 Georg Spalatin (1484–1545) prepared a German translation at Luther's request, and five editions in all (at Wittenberg, Leipzig, and Augsburg) were printed, with two additional printings in 1522 and 1525.[5] There were also translations into Dutch (1521), French (1534), and English (1538).[6]

Luther himself oversaw a 'revised' Latin edition in 1536, in which he claims to have restored the sense of his original (which he felt had been mutilated by the many subsequent editions).[7] He refused to update anything, so as to preserve the document's historical meaning. Luther claimed in the 1536 Preface that the thought contained in the present edition reflected his thoughts at that earlier time (1519) and, when viewed nearly two decades later, would thus provide "proof of my progress and also please my adversaries by giving them something on which they can vent their malice" (*WA* 6:104.12–13).[8]

Also omitted until 1536 in the Latin printings, but included in all the German editions, is the Letter of Dedication (*LW* 42:121–124; *WA* 6:104–106). While not originally included (and therefore not available to Frederick), Luther's piece provides us a glimpse of his theology of caregiving. We read arguments from Scripture about what believers are to do when they discover people in need, this information coming to us in the context of Luther's relationship with, and responsibility to, his prince. An outline of the dedication's organization can be seen as a series of five steps: (1) Christ commanded us to minister to others, and in the incarnation he also set an example of ministering to others; (2) Christ himself suffers when anyone—especially a Christian—is sick; so fulfilling our duty by ministering to a sick brother is ministering to Christ; (3) The significant role of Frederick as head of state means his fate is to be shared by his subjects, of whom Luther is one; (4) All subjects have a duty not only to suffer along with their head, but also

---

[3] Benzing Nr. 592–95 ('B'–'D' in *WA* 6:101).

[4] Benzing Nr. 596 ('E' in *WA* 6:101).

[5] Benzing Nr. 598–604 ('a'–'g' in *WA* 6:102f.). I have examined a modern German version, *Vierzehn Trostmittel für Mühlselige und Beladene*, edited by G. Kawerau, in *Luthers Werke für das christliche haus*, ed. G. Buchwald et al., vol. 7, *Erbauliche Schriften* (Braunschweig, 1891), 5–60.

[6] Benzing Nr. 605–608.

[7] Wittenberg: Josef Klug; Benzing Nr. 597 ('F' in *WA* 6:101).

[8] "...testimonium ostendere mei profectus et gratificari Antilogistis, ut habeant quo suam malitiam exerceant."

to pray for his health; this book is a special consolation to that end; (5) Luther explains the book's structure, with its parallels to (and contrasts with) the 'fourteen saints.' As it happens, Luther's manner of arguing in the Preface (and also in the Introduction) provides a preview of some of his style in the body of the document—in other words, nearly two decades later much of his style still persists: in his use of superlatives, crafted dialogue, and a 'how much more' strategy.

In the first two steps Luther sets a pattern begun in the Preface and salutation:[9] he speaks in a language of superlatives, for which he finds sanction in his topic and in Scripture. He writes for the 'most excellent [*ad optimum*]' prince, citing the 'brightest example [*illustrissimum exemplum*]' of Jesus in descending from the bosom of the Father, taking on our 'most wretched [*calamitosissimam*]' life. However, the power of Jesus' 'illustrious example [*illustre exemplum*]' resides not only in its pattern fit for a leader of Frederick's stature; all Christians have been given a commandment (*mandatum*; later, 'divine commandment [*divini mandati*]') to perform 'humanitarian services [*officia humanitatis*]' or 'works of mercy [*misericordiae*]' for those 'afflicted and in a state of calamity [*afflictis et calamitosis*]' (*WA* 104.21–105.6). Luther's use of superlatives plays a strong role at various points throughout the entire document, and it seems consistent here with the high style of a letter of dedication.

Moreover, this language also helps do justice to the urgency of the topic, and Luther's agenda—at least here in the Letter of Dedication—can be seen in his attempt to capture the thrust of Matt. 25:41–45, where, following his quote of v. 41a ("Depart from me, you cursed ones, into everlasting fire") and 43b ("I was sick, and you did not visit me"), he elaborates on his own: "With gross ingratitude [*extreme ingratus*] for the supreme blessings [*summis benefitiis*] bestowed by me upon you and the whole world, you have not by even the smallest service [*levissimis*] come to aid your brethren—no, me—Christ, your God and Savior, in the brethren" (*WA* 6:105.7–11). Luther's warrant for—i.e., major premise—authorizing the command to serve the sick comes from the

---

[9] The Salutation reads: "ILLVSTRISSIMO PRINCIPI ET DOMINO DOMINO FRIDERICO, || SAXONIAE DVCI, SACRI ROM. IMP. ARCHIMARSCHALCO, || ET ELECTORI, LANDGRAVIO TVRINGIAE, MARCHIONI, || MISNAE, DOMINO SVO CLEMENTISSIMO" (104.16–19). Luther uses 'Most Illustrious Prince' [*Illustrissime Princeps*] once more, as direct address, in the letter of dedication (105.12). He uses 'your Lordship' [*tua dominatus*, etc., often abbreviated *tua D.* or *TD*] in indirect speech roughly 15 times in the letter of dedication.

Scriptures, namely the Matt. 25 passage, but also from Luke 6:36.[10] There Jesus names them (Luther uses *vocat*) works of mercy (*misericordiae*) that he commands others to perform, precisely because the Father in heaven is merciful (*misericors*). In Isa. 43:24, the only text Luther actually cites, we find more of the strong language that inspired him to attribute the urgency of superlatives to this matter of one's obligation to the sick (*morbo*), the captives (*captives*), the neighbor (*proximo*): "You have burdened me with your sins, and you have wearied me with your iniquities" (*WA* 6:105.3f.).[11] Luther found the 'infinite love [*immensum amorem*]' that Christ had for all people (*genus humanum*) to be a fact that merited all the linguistic resources he could muster in its explication and defense.

Luther takes seriously the 'grave illness [*gravi morbo*]' of Frederick, which is accompanied by Christ's sickness (*aegrotare*). Using crafted dialogue, Luther argues that Christians do not bear (*patitur*) such evils that others suffer but that Christ himself bears them: "I cannot pretend that I do not hear the voice of Christ as it cries out to me out of your Lordship's body and flesh, saying, 'Look, I am sick [*Ecce infirmor hic*]'" (*WA* 6:105.15f.). Since Christians live in Christ, 'we' have a duty to visit and console (*visitemus et consolemur*) those who are afflicted with sickness (*adversa*), especially to the 'household of faith [*domesticis fidei*].' Thus, Luther has cogently explicated the logic in Matt. 25 (to minister to Christ's own is to minister to Him, since they are *in Him*). Quoting Matt. 25:40 ('unto the least [*minimo*] of mine') and citing Paul at Gal. 6:10, Luther argues that because Christians are obligated to "those bound to us by intimate ties [*necessitudine nobiscum coniunctos*]," he has a duty (*offitii*) to produce this 'little writing [*aliquo scripto*]' (*WA* 6:105.17–23).

Steps three and four find Luther acknowledging 'other reasons [*alias . . . rationes*]' for writing this book; the focal object shifts from Christ to Frederick. Unlike his lateral relationship with—and responsibility to—other believers, Luther's role as his prince's subject prompts him to see Frederick as a God-appointed national protector. Seeing himself and his prince as a 'member with its head [*membrum cum capite*],' Luther argues that he himself shares with all subjects the blessings of "all our

---

[10] *LW* 42:122 cites Luke 6:36, whereas *WA* 6:104 cites both Luke 6:36 and Matt. 25:34ff.

[11] "In peccatis tuis fecisti me laborare et in iniquitatitibus tuis mihi fecisti negotium &c." It is clear from the '&c.' that Luther had the entire context in mind; despite Israel's sin, God came to save them.

fortunes, all our safety and happiness [*omnes nostrae fortunae, omnis incolu-mitas et foelicitas nostra*]" and that they 'suffer with you [*quasi aegrotare*]' (*WA* 6:105.26–28). Whether this is the flattering style of the letter of dedication or the sincere assessment due the times, Luther declares the special position that Frederick holds for his subjects. He suggests to his prince that he holds a responsibility to his country not only to protect but also to lead, by obeying God. Luther claims that this duty is to 'much more [*multo magis*]' than offering consolation and of making Frederick's condition 'our own [*familiariter*]' (*WA* 6:105.34–38). Apparently Luther counts people's prayers as more effectual than their ability to console their prince. But as a writer, he can do something more, explaining his duty to render 'special service [*singulari aliquo*].' Acknowledging the request by Spalatin, one of Frederick's chaplins (*a sacris*), to present a 'spiritual consolation [*consolationem aliquam spiritualem*],' Luther accepts this 'friendly counsel [*amici consilio*].' He trusts (*spero*) that the book will be a great help (*maxime fore utilem*) to "uplift and strengthen the pious heart [*mens pia erigenda ac confirmanda est*]." He offers it for "diligent reading and contemplation [*diligenti lectione et consideratione*]," in order to bring 'some comfort [*nonnihil acquiescat*],' closing with the signature of 'your subject, Martin Luther, Doctor' (*WA* 6:106.1–19).[12]

Step five of the Letter of Dedication, obviously, precedes the closing signature, and is Luther's account of the book's purpose and structure. Since this material is an expansion of what he had put into the Introduction in 1519, I will simply state Luther's directions here; when they occur again in the Introduction, I shall analyze both Luther's directions and the deviations from his plan.

In a few short lines he explains how he has composed fourteen chapters (*quatuordecim capita*) 'after the fashion of an altar screen [*in tabula digesta*].' He names the chapters Fourteen Consolations (*tessaradecados*). Such a designation is interesting, especially when one hears Luther out. For *tessaradecados* (accusative plural) is from Greek denoting 'fourteen,' but *tessara* (Greek, 'four') also may trigger associations with *tessera* (Latin, a 'token,' 'sign,' or even 'mosaic'). By using the term *Tessaradecas* (nominative plural), as he does here and in his title, Luther may be calling attention, not only to the number (fourteen) but also to the 'sign' nature of his book, its visual function as a mnemonic, meditative device. As he

---

[12] Luther's signature on the title page ('Martin Luther, Augustinian at Wittenberg') reflects the broader audience in view.

continues, Luther calls his structure a spiritual screen (*spiritualis tabula*), not one of silver (*argentea*), as would hang above the altar. Indeed, a limewood panel of 84 cm by 127 cm (33 inches by 50 inches) depicting the Fourteen Holy Helpers (*Vierzehnheiligen*)—dating from ca. 1505 and painted by Lucas Cranach the Elder (1472–1553)—still hangs above the altar in the *Marienkirche* at Torgau, Frederick's electoral residence.[13]

The physical screen is meant merely 'to adorn the walls of churches [*templorum parietes ornandi*].' As he says, Luther would have his 'fourteen chapters' (which he elaborates in his book's title, *Tessaradecas consolatoria pro laborantibus et oneratis*)[14] "replace [*loco*] the fourteen saints [*Divorum*] whom our superstition has invented [*fecit*] and called 'The Defenders Against All Evils' [*omnium malorum depulsores*]" (*WA* 6:106.6–9). Luther wants his book to perform a function different from (and superior to) the false function of the altar screen and its tradition of 'auxiliary' or 'helper in need [*Nothelfer*]' saints, who supposedly could help 'drive away [*depulsores*]' evils. In order to facilitate such a dramatic and fundamental shift in how Christians should approach their troubles, Luther dismantles the fourteen-saints structure and replaces it with a two-part arrangement to his book: the first part deals with 'seven images of evil [*septem imagines malorum*],' a contemplation of which "will make the troubles

---

[13] Max J. Friedländer and Jakob Rosenberg, *The Paintings of Lucas Cranach*, rev. ed. (Ithaca, 1978), 18–19, 68–70; Werner Schade, *Cranach: A Family of Master Painters*, transl. Helen Serba (New York, 1980), plate 37. The painting depicts the saints surrounding the Christ child. Anonymous woodcuts, ca. 1500, depict the saints, surrounding Christ on the cross; Brad S. Gregory, *Salvation at Stake: Christian Martyrdom in Early Modern Europe* (Cambridge, Mass., 1999), 36. Each saint was invoked for protection from (or during) a particular situation—i.e., emergency, disease, or condition. Three were bishops: Denis of Paris (invoked against headache and rabies), Blaise (invoked against throat troubles), Erasmus, called Elmo (invoked against colic and cramp). Three were virgins: Barbara (invoked against lightning, fire, explosion, sudden death), Margaret (invoked against possession and by pregnant women), Catherine of Alexandria (invoked by philosophers, students, wheelers, etc.). Three were knightly patrons: George (protector of soldiers), Achatius and Eustace (invoked by hunters). The physician Pantaleon (invoked against tuberculosis); the monk Giles (invoked against epilepsy, insanity, and sterility); the deacon Cyriac (invoked against demonic possession); the martyr Vitus (invoked against epilepsy and 'Vitus dance'); and the giant Christopher (invoked by travelers in difficulties). For a discussion of the history of the 'Fourteen Holy Helpers' (feast, 8 August) and its cult, see *New Catholic Encyclopedia*, 2nd ed. (2003), s.v. "Fourteen Holy Helpers," by J. Dünninger; cf. Bernd Moeller, "Religious Life in Germany on the Eve of the Reformation," in *Religion and Society in Early Modern Europe 1500–1800*, ed. Kaspar von Greyerz (London, 1984), 13–42. For important background on Luther's document, see R. Guy Erwin, "Flesh Made Words: Luther's Reform of Piety," North American Luther Forum, Luther Seminary, St. Paul, MN, 28–30 April 2006.

[14] "[F]or those who labor and are heavy laden" (Matt. 11:28).

of the present lighter [*praesentia incommoda mitigantur*]"; the second part's seven images are images of blessings (*bonorum*), "gathered together for the same purpose [*ad eundem usum collectas*]" (*WA* 6:106.8–14). This structure is then explained more thoroughly in the Introduction.

In a brief Introduction (*Praefatio; LW* 42:124f.; *WA* 6:106f.) Luther lays out a rationale and authority for consolation. In the Letter of Dedication he had argued that the mandate for consoling others in their need comes from the command of Scripture and the example of Christ. Here Luther explains what consolation is and from whence it originates. Using just two scriptural texts, he argues that one must use the mind to help one turn attention from the thing (*rem*) to the Word (*verbo*). The authority of our consolation—that is, its source—is the Scriptures. Citing and quoting Paul at Rom. 15:4, Luther adds the vocative 'Brothers [*Fratres*]' to his verbatim quotation that stipulates that "whatever was written was written for our instruction [*doctrinam*], so that through patience and comfort [*patientiam et consolationem*] of the Scriptures we might have hope [*spem*]," and he interprets that text to mean that it plainly teaches (*aperte docet*) that consolations (*solatia*) are 'to be drawn from [*petenda*]' Holy Scriptures (*WA* 6:106.21–24).

The rationale for comfort (*consolationis*), or consolation (*solatia*)—Luther seems not to distinguish them here—derives from his exegesis of Ecclus. 11. Here he found the two-fold structure of evils and blessings[15] presented by the 'wise Preacher [*Ecclesiasticus sapiens*]':[16] "In the day of evil be mindful of the good, and in the day of the good be mindful of the evil": *In die malorum* [a] *memor esto bonorum* [b] *et in die bonorum* [b] *memor esto malorum* [a]" (*WA* 6:106.27f.). In this statement Luther has reworked the biblical text of v. 25 ("In the day of prosperity, adversity is forgotten, and in the day of adversity, prosperity is not remembered"), while retaining its structure as chiasmus: (1) he changes observations of negative behavior into commands of positive actions; (2) he reverses the order of ideas, probably because his topic is 'evils' and the biblical text begins with 'prosperity.' Luther will later employ this same chiastic structure when he summarizes his point.

Meanwhile, he proceeds to interpret the important rationale he finds here, arguing that a thing (*rem*) has only the value and meaning (*qualis*

---

[15] Probably following the order in Ecclus. 11:25 (LXX), *LW* 42:124 erroneously reads 'blessings and evils.'
[16] *LW* 42:124 omits 'wise.'

et quanta) that the mind in its thoughts (*opinio*) assigns. He illustrates this cognitive power in one direction only: the mind's ability to reduce in magnitude life's powerful experiences: "Whatever he regards [*ducitur*] as trivial and of no value [*vile et nihili*] will affect him only slightly, whether it be love [*amore*] when it comes to him or pain [*dolore*] when it goes away" (*WA* 6:106.19–21). This ability to neutralize that which moves (*afficit*) us is best effected (*potissimum fiat*) through the Word, turning our thoughts from debilitating experiences in the present onto that which is "either absent or does not move us at the moment [*absens est vel non afficit praesens*]." Therefore, Luther concludes, consolation comes *only* from the Scriptures (*non nisi per scripturarum*).[17]

Luther then concisely explicates his organizational structure for the book: two series of pictures or images (*spectra et imagines*), each divided into seven parts (*partes*). He then enumerates the first part (or image [*imago*]), which deals with the evils: All of the evils *appear to be* spatially oriented: within [*intra*], before [*ante*], behind [*post*], left [*sinistro*], right [*dextro*], beneath [*infra*], above [*supra*] (*WA* 6:107.1–3). In actuality, the second (before) and third (behind) are temporally ordered. Moreover, the apparent physical directions are only for visualization and concentration, and after the first three images Luther even deviates from his stated plan. He moves the evil beneath from sixth to fourth position. Thus, he previews one order (within, before, behind, left, right, beneath, above) yet follows another order (within, before, behind, beneath, left, right, above).

However, the discrepancy between stated plan and followed plan should not bother any reader, for the immediate connections and transitions are more naturally followed than the synchrony between a plan stated on one page and a deviation from it many pages later. Moreover, the rationale for the deviation can be discerned. The logical components Luther has chosen are not cryptic, for he uses three pairs of orientation points along three axes or dimensions. We can envision two pairs as *horizontal* (before/behind, left/right), and a third as *vertical*

---

[17] Notice the chiasmus again, from Ecclus. 11:25, and in the indicative: "It is thus very true that we shall find consolation only through the Scriptures, which in the days of evil [a: *die malorum*] call us to the contemplation of our blessings [b: *spectanda bona*], either present or to come, and in the days of blessing [b₁: *die bonorum*], point us to the contemplation of the evils [a₁: *spectanda mala*]" (*WA* 6:106.34–37). The verb is the same (*avocat*, 'call' or 'point') in both 'a' and 'b' elements of the chiasmus. Luther argues that this diversionary power of the Word is necessary, or we would simply be thinking about and being affected (*opinio et affectu*) by the experiences or things (*rerum*) themselves, thus held captive by them and not by the Word of God, finding no consolation.

(below/above), plus a fourth single point (within). But whether he will proceed from one axial pole to its opposite, or whether he finds other connections, from one axial pole to a different axial pole, is not self-evident. In fact, for both parts—evils and blessings—he starts at 'within' and ends with 'above.' So we know what is first and last (seventh). Thus, the first important transition is from 'within' to 'before' (meaning the future). From before (future) he proceeds to behind (past). Then, the next important transition is which axis to take up next; Luther moves to his 'vertical' axis (beneath/above), taking up 'beneath' (infernal evil), and then proceeding to the other horizontal axis (left/right), seeing an important connection between 'beneath' and 'left.' Next, he goes from left to right, and now he can end with 'above' as seventh.

By considering these three bipolar axes, we can also understand why, perhaps, Luther's parallel language—doublets and chiasms—seems fitting. Some figures are oppositional ('present or to come'; 'evils and blessings'; 'day of evil/day of good'; 'whether love…or pain'), others are synonymous or incremental ('value and meaning'; 'trivial and of no value'; 'absent or does not move us at the moment'; 'pictures or images'; 'thinking about…being affected by'). When we reckon with the decisions Luther had to make about the order in which to explicate the seven images, we recall that he claimed that the Scriptures present to our view (*videlicet*) both evils and blessings wholesomely intermingled (*saluberrima temperie mixtas*). And when we recall his strong conclusion that the Scriptures are the necessary and sufficient source of comfort, his use of just one superlative ('best effected') and an epithet of the 'wise' preacher functions to persuade the reader of this unique insight into consolation, which all people long to find.

II. *Analysis of "Fourteen Consolations"*

A. *The First Image: The Evil Within Us* [malum internum]

With just his first sentence of this chapter (*LW* 42:125–127; *WA* 6:107f.), Luther makes clear why he has begun with the internal position, as well as why he ends with the 'above' position: he proceeds from worst to best.[18] To Frederick (and anyone else gravely ill), Luther offers perspective on one's illness: "[I]t is most certain and true [*ratum est et verissimum*]

---

[18] Later, in chapter four of part two (see p. 33), we discover quite clearly another reason for this organization.

that no torture [*cruciatum*] can compare with the worst [*pessimum*] of all evils, namely, the evil within man [*in ipso*] himself. The evils within him are more numerous and far greater [*longe plura et maiora*] than any which he feels [*sentit*]" (*WA* 6:107.6–8). Luther's strategy in this chapter is to argue that: (A) The worst evils are spiritual and within, and God shields us from most of these; (B) When understood, this situation itself can be turned into consolation; (C) Yet evils, both physical and mental, are real and vexing, so whether we 'feel' them or not, our minds must understand them as sent by God.

Luther's authorities in these arguments (in step A) are scriptural: 'the prophet' (= psalmist), 'the Apostle' (= author of Hebrews epistle), 'the Preacher' (= author of Ecclus.), Job, David, and, of course, God. Luther's stylistic resources are varied: (1) to drive home the claim that the evil within man—what he cannot feel—is the worst, Luther advances a progression, twice using 'feel [*sentiret*],' twice using 'hell [*infernum*],' the latter a striking rhyme with *internum*; (2) Luther turns to ratiocinatio (a short question and its answers), quoting portions of Ps. 116:11 (= 115:11 Vulgate) and Ps. 39:6 in such a way as to craft a chiasmus, only apparent by altering the translation;[19] (3) following that, Luther employs sorites (a progression formed by a series of enthymemes or truncated syllogisms having a suppressed major premise). His chain of doublets is linked by repeated copulas (to be [*esse*]);[20] (4) in summarizing God's parental, disciplinary action, Luther uses six imperatives in succession, three for each of the two contemplations he invites.[21]

Luther's second, brief move (B) in this chapter is to try to illustrate and apply the truth he argued previously, transforming the evil into consolation (*consolatoria*). He does this all in third person singular, using more language of comparison and contrast (superlatives and compara-

---

[19] "Every man [a] is a liar [b]...Nothing but vanity [b₁] is every living man [a₁]" [*Omnis homo mendax...Universa vanitas omnis homo vivens*] (*WA* 6:107.10f.).

[20] "[T]o be a liar and a vanity [*mendacem et vanum*] is to be without truth and reality [*vacuum veritate et re*]. And to be without truth and reality [*sine veritate et re*] is to be without God and to be nothing [*sine deo et nihil*]. This condition in turn is to be in hell and to be damned [*in inferno et damnatum*]" (*WA* 6:107.11–13).

[21] "Therefore, in the day of evils remember the day of blessings [*memor esto bonorum*] (Ecclus. 11:25). Just see [*Vide*] what a great good it is not to know the whole of our evil. Be mindful of this good [*esto boni memor*], and the evil that you feel will torment you less. On the other hand [*Ita rursus*], in the day of good be mindful of the evil [*memor esto malorum*]. That is to say, while you do not feel [*indolens*] the true evils, be grateful [*gratus esto*] that you do not feel, but keep [*memorare*] the true evils in mind" (*WA* 6:107.28–32).

tives, doublets), adding a feature we have not yet fully seen since the Letter of Dedication—dialogue, the invented soliloquy of those who understand God's strategy. Thus, the dialogue models how Luther would have Christians respond to his teaching:

> 'Not yet, O man, do you feel [*sentis*] your evil. Be glad and grateful [*gaude et gratius age*] that you do not have to feel [*sentire*] it.' When compared [*comparatione*] with the greatest [*maximi*] evil, the small evil [*malum parvum*] thus becomes light [*leve*]. It is this that others mean when they say, 'I have deserved something far worse [*longe peiora*], even hell itself'—a thing so easy [*facile*] to say, but horrible [*intolerabile*] to endure [*sensu*]' (*WA* 6:108.3–7).

B. *The Second Image: The Future Evil or the Evil Before Us* [ante se]

In this chapter (*LW* 42:127–130; *WA* 6:108–110) Luther argues that much evil (meaning harm and misfortune) awaits us in this life but that God protects us from much of this; accordingly, the greatest evil—death—is the most fearsome. Yet even death has a way of reminding us of God's goodness. Luther argues these claims in four steps, the first two of which address evils; the latter two speak of death: (A) the future of us all—particularly for those of social stature—holds great dangers; (B) when we are spared all or part of these future evils we should count it as gain; (C) the greatest future evil is death, yet properly fearing it can provide comfort from God; (D) We should adopt God's hatred of sin—the cause of evils—and not fear death.

The purpose behind Luther's argument (A) is his striking claim that turning the mind (*vertas animum*) toward the future will "lighten your present evil in no small degree [*Non parum levabit praesens quodcumque malum*]." However, it is clear that Luther is not doing what so many of us today attempt: to divert attention from present difficulties by thinking about a *brighter* future! For he continues with the relative pronoun *quae*, referring to understood future evils (*mala*), which will be greater than what one now faces (*malum*)![22] Indeed, Luther then provides a definition of fear ('the emotion that is caused by a future evil') from an unknown (*incertius*) authority. His objective is to urge that one should

---

[22] *LW* 42:127 includes the understood noun ('evils') in its translation. To express how much worse they will be, Luther uses a rhyming, polysyndetic, progressive triplet: 'so numerous, so varied, and so great [*tot et talia et tanta*],' and to describe their outcome of fear (*timor*), he uses a doublet epithet: 'one of the great and principal emotions [*magnus ille et unus principalium affectuum*].'

soberly consider these ineluctable problems, and he quotes Paul precisely
at Rom. 11:20b: "Be not proud, but rather fear [*Noli altum sapere, sed
time*]." This concise antithesis makes sense, given what Luther provides
next—a common saying (*Vulgateo quoque proverbium*) that "No age is proof
against the itch [*Non est ulla aetas scabiei etiam superior*]." Luther's verbs
make evident how susceptible all humans are to both physical and
emotional torment ('misery, shame, and all indignity [*inopia, ignominia et
omnia indigna*]'). As he had argued in the previous chapter, Luther urges
his reader Frederick (and others to whom it may apply) that for those
of higher dignity and rank (*maior…dignior status*), the potential losses
are much greater. Thus, Luther's strategy in this first point has been
to move from the inevitable, but lesser, maladies to the catastrophic
(*WA* 6:108.31–109.13).

Luther's second move (B) in this chapter is to argue that such evils,
should they somehow not befall us,[23] should give us no small comfort
(*non parvo solatio*). This bit of meiosis (understatement)—that complements Luther's use of several superlatives later in this chapter—precedes
three Scripture texts (from Jeremiah, Luke, and Job) that he employs
to establish that God's intervening protection shields us from Satan's
fury. With minimalist language—only a single doublet captures Satan's
actions—Luther suggests we invoke Jeremiah's declaration, "It is of the
Lord's mercies that we are not consumed [*misericordiae domini, quod non
sumus consumpti*]," a nearly verbatim quote of Lam. 3:22. Luther then
slides to Job, as he understands both Luke's and Job's comments to be
from God: "To this place shall you come and here shall your proud
waves be stayed [*huc pervenient et confrigentur tuamentes fluctus tui*]" (Job
38:11). Now it is clear to us that Luther's earlier embellished reference in
chapter one (the first evil) to 'the sea of this world,' had Job 38:11, with
God's protective hedge about Job, clearly in mind (*WA* 109.14–24).

In Luther's third step (C) of this chapter (*LW* 42:129f.; *WA* 6:109.25–
110.14), he considers death, and in so doing he lays some groundwork
that he will build upon later, in the fourth chapter—on the infernal
evil. Since he considers God, whether permitting evil or protecting from
it, to be providing just what his people need, Luther uses a variety of
tactics to establish death's formidability. Even if one is spared all harm,
death is 'the greatest of all terrors [*omnium terribilium maximum*]' certain
to come and, as Luther argues, always at an uncertain time.

---

[23] Twice in *WA* 6:109.14f. Luther uses verb forms of *accido* (*acciderit, accidit*).

Thus, to this point in the book Luther has joined this chorus of 'consoling' literature, and as he promises to argue later (*ut videbimus infra*), says that divine mercy (*misericordia divina*) is most concerned about comforting faint hearts (*curarit pusillanimes confortare*) in their fear of and preparation for death. Lastly, in this step, Luther cites Cyprian, the first African martyr (d. 258), suggesting that he and others have argued that because these evils pose such a threat to our spiritual well being, we should do whatever is necessary to protect ourselves, even to seek death as a quick means of escape (*volocem ad evadenda*).[24] In interpreting and summarizing not only Cyprian but also other 'highminded men [*bonicordes hii homines*],' Luther declares the two reasons for desiring to die and be delivered: (1) to escape the evil of the sins in which they are now held (*malo peccatorum, in quo sunt*); and (2) to avoid the evil of the sins into which they are still able to fall (*quod cadere possunt*) (*WA* 6:110.10–14).[25] Thus he has covered both chapters one and two.

Luther's brief fourth and concluding step (D) in this chapter is to summarize how evils and death are threats and to offer sound advice for facing them. His conclusion is that we should follow the example of Paul (Rom. 7:24f.) and the desire and grace of God. Clearly death ends sin's grip on a person's life, but death is also 'the minister of life and righteousness [*ministra vitae ac iustitiae*].' To explain fully and demonstrate this last claim, Luther defers until later (*infra*), which is not taken up in the next but instead in the fourth chapter, the evil below (*infra*).

C. *The Third Image: The Past* [preteritum] *Evil or the Evil Behind Us* [post nos]

In this chapter (*LW* 42:130–132; *WA* 6:110–112) Luther turns much more strongly to contemplation and praising God for his wonderful

---

[24] In its twenty-six chapters, Cyprian's *On Mortality* argues that death, especially martyrdom, should be welcomed and highly prized. Chapter 26 begins: "We should consider, dearly loved brethren—we should ever and anon reflect that we have renounced the world, and are in the meantime living here as guests and strangers. Let us greet the day which assigns each of us to his own home, which snatches us hence, and sets us free from the snares of the world, and restores us to paradise and the kingdom"; John Brubaker and Gary Bogart, "Internet Christian Library," <http://www.ewtn.com/library/SOURCES/MORTAL.TXT> (accessed 25 September 2006).

[25] Clearly Luther understood—and argued—what Cyprian was advocating; a similar thought comes recently from Joseph Bayly: "And death, not healing, is the great deliverance from all pain and suffering. Death delivers God's people from the hands of persecuting governments, from the ravages of disease, and from every evil affliction"; *The Last Thing We Talk About*, 87.

protection in the past, claiming that in this image (*In hoc eximie*) God the Father's sweet mercy (*dulcis misericordia*) shines more brightly than in any other chapter (so far). In fact, three times in the opening two sentences he emphasizes this superiority: (a) 'shines more brightly than in the others [*prae caeteris lucet*]'; (b) 'able to comfort us in every distress [*potens nos consolari in omni angustia nostra*]'; (c) "Never does a man feel... more closely than [*Neque enim... quilibet sentit*]." In addition to his own assertions, Luther quotes Augustine's *Confessions* for evidence that reliving one's past life, with its great dangers and evils (*tanta et pericula et mala*), would be worse than dying.[26] Following this introduction, Luther's overall strategy in this chapter unfolds in five steps: (A) God's hand of protection has operated despite our ignorance of it; (B) our awareness of God's protection should make us grateful; (C) gratitude to God compels us to trust Him to continue this protection; (D) Prolepsis (anticipating and refuting a potential objection): God's permission of our trials is to show His goodness; (E) our trust should take comfort, not anxiety, in trials, and we should ponder God's works (= care for us).

In his initial step (A) Luther first expounds upon our ignorance of how God was protecting us in the past and how we had no hand in this protection; it was all God's doing. He uses soliloquy and two Scriptures to document this; to emphasize man's inaction Luther uses doublets (sometimes with anaphora, the use of repeated initial words) and triplets in exploring all possibilities. His quotation of Prov. 16:9 alters the Vulgate enough to make an even more strikingly concise, antithetical

---

[26] *Confessions* 10.28.39: "When I shall with my whole self cleave to Thee, I shall nowhere have sorrow or labour; and my life shall wholly live, as wholly full of Thee. But now since whom Thou fillest, Thou liftest up, because I am not full of Thee I am a burden to myself. Lamentable joys strive with joyous sorrows: and on which side is the victory, I know not. Woe is me! Lord, have pity on me. My evil sorrows strive with my good joys; and on which side is the victory, I know not. Woe is me! Lord, have pity on me. Woe is me! I hide not my wounds; Thou art the Physician, I the sick; Thou merciful, I miserable. *Is not the life of man upon earth all trial?* [Job 7:1]. *Who wishes for troubles and difficulties? Thou commandest them to be endured, not to be loved. No man loves what he endures, though he love to endure. For though he rejoices that he endures, he had rather there were nothing for him to endure. In adversity I long for prosperity, in prosperity I fear adversity. What middle place is there betwixt these two, where the life of man is not all trial?* Woe to the prosperities of the world, once and again, through fear of adversity, and corruption of joy! Woe to the adversities of the world, once and again, and the third time, from the longing for prosperity, and because adversity itself is a hard thing, and lest it shatter endurance. Is not the *life of man upon earth all trial:* without any interval?" transl. E. B. Pusey, <http://ccat.sas.upenn.edu/jod/Englishconfessions.html> (Accessed 22 August 2006); italics are mine. Augustine (354–430) is thus far the first authority that Luther has designated as 'Blessed' [B = *Beatus*]; text 'F' (1535) reads 'S. Augustinus' [= *Sanctus*].

statement: "Man proposes, but God disposes [*Homo proponit, deus autem disponit*]." Luther is probably quoting from Thomas à Kempis' *Imitatio Christi* (1.9), which uses the concise form.[27]

What I have called Luther's second (B) step (*WA* 6:111.9–14) is virtually an extension—into feeling—of the claim he has just argued. That is, by continuing with the intimate first person plural, Luther amplifies the emotion that should be elicited when we realize the extent and goodness of God's protection and care; our own past lives, he says, are sufficient testimony to this care. Luther executes this amplification through several doublets (including two superlatives) and a rich paraphrase from Deuteronomy. Recalling again the role of consoling literature—to which Luther is now making a contribution—we see him argue that even if there were no 'books or sermons [*libri neque sermones*],' our very lives (*ipsa nostra vita*) and their many 'evils and dangers [*mala et pericula*]' commend to us the 'ever present and most tender [*praesentissimam et suavissimam*]' goodness of God that exceeds 'our thought and feeling [*consilium et sensum nostrum*]' and has carried us in his bosom. Next, he paraphrases Moses in Deut. 32:10f.: "The Lord kept [*custodivit*] him as the apple of his eye [*pupillam oculi sui*], and led him about [*circumduxit*], and carried him on his shoulders."[28]

Luther's third step (C) in this chapter takes his readers a step farther along the path of finding comfort. He builds this comfort-taking action from four scriptural paraphrases and a dialogue series of rhetorical questions. The first three quotes, given in quick succession, come from the Psalms. The three quotes are all anaphoric in their initial phrases: 'I remember [*Memor fui*]....' (Ps. 143:5 = 142:5 Vulgate); 'Surely I shall remember [*Memor ero*]...' (Ps. 77:11 = 76:12 Vulgate); 'I have remembered [*Memor fui*]...' (Ps. 119:52 = 118:52 Vulgate). These verbal phrases also have parallel objects ('days of old'; 'all your works'; 'the work of your hands'; 'your wonders of old'; 'your judgments').

---

[27] Thomas à Kempis (c. 1380–1471) is the presumed author of this work, which was the most popular devotional book of the late Middle Ages. The proverb, "Man proposes, but God disposes," appears in a book of John Bartlett (1820–1905), *Familiar Quotations*, 10th ed., 1919, noting: "This expression is of much greater antiquity. It appears in the *Chronicle of Battel Abbey*, p. 27 (Lower's translation), and in *The Vision of Piers Ploughman*, line 13994, ed. 1550. A man's heart deviseth his way; but the Lord directeth his steps—*Proverbs xvi. 9.*"

[28] While 'carried' is not part of v. 10 or 11, the motif of protection certainly is, for vv. 10–11 describe God's care as that of an eagle for her young, and *in humeris suis* ('on his shoulders') is identical to v.11, translated 'on its pinions' in RSV.

Further, in its second and third clauses, the first quoted Scripture is chiastic.[29] These references to God's *works* will again proliferate in the final paragraph of this chapter.

In his fourth (D) step (*WA* 6:111.31–40) Luther fully addresses, proleptically, this little matter of God's leaving us to ourselves only 'rarely' or 'for a brief moment.' This is important to Frederick or any reader who would naturally see one's self *at the time* as forsaken, or at least tested, by God. Luther stays in the inclusive, first person plural, arguing that when God does indeed leave us to our own care (*nostro consilio*), it is only briefly, for little things, and that when he does so his purpose is to test (*tentet*) us to see if we are willing to trust (*credere*) in his care and compare the difference between His care and ours. Luther's evidence that the trials are slight: we cannot even heal a "small pain in the leg [*unicum dolorem cruris*] for even the shortest span of time [*parvissimo tempore*]," as he himself had learned first hand in 1503.[30]

Luther's fifth (E) and final step (*WA* 6:111.40–112.6) in this chapter returns—in first person plural—to the notion of God's works, arguing that the testing He permits should elicit comfort, not anxiety; it ends—in third person plural—with sober warnings against failing to trust him. Thus Luther closes with the emphasis on God's care, which is His work, and with the comparative abundance of it alongside our own paltry and ineffective efforts to look after ourselves.

D. *The Fourth Image: The Infernal Evil or the Evil Beneath Us* [infra nos]

In this chapter (*LW* 42:133f.; *WA* 6:112f.) Luther is now at the midpoint of the seven evils, so he takes time to summarize his perspective on the three evils covered thus far, and how such a perspective lends comfort. In covering the material of this chapter—death and hell—he spends equal time on each, and his summary conclusion is consistent with his summary thus far: when looking to the evils we suffer, they are nothing compared to those (even death and hell) from which God protects us.

---

[29] "I meditate on all your works, and in all your hands have wrought I muse" [*meditatus sum* (a) *in omnibus tuis* (b) *et in factis manuum tuarum* (b₁) *meditabar* (a₁)]."

[30] *LW* 42:132, note 12, reports the incident near Erfurt. In *LW* 54:14f. (*WATr* 1, #119; cf. *WATr* 5, #6428), Luther recalls that the severed artery bled profusely and a surgeon was needed. The wound even reopened during the night, and Luther recounts, telling the story in 1531, that his cries to Mary for help were to no avail; cf. Brecht, *Martin Luther*, 1:46f.; John Wilkinson, "The Medical History of Martin Luther," *Proceedings of the Royal College of Physicians of Edinburgh* 26 (1996): 115–134, here at 120.

Yet such an optimistic outcome emerges from an extremely sobering context, for this chapter is frighteningly humbling. The strategy is: (A) introductory summary of the evils thus far surveyed (*WA* 6:112.9–17); (B) Death: we usually get off easier than we deserve, since God's justice contains mercy (*WA* 6:112.18–113.2); (C) Hell: all are condemned, in keeping with God's mercy and grace (*WA* 6:113.3–24); (D) summary (*WA* 6:113.24–26).

Luther's introductory (A) summary (*WA* 6:112.9–17) continues the inclusive style of first person plural and is fairly concise, yet it introduces a stylistic device seldom used thus far, but which will become more prominent later: anthypophora—asking questions, then answering them; this device is particularly suited to render strong agreement to the summary, something necessary for a summary and absolutely crucial to this one. Luther's first new (B) topic (*WA* 6:112.18–113.2) in the chapter is death,[31] which he has addressed to some extent in chapter two, where he called it the *omnium terribilium maximum* and where he assured his readers that here was the matter of God's greatest concern for comforting faint hearts (*pusillanimes confortare*).[32] In the second new (C) topic (*WA* 6:113.3–24) of the chapter (hell), which Luther has not previously addressed, his strategy is the same as with the previous topic (death). He first enumerates categories of sinners for readers to compare themselves to (Luther's first two sentences are in first plural), expecting that they will feel guilt for still surviving while those others, more righteous, languish in 'true hell and eternal damnation [*inferno vero et aeterna damnatione*]' (note the chiasmus).[33] Luther's concise summary (D), in first plural again, turns to praise and love (*laudis et amoris*) that "we owe our gracious God in every evil of this life [*debeamus optimo deo nostro in quocunque malo huius vitae*]," since each evil is scarcely a drop (*stilla una*) of what we deserved (*WA* 6:113.25f.).

---

[31] Prior to beginning his exposition of death, and unlike any of the other thirteen chapters in this work, Luther here provides a one-sentence distributio, set off as a distinct paragraph in *WA* 6:112.18f.: "Of the evils beneath us the first is death and the other is hell" (*LW* 42:133). He precisely places the two topics in final position (*Primum...mors, alterum infernus*).

[32] *Confortare* might better be translated 'strengthening' or 'encouraging'; cf. Leo F. Stelten, *Dictionary of Ecclesiastical Latin* (Peabody, Mass., 1995).

[33] *LW* 42:133 omits 'true' before 'hell.'

E. *The Fifth Image: The Unfavorable* [sinistrum] *Evil on Our Left Hand*
[sinistram]

In this chapter (*LW* 42:134–137; *WA* 6:113–115) Luther turns straight-
forwardly to the plight of the wicked; that is, not to their future outcomes—death and hell—as with chapters two and four, but to the
people themselves, the vast multitude of 'adversaries and wicked men
[*adversariorum et malorum hominum*].' Having twice already pointed out
to readers (especially Frederick) that leaders often experience greater
'evils,' Luther's argument here about one's enemies has a powerful irony
to it, in that he aims to persuade his readers to feel pity (*compatiamur*)
for those enemies. With little introduction he embarks on a four-step
strategy, then summarizes: (A) Many enemies are out there, but they are
hindered by God from seriously harming us; (B) Their evil sufferings
are worse than ours, and that should elicit our pity; (C) Taking Christ's
examples, we should pray for our enemies; (D) The evils of the wicked
are terrible; (E) Summary. Luther quotes one Scripture each for steps B
and C, two in step D, and in the summary he alludes to three others.
There is no dialogue and only one small anaphora; the primary stylistic
tactics are doublets and triplets. Nearly all the argumentation, except
for use of scriptural material, is in first person plural.

Luther's concluding summary is signaled (*Breviter*) and provides
not only clear conclusions as to what to believe about, how to feel
about, and how to act in regards to the wicked but also supplies three
biblical authorities (Moses, Paul, Christ)—with allusions to their scriptural sources—as examples.[34] He does all this through parallel verbs,
anaphora, doublets, and two triplets. All the evils of the wicked (*mala
malorum omnia*)—numerous and both physical and spiritual, when viewed
(*videret*) rightly (*digno affectu*)—will make a man forget (*oblivisceretur*) his own
evil, and it will even seem (*videretur*) like one is not suffering at all.

F. *The Sixth Image: The Favorable Evil* [malum dextrum][35] *on Our Right*
[dextram] *Hand*

This chapter (*LW* 42:137–140; *WA* 6:115–117) is the longest of the
seven chapters of evils, and with good reason, for here Luther tackles
directly the cult of the saints. While he used saints (*sancti*) only once

---

[34] Exod. 32:32 and Rom. 9:3.
[35] *LW* 42:137 does not translate the adjective *dextrum*.

each in chapters two and five, in his attempt here to distinguish (from superstition) their proper role, Luther uses the term eleven times.[36] He draws a powerful example of undeserved suffering and death from one saint (John the Baptist), to argue that, from this example Christians can learn a willingness to suffer. Accordingly, there is no mention of special assistance for avoiding or relieving suffering; nothing is said about Mary or patron saints and their intercession. At the same time, however, one can still find traces of merit theology here. Luther's organizational plan is as follows: (A) Thesis: The Proper Function of the Cult of the Saints; (B) The Improper Function of the Cult of the Saints; (C) Scriptural Teaching Supporting the Proper Use of the Cult of the Saints; (D) Specific Saints' Suffering Testified in Scripture; (E) Prolepsis: About Suffering for Sin; and (F) Conclusion.

Luther begins (A) by identifying the 'favorable' evil on the right hand as that of our friends (*amici nostri*), which he says makes our own evil lighter (*mitigari*) and is taught in 1 Peter 5:9, which he then quotes.[37] In his claim that the church's prayers petition (*orat*) and urge (*provocati*) us, by the example of the saints, to imitate (*imitemur*) the virtue of their sufferings, it is clear that by 'saints' Luther is using the term in its orthodox sense of those Christians who have died, for he distinguishes 'saints' from 'the church.' In attaining the martyr's palm, these who were already saints—according to New Testament usage[38]—have something special to offer those still living here below, according to an antiphon in the Roman breviary that Luther quotes. So the sufferings and torments of martyrs offer example and encouragement (*WA* 6:115.20–29).

In what I call step B, The Improper Function of the Cult of the Saints (*WA* 6:115.29–31), Luther provides a bit of commentary on the 'superstition' he has just mentioned. He observes that many manage to miss the evil that the 'example and memory [*exemplo et memoria*]' of the saints teach us should be borne (*ferendum docent*): "They thus

---

[36] In the Letter of Dedication Luther refers to the 'fourteen saints' [*quatuordecim Divorum*], who he says were invented by superstition and which he is replacing with these *tessaradecados* (*WA* 6:106.8).

[37] "Resist the devil in firm faith [*Resistite diabolo fortes in fide*], knowing that the same sufferings [*easdem passiones*] are inflicted [*fieri*] on your brethren [*fraternitati*] in the world."

[38] The vast majority of usages of 'saints' [*sancti*, ἅγιοι] in the New Testament, especially by Paul, refers to the living Christians of the church on earth. Of the 60 NT usages, 40 are Pauline, 5 are in Gospels-Acts, 17 are in Hebrews-Revelation. In Matt. 27:52 the author qualifies 'saints' by the addition of the phrase 'who had fallen asleep'; in Rev. 17:6 'saints' and 'martyrs' are separately named.

become unlike those whose feasts they celebrate to become like them
[*ferant fiantque dissimiles eis, quorum festa habent ut similes fierent*]." This
warning should be sobering—yet hopefully not off-putting—to those,
like Frederick, who invest such belief, time, energy, and money in the
cult and its relics (in 1493 he made a pilgrimage to the Holy Land,
and by 1520 his collection was one of the most well known in the
Holy Roman Empire, numbering 19,013 items).[39] Therein, Luther
has argued that one ought look to the saints in order to embrace, not
avoid, one's suffering.

The next two steps (C and D) both offer biblical evidence of the
role of suffering as chastisement (*disciplina*). That Luther has turned to
Scripture rather than tradition is a fundamental component of his argument. Step C (*WA* 6:115.32–116.19) begins with a lengthy quotation
from Hebrews 12 [:4–11]. We cannot escape the fact that Luther's text
contains such an assortment of disciplinary terms and that it contrasts
temporary pain with enduring reward; the antithetical doublet 'not for
our pleasure but to our sorrow' captures the contrast.[40] We can also see
that Luther has skipped v. 7a and v. 10; in the latter omission he has
streamlined the direct comparison between our fathers in the flesh (*patres
quidem carnis nostrae*) and the Father of spirits (*patri spiritum*), a comparison
of *multo magis*—'even more,' or better, 'how much more'—the kind of
comparison the Hebrew exegetes call '*qal wachomer*.'[41]

Luther's fourth (D) step (*WA* 6:116.19–117.5) turns to specific examples of deceased saints suffering, the chief of which is blessed John the
Baptist (*B. Iohannes Baptista*). To add authority to his own argument about
one of the chief saints, John the Baptist, Luther quotes Jeremiah 49:12
exactly, where the Lord is making the *qal wachomer* argument, which
He does chiastically.[42] Then, with much detail, Luther elaborates upon

---

[39] *OER*, s.v. "Frederick III of Saxony," by Ingetraut Ludolphy; s.v. "Saints: Sainthood," by Franz Courth, who counts Frederick's collection as one of the most famous.
Martin Brecht, *Martin Luther*, 1:117, says that the relic collection in Halle was twenty
times larger than Frederick's.

[40] Luther's syntax, forming the antithetical doublet, follows GNT but not Vulgate.
Verse 6 also presents a series of verbs, whose relationship is chiastic: [a] loves (*diligit*),
[b] chastens (*castigat*): [b₁] scourges (*flagellat*), [a₁] receives (*recipit*).

[41] The first exegetical rule of Rabbi Hillel (light to heavy), πόσῳ μᾶλλον in Greek,
translated 'how much more' by KJV and RSV in Matt. 7:11; 10:25; Luke 11:13; 12:24,
28; Rom. 11:12, 24; Heb. 9:14; cf. Richard N. Longenecker, *Biblical Exegesis in the Apostolic
Period* (Grand Rapids, 1975), 68f. Hillel flourished in the 1st Century C.E.

[42] "Look...if those whose judgment was (a) not to drink the cup [*non erat iudicum, ut
biberent calcem*] did (b) drink it [*bibentes bibent*], will you then (c) be free to go unpunished

aspects of John s character and his death; the purpose is to show how undeserving John was of such suffering and that this example puts to shame any tendency to find merit in our own suffering.[43]

Step E (*WA* 6:117.6–17) is a prolepsis that reckons with the potential objection that some suffering Christians endure is deserved punishment for their sins. Indeed, we observed that Luther has just acknowledged both the Lord's chastening (*disciplina domini*) and the persecutions of the devil, the latter of which we understand him to mean especially in the context and example of John the Baptist, whose sufferings evoke the superlative *gravissimas* are undeserved, and distinct from the former. But, when in the midst of suffering, one cannot always be so confident of the type of suffering she is experiencing. However, Luther argues here that identifying which type of suffering one experiences is not important; what matters is that one bears the suffering patiently and that one confess one's sins. To advance this argument, Luther articulates the objection with invented dialogue, stating the comparison with the suffering of the saints that bothers our objector: I am a sinner [*peccator sum*] and do not deserve [*dignus*] to be compared with them. They suffered for their innocence [*innocentia sua*], but I suffer for my sins. As he begins to argue his rebuttal, Luther makes use of rhetorical questions with his responses containing biblical examples, and doublets; hence, anthypophora. Both examples are extreme and thus drive the objector to reconsider; thus, Luther's response to the question is concise: You are not (*Non es*) a sinner like them if you have patience (*si patiens fueris*).

Luther's conclusion (*WA* 6:117.17–25) to the chapter begins with a concluding argument of the prolepsis, an explanation of how suffering *pro peccatis* can cleanse. All that remains now is to summarize and conclude the entire chapter, showing how the suffering of the saints is a consolation, not a condemnation. Here he uses saints three times in a progression of benefits, capping them off with asyndeton, a series lacking conjunctions, and anaphora; together they assist one in unleashing a list that gives readers a stronger impression of a singular idea with several facets (*WA* 6:117.23–25). Thus Luther has ended on a strong

---

[*et tu innocens relinqueris*]? (c) You shall not go unpunished, but (b) shall surely drink of it [*non relinqueris innocens, sed bibens bibes*]."

[43] The commemoration of John's beheading (29 August) was being observed (*recordamur*) on the day Luther was writing this section, so a rhetorical question expecting an affirmative answer (*Nam . . . nonne*) is quite appropriate for suggesting that his death should "shame and amaze us all [*none stupore nos omnes confundit*]."

note about the unifying and exemplary role of properly imitating the suffering of the saints. Further, in the *apparatus criticus* of *WA* 6:117 we can observe Luther's attempt in 1535–36 to fix some of this merit theology by inserting faith at important places in the text.

G. *The Seventh Image: The Supernal Evil, or the Evil Above Us* [supra nos]

In this chapter (*LW* 42:141–144; *WA* 6:117–119) Luther turns to Christ as the sole epitome of suffering, and thus of healing through suffering.[44] He returns, in the opening section, to the Wisdom literature for authoritative texts and allusions. The style of this chapter is elevated from all previous ones, for in his execution of *qal wachomer* strategy Luther incorporates ubiquitous doublets and larger series, anaphora, rhetorical questions and anthypophora, and several superlatives. The plan of the chapter is: (A) Introduction and Thesis (*WA* 6:117.28–35): Christ alone is the supreme example of suffering and the source of consolation; (B) Scripture teaches Christ's sweetening passion (*WA* 6:117.35–118.7); (C) His passion sweetens by having transformed all suffering into joy (*WA* 6:118.8–26); (D) The paradoxical reality of Christ's victory is analogous to Moses' bronze serpent (*WA* 6:26–37); (E) Application and Exhortation (*WA* 6:118.38–119.6): Christ's superior transforming power is greater than the relics and thus banishes them; (F) The Challenge (*WA* 6:119.13–16): To keep Christ's passion before us; (G) Summary of the seventh, and of all, evils; preview of part 2, the seven blessings (*WA* 6:119.17–32).

In (A) the Introduction and Thesis (*WA* 6:117.28–35), Luther incorporates language from five different Old Testament texts, three of which come from Song of Solomon (*Canticles*). Using the imagery of bride and lamb, he blends much alliteration and repetition as he applies doublets and a series to argue that Jesus is the goal of all contemplation for consolation in suffering. In order to accomplish this, Luther must establish the superiority of Jesus, whose beauty and majesty even reflects upon his bride. This seventh chapter indeed is the capstone—seven representing completion in Scripture—for Luther begins with 'Finally

---

[44] Joseph Bayly comments on the well-known text in James 5:15 ("and the prayer of faith will save the sick man"). Speaking of a friend, Bayly adds that his friend, who did not recover from cancer, nevertheless believes his prayer was answered: "I prayed for healing, and God healed me. He didn't heal my body, but He healed my mind and my spirit. He healed me of fear, of resentment, of bitterness, of worry for my family. This is God's answer to my prayer"; *The Last Thing We Talk About*, 87.

[*Ultimo*],' a superlative that can mean not only 'last,' but also 'ultimate.'[45] Having thus attempted to weave a chain of key signs of royalty and supremacy—the most unique sign being the epithet, the 'blood of the lamb'—Luther has set the groundwork for identifying Christ as the royal lamb, the bridegroom to whom the bride is sealed—subservient, yet wedded—the superb, sweetening substance that nullifies the worst suffering. Luther will now expand this material.

Luther's task in the second (B) step (*WA* 6:117.35–118.7) of this chapter is to establish the consoling power of the bridegroom. To do so, he returns to his most basic tools for describing an entity of uniqueness—superlatives, doublets, and a quadruplet series—supplying to these forms lavish images from an allegorical interpretation of Song of Sol. 5:13b. A new argumentative feature Luther uses here is a form of clarification by negation—that is, expanding a claim by then denying a putative exception.

In the third (C) step (*WA* 6:118.8–26) of this chapter, Luther attempts to explain how Christ's sweetening power works. He uses an abundance of doublets and series, anaphora, and one New Testament text in this argument. He employs anthypophora, some use of the second person singular for intimacy or confrontation, and a new tactic—oxymoronic terms. Moreover, Luther has not exhausted his attempt to amplify the capacity of Christ and to exhort his readers to apply it to themselves. Notice the emphasis, through repetition, on the terms *all* and *every* as Luther enumerates the manner in which, and extent to which, Christ has made available his power; he makes, once again, the *qal wachomer* argument: For if Christ by the touch (*Si enim tactu*) of his most innocent flesh (*suae mundissimae carnis*) has hallowed "all waters [*omnes aquas*], yes, even all creation [*immo omnem creaturam*]" through baptism, "how much more has he by the same touch [*quanto magis tactu*]" of his most innocent flesh and blood (*mundissimae carnis et sanguinis*) sanctified "every form of death [*omnem mortem*], all suffering [*omnes passiones*], all loss [*omnes iniurias*], every curse [*omnia maledicta*], every shame [*omnem ignominiam*]" for the baptism of the Spirit or the baptism of blood (*WA* 6:118.16–20).

---

[45] See George Tavard, "Luther's Teaching on Prayer," *LTSB* 67 (winter 1987): 3–22, here at 8, for comments on the use of a golden number in constructing meditative writings: Such models were often featured in medieval sermons. They were all the more effective aids to meditation as they were commonly seen in the gothic architecture and ornamentation of churches, in which everything fell into place, in uneven symmetry, around a golden number.

In Luther's fourth (D) step (*WA* 6:118.25–37) of this chapter, he introduces the bronze serpent of Moses (Num. 21:8f.), which, at God's order, was built to allow the Israelites to gaze upon—and thereby survive the otherwise fatal bites of—the fiery serpents God had sent as punishment for Israel's speaking against Him and Moses. Using the analogy of the bronze serpent, Luther shifts his style, dropping the heavy use of doublets and resorting to other devices for stressing the appearance/reality pair. For if death and suffering really are *blessings* for the Christian, readers need instructive tactics for appreciating them. The bronze serpent and Luther's assortment of expressions distinguishing between the real and the apparent provides the rationale, while three other Scriptures (Wisd. of Sol. 3; John 8; Ps. 139:12b [= 138:12b Vulgate]) provide the authority.

In step E (*WA* 6:118.38–119.16) Luther makes an application of the truth that Christ's power is superior to suffering and death, transforming them into victory and life. He exhorts his reader to transfer one's attachment to relics over to the sufferings of this life and their concomitant transforming power in Christ. The exhortation, however, is not strongly explicit—although it is all in second person singular—for no overt instructions or commands are given. The persuasive power is rather in the compelling nature of the comparison, with Luther's abundant use of series for making comparisons (including superlative language) that serve the *qal wachomer* strategy. With a rhetorical question designed to force deep contemplation, even shame, Luther addresses his readers' tendencies ('If you [*Proinde si*]')[46] to revere relics—Frederick being a master relic collector—by first naming the objects (type of relic) and then specifying their actions toward them. Next he argues that they should <u>even more</u> apply these actions to the sufferings of this world. Thus, in Luther's German syntax four sets of lists form an antithetical chiasmus—[a] inferior objects, identified according to association with Christ, [b] improper actions toward those objects: [b₁] proper objects, [a₁] superior actions):

> If you kiss, caress, embrace [*exoscularis, diligis, amplecteris*] as sweetest relics the robe of Christ, the vessels, water jugs, and anything Christ [*tunicam Christi, vasa, hydrias et quaecunque tandem Christus*] touched or used or hallowed by his touch [*tetiget et quibus usus…tanquam suo tactu consecratis*] [*dulcissimus*

---

[46] Better translated, 'Just as if …'; the presumption is that readers do revere the relics.

reliquiis], <u>why will you not much more rather</u> [*Cur non multo magis*] love, embrace, kiss [*diligis, amplecteris, oscularis*] the pain, evils of this world, the disgrace and death[47] [*poenas, mala mundi, ignominiam et mortem*] which He <u>not only</u> [*non solum*] hallowed by his touch [*tactu consecrata*] <u>but also</u> [*sed etiam*] sprinkled and blessed [*tincta et benedicta*] with his most holy [*purissimo*] blood, yes, even embraced [*amplexata*] with a willing heart and a supreme constraining love [*voluntate cordis et summa coartante charitate*]? (*WA* 6:118.38–119.2).

In the sixth (F) step of the chapter Luther breaks off suddenly in a display of emotion as he continues this implicit exhortation—a type of modeling before his reader of the kind of feeling and action one ought to have in keeping Christ's passion ever before him, especially when one is suffering. Luther uses abundant doublets. Finally (G), Luther summarizes this seventh evil and all the preceding ones, mildly exhorting his reader—in the subjunctive—to heed the lessons, especially of this final evil, whose power derives from the suffering Christ. Using many doublets and one quadruplet series, Luther does all this in first person plural. The key to application, he argues, is to have learned from the preceding images, 'those beneath and near us [*infra et iuxta*],' and to bear evils with patience.

Prior to beginning the second part of the book (seven blessings), Luther provides a succinct preview, of which I summarize as follows: The second part also contains seven images, opposite to the seven in the first part. First is the internal blessing; second is the future blessing; third is the past; fourth, the infernal; fifth, the left hand; sixth, the right hand; seventh, the supernal.

H. *The First Image: The Blessing Within* [bonum internum]

In analyzing the First Blessing, I must consider the possibility that Luther's *inventio*—the discovery of arguments and appeals—reaches not only into Scripture but also draws from classical sources of consolation. This is pertinent in part because Luther turns to pagan evidence but especially due to the very nature of that evidence. On first glance, it appears that Luther's arguments resemble the stock Epicurean topics of *avocatio* (turning one's mind away from what is painful) and *revocatio* (dwelling upon what is pleasant). Cicero discusses these topics in book

---

[47] *LW* 42:142 wrongly translates the doublet *ignominiam et mortem* as 'disgrace and shame.'

3 of the *Tusculan Disputations* (3.13.28–22.52).[48] We shall note Luther's use of pagan proverbs, and when concluding our analysis of the document we shall assess to what extent Luther may be following classical strategies.

In this chapter (*LW* 42:144–147; *WA* 6:119–122) Luther explores the blessings one has within his own self, and then he argues that all these far exceed the suffering one occasionally endures. He takes inventory of gifts material and spiritual, physical and intellectual, while for the most part considering only the individual believer; family and other external blessings are only briefly mentioned.[49] This chapter is longer than any of those on the evils, and it is second longest of this part on blessings; in both parts, the second chapter (future evils and future blessings) is the longest. Luther turns to a vast array of Scripture for authority, but he first cites several cultural proverbs. The organization of the chapter is as follows: (A) Introduction (*WA* 6:119.34–120.6): physical blessings far outweigh a few short evils; (B) Material abundance and influence far outweigh small evils (*WA* 6.120.7–14); (C) Blessings of character and intellect are properly distributed by God (*WA* 6:120.15–18); (D) All these blessings are more enjoyable when commingled with occasional troubles (*WA* 6:120.19–32); (E) Exhortation (*WA* 6:120.33–121.23): God's word teaches us to praise Him for these blessings; (F) The Christian has an even greater blessing (*WA* 6:121.24–32): Faith in Christ; (G) Prolepsis: We are not able to comprehend the fullness of these blessings (*WA* 6:121.33–122.6).

In introducing this (A) chapter (*WA* 6:119.34–120.6) Luther proceeds by anthypophora. He begins with a question and ends with an affirmation; both questions and responses are loaded with language that denotes: (1) gifts of abundance; (2) slight experiences of trouble. Luther is writing with Frederick in mind, and he makes clear that he is addressing male readers, for these bodily gifts thus enable men (*in masculo*), who are superior (*nobilissimus sexus*), in many things, 'both in private and public life [*tum privates tum publicis*],' as well as other things that are excluded (*aliena*) to a woman. He is then able to quote two German proverbs ('a saying current among scoundrels [*Nebulones proverbio*]') that capture this observation: "It is merely a matter of one bad

---

[48] Paul A. Holloway, "*Bona Cogitare*: An Epicurean Consolation in Phil 4:8–9," *HTR* 91 (1998): 89–96.

[49] Frederick was unmarried, yet he had three children by his mistress Anna Weller of Molsdorf; cf. Brecht, *Martin Luther*, 1:111.

hour" and "One good hour makes up for a bad one."[50] With more anthypophora, Luther then concludes his introductory thesis on the comparative abundance of God's goodness.

In step B (*WA* 6:120.7–14) of this chapter Luther pursues a form of *qal wachomer* strategy, building upon what he has established in the introduction; he will build upon it even more in step C. He has tried to emphasize how brief and slight are one's struggles, when set against all the gifts of God. He even offers an admonition to his wealthier readers—of which his fellow bachelor Frederick certainly was one (and Luther was not)—with the rationale that it is not as comforting to have "great wealth as [it is to have] a cheerful mind [*multae divitiae quam iucundus animus*]"; however, in his sovereign plan God provides both. In step C (*WA* 6:120.15–18) of this chapter Luther continues his grammar of values, arguing that character, what he calls the blessings of the mind (*Animi bona*; in first position), are truly more excellent than all the preceding blessings. These include—and seem not to be ordered: 'reason, knowledge, judgment, eloquence, prudence [*ingenium, scientia, iudicium, facundia, prudentia*].'[51]

In step D (*WA* 6:120.19–31) of this chapter Luther returns to prover-bial wisdom and doublets—he uses no Scripture—as he summarizes the attitude he wants his readers to have toward their inventory of internal blessings as they stack up against infrequent suffering. Accordingly, the way he juxtaposes blessing and bitterness, one may form an impression that Luther is advising a Stoic resignation; he even interjects a personal reflection, which in this book is unusual. However, his recommendation is not resignation, as is apparent from the relative imbalance of good over bad that he has been stressing, and a couple of key statements in this step make that clear. In the steps that follow it is overwhelmingly plain. He reasons that all meats taste better with salt, and that every palatable dish has a certain bitter taste (*acerbiore quopiam sapore*)—which he means as a positive trait. These kinds of proverbs consolidate rea-soning into compact wisdom.[52]

In step E (*WA* 6:120.32–121.23) of this chapter—by far the longest step—Luther returns to Scripture as his storehouse of authority and wisdom, as he crafts an exhortation that is more of teaching than

---

[50] "Es ist umb ein bose stund zuthun"; "Ein gutt stund ist eyner posen werdt."

[51] *LW* 42:145 wrongly reverses items two and three in the list.

[52] H. G. Haile, "Luther and Literacy," *Publications of the Modern Language Association* 91 (1976): 816–828, here at 820.

of urging. Using doublets and eleven quotations—all from the Old Testament[53]—Luther returns to his use of anthypophora to converse with his readers about God's rich blessings, which can only be properly understood and appreciated when one recognizes the value of His chastisement. So, through numerous Scriptures, he has argued in this step—and strongly implied that one should thank God—that God's blessings far outweigh the sorrows he permits, yet we must thank Him for both and must recognize both as blessings for our good. Step F (*WA* 6:121.23–26) of this chapter is a very short interpretation, whereby Luther clarifies the difference between the bodily blessings—which he has been discussing—and Christian faith. The former, he argues, are given to all, while the latter is superior, for a Christian has 'other and far better [*aliis longe melioribus*]' blessings within. The superiority of this faith is verified (*dictum*) for Luther in Psalm 45:13 (= 44:14 Vulgate), which he paraphrases.[54]

The final (G) step (*WA* 6:121.26–122.6) is a type of prolepsis that Luther uses to explain further how the Christian's greatest internal blessings are not always apparent. This argument likens the situation to that of the first evil, claiming that the body's limitations prevent us from perceiving the full extent of what is nevertheless now within, albeit in potentiality.

I. *The Second Image: The Future Blessing* [bonum futurum] *Before us* [ante se]

In this chapter (*LW* 42:148–152; *WA* 6:122–124)—easily the longest[55] of the book—Luther reflects upon what happens in the future, for both Christian and nonChristian. His emphasis, of course, is on the blessings awaiting Christians, which are, for the most part, wrapped up not only in their future death but also in their present deadness to the world and to sin. In this chapter Luther uses 22 Scriptures, the most of any chapter in the entire book; twice as many come from the Old

---

[53] Wisd. of Sol. 8:1; Deut. 32:10; Ps. 33:5b (= 32:5b Vulgate); Ps. 104:24b (= 103:24b Vulgate); Hab. 3:3c; Ps. 92:4 (= 91:5 Vulgate); Isa. 6:3b; Gen. 1:31; Psalm 106:24a (= 105:24a Vulgate); Job 2:9–10.

[54] "The king's daughter is all glorious within; her clothing is of wrought gold [*Omnis gloria eius filiae regis ab intus in fimbriis aureis circumdata varietate*]." The syntax of this verse suggests a chiastic form to the content, whereby the center pair (within/without [= clothing]) is surrounded by the outer pair (all glorious/wrought gold).

[55] At 107 lines in *WA* 6, this chapter is 16 lines longer than the one before it—which is the next longest—and 23 lines longer than the longest chapter of part I.

Testament as from the New.[56] The stylistic features he uses most often are doublets, superlatives, and a couple of series. The organization of the chapter is as follows: (A) Introduction (*WA* 6:122.9–18): The nonChristian is deceived in desiring material goods and not realizing his uncertainty before God; (B) NonChristians have a two-fold blessing of realizing that evils will pass and good things will come (*WA* 6:122.19–26); (C) A Christian's greatest future blessing is that death will end all suffering—the evils of the body (*WA* 6:122.27–123.26); (D) For the Christian, death ends all sin and vice—the evils of the soul (*WA* 6:123.27–124.4); (E) Thus, we should love death, which God provided for our good, as many Scriptures teach (*WA* 6:124.5–36); (F) Conclusion: Exhortation to meditate on Christ's power and grace and how our meditation can defeat the effects of stress (*WA* 6:124.37–39).

In (A) Luther's introduction (*WA* 6:122.9–18) to this chapter he prepares his Christian reader to realize his blessings, yet—quite unusual for this book—the entire introduction of this chapter, as well as all of the second and well into the third step, is written in third person.[57] Luther uses forms of 'hope,' but both uses clearly connect it with a vain quest. Jesus' comment in Luke 18:21 dictates the meaning to be appropriated: "So is he who lays up treasures [*thezaurisat*] and is not rich toward God" (*WA* 6:122.9–18). In step B (*WA* 6:122.19–26) of this chapter Luther stays with the third person; in addition to two Scriptures (Rom. 2:4; Isa. 46:8), he uses frequent antithetical or progressive doublets—several of which contain intervening terms or phrases—to argue that nonChristians, the sons of men, have not been forsaken (*reliquerit*) but rather are comforted (*soletur*) by God. He provides them with what Luther later calls a 'twofold blessing'—namely, a hope (*affectu*) that "evils will pass and that good things shall come." Thus, in both of these first two steps, Luther has tried to show God's generosity (*donum dei*) and grace in permitting all people a comforting hope that, although anything but certain, can still lead them to a more sure hope, through their leaning on God alone.

In C, a much longer step (*WA* 6:122.27–123.26) of this chapter, Luther turns to the blessings of Christians, which exceed even those

---

[56] Luke 12:18–21; Rom. 2:4; Isa. 46:8; Ps.116:15 (= 115:15 Vulgate); Ps. 4:8; Wisd. of Sol. 4:7; Ps. 34:21 (= 33:22 Vulgate); Ps. 140:11 (= 139:12 Vulgate); Phil. 1:21; Rom. 14:8; Ps. 23:3 (= 22:4 Vulgate); Nu. 21:8f.; Wisd. of Sol. 4:10–14a; Gen. 3:19; Matt. 6:10; Ps. 30:5 (= 29:5 Vulgate); 1 Sam. 17:51.

[57] Twice Luther uses 'we' in the introduction, but it is strictly editorial.

blessings of all men previously discussed—for at death all suffering will end. He engages the language of comparison—superlatives and *qal wachomer*. Moreover, at the beginning he continues in the third person, until he reaches his Scripture quotations, which are many; most of the first few, however, are from the Old Testament (Psalms and Wisd. of Sol.) and themselves in third person. It is not until he reaches the Pauline quotations and Psalm 23 that Luther begins to celebrate, in first person plural, the blessings of Christians. In step D (*WA* 6:123.27–124.4) of this chapter Luther renames succinctly the first blessing of death: it puts an end to the evils of this life's punishments or what he also called 'the whole tragedy of this world's ills'; then he turns to the other blessing of death. Contrary to what some people today consider the two so-called blessings of death (heaven and the end of suffering), Luther calls this second blessing even more excellent (*praestantius*), for it puts an end to all 'vices and sins.'[58]

In step E (*WA* 6:124.5–39) of this chapter, Luther concisely summarizes how death has been defanged for the Christian. Then he develops a lengthy argument that Christians should therefore love death, which God provided for our good. The argument is sustained chiefly through metaphor, doublets, scriptural allusions, quotes, and examples, the chief of which is the story of the Fall (Gen. 3). To support this argument, he invokes the Edenic story, placing the initiative in God's hands: God appointed (*ordinarit*) death to destroy death, in that he imposed death on Adam immediately after his sin. He elaborates on how sin is destroyed, "not by that of another, but by its own work [*non alieno sed suo proprio opere*]," how it is stabbed (*iugulatur*) with its own sword, "as Goliath is beheaded by his own sword." Completing the allegorical exegesis, Luther plainly applies the text of 1 Sam. 17:51 to Christ, finishing with a progressive <u>triplet</u> of verbs:

> Goliath also was a kind of sin [*figura fuit peccati*], a giant terrifying [*terribilis gygas*] to all except the young boy David, that is, to Christ [*id est Christo*], who singlehandedly laid him low [*qui solus eum <u>prostravit</u> et*], beheaded him with his own sword [*<u>absciso</u> capite proprio illius gladio*], and in 1 Samuel 21 [:9] said that there was no better sword than the sword of Goliath [*iam meliorem non esse gladium <u>dicit</u> quam Goliath. I. Reg. xxi.*] (*WA* 6:124.20–36).

In F, his last step (*WA* 6:124.37–39) of this chapter, Luther concludes—concisely and creatively, with a single rhetorical question, in first person

---

[58] *LW* 42:150 erroneously reverses the last doublet.

plural—that we should meditate on "joys of the power of Christ and the gifts of his grace." If we thus meditate, Luther says, how can any small evil distress (*torquebit*) us when in the great evil to come [i.e., death] we see such great blessings? As written by Luther, and as translated by Martin Bertram, the sentence forms a chiasmus of comparison: (a) joys and gifts; (b) small evil: (b₁) great evil; (a₁) great blessings.[59] Therefore, in this chapter, especially with the fourth step, Luther has anticipated the substance of John Donne's *Death Be Not Proud*, particularly its final line: "Death, thou shalt die."

J. *The Third Image: The Past Blessing* [bonum praeteritum] *Behind Us* [post se]

This chapter (*LW* 42:152–155; *WA* 6:125f.) is a contrast (*contrario*) to its corresponding chapter, the evil of the past (*praeterito malo*). Luther claims that consideration of this image should be easy, but that he will help (*iuvemus*)[60] with the consideration. Indeed, help he does, for not only does he advance many of the same type of arguments—namely, look at all God has done for us, especially as seen in our weakest state: birth and infancy. But in exploring God's blessings in one's past, Luther goes farther in his appeals to guilt and shame than he did in the corresponding chapter on all of God's previous protections from dangers. He uses approximately a dozen Scripture texts, two-thirds from the Old Testament, especially the Psalms. As he did with the past evils, Luther cites Augustine's *Confessions* and also his Commentary on the Psalms. The chapter is organized in the following way: (A) Introduction/Thesis (*WA* 6:125.3–13): All our blessings, as we reflect on our past, were ordered by God for our good; (B) Our experience teaches us that God continues to care for us, so why don't we trust him to do that? (*WA* 6:125.14–31); (C) When we doubt God's providence, Scripture and our own reason correct us (*WA* 6:125.32–126.28); (D) Prolepsis (*WA* 6:126.28–37): Failure to trust in and depend on God will create misery; (E) Conclusion (*WA* 6:126.37–40).

---

[59] The final phrase (*magna bona videmus*) makes clear that—contrary to *LW* 42:152, which translates *magna bona* as a singular—Luther had both blessings in view here: (2) *alterum*, the end of sin and (1) *primum*, the end of suffering and the rectifying of wrong. Steinhaeuser (PE 1:151) correctly translates the term as plural, though his translation of the entire last sentence disrupts Luther's chiasmus.

[60] Luther uses the first person plural (*iuvemus*) here editorially.

In introducing this chapter (A), Luther turns immediately to 'Blessed Augustine,' praising him as an excellent master (*eximius est artifex*) who, in the *Confessions* (1.6) speaks so beautifully (*pulcherrime recitat*) about God's provision in infancy (*ab utero matris suae*). However, Luther's praise is not toward Augustine per se but for God—the benefits of God and the goodness of God—for he spends much more time paraphrasing (and citing) Psalm 139 (= 138:1ff. Vulgate) and commenting on the text through his own interpretative dialogue. In step B (*WA* 6:125.14–31) of this chapter, Luther uses three Scriptures (Wisd. of Sol. 7:16; 1 Cor. 12:6; Ps. 40:17a [= 39:17a Vulgate]) and Augustine's commentary on Psalm 40 to argue that our own experience teaches us that we have been under God's providential care in the past, and that this is for our good. Luther is not lauding the trustworthiness of experience so much as our solidarity with Augustine—that his experience is also ours. With strong language—containing rhetorical questions and doublets—Luther admonishes his reader to feel shame for not realizing God's care and not trusting him during difficult times.

Luther's step C (*WA* 6:125.32–126.27) in this chapter is to build a scriptural case for showing how faulty human 'wisdom and judgment' really are. He says those faculties blind (*obstant*) us to God's providence, wherein, by chance, frequent circumstances develop (*evenerint*) in accordance with our plans. Luther uses a flurry of doublets to heap more shame and guilt, as he prepares his reader for more Scripture, this time from 1 Peter. He seems to be pitting Scripture against failed human reason, in order to show the superiority of the latter, when looked at humbly and responsibly. The argument is still the same: that one should depend on God for everything (= claim/conclusion of policy), because God cares—past, present, future—for us (= datum/minor premise), given that whomever God cares for is well cared for, and we desire to be well cared for (= implicit motivational warrant/major premise).

In step D (*WA* 6:126.28–37) of this chapter, Luther launches a prolepsis that does not test—in the sense of object to—his argument, as much as it presents outcomes and consequences of failing to heed his argument—that is, failing to depend fully on God. Luther describes a scenario that would presumably be objectionable to his reader, for the reader is not recalcitrant but cautious—that is, wanting to depend on God, but finding it difficult. Luther then invokes the entire book of Ecclesiastes for its treatment (*loquitur*) of his subject, arguing that its author himself experienced the life of trying out (*tentaverit*) many things, only to discover (*invenerit*) them all to be only 'toil, vanity, and affliction of the spirit.' Luther concludes (E) this chapter (*WA* 6:126.37–40) very succinctly with a rich expression: Therefore, "we ought to have no other care for ourselves" than this—namely, we should not care for ourselves or rob God of his care for us. Then, for further contemplation he—again (*ut dixi*)—refers his reader back to the corresponding image (*spectro contrario*) of evil—part one, chapter three—and he still recommends introspection into one's past life (*recordatione totius vitae praeteritae*). For Luther has been implying that one's judgment is clouded in the present; but in later reflection on the past, especially when viewing life through scriptural lenses, one more readily sees God's providential care *and* the futility of our own fussing.

K. *The Fourth Image: The Infernal Blessing* [bonum infernum] *Beneath Us* [infra nos]

In this chapter (*LW* 42:155–157; *WA* 6:127f.) Luther argues that what God is doing with the dead and damned offers a strange but powerful blessing, when one considers His justice and mercy toward them and us. In broadening the scope of one's affliction, Luther opens the consideration of the unrighteous and the role they, and their outcome, play for the righteous. As the chapter closes Luther twice mentions the 'saints,' once speaking of their goodness and the other of their injuries. He uses several Scriptures, all from the Old Testament, and one sententia from Gregory the Great (540, 590–604). In this rather sobering examination of God's punishment of the wicked, one finds Luther concluding this chapter with a strategy he seldom uses in this book: extended exhortation in the second person singular; he seems to be offering Frederick a lesson in humility and gratitude. Normally in this work, Luther exhorts in the first person plural, and he does so without heavy-handed confrontation or forceful urging. Perhaps here he seeks to incorporate a greater measure of the admonitory to blend well with the comforting.[61] The chapter is organized as follows: (A) Recapitulation of blessings already—and yet to be—considered and

---

[61] An instructive text in Scripture is Acts 9:31, which summarizes the effect upon the early church that resulted from, among other things, the early activities of the newly converted Saul of Tarsus. It shows a healthy blend of fear and comfort, as though they are complementary, not antithetical: "So the church throughout all Judea and Galilee and Samaria had peace and was built up [*aedificabatur*]; and walking in the fear [*timore*] of the Lord and in the comfort [*consolatione*] of the Holy Spirit it was multiplied [*replebatur*]."

Thesis for this (*infernal*) blessing (*WA* 6:127.3–7); (B) A comparison of our lot to that of the damned should cause us to rejoice and be instructed (*WA* 6:127.7–31); (C) A comparison of what the damned receive to what they justly deserve motivates us to celebrate God's judgment (*WA* 6:127.32–128.17); (D) Concluding exhortation: Rejoice at God's righteous punishment of our enemies, both without and within (*WA* 6:128.17–29). In our closer scrutiny below, we will not examine every step.

In step B (*WA* 6:127.7–31) of this chapter Luther explains how a comparison of our lot with that of the damned should bring gratitude and sober warning. The language of comparison, invoking *qal wachomer* reasoning, includes superlatives, doublets, triplets, chiasmus, an extended Scripture quotation, a pithy *sententia* from Gregory, and—in the recapitulation and first half of this step—a high frequency of *seeing* terms, seven of them in the first 13 lines of this chapter. In step C (*WA* 6:127.32–128.17) of this chapter Luther attempts to bolster the case for how God's judgment of sinners becomes a blessing—and hence, also a subject for thanksgiving and praise—for his Christian reader. Luther does not speak in such a way as to signal this section as prolepsis, but it does serve that function somewhat. The argument compares the treatment described in Isa. 65 with Luther's attributions of God's character. He uses repetition of terms for justice, righteousness, mercy, etc., several doublets, a triplet, superlatives, chiasmus, and turns to more Scriptures (Ps. 58:10 [= 57:11 Vulgate]; 1 Sam. 16:1; 2 Sam. 19:6). Luther's last (D) step (*WA* 6:128.18–29) in this chapter is a concluding exhortation in second person singular; 23 times in 12 lines 'you' is found, either as pronoun or as included in the verb form.[62] Here he continues what he had begun earlier in first plural—the invocation to rejoice at God's justice for all, and to guard against resisting it—by using numerous doublets, rhetorical question, antithesis, superlatives, and a quotation of 2 Sam. 19:6 a second time. In his final sentence Luther returns to the inclusive first person plural.

---

[62] Five expressions that signal conclusion-drawing are present in these lines: 'Thus you see' [*Atque ita vides*]; 'What wonder, therefore' [*Quid ergo mirum*]; 'Therefore, you should be rejoicing' [*immo gaudendum tibi*]; 'Therefore…you ought' [*Sicut ergo…debes*]; 'Thus you see' [*Vides itaque*].

L. *The Fifth Image: The Adverse Blessing on Our Left Hand*
[bonum sinistrum seu ad sinistram]

In this chapter (*LW* 42:157–160; *WA* 6:128–130), Luther completes his discussion of his reader's *adversarii*, having already covered—in the previous chapter—those who are "already damned and given over to the devils." His present subject is those adversaries still living, and in them Luther offers a twofold blessing,[63] if his reader will consider his living adversaries with other feelings (*alio affectu intueri*). By that, we presume he means other than with negative feelings only. While this chapter is virtually equal in length to the previous one, here Luther will use double the number of Scriptures; they come in equal proportions from both testaments. The argument is chiefly one of *qal wachomer* and, after the initial introductory sentences that I have already explained, its structure is simple: (A) The First Blessing (*WA* 6:128.34–129.19): The abundance of our adversaries helps us see our greater blessings; (B) The Second Blessing (*WA* 6:129.20–37): Trials make us stronger; (C) Persecution is strong, but it too turns into our blessing (*WA* 6:129.37–130.14); (D) Conclusion: God works all things for our good (*WA* 6:130.15–23).

The First Blessing (A) begins not simply with the obvious observation that the ungodly abound in temporal goods. Rather, Luther takes his remark to its natural *telos*: even the prophets are almost envious (*prope commoti sint ad invidiam*). We note here that—unlike his typical strategy of announcing the blessing or evil fully in advance—Luther lures his reader into agreement with the problem, with little hint of its solution; hence, the argument here is somewhat inductive. That is, without rhetorical question or anthypophora, Luther delays revealing the blessing until later. In step B (*WA* 6:129.20–130.15) Luther takes up the second blessing, which he says is even more marvelous (*multo mirabilius*). This blessing is but an extension of the first, wherein the prior step begins where the reader—or anyone, including 'the prophets'—presently remains: namely, that in the prosperity of his enemies and in their escaping of trials one does not recognize his own blessings, but that is what God is doing, nonetheless. Here Luther takes his examination farther and deeper, no longer exploring others' blessings but our trials,

---

[63] The twofold blessing actually turns into threefold, although Luther does not make this very clear, for midway through the second blessings he turns from the temptations and trials of the world to its persecution.

which often originate with our enemies, arguing that—in the providence
of God (*deo sic nos curante*)—trials make us strong.

At *WA* 6:129.38, Luther makes a third step (C), which takes up
another side of the world's evils, namely *adversitas*, by which he means
persecution. Here he spends the first half of his time describing the
ferocity of persecution and the second half focusing on how it is turned
into blessing. He supplies two historical examples, the first being Blessed
Augustine's comment on the innocents murdered by Herod (Matt.
2:16–18), to the effect that Herod accomplished more good with his
hatred (*odio*) than with his favor (*obsequio*). The second example is Blessed
Agatha,[64] who Luther says commented to her captors, 'pleading in this
manner.' Her remarks (quoted below) epitomize the claim that persecution can result in great blessing, provided one recognizes and cooperates
with this fact. To the religious conservative Frederick, the dialogue that
Luther puts into Agatha's mouth should be very meaningful:

> Unless you cause my body [*corpus*] to be broken [*contrectari*] by your execu-
> tioners [*carnificibus*], my soul [*anima*] will not be able to enter paradise
> bearing the Victor's palm, even as a grain of wheat, unless it is stripped
> of its husk and harshly beaten on the threshing floor and is gathered into
> the barn [*non reponitur in horreum*] (*WA* 6:130.10–14).[65]

---

[64] Reportedly martyred during the persecution under Decius (250–253); the feast
day is February 5.

[65] These remarks are likely from the account of St. Agatha in Jacobus de Voragine,
The Golden Legend: Readings on the Saints, 2 vols., trans. William Granger Ryan (Princeton,
1993), 1:155: "And Agatha said: 'These pains are my delight! It's as if I were hearing
some good news, or seeing someone I had long wished to see, or had found a great
treasure. The wheat cannot be stored in the barn unless it has been thoroughly threshed
and separated from the chaff: so my soul cannot enter paradise...unless you make
the headsmen give my body harsh treatment'" [dixitque Agatha: ego in his poenis ita
delector, sicut qui bonum nuntium audit aut qui videt, quem diu desideravit, aut qui
multos thesaurus invenit. Non enim potest triticum in horreum poni, nisi thcca fuerit
fortiter conculcata et in paleis redacta. Sic anima mea non potest intrare in paradisum
cum palma martirii, nisi diligenter feceris corpus meum a carnificibus attrectari]. I have
placed an ellipsis to indicate a phrase ('with the martyr's palm' [cum palma martirii])
omitted by Ryan's translation but included in *The Golden Legend* of Jacobus de Voragine,
trans. William Granger Ryan and Helmut Ripperger (New York, 1941; reprint ed., New
York, 1969), 159, and in the critical edition, from which I have quoted above: Jacobi
a Voragine, *Legenda Aurea: Vulgateo Historia Lombardica Dicta*, 3rd. ed., ed. Th. Graesse
(Leipzig, 1890; reprint, Melle, 2003), 171. For background on this important medieval
work, see Sherry L. Reames, *The Legenda aurea: A Reexamination of Its Paradoxical History* (Madison, 1985). The *Legenda* was compiled by the Dominican friar Jacobus de
Voragine (ca. 1229–1298). It was a bestseller in many languages throughout England
and the Continent, until its publication came to a virtual stop in 1613. Ryan (1:xiii) says
some one thousand manuscripts have survived, and he reports that "it has been said
that in the late Middle Ages the only book more widely read was the Bible." *Legenda*

The final (D) step (*WA* 6:130.15–23) of the chapter is Luther's conclusion, where he argues that additional evidence is unnecessary: Why waste words (*modica loquimur*), he says, when we see that members of the following triplet all agree: (1) All of Scripture; (2) The writings and statements of all the fathers; (3) The lives and deeds of all the saints. Judging by what Luther has been practicing in this book, we must say that the triplet of witnesses is in descending order of authority.

M. *The Sixth Image: Favorable Blessings on Our Right Hand*
[bonum dextrum seu ad dextram]

In this chapter (*LW* 42:160–163; *WA* 6:130–132) Luther engages the topic of this chapter's correlative—part one, chapter six, the evil on our right hand—where he addressed the cult of the saints—almost exclusively their suffering—and argued against a superstitious attachment to them and their relics. However, here the blessing on the right hand is the church of the saints (*Ecclesia sanctorum*), for the two are brought together powerfully. So, in an important sense, this is another look at the saints (the term in the plural appears nine times), often in connection with the church—but a look more at the blessings they enjoy, and in which we can share, than at their sufferings, which was the focus in part one. Here, when Luther speaks of the saints' suffering, he stresses its mutuality with—and benefits to—living Christians. His style is more elevated, too, for—almost always in first person plural—Luther employs nearly every one of his strategies found earlier in this book. Particularly

---

is "almost universally regarded as a kind of *summa hagiographiae*, a book presenting the essence of what medieval people knew, or thought they knew, about the saints. And its spectacular fall from esteem during the Renaissance has been explained in effect as a mistake, the result of critics' prejudices or reformers' zeal" (Reames, 5). Reames seeks to discover the "real story behind the rise, reign, and fall of the *Legenda*." We have evidence from as early as 1516 that Luther was familiar with the Golden Legend. In a letter (24 August 1516) to Georg Spalatin Luther says, "I am quite annoyed with the nonsense and the lies to be found in the *Catalogue* and *The Golden Legend*" (*WABr* 1:50); 'Catalogue' refers to *Catalogue of the Saints* by Peter Natalibus (Lyons, 1508); see Franz Posset, *Pater Bernhardus: Martin Luther and Bernard of Clairvaux*. Cistercian Studies 168 (Kalamazoo, Mich., 1999), 74. Yet here, with Agatha, we find Luther using favorably material he might well have gotten from the *Legend*. The same is true of stories about Bernard of Clairvaux (1090–1153); cf. Posset, *Pater Bernhardus* 74f., 313f.; "St. Bernard's Influence on Two Reformers: John von Staupitz and Martin Luther," *Cistercian Studies Quarterly* 25 (1990): 175–187; "*Divus Bernhardus*: Saint Bernard as Spiritual and Theological Mentor of the Reformer Martin Luther," in *Bernardus Magister: Papers Presented at the Nonacentenary Celebration of the Birth of Saint Bernard of Clairvaux, Kalamazoo, Michigan*, ed. John R. Sommerfeldt (Kalamazoo, 1992), 517–532.

in its manner of engaging the reader through questions and answers, the chapter has more of a sermonic feel to it—even to the point of ending with 'Amen.' The organization of the chapter is as follows: (A) Introduction and Thesis (*WA* 6:130.26–131.4): The Church is a blessing, and the first blessings are visible; (B) The best blessings come through the communal relationship one has in the church (*WA* 6:131.4–132.10); (C) Applying the reality of the communion (*WA* 6:132.11–24).

In step A (*WA* 6:130.26–131.4) Luther identifies the subject of the chapter and narrows his focus in this step to the visible, material blessings of the church; early on there is an *optical* emphasis. In identifying his subject, Luther uses doublets, an asyndetic triplet, and anaphora. He is speaking of "the church of the saints, the new creation of God, our brothers and our friends." Luther's step B (*WA* 6:131.3–132.24) is not clearly signaled, since he has already been comparing material to nonmaterial blessings. So I pick up his summary of the material blessings, in which he uses doublets and an asyndetic series to wrap up one form of blessing and move on to the next, providing an explanation for how these blessings to others can be a comfort to us. The purpose of God's giving (*Dat*, in first position in the sentence) worldly wealth—in whatever form—to his people is that He wants to 'comfort them and others.' However, these are not true (*propria*) blessings but only 'shadows and signs [*umbra et signa*]' of the real blessings which are 'faith, hope, love, and other graces and gifts,'[66] which are shared with all through love.

In the last step (C) in this chapter (*WA* 6:132.8–24), Luther returns to the communal first person plural, using doublets and triplets, with anaphora, to exhort his reader to partake of the consoling resources of 'Christ and the church.' As his journey language turns into more lively metaphor, Luther leads his reader into Scripture—the story of Elisha (2 Kings 6). The writer's goal in using this text (notice the Scripture speaks directly, in second person and third person singular) is to assist the reader in transferring his own fear into the resourceful hands of the church, for Luther begins: "Actually, the church bears it more bravely [*fortius*] than we do. Thus truthfully we can apply to ourselves the words Elisha in 2 Kings 6[67] spoke to his fearful servants"

---

[66] *LW* 42:161 mistakenly reverses the final pair in the series.
[67] While citing the Scripture text in their notes, both *LW* 42:163 and PE 1:167 neglect to translate *iiij. Reg. vi.* (*WA* 6:132.16) in their translation.

(*WA* 6:132.11–16). Luther's quote of v. 16f. is nearly exact and begins with an imperative (*WA* 6:132.17–20).[68]

Luther's closing exhortation, which—as is typical in this book—does not use imperatives, makes a direct application (in first person plural) of the Elisha text to the current situation: the need for consolation in the face of overwhelming need. The journey language and the visual motif will become even more prominent in the following, final chapter, where it turns into lively metaphor.

N. *The Seventh Image: The Supernal Blessing Above Us*
[bonum supernum seu super nos]

The final chapter (*LW* 42:163–165; *WA* 6:132–134) is the shortest of all the blessings chapters and the third shortest of the entire book. The subject is not the future heaven but the Christ—past, present, and future—especially his righteousness (11 occurences of *iustitia*). Nearly all the Scripture texts Luther uses (7 of 9) come from the New Testament, and all are Pauline—from Romans or 1 Corinthians. He emphasizes the blessings to the individual Christian, even though the speaker stance is predominantly communual, using first person plural, for the tone of this chapter is highly celebratory—to the extent that there are not one but two 'Amen's here. In this chapter Luther uses the image of the 'wagons' Joseph took to Canaan in order to bring back his father Jacob and all his family to Egypt (Gen. 45); he applies the image to Christ's redemption and blessings. The wagon metaphor may also derive from the 'Fuhrwagen' illustration of Luther's Wittenberg colleague, Andreas Bodenstein von Karlstadt (1486–1541), which depicted two wagons leading to heaven and hell respectively. As with the limewood panel of the *Vierzehnheiligen* above the altar at Torgau, drawn by Lucas Cranach the Elder, in advance of the Leipzig Debate, Karlstadt was characterizing the triumph of the Gospel at Leipzig, soon after which Luther wrote this book.[69] In Karlstadt's 'two-frame cartoon,' the top

---

[68] The style of this text, with its syntactic, coordinating conjunctions (*Cumque… et…et…Et*), preserves the Hebrew style and its waw consecutive; hence, a chain of events is strung together in order to convey a sense of inevitability—not an ineluctable fatalism that resists understanding or supplication, but rather God's great power that is responsive to the 'effectual fervent prayer of a righteous man' (Jas. 5:16).

[69] Martin Brecht, *Martin Luther*, 1:354; Ulrich Bubenheimer, "Andreas Rudolff Bodenstein von Karlstadt: Sein Leben, seine Herkunft und seine inner Entwicklung," in *Andreas Bodenstein von Karlstadt, 500-Jahr-Feier: Festschrift der Stadt Karlstadt zum Jubiläumsjahr 1980*, ed. Wolfgang Merklein (Karlstadt, 1980), 19–28. The more common

frame presents the wagon of an Evangelical moving 'in God's name' toward Christ, in spite of the demon attempting to brake the wheels. The bottom frame depicts the wagon of the scholastics proceeding to hell, its wheels greased by the theology of 'doing one's best.'[70] In his culminating chapter here, however, Luther makes use of only the former image. The chapter is organized as follows: (A) Introduction (*WA* 6:132.27–37): Declaration of what this blessing is; (B) Resurrection blessings (*WA* 6:133.1–29); (C) Summary of Resurrection blessings and Righteousness of Christ, our resting place (*WA* 6:133.30–134.4); (D) Conclusion (*WA* 6:134.5–9).

In his introduction (*WA* 6:132.27–37) to the subject of *supernal* blessings, Luther first clarifies what his subject is and then proceeds to characterize and praise it through several stylistic devices—doublet, triplet, anaphora, superlatives, metaphor, and two Scripture quotations. He begins by stipulating that his subject is not the 'eternal and heavenly' blessings enjoyed by the blessed (*beati*) in the perfect vision of God.[71] In the main argument of the chapter—step B (*WA* 6:133.1–29)—Luther articulates the resurrection blessings, showing the transporting upward by Christ's righteousness. In this step he introduces the 'wagon' metaphor, turning to Scripture for an example of such incredulity and finding it in Jacob (Gen. 45). Luther's recounting of the story's highlights emphasizes how hard it is to believe (*non credebat* is in first position) and the convincing evidence that was sent (*missa a Ioseph* is in final position). Jacob was one who heard it told—by his own sons, though Luther does not mention it—that Joseph ruled Egypt, yet he seemed (*quasi*) to be awakening from a deep sleep and did not believe. Despite repeated tellings in Joseph's words, it took the sight of the wagons (*plaustra*) sent by Joseph to convince Jacob. Luther then explicitly likens Jacob's dilemma-turned-joyful-outcome to his (and his reader's) situation, and also to that of Christ's disciples. For those of us who truly

---

designator in German of Karlstadt's drawing is Der 'Himmel- und Höllenwagen.' On 24 June 1519 the Wittenberg party arrived in Leipzig, the lead wagon (*Fuhrwagen*) bearing Karlstadt and his many books, while the second carried Luther, Melanchthon, Duke Barnim of Pomerania, and the rector of the University of Wittenberg. To the delight of Johann Eck (1486–1543) and his supporters, Karlstadt's wagon crashed at the city gate, flinging him into the muck and injuring him to the point of his needing medical attention; cf. Ernst Schwiebert, *Luther and His Times: The Reformation from a New Perspective* (St. Louis, 1950), 391.

[70] Carter Lindberg, *The European Reformations* (Oxford, 1996), 84–88.

[71] For *visione clara dei LW* 42:163 reads 'perfect wisdom of God'; PE 1:168 reads 'perfect vision of God,' but has different mistakes—probably errors of copy editing—in the sentence.

find it hard to believe (*credere*) that in Christ such great blessings have been bestowed on 'us unworthy creatures [*nobis indignis*],'[72] we have, Luther argues, been taught by Christ through 'many words, and by the evidence of our own experiences,'[73] whereas Christ's disciples had his many appearances.

Luther likens our instruction to the wagons Joseph sent. More precisely, however, Luther characterizes our wagon (*Plaustrum*, in first position) as certainly the most precious wagon (*sane suavissimum plaustrum*), one made by God 'for our righteousness, sanctification, redemption, wisdom' (1 Cor. 1:30b). This section may very well serve a proleptic function, given how hard it is to believe—as Luther has already noted—that Christ would come for us. Note the locomotive verbs, the juxtaposed predications assigned to 'I' and 'his,' and how 'I' is totally passive, for Christ 'does the driving for us,' so to speak:

> I am a sinner, but I am borne by his righteousness, which is given to me. I am unclean, but his holiness is my sanctification, in which I ride gently [*vehor suaviter*]. I am an ignorant fool, but his wisdom carries me forward [*vehit me*]. I deserve condemnation, but I am set free by his redemption [*libertas eius*], which is a safe wagon for me [*plaustrum securissimum*] (*WA* 6:133.1–15).

To finish this step, Luther turns to Paul's confident taunt in 1 Cor. 15:55–57. First he claims the verse for every reader: "Say, therefore, Christian, in full confidence [*Dicat ergo Christianus cum fiducia*]."[74] As I quote the remainder of Luther's argumentation, notice the parallelism: in clauses, each ending with a present participle; in homoioptoton—three verbs in final position, all with similar case endings (*habemus... implemus... superamus*). Notice also the doublets, the closing triplet, the frequent 'his' juxtaposed with 'our':

> No, but it was Jesus Christ, from the dead rising [*a morte resurgens*], sin and death condemning [*peccatum et mortem damnans*], his righteousness to us imparting [*suam iustitiam nobis impartiens*], his merits on us bestowing [*sua merita nobis donans*], his hand over us holding [*suam manum super nos ponens*]. And now all is well with us and the law we fulfil [*et bene habemus et legem implemus*], and the sin and death we vanquish [*et peccatum mortemque superamus*]. For all of this let there be honor, praise, and thanksgiving [*honor, laus, et gratiarumactio*] to God for ever and ever. Amen (*WA* 6:133.25–29).

---

[72] *LW* 42:164 fails to include *indignis* in its translation, as PE 1:169 correctly does.

[73] Translation by A. T. W. Steinhaeuser at PE 1:169.

[74] PE 1:169 also translates properly the imperative and vocative as singulars.

Besides all else we observed above, we also notice the terms Luther uses that connote—some even denote—pictures of verticality, power, and protection. Luther's step C (*WA* 6:133.30–134.4) summarizes the resurrection blessings and argues that the righteousness of Christ is our resting place.

In his conclusion (*WA* 6:134.5–9) to this chapter—and in a way, to the entire book—Luther returns to the prospect of 'firmly believing,' which preceded the warning above. With doublets, a flurry of first person plural pronouns, and *qal wachomer* reasoning—and without resorting to imperative—Luther exhorts his reader to be instructed (*erudiat*). He begins by designating this one image by itself as sufficient to fill us with such comfort—if considered 'properly and with an attentive heart'—that "not only over our evils should we not grieve, but even should we glory in our tribulations." Further, Luther argues that these tribulations—"for the joy that we have in Christ"—we should scarcely feel. He closes with a doxological benediction: "In which glorying may Christ Himself instruct us, our Lord and God, blessed forevermore. Amen" (*WA*:134.5–9).[75]

Postscript

Luther ends[76] the book with a personal message to the Elector (*WA* 6:134.11–20). The message takes on the customary deferential stance toward an addressee of royalty and thus is somewhat parallel to the Letter of Dedication, where the use of superlatives and epithets of distinction are abundant. However, here Luther's only superlatives are the three instances of acknowledging his "Most Illustrious Prince" in the first and fourth lines, and the closing signature, "Your Most Illustrious Lordship" (*Illustrissimae D.T.*). The stance Luther takes mostly is reflexive, where he calls attention to his own role (*officium*) of service, signing off as his prince's "Intercessor [*Orator*]. Brother [*Frater*] Martin Luther, Augustinian at Wittenberg." Luther's final remark expresses concisely the argument he has sustained throughout the book—that is, without any explicit mention of blessings or evils, that the Christian is ever safe in God's hands.

---

[75] The final sentence follows the translation of Steinhaeuser at PE 1:170.

[76] Following the 'Amen' and prior to the postscript (which is untitled), Luther adds the Greek word Τέλος, which is printed in *WA* 6:134.10 without final sigma. In addition to 'end' or 'conclusion,' Τέλος can mean 'goal' or 'completion' and is thus a more fitting epithet for this book of Luther's than the traditional *finis*.

III. *Conclusion*

Using abundant scriptural quotations and constructed dialogue, Luther creates a strong presence for each image (*spectrum*), both of evil and blessing. In contrast to many of his vernacular texts, Luther's argumentation in Latin employs a few more stylistic devices. With ample use of these devices, including a strong reliance on comparatives, superlatives, and anthypophora, Luther follows a 'how much more' (*qal wachomer*) argumentative strategy.

What authorities drive Luther's consolation? While he has used profane proverbs, and cited or alluded to classical texts (Dyonisius, Homer) and patristic sources (Cyprian, Augustine, Jerome, Gregory) only sparingly, Luther has used most often the Word of God to argue that Christ's resources are sufficient for consolation. In 480 lines of text he used Scripture 167 times (99 from OT, 68 from NT). Of those OT texts, 52 come from the Wisdom Literature (Job, Psalms, Proverbs, Ecclesiastes, Ecclesiasticus, and Wisdom of Solomon). While Luther has not shrunk from employing the rationale of human reason, his sources are older than most of Cicero's authorities. He advocates turning away from pain and suffering only after closely examining it to identify what can be celebrated therein. As he argues in the Introduction, a thing has only the value and meaning (*qualis et quanta*) that the mind in its thoughts assigns: "Whatever he regards as trivial and of no value [*vile et nihili*] will affect him only slightly, whether it be love when it comes to him or pain when it goes away" (*WA* 6:106.19–21). Luther claims this ability to neutralize that which moves us is best effected through the Word, turning our thoughts from debilitating experiences in the present onto that which is "either absent or does not move us at the moment." Therefore, Luther concludes, consolation comes *only* from the Scriptures. Christian duty (to comfort ourselves and others) is empowered by the Word of God, through the Comforter, the Holy Spirit. As George Tavard points out, Luther strategically used formal patterns to organize his own efforts to channel the Spirit's consoling thoughts to suffering people and to help people "find a structure for their prayer of meditation."[77]

---

[77] George Tavard, 8. Besides "Fourteen Consolations," Luther used formal patterns (*LW* 43:202) in the "Letter to Peter Beskendorf: A Simple Way to Pray" (1535); *Eine einfältige Weise zu beten für einen guten Freund* (*WA* 38:358–75).

CHAPTER TWO

"I HAVE OVERCOME THE WORLD": LUTHER'S "SERMON ON PREPARING TO DIE" (1519)

Despite the fact that Elisabeth Kübler-Ross's *On Death and Dying* (1969) has sold over a million copies, and that her five stages of dying are manifest in all nursing textbooks,[1] today there are virtually no contemporary books on how to die that are written for the dying.[2] For caregivers

---

[1] Tony Walter, *The Revival of Death*, 70–76. For critiques of the limitations and influence of the stage theory of dying by Kübler-Ross, see the work of Dennis Klass, who worked with her in Chicago: "Elisabeth Kubler-Ross and the Tradition of the Private Sphere: An Analysis of Symbols," *Omega* 12, no. 3 (1981–1982): 241–267; Dennis Klass and Richard A. Hutch, "Elisabeth Kubler-Ross as a Religious Leader," *Omega* 16, no. 2 (1985–1986): 89–109; Richard Schulz, *The Psychology of Death, Dying, and Bereavement* (Reading, Mass., 1978), 69–76; Robert J. Kastenbaum, *Death, Society, & Human Experience* (St. Louis, 1977), 208–216; Richard Schulz and David Aderman, "Clinical Research and the Stages of Dying," *Omega* 5 (1974): 137–143; Jane Littlewood, *Aspects of Grief: Bereavement in Adult Life* (London, 1992); Roy Branson, "Is Acceptance a Denial of Death? Another Look at Kübler-Ross," *ChrCent* 92 (1975): 464–468; Joan Retsinas, "A Theoretical Reassessment of the Applicability of Kübler-Ross's Stages of Dying," *DS* 12 (1988): 207–216. The Kübler-Ross theory of the stages of dying (denial, anger, bargaining, depression, acceptance) is based on her observations of 20 terminally ill cancer patients, all of whom—Tony Walter infers—had not reached their 'three-score and ten.' Yet the theory was generalized to represent the emotional trajectory of dying persons of all ages. Walter calls her legacy—which has stubbornly persisted—a meta-story: "It is a story in a 150-year-old American romantic tradition that elevates female over male, feeling over technique, home over hospital—a story of the triumph of ordinary people and their experience, championed by a caring woman, over the depersonalization of male technological rationality. In conflating hard data, personal involvement and a message that will save the world, Kübler-Ross has written not so much a scientific monograph offering testable hypotheses as a persuasive political/religious tract [Klass]. It is also true to the times in being secular. Death is portrayed not as a spiritual transition but as a return to the acceptance of infancy—a comforting message to a neurotic generation thirsting for self-help books on unconditional acceptance. (Later, Kübler-Ross did re-cast dying as a spiritual transition, and found a substantial following, but many more felt she had gone off the rails.)"; *The Revival of Death*, 71. To many scholars and theologians her 'spiritual transition' had almost nothing to do with traditional religion and was thoroughly, and presciently, New Age.

[2] Anne Hunsaker Hawkins, "Constructing Death: Three Pathographies about Dying," *Omega* 22 (1990–1991): 301–317, however, attempts "three potential versions of an art of dying for our time," a 'contemporary *ars moriendi*' (here at 301); cf. LeRoy Aden, *In Life & Death: The Shaping of Faith* (Minneapolis, Minn., 2005); Austra Reinis, *Reforming the Art of Dying: The Ars Moriendi in the German Reformation (1519–1528)*. St. Andrews Studies in Reformation History (Aldershot, U.K., 2007).

and observers, works on eschatology and grief abound, but we have
no contemporary Art of Dying. Such was not the case in late medieval
and early modern Europe. For those generations that followed closely
on the heels of massive mortality due to plague, a strong 'market' for
aids in dying—that prepare one for death without a priest—apparently
sprang up quickly and persisted for some time. As he found opportunity,
Luther also contributed to that literature. As Martin Brecht attests,
"Luther's Reformation theology had to pass the test of whether it was
able to stand up to the last human fear."[3]

I. *Orientation to Luther's Document*

Luther's 1519 *Ein Sermon von der bereitung zum sterben*, a brief tract of eight
quarto pages, was unquestionably a 'bestseller,' seeing 26 editions in
six years: 22 in German, 2 in Latin, 1 each in Dutch and Danish.[4] He
wrote it in mid-October, in response to an earlier request in May by
Markus Schart, via the Elector's secretary, Georg Spalatin (*LW* 42:97).[5]
Luther was able to delay Spalatin until after the Leipzig Disputation,
in the interim recommending "The Imitation of the Willing Death of
Christ" (1515) of Johann Staupitz (ca. 1470–1524).[6] Gottfried Krodel

---

[3] Martin Brecht, "Luthers reformatorische Sermone," in *Fides et Pietas. Festschrift
Martin Brecht zum 70. Geburtstag*, ed. Christian Peters and Jürgen Kampmann. Historia
profana et ecclesiastica 8 (Münster, 2003), 15–32, here at 28; cf. the synopsis of Rudolf
K. Markwald in *Luther Digest* 14 (2006): 12–19, my quotation in English above is on
page 16.

[4] Werner Goez, "Luthers 'Ein Sermon von der Bereitung zum Sterben' und die
spätmittelalterliche ars moriendi," *LuJ* 48 (1981): 97–114, here at 97. *Martin Brecht,
Martin Luther*, 1:354 says writings of comfort were best sellers in the sixteenth century.
On the publication history of *Ein Sermon*, see Benzing, Nr. 435–460, pp. 54–57. The
following lists the editions by language, year, city, and Nr. in Benzing: (I. German)—in
1519, 10 editions, in Wittenberg (435–436), Leipzig (437–439), Nürnberg (440–441), and
Augsburg (442–444); in 1520, 7 editions, in Wittenberg (445), Leipzig (446), Erfurt (447),
Augsburg (448–450), and Basel (451); in 1522, 1 edition (Wittenberg, 454); in 1523, 3
editions, in Straßburg (452–453) and Basel (455); in 1525, 1 edition (Altenburg, 456);
(II. Latin)—in 1520, 2 editions, in Leipzig (458) and Antwerp (459); (III. Dutch)—in
1522, 1 edition (Antwerp, 460); (IV. Danish)—in 1538, 1 edition (Copenhagen, 457).
WA 2:680ff. assigns a letter designation to each German edition, lettered respectively
according to the Benzing enumeration as follows: 1519 (A–K), 1520 (L–R), 1522 (U),
1523 (S, T, V), 1525 (W). The two Latin editions of 1520 are designated as: 'a' (Leipzig,
458) and 'b' (Antwerp, 459). Text and commentary on *Ein Sermon von der bereitung zum
sterben* can be found in Ottfried Jordahn, "Sterbebegleitung und Begräbnis bei Martin
Luther," in *Liturgie im Angesicht des Todes: Reformatorische und katholische Traditionen der Neuzeit*,
ed. Hansjakob Becker and Michael Fischer (Tübingen, 2004), 1–22.

[5] Martin Brecht, *Martin Luther*, 1:354.

[6] *Ein buchlein von der nachfolgung des willigen sterbens Christi*, entitled in Latin, *De imitanda*

calls Luther's little book "an evangelical version of the popular late medieval *ars moriendi* books."[7] Werner Goez,[8] Jared Wicks,[9] and Dick Akerboom[10] have examined Luther's book in its context of the *ars*, while Richard Marius gleans from the work only corroboration of his thesis of Luther's 'obsession with death.'[11] Drawing on these secondary studies, and employing close rhetorical analysis to Luther's document in German, we can only modestly engage the extent to which Luther's work intersects with the late medieval *ars moriendi* literature;[12] we shall concentrate instead on the style in which Luther argued. While I specifically show how the sermon regards the sacraments that are relevant

---

morte Jesu Christi libellus (1515) in *Johann von Staupitzens Sämmtliche Werke*, ed. J. F. K. Knaake, vol. 1, *Deutsche Schriften* (Potsdam: Krausnick, 1867), 52–88. Staupitz's book has 15 chapters. On the circumstances of Luther's writing of his *Ein Sermon*, see *LW* 42:97f.; David C. Steinmetz, *Luther and Staupitz: An Essay in the Intellectual Origins of the Protestant Reformation*. Duke Monographs in Medieval and Renaissance Studies 4 (Durham, N.C., 1980), 75–78.

[7] Gottfried G. Krodel, "Luther's Work on the Catechism in the Context of Late Medieval Catechetical Literature," *Concordia Journal* 25 (1999): 364–404, here at 398, footnote 105; Friedrich Gerke, "Die satanische Anfechtung in der ars moriendi und bei Martin Luther," *Theologische Blätter* 11 (1932): 321–332; Austra Reinis, "Evangelische Anleitung zur Seelsorge am Sterbebett 1519–1528," *Luther* 73 (2002): 31–45; idem, "How Protestants Face Death: Johann Gerhard's Funeral Sermon for Kunigund Gotsmännin, Widow of Hans Dietrich von Haßlach zu Stockheim (d. 1616)," *Theological Review* 25 (2004): 24–45, especially 29ff.

[8] Werner Goez, "Luthers 'Ein Sermon von der Bereitung zum Sterben und die spätmittelalterliche ars moriendi.'" *LuJ* 48 (1981): 97–114.

[9] Jared Wicks, S.J., "Applied Theology at the Deathbed: Luther and the Late-Medieval Tradition of the *Ars Moriendi*," *Gregorianum* 79 (1998): 345–368; cf. Hans-Martin Barth, "Leben und Sterben können: Brechungen in der ars moriendi 'ars moriendi' in der Theologie Martin Luthers," in *Ars Moriendi: Erwägungen zur Kunst des Sterbens*, ed. Harald Wagner (Frieburg, 1989), 45–66; Reinhard Schwarz, "Das Bild des Todes im Bild Lebens überwinden: Eine Interpretation von Luthers Sermon von der Bereitung zum Sterben," in *Gewißheit angesichts des Sterbens*. Veröffentlichungen der Luther-Akademie e. V. Ratzeburg 28, ed. Reinhard Schwarz (Erlangen, 1998), 32–64; Alois M. Haas, "Didaktik des Sterbens: Zur Botschaft der spätmittelalterlichen Sterbebüchlein," in *Gewißheit angesichts des Sterbens*, 13–31.

[10] Dick Akerboom, "'Only the Image of Christ in Us': Continuity and Discontinuity between the Late Medieval ars moriendi and Luther's Sermon von der Bereitung zum Sterben," in *Spirituality Renewed: Studies on Significant Representatives of the Modern Devotion*, ed. Hein Blommestijn, Charles Caspers, and Rijcklof Hofman (Leuven, 2003), 209–272.

[11] Richard Marius, *Martin Luther: The Christian Between God and Death* (Cambridge, Mass., 1999), 213–214. Marius had published his first book on Luther in 1974; *Luther, A Biography* (Philadelphia).

[12] In a review of Marius's *Martin Luther* (1999), Heiko Oberman claims that a popular version of the *ars moriendi*, one written by Jean Gerson (1363–1429), was typeset in the cellar of Luther's own monastery in Wittenberg in 1513; Heiko A. Oberman, "Varieties of Protest," *New Republic*, 16 August 1999, 40–45, here at 43. Brian Patrick McGuire, *Jean Gerson and the Last Medieval Reformation* (University Park, Penn., 2005), is silent on this claim.

and useful for the dying, how it frequently mentions the saints' role in the dying process, and how it strategically addresses the three images (*Bilder*) of death, sin, and hell, my principal focus is on how Luther uses such strategies as scriptural quotation and elaboration, and on how dialogue, rhetorical question and imaginary direct speech produce an intimate enactment of encouraging instructions and exhortations to the dying. Luther grounds his arguments in the "saving work of Christ *for us*, now offered to us to be appropriated in sacraments of assurance."[13] His language of conquest dominates the second half of the book.

II. *Context of Luther's Book*

Wicks's study compares the motifs in Luther's "Sermon on Preparing to Die" with those of similar vernacular works such as that of Thomas Peuntner (written in 1434), Jean Gerson, Johann Geiler of Keisersberg (d. 1510), and Johann von Paltz (d. 1511), some of which were undoubtedly the predecessors of "The Art of Dying," a genre that flourished on the European Continent and in Britain until well into the seventeenth century. Still existing in at least 300 manuscripts in Latin and the Western vernaculars, it is a "complete and intelligible guide to the business of dying, a method to be learned while one is in good health and kept at one's fingers' ends for use in that all important and inescapable hour."[14] There is little stress upon hell, only hope of heaven; the dying person (*Moriens*) is always encouraged and consoled. The book is entirely orthodox, and may have been intended for those to whom the ministrations of the clergy were not available, probably in times of plague.

The longer (yet earlier) version of the text consists in six parts. In the first Moriens is coached—through a collection of ecclesiastical utterances on death—in giving up his soul gladly and willfully; the second takes up the meeting of five temptations with which, one after another, the devil will put him to the test (Unbelief, Despair, Impatience, Vainglory, and Attachment to Relatives and Material Possessions). In the third are given two series of questions which, answered rightly, will

---

[13] Jared Wicks, S.J., "Facts and Fears in and around Martin Luther," *Moreana* 37/141 (2000): 5–32, here at 25.

[14] Sister Mary Catherine O'Connor, *The Art of Dying Well: The Development of the Ars moriendi* (New York, 1942), 5.

insure his salvation; in the fourth, rules of conduct which will pattern his dying upon that of Christ on the cross. The fifth and sixth parts address those who stand by the bedside, to aid the dying and to offer prayers for his safe departure. Included in the text is a series of eleven woodcut illustrations, each of which pictures the five temptations, then five inspirations corresponding to each temptation, and a final picture of death that shows the demons vanquished and the angels and bystanders triumphant.

III. *Analysis of Luther's "On Preparing to Die"*

While others will have to make a more thorough study, some comparisons of Luther's sermon and the *ars* are in order. One scholar suggests that Luther's sermon was probably inspired by the shorter version of the *ars*.[15] The sermon addresses each of the five temptations, but not very directly. Instead, Luther's message is organized in twenty Articles, with the first five serving as introduction; the remaining fifteen Articles divide into two sections. The introduction counsels first (not last, as in the *ars*) the regulating of earthly goods, then the seeking of forgiveness of others, then to understand death as a glorious birth, and finally to confess and seek the sacraments. The body of the sermon focuses on the sacraments and their virtues, the latter taken up first (in Articles 6–14), and the former discussed last (in Articles 15–20). Instead of referring to five temptations, Luther repeatedly proclaims that three images (*Bilder*) sent by the devil must be overcome: death, sin, and hell. He mentions the three images in list form 29 times:[16] A. <u>Short Lists</u> of just three words (or with one conjunction added, or with pronouns added) have the predominant order of 'death, sin, hell' (19 times),[17] with 'sin, death, hell' (twice) and 'hell, sin, death' (once); B. <u>Extended Lists</u>, or using the terms in the same clause, 7 times, all but three coming in the 'death, sin, hell' order.

There is no mistaking what the dying person is up against. In fact, other than the first short list occurrence in Article 5 (sin, death, hell), Luther's introduction of the three as what we might call a 'triple threat,'

---

[15] Ibid., 190.
[16] In 13 of these the *LW* 42 translator gives the wrong order, by inverting the first two terms.
[17] Article 7 (1), Article 13 (1), Article 14 (4), Article 15 (2), Article 16 (4), Article 17 (2), Article 18 (1), Article 20 (4).

seems to establish the 'death, sin, hell' order, by virtue of progressive triplet; Luther constructs each image more powerfully than the one before:

> There are three such evils: first, the terrifying image [*erschrockliche Bild*] of death; second, the awesomely manifold image [*graulich manichfeltig Bilde*] of sin; third, the unbearable and unavoidable image [*untreglich und unvormeydliche Bild*] of hell and eternal damnation [*Hellen und ewiges Vordamnüsz*]. Every other evil issues from these three and grows large and strong as a result of such mingling (*WA* 2:686.32–36).[18]

In contrast to the *ars*, the family of the dying person is virtually absent from the scene of Luther's document, except as one might want to make amends with these, as indicated in Article 2. In addition, Luther's perspective on one's focus on personal sin at time of death sharply diverges from the medieval *ars* in that he argues against meditating on one's sin, something he says should be done during one's lifetime. Indeed, in Articles 7–9 Luther argues that contemplation on 'death, sin, hell' should be done well before death is imminent.

However, there are still apparently orthodox elements of the sermon, for Luther advocates receiving the sacraments and extreme unction, and the saints (including Mary) play a role—not only as intercessors but also, in Wicks' words, as 'sharers in [Christ's] life and grace.'[19] I take up the meaning and function of the sacraments below, but let us here briefly examine what Wicks calls 'isolation overcome in the communion of saints,'[20] to see to what extent Luther recommends invoking the saints and angels in one's prayers. I quote from Article 19:

> [L]et no one presume to perform such things by his own power, but humbly ask God to create and preserve [*schaff und erhalt*] such faith in and such understanding of his holy sacraments in him. He must practice awe and humility [*Furcht und Demut*] in all this, lest he ascribe these works to himself instead of allowing God the glory. To this end he must call upon the holy angels, particularly his own angel, the Mother of God, and all the apostles and beloved saints, especially since God has granted him exceptional zeal for this (*WA* 2:696:20–26).[21]

---

[18] "Der seyn drey: die erste das erschrockliche bild des todts, die ander das graulich manichfeltig bilde der sund, die dritte das untreglich und unvormeydliche bild der hellen und ewiges vordamnüsz. Nu mucht win yglichs ausz diszen dreyen und wirt grosz und starck ausz seinen zusatzen."

[19] Wicks, "Applied Theology at the Deathbed," 362f.

[20] Ibid.

[21] "Soll aber niemant sich vormessen solch dingk ausz seynen crefften zu uben, sondern gott demutiglich bitten, das er solchen glauben und vorstant seyner heyligen

This emphasis on the mediating role of the saints, I argue, is deeply traditional yet represents a developing view of Luther's, regarding the identity and function of the saints. So, then, is his call for praying to them grounded in the treasury of merit or upon their participation in the body of Christ? Since his Lectures on Romans (1515–16), Luther had been moving towards a distinction between a traditional identification of the saints—as dead Christians, "those who are blessed and participating in glory"—and a more biblical identification—'all those who believe in Christ' (*LW* 35:51).[22] By the end of the year 1519, Luther will argue for a stronger connection between living and dead believers, in the 'fellowship of all the saints,' as grounded in the sacrament.[23]

---

sacrament yn unsz schaff und erhalt, auff das alszo mit furcht und demut zu gehe, und wir nit unsz solch werck zu schreyben, sondern gott die eere lassen. Darzu soll er alle heyligen Engell, bszonder seynen Engell, die Mutter gottis, Alle Aposteln unnd lieben heyligen anruffen, szonderlich da yhm gott bszondere andacht zu geben hatt." *LW* 42:113 omits 'beloved' from *lieben heyligen*. For information on Luther and angels, see Susan Schreiner, "Unmasking the Angel of Light: The Problem of Deception in Martin Luther and Teresa of Avila," in *Mystics, Presence, and Aporia*, ed. Michael Kessler and Christian Sheppard (Chicago, 2003), 118–137; Scott Hendrix, "Angelic Piety in the Reformation: The Good and Bad Angels of Urbanus Rhegius," in *Frömmigkeit—Theologie—Frömmigkeitstheologie: Contributions to European Church History. Festschrift für Berndt Hamm zum 60. Geburtstag*, ed. Gudrun Litz, Heidrun Munzert, and Roland Liebenberg. SHCT 124 (Leiden, 2005), 385–394.

[22] In his *Lectures on Romans: Glosses and Scholia* (*LW* 25), Luther makes no gloss on Rom. 1:7a ("To all God's beloved in Rome, who are called to be saints"), but on 12:13 (contribute to the needs of the saints) he glosses: "saints, that is, the believers" (*LW* 25:107). In the Scholia, he comments at length (*LW* 25:257–278) on Rom. 4:7 ("Blessed are those whose iniquities are forgiven, and whose sins are covered"). He begins (257) by saying, "The saints are always sinners in their own sight, and therefore always justified outwardly." One page later he adds, "'God is wonderful in His saints' (Ps. 68:35). To Him they are at the same time both unrighteous and righteous" (258). Near the end he says, "You say, 'Then why is there so much preaching about the merits of the saints?' I reply, 'Because these are not the merits of the saints but the merits of Christ in them, for whose sake God accepts their works, which otherwise He would not accept. Hence the saints themselves never know that they perform and possess meritorious works, but they do all those things only that they might find mercy and escape judgment, praying for forgiveness with loud groaning rather than presumptuously looking for the crown'" (*LW* 25:277).

[23] Paragraph 4 of "The Blessed Sacrament of the Holy and True Body of Christ, and the Brotherhoods": "The *significance* or effect of this sacrament is fellowship of all the saints [*gemeynschafft aller heyligen*]. From this it derives its common name *synaxis* [Greek] or *communio* [Latin], that is, fellowship [*gemeynschafft*]. And the Latin *communicare* [commune or communicate], or as we say in German, *zum sacrament gehen* [go to the sacrament], means to take part in this fellowship [*gemeynschafft empfahen*]. Hence it is that Christ and all saints are one spiritual body [*eyn geystlicher corper*] [cf. Rom. 12:5; 1 Cor. 12:5], just as the inhabitants of a city are one community and body, each citizen being a member of the other and of the entire city. All the saints, therefore, are members of Christ and of the church [*Christi und der Kirchen glid*], which is a spiritual and eternal city of God [cf. Isa. 60:14; Heb. 12:22; Rev. 3:12].... To receive this sacrament in

While his meaning of 'saints' here in 1519 still predominantly means Christians who have died, by 1532 Luther will insist on the biblical meaning of 'saints' as 'every Christian.'[24] A brief tracing of Luther's 17 uses of 'saints' here in "On Preparing to Die" reveals how he uses the term, both as to identity and function.

In Article 10 Luther tells his reader not to dwell on death in one's self but rather to focus intently on only those who died in God's grace and who have overcome death, "particularly in Christ and then also in all his saints.... For Christ is nothing other than sheer life, as his saints are likewise" (*WA* 2:689.9–12).[25] In Article 11 Luther says that one should look at sin only within the "picture of grace, which is nothing else but that of Christ on the cross and of all his dear saints" (*WA* 2:689.28f.).[26] He says Christ on the cross takes our sin, bears and destroys it. "Likewise, all the saints who suffer and die [*leyden und sterben*] in Christ also bear your sins and suffer and labor [*leyden und erbeytet*] for you" (*WA* 2:689.33–35).[27] In Article 12 Luther advises his reader not to fret about predestination (*Vorsehung*), but rather to "look at Christ and all his saints and delight in the grace of God, who elected them, and continue steadfastly in this joy, ... However, if you do not adhere solely to this but have recourse to yourself, you will become adverse [*Unlust*] to God and all saints, and thus you will find nothing good in yourself" (*WA* 2:690.26–31).[28] In Article 13 he says 'death, sin, hell' will flee if we gaze on the "glowing picture of Christ and his saints and abide in the faith" (*WA* 2:690.36–38).[29] In Article 15 Luther assures readers

---

bread and wine, then, is nothing else than to receive a sure sign of this fellowship and incorporation with Christ and all saints [*diszer gemeynschafft und eyn leybung mit Christo und allen heyligen*]" (*WA* 2:743.7–22)

[24] ...in iglicher Christen (*WA* 36:258.33); *LW* 51:258.

[25] "...furnemlich yn Christo, darnach yn allen seynen heyligen.... Dan Christus ist nichts dan eytell leben, seyn heyligen auch."

[26] "Der gnaden bild ist nit anders, dan Christus am Creutz und alle seyne lieben heyligen."

[27] "Desselben gleichen alle heyligen ynn yhrem leyden und sterben auch auff yhn tragen deyne sund und fur dich leyden und erbeyten." Luther then quotes Gal. 6:2, which is the only Scripture from this sermon that he uses again in "The Blessed Sacrament of the Holy and True Body of Christ, and the Brotherhoods" (*LW* 35:54).

[28] "Alszo wan du Christum und all seyne heyligen ansihist, und dir woll gefellet die gnad gottis, der sie alszo erwelet hatt, und bleybst nur fest yn dem selben wolgefallen,.... Hafftestu aber nit hir auff alleyn, und fellest yn dich, szo wirt dir eyn unlust erwachen gegen gott und seyne heyligen, und alszo yn dir nichts guts finden."

[29] "Alszo fleugt tod, sund und hell mit allen yhren crefften, szo wir nur Christi und seyner heyligen leuchtende bild yn unsz uben yn der nacht, das ist ym glauben."

that God grants blessings found in Christ, and that the sacraments are sign and testimony (*Wartzeichen und Urkund*) that 'death, sin, hell' are overcome in Him. Through the same sacraments—and he has just listed confession, absolution, eucharist, and extreme unction—one is "included and made one [*eyngeleybet und voreyniget*] with all the saints. You thereby enter into the true communion of saints so that they die with you in Christ, bear sin, vanquish hell" (*WA* 2:692.33–35).[30]

In Article 17 Luther discusses the benefits of the sacraments, asking the following rhetorical question (his fifth successive rhetorical question): "Why do people not hold to the sacraments, which are sure and appointed signs, tested and tried [*probirt und vorsucht*] by all saints and found reliable by all who believed and who received all that they indicate?" (*WA* 2:694.38–695.3).[31] In Article 18 he refers several times to the saints, arguing that the dying Christian is surely not alone; rather, upon him are the eyes of God and Christ himself, the eyes "of the dear angels, of the saints, and of all Christians.... In that hour the work of love and the communion of saints are seriously and mightily active" (*WA* 2:695.20–24).[32] Further commenting on the fellowship and assistance of the saints, and using asyndetic triplet and quintuplet series—plus anaphora—Luther says,

> He who doubts this does not believe in the most venerable Sacrament of the Body of Christ, in which are pointed out, promised, pledged [*gezeugt, zugesagt, vorpflicht*] the communion, help, love, comfort, and support [*Gemeynschafft, Hulff, Lieb, Trost und Beystand*] of all the saints in all times of need.... If God looks upon you, all the angels, all saints, all creatures will fix their eyes upon you (*WA* 2:695.26–33).[33]

In Articles 19–20 Luther urges his reader to call upon God for assistance, and to include all the saints in one's plea. In seeking faith and

---

[30] "Darzu wirstu durch sie selben sacrament eyngeleybet und voreyniget mit allen heyligenn und kumist yn die rechte gemeynschafft der heyligen, alszo das sie mit dyr in Christo sterben, sunde tragen, hell ubirwinden."

[31] "Warumb halten sie sich nit an die sacrament, wilchs gewisse und eingesetzte zeychen sein, durch alle heyligen probirt und vorsucht, gewisz ersunden allen denen, die do glaubt haben, und ubirkummen als wasz sie zeichent?"

[32] "...darnach die lieben engel, die heyligen und alle Christenn, ...Da geht das werck der liebe und gemeynschafft der heyligen ym ernst und gewaltiglich."

[33] "...der glaubt aber nicht an das hochwirdig sacrament desz leychnams Christi, Jn wilchem gezeygt, zugesagt, vorpflicht wirt gemeynschafft, hulff, lieb, trost und beystand aller heyligenn yn allen noten.... So aber got auff dich sicht, szo sehen ym nach alle engele, alle heyligen, alle creaturen, und szo du yn dem glauben bleybst, halten sie alle die hend unter."

understanding of the sacraments, one must "call upon the holy angels, particularly his own angel,[34] the Mother of God, and all the apostles and dear saints"[35] (*WA* 6:696.25).[36] Luther further urges that one "implore God and his saints our whole life long for true faith in the last hour" (*WA* 2:697.5f.).[37] Finally, Luther declares that God "commands his angels, all saints, all creatures to join him in watching over you, to be concerned about your soul, and to receive it" (*WA* 2:697.22–24).[38]

This survey of Luther's use of the term 'saints' reveals that he brings a strongly traditional sense of the fellowship and function of the saints, despite the fact that he draws the Christian into these in the sacrament. It will be in other writings in the next two years that Luther will abandon some of these teachings.

A. *Using Scripture*

How does Luther encourage the dying person to combat the images of 'death, sin, hell' and overcome fear, unbelief, and despair? One principal way is by wielding the Word of God—i.e., Scripture, something not much used in the *ars*, in a personal and intimate manner: 72 lines are Scriptures directly quoted or paraphrased or alluded to, from 34 different texts (14 from OT and 20 from NT, 13 of which are from the Gospels). Approximately 60 percent of these lines derive from the OT. The most frequently cited source is the Psalter; the second is the passion narratives, Matthew's being the favorite text. In all but one of the quotations from the Gospels, Luther has chosen the words of Christ and attributed them to him, rather than citing the scriptural writer of the text. Only three pauline texts are used. While Luther summons the words of Mary, Paul, Isaiah, Peter, Elisha, the psalmist (also called 'the prophet'), and 'the Apostle' (writer of Hebrews)—all of whom declare positively the Lord's words and works—the dominant voices of the

---

[34] On guardian angels, *LW* 42:113, note 13 cites Gal. 1:8; 1 Tim. 3:16, and 1 Pet. 1:12.

[35] *LW* 42:113, note 14 reads: "On Luther's later opposition to the invocation of Mary and the saints, see "On Translating: An Open Letter" (1530); *LW* 35:198–200.

[36] "Darzu soll er alle heyligen Engell, bszonder seynen Engell, die Mutter gottis, Alle Aposteln unnd lieben heyligen anruffen." *LW* 42:113 omits translating 'dear' saints.

[37] "Darzu solt man das gantz leben lang bitten gott und seyne heyligen umb die letzten stund fur eynen rechten glauben." *LW* 42:114 wrongly translates *seyne heyligen* as 'his dear saints.'

[38] "Er befelht seynen Engeln, allen heyligenn, allen creaturen, das sie mit yhm auff dich sehen, deyner seel warnemen und sie entpfahen."

Scriptures Luther quotes are those of God or the Lord or Christ. One exception is 'the Jews,' whom Luther quotes as they deride Christ on the cross. He does not cite a single father of the church.[39] Moreover, while his authority is clearly God himself, Luther indirectly attributes authority to Scripture, for in roughly equal measure he mixes quotations or paraphrases of a biblical speaker with that of the biblical book and chapter reference. Many of these documented statements affirm the promises of God.

Luther invokes the great majority of his Scripture texts responsibly. Evidence for that claim is found: (1) in the accuracy of his quotations; (2) in how often he cites the reference (book and chapter) and attributes the quote to a speaker; and (3) in his willingness at times to quote a portion of the text in the original. He did this in Article 12, quoting Jesus on the cross: "'Eli, Eli lama sabachthani!'—'O my God, O my God, why hast thou forsaken me?'" (*WA* 2:690.20f.).[40] He does a similar thing in Article 18, quoting Ps. 32:8, where he begins in Latin ('Firmabo, etc.'), then quotes the entire verse in German (*WA* 2:695.30f.).[41]

Yet Luther is not reluctant to add his own interpretation to a scriptural quote: First, in Article 5, having twice already used a quote from Christ in the two preceding Articles (John 16:21, Article 3; Mark 9:23, Article 4), Luther introduces the sacraments, what they mean (*bedeuten*), all that God declares and indicates (*sagt und anzeygt*) in them, and how God speaks and acts (*redt und zeychnet*) through the priest. In the midst of this explanation Luther quotes Mary at Luke 1:38, "Let it be to me according to your words and signs [*Worten und Zeychen*]." In fact, all that Luke has Mary say to the angel is 'according to your word.'[42] Luther's argument about sacraments, informed by his doublet style and the hermeneutic it embodies, no doubt prompted him to embellish Luke's reading. Second, in Article 10 Luther's argument is that, in order to find peace about one's death, one must look away from self—and one's own anxiety—and onto Christ and his death. Luther

---

[39] Staupitz's *Ein buchlein von der nachfolgung des willigen sterbens Christi* cites St. Augustine once (chap. 3 [p. 57]) and St. Bernard twice (chap. 14 [p. 87]).

[40] "Eli, Eli, lama sabathani, O meyn gott, o meyn gott, Warumb hastu mich vorlassen?" *LW* 42:104 follows the standard transliteration 'sabachthani' (cf. Vulgate 'sabacthani') and omits Luther's double interjection 'O … O.'

[41] "Firmabo 2c. Jch will meyn augen stet auff dich haben, das du nit untergehest."

[42] The GNT reads κατὰ τὸ ῥῆμά σου, and in *SeptBib* Luther himself translates this phrase as *wie du gesagt hast*, 'as you have said.'

quotes two passages that teach this looking to God: the bronze serpent (Nu. 21:6–9)[43] and the blessedness of those who die 'in the Lord'
(Rev. 14:13). Finally he adds a quote from Christ (John 16:33), in the
middle of which Luther adds his own parenthetical interpretation: "In
the world (that is, in yourselves) you have unrest, but in me you will
find peace."[44] The insertion is consistent with Luther's point, and to
him it may have seemed required. Fourth, in Article 11 Luther adds
terms to his quotation of 1 Cor. 15:57: to the first word of the opening
clause ('thanks be to God') Luther adds 'and praise'; to the ending of
the "final clause" he adds 'over sin and death,' which are the subjects,
in reverse order, of the argument in Articles 10 (death) and 11 (sin).
Finally, Luther is not averse to altering the syntax of a Scripture text
as he quotes it. He does this in Article 20, quoting Ps. 111:2 (= 110:2
Vulgate), "Great are the works of the Lord, selected according to his
pleasure," which Luther inverts into, "The works of God are great and
selected according to all his pleasure" (*WA* 2:697.29f.).[45]

B. *Using Dialogue*

In his "An Exposition of the Lord's Prayer for Simple Laymen" (*LW*
42:15–82), written in April 1519, Luther concluded his exposition with
a 'summary and arrangement' of the seven petitions of the *Vaterunser*
(78–81).[46] Here, Luther puts the petitions into dialogue form, where 'The
Soul' (i.e., Christians, for the pronouns are plural) and God participate
in a sequential conversation. The dialogue style not only helps reveal
how the petitions proceed in sequence, but it also renders the action
more dramatic, the content more vivid. By including God's explicit
responses, Luther gives the petitions a dramatic context; they *make more
sense*. In *Ein Sermon* Luther uses dialogue quite sparingly, compared to
many of his other writings. In Articles 14 and 16 he quotes voices
from Scripture in such a way as to test the dying Christian, as the devil
(and 'the Jews') taunted Christ on the cross. Fourteen lines of scriptural

---

[43] *LW* 42:104 has Luther mistakenly citing Exodus 21, correcting the citation in brackets. However, Luther correctly cites *Numeri 21*. (*WA* 2:689.17).

[44] "Jn der welt (das is auch yn unszselb) werdet yhr unruge haben, Jn mir aber den friden" (*WA* 2:689.21–23). Instead of the parenthetical insertion, *LW* 42:104 uses hyphens.

[45] "Die werck gottis seyn grosz und auszerwelet nach allem seynenn wolgefallenn."

[46] "Auslegung deutsch des Vaterunsers für die einfältigen Laien" (*WA* 2:74–130), which saw twelve German editions (Benzing Nr. 265–276) by 1521.

dialogue dramatize the power of such temptations, so that the dying Christian can be ready, armed in advance with the knowledge of what she or he will face. In each case Luther follows the testing statements with his own expansion of them, in the form of additional, invented dialogue, so as to interpret the test and amplify its intensity. In Article 14 he argues that Christ has defeated 'death, sin, hell' by first suffering and overcoming the temptations entailed in 'these pictures [*diszen Bilden*].' To demonstrate that this happened, and to make vivid and real what it was like, Luther quotes, then explains, the Jews' taunt of Christ: "'Let him come down from the cross; he has healed others, let him now help himself' [Matt. 27:40–42]. They said as it were, 'Here you are facing death; now you must die; nothing can save you from that'" (*WA* 2:691.27–29).[47] Luther employs the same tactic for the images of sin and hell. In only one instance, though (Article 16), does the temptation dialogue not originate in Scripture but consist in words Luther puts into the devil's mouth, to be whispered to the dying: "But then the devil comes along and whispers into your ear, 'But suppose I received the sacraments unworthily and through my unworthiness robbed myself of such grace?'" (*WA* 2:693.35–36).[48]

Yet Luther also creates dialogue for the dying person to say, and there is twice as much of this discourse as was given to the devil. This dialogue is found in Articles 15–17. The first instance, in Article 15, argues that the sign of the words of the priest is the only help in death's agonies (*Tods Noten*). When faced by the image of 'death, sin, hell,' we are to use Luther's words below; the pronouns—'his' (= Christ) and 'me/mine' (= the dying believer)—emphasize the crisis-opportunity.[49] At the center of the dialogue are three <u>pivotal phrases</u> that identify the promise:

> God promised and in his sacraments he gave me a sure sign of his grace that Christ's life overcame [*ubirwunden*] <u>my death in his death</u>, that his obedience blotted out [*vortilget*] <u>my sin in his suffering</u>, that his love destroyed [*zustort*] <u>my hell in his forsakenness</u>. This sign, this promise of my

---

[47] "Er steig nu herab vom Creutz, Er hatt ander gesund macht, er helff yhm nu selbs, als sprechen sie, 'Da, da sihstu den todt, du must sterben, da hilfft nichts fur.'"

[48] "Szo kompt dan der teuffell und blysset dir eyn 'ja wie, wan ich dan die sacrament hett unwirdig empfangen und mich durch meyn unwirdickeit solcher gnaden beraubt?'"

[49] (1) Opportunity—as the source of promise: *God, Christ, God, God*, and 5 'his' pronouns; as the recipient of the promise: 6 'my/mine' pronouns; (2) Crisis—*death... sin...hell.*

salvation will not lie nor deceive me. It is God who has promised it, and God cannot lie either in words or in deeds (*WA* 2:693.8–13).[50]

A second discourse given to the dying believer is found in Article 16 (*LW* 42:110; *WA* 2:693:8–13), but I comment on it in the next section.

So I turn now to the third discourse, in Article 17 (*LW* 42:111). This speech is longer than the other two and celebrates the advantage that one receiving the Sacrament of the Altar has over those who can still obtain the benefits but who must operate solely on faith and the desires of their hearts. Notice how Luther uses doublets and a long series, and how intensely personal ('I/me/my') the discourse is. The tone is progressive; it moves from the conditional ('If,' meaning virtually, 'since'), to the boldly assertive ('I will'), to the demanding ('Away with you'):

> Thus you must also say with regard to the Sacrament of the Altar, 'If the priest gave me the holy body of Christ, which is a sign and promise of the communion of all angels and saints that they love me, provide for me, pray and suffer for me, die, bear my sin and overcome hell [*sterben, Sund tragen und Hell ubirwunden*], it will and must therefore be true that the divine sign does not deceive me. I will not let anyone rob me of it. I would rather deny all the world, myself, than doubt my God's trustworthiness and truthfulness in his signs and promises.[51] Whether worthy or not, I am, according to the text and declaration of this sacrament, a member of Christendom. It is better that I be unworthy than that God's truthfulness be questioned. Away with you, Devil, if you advise me differently' (*WA* 2:694:22–32).[52]

---

[50] "'Got hat myr zugesagt und eyn gewisz zeichen seyner gnaden yn den sacramenten geben, das Christus leben meynen tod yn seynem tod ubirwunden hab, seyn gehorsam meyne sund yn seynem leyden vortilget, sey lieb meyn hell ynn seynem vorlassen zustort habe, das tzeichen, das zusagen meyner selickeit wirt myr nit liegen noch triegen, Gott hat es gesagt, gott mag nit ligen, noch mit worten noch mit wercken.'"

[51] The pairing of 'signs and promises' is an alliterative rhyming doublet (*zeychen und zusagen*) that occurs 4 times, in addition to 3 other pairings of the two terms (in some form). The rhyme helps bond the two ideas.

[52] "Alszo soltu auch sagen ubir dem sacrament des Altars 'Hat mir der priester geben den heyligen laychnam Christi, das eyn zeychen und zusagen ist der gemeynschafft aller Engel und heyligen, das sie mich lieb haben, fur mich sorgen, bitten und mit mir leyden, sterben, sund tragen und hell ubirwunden, Szo wirt es und musz alszo seyn, das gottlich zeychen treugt mich nit, und las mirs nit nhemen, ich wold ehe alle welt, mich selb vorleugnen, he ich dran zweyffelt, Meyn gott der sey mir gewisz und warhafftig yn dissem seynem zeychen und zusagen, Jch sey seyn wirdig odder nit, szo byn ich ein glid der Christenheit nach laut und anzeygung diszes sacraments. Es ist besser, ich sey unwirdig, dan das gott nit warhafftig gehalten werden, heb dich, teuffell, szo du mir anders sagst.'"

C. *Intimate Language*

One cannot help but notice how personal Luther's language in this last dialogue is, especially driven home through all the first and second person singular pronouns. He words the argument in such a way so as to be intimately conversing with the dying one. Notice his recommendation for responding to the devil's whisper—worded above in the dying one's own perspective. The devil's implanted worry is then countered by Luther's strong correction about worthiness, and his subsequent, comforting claims:

> In that event cross *yourself* and do not let the question of *your* worthiness or unworthiness assail *you*. Just see to it that *you* believe that these are sure signs, true words of God, and then *you* will be indeed be and remain worthy. Faith makes [one] worthy; doubt makes [one] unworthy. The evil spirit brings up the question of worthiness and unworthiness to stir up doubts within *you*, thus nullifying the sacraments with their benefits and making God a liar in what he says. God gives *you* nothing because of *your* worthiness, nor does he build his Word and sacraments on *your* worthiness, but out of sheer grace he establishes *you*, unworthy one, on the foundation of his Word and signs (*WA* 2:693:36 694:8, my emphasis).[53]

Luther also uses dialogue not only to invoke and enlarge God's promises—and to verify and amplify temptations—but sometimes he puts words into the mouth of the dying also, thus giving her or him a seemingly tailor-made speech, a *credo* of confidence. Twenty-seven German lines of such prepared direct speech can be found, in Articles 15–17 and 19. In Article 16 Luther combines his use of pronouns of intimacy (first person singular) with balanced <u>triplet phrasing</u>, as he completes his prolepsis—anticipating reader objections and then refuting them—which he does in each instance of allowing the devil to express a doubt the dying Christian might have:

> Hold fast to that [the foundation of his Word and signs] and say, 'He who gives *me* and has given *me* his signs and his Word, which assure *me* that Christ's <u>life, grace, and heaven</u> have kept *my* <u>death, sin, and hell</u> from harming *me*, is truly God, who will surely preserve these things for

---

[53] "Hie mach das Creutz fur dich, las dich wirdickeit, unwirdickeit nichts anfechten, schaw nur zu, das du glaubst es seyn gewisse zeychen, ware wort gottis, szo bistu und bleybst wol wirdigk: glaub macht wirdig, zweyffel macht unwirdigk. Darumb will der bösze geyst dir an der wirdickeit und unwirdickeit furwenden, das er dir eynen zweyffel unnd da durch die sacrament mit yren wercken zu nichte und gott yn seynen worten eynen lügner mache."

me. When the priest absolves *me*, *I* trust in this as in God's Word itself. Since it is God's Word, it must come true. That is *my* stand, and on that stand *I* will die' (*WA* 2:694.9–14).[54]

Before we respond to the question *To whom is the dying one reciting?*, we note that the worthy/unworthy theme is an important issue in the sermon, particularly when Luther instructs the dying person as to how she can overcome fear that she is not one of the elect, or to doubt the efficacy of the sacraments. The prepared speech in Article 17 (see above) contains a series of affirmative declarations, collectively intended to forestall any objection to receiving the benefits of the sacrament, and heavily expressed in first person singular.

It appears that the above two speeches are addressed to the devil, or to that aspect of one's consciousness that is entertaining doubts. Article 19 includes two brief utterances the dying one can use to thwart the devil, but these remarks are instead directed toward sources of hope and assurance. First, the dying one has every right to implore God's attention: "My God, *you* have commanded *me* to pray and to believe that *my* prayer will be heard. For this reason *I* come to *you* in prayer and am assured that *you* will not forsake *me* but will grant *me* a genuine faith" (*WA* 2:697.2–4).[55] Second, Luther quotes a familiar prayer sung at Pentecost, one reflecting a communal solidarity of faith: "Now let *us* pray to the Holy Ghost for the true faith of all things the most, when *we* go home from this misery, etc." (*WA* 2:697.7–8, my emphasis).[56] So Luther provides practical discourse—much of it originating in Scripture itself—as weapons to be used to suppress doubt and nourish faith, weapons that are words.

D. *Sacraments as Signs*

Early on in *Ein Sermon* it is evident that Luther was still recommending that the dying one provide oneself with the sacrament. However, he

---

[54] "Daran halt nur fest und sprich 'Der mir seyn zeychen und wort gibt und geben hatt, das Christus leben, gnad und hymel meynen tod, sund, hell mir unschedlich gemacht hab, der ist gott, wirt mir die ding woll halten. Hatt mich der priester absolvirt, szo vorlasz ich mich drauff als auff gottis wort selber. Seynd es dan gottis wort, szo wirt es war seyn, da bleyb ich auff, da stirb ich auff.'"

[55] "'Meyn gott, du hast gepoten zu bitten unnd zu glauben, die bitt werd erhört, drauff bitt ich und vorlas mich, du werdest mich nit lassen und eynen rechten glauben geben.'"

[56] "Nu bitten wir den heyligen geyst umb den rechten glauben aller meyst, wen wir heim faren ausz dissem elende 2c."

does not make it mandatory, and by the end of 1519 he began writing about his changing views of the sacrament of penance,[57] of baptism,[58] and the sacrament of the altar.[59] It is to the sacrament of the altar, also called the blessed sacrament, that Luther refers in *Ein Sermon*. It was in his "Sermon on the Blessed Sacrament" that he suggested that the laity[60] receive both cup and bread, for which by late December he had aroused the wrath of Duke George of Saxony.[61] By the following summer Luther was condemned for this in the papal bull of 15 June 1520, and by the fall of 1521 communion 'in both kinds' became a major issue of the so-called 'Wittenberg Movement.' Here, in first mentioning the sacraments (Article 4), Luther says readiness for dying can be had through confession, the holy Christian sacrament of the holy and true body of Christ, and with the unction. "If these can be had, one should devoutly desire them and receive them with great confidence [*groszer Zuvorsicht*]. If they cannot be had, our longing and yearning for them should nevertheless be a comfort and we should not be too dismayed by this circumstance" (*WA* 2:686.13–16).[62]

The unction, however, virtually disappears from consideration, for Luther speaks only of the sacrament of the altar, mentioning unction only once more. Quoting Jesus' reassurance to a distraught father (Mk. 9:23), "All things are possible to him who believes," Luther proceeds to argue that the sacraments "are nothing else than signs which help and incite [*dienen und reytzen*] us to faith" and that without faith they

---

[57] "The Sacrament of Penance" (1519) in *LW* 35:9–22; *Ein Sermon von dem Sakrament der Buße* (*WA* 2:714–723); Benzing Nr. 462–478 (17 editions in Wittenberg, Leipzig, Nürnberg, Augsburg, Straßburg, Erfurt, and Halberstadt [Niederdeutsch] in 3 years).

[58] "The Holy and Blessed Sacrament of Baptism" (1519) in *LW* 35:29–43; *Ein Sermon von dem heiligen hochwürdigen Sakrament der Taufe* (*WA* 2:727–737); Benzing Nr. 479–496 (17 editions in Wittenberg, Leipzig, Nürnberg, Augsburg, Straßburg, Erfurt, and Colmar in 5 years).

[59] "The Blessed Sacrament of the Holy and True Body of Christ, and the Brotherhoods" (1519) in *LW* 35:49–73; *Ein Sermon vom Sakrament des Leichnams Christi und von den Brüderschaften* (*WA* 2:742–758); Benzing 497–515 (19 editions in Wittenberg, Leipzig, Nürnberg, Augsburg, Straßburg, Zwickau, Basel, Leiden in 6 years, including editions in Latin and Czech. *LW* 42:100, note 2; Brecht, *Martin Luther*, 1:358–364.

[60] Luther addressed the book specifically to laymen (the subtitle reads, "Fur die Leyen" [*WA* 2:739]) and dedicated it to Margaret, duchess of Brunswick; cf. *LW* 35:47.

[61] *LW* 35:47.

[62] "...die selben andechtig begere und mit grosser zuvorsicht empfahe, szo man sie haben mag. Wo aber nit, soll mit defte weniger das vorlangen und begere der selben trostlich seyn und nit darob zu seher erschrecken."

serve 'no purpose [*nichts Nutz*]' (*WA* 2:686.17–18).[63] This statement is thoroughly consistent with what Luther writes a few months later in "The Blessed Sacrament,"[64] and it is these two claims that he declares he will support later in this Sermon ('as we shall see'). As it happens, he uses the term *sacrament* 37 times, 24 of which are in Articles 15–17. In Articles 4–6 he begins his explanation, using the word 6 times.[65]

As he begins to explain how the sacraments help us in the dying process, Luther argues that they can overshadow our sins. A proper understanding of their virtues includes truly receiving what the sacraments signify and all that God declares and indicates in them (*WA* 2:686.25).[66] "When one rightly honors the sacraments, one can say with Mary [the mother of God, omitted in *LW*], 'Let it be to me according to your words and signs' [Luke 1:38]" (*WA* 2:686.26–27).[67] Luther is enumerating auditory and visual signification, which employ both the verbal and nonverbal. The dual functions of word and sign are then fleshed out: "Since God himself here speaks and acts [*redet und zeychnet*] through the priest, we would do him in his Word and work [*Wort und Werck*] no greater dishonor than to doubt whether it is true. And we can do him no greater honor than to believe that they are true and to rely firmly on them" (*WA* 2:686.27–30).[68]

Although Luther does not explicitly mention the sacrament in Articles 7–14, he nevertheless develops the theme of their function as signs and their function of signifying positively, in opposition to the negative signification of 'death, sin, hell': Man "seeks signs of God's will" (*WA* 2:688.7);[69] our foes "boldly rush in...with their image, their arguments,

---

[63] "Dan die sacrament auch anders nit seyn, dan zeychen, die zum glauben dienen und reytzen, wie wir sehen werden, An wilchen glauben sie nichts nutz seyn."

[64] Paragraph 17: "So it is clear from all this that this holy sacrament is nothing else than a divine sign, in which are pledged, granted, and imparted Christ and all saints together with all their works, sufferings, merits, mercies, and possessions, for the comfort and strengthening of all who are in anxiety and sorrow, persecuted by the devil, sins, the world, the flesh, and every evil. And to receive the sacrament is nothing else than to desire all this and firmly to believe that it is done" (*LW* 35:60).

[65] There are also 7 occurrences of *sacrament* in Articles 18–20.

[66] "...was die sacrament bedeuten, und alls, was gott darynnen sagt und anzeygt."

[67] "...das man mit Marien, der mutter gottis, yn festem glauben sprech: Mir geschech nach deynen worten und zeychen."

[68] "Dan die weyl da selbst gott durch den priester redt und zeychnet, mocht man gott kein grosser uneehr yn synem wort und werck thun, dan zweyfelen, ab es war sey, und kein grosser eehre thun, den glauben es war seyn und sich frey drauff vorlassen."

[69] "...er sucht zeychen gottlichs willen."

and their signs" (*LW* 42:103).[70] Some of these signs are <u>visual or mental</u>, and Luther calls them *Bilder*, 'pictures' (*disze Bilde*, *drey Bild* [3×], *dreyfeltig Bild*) or 'images' (9×): [1] death as being killed by God's wrath (2× in *LW* 42:104), or [2] as sin in sinners, which must be fought off by the picture of grace (2× in *LW* 42:104f.) or [3] as hell and eternal pain, to be countered by the heavenly picture of Christ (*LW* 42:105). Thus, three pictures of harm ('death, sin, hell') are countered by three images of victory, which Luther amplifies from Scripture, claiming that these conflicts are foreshadowed in Judges 7 (Gideon and the Midianites) and ultimately by Christ, as cited in Isa. 9 and completed on the cross. In a powerful argument, initiated by question and answer (anthypophora)[71] and completed by anaphora (repetitions of statements beginning with '*He is…*'), Luther declares a creedal utterance:

> And when did Christ do this? On the cross! There he prepared himself as a threefold picture for us, to be held before the eyes of our faith against the three evil pictures with which the evil spirit and our nature would assail us to rob us of this faith. *He is* the living and immortal [*lebendig und unsterblich*] image <u>against death</u>, which he suffered, yet by his resurrection from the dead he vanquished death in his life. *He is* the image of the grace of God <u>against sin</u>, which he assumed, and yet overcame by his perfect obedience. *He is* the heavenly image, the one who was forsaken by God as damned, yet he <u>conquered hell</u>, through his omnipotent love, thereby proving that he is the dearest Son, who gives this to us all if we but believe (*WA* 2:691.12–21, my emphasis).[72]

In article 15 Luther returns to the notion of sacraments operating as signs, and he deals with both visual and oral aspects of their signification: In the sacraments your God, Christ himself, deals, speaks, and

---

[70] "…sie werden selbs alzustarck hereyn…mit yhrem ansehen, disputirn un zeygen" (*WA* 2:688.25).

[71] Here Luther uses the question to anticipate his readers' thoughts, and then to answer them. In his work on the catechisms Luther employed a strong pattern of question and answer (*Was ist das? Antwort*); see Charles P. Arand, *That I May Be His Own: An Overview of Luther's Catechisms* (St. Louis, 2000), 101–107; Gottfried G. Krodel, "Luther's Work on the Catechism," "Appendix," 380–383.

[72] "Wen hatt er das than? Am Creutz, dan doselb hatt er unsz sich selbs bereyt eyn dreyfeltig bild unszerm glauben furzuhalten widder die drey bild, da der bösze geyst und unszer nature unsz mit ansicht ausz dem glauben zu reyszen. Er ist das lebendig und unsterblich bild widder den tod, den er erlitten, und doch mit seyner ufferstand von todtenn ubirwunden yn seynem leben. Er ist das bild der gnaden gottis widder die sund, der er auff sich genommen und durch seynen unubirwindlichen gehorsam ubirwunden. Er ist das hymelisch bild, der vorlassen von gott, alsz eyn vordampter, und durch seyn aller mechtigist liebe die hell ubirwunden, bezeugt, das er der liebst sun sey und unsz allen dasselb zu eygen geben, szo wir alszo glauben."

works with you through the priest. His are not the works and words of man.... God wants the sacraments to be a sign and testimony [*Wartzeichen und Urkund*]...(*WA* 2:692.28–30).[73] [T]he sacraments, that is the external words of God as spoken by a priest are a truly great comfort and at the same time a visible sign of divine intent [*sichtlich Zeichen gotlicher Meynung*] (*WA* 2:692.36f.).[74] Everyone who is saved:

> is saved only by that sign. It points [*weyszet*] to Christ and his image, enabling you to say..., 'God promised and in his sacraments he gave me a sure sign [*gewisz Zeichen*] of his grace.... This sign, this promise [*das Tzeichen, das Zusagen*] of my salvation will not lie to me or deceive me. It is God who has promised it, and he cannot lie either in words or in deeds' (*WA* 2:693.6–13).[75]

The sacraments contain nothing but "God's words, promises, and signs. This means that we have no doubts about the sacraments or the things of which they are certain signs" *WA* 2:693.17–19).[76] The sacraments will be completely fruitless if we do not believe the things that are 'indicated, given, and promised there [*anzeygt, geben und vorsprechen*]' to us (*WA* 2:693.25). To disbelieve makes God a liar in his "Word, signs, and works, as one who speaks, shows, and promises [*redt, zeyge, zusage*] something which he neither means nor intends to keep" (*WA* 2:693.27–29).[77]

Clinging to the signs and promises of God takes faith (*LW* 42:110; *WA* 2:693.30). While later, in "The Blessed Sacrament," he will explicate faith's role more clearly,[78] here Luther admonishes the dying to believe

---

[73] "...dann yn den Sacramenten handelt, redt, wirckt durch den priester. Deyn gott Christus selbs mit dyr und geschehen da nit menschen werck oder wort...will die sacrament eyn wartzeichen und urkund seyn."

[74] "...die sacrament, das ist die euszerliche wort gottis, durch eynen priester gesprochen, gar eyn grosser trost seynt und gleich eyn sichtlich zeichen gotlicher meynung."

[75] "...dan mit dem tzeichen werden all erhalten, die erhalten werden. Es weyszet auff Christum und sein bild, das du magst widder des tods, sund und hell bild sagen 'Got hat myr zugesagt und eyn gewisz zeichen seyner gnaden yn den sacramenten geben, das Christus leben meynen tod yn seynem tod ubirwunden hab, seyn gehorsam meyne sund yn seynem leyden vortilget, seyn lieb meyn hell ynn seynem vorlassen zustort habe, das tzeichen, das zusagen meyner selickeit wirt myr nit liegen noch triegen, Gott hat es gesagt, gott mag nit ligen, noch mit worten noch mit wercken.'"

[76] "...eytel gottis wort, zusagen, zeichen geschehen, hoch achte, yn ehren halt, sich drauff vorlasse, das ist, das man widder an den sacramenten noch an denn dingen der sie seynd gewisse tzeichenn."

[77] "...wort, zeychen und werck als ein lugner geachtet wirt, alls der ettwas redt, zeyge, zusage, das er nicht meyne, noch halten wolle."

[78] Paragraph 1: "The holy sacrament of the altar, or of the holy and true body of

the sacraments are 'sure signs, true words of God' (*WA* 2:694.2–3). God builds his Word and sacraments on sheer grace on the foundation of his 'Word and signs.' One who receives the sacraments "has received a sign [*Zeychen*] and a promise [*Zusag*] from God" (*WA* 2:694.17f.). Having to go 'without these signs' means one's faith must even more strongly persevere (*WA* 2:694.20). Notice, in the discourse below, that Luther has created more dialogue for his reader to use, a soliloquy that is intensely personal (with numerous first person singular <u>pronouns</u>):

> Thus you must also say with regard to the Sacrament of the Altar, 'If the priest gave <u>me</u> the holy body of Christ, which is a sign and promise of the communion of all angels and saints that they love <u>me</u>, provide and pray for <u>me</u>, suffer and die with <u>me</u>, bear <u>my</u> sin and overcome hell, it will and must therefore be true that the divine sign does not deceive <u>me</u>. <u>I</u> will not let anyone rob <u>me</u> of it. <u>I</u> would rather deny all the world and <u>myself</u> than doubt <u>my</u> God's trustworthiness and truthfulness in his signs and promises. Whether worthy or unworthy of him, <u>I</u> am, according to the text and declaration of this sacrament, a member of Christendom (*WA* 2:694.21–30).[79]

The signs still require faith: People want to be certain (*gewisz*) or have a 'sign from heaven' telling whether they are elected. Luther challenges this position with five successive rhetorical questions—replete with the repetitive *Zeychen*—the final one of which emphasizes the reliability of what those signs indicate:

> But what help would it be to them to receive such a sign if they would still not believe? What good are all the signs without faith? How did Christ's signs and the apostles' signs help the Jews? What help are the venerable signs [*hochwirdigen Zeychen*] of the sacraments and the words of God even today? Why do people not hold to the sacraments, which are

---

Christ, also has three parts which it is necessary for us to know. The first is the sacrament, or sign. The second is the significance of this sacrament. The third is the faith required with each of the first two. These three parts must be found in every sacrament. The sacrament must be external and visible, having some material form or appearance. The significance must be internal and spiritual, within the spirit of the person. Faith must make both of them together operative and useful" (*LW* 35:49).

[79] "Alszo soltu auch sagen ubir dem sacrament des Altars 'Hat mir der priester geben den heyligen leychnam Christi, das eyn zeychen und zusagen ist der gemeynschafft aller Engel und heyligen, das sie mich leib haben, fur mich sorgen, bitten und mit mir leyden, sterben, sund tragen und hell ubirwunden, Szo wirt es und musz alszo seyn, das gottlich zeychen treugt mich nit, und las mirs nit nhemen, ich wolt ehe alle welt, mich selb vorleugnen, ehe ich dran zweyffelt, Meyn gott der sey mir gewisz und warhafftig yn dissem seynem zeychen und zusagen, Jch sey seyn wirdig odder nit, szo byn ich ein glid der Christenheit nach laut und anzeygung diszes sacraments."

sure and appointed signs [*gewisse und eingesetzte Zeychen*], tested and tried by all saints and found reliable by all who believed and who received all that they indicate [*zeichent*]? (*WA* 2:694.37–695.3).[80]

Luther follows his series of rhetorical questions with a final summary of the sacraments' function:

> The right use of the sacraments involves nothing more than believing that all will be as the sacraments promise and pledge through God's Word. Therefore, it is necessary not only to look at the three pictures in Christ and with these to drive out the counter-pictures [*gegen Bild*], but also to have a definite sign which assures us that this has surely been given to us. That is the function [*das seyn*] of the sacraments (*WA* 2:695.10–15).[81]

From Article 18 on Luther's main objective is not to teach what the sacraments mean or do, but to encourage the dying to recognize and depend on others for support: God and Christ, the angels, saints, and all Christians. But he keeps returning, on occasion, to the signifying power of the sacraments (and of the Word) to remind us of this assistance. "He can be certain, as the sacraments point out that a great many eyes are upon him" (*WA* 2:695.17f.).[82] There is no doubt, as the Sacrament of the Altar indicates [*weyszet*], that all of these…run to him (*WA* 2:695.22).[83] He who doubts this does not believe in the most venerable Sacrament of the Body of Christ, in which are pointed out, promised and pledged [*gezeygt, zugesagt, vorpflicht*]…(*WA* 2:695.26f.).[84] Therefore, we must know that even though the works of God surpass human understanding, God yet effects all of this through such insignificant signs [*cleynen tzeichen*] as the sacraments to teach us what a great thing a true faith in God really is (*WA* 2:696.16–19).[85] We have two reasons

---

[80] "as helffen noch heut die hochwirdigen zeychen der sacrament und wort gottis? Warumb halten sie sich nit an die sacrament, wilchs gewisse und eingesetzte zeychen sein, durch alle heyligen probirt und vorsucht, gewisz erfunden allen denen, die do glaubt haven, und ubirkummen als wasz sie zeichent?"

[81] "Der prauch ist nit anders, dan glauben, es sey alszo, wie die sacrament durch gottis wort zusagen und vorpflichten. Drumb ist nott, das man nit alleyn die drey bild in Christo ansehe und die gegem bild damit ausztreyb und fallen lasse, sondernn das man eyn gewisz tzeichen hab, das unsz vorsichere, es sey alszo unsz geben, das seyn die Sacrament."

[82] "…gewisz seyn, das noch antzeigung des sacraments auff yhn gar viel augen sehen."

[83] "…da ist keyn zweyffell, wie das sacrament des altaris weyszet, das die allesampt alsz…zu seynem glidmas zu lauffen."

[84] "…wer dran zweiffelt, der glaubt aber nicht an das hochwirdig sacrament desz leychnams Christi, Jn wilchem gezeygt, zugesagt, vorpflicht wirt."

[85] "…darumb soll man wissen, das gottis werck seyn, die grosser seyn dan jemand

for believing our prayer is heard: The first one is that he has just heard from the Scriptures how God commanded the angels to give love and help to all who believe and how the sacrament conveys [*gibt*] this (*WA* 2:696.28f.).[86] Luther puts together, in the final Article, how the images and the sacraments function. While obscured in *LW* 42:114 (but clear in German), notice how he uses <u>anaphora</u> and asyndetic repetition (especially in repeating second singular personal pronouns) to build a cumulative celebration of God's *pro me* provision:

> <u>He offers</u> you [*Er weyst und gibt deynen*] in Christ the image of life, of grace, of salvation [*des lebens, der gnade, der selickeit*] so that you [*du*] may not be horrified by the images of death, of sin, of hell. <u>He lays</u>, furthermore [*Er legt dartzu*], your death, your sin, your hell on his dearest Son, and vanquishes them, renders them harmless for you. <u>He lets</u>, in addition, your trials [*Er leszt dartzu deyne anfechtung*] of death, of sin, of hell also assail his Son and teaches you how to preserve yourself in the midst of these and how to make them harmless and bearable. <u>He grants</u> you, [*Er gibt dyr*] to relieve you of all doubt, a sure sign [*gewisz Wartzeichen*], namely, the holy sacraments. <u>He commands</u> [*Er befelht*] his angels, all saints, all creatures to join him in watching over you, to be concerned about your soul, and to receive it. <u>He commands</u> you [*Er gepeut, du*] to ask him for this and to be assured of fulfilment (*WA* 2:697.15–25).[87]

E. *Visual Narration, Description, and Exhortation*

Luther may have been consciously trying to build on the notion that the woodcut illustrations of the *ars moriendi* were an aid to illiterate dying people who needed help in appreciating—through visualizing—the spiritual temptations of 'death, sin, hell,' and especially the spiritual assistance of God, the angels, the saints, the sacraments, etc.[88] Notice

---

dencken mag, und sie doch wircket ynn solchen cleynen tzeichen der Sacrament, das er unsz lere, wie grosz dinck sey eyn rechter glaub tzu Gott."

[86] "Die erste, das er itzt gehort ausz der schryfft, wie gott yhnen befolen hat, und wie das sacrament gibt."

[87] "Er weyst und gibt dyr in Christo des lebens, der gnade, der selickeit bild, das du fur des tods, der sund, der hell bild nit dich entsetzist. Er legt dartzu deynen tod, deyne sund, deyn hell auff seynen liebsten sun und ubirwindt sie dyr, macht sie dyr unschedlich. Er leszt darzu deyne anfechtung des tods, der sund, der helle auch ubir seynen sun gehen, und dich darinne tzu halten leret und sie unschedlich. Darzu treglich macht. Er gibt dyr des alles ein gewisz wartzeichen, das du yhe nit dran zweiffelest, nemlich die heyligen sacrament. Er befelgt seynen Engeln, allen heyligenn, allen crea-turen, das sie mit yhm auff dich sehen, deyner seel warnemen und sie entpfahen. Er gepeut, du solt solchs von hym bitten und der erhorung gewisz seyn."

[88] Perelman emphasizes the role of 'presence' in persuasion; cf. Chaim Perelman and L. Olbrichts-Tyteca, *The New Rhetoric: A Treatise on Argumentation*, trans. John Wilkinson

especially what I call Luther's *vision talk* and the phrases (both verbs and objects) that describe or prescribe sensual, particularly visual, action and contemplation. Although the actions take concentrated effort to perform, they do not necessarily connote physical movement (which is not easy for a dying person). Neither do the actions require explanation, for the notions of seeing, looking, viewing, gazing, etc., are self-explanatory. Vision talk is required because the enemy also uses this tactic.

We must 'turn [*richten*]' our eyes to God (*WA* 2:685.20). Death 'fixes its gaze [*zu seher vor Augen hatt*]' (*WA* 2:687.4–17). The devil presses man to 'look closely [*betrachten*]' at the image of death (*WA* 2:687.5). Indeed, he "conjures up before man's eyes [*die eyn Mensch yhe gesehen*] . . . all kinds of death ever seen, heard, or read" by man (*WA* 2:687.6f.). We 'must refuse to see [*nit sehen wollen*]' death. Death's power and might are rooted in our 'undue viewing and contemplating [*ansehen odder betrachten*]' of it (*WA* 2:687.17). We tend to "dwell on [sin] and brood over it too much [*ansehen und zu tieff bedencken*]" (*WA* 2:687.18f.). We should constantly "have our eyes fixed [*stetig vorauген haben*]" on the image of 'death, sin, hell' (*LW* 42:102; *WA* 2:687.32f.). The devil "closes our eyes and hides these images [*thut er unsz die Augen zu und vorbirget die selben Bild*]," the images being the words of Ps. 51:3, "My sin is ever before [*alzeit voraugen*] me." But in the hour of death, when our "eyes should see only [*voraugen haben nur*]" life, grace and salvation, he at once "opens our eyes [*thut er unsz dan aller erst die Augen*] . . . so that we shall not see the true ones" (*WA* 2:687.34–36). We must strive "not to open [*lade*] our homes to any of these images and not to paint the devil over the door" (*WA* 2:688.22–24).[89] The only thing to do with these pictures is

---

and Purcell Weaver (Notre Dame, 1969). For a brief discussion of presence, see Neil R. Leroux, "Perceiving Rhetorical Style: Toward A Framework for Criticism." *Rhetoric Society Quarterly* 22 (fall 1992): 29–44.

[89] Here Luther has used a proverb he uses several times later, in other works, according to James C. Cornette, Jr., *Proverbs and Proverbial Expressions in the German Works of Martin Luther*, ed. Wolfgang Mieder and Dorothee Racette. Sprichwörterforschung 19 (Bern, 1997), 107. See *WA* 9:154.12; 16:319.10f.; 18:72.29; 30(2):644.25f.; 32:112.32; 37:577.22; 46:177.23; 47:137.14; 50:445.16; 54:235.1. This proverb is catalogued as No. 356 in 'Luthers Sprichwörtersammlung' (*WA* 51:657, 712). The proverb, "mahle den Teuffel nicht uber die thuer, er kompt dir sonst wohl," Luther here renders as: "[I]n this affair we must exercise all diligence not to open our homes to any of these images and not to paint the devil over the door. These foes will of themselves boldly rush in and seek to occupy the heart completely . . ." (*LW* 42:103); "Nu musz man yn diszem handell allen vleysz ankeren, das man dyszer dreyer bild keyns zu hausz lade, noch den teuffell ubir die thur male, sie werden selbs alzustarck hereyn fallen und das hertz mit yhrem ansehen" (*WA* 2:688.23–26).

'to combat and expel them.' We must 'look [*ansehen*]' at death while alive and 'see [*ansehen*]' sin in the light of grace and hell in the light of heaven, permitting nothing to divert us from that 'view [*Blick*]' (*WA* 2:688.27–36).

In Article 10 (*LW* 42:104; *WA* 2:689.3–24) Luther argues that one must not 'view or ponder [*ansehen odder betrachten*]' death as such. Rather, we must resolutely "turn your gaze [*Sondern deyn Augen*]...and look [*ansehen*] at death closely and untiringly [*starck und emfig*]." The more profoundly we impress that image upon our heart and 'gaze [*ansihest*]' upon it, the more it will 'vanish [*vehter*].' The children of Israel had merely to 'raise their eyes [*ansehen*]' to the dead bronze serpent and not 'look [*ansihest*]' at death. In Article 11 (*LW* 42:104f.; *WA* 2:689.25–690.3) Luther urges readers: "[Y]ou must not look [*ansehen*] at sin in sinners"; you must "turn [*abkeren*] your thoughts away from that and look [*ansehen*] at sin only within the picture of grace." "Engrave that picture...keep it before your eyes [*vor Augen haben*]." He urges readers to keep the cross 'before your eyes [*vor Augen haben*],' which means to "view the picture of grace and engrave it in yourself." Readers may view (*ansehen*) their sins in safety; they may see (*ansihest*) their death taken upon Christ. In Article 12 (*LW* 42:105; *WA* 2:690.13–26) Luther urges readers to "keep your eyes closed tightly to such a view [*die Augenn fest zuhaltenn fur solchem Blick*]" as hell and damnation. Instead, gaze (*ansich*) at the heavenly picture of Christ, and don't allow it to be 'erased from your vision [*las dirs nur nit ausz den Augen nhemen*].' 'Seek yourself [*Suche dich*]' only in Christ and you will find; when you 'look [*ansihist*]' at Christ you are already elected.

In Article 13 (*LW* 42:106; *WA* 2:690.37–691.13) Luther urges readers to concentrate on the 'glowing picture [*leuchtende Bild*]' of Christ and his saints, abiding in faith, which "does not see and does not want to see the false pictures." Luther implores readers that Christ 'be held before the eyes of our faith.' In Article 14 (*WA* 2:691.28–692.19) Luther claims the Jews "held the image of sin before Christ's eyes [*Der Sund Bild hilten sye ym fur*]"; they pressed the picture of hell before Christ's eyes (*Bild trieben sie zu yhm*), saying 'let us see' if God will deliver him now. Luther argues that 'now we mark [*wyr nu sehen*]' that on the cross Christ acts as though he does not hear or see them. So also we must 'let these images slip away [*lassen her fallen und abfallen*],' cling to God's will—meaning hold (*hafften*) and firmly believe (*festiglich gleuben*). In Article 15 (*LW* 42:109) Luther says we must "carefully walk with open eyes [*eyn Aug auff haben soll mit allem vleysz*]" (*WA* 2:693.3). In Article 16 (*LW* 42:110) he says,

"Just see to it [*Schaw*] that you believe" (*WA* 2:694.2). In Article 17 (*LW* 42:111; *WA* 2:694.32–695.14) Luther says, 'Just see [*Nu sihe*]' how many people want to be certain; the signs are believed by all who received all that they indicate (*zeichent*). 'Look [*ansehe*]' at the three pictures in Christ, and 'drive out the counter-pictures [*die gegem Bild damit ausztreyb*].' In Article 18 (*LW* 42:112; *WA* 2:695.18–37) Luther claims a great many eyes are fixed (*gar viel Augen sehen*) upon the dying Christian: first, the eyes of God and of Christ himself; then also those of the dear angels. A Christian must see this for himself; God's 'eyes rest upon you.' Psalm 32:8, which Luther quotes, reads, "my eyes will constantly be upon you lest you perish." Luther continues to say that if God 'looks upon you,' all will 'fix [*sehen*]' their eyes upon you, as with the Israelites, who could see nothing but their surrounding enemies. Then the Lord opened the eyes of Elisha's servant. In Article 19 (*LW* 42:113) Luther says God can make our faith stronger as we face death. In Article 20 (*LW* 42:114) he declares that all creatures join God in 'watching over you,' and then we can see God is true (*WA* 2:697.23–26).

F. *Physical Action and Thought in Luther's Language*

In addition to *vision talk*, Luther's concrete language also incorporates many phrases evoking physical action, or at least offering a degree of vividness, not only the verbs but also the nouns that elicit them—by providing a scene for, or an object of, action. These phrases often establish a pattern of dynamic action, especially in describing God's active, physical provision, which in turn leads naturally to admonishing the dying person to 'fix [his] eyes' on Jesus. Often these phrases—noun or verb—are doublets, and they are frequently constructed in close parallelism, sometimes in rhyme. The working of not one but two terms enhances the prospects of Luther's communication being more compelling. There are roughly five categories of such language.

A. Spatial Description: The Birth Analogy. In Article 3 (*LW* 42:99f.), upon the first use of a visual command ('turn our eyes to God,' which is not very literal or explicit in German),[90] Luther constructs the analogy between dying and being born, calling death a new birth (*new gepurt*). He derived the analogy from John 16:21, which he quotes. The path of death 'leads and directs us' to God. In Him we find the 'narrow

---

[90] "Soll man sich dan alleyn zu gott richten" (*WA* 2:685.20f.).

gate and straight path' to life, on which all must joyfully venture forth, because the path is not long, though the gate is quite narrow.[91] Observe Luther's use of assonant rhyme (*cleynen/weyten*) to stress the comparison: there are pain and peril (*Gefar und Engsten*) that accompany the infant from the small abode (*cleynen Wonung*) of the mother's womb, but then begins life in an 'immense heaven and earth.' All then depart life through the narrow gate of death (*enge Pforten des Todts*). During life, heaven and earth seem 'large and wide' but are really 'narrower and smaller' than the womb, when compared to the future heaven. Luther's first proof is the feast day called *Natale* in Latin, commemorating the death of saints but literally meaning birth. Reasoning that death makes us think of this life as expansive and the life beyond as confined, Luther argues that a child's physical birth should teach us what Christ has declared in John 16:21 about the forgotten sorrow of childbirth's travail, once the child is born. In dying, anguish must be borne in the belief that expansive joy follows: the path of death leads and directs us, yet all must joyfully venture forth (*frölich erwegen*). Following his quote of John 16:21, Luther argues that, as with the travail (*Angst*) of childbirth, the anguish (*Angst*) of dying is what we must bear, for not only is the anguish forgotten; a 'large mansion and joy' will follow.[92]

B. The Devil and Our Conscience. In Articles 6–8 (*LW* 42:101f.) Luther uses the concrete language—of noun, verb, adverb, and adjective—and the series (doublet, triplet) to argue that the devil attacks the consciences of Christians, using the images of 'death, sin, hell' to

---

[91] Luther uses two balanced, parallel clauses (6 syllables each) for this anaphoric antithesis: "er ist woll fast enge, er ist aber nit langk" (*WA* 2:685.23f.).

[92] "Man szo yderman urlaub auff erden geben, Soll man sich dan alleyn zu gott richten, da der weg des sterbens sich auch hin keret und unsz furet. Und hie hebt an die enge pforte, der schmale steyg zum leben, des musz sich eyn yglicher frölich erwegen, dann er ist woll fast enge, er ist aber nit langk, und geht hie zu, gleych wie ein kind ausz der cleynen wonung seyner mutter leyb mit gefar und engsten geboren wirt yn diszenn weyten hymell und erden, das ist auff disze welt. Alszo geht der mensch durch die enge pforten des todts ausz diszem leben, und wie woll der hymell und die welt, da wir itzt yn leben grosz und weyt angesehen wirt, Szo ist es doch alles gegen dem zukunfftigem hymel vill enger und kleyner, dan der mutter leyb gegenn diszem hymell ist, darumb heyst der lieben heyligen sterben eyn new gepurt, und yhre fest nennet man zu latein Natale, eyn tag yhrer gepurt. Aber der enge gangk des todts macht, das unsz disz leben weyt und yhenes enge dunckt. Drumb musz man das glauben unnd an der leyplichen gepurt eyns kinds lernen, als Christus sagt: Eyn weyb, wan es gepirt, szo leydet es angst, man sie aber geneszen ist szo gedenckt sie der angst nymmer, die weyll eyn mensch geporn ist von yhr yn die welt, alszo ym sterben auch musz man sich der angst erwegen und wissen, das darnach eyn groszer raum und freud seyn wirt" (*WA* 2:685.20–686.8).

condemn believers. Residing in the cognitive and psychological realms, this language—all along the figurative-literal continuum—is less *physical* than the birth-analogical diction; yet it still is dynamic. Luther claims our nature has etched death's image too vividly within itself; that the devil presses (*steuret*) man so that the 'mien and image [*Geperd und Bild*]' of death adds to his 'worry, timidity, and despair'; that the devil had 'tormented and destroyed [*geplagt und vorterbet*]' sinners; that the devil sees that man 'flees and abhors' death and thus 'is and remains disobedient [*erfunden werde und bleybe*].' In order to combat this onslaught when one is dying, Luther boldly argues that we should familiarize ourselves with death, "inviting death into our presence when it is still at a distance and not on the move." At the time of dying, however, we must put the thought of death out of mind.[93] Regarding sin (Article 7), we should not 'dwell on it and brood over it too much [*ansehen und zu tieff bedencken*]' or else our conscience is 'ashamed before God and accuses itself terribly.' The devil wants us to "despair or die reluctantly, thus forgetting God and being found disobedient" (*WA* 2:687.18–24).[94] In Article 8 (*LW* 42:102f.) Luther says hell looms large for us because of 'undue scrutiny and stern thought.' In a vivid expression (not fully apparent in *LW* 42:103), the devil tries to blast God's love from a man's mind (*Gottis Lieb mit eynem Sturm wind auszuleschen*) and to arouse thoughts of God's wrath. In the end, the imperiled man who accepts the devil's thoughts falls prey to 'hatred and blasphemy' of God. The devil is always reminding us of the lost, "agitating such dangerous and pernicious thoughts so violently" that man, who would otherwise gladly die, "now becomes loath to depart this life."[95]

C. Scriptural Images of Conflict. In Article 13 (*LW* 42:106f.) Luther uses two OT Scriptures (plus the event of Christ's crucifixion in the NT) as *figur*, wherein he argues that the triple threat ('death, sin, hell') has been anticipated by God and conquered by Gideon (Judges 7:16–22; Isa. 9:4) and by Christ. Having already discussed the two Scriptures briefly, here I want simply to highlight Luther's concrete

---

[93] *WA* 2:686.31–687.17.

[94] "Die sund wechst und wirt grosz auch durch yhr zuvill ansehen und zu tieff bedencken. Da hilfft zu die blodickeit unszers gewissen, das sich selbs vor gott schemet und grewlich strafft. Da hatt der teuffell dan dyn bad sunden, das er gesucht, da treybt er, da macht er die sund szo vill und grosz, da soll er alle die fürhalten, die gesundet haben, und wie vil mit wenigern sunden vordampt seyn, Das der mensch aber musz vorzagen odder unwillig werden zusterben gottis vorgessen und engehorsam ersunden."

[95] *WA* 2:688.1–21.

and vivid language, especially through verbal and nominal doublets (and a triplet), in which he narrates these stories. Three 'pictures or conflicts' appear in Judges 7: Gideon attacked the Midianites at night with three hundred men in three different places but did no more than have 'trumpets blown and glass fragments smashed'; the foe then 'fled and destroyed himself [*feynd flohen und selbs erwurgten*].' Similarly, 'death, sin, and hell' will flee with might. We must 'encourage and strengthen' ourselves with God's Word as with the sound of trumpets. Isaiah 9 uses this figure and three images: the yoke of his burden, the staff for his shoulder (*Ruthe seynes Rucken*), the rod of his oppressor (*Scepter seynes Trebers*) were broken (*ubirwunden*), were overcome (*ubirwand*) by Gideon. Luther then repeats these images with his interpretation of Isaiah 9. In this interpretation, Luther uses a form of dialogue, wherein he puts his interpretation into the mouth of Isaiah (*WA* uses quotation marks). Further, Luther foregrounds sin, by placing it first in the list and by finishing the interpretation with another reference to sin. Luther uses parenthesis to comment on each of the three applications; the three parentheses are virtually anaphoric:

> He says as it were: 'The sins of your people (which are a heavy "yoke of his burden" for his conscience), and death (which is a "staff" or punishment laid upon his shoulder), and hell (which is a powerful "rod of the oppressor" with which eternal punishment for sin is exacted)—all these you have defeated. This came to pass in the days of Midian, that is, when Gideon, by faith and without wielding his sword, put his enemies to flight' (*WA* 2:691.5–11).[96]

D. <u>Scriptural Images of Hope and Strength</u>. In Article 18 (*LW* 42:112f.) Luther employs five different OT Scriptures, all for the purpose of bringing comfort in the hour of death. The message is that one is not alone, that the *eyes* of many—God, Christ, the angels, the saints, and all creatures—are upon the dying one. In contrast to the previous section's emphasis on Luther's visual narration, depiction, and description—where the dying one is doing the looking—here Luther describes the looking down of others. Two things are evident here: (1) Luther's

---

[96] "Als sprech er 'Deyns volcks sund (das do ist eyn schwere last seyner burden yn seynem gewissen) und den tod (der do ist dyn ruthe odder straff, der do druckt seynen rücken) unnd die hell (die eyn scepter und gewalt ist des treybers, do mit gefodert wirt ewiges betzalen fur die sund). Hastu alls ubirwunden wie es dan geschehen ist zu den zeyten Madian, das ist durch den glaubenn, da durch Gedion an all schwert schlag die feynd vorjagt.'"

emphasis upon the eyes which look down 'upon him'—'upon you,'—is prevalent in the Scriptures quoted; (2) the concrete language of persons and places that the quoted Scriptures bring.

First, in the hour of death one can be certain (*gewisz*), as the sacraments point out, that a great many eyes are on him: initially, the eyes of God himself and of Christ; also, the eyes of the dear angels and of the saints, and all Christians. These eyes 'in a body' help him to overcome and bear all things. God's eyes rest upon you, as Ps. 32 says: "*Firmabo, etc.*, my eyes will constantly be upon you lest you perish." Luther argues that if God looks upon you (*auff dich sicht*), "all the angels, [all the] saints, and all creatures...all of them will uphold you with their hands." While not strictly speaking of 'eyes,' Luther nevertheless cites 2 Kings 6 [:16f.] to explain how the Lord opened the eyes of the young man Elisha.

Second, what the young man saw was the huge mass (*groszer Hauff*) of horses and chariots (*Wagen*) of fire, even though, at first, all Elisha could see was that enemies surrounded him. Those who are with us are more than those who are with them, Luther says. He then notes the words of Ps. 34:7 (= 33:8 Vulgate), telling of the angel that will encamp around those who fear him and deliver them. In Ps. 125:1–2 (= 124:1–2 Vulgate) those who trust in God cannot be moved (*unbeweglich*) and are like Mount Zion, which abides forever. As the mountains encircle (*umbring*) Jerusalem, so the Lord encircles (*umbringet*) his people, 'from this time forth and forevermore.' Luther then paraphrases from Ps. 91:11–16 (= 90:11–16 Vulgate.), a fascinating text, from which (vv. 11–12) the devil quoted to Jesus in his wilderness temptation (Matt. 4:6; Luke 4:10f.). The psalm has a narrator tell of all the protections God (vv. 1–10) and his angels (vv. 11–12) will provide the reader, who is directly addressed as 'he' (vv. 1–3) and 'you' (singular, throughout). Then in vv. 14–16, God's voice interrupts the narrator and repeatedly pledges his own protection ('I will') to the reader. Note Luther's interpretive paraphrase and the blend of comforting terms with concrete dangers, which ends with the <u>anaphora</u> of God's own promise:

> For he has charged his angels to bear you on their hands and to guard you wherever you go lest you dash your foot against a stone. You will tread on the adder[97] and the lion, the young lion, and the serpent you will trample under foot (this means that all the power and the cunning

---

[97] *LW* 42:113 reverses the doublet.

[*Stercke und List*] of the devil will be unable to harm you), because he has trusted me and I will deliver him.[98] I will be with him in all his trials, I will rescue and honor him. With eternal life I will satisfy [*machen*] him, and I will show [*offenbaren*] him my eternal grace (*WA* 2:696.5–13).[99]

E. Actions That Exercise Faith. Having just acknowledged that such great matters—the legion of angels, God's ministering spirits (*Dinstpar*), sent to those who are to be saved—are, without the sacraments, hard to believe, Luther declares that a true faith is a great thing. Moreover, in Article 19 (*LW* 42:113f.) he suggests ways Christians can ask God to 'create and preserve' this faith, especially at the hour of death. Luther's language is vivid, his tone is urgent, and we note his call for intermediaries. He urges: (1) that one practice 'awe and humility,' lest one ascribe these things to himself, denying God the glory (*eere*); (2) that one call upon the holy angels, particularly his own angel, the Mother of God, and all the apostles and dear saints, since God has granted exceptional zeal (*bszondere Andacht*) for this; (3) that one believe one's prayer will be heard, because God commanded the angels to help; (4) that we (Luther shifts from third singular to first plural here) must hold (*fürhalten*) this before them and remind (*auffrucken*) them, so as to make our 'faith and trust' in them and God 'stronger and bolder'; (5) that God has enjoined (*gepoten*) us firmly to believe in the fulfilment of our prayer, that it is truly an Amen; (6) that we bring this command (*Gespott*) to his attention (the prayer uses first person singular): "My God, you have commanded me to pray and to believe my prayer will be heard. I come assured you will not forsake but will grant me a genuine faith";[100] (7) that we should implore God and his saints our whole life long for true faith in the last hour, as we sing on Pentecost: "Now let us pray to the Holy Spirit for the true faith of all things the

---

[98] *LW* 42:113 inserts the following words, from Ps. 91:14b–15a, into Luther's quote: "I will protect him because he knows my name: When he calls to me, I will answer him"; these words are absent in *WA* 2:685.

[99] "Er hat seynen Engelen dich befolen, Auff den henden sollen sie dich tragen und dich bewaren, wo du hyn gehest, das du nit stoffest deynen fusz an yrgend eynen steyn, Auff den schlangen und basiliscken soltu gehen, und auff den lawen und drachen soltu treten (das ist alle sterck und list desz teuffels wreden dyr nichts thun), dan er hat yn mich vortrawet, Jch wil yhn erloszen, ich wil bey ym seyn yn allen seynen anfechtungen, ich will yhm ausz helffen und zu ehren setzen, Jch will yhn soll machen mit ewickeit, Jch will yhm offenbaren meyne ewigen gnade."

[100] "'Meyn Gott, du hast gepoten zu bitten unnd zu glauben, die bitt werd erhört, drauff bitt ich und vorlas mich, du werdest mich nit lassen und eynen rechten glauben geben'" (*WA* 2:697:2–4).

most, and as home we go, etc." (*WA* 2:697.7f.).[101] Luther closes Article
19 with the following plea:

> When the hour of death is at hand one must offer this prayer and, in
> addition, remind God of his command and of his promise and not doubt
> that one's prayer will be fulfilled. After all, if God commanded us to pray
> and to trust in prayer, and, furthermore, has granted the grace to pray,
> why should one doubt that his purpose in this was also to hear and to
> fulfil? (*WA* 2:697.8–13).[102]

G. *Overcoming the Enemy*

In this pamphlet on preparing for dying Luther frequently turns to the
language of conquest. One of the strong terms he uses for characterizing Christ's (and the Christian's) victory at death is *uberwunden*—all
but once as verb. This conquest language is not as ubiquitous as the
vision talk, but for the most part it occurs in the same places: The
conquest language begins at Article 8; the vision talk is also heard
only sparingly in the earlier articles. In his 26 uses of *uberwunden* (and
its variants), Luther makes victory seem certain. While he most often
uses *uberwunden* as an active verb, he occasionally uses the passive voice
to feature how the enemy (usually 'death, sin, and hell') is overcome.[103]
Only 3 times does he use the verb *uberwunden* to remind readers of
the dangers of 'being overcome.' *LW* 42:99–115 translates *uberwunden*
as some form of 'overcome' (15×), 'vanquished' (5×), 'defeated' (4×),
'broken' (1), and 'victory' (1). Moreover, alluding to Hebrews 5:8–9,

---

[101] "Nu bitten wir den heyligen geyst umb den rechten glauben aller meyst, wen wir
heim faren ausz dissem elende 2c." *LW* 42:114 adds words to the hymn that Luther
did not utter here, but which were indeed part of the German text (first verse) of
this well-known hymn, "Sancti Spiritus adsit nobis gratia, quaecorda nostra sibi faciat
habitaculum," an eleventh-century song appointed for use following the reading of the
Epistle for Pentecost. The song is attributed to Notker Labeo (d. 912); cf. *LW* 53:25.
In 1524 Luther added three stanzas. The English translation of the hymn is "Now
Let Us Pray to the Holy Ghost" (*LW* 53:263f.).

[102] "Und wan die stund kommen ist zusterben, soll man gott desselben gepeets
ermanen neben seynem gepot und zusagenn an allen zweyffell, es sey erhoret, dann szo
er gepoten hat tzu bitten und zu trawen ym gebet, dartzu gnad geben zu bitten, Was
solt man zweiffellnn, er habs drumb alls than, das er es erhoren und erfullen will?" *LW*
42:114 includes several first plural pronouns that are not explicit in Luther's text.

[103] The list of 19 short-list occurrences of 'death, sin, hell' is strikingly parallel
to the 26 occurences of *uberwunden*. Not counting Articles 10–12, in which we find
uberwunden used 8 times, the two lists are practically identical. In other words, Luther
(unintentionally, no doubt), used an equivalent number of 'conquest' verbs as he did
'death, sin, hell' short lists. He saw to it, that is, that the *triple threat* of 'death, sin, hell'
was thoroughly vanquished.

Luther uses *unubirwindlichen* to describe the 'perfect' obedience of Christ, which 'overcame' sin.

Article 8 (*LW* 42:103): "He who surmounts this temptation [over whether I am elected] has vanquished [*ubirwunden*] hell, sin, and death all in one."[104] In Article 10 Luther argues:

> [Y]ou must not view or ponder death as such, not in yourself or in your nature, nor in those who were killed by God's wrath and were overcome [*ubir wunden*] by death. If you do that you will be lost and defeated [*ubir wunden*] with them. But you must resolutely turn your gaze, the thoughts of your heart, and all your senses away from this picture and look at death closely and untiringly only as seen in those who died in God's grace and who have overcome [*ubir wunden*] death, particularly in Christ and then also in all his saints" (*WA* 2:689.3–10).[105]

In Article 11 we find: Thus you must not look at sin in sinners, or in your conscience, or in those who abide in sin to the end and are damned. If you do, you will surely follow them and also be overcome [*ubirwunden*] (*WA* 2:689.24–26).[106]

> Here [when borne by Christ] sins are never sins, for here they are overcome [*ubirwunden*] and swallowed up in Christ. He takes your death upon himself and strangles it so that it may not harm you, if you believe that he does it for you and see your death in him and not in yourself. Likewise, he also takes your sins upon himself and overcomes [*ubir windt*] them with his righteousness out of sheer mercy.... 1 Cor 15 [:57]: 'Thanks and praise be to God, who through Christ gives us the victory [*Ubirwundung*] over sin and death' (*WA* 2:689.38–690.9).[107]

---

[104] "Wer hie gewinnet, der hat die hel, sund, todt auff einem hauffen ubirwunden" (*WA* 2:688:21f.).

[105] "Du must den todt nit yn yhm selbs, noch yn dir odder deyner nature, noch yn denen, die durch gottis zorn getodtet seyn, die der todt ubir wunden hatt, ansehen odder betrachten, du bist anders vorloren und wirst mit yhn ubir wunden, Sondern deyn augen, deyns hertzen gedancken unnd alle deyne syn gewaltiglich keren von dem selben bild, und den todt starck und emfig ansehen nur yn denen, die yn gottis gnaden gestorben und den todt ubir wunden haben, furnemlich yn Christo, darnach yn allen seynen heyligen." There is a pregnant phrase facilitated by alliterative consonance in *Gottis Gnaden gestorben* above.

[106] "Also mustu die sund nit ansehen yn denn sundern, noch yn deynem gewissen, noch yn denen, die yn sunden endlich bliben und vordampt seyn, du ferest gewiszlich hynach und wirst ubirwunden."

[107] "...da seynd sund nymer sund, da seynd sie uberwunden und yn Christo vorschlunden: dan gleych wie er deynen tod auff sich nympt und yhn erwurgt, das er dir nit schaden mag, szo du anders gleubst, das er dyr das thut, und deynen todt yn yhm, nit yn dyr ansihest, alszo nympt er auch deyn sund auff sich und yn seyner gerechtickeit ausz lauter gnaden dir ubir windt:...das sagt Paulus 1. Corin: 15. Gott

In Article 12: "In that picture [of Christ, forsaken, on the cross] your hell is defeated [*ubirwunden*] and your uncertain election is made sure" (*WA* 2:690.21).[108]

Luther's conquest language is most prolific in Article 13. Quoting Isa. 9:4, Luther says, "For the yoke of his burden, and the staff for his shoulder, the rod of his oppressor, thou hast broken [*ubirwunden*] as in the days of the Midianites, who were overcome [*ubirwand*] by Gideon....all these you have defeated [*ubirwunden*]" (*WA* 2:691.3–9).[109] Incorporating <u>anaphora</u>, Luther declares:

> <u>He</u> [Christ] <u>is</u> the living and immortal image against death, which he suffered, yet by his resurrection from the dead he vanquished [*ubirwunden*] death in his life. <u>He is</u> the image of the grace of God against sin, which he assumed, and yet overcame [*ubir wunden*] by his perfect [*unubirwindlichen*] obedience. <u>He is</u> the heavenly image, the one who was forsaken by God as damned, yet he conquered [*ubirwunden*] hell through his omnipotent love, thereby proving that he is the dearest Son, who gives this to us all if we but believe (*WA* 2:691.15–18).[110]

Note the opening prepositional phrase as Luther begins Article 14: "[B]eyond [*Zu Ubirflusz*] all this he not only defeated [*ubirwunden*] sin, death, and hell in himself and offered his victory to our faith, but for our further comfort he himself suffered and overcame [*ubirwunden*] the temptations which these pictures entail for us" (*WA* 2:691.22–25).[111] We see another passive use of our conquest verb in the following: "We must, similarly, let these images slip away from us to wherever they wish or care to go, and remember only that we cling to God's will, which

---

sey lob und danck, das er unsz yn Christo geben hatt ubirwindung der sund und des todts."

[108] "Sich, yn dem bild ist ubirwunden deyn helle und deyn ungewisz vorsehung gewisz gemacht."

[109] "Die last seyner burden, die ruthe seines rucken, das scepter seines treybers hastu ubirwunden gleych wie zu den zeyten der Madianiten, die Gedeon ubirwand.... Hastu alls ubirwunden."

[110] "Er ist das lebendig und unsterblich bild widder den tod, den er erlitten, und doch mit seyner ufferstand von todtenn ubirwunden yn seynem leben. Er ist das bild der gnaden gottis widder die sund, die er auff sich genommen und durch seynen unubirwindlichen gehorsam ubirwunden. Er ist das hymelisch bild, der vorlassen von gott, alsz eyn vordampter, und durch seyn aller mechtigist liebe die hell ubirwunden, bezeugt, das er der liebst sun sey und unsz allen dasselb zu eygen geben, szo wir alszo glauben."

[111] "Zu ubirflusz hatt er nit allein yn yhm selbs die sund, todt, hell ubirwunden und unsz furgehalten zu glauben, Sondern zu mehrem trost auch selbst die anfechtung erlitten und ubirwunden, die wir yn diszen bilden haben."

is that we hold to Christ and firmly believe our death, sin, and hell are overcome [*ubirwunden*] in him and no longer able to harm us" (*WA* 2:692.16–20).[112] In Article 15:

> God wants the sacraments to be a sign and testimony that Christ's life has taken your death, his obedience your sin, his love your hell, upon themselves and overcome [*ubirwunden*] them. Moreover, through the same sacraments you are included and made one with all the saints. You thereby enter into the true communion of saints so that they die with you in Christ, bear sin, vanquish [*ubirwinden*] hell (*WA* 2:692.29–35).[113]

Giving them dialogue they can recite when facing the image of death, sin, and hell, Luther also assures his readers that "God promised and in his sacraments he gave me a sure sign of his grace that Christ's life overcame [*ubirwunden*] my death in his death, that his obedience blotted out my sin in his suffering, that his love destroyed my hell in his forsakenness" (*WA* 2:693.8–12).[114]

The last five occurrences of *uberwunden* are scattered within Articles 16–20. In Article 16: What will it profit you to assume and to believe that death, sin, and hell are overcome [*ubirwunden*] in Christ for others, but not to believe that your death, your sin, and your hell are also vanquished [*ubirwunden*] and wiped out and that you are thus redeemed? (*WA* 2:693.21–24).[115] Article 17 (more soliloquy Luther gives his reader): If the priest gave me the holy body of Christ, which is a sign and promise of the communion of all angels and saints that they love me, provide and pray for me, suffer and die with me, bear my sin and overcome [*ubirwunden*] hell, it will and must therefore be true that

---

[112] "Alszo solnn wyr die selben bild auch lassen her fallen und abfallen, wie sie wollen oder mugen, und nur gedencken, das wyr an dem willen gottis hangen, der ist, das wir in Christo hafften und festiglich gleuben, unszer tod, sund und hell sey unsz yn yhm ubirwunden und mug uns nit schaden."

[113] "Da geredt dyr gott selbs alle ding, die itzt von Christo gesagt seyn, und will die sacrament eyn wartzeichen und urkund seyn, Christus leben soll deynen tod, seyn gehorsam soll deyn sund, seyn liebe deyn helle auff sich genommen und ubirwunden haben. Darzu wirstu durch die selben sacrament eyngeleybet und voreyniget mit allen heyligenn und kumift yn die rechte gemeynschafft der heyligen, alszo das sie mit dyr in Christo sterben, sunde tragen, hell ubirwinden."

[114] "'Got hat myr zugesagt und eyn gewisz zeichen seyner gnaden yn den sacramenten geben, das Christus leben meynen tod yn seynem tod ubirwunden hab, seyn gehorsam meyne sund yn seynem leyden vortilget, seyn lieb meyn hell ynn seynem vorlassen zustort habe....'"

[115] "Was hulffs, das du dyr vorbildest und gleubest, der tod, die sund, die hell der andernn sey in Christo ubirwunden, Wan du nit auch glaubst, das deyn tod, deyn sund, deyn hell dyr da ubirwunden und vertilget sey, und alszo erloszet seyest?"

the divine sign does not deceive me (*WA* 2:694.22–27).[116] Article 18: There is no doubt, as the Sacrament of the Altar indicates, that all of these [the eyes of angels, saints, Christians] in a body run to him as one of their own, help him overcome [*ubirwinden*] death, sin, and hell, and bear all things with him (*WA* 2:695.20–23).[117] Article 20: Furthermore, he lays your sin, your death, and your hell on his dearest Son, vanquishes [*ubirwindt*] them, and renders them harmless for you (*WA* 2:697.17–19).[118]

IV. *Conclusion*

Already in 1519 we see clear evidence in "Sermon on Preparing to Die" of Luther's rhetorical artistry, homiletical power, and consolatory effectiveness. Martin Brecht calls 'graphic' Luther's descriptions of the images of 'death, sin, hell'; he aptly characterizes Luther's argument that, "One's gaze should be directed toward another concrete image, namely, toward Christ who has overcome death and is pure life, who on the cross has throttled and annihilated sin and has vanquished hell." Brecht has captured most of the themes that my rhetorical analysis has uncovered. He argues that the significance 'for the reformatory concept' of Luther's 1519 writings on comfort and death may now be underestimated. "At that time the crucial test for it was not least whether one could not only live with it, but also die with it."[119] My hope is that, with continued study of this and other consolatory writings of Luther, we may more clearly understand what it meant (and means) to *die well*.

---

[116] " 'Hat mir der priester geben den heyligen leychnam Christi, das eyn zeychen und zusagen ist der gemeynschafft aller Engel und heyligen, das sie mich lieb haben, fur mich sorgen, bitten und mit mir leyden, sterben, sund tragen und hell ubirwunden, Szo wirt es und musz alszo seyn, das gottlich zeychen treugt mich nit, und las mirs nit nhemen…' "

[117] "…da ist keyn zweyffell, wie das sacrament des altaris weyszet, das die allesampt alsz eyn gantz corper zu seynem glidmas zu lauffen, helffen yhm den tod, die sund, die hell ubirwinden und tragen alle mit yhm."

[118] "Er legt dartzu deynen tod, deyne sund, deyn hell auff seynen liebsten sun und ubirwindt sie dyr, macht sie dyr unschedlich."

[119] Martin Brecht, *Martin Luther*, 1:355.

CHAPTER THREE

"OF WHOM THE WORLD WAS NOT WORTHY": LUTHER'S MARTYROLOGICAL LITERATURE

A *martyr* is not one who merely expires, not even a 'good person' about whom words are inadequate to express our love, respect, and admiration (particularly so, now that the person is dead). The term is not assigned consensually to one whose aim in dying is to kill as many others as possible. Rather, a martyr is said to have died for the faith; a Christian martyr has died for 'the faith once for all delivered to the saints' (Jude 3). The first definition offered in today's English dictionaries seeks to capture the meaning of the Greek *martys/martyros* (= witness): "a person who voluntarily suffers death as the penalty of *witnessing to and refusing to renounce a religion*." While some scholars argue that the operational definition of martyr ought also to include 'refusing to accept aid or escape,' nevertheless it is clear that true martyrs are a minority, and they are generally esteemed by those in their faith community because they testify to something of immeasurable worth for which few can imagine themselves capable of standing firm.[1] But are martyrs like heroes, or does their cause deserve greater credit than their deed?

Discourse that promulgates cultural discussion about martyrs is yet another genre to which Luther put his pen: martyrology. As happened with the advance of European Christianity, opportunities for martyrdom had dwindled,[2] and yet the sixteenth century saw a

---

[1] William C. Weinrich, "Death and Martyrdom: An Important Aspect of Early Christian Eschatology," *CTQ* 66 (2002): 327–338, here at 327; Peter Burschel, *Sterben und Unsterblichkeit: Zur Kultur des Martyriums in der frühen Neuzeit*. Ancien Régime Aufklärung und Revolution 35 (Münich, 2004). J. Warren Smith, "Martyrdom: Self-Denial or Self-Exaltation? Motives for Self-Sacrifice from Homer to Polycarp, A Theological Reflection," *Modern Theology* 22 (2006): 169–196; Keith L. Sprunger, "Dutch Anabaptists and the Telling of the Martyr Stories," *MQR* 80 (2006): 149–182.

[2] According to Thomas A. Fudge, the early fifteenth century saw Germany serve "as a killing field for wandering Hussites: Hus, Jerome of Prague, Nicholas of Dresden, etc. Johannes Drändorf, a Hussite emissary, together with his companion Martin Borchard, were put to death at Heidelberg on 17 February 1425 with the approval of the Bishop of Worms and a number of the professors at the University of Heidelberg.... Peter Turnow was burnt at Speyer in 1426. In 1458 Matthäus Hagen was burned at Stettin for claiming that Hus and Jerome were saints"; "'The Shouting Hus': Heresy

'stunning renaissance' of men and women who died for their faith.[3] The situation had shifted from the prospect of dying for the faith being seldom more than a fantasy, 'except for the missionaries,' to the reality of approximately five thousand martyrs among Anabaptists, Protestants, and Catholics in the sixteenth century.[4] Brad Gregory argues that the late medieval context of attitudes toward patient suffering and death, informed by discourse such as the *Golden Legend* and the *ars moriendi*, provided the fertile soil of desire and readiness for death, to which the Reformation's emphasis on *sola scriptura* added opportunity and justification for persecution by fellow believers.[5] Luther himself, under imperial ban by the Edict of Worms, was rumored to have been murdered in the spring of 1521. From his seclusion at Wartburg castle he was profoundly conscious of being part of the persecuted church (cf. "A Letter of Consolation to All Who Suffer Persecution" [1522; *LW* 43:61–70]), and he said in a letter to Staupitz (June 1522) that 'the sophists' were planning to burn him, just as he believed that Jakob Propst (ca. 1495–1562) and two other Augustinians at Antwerp had already been burned.[6] While Luther had been misinformed about the fate of Propst and the others, a little over a year later—in midyear 1523—he expressed similar thoughts about the positive value of martyrdom in "To the Christians in the Netherlands" (August 1523), which we shall analyze later.

Appropriated as Propaganda in the Sixteenth Century," *Communio Viatorum* 38 (1996): 197–231, here at 200.

[3] Brad S. Gregory, "Late Medieval Religiosity and the Renaissance of Christian Martyrdom in the Reformation Era," in *Continuity and Change: The Harvest of Late Medieval and Reformation History. Essays Presented to Heiko A. Oberman on his 70th Birthday*, ed. Robert J. Bast and Andrew C. Gow (Leiden, 2000), 379–399, here at 379.

[4] Richard Kieckhefer, *Unquiet Souls: Fourteenth-Century Saints and Their Religious Milieu* (Chicago, 1984), 66, cited in Gregory, "Late Medieval Religiosity," 380. Gregory, ibid., 379 (note 1), supplies documentation for the frequently mentioned figure of 5000. William Monter, "Heresy Executions in Reformation Europe, 1520–1565, in *Tolerance and Intolerance in the European Reformation*, ed. Ole Peter Grell and Bob Scribner (Cambridge, 1996), 48–64 (here at 49), lists the figure of approximately 3,000 'legally sanctioned deaths across Latin Christendom.'

[5] Gregory, "Late Medieval Religiosity," passim.

[6] *LW* 48:13, Letter # 124, "To Johann Staupitz" (27 June 1522); *WABr* 2:567–568.

I. *A Letter of Consolation to All Who Suffer Persecution Because of God's Word, Addressed to Hartmuth von Cronberg (1522)*

A little more than a year before the first two martyrs were burned at Brussels (1 July 1523), Luther received two writings from a young Franconian nobleman, Hartmuth von Cronberg (1488–1549). Von Cronberg had participated in the Diet of Worms in 1521 (Luther's hearing was on 17–18 April) and soon became an ardent supporter of the reformation. After the Edict of Worms was signed (8 May 1521), von Cronberg renounced in protest an imperial stipend of 200 gulden, and he began writing on behalf of the reformation cause, thus becoming one of a number of laity who authored a significant (though minority) portion of the religious tracts in the early 1520s.[7] Luther's response to von Cronberg, *Eyn missive allen den, szo von wegen des wort gottes verfolgung leyden an Hartmutt von Cronberg geschrieben* (*WA* 10^II:53–60), was probably written from the Wartburg in early 1522. While Luther had not intended it for publication, von Cronberg published *Eyn missive*, together with some of his own writings (Wittenberg: Johann Rhau-Grunenberg, 1522). By the end of the year, the work was also printed in Straßburg (two editions) and in Augsburg.[8]

Explanations for the work's popularity can certainly be found in the general notion that anything from Luther during this period was bound to sell. However, we shall see that the subject matter and style of the document make it not only exciting reading but also useful to anyone who supported the reformation cause, for the letter speaks boldly and aggressively about the rightness of the cause. Luther fills his letter with scriptural evidence designed to explain to his new 'partner' in the cause how normal it is to expect persecution when proclaiming Christian truth.[9] While there were no actual martyrs for the Luther movement yet, the Edict of Worms made the prospect of such very real to Luther. Consequently, although we find scarcely any reference

---

[7] "Luther to Melanchthon," 12 May 1521 (no. 77), *LW* 48:215–217; *WABr* 2:232–233; *OER*, s.v. "Laity," by Lorna Jane Abray.

[8] *LW* 43:59–60; Benzing, Nr. 1168–1171.

[9] We note that while he has just joined the reformation effort, von Cronberg is only five years younger than Luther. Regardless of age, however, Luther had to have felt affection for this man, and the risks that von Cronberg would face made any prospect of losing him not an easy thought for Luther. On the notion of concern for a 'fellow worker and fellow soldier' whose illness made very real the prospect of his death, hence 'sorrow upon sorrow,' see Phil. 2:25–30 (Paul and Epaphroditus).

to *blood, murder,* or *martyrs* per se, Luther argues back and forth among three themes: (1) persecution (trials and testing) is a real fact that must be expected and prepared for; (2) we can be strong in Christ; and (3) we must pray for our enemies.

The letter's overt structure is not easy to discern, but the following should prove helpful for presenting the analysis: I. *Salutatio* (2 lines); II. *Benevolentiae captatio/narratio* (*WA* 10^{II}:53.7–55.29); III. *Petitio* (55.29–60.10); IV. *Conclusio* (60.1–9); V. Pauline postscript (60.10–20); VI. Benediction and Signature (3 lines). In such an order Luther's greeting and closing are ritualistic and parallel, and the *benevolentiae captatio* and postscript have similar functions. The bulk of the letter's body, then, gradually invites the reader to hear favorably a message about the prospect and meaning of persecution—to consider such a situation with resolve and hope. In this document one cannot miss the sense of joy Luther feels in learning of how God is working faithfully in others who have caught the spirit of reformation faith.

I. *Salutatio*: Luther's eloquent greeting is noteworthy, not simply in itself but also for what will follow it. In itself, (1) unlike all other (later) documents we have examined thus far, here he still uses the 'Jhesus' heading, which he had used consistently up until 1522 but not thereafter;[10] (2) instead of the Pauline 'grace and peace' that Luther comes to use so often, here he wishes his reader the "favor and peace of God the Father and of our Lord Jesus Christ" (*LW* 43:61). 'Favor [*Gunst*]' is especially appropriate in light of von Cronberg's recent rejection of an annual monetary stipend (200 guldens) and is repeated in the following line as well as in the Benediction.[11]

II. *Benevolentiae captatio/narratio*: Since the *salutatio* was expressed as a wish (optative) rather than a granting (imperative), it has absorbed the next function—expressing one's good intentions toward the reader. In this case Luther combines this function with that of *narratio*, revealing the circumstances that prompt him to write. Luther's 'great joy' at receiving von Cronberg's writings prompts him to write back a letter of encouragement.[12] What has prompted this feeling in Luther is his conclusion

---

[10] Timothy J. Wengert, "Martin Luther's Movement toward an Apostolic Self-Awareness As Reflected in His Early Letters," *LuJ* 61 (1994): 71–92, here at 75.

[11] One also notices the repetitive, hard 'g' sound in which this greeting is expressed: 'wish [*gewunscht*],' followed by 'kind sir [*Günstiger*]' and, two words later, 'favor [*Gunst*],' which comes (in the preceding line) from God [*von Gott*] (*WA* 10^{II}:53.5–7).

[12] *WA* 10^{II}:53.9, 24. Twice in the initial sentences of the first two paragraphs of this section Luther uses this word *joy* as justification for writing and for explaining

that von Cronberg has been gifted by the word of God with the truth of the Gospel. This strategy is similar to Paul's in several epistles: first thanking God for what he finds praiseworthy in his readers.[13]

In the next paragraph Luther reveals how his thankfulness for von Cronberg's spiritual gift relates to persecution. The language is personal, in the 'I/you' style, but it does not preclude a wider audience. Twice in this paragraph Luther says he finds 'comfort' when he realizes that his reader recognizes the truth and openly confesses it. His argument now extends his explanation of how persecution fits into God's plan. His reasoning is clear: God's word is truth, which makes one thirsty to proclaim truth, in order to save others (what Paul desired and what Christ taught). With this thirst comes also persecution: one is linked to Christ through faith and persecution; those without faith—who persecute the faithful—are not linked to Christ but to the villains who crucified him.

In the next paragraph of the *narratio* Luther contrasts the persecutors' state with that of believers (note the double use of the contrastive conjunction, *tzonder*).[14] Arguing that death puts an end to sin, by reason

---

why he feels this way, when the circumstances prompting joy do not seem *to us* to be 'happy.'

[13] E.g., Rom. 1:8; 1 Cor. 1:4; Eph. 1:16; Phil. 1:3, 5; Col. 1:3; 1 Thess. 1:2; 2 Thess. 1:3; 2 Tim. 1:3; Philem. 1:4. Again, following Luther's greeting in the *Salutatio*, the 'g' sound of alliteration reverberates in the next three lines: "Two of your letters, the one...the other given [*gethan*]...came to my attention and were read [*geleszen*] by me with great joy [*mit grosser Freud*]. I thank my God [*Gott*] for the favor [*Gunst*] and gift [*Gabe*] of the knowledge of Christian truth bestowed [*geben*] on you and in addition for your delight and active love in it" (*LW* 43:61) ["Ich hab ewer schrifften zwo, eyne an Keyszerliche Maiestat, die ander an die bettel ordenn gethan, mit grosszer freud erfarenn unnd geleszen und danck meynem gott fur die gunst und gabe, szo euch geben ist an der erkentnisz der Christlichen warheyt, dar tzu auch die lust unnd thetige liebe tzu der selbigen"] (*WA* 10^II:53.7–11).

[14] Luther s own argumentation here contains interesting rhetorical style: [A] ironic, almost comic, ridicule, via *chiasmus* [a.b:b^1.a]—"They threaten us with death. If they were as smart as they are stupid, they would threaten us with life" [*Sie drauwenn* (a) *uns mit dem Todt* (b). *Wenn sie szo klug weren, als thoricht sie sind, sollten sie uns mit dem Leben* (b^1) *drawen* (a)] (*WA* 10^II:55.3–4); [B] simile, with consonance between subject and verb—"It [threatening Christians with death] is just like [*Gleych als wenn*] trying to frighten a man by bridling and saddling his horse [*Rosz*] and bidding him to ride [*reytten*] on it" (*WA* 10^II:55.6–8); [C] epithet; whereas earlier Luther quoted Scripture calling men 'gods [*Gotter*],' here he uses a different word to designate Christians as he does Christ—"they are lords and victors [*Hern unnd Sieg*] over death.... Christ rose from the dead and is a Lord [*Herr*] over life and death" (*WA* 10^II:55.6–10); [D] doublet, coupled with maxim—"But we are confident and happy [*trotzen und sind freydig*] because we know that Christ rose and that death is no more than the end of sin and the end of itself" [todt nichts mehr sey denn syn ende der sunde und seyn selbs] (WA^II:55.10–12).

of the flesh, Luther resorts to apostrophe—direct address—much like John Donne's "Death Be Not Proud," in that his cry ("Come, death and Judgment Day, and put an end both to sin and death. Amen") not only models a defiance of death but also invokes, through interpretatio, Paul's words, '*Wie sanctus Paulus Roma. 7. und 8. Schreybt.*'

III. *Petitio*: Luther begins his exhortation to von Cronberg in the first person singular language that Paul often uses in his epistles).[15] As he urges that his reader pray for Duke George, Luther tries to alert von Cronberg to scriptural teaching on formidable enemies of the Gospel, who, although they are destined for wrath—unless they repent—also have great power and potential for good. To clarify and test—and thus strengthen—the exhortation to be kind and loving toward enemies (especially Duke George), Luther shifts to discussing how he has handled some of his enemies. In the next twelve lines he ventures deeper into personal speculation, thinking aloud to his reader—who deals with similar issues—about the possibility that resistance, harassment, and persecution are a deserved punishment. For the remainder of the *petitio* (and the document), Luther frequently returns to the issue of the Diet at Worms—in which von Cronberg participated and because of which both his and Luther's lives, and that of the German nation, were forever changed. The dilemma for Luther, in hindsight, is whether he acted properly at Worms; the issue for his chief patrons (particularly the Saxon Elector, Frederick the Wise) is whether they themselves have yet demonstrated sufficient courage and faith. The first person singular pronouns are telling: two refer to his chief patrons (*meynen gonnern*); ten refer to his own conduct (*WA* 10^{II}:56.13–24).[16]

Luther's exhortation of gratitude and prayer for a strong Christian faith and a stable German society then returns to expressions of fear for what may happen to the nation. In 15 lines Luther mentions the *nation* three times explicitly, even more through relative pronouns; he

---

[15] 'I ask you [*Ich bitt, yhr*]'; 'I would exhort you [*Ich wollt euch woll ermanen*]'; "I know of nothing else to do in his behalf than to pray for him [*ich nichts denn das gebett weysz fur yhn tzuthun*]" (*WA* 10^{II}:55.29–37). In Paul (according to *SeptBib*): "I ask [*bitte*] you' (Eph. 3:13; Phil. 4:3); 'I beg [*bitte*] you' (2 Cor. 2:8); 'I beseech [*bitte*] you' (Gal. 4:12); 'I urge [*ermahne*] you' (1 Cor. 4:16; 16:16); 'I appeal to [*ermahne*] you' (Rom. 12:1; 15:30; 16:17; 1 Cor. 1:10; Philem. 1:10).

[16] We should also call attention to the Luther's four references to the Word (in 8 lines): 'God's word [*Gottes Wortt*]'; 'divine truth [*gotlich Warheytt*]'; 'precious word [*thewr Wort*]'; 'God's word [*Gottes Wort*]' (WA^{II}:57.20–27).

names *Worms* twice; he uses forms of the explicit terms *blood* (four times) and *murder* (twice). He puts these graphic terms in an argument from historical examples that purportedly add up to an indictment of Germany for a fate similar to that of the people of Judah in 2 Chron. 36—the fall of Jerusalem in 586 B.C.: (a) Germany's crimes occurred all over the land in the preceding century;[17] (b) "The nation is tempting God too often";[18] and (c) "In their hearts they are continually murdering me. You unhappy nation! Why must you more than others be the Antichrist's jailer and his hangman of God's saints and prophets?" (*WA* 10^{II}:59.33–35).[19]

IV. *Conclusio*: Luther's remarks neatly summarize the exigence prompting this letter, both what caused him to write and what he hopes to accomplish in writing. His words begin as apology for wordiness and conclude with a blessing. In between, he takes a scriptural story from the Nativity narrative (Luke 1:39–41) to characterize his feelings toward von Cronberg, feelings he hopes are mutual. While the language of these ten lines is in the intimate first and second person singular (three pronouns each), the feelings expressed are not merely at the 'personal' level but rather center in the actions each has taken. That is, Luther's joy—and, he hopes, von Cronberg's also—is rooted in the letters he received; each man's spirits can soar because of the reformation in which they are participating. Luther's remarks are, of course, intended to strengthen and comfort von Cronberg, and they

---

[17] (1) Shedding the 'innocent blood [*unschuldig Blutt*]' of [Jan] Hus and Jerome [of Prague at the Council of Constance] (1415); (2) at Worms and in Heidelberg [Johannes] Dramsdorf [von Schlieben] and others [were burned at stake in 1425]; (3) Mainz and Cologne, both of which are sites of an archbishopric, are also named, without detail; (4) the entire Rhine 'is bloody'; (5) finally, Worms again [at the Diet in 1521] is the scene of the nation's condemnation; through two highly metaphorical statements that surround one concise, sobering declaration, Luther's denunciation of all these is strikingly blunt: "The entire Rhine [*Reynstrom*] is bloody and will not be cleansed [*reynigen*] of the blood, but unceasingly fetes the murderers of Christians, the inquisitors, until God intervenes, and then the time of help will be past" [der gantz Reynstrom ist bluttig und will noch nicht sich reynigen lassen von dem blutt vergissen, szonder feyret die Christ mörder, die ketzer meyster an aufhören, bisz das gott hereyn platz unnd auch keyn hülff mehr da sey] (*WA* 10^{II}:59.28–31).

[18] "Sie versucht gott tzu offt" (*WA* 10^{II}:59.31).

[19] "und mördern mich noch on underlasz ynn yhrem hertzen. Du unselige Nation, mustu denn vor allen andern des Endchrists stockmeyster und hencker seyn uber gottes heyligen und Propheten?"

attempt to do that in several ways.[20] Franz von Sickingen (1481–1523)[21] had been introduced to Luther and the theological debates by Ulrich von Hutten (1488–1523), a humanist poet and antipapalist.[22] Luther asks that both men be greeted in the faith.

VI. Benediction and Signature: Luther's closing remark ("May God's favor [*gunst*] rest upon you. Amen") neatly matches the *salutatio*. His signature is a simple "Martinus Luther."

II. *To the Christians in the Netherlands (1523)*

Early in 1523 Luther had already expressed indignation against the imprisonment of a young master, Arsacius Seehofer (1505–1545), by the University of Ingolstadt, and he had strongly objected to the canonization (on 31 May in Rome) of Benno, Bishop of Meisen (1066–1106). Luther claimed that the "popes kill the true saints and elevate the counterfeit ones; they condemn God's Word and set up their own human teachings."[23] In the early 1520s the Low Countries were under strict control of Margaret, regent of Emperor Charles V. In October 1522 she had all of the monks of the Observant Augustinian monastery in Antwerp arrested on suspicion of Evangelical sentiments. On 1 July 1523 Hendrik Vos and Johann van den Esschen were burned at stake on the Grote Markt in Brussels—the Reformation's first martyrs—who were from the Augustinian monastery in Antwerp, all of whom adopted

---

[20] (1) The disclosure about Wittenberg reveals insight into Luther's own struggles with resistance and persecution, to which the reader can relate; (2) information about Luther's other literary projects—Bible translation, the book on confession (dedicated to von Sickingen), the books of postils on the Gospels and Epistles—are all discussed so that von Cronberg can know what works of Luther are available, so he can purchase them. Luther adds that the postils, when finished, will contain (he hopes) "all that is necessary for a Christian to know" (*WA* 10^{II}:60.20); (3) brief remarks about Francis von Sickingen and Ulrich von Hutten, and other 'friends in the faith,' consistent with Pauline epistolary practices, strive to solidify the reader's faith and confidence by reminding him of the community of Christians, especially those older in the faith and of similar situation—including great personal and professional risk, and persecution: e.g., Rom. 16:1–23; Phil. 4:21f.; Col. 4:9–17; 2 Tim. 4:19–21; Philem. 1:23f. In Phil. (2:19–30) Paul conveys news about Timothy and Epaphroditus in the middle of the letter also.

[21] Franz von Sickingen, an imperial knight, saw himself as 'the Protector of the Reformation' and was the first secular follower to declare his support for Luther, having—a couple years earlier—offered him protection at his home, the Ebernburg castle. *OER*, s.v. "Sickingen, Franz von," by Ulman Weiß.

[22] Ibid., s.v. "Hutten, Ulrich von," by Eckhard Bernstein.

[23] Martin Brecht, *Martin Luther*, 2:88–89.

Lutheranism, only later to recant. The exceptions were Vos and van den Esschen.[24]

The first responding publication, *Der actus vnd handlung der degradation vnd verprenung der Christlichen Ritter vnd merterer Augustiner ordens geschen zu Brussel . . .*, saw sixteen editions by year's end, produced by at least eight separate printers working in seven different German cities.[25] Luther joined others in the mass media uproar.[26] "Instead of pitying these men for the sacrifice which they had been forced to offer, he considered their faithfulness a victory and their martyrdom an honor" (*LW* 53:211). Upon learning of the burning, he is reported by an eyewitness to have lamented the fact that he had thought that he would be the first to be martyred but was not worthy of it.[27]

Ein Brief an die Christen im Niederland (1523) was published in six different German cities, in eleven editions in its first year.[28] Luther intended this letter to be read by *groups* of reformation believers, however and

---

[24] Luther an Spalatin in Kolditz, 22. oder 23. Juli 1523 (*WABr* 3:114–116 [Nr. 635]). In December 1521 Jakob Probst (James Propst), the prior of Antwerp's Observant Augustinians, was imprisoned on suspicion of heresy. When pressured, he publicly recanted and was released; *Corpus documentorum inquisitionis haereticae pravitatis neerlandicae*, ed. Paul Dredericq (Ghent, 1889–1902), 4:80–81, 88–96, cited by Brad S. Gregory, *Salvation at Stake Christian Martyrdom in Early Modern Europe* (Cambridge, Mass., 1999), 79. Martin Brecht, *Martin Luther*, 2:102, has the date that Propst allegedly recanted as February 1522. Propst was then transferred to Ieper and there preached in an evangelical way so that he was again imprisoned in the summer of 1522. He escaped, coming to Wittenberg, and in 1523 he became the leader of the Reformation in Bremen.

[25] Gregory, *Salvation at Stake*, 3. The document is found in *Bibliotheca Reformatoria Neerlandica. Geschriften uit den tijd der hervorming in de Nederlanden*, ed. S. Cramer and F. Pijper (The Hague, 1903–14), 8:13–19.

[26] Tappert, 192–194; *OER*, s.v. "Books of Martyrs," by Jean-François Gilmont, speaks of four pamphlets, disseminated in over twenty editions, that proclaimed the perception that the two men were martyrs, not heretics. Bernd Moeller, "Inquisition und Martyrium in Flugschriften der frühen Reformation in Deutschland," in *Ketzerverfolgung im 16. Und frühen 17. Jahrhundert*, ed. Silvana Seidel Menchi. Wolfenbütteler Forschung 51 (Wiesbaden, 1992), 45–71 (here at 46), catalogs five documents (two of which are Luther's and were published together) and more than 25 editions.

[27] *WABr* 3:238.18 (note 3): "Joh. Keßler in seinen Sabbata (Neuausgabe 1902, S. 131, 27ff.): 'Wie ich zu der Zeit in Wittenberg war in Sachsen [am 9. November 1523 langte er wieder in St. Gallen an], sagt man mir, daß Martinus Luther, als er die Histori von diesen zweien obgemendten Märtyrern gschriftlich vernommen, hat er angefangen innerlich zu weinen und gesagt: Ich vermeint, ich sollte ja der erste sein, der umb dies heilig Euangelion wegen sollte gemarteret werden; aber ich bin des nit wirdig gewesen.'" Also cited by Brecht, *Martin Luther*, 2:103.

[28] *WA* 12:77–79, Benzing, Nr. 1658–1668. Hildegard Hebenstreit-Wilfert, "Märtyrerflugschriften der Reformationszeit," in *Flugschriften als Massenmedium der Reformationszeit: Beiträge zum Tübinger Symposion 1980*, ed. Hans-Joachim Köhler (Stuttgart, 1981), 397–446.

wherever they could get their hands on the document or hear it read ("To all my dear brethren in Christ living in Holland, Brabant, and Flanders, together with all believers in Christ"). When read by individuals, its effectiveness will be diminished, for the appeal is to support and strengthen one another. The letter brings comfort and encouragement for those affected by the martyred deaths of 'Henry and John.'

Because Luther wrote this letter[29] soon after Louvain theologians executed the two Augustinian brothers for heresy, we may consider that he had perhaps two goals in mind: (1) to prevent his readers from becoming discouraged due to their drawing false conclusions—e.g., that the punishment was deserved, a just retribution for sinning against God and his church, since even Jesus' disciples surmised that suffering may be a sign of God's disfavor upon someone's sin, either 'this man or his parents' (John 9:2); (2) to embolden sympathetic readers who may fear repercussions. In this short correspondence Luther's objective is not to produce a detailed account of what happened, nor does he graphically describe the means of execution. The word 'burned [*verprandt*]' is not found in the letter but in the appendix (*Die Artickel*) that follows; the word 'blood' occurs but twice, and 'martyrs' only once.[30] There is no list of charges, for *Die Artickel* are appended to the letter, listing three concise questions put to the defendants, along with their equally concise responses.[31] The tale of what happened is reserved for his very first hymn, "A New Song Here Shall Be Begun" (August 1523) [*Eyn newes lyed wyr heben an*], which we shall examine next in turn.

In typical humanist fashion Luther attaches his name at the head of the *salutatio*, followed by the initials 'E.W. [Ecclesiastes Witebergensis].' The epithet, which he uses in several martyrological writings, foregrounds his position as preacher (spokesman) in Wittenberg, where the reform movement had begun, not only within the University but especially within Luther's own Order, the Observantist Order of the Hermits of St. Augustine. Moreover, Luther's signature downplays his

---

[29] *Brief*; two editions (Benzing Nr. 1663, 1665) have *Sendbrief*.

[30] Tappert, 193; *WA* 12:78.7, 13, 18.

[31] *WA* 12:79f. The questions and responses occur in third person, for this document is not a transcript of the legal proceedings but rather a report by a biased party, Luther, followed by a twenty-five line 'judgment [*Urteyl*].' Apparently there were sixty-two articles that they refused to recant. For discussion of the several pamphlets defending the boys' sixty-two articles and for the documents pertaining to the suppression of the monastery in Antwerp, see Gregory, "Late Medieval Religiosity," 380f.

own particular function as avowed monk in that Order, for it is his fellowship with his readers (both lay and religious) that he promotes.[32] If we consider the two parts of the letter's 'body' as *narratio* and *petitio*, they are roughly equal in length and do not provide concrete information about the event itself, but rather characterize the event and its significance as something God will use to bring joy. The *narratio* portrays what happened to Henry and John (the names are only mentioned once in the letter)—the 'shame and injury, anxiety and distress, imprisonment and death'—as 'joy and pleasure' producing 'strong and productive' Christians of their friends (Tappert, 193; *WA* 12:78.2–5).

To persuade his readers that everything that happened is consistent with God's design and will result in his glory, Luther weaves a kind of legal case in the *narratio*. Efficiently, he compiles six categories of witness that seem to testify for his case: (1) Henry and John themselves are 'two precious jewels of Christ'; (2) their condemnation was 'unjustly conducted' but will eventuate in their returning with Christ to 'judge justly' those who killed them; (3) Scripture itself calls their blood 'precious' and their death 'dear' in God's sight (cf. Ps. 9:13; 116:15); (4) the angels look upon these souls with 'gladness and joy'; (5) the Germans—and surely this means, first of all, Luther himself—would like to count themselves "deserving to become so precious and worthy an offering to Christ"; and (6) the great 'signs and wonders' God has begun to do. Not only does he bring witnesses, but Luther also lets them help argue his case: He interprets the motives of the victims ('held their lives of no account'), making their martyrdom available for others to appreciate and emulate; he suggests the intentions of the persecutors, for readers to hate and take as a sign of evil, not righteous, zeal; he downplays the significance of bodily death, bolstering his argument with Scripture as proof of God's acceptance of these men's commitment; he claims that what the Germans see in Henry and John are 'real saints and true martyrs [*rechte Heyligen und warhafftige Merterer*],' a welcome contrast to the many 'false saints' they have known and worshiped for too long (Tappert, 193; *WA* 12:78.6–23).

We find most of Luther's scriptural evidence in the *petitio*, in a compact series of quotations, all meant to encourage readers to know

---

[32] Luther wore his Augustinian cowl until October 1524; Brecht, *Martin Luther*, 2:95; Eric L. Saak, *High Way to Heaven: The Augustinian Platform between Reform and Reformation, 1292–1524*. SMRT 89 (Leiden, 2002), 3–4; *LW* 54:337–339; *WATr* 4 (Nr. 4414).

God understands their plight and will make things right. Luther also provides a small prolepsis, acknowledging that charges of 'Hussites, Wycliffites, and Lutherans' will abound but that Christ's cross will always be slandered, yet He will pass a just judgment.[33] Coming near the end of the letter, this assurance of Luther that 'This we know for certain' summarizes his case that Henry and John are legitimate martyrs and that readers should take heart from this, making ready to join them, if necessary.[34]

Finally, we must acknowledge several stylistic tactics Luther uses. One I call endearment, a combination of inclusive, first person plural, pronouns (where they matter most—in the early and late parts of the letter) and direct address ('dear brethren,' etc.). Luther uses direct address not only in both *salutatio* and *conclusio* but twice also in the body. When he says, 'let us thank him' (*WA* 12:78.23) or "Pray for us and for one another, dear brethren, that we may uphold one another with faithful hands and all of us may cling in unity of spirit to our Head, Jesus Christ" (*WA* 12:79.8–10),[35] Luther is intensifying the solidarity with—not isolation from—other followers of the reformation faith that he wants his readers to feel; he does not treat Henry and John as pitiful victims.

A second tactic is juxtaposition, where he aligns opposing terms within the same section, or even sentence. Notice how the following two lists I have selectively compiled from the *narratio* (21 lines in *WA* 12:78) highlight the paradoxical nature of the execution's event, attempting to transform apparent defeat into real victory: (1) *shame* (2 times), *slain, injury, anxiety, distress, imprisonment, condemned* (2 times), *death, false saints, persecution, ignominy, fire, blood;* (2) *joy* (4 times), *pleasure, privilege, strong, productive, watered, strengthened, deserving, precious, worthy, dear, gloriously, everlasting glory, eternal life.*

---

[33] Two years later Luther would argue that Hus 'should be canonized'; Robert Kolb, "'Saint John Hus' and 'Jerome Savonarola, Confessor of God': The Lutheran 'Canonization' of Late Medieval Martyrs," *Concordia Journal* 17 (1991): 404–418, here at 404.

[34] Marius, *Martin Luther*, quotes assorted remarks of Luther, calling attention to the "tone of jubilation in the letter." He uses this observation as evidence that Luther had now 'backed away' from a previous position, "that no one could know the state of another's soul, that even if the apostle Peter were among us, we could not know if he were among the redeemed" (394).

[35] "Bittet fur uns, lieben bruder, und unternander, auff das wyr die trewe hand eyner dem andern reichen, und alle ynn eynem geyst an unserm heubt Jhesu Christo hallten."

In a third tactic, metaphor, that occurs in the section between *salu-tatio* and *narratio*—a kind of Pauline *benevolentiae captatio* that praises the Father, not the reader—Luther evokes images of flora and fauna from Song of Solomon 2:12. The 'voice of the turtledove [*Dordel tauben Stym*]'[36] and 'flowers [*Blumen*]' appearing signal, for him, a promised awakening of the earth to God's 'wonderful light' that had been long hidden; he will employ the springtime motif again in stanza ten of "A New Song" (*WA* 12:77.7–11). These images of darkness/light and of signs of springtime (or even a new, post-deluvian world) are extended in the opening lines of the *narratio* when Luther suggests that the newly released Gospel has allowed the Netherlanders to become strong and productive: They have "watered and strengthened the cause with your very blood"; Henry and John are two 'precious jewels of Christ.'

Luther implies that the God who made light and seasons and crea-tures and causes finds the blood of the two martyrs as pleasing, rather than crying out for justice from the ground, as with Abel (Gen. 4:10). These metaphors, while strictly speaking 'mixed,' nevertheless are quite consistent with Luther's personal background and with the flowing context of the *narratio* and its six 'witnesses.'[37] Accordingly, the need to spread the news of what God was now doing provoked Luther to turn next to the medium of song.

III. *A New Song Here Shall Be Begun (1523)*

Not only did the execution of Henry and John at Brussels on 1 July 1523 inaugurate the first of the Reformation's martyrs in the sixteenth century, but the event also proved to be the launching of Martin Luther's career as hymn writer. Not as musically proficient as Huldrych Zwingli (1484–1531), Luther nevertheless was both gifted and thoroughly trained in music: from his earliest days at the Mansfeld Latin school, where he learned Latin and singing, to the Quadrivium at the St. George's school at Eisenach, to the University at Erfurt, he was well grounded in music theory and singing. He played proficiently both flute and lute; testimonies abound to his melodic tenor voice, tracing back to choir at Eisenach and forward to his legendary table talk sessions at the

---

[36] Tappert, 192, translates *dordel tauben* as 'turtle.'
[37] His father was a miner, and Luther himself had just spent nearly a year at Wart-burg castle, listening to the birds of the Thüringian hills above Eisenach.

Black Cloister, which Elector Frederic the Wise gave the Luthers to be their home.[38] Moreover, he was clearly the only one of the magisterial reformers who did not completely remove music (as did Zwingli) or severely limit it from the worship service (as did Calvin).[39] Indeed, 'the Wittenberg nightingale'—as Luther is called in a 1523 poem by Hans Sachs (1494–1576), the famous Meistersinger of Nürnberg—promulgated a flowering of music in the life of the church, which was to see its culmination in the career of J. S. Bach at Leipzig in the eighteenth century.[40] Luther believed music was a divine gift, second only to theology, and he insisted that singing—the most important of the fine arts—be given back to the congregation.[41] This first of his thirty-six hymns,[42] the vast majority of which were composed within two years, is

---

[38] Carl F. Schalk, *Luther on Music: Paradigms of Praise* (St. Louis, 1988), 11–15; Dennis Marzolf, "Luther and Music Education," *Lutheran Synod Quarterly* 46 (2006): 68–105.

[39] Markus Jenny, "The Hymns of Zwingli and Luther: A Comparison," in *Cantors at the Crossroads: Essays on Church Music in Honor of Walter E. Buszin*, ed. Johannes Riedel (St. Louis, 1967), 45–63 (here at 45), says Calvin wrote no hymns, and Zwingli has only three preserved hymns.

[40] *Die Wittenbergisch Nachtigall, die man jetzt höret überall* has 700 lines.

[41] Robin A. Leaver, "The Lutheran Reformation," *The Renaissance: From the 1470s to the End of the Sixteenth Century*, ed. I. Fenelon (Englewood Cliffs, N.J., 1989), 263–285 (here at 265). In his famous letter of 4 October 4 1530, to the well known Catholic composer, Louis Senfl (ca. 1486–1543), chief conductor and court composer to Duke William of Bavaria, Luther wrote: "Indeed I plainly judge, and do not hesitate to affirm, that except for theology there is no art that could be put on the same level with music, since except for theology [music] alone produces what otherwise only theology can do, namely, a calm and joyful disposition. Manifest proof [of this is the fact] that the devil, the creator of saddening cares and disquieting worries, takes flight at the sound of music almost as he takes flight at the word of theology. This is the reason why the prophets did not make use of any art except music; when setting forth their theology they did it not as geometry, not as arithmetic, not as astronomy, but as music, so that they held theology and music most tightly connected, and proclaimed truth through Psalms and songs" (*LW* 49:428); "Et plane iudico, nec pudet asserere, post theologiam esse nullam artem, quae musicae possit aequari, cum ipsa sola post theologiam id praestet, quod alioqui sola theologia praestat, scilicet quietem et animum laetum, manifesto argumento, quod diabolus, curarum tristium et turbarum inquietarum autor, ad vocem musicae paene similiter fugiat, sicut fugit ad verbum theologiae. Hinc factum est, ut prophetae nulla sic arte sint usi ut musica, dum suam theologiam non in geometriam, non in arithmeticam, non in astronomiam, sed in musicam digesserunt, ut theologiam et musicam haberent coniunctissimas, veritatem psalmis et canticis dicentes" [*WABr* 5: 639.12–21]. Luther also admired the music of Josquin des Prés and Pierre de la Rue; Robert M. Stevenson, *Patterns of Protestant Church Music* (Durham, N.C., 1953), 5.

[42] Among scholars, the number varies between 36–37; Herbert R. Pankratz, "Luther's Utilization of Music in School and Town in the Early Reformation," *Andrews University Seminary Studies* 22 (1984): 99–112, here at 100. Kyle C. Sessions, "Luther In Music and Verse," in *Pietas et Societas: New Trends in Reformation Social History. Essays in Memory of Harold J. Grimm*, ed. Kyle C. Sessions and Phillip N. Bebb. SCES 4 (Kirksville, Mo.,

one of the handful for which Luther composed both lyrics and melody, and it is virtually the only one not intended for the worship service.[43]

While *Ein Brief an die Christen im Niederland* was intended to support and embolden evangelical believers through 'witnesses' and arguments, *Eyn newes lyed wyr heben an* provides evidence to Germans of what took place there ('in Brussels in the Netherlands,' first stanza, 5th line) by spreading the news through mass media—the broadsheet and popular song,[44] both of which were popular, despite the fact that in many regions they were subversive and illegal.[45]

1985), 123–139, maintains the number of Luther's hymns at 37, as does Helen Pietsch, "Luther's Attitude to Music in Worship and Implications for Today," in *Perspectives on Martin Luther*, ed. M. W. Worthing (North Adelaide, So. Australia, 1996), 141–154 (here at 143), who cites recent work of Markus Jenny, considered to be a definitive source on Luther's music. Jenny's "The Hymns of Zwingli and Luther" (45) has the number of Luther's hymns still at 36, as does Gerhard Hahn, ed., *Martin Luther: Die geistlichen Lieder* (Tübingen, 1967).

[43] Luther completed twenty-three hymns within the space of twelve months; Johannes Riedel, *The Lutheran Chorale: Its Basic Traditions* (Minneapolis, 1967), 37. Luther D. Reed, *Luther and Congregational Song*. Papers of the Hymn Society 12 (New York, 1947), 9, lists five entirely original songs. "When a melody or a whole composition is reused, altered, or unaltered, the result is a parody or a contrafactum, depending largely on when it was borrowed. If the borrower is a poet or musician who lived before about 1500, what is produced is likely called a contrafactum; if an eighteenth-century musician is borrower, it is usually called a parody"; cf. Robert Falck, "Parody and Contrafactum: A Terminological Clarification," *The Musical Quarterly* 65 (1979): 1–2. Most studies of Luther's hymns and hymnology pass over *Ein neues Lied* and concentrate on the choral hymns. A few studies provide comment, however: Rolf Wilhelm Brednich, *Die Liedpublizistik im Flugblatt des 15. Bis 17. Jahrhunderts, bd. 1, Abhandlung* (Baden-Baden, 1974), 79–87; Gerhard Hahn, *Evangelium als literarische Anweisung: Zu Luthers Stellung in der Geschichte des deutschen kirchlichen Liedes* (Munich, 1981), 98–109; Markus Jenny, *Luther—Zwingli—Calvin in ihren Liedern*, (Zürich, 1983), 15–29 ["Luthers Lied"], 97–101 [Ein neues Lied]; Christine Helmer, *The Trinity and Martin Luther: A Study on the Relationship between Genre, Language and the Trinity in Luther's Works (1523–1546)*. Veröffentlichungen des Instituts für Europäische Geschichte Mainz, Abteilung abendländische Religionsgeschichte 174 (Mainz, 1999), 123–131; Christian Möller, "'Ein neues Lied wir heben an': Überlegungen zum 'neuen' geistlichen Lied," in *Der heilsame Riss: Impulse reformatorischer Spiritualität*, ed. Christian Möller (Stuttgart, 2003), 257–273; Gracia Grindal, "The Rhetoric of Martin Luther's Hymns: Hymnody Then and Now," *WW* 26 (2006): 178–187.

[44] *Lied*, the union of lyric poetry with music; Hugo Riemann, *Dictionary of Music*, 2 vols., trans. J. S. Shedlock (New York, 1970), s.v. "Lied." Leaver, "The Lutheran Reformation," 268, says these freely composed hymns took as their model the *Hofweise*, the art song of the day.

[45] Sessions, "Luther In Music and Verse," 125, claims that the "practice of broadsheet dissemination was initiated with 'A New Song' and was continued with three more early compositions...." Hebenstreit-Wilfert, "Märtyrer Flugschriften der Reformationszeit," 404–406, provides a brief summary of the song. Robinson-Hammerstein argues that this form of narrative song (*Zeitungslied*) was a solo song to be sung as 'news' to an audience, "in the manner of the *Bänkelsänger*, who normally operated out-of-doors in

Eyn newes lyed can rightly be called a propaganda song, for it is a folk ballad of twelve, nine-lined stanzas (566 words) that tell the heroic tale of the trial and execution of Vos and Van den Esschen. *Eyn newes lyed* is not the song's title but rather, like many songs, the opening phrase of its first stanza, which follows a characteristic folk song phrase of the day, "What shall we now take up and sing? [*Was wollen wir singen und heben an?*]." The language and monophonic melody are simple and easily learned, despite the fact that the melody was probably new to listeners.[46] In keeping with the composition, I shall analyze the verbal message and the vocal features in close coordination.

The song is essentially simple poetry set to music, following the traditional bar form (*Barform*: AAB: the first four lines are two *Stollen* [A], the final five lines the *Abgesang* [B], making the specific pattern a serial bar form).[47] The poetic pattern of the stanzas is as follows: (1) 43–52 words per stanza, the majority (64%) of which are monosyllables; (2) each stanza averages 66–68 syllables; (3) the pattern of meter is 8.7.8.7.8.7.8.7.6; and (4) the end rhyme pattern is a.b.a.b.c.d.c.e.f.[48] A stirring and robust hymn of faith, the melodic line maintains familiar territory, written in Ionian mode, "with all but one note remaining within the span of an octave, and all cadences but one ending on C or F."[49] With the melody

---

the controlled social environment of the marketplace.... It can even be shown that an audience, after absorbing the news, was encouraged by the tied form of rhyme and familiar tune to internalise and repeat what had been communicated and thus to become informed communicators themselves as singing individuals or as a singing group"; Helga Robinson-Hammerstein, "The Lutheran Reformation and its Music," in *The Transmission of Ideas in the Lutheran Reformation*, ed. Helga Robinson-Hammerstein (Dublin, 1989), 141–171 (here at 155).

[46] At least, scholars have not yet identified any precursors and give Luther credit for composing new music.

[47] Riedel, *The Lutheran Chorale*, 45.

[48] Ernst Sommer, "Die Metrik in Luthers Liedern," in *Jahrbuch für Liturgik und Hymnologie*, bd. 9, ed. Konrad Ameln, Christhard Mahrenholz, and Karl Ferdinand Müller (Kassel, 1965), 29–81, here at 56.

[49] Rebecca W. Oettinger describes the tempo, or note value, as follows: "In the opening phrase, a very simple rhythmic pattern of minim [eighth note] followed by seven semibreves [quarter notes] is established; the minim upbeat keeps the rhythm from becoming too monotonous. The rhythm of the first line repeats for all seven remaining phrases, with slight variation at the end of two internal cadences on the sixth and eighth lines, and all nine phrases use the eighth note pick-up beginning. Such a simple vocal line facilitates quick memorization"; *Music as Propaganda in the German Reformation* (Aldershot, 2001), 62. Oettinger continues: "In Luther's original melody that presumably appeared in the now-lost broadside, the final phrase returned to the starting pitch of F." In a footnote she adds, "However, the better known version of the melody,

starting and ending on the same note, untrained singers can easily continue singing stanza after stanza.

The melody essentially allows one note per syllable, except for the cadential figures at the end of some lines, where a syllable in the final word of the line may encompass 2–4 notes. The melodic line pattern of each stanza (a.b.a.b) follows quite closely the poetic end rhyme pattern of the *Stollen* (a.b.a.b). However, the *Abgesang* departs from the poetic repetition (c.d.c.e.f), allowing the final line's melodic ascendance to climax (c.d.e.f.g.), drawing emphasis to its verbal message.[50] In fact, the opening three-note pickup (all the same note) functions like a trumpet call, and is the same pattern used in Luther's most famous hymn, *Ein feste Burg* (1528). Riedel summarizes three important musical characteristics of Luther's four 'personal hymns'—"A New Song," "A Mighty Fortress," "From Heaven Above" (1535) and "Our Father in Heaven" (1539): (1) Unlike his other Ionian hymns, a close similarity exists among all the phrases; (2) The four tunes begin with the upper tonic in order to descend to its lower equivalent within the space of two phrases;[51] and (3) Luther's robust melodies differ from their progenitors (in the descending line feature) in that they are not meant to be passively heard; rather, they invite people to join actively in singing them. "They are extroverted optimistic manifestations of Lutheran faith."[52] The tale the song tells is worth tracking, for we can identify significant features of the story and hence construe it as argument.

The first stanza emphasizes God's initiative and work in the deaths, thus suggesting that one purpose for the entire song is to bring praise to God, who deserves it even more than the two martyrs; that God has done a wonder in this act; that this blessed act involved two young boys in Brussels; and (final line) that dying for God is a blessing and not a curse. The second stanza names the two (John and Henry) who thereafter are called 'boys [*Knaben*]' or referred to with pronouns. Their character is deemed innocent, in God's favor, and their decision to disdain this life gains them a crown. By using the word 'martyrs' in the

---

which first appeared in the tenor voice of Johann Walther's *Geistliches Gesangbüchlein* of 1524, ends on C." Modern melody is normally written for the soprano voice, but the sixteenth century and earlier centuries wrote it for the tenor.

[50] Ibid.

[51] "Some musicologists see in this octave-space treatment a personality-tinged feature of Luther's own style of musical production"; Riedel, *The Lutheran Chorale*, 51.

[52] Riedel, *The Lutheran Chorale*, 50f.

final line, Luther argues thus far for a redefinition of the term, omitting from jurisdiction any ecclesiastical decision, in favor of "God's good children [who] *For his word* life disdained." Luther's song clearly challenges the prevailing understanding of sainthood, recasting it as a part of early Christianity's pattern of recognizing, without official committee decision, those who were willing to die for their faith.[53]

Stanzas three through five describe the legal proceedings: The third stanza assigns blame to named perpetrators, identifying their motive and strategy: to entrap the boys into heretical admissions against the Word.[54] With both devil and theologians named here, it is clear that they are collaborating.[55] Luther calls this a 'trick [*Kunst*]' that backfires, drawing the sophists themselves into their own 'game,' only to be made fools of by the Spirit, gaining them (final line) nothing at all; herein the punch line indicates the innocence of the two men. Stanza four sings sarcastically (with rhyme) of various tactics by the prosecution ('sang sweet…sang sour'), upholding the 'boys'/'youngsters' as courageous, which only elicited more hatred. The wrath of the perpetrator quickly led to plans for burning. The wrath's greatness conjures up thoughts of the three men in the Book of Daniel who were cast into the fiery furnace, for one translator renders *er wart vol zorn von stunden* as 'His wrath grew sevenfold heated' (*LW* 53:215).[56] Stanza five completes the proceedings by characterizing the 'boys' as thanking God for their 'rescue,' though there is no hint of escape, release, or acquittal. The boys are stripped of their 'vestments' and 'consecrations:' The final line emphasizes the deception for which (*betreuget* is the emphatic final word) the world has fallen.

Stanza six is a bold redefinition of the priesthood! It argues that God alone is the grantor of martyrdom, and only for a 'true priesthood,' not

---

[53] Oettinger, *Music as Propaganda*, 51–69, argues that Luther's song, published in the midst of a polemical battle with Hieronymus Emser (1477–1527) over the canonization of Benno, fired the first musical shot in the battle over 'true sainthood' and that Luther's song was so successful that Emser is, to her knowledge, one of only two Catholic theologians (the other being Thomas Murner [1475–1537]) to use propagandistic song as a defense of the faith in the early decades of the reformation (52).

[54] The 'old arch-fiend [*allte Feynd*],' line one; *Sophisten* from Louvain, line five; *Sophisten* appears again in stanza eight.

[55] Oettinger, 66, translates the subjects of lines 1, 3, 5 as all plural, thus overlooking the devil and seeing only the theologians as blamed: "Luther departed from Catholic belief in the second [*sic*] strophe, when he named the ancient enemy not as the Devil, but as the Catholic theologians, or 'sophists' from Louvain, who belittled Scripture."

[56] Oettinger, 66.

for a 'falsehood made a schism.' 'Christ's own order' is what these two achieve, thus correcting the usual Catholic terminology for holiness on earth (priest, holy orders).[57] They come to heaven 'all pure and white.'[58] Stanza seven explains how the formal charges were assigned, making clear how unscriptural the condemnation was. The stanza describes the articles of condemnation, citing only one of the three *Die Artickel*, the final one that includes explicit denial of papal and patristic authority. Yet the actual wording of lines 6–8 excludes those entities, juxtaposing only God and man. The result is to diminish all but God, and the German syntax brings that out far better than English does.[59] The final line (*Des musten sie verbrennen*) is highly repetitious from the final line of stanza four (*Gedacht sie zuuerbrennen*), as though the 'trial' was but a hesitation in the plan, that the plan is now become necessity, which in the following stanzas is proclaimed.

Stanza eight describes the actual burning, the opening three F notes of line 1 intensifying the fire image, while the corresponding phrase of line 3, its poetic-melodic mate, stresses the attitude of bystanders at the resignation of the condemned: they had contempt for the pain, and with joy, offer praise to God. With singing, they faced their deaths.[60] Meanwhile, the *Sophisten* are taking notice (final line) of what God is revealing, reminiscent of stanza one. Stanza nine (eleven in *LW*)[61] argues that the perpetrators spread lies that the boys had recanted with their last breaths, a serious claim that could be devastating to the story.[62] With the final line saying that 'they recanted their statements,' this stanza—and the next one—functions much like a prolepsis, raising

---

[57] Ibid., 67.

[58] "frey und reyn" is the rhyming phrase of the rich melodic cadence at the end of line 7. The following line begins with *Müncherey*, which rhymes with the previous phrase, and prepares for the final line, which throws one more slap at the traditional clergy.

[59] "Mann musz alleyn Gott glawben/der mensch lewgt und trewgt ymmerdar/dem soll man nichts vertrawen."

[60] One might be reminded of Paul and Silas singing in the Philippian jail (Acts 16:25).

[61] I shall follow the order of stanzas in *WA* 35:487f., which follows the 'A' print (Wittenberg: Hans Lufft, 1523). *LW* 53:216 orders stanzas 9–12 differently. The issue is due to textual variations wherein two stanzas are omitted from some texts. Martin Rössler, "Ein neues Lied wir heben an: Ein Protestsong Martin Luthers," in *Reformation und praktische Theologie: Festschrift für Werner Jetter zum siebzigsten Geburtstag*, ed. Hans-Martin Müller and D. Rössler (Göttingen, 1983), 216–232, orders the stanzas as I do: 1–8, 11–12, 9–10.

[62] Indeed, all but three from the monastery had earlier renounced Lutheran teaching (*LW* 53:211). Such rumors no doubt played a significant role in prompting Luther to write the song.

an objection to the tale of righteous martyrdom. Stanza ten (twelve in *LW*) complements the previous stanza in that, as prolepsis, the objection is strongly answered. No evidence is given, save that—as in "A Letter to the Christians in the Netherlands"—believers can celebrate the reappearance of God's Word, though lies abound. Luther returns to the springtime motif of the Letter, adding to those metaphors from Song of Solomon 2:12: at *Wynter*'s end *Sommer* appears, bringing with it 'tender flowers,' all reliable signs that (final two lines), "His hand when once extended/Withdraws not till he's finished."[63]

Stanzas eleven and twelve extend the rebuttal by arguing that, in addition to God's own sanction, we now have the regrets of the perpetrators themselves. First, in shame they tried to hush up the deed, which 'In their hearts gnaweth infamy,' even deploring it to their friends.[64] Yet the 'Spirit cannot silent be,' and the final two lines invoke the Cain and Abel example, with the stigma of Cain's mark (final line) looming ominously on Catholic consciences, as did Abel's blood 'cry out' to God (Gen. 4:10): "Good Abel's blood out-poured/Must still besmear Cain's forehead" (Gen. 4:15).[65] Stanza twelve closes the song with two images: (1) the ashes of the two inexorably scattering into all lands in testimony to the shame of their murderers who silenced them. No natural disposal place will suffice;[66] (2) the singing tongues of the dying (now dead) are multiplied in the voices of all who will sing this song, perhaps a precursor to the final revelation that will cause "every tongue [to] confess that Jesus Christ is Lord, to the glory of God the Father" (Phil. 2:11). Luther's final line provides a satisfactory antiphon to the song's opening line, for there now really is a *New Song* we *have here begun.*

The majority of Luther's hymns were intended for congregational worship, and for most of them he adapted known tunes. He wanted to enlist the aid of poets in setting to music many of the Psalms, and at the end of 1523 he wrote to the Elector's secretary, Georg Spalatin, for help in this project. The brief letter is very important for under-

---

[63] "...der das hat angefangen,/der wirdt es woll volende."

[64] Die schand ym hertzen beysset sie" (Stanza eleven, line 50).

[65] "...des Aabels blut vergossen,/Es mus den Cain melden." Oettinger (68) claims that the 'figure of Cain' appears in several songs, most prominently in Johann Walther's 'Cain sich aber regen thut,' published in *Wittembergisch deudsch Geistlich Gesengbüchlein. Mit vier vnd fünff stimmen* (Wittenberg: Georg Rhau, 1544), Part II, no. 28."

[66] Note the rhyme of the four sites ('Stream, hole, ditch, grave [*Bach, Loch, Grub noch Grab*]').

standing Luther's understanding of, and agenda for, the use of music in worship.[67] However, as we have seen with "A New Song," even before that Luther was writing 'news' hymns.[68] And the news he wanted to convey was the Good News of the Gospel, to 'sing a new song,' as the Psalms and Prophets had foretold.[69] With the martyrdom of Henry and John, it was obvious to Luther that the Gospel had been unleashed once again.[70]

IV. *To the Christians in Riga, Tallinn, and Tartu (August 1523)*[71]

More than twenty years ago, and just a few weeks after the death of our teenage son, an acquaintance of mine—also a preacher—said, in response to my complaint that I was not doing very well, that "You're probably doing some of your best preaching." While we cannot now discuss the complexities of that remark, it is worthwhile to examine briefly another epistle Luther wrote in mid-1523, to Christians also living well north of Wittenberg, for we can see that the recent deaths of Henry and John were on his mind, perhaps helping him produce 'some of his best preaching.' Although he made only brief mention of those two men in this composition, Luther offers a compelling letter of exhortation (*Ermanung*) that outlines a threefold teaching about what is most important in the Christian life, in view of the seriousness of the times—the proliferation of the Gospel and its concomitant persecution.

In August 1522 Luther had received a letter from John Lohmüller, secretary of the town council in Riga,[72] asking for a letter of encouragement for two Evangelical clergymen there. Luther directed his response to reformation followers not only in Riga but also in Tallinn[73] and Tartu, another city in Estonia. Luther's *Brief an die Christen in Riga, Reval und*

---

[67] *LW* 49:68–70; *WABr* 3:220.

[68] Robinson-Hammerstein, 152, 155.

[69] Ps. 33:3; 40:3; 96:1; 98:1; 144:9; 149:1; Isa. 42:10; Rev. 5:9; 14:3.

[70] Dick Akerboom, 'Ein neues lied wir heben an': Over de eerste martelaren van de Reformatie en het ontstaan van het eerste lied van Martin Luther," *Luther-Bulletin* 14 (2005): 27–43, which I have just recently come across, argues that Luther's song "shows clear parallels with the martyrs' hymns of the first century of the Church," here at 43.

[71] Tappert, 194–197.

[72] Located on the Baltic Sea, in present-day Latvia.

[73] Also on the Baltic Sea, in present-day Estonia, and its capital.

Dorpat (1523) saw three editions in 1523.[74] What may account for its popularity is not so much the conditions of immediate persecution but rather its ability to synthesize, for struggling new Evangelicals (especially those outside of Electoral Saxony), the essence of the Christian faith, what—in the first of the Invocavit Sermons (9 March 1522) and again here—Luther called the 'chief thing [*Heubstuck*].' In responding to a request for a letter of encouragement, under the same signature used to address those in the Netherlands,[75] he consolidates the four 'chief things' down to three: he takes the faith, hope, and love of 1 Cor. 13 and reorders them (faith, love, hope). By ending with hope, Luther tries to provide encouragement for believers to withstand persecution and false teachers.

As with "To the Christians in the Netherlands" (1523), Luther's *narratio* (combined with *benevolentiae captatio*) declares that the reception of the 'gracious light of his [God's] truth' has produced reliable signs that He is at work: fruit has been produced, and resistance is encountered. As evidence of the latter, he announces that 'recently they have burned two,' arguing that his readers are those at the ends of the world who are receiving the 'true Word' and the 'saving Word,' despite this kind of opposition. As he begins the *petitio*, the substance of the letter, Luther *reminds* readers what they need to know, believe, and do, with three paragraph-initiating leads: 'You have heard and learned'; 'From this you have gone on and learned'; 'Afterward you heard that.'[76] He appeals to them to: (1) be thankful for God's grace, and (2) be responsible to God's grace. The style of this section uses the second person pronoun much more heavily than in the *narratio*. In warning readers to be vigilant,[77] Luther uses a long, asyndetic list of titles for Christ, a list intended to convey a notion of confidence in Christ's sufficiency, so that no one will resort to works for his own righteousness: "he, alone

---

[74] *WA* 12:147–50 (Benzing 1681–1683). See Leonid Arbusow, Jr., *Die Einführung der Reformation in Liv-, Est- und Kurland*. Quellen und Forschungen zur Reformationsgeschichte 3 (Aalen, 1964), 271–279; Janis Matulis, "Die ersten Schritte der Reformation in Riga," in *Luther und Luthertum in Osteuropa: Selbstdarstellungen aus der Diaspora und Beiträge zur theologischen Diskussion*, ed. Gerhard Bassarak and Günter Wirth (Berlin, 1983), 354–363; Reinhard Slenczka, "Luther's Care of Souls for Our Times," *CTQ* 67 (2003): 33–63, here at 58–63.

[75] "Mar. Luther, Eccl. Wyttem."

[76] "Denn also habt...Aus disem yhr weytter gelernt habt...Darnach habt yhr gehört" (*WA* 12:148.21; 149.3, 13).

[77] Similar to Paul's admonition to the Ephesian elders in Acts 20:21ff.

and always, is our Lord, Priest, Teacher, Bishop, Father, Saviour, Helper, Comforter, and Protector in all sins, in death, in necessity, and in every need, whether temporal or eternal."[78]

In a second warning of the *petitio*—urging readers to be faithful, not succumbing to works' righteousness—Luther stresses the body life of the church, and he does so by shifting to a predominance of first plural pronouns. This admonition stresses the first of the triad (faith), yet he uses that term (*Glawben*) only twice: as verb, just before quoting Rom. 3:28 (which he says is Rom. 4) and, near the end of the section, as noun.[79] This faith binds Christians together, providing such blessings and peace that they can be unafraid of misfortune. Indeed, such faith is a necessary component of being a Christian, and persecution is a reliable indicator that one has such faith.[80]

A third teaching of the *petitio* (and the completion of the 'faith' section) urges readers to avoid actions that would undermine faith. Luther here presents another asyndetic list, which complements the first one. The set of behaviors to avoid contains much alliteration, especially two types of end-rhyme.[81] A fourth teaching of the *petitio* consists in the Christian's only true obligation: to love his neighbor, meaning that good works are to be done for others, not self. Unlike his speaking on 'faith' (which was twice as long as this section), Luther here uses the verb 'love' five times, and he calls it the 'second chief thing' in the Christian life. The final teaching of the *petitio* brings the third element of the triad ('hope') into view. The teaching is a warning that persecution is imminent, and the arguments supporting it appeal to logic: that the enemy feels compelled to resist and that we should fare no better than

---

[78] "...das er alleyn ist unser herr, priester, lerer, bischoff, vatter, heyland, helffer, trost und beystand ewiglich ynn allen sunden, tod, nott und was uns seylet, es sey zeyttlich odder ewiglich" (*WA* 12:148.17–20).

[79] Clearly 'faith' is the subject, for not only has Tappert, 195f., inserted the noun 'faith' five additional times (where the context justifies it), but Luther himself confirms it, in his summary of the three terms at the end of the *petitio*.

[80] Note the regressive triplet of clauses in Luther's comment, the triplet expediting the meaning, so that the last item, the one left standing, seems more blatant: Where such [faith] is wanting there is blindness, there are no Christians, there is not even a spark of God's work and favor.

[81] (1) plural nouns that end with -*en*; (2) singular substantives ending with -*erey*: the appointed fasts, prayers, pilgrimages, Masses, vigils, charitable endowments, monkery, nunnery, priestcraft [*die gesatzten Fasten, Beten, Wallen, Messen Vigilien, Stifften, Moncherey, Nonnerey, Pfafferey*] all such things are devilish doctrine [*Lere*] and blasphemy [*Lesterung*] (*WA* 12:149.5f.).

Christ. Accordingly, Luther argues that the cross is necessary, but he also argues somewhat paradoxically—that the cross brings hope (*Hoffnung*), a term he uses twice in this, the shortest section on the triad.

So faith, love, hope are what Luther says are 'prepared and perfected' by the cross. He urges his readers not to depend on Rome, or on priests and bishops, for Christ is their 'Lord and Bishop.'[82] The heavily Pauline material that Luther uses for teaching on faith and love, the warnings of false teachings (Paul at Acts 20:21), and the persecution motif of 1 Peter all provided material for exhortation in this letter. Luther found a way to generate some of his best preaching in this letter of exhortation to isolated Evangelicals—God's 'elect [*Auszerwelten*]'—in the northern regions on the Baltic.[83]

V. *Letter to Lambert Thorn (19 January 1524)*

In the summer of 1523 a third Augustinian from Antwerp was scheduled for execution, along with Vos and van den Esschen. However, Lambert Thorn was not burned but thrown into prison, where he died five years later without recanting (Tappert, 197–199). Luther's letter to him (in Latin) is a short (41 lines) but moving personal message that not only attempts to comfort and encourage the reader; it also provides evidence of Luther's attitudes toward aspects of martyrdom at the time. A modern critical edition of the text of *Luther an den eingekerkerten Augustiner Lambert Thorn (Wittenberg, 19. Januar 1524)* is printed in *WABr* 3:238–239—with lines numbered consecutively across both pages—and is organized in the following way: I. Heading and *salutatio* (3 lines); II. *Benevolentiae captatio* (lines 3–12); III. *Petitio* (12–22); IV. *Exhortatio* (22–33); V. *Narratio* and benediction (34–39); VI. *Conclusio* (40–41). Luther's goal is to bolster Thorn's Christian hope by assuring him that he is suffering for Christ and the Gospel and by reminding him of the support he has in the fellowship of the Lord and his church.

This goal is consonant with the situation, for Thorn may have been experiencing what today resembles so-called 'survivor guilt.' Six months had passed since his two Augustinian brothers (Henry and John) were

---

[82] *Twice* in this *Brief* Luther has referred to Christ as *Bischoff*, a biblical epithet used only by Peter (1 Pet. 2:25) and consistent with Luther's quoting of 1 Pet. 5:10 near the end of the letter.
[83] From the *salutatio* (*WA* 12:147.1).

burned at stake in Brussels, and Thorn was probably wondering why he escaped the flames, or how long it might be before the same fate befell him. On the other side of the exigence is fellow Augustinian Luther and his own feelings as to why he has been spared the honor of martyrdom. In some ways this letter is an "inverted" image of Paul's prison epistle to the Philippians: instead of an incarcerated apostolic writer consoling and encouraging his concerned congregation, a free Luther writes to a chained follower on the inside of prison walls.

I. Heading and *salutatio*: Luther's address and greeting follow classical conventions more closely than in his public letters, yet the content is thoroughly Christianized. That is, the names of both addressee and sender appear at the letter's beginning, and the epithets remind the addressee (and all other readers) of whose cause it is in which they share fellowship and service.[84] The endearing salutation of Tappert's translation ('Dear Brother Lambert') is actually embedded as apostrophe ('greatest Brother Lambert'), following the first sentence of the next section. Thus Luther foreshadows the major themes of the letter.

II. *Benevolentiae captatio* (3–12): This section goes beyond a mere well wishing, yet it functions to put the reader at ease, in that it argues that Thorn is thoroughly grounded in Christ and that he technically 'needs' no consolation. Yet by sending this letter, and by Thorn's reading it, Luther encourages him in his plight: the exigence of imprisonment cannot be altered, but Thorn's attitude can be addressed. That this section is not about Luther but about Thorn and Christ is clear from the pronouns alone.[85] In lines 5–6 he explains what he means by 'Christ, who is in you' and what accomplishments He has obtained; these accomplishments then enable Thorn to be strengthened by his

---

[84] The first words of the heading are 'Disciple of Christ'; in the critical notes is acknowledged a variant reading that adds the word 'faithful [*fideli*].' In second position comes 'brother Lambert Thorn,' followed by terms acknowledging the reader's present plight and affirming the writer's affection: "bound in chains on account of the gospel, my beloved friend in the Lord, Martin Luther [*in vinculis euangelii posito suo in Domino chariss[imo]. Martinus Lutherus*]." The greeting ('*Gratiam et pacem in Domino!*') is thoroughly Pauline, yet it is the one Luther has consistently used since 1522; cf. Wengert, "Apostolic Self-Awareness," 71.

[85] Once Luther has asserted that Christ "has given me abundant testimony [*Quanquam satis mihi…testatur*]," only three times do we find the first person singular pronoun 'my,' where Luther says "you do not need my [*meis*] words….. Thus both they and you are to me [*mihi*] a great consolation….. There is little need to burden you with my [*mea*] consolation" (lines 4, 11); eight instances of 'you' in pronouns [*te, sis*], with numerous others implicit in the inflected verbs or understood from the main clause, remind reader Thorn of his position. As he explicates, Luther piles up doublets of verbs.

Spirit and consoled by the double example of brothers John and Henry. Luther argues that the three Augustinians' witness brings him great 'consolation and strength' and bring to the whole world a 'sweet savor [*suavissimo odori*],' a phrase from the language of sacrifice and burnt offerings of the Old Testament.[86] As he finishes this section, Luther pointedly addresses Thorn's concern for why he lives on, offering him the prospects of something better, by reminding him that the matter is out of his (own) hands: "Who knows why the Lord was unwilling to have you die with the other two? Perhaps you were saved for another miracle."[87]

III. *Petitio* (12–22): Luther injects more of his own persona—feelings, concerns, teachings—in this section, focusing on how to encourage Thorn by helping him realize that his imprisonment is a good thing. Luther confesses a certain amount of envy, clearly speaking of the prospect of Thorn's likely martyrdom: "Alas, though I am the first to teach these things, I am the last to share your chains and fires, and perhaps I shall never be found worthy to share them."[88] So by turning from Thorn's likely martyrdom to his own lack thereof, Luther seems to have slipped into a preoccupation with himself. However, what we must not miss is the *shared* nature of this business of suffering for Christ: Luther emphasized earlier that it was 'grace' that was given to Thorn and that knowledge of the Word and the Spirit were 'given [*donavit*]' to him (Luther). So, to whatever extent Luther (or even others) can share in these sufferings (the outcome), it is possible, provided he (or they) share in the task of confessing and preaching and rejoicing with those

---

[86] *WABr* 3:239 and Tappert, both cite Exod. 29:18 for the phrase 'sweet savor [*suavissimo odori*],' but it occurs over forty times in the Old Testament, and Thorn surely would recognize the term and its context of sacrifice.

[87] "Quis scit, cur te Dominus noluerit cum duobus istis perire? Servaris in aliud miraculum" (*WABr* 3:238.11–12).

[88] Me miserum, qui primus ista docuisse iactor et novissimus et forte nunquam vestrorum vinculorum et ignium particeps esse dignus sum! (*WABr* 2:238.16–18). As we notice that Luther placed himself (*sum*) in final position in that sentence, he begins the next with himself, offering a more positive attitude on how he should handle the way things have gone: "Nevertheless, I shall avenge myself for this unhappiness of mine and console myself with the thought that your chains and prisons and fires are all my own, as indeed they are so long as I confess and preach these doctrines and sympathize with you and rejoice with you [Vindicabo tamen hanc meam miseriam et consolabor me, quod vestra vincula mea sunt, vestri carceres et ignes mei sunt. Sunt vero, dum et ego eadem confiteor et praedico vobisque simul compatior et congratulor]" (*WABr* 3:328.18–21).

who suffer. Thus we note that Luther has begun this section with con-
gratulations and thanks, and he ends it with sympathy and rejoicing.

IV. *Exhortatio* (22–33): While we could call it *petitio*—for in it Luther
makes a request of his reader ('pray for me')—the section is devoted
almost entirely to offering encouragement ('pray for me *as I do for you*')
through scriptural quotations (without citations) that remind the reader
of his resources from the Lord. He reminds Thorn that he is not suffering alone. This stress on the inclusiveness of the fellowship Thorn
has with others is seen in the presence of several first person plural
pronouns, which Luther has used only in this section, as he emphasizes
the Lord's presence and power which are available for Thorn: "Do
not argue with Satan but fix your eyes on the Lord, relying on simple
faith on Jesus Christ, and know that by his blood we are saved. Just
as our works and human laws cannot be the blood of Christ, so they
can neither take away *our* sins nor justify *us*, can neither condemn *us*
nor accuse *us*" (29–33, my emphasis).[89] It is in this section of the letter (24–30) that Luther uses promises from Scripture, knitting them
together with pledges and exhortations of his own, into a seamless
encouragement that reminds Thorn of the strength he can draw from
the Lord and his people.[90]

V. *Narratio* and benediction (34–39): Luther's final section of the
letter conveys news updates about what is happening on the outside.
It appears to be all 'bad news,' which generally one is cautious about
divulging, lest it discourage the inmate. However, these generalizations
with which Luther characterizes the state of affairs are meant further to

---

[89] "Ne disputes cum Sathana, sed ad Dominum stent oculi tui, simplici fide innixus.
Solum Iesum Christum esse scito, cuius sanguine nos salvi erimus. Opera nostra et
humana statuta, sicut non possunt esse sanguis Christi, ita nec peccata tollere nec
iustificare, ita neca damnare nec reum tenere." The italicized pronouns are all neces-
sitated by the correlative conjunctions (*nec...nec...nec...nec*), which hark back to the
pronoun *nostra*.

[90] Paraphrasing Psalm 91:14f. (90:14f. Vulgate), Luther reminds Thorn that the
Lord is with him in trouble, that "I will deliver him: I will set him on high because he
hath known my name [*liberabo eum, protegam eum, quoniam cognovit nomen meum*]." Prior
to quoting John 16:33, Luther makes his own declaration (two imperatives that surround a promise of future benefit) that paraphrases Psalm 27:14 (26:14 Vulgate): "Be
of good courage and he will strengthen your heart; wait on the Lord [*Tantum viriliter
age, confortetur cor tuum et sustine Dominum!*]," which he follows with this comfort from the
Lord's own words ("He has said: 'In the world ye shall have tribulation, in me you have
peace, but be of good cheer; I have overcome the world' [*Ipse dixit: 'In mundo pressuram
habetis, in me autem pacem, sed confidite, ego vici mundum!*']").

verify his contention that persecution is a reliable sign that the Lord is at work, that the Gospel is effective, and perhaps that the judgment—or even the return—of the Lord is at hand. Hence, 'bad news' should be reassuring to Thorn.

VI. *Conclusio* (40–41): Luther's closing is both classical and Christian (especially Pauline): "Farewell, my brother in Christ. Greetings to you from all our friends and our whole church" (40–41). 'Farewell' is a typically classical close; 'greetings to you' from the church or churches is a common close in the Epistles.[91]

VI. *To the Christians of Miltenberg (14 February 1524)*

Miltenberg was a small town near Heidelberg, in the jurisdiction of Albert of Mainz, who opposed the Luther reformation. When they called an Evangelical pastor, John Drach, in the spring of 1522 (roughly coinciding with Luther's return to Wittenberg from Wartburg castle), many in the town responded to his preaching. Opposition also spread, and Drach was excommunicated; in the fall of 1523 he fled. Some of his followers were later beheaded, and the reformation was suppressed in the town. Having been kept informed by Drach, Luther wrote a letter of encouragement (*Christlicher trostbrieff*) in February 1524. In this document (Tappert, 199–208) we find similar themes from the previous two letters written a few months earlier, and we begin to comprehend their significance.[92] Luther's understanding of the Miltenbergers' situation and needs, then, is more that of their need for comfort from false accusations of sedition—and in the midst of persecution, of their beliefs—than it is about assuaging their grief over specific losses they have suffered.[93]

---

[91] 1 Cor. 16:19–20; Col. 4:15; 2 Tim. 4:21; Titus 3:15; Philem. 1:23; Heb. 13:24; 1 Pet. 5:13.

[92] *Eyn Christlicher trostbrieff an die Miltenberger, Wie sie sich an yhren feynden rechen sollen, aus dem 119. Psalm* (*WA* 15:69–78) appeared in seven editions, from five German cities, in 1524 (Benzing Nr. 1888–1894). In a letter to Archbishop Albert (dated the same day, 14 February), Luther explains that he published this document as an open letter of consolation in order to reach poor people who cannot receive letters and so that he would not be guilty of being condemned by Christ on the last day, "I was in prison and ye visited me not" (Matt. 25:35–39); Tappert, 199.

[93] Indeed, the term 'martyr' does not appear, although 'murderers of souls [*Seel Mörder*]' does occur once (*WA* 15:70.14).

In the role indicated in the *salutatio*'s signature in all letters thus far—'*preacher* in Wittenberg' (my emphasis)—Luther stresses the authority of God's word and its stake in this situation: it is preaching that is needed. Although the *salutatio* seems like his typically Pauline greeting, the phrase 'from God' proves revealingly important.[94] The distinction Luther makes, then—and it is one with which he begins the body of the letter and uses as an organizing principle throughout the piece—is between the comfort of men and the comfort 'of God.'[95] The *Trostbrieff* itself is an example of an attempt to comfort others with God's comfort.

His proof of God's comfort is a dichotomy between false (worldly) and true (Christian) comfort. The evidence—or rather, definition—of comfort from God is found in Rom. 15:4, which links patience and comfort *of the Scriptures* with hope. He tells readers that the world's comfort is based only on what the afflicted 'desire [*Begerd*],' which is contrasted to hope, which can neither be seen nor felt (Rom. 8:24f.). But what really convinces Luther about 'God's comfort' is what he finds Paul *doing* throughout the Second Epistle to his Corinthians:[96] (A) "telling them [the Corinthians] that they are a letter of Christ prepared by the preaching of the gospel and written by the living Spirit"; (B) then praising the office of preaching[97] and boasting of the gospel by offering a 'psalm of praise to the Gospel.' Acknowledging that a carnal man may find this approach to consolation absurd (what comfort does one bring by failing to affirm the plight of the bereaved and by mouthing scriptural platitudes to him?), Luther appeals to his readers to discover the genius and sovereignty of God in such a strategy. And Luther himself then sets out to follow that strategy.

He begins step (A) by acknowledging the plight of his readers (the Miltenbergers), in a sort of mini *narratio* that uses many first and second person pronouns to aid in conveying to them that ('I') recognize the

---

[94] He will use similar phrases ('from God,' 'of God,' 'for God's sake,' etc.) 15 times in the first 120 lines, where he then narrows to a fairly consistent focus on the Word of God ('God's word,' 'his word,' 'the Word,' etc., another 19 times).

[95] That is to say, instead of starting with a *narratio*—facts from the situation of the readers and about the writer's perspective and purpose—Luther begins by completely quoting 2 Cor. 1:3–4, using the final clause ("comfort wherewith we ourselves are comforted of God [*mit dem Trost, da mit wyr gestrostet werden von Gott*]"; *WA* 15:69.14f.) as his thesis, what he wants his readers to find (God's comfort) and which he himself wants to provide in the letter.

[96] Tappert, 200, misses the *seynen* in translating *WA* 15:69.28.

[97] Tappert, 200, says 'praises himself and his preaching.'

harm ('you') have suffered. Second, following that brief section, Luther
starts a lengthy discussion of how to draw comfort from this plight. In
function, this section operates like a rhetorical contrarium, which offers
a counter-example, or as in this case, considers *unhelpful* responses, such
as complaining, scolding, even revenge. Such counter-examples are quite
consistent with arguing from definition, for definitions often include
what is *not fitting*.[98] This section is rich with second person pronouns,
not of confrontation but of exhortation, a kind of Pauline praise of
the audience for what God (not the enemy) is doing in them.[99]

Yet Luther does grant a concession to his audience, an avenue along
which they can direct their revenge: it can be heaped upon the devil.
Moreover, Luther begins to deal with step (B) of Paul's two-fold strategy
in 2 Corinthians, namely: praising the office of preaching and boasting of the gospel by offering a 'psalm of praise to the Gospel.' This
is where Luther takes Scripture—in this case a 'little verse' from the
Psalter—exegetes, expounds, and applies it to the case at hand, therein
thwarting the devil's plan.[100]

But what if speaking the Word is forbidden? That objection, a real
problem in Albertine Saxony, Luther next takes up, in his prolepsis.
He uses dialogue to allow the objection to have voice, and he answers
it with brief dialogue. Toward the goal of supplying strength to the
weak to meet this task, Luther next offers his German translation of

---

[98] Luther returns to the comfort from God, employing several of the key phrases
linking suffering to God and his word—especially the phrase 'for the sake of [God,
God's word, etc.].' 'Suffering [*leydet*]' is repeatedly used in this section (six times in fifteen lines), along with seven instances (in nine lines) of terms such as 'sure' or 'certain
[*gewis*],' 'know [*wissen*],' 'conscience [*Gewissen*].' Luther's German syntax twice places
umb yhr gottis immediately after *gewiss*. In one instance Luther uses the opposite term
ungewissen.

[99] The 'you's and 'your's are juxtaposed to 'they's and 'them's, as Luther distinguishes
between what benefits the Miltenbergers enjoy (salvation, good conscience, righteous
cause, "the consolation of God with patience and hope out of the Scriptures"), compared to the harms suffered by their persecutors (misery, bad conscience, blind cause,
"the devil's consolation in revenge and visible tyranny" [Tappert, 202]). In employing
pronoun and descriptive juxtaposition, Luther entices these answers from his readers
through rhetorical question and *argumentum ad absurdum*, ending the one section of exhortation with a striking chiasmus (a.b.c:c_1.b_1.a_1): If you had the power to choose between
their lot and your own, ought you not flee from theirs as from the devil himself, even
though it were a kingdom of heaven that they had, and hasten to choose your own lot,
even though it were a hell? For heaven [a] cannot be glad [b] if the devil [c] reigns
there, and hell [c_1] cannot be sad [b_1] if God [a_1] reigns there (Tappert, 202).

[100] In *Ein feste Burg* the final line of stanza three explains the principle: "One word
can overturn him" (*LW* 53:285), or as another translation puts it, "One little word
shall fell him."

Psalm 120 (119 Vulgate), which he says fits their situation perfectly.[101] In order to see how Luther finds the existential *Sitz im Leben* of the Miltenbergers and the Word of God in this Psalm, his exposition of its seven verses is worth examination.

Psalm 120 (119 Vulgate), one of the Lament Psalms, shows the human battle under persecution, and it identifies God's answers and assistance.[102] Luther offers a translation of each verse, and then he expounds each verse in turn. Structurally, the psalm progresses rapidly from questions (vv. 1–3) to answers (vv. 4–7).[103] His exposition of v. 1 covers both clauses, starting with the first, for Luther's emphasis is on the source to which we cry out for help. Using expeditio—dispatching wrong answers in order to get to the correct one, thus leaving it standing alone, triumphantly—he offers three wrong sources (emperor, sword, our own devices and wisdom) before he turns distinctly (*sondern*) to emphasize the right answer: the Lord. By completing the exposition with a paraphrase, Luther finds God's pleasure in being sought and in acting to 'hear and help.' In verse two, the imperative (vocative), Luther argues that the cry functions not to inform God of our need but to motivate us to pray more diligently. He then identifies the Miltenbergers' enemies as revealed in the Psalm, showing how applicable Scripture is to human situations (God's comfort). In verse three, Luther finds the distressed person's thoughts about how to respond to the persecution, indicating that the person feels weak, needing help, and is considering compromise. Luther says the Spirit rejects these proposals.

Luther spends the most time with the two metaphors of verse four, and the images of this verse are crucial to understand. The coherence of this Psalm with the body of the letter now emerges, for the preaching of the word is 'help that comes from God,' sharp arrows that pierce human opinion. So both preaching truth and loving life are needed, and these stand out in stark contrast to the impotent sermons and cold

---

[101] In his lectures on the Psalms (1513–1516) Luther plainly declares that this psalm is "speaking about the trouble of treachery, not the trouble of torments" (*LW* 11).

[102] In the Vulgate and German Bibles the first verse has attached to it at the beginning: 'A pilgrimage song,' and here Luther includes as heading the Latin 'first line title' (*Ad dominum, cum tribularer, clamavi*).

[103] The first three verses get brief exposition (7 lines, 7 lines, 5 lines); the fourth verse—the center—gets the longest treatment (18 lines); the final three verses are more treated more concisely (11 lines, 8 lines, 8 lines). In five of the seven verses Luther interprets the meaning as dealing with the Word of God, a seemingly rather strange connection to find in this Psalm, for the only obvious link are terms that indicate speaking: *cried, heard* (v. 1); *lips, tongue* (v. 2, 3); *speak* (v. 7).

love of many preachers. In the fifth, sixth, and seventh verses Luther
explains the treatment preachers of God's Word receive. The final verse
continues the cry of the righteous, confessing their love for peace, all the
while being charged with sedition when they speak Christian doctrine.
Luther bolsters his exposition with the historical example of Ahab's
false charge against Elijah for troubling Israel (1 Kings 8:17f.).

Following his brief exposition of Psalm 120, Luther then returns to
a more direct conversational exhortation with his readers as he tries
to show them how the psalm applies to their present situation. Following that, he concludes the entire letter. He asks that confident and
abundant prayers be offered for Miltenberg and elsewhere, to fan the
flames which the Word has ignited.[104] Luther's closing is thorough and
very gracious in its fullness, invoking God's name (not once but three
times) so that Christ will be preached.[105]

---

[104] In his final paragraph of application and exhortation, Luther shifts to first person
plural, turning attention onto himself as well as his readers, as he continues using the
fire metaphor to urge steadfastness and passion in prayer. The exhortation concludes
(set off as an independent paragraph in *WA*) with three successive 'Let us...' clauses:
"So let us be up and about. The time is here. The devil is playing evil tricks on us
everywhere. Let us for once do something to vex him and revenge ourselves on him.
In other words, let us pray God without ceasing until he sends us enough instruments,
marksmen, sharp arrows, and coals" (Tappert, 207) [Darumb lasst uns auff wachen
und frisch seyn, die zeyt ist hie. Er thu(o)tt uns allenthalben viel böser tück, last uns
doch auch eyn mal yhm etwas beweysen, das yhn verdreuffet, und uns rechen, das ist,
lasst uns bitten zu Gott on unterlas, bis er uns gerüfte schützen mit scharffen pfeylen
und kolen gnüg sende] (*WA* 15:77.30 78.2).

[105] "Hie mit will ich euch, lieben freunde, Gott ynn seyn gnad und barmhertzickeit
befollen haben, und bittet auch Gott fur mich armen sunder, und lasst euch ewer
prediger befollen seyn, so Christum und nicht den bapst odder die Meyntzischen
tempeljunckern predigen. Gottis gnade sey mit euch. Amen" (*WA* 15:78.19–22). Such
a closing allows us to call brief attention to how similar this document is to Luther's
sermons, especially the Invocavit sermons of March 1522: (1) in its strategic use of
pronouns for shifting attention to subjects and for maintaining reader communion with
speaker; (2) in its frequent use of the 'endearment' (*lieben Freunde*), seven times in all;
(3) in its emphasis on the 'chief things' of the Christian life, which must be constantly
returned to during times of stress, such as rapid innovation (March 1522) or heavy
persecution (February 1524); (4) in its singular focus on the Word of God as the source
of life, with preaching as the vehicle through which the Word is made effective, and
with the importance of allowing the Word to have free course; (5) in its exhortation
to maintain good works of love, not for righteous merit but for demonstrating faith
and for fanning the flames kindled by the Spirit.

VII. *The Burning of Brother Henry (1525)*

Hendrik van Zutphen (Heinrich von Zütphen) was a Dutch Augustinian who had been educated in Wittenberg (Master's degree, 1511) and
had served as prior of his order at Cologne in 1514 and at Dort in
1515. In 1522 he left Wittenberg, where he had resumed his studies
(Bachelor of Divinity, 1521), to serve as prior at Antwerp, where he
was arrested. As it happened, though, 'Henry' was helped to escape the
country—on his way, presumably, back to Wittenberg. However, having
been persuaded at Bremen to stay there and preach, Henry never got
out of Holstein. In the fall of 1524 he accepted a potentially dangerous, but also compelling, call to Meldorf in Dithmarschen,[106] where
he was later kidnapped and eventually tortured and murdered on 10
December by a mob at Hemmingstedt.[107] Luther was asked to write
a letter of consolation to the congregation in Bremen, and he did so,
joining others who memorialized Henry's martyrdom in print.[108]

"The Burning of Brother Henry in Dithmarschen, Including an
Explanation of the Ninth Psalm" (*LW* 32:265–286)[109] was written in
February or March of 1525, based on reports of witnesses.[110] It is
Luther's second attempt at writing about the death of a martyr, and as
a consolatory letter that includes an exposition of a psalm, the docu-
ment also includes something new—Luther's first literary 'martyrology.'
"The Burning of Brother Henry" differs from "A New Song Here Shall
Be Begun" (1523) in several respects: (1) since this 'execution' had no
official ecclesiastical sanction; there are no *Acta* that outline the charges

---

[106] Near the mouth of the Elbe river, at the North Sea.

[107] A half mile outside of the village of Meldorf.

[108] Bernd Moeller, "Inquisition und Martyrium," 47, catalogs four different *Flugschriften*, including Luther's, which responded to the *Prozeß* against Heinrich von
Zütphen, which were issued in ten total editions. Martin Brecht, *Martin Luther*, 2:349,
says the request of Luther that he write to Henry came from Jakob Propst; cf. *WABr*
3:400–403.

[109] Tappert, 208–211, omits both the explanation of Psalm 9 and the 'history.'

[110] Luther's *Von Bruder Henrico in Ditmar verbrannt samt dem zehnten Psalmen ausgelegt* (*WA*
18:224–240) was published in seven German editions (including one in Niederdeutsch) in
five German cities, all in 1525 (Benzing, Nr. 2107–2113). Three authors of *Flugschriften*
that Moeller, "Inquisition und Martyrium," cites were Jakob Propst, Henry's predeces-
sor at Antwerp, Johannes Lang (1488–1548), and Wenceslaus Linck (1482–1547), all
Augustinians, followers, and friends of Luther. Linck was on the theology faculty at
Wittenberg, and Lang had been at Erfurt with Luther. For background on the Augustinian order, see David Gutierrez, *The Augustinians from the Protestant Reformation to the Peace
of Westphalia 1518–1648*. History of the Order of St. Augustine 2 (Villanova, 1979).

and sentence; (2) Luther's is one of four documents—all Lutheran—to chronicle the story;[111] and (3) that its prose provides far more detail and evidence, purporting to present an historical, journalistic account of the events.

Luther's document devotes approximately one-third to consolatory letter and psalm exposition, two-thirds to the *Geschichte* of Henry's murder. The structure is roughly as follows: (A) *Salutatio* (*LW* 32:265; *WA* 18:224.1–2); (B) *Narratio* (*LW* 32:265; *WA* 18:224.4–11); (C) Exposition and exhortation on the meaning of martyrdom, plus a short justification for including the psalm exposition (*LW* 32:265–268; *WA* 18:224.12–226.11); (D) Exposition of the Ninth Psalm, including an exhortation on how believers should respond to the burning (*LW* 32:268–272; *WA* 18:226.17–229.17); (E) *Conclusio* (*LW* 32:272; *WA* 18:229.17–21); (F) Narrative of the murder of Henry (*LW* 32:272–286; *WA* 18:229.22–240.33).

As a multi-layered discourse responding to a violent and unofficial killing—rather than a clerically sanctioned trial and execution—several distinctive features of rhetorical style can be found in the overall document: (1) Luther uses abundantly the words *blood, murder, martyr,* and *martyrdom,* along with vivid descriptions of these deeds; (2) he is endearing to his audience, as he offers ubiquitous and praiseworthy references to *Henry,* the victim; (3) the *Word of God,* and the preaching and teaching of it, are repeatedly emphasized, including detailing topics Henry preached and the favorable responses to them; (4) guilty perpetrators are described—names are given and actions told; and (5) Luther frequently inserts dialogue into the narrative, in order to demonstrate the clear difference between Henry's innocence and the persecutors' guilt.

(1) Unlike the few explicit references to *blood* and *martyrs* in the 1523 documents, nearly two years later Luther is more direct and concrete: he mentions *blood* fourteen times, nearly all of them in the letter and exposition section (three of those uses come from Scriptures quoted).[112]

---

[111] The titles of documents catalogued by Moeller, "Inquisition und Martyrium," 47, all claim to be 'histories': Nr. 1 (Jakob Propst): "Ain erschrockliche geschicht…"; Nr. 2 (Johann Lang): "Eyn Hystorie odder geschicht…"; Nr. 3 (Johann Lang-Wenceslaus Linck): "Historia wie S. Heinrich zon Zutphan…"

[112] While Psalm 9:12 is the only verse to use the word *blood,* Luther's explanation for the meaning of this psalm invokes its title ("A Psalm of David, to be sung with voice uplifted, about the youth of the son"), the latter phrase of which Luther interprets as referring "to the martyrs of Christ the Son of God." These are his "young and strong

Virtually all of the time, when Luther mentions *blood*, he speaks of it positively.[113] At the same time, such an act is *murder*, which stained (*befleckt*) the hands of those who shed it. Luther calls those who do such things 'murderers,' and he uses these terms four times, all in the early part of the letter. In addition to speaking of the biblical and legal synecdoche for life (blood), Luther's *Geschichte* of Henry's murder describes the events candidly, concretely, and vividly enough to characterize the murders (and murderers) in unmistakably derogatory terms. The mob who attacked Henry were peasants, about five hundred of them, drunk on three barrels of Hamburg beer.[114]

(2) Not surprisingly, Luther's references to Henry are affectionate and praiseworthy.[115] Here was a fellow Augustinian, trained at Wittenberg, with whom Luther had a lot in common. Moreover, the discourse directly addresses the bereaved congregation at Bremen, and more indirectly, all Evangelicals. Accordingly, Luther is gentle and affectionate with his readers in the letter, as we have come to expect.[116] Yet the complimentary references are strategic, in that they vary according to audience and context of the discourse.

---

followers who by faith are made perfect in death" (268). No hint of such an interpretation is found in his Psalm lectures of 1513–1515 (*LW* 10:91), so we may conjecture that events subsequent to that time have influenced Luther to read this Psalm differently than he did then, although he may have also been influenced by Jewish sources and by Jerome (cf. 268, note 7).

[113] Whether it is Henry's 'precious [*theure*]' blood or the saints' blood, having innocent blood (*unschuldigen Blute*) shed for the cause of Christ is an advantageous event for the sufferers, because it confirms (*bezeuget*), certifies (*gewis machten*), and seals (*versigelt*) the Gospel.

[114] "They broke into the parsonage and, in the manner of drunken, senseless peasants, smashed everything in sight—cans, pots, clothing, cups" (*LW* 32:283). These 'wretched creatures,' these 'poor, miserable, drunken people' bind Henry, drag him away, beat him over the skull with a rapier, stab him "in the sides, the back, the arms, and wherever they could get at him, not just once, but as often as he attempted to speak" (286). They tied him to a ladder, raised him up to the fire, and 'roasted him on the coals' (286).

[115] In the letter Luther stresses relationship—of Henry to his fellow believers: usually he simply calls him 'Henry' but also "the sainted Brother Henry of Zütphen, your evangelist"; later 'your Henry,' and again, 'the sainted Henry.' Luther does not mention him at all in the Ninth Psalm exposition, but in the *Geschichte* he usually calls him 'Brother Henry' (seven times), 'the good Henry' (seven times), 'good Brother Henry' (twice), and on the last page he calls him 'the good martyr of Christ' (three times), 'the martyr of Christ,' the 'holy martyr' (twice).

[116] The *petitio* is directed to "dear friends in Christ, at Bremen"; the *narratio* begins, 'Dearly beloved in Christ'; the exhortation, at the end of the letter, to take the Ninth Psalm as comfort, is directed to 'my dear sirs and friends.'

(3) Throughout the entire document Luther stresses the role of the Word of God. Not only does he use the phrase with abandon, but as we trace how he uses it we find this discourse consistent with previous documents: First, Luther sees the times[117] as an exciting period of the demonstration and confirmation of the Word with great deeds, so that (alluding to Acts 2:47) people are shedding their blood, suffering imprisonment, being driven from their homes. The pattern 'of a true Christian life' has reappeared, which is costly and precious in God's sight.[118] The sheer number of times Luther uses the phrases *Word of God*, *God's Word*, *his Word*, *thy word* (when paraphrasing Scripture), *the Word*, *Scripture*, and *holy Scripture* is itself telling of his emphasis: 5 times in the letter, 11 times (out of 20 verses) in the psalm exposition; 27 times in the *Geschichte*.[119] In Luther's account of the actual kidnapping, torture, and murder (*LW* 32:283–286), the Word or the Scriptures are scarcely mentioned. That is true not only because the punishment has begun but also because Luther has previously established, in some detail, what topics Henry had preached and how his congregation had responded.[120]

---

[117] '[I]n this time [*dieser Zeyt*]'; 'in our day [*Und nu widder*].'

[118] Luther's proof texts offer a clever rhetorical tactic: in the first text (Ps. 116:15) his German syntax alters the Vulgate's, using hyperbaton to emphasize the predicate ("Costly in the Lord is the death of his saints [*Köstlich ist fur dem Herrn der Todt seyner Heyligen*]"); in the second (Ps. 72:14) Luther also alters the Vulgate syntax (Their blood is precious in his sight. [*Yhr Blut ist köstlich fur seynen Augen*]"), thereby creating a chiasmus—costly, death: blood, costly (*WA* 18:224.21–24).

[119] When we look carefully at the context of these uses, we learn more: we have, hear, and read the pure [*lauter*] Word of God (*LW* 32:265); martyrdom is suffered for the sake of God's Word (266); to preserve the Word of God (266); only for God's Word will God's martyrs [*Gottes Marterer*] die (267). In the psalm exposition Luther argues that the Word of God is the just cause which the godless oppose (v. 4); thy Word punishes and converts the godless (v. 5); His Word and kingdom will stand (v. 7); through his Word he leads and teaches the world justly (v. 8); those who seek Him will hold fast to his Word (v. 10); his Word must be preached (v. 11); God uses persecution and martyrdom to strengthen his Word (v. 15); the Lord does not forsake his Word (v. 16); one should judge circumstances only according to his Word (v. 18); let thy Word be heard (v. 19); dependence upon God alone is learned only from the public preaching [*eusserlich gepredigt*] of the Word (v. 20).

[120] In about a dozen lines Luther takes one-third of the space to report on four different sermons, preached on two different occasions, giving their titles or scriptural basis (in Latin), devoting twice as much space then to describe how Henry argued these texts and with what degree of persuasion: "He preached with such spirit that everyone was astonished and prayed God earnestly to let them keep such a preacher a long time.... All this he taught with such spirit that everyone marveled and thanked God fervently for sending them such a preacher. For they now saw plainly how they had been duped by the monks and priests" (*LW* 32:281).

(4) Luther offers the names of many attackers and plotters, giving details of their actions. The first group named, as sharing the overall blame, is 'the monks' (*LW* 32:272) and sometimes 'the papists' (276) and 'the devil and his followers' (278). To this group Luther adds the 'canons' and 'priests,' later the 'bishop,' two of his councilors, one of which was the suffragan bishop, and a Dominican (274). Then he mentions Lady Margaret, a provincial synod at Buxtehude, the monks of the Black Cloister (called Jacobins), stirred up by Augustine Torneborch and Master John Snicken (278).[121] Moreover, amongst all the specific perpetrators fingered, Luther also describes valiant defense actions on Henry's behalf carried out not only by the 'wise and honorable council' at Bremen, but also a small handful of others.[122]

(5) Luther uses dialogue very sparingly, but when he does it supplies not only liveliness to the narrative but also 'evidence' that would be far less potent in non-dialogue form. Of course, his most common form of dialogue is when he quotes Scripture, and in preaching he frequently quotes unnamed objectors or listeners, both of which serve as sounding boards for the audience's ideas to be considered. But in the *Geschichte* Luther also occasionally inserts language into the mouths of characters in his narrative. Near the end of the section detailing the proceedings, he uses a second bit of dialogue—this one another attempt at reasoned argument, this time by the prior, who would have nothing of delays. By

---

[121] Accusations were supported by Master Günter and Peter Hannen (*LW* 32:279), a Dominican, Doctor William (281), the 'gray monks,' who summoned several regents—Peter Nannen, Peter Swin, Claus Roden (only Nannen is identified as a culprit; Swin later intervened on Henry's behalf, and nothing precise is said of Roden). As ringleaders (*heubt leute*), Luther named: Peter Nannen, Peter Swin's son, Henning of Lunden, John Holm, Lorenz Hannemann, Ludwig Hannemann, Bostel John Preen, Claus of Weslingburen, Brosi John of Wodkenhausen, Marquard Kramer of Henstedt, Ludecke John of Wessling, and Peter Grossvogt of Hemmingstedt (282). During the actual capture and torture there was a traitor (Henning's Hans); one who dragged Henry along (John Balke); a cooperating priest named Reimer Hozek; other priests—Simon, of Altenworden, and Christian, of Neuenkirchen (284); and a magistrate Schoesser Maes, who pronounced sentence (285). Finally, one of the ringleaders, John Holm, is named twice as inflicting blows, including the final lethal blow (286).

[122] 'Pastor Nicolas Boye and other good Christians' of Meldorf, who called Henry to preach (*LW* 32:276); Peter Detlefs, one of the Bremen council, who spoke up at the proceedings at Heide, that there was insufficient evidence against Henry at that time (280); Peter Swin, who tried to support allowing the congregation to hold Henry accountable to the Word (282); an unnamed woman who wept at the dragging off of Henry (285); Claus Jungen's wife (who was also a sister of one of the ringleaders!), who offered to take Henry's place at the fire and also promised to pay a bond of a thousand gulden if the execution could be delayed until a proper trial was conducted (285).

including this little 'speech' of the prior, Luther supplies a potent piece of evidence for Henry's innocence and persuasiveness, for the prior's remark seems to confirm previous conclusions Luther shared.[123]

Luther put his most damning dialogue in the account of the killing itself. Thirteen separate statements are recorded, most of them spoken by Henry's attackers. As with some Gospel accounts of Jesus' crucifixion, Luther often juxtaposes Henry's own comments (or that of a sympathetic onlooker) to the vicious remarks of mob members. When heard together, each remark draws sharper clarity from its opposite—in the presence of reason and innocence, a harsh remarks seems even more callous and brutal; seen against cruelty, gentle responses shine more brightly.[124]

While the document ends with the *Geschichte*, we must recall Luther's words at its beginning, following the exposition of the psalm. He wanted no retribution, no desire for revenge. Much as with previous documents we have examined, Luther speaks of the good that Henry's death can accomplish: (1) with the metaphors of spark (*Funke*) and fire (*Fewr*) to speak of the increasing benefit that can come from this event, Luther urges friendship and kindness toward those in Dithmarschen; (2) he says many there are sorry this happened in their land, and they should be

---

[123] "[A] majority of the younger clergy they sent admitted that such doctrine and preaching were the truth and were from God, which no one could oppose. They added that they had never in their lives heard such teaching from any man" (*LW* 32: 276) [das der meyste hauffen yhrer Capellan, die sie hin fandten, bekant haben, das solche lere und predigt die warheyt und von Gott sey, der niemand widerstehen könde, denn sie hyr leben lang von keynem menschen solche lere gehöret hetten] (*WA* 18:232.10–13). "He preached with such spirit that everyone was astonished and prayed God earnestly to let them keep such a preacher a long time.... All this he taught with such spirit that everyone marveled and thanked God fervently for sending them such a preacher" [mit solchem geyst, das sichs yderman verwundert, und Gott mit vleys betten, yhn solchen prediger lang zu lassen.... und das alles mit solchem geyst, das yderman sich verwundert, und Gott vleyssig danckten, das er yhn solchen prediger zugeschickt hette (*WA* 18:236.15–16, 20–22). The prior's statement is also highly reminiscent of similar remarks by Jewish leaders who resented the success of Jesus with the common people (John 7:46).

[124] "'Kill him! Kill him!'.... But others shouted, 'Let him go! We have no orders to capture him'" [schlah todt, schlah todt..... Dan ander teyl schrey, man solt yhn gehen laffen, denn sie hetten keynen befelh, yhn zu fangen] (*WA* 18:238.9–13). In response to a lose-lose question of venue, "Henry answered, 'If I have taught or done anything un-Christian you may indeed punish me for it. God's will be done!' Master Günther replied, 'Listen to him, dear friends, he wants to die in Dithmarschen'" [Antwort Henricus: hab ich was unchristlichs geleret odder gehandelt, künden sie mich wol drumb straffen, der wille Gottes geschehe. Antwort M. Günter: hört, lieben freunde, er will ynn Diedmar sterben] (*WA* 18:239.5–7).

comforted and helped; and (3) the people of Bremen are to comfort themselves with the psalm. Luther uses his typically Pauline *conclusio*, adding boldly that Henry's blood has sealed the doctrine to which they should hold fast, and that they should follow gladly in Henry's footsteps, "if God should demand it" (*LW* 32:272). Meanwhile, in Freiburg in Ducal Saxony, Luther's letter was read in public. It touched off violent reactions by the old believers, who "were outraged that the heretic had been called a saint."[125]

VIII. *A Letter of Consolation to the Christians at Halle (1527)*

In May 1527 Luther learned of the sudden death of a young pastor friend, George Winkler, living near Halle. By this time he had written several documents that responded to executions and murders of Evangelicals, which he identified as Christian martyrs. The Peasant War was over, Luther and Katy had been married for two years and had one child, Hans, with another, Elizabeth, on the way. Plague had broken out in Wittenberg, and the University was moved to Jena; however, Luther refused to leave town, choosing instead to stay and minister to the sick. Moreover, he himself was not well, and illness delayed his response to the death of his friend. Winkler, formerly a zealous papist, now turned to Luther's teaching and was canon of the *Stiftkirche* in Halle. Earlier in 1527 he had been charged with administering the sacrament in both kinds (bread and cup) but was then released by his friend, Archbishop Albrecht of Mainz (1490, 1514–1545). Lured away from his companions on the return trip to Halle, Winkler was murdered on 23 April.[126]

While we do not know precisely what Albrecht's attitude toward Winkler was, Luther believed that Albrecht was implicated in the murder, the responsibility for which he attributed directly to the cathedral chapter at Mainz. Yet Luther and others did not want to accuse the Archbishop directly, and he still hoped to influence Albrecht for the Reformation cause. However, because the doctrinal issue of sacrament in both kinds was involved, Luther's response was particularly blunt. *Tröstung an die Christen zu Halle über Herr Georgen ihres Predigers Tod* was printed in Wittenberg by Hans Lufft in 1527, and in five subsequent

---

[125] Martin Brecht, *Martin Luther*, 2:349.
[126] *LW* 43:141.

editions the same year.[127] Luther's *Tröstung* can be seen as follows:
I. *Salutatio* (*LW* 43:145; *WA* 23:403.3–4); II. *Narratio* (*LW* 43:145–146;
WA 23:403.5–404.31); III. *Petitio* (*LW* 43:146–151; *WA* 23:403.32–
413.2); IV. *Apologia* on Communion in Both Kinds [not included in my
analysis that follows] (*LW* 43:151–160; *WA* 23:413.3–423.5); V. *Petitio*,
continued (*LW* 43:160–164; *WA* 23:423.6–429.24); VI. *Exhortatio* (*LW*
43:164–165; *WA* 23:429.25–431.27).

I. Luther's *salutatio* is typically Pauline, but it has two dissimilarities
from others we have seen him use in previous comforting and martyrological documents: (1) The signature, 'Martinus Luther,' does not
include the epithet of 'preacher at Wittenberg.' Without further research,
one can only guess why that is so, but we do note that Luther does
not as frequently mention preaching or the Word, not even where we
might expect it more—in the *apologia* on both kinds in the sacrament.
However, he does stress the preaching of the Word in the *narratio*, as
we shall see below. Further, it is now four years after the first martyrs,
and Luther does not dwell as much on the flowering or flaming of
the Gospel in these times as he did earlier. Yet we will see later an
apocalyptic motif; (2) Luther includes the epithet 'our Lord and *Savior*,'
which is unusual, *Savior* being found in only 10–15% of the letters of
consolation in Tappert.

II. The *narratio* notes circumstances for writing the letter of comfort,
for which Luther has dual outcomes in mind, both to 'admonish and
comfort' (*LW* 43:145; *WA* 23:403.6), and he identifies what happened to
Magister Georgen (as he typically calls him) as murder five times in these
21 lines. Yet even before he mentions the victim by name, Luther first
identifies the villain: *der Satan* (three times mentioned). Moreover, his
admonition and comfort is for the loss of a 'good and excellent man'
and a 'steadfast preacher of God's word,' and after a lapse of several
months he writes because he can no longer delay. In these remarks
of Luther we note several expressions for how truth must be uttered
orally.[128]

---

[127] *WA* 23:403–434 prints, on alternating pages, a critical edition of the text of the
original manuscript and that of the printed editions. I shall follow the printed editions,
because the text of the manuscript is fragmentary. Therefore, succeeding pages of the
text will skip a page in between; i.e., 403, 405, etc.

[128] Luther could not 'remain silent [*zu schweigen*]'; Winkler's blood allows the holy
word of God to be 'declared and made known [*bezeuget und bekand*]'; Luther wants to
use his writing to help 'shout out to the heavens [*ruffen und schreien gen Hymel*]' to prevent 'concealment [*geschwigen*]' of the murder; so that God will 'hear our cry [*geschrey*

III. The *petitio*, or the content of the purpose section, tries to provide information to readers that will bring comfort and satisfaction for them, a 'knowledge is power' ('Demons live in the dark') strategy that counselors often invoke.[129] Luther's goals in this section are: (A) to implicate Satan as the chief villain, through explaining how his dominion operates, and to speculate, through argument and evidence, upon what persons might have been involved in the murder of Winkler; (B) to establish and celebrate Winkler's innocence of wrongdoing against authority, thereby attempting to refute any allegations of heresy or sedition; (C) to explore the circumstances surrounding and motives for the killing, asserting that it was for a reformation doctrine (communion in both kinds), upon which he will later expound; (D) to persuade readers to realize that George is better off now and that they should pray for the perpetrators; and (E) to convince readers that these killings are signs that God is removing his elect before calamity comes to unbelievers.

For goal (A) Luther addresses his readers as 'dear friends'—already the third such endearment thus far—offering to provide 'comfort and satisfaction' for both them and his own people.[130] His explanation tries to show how Satan controls this world, primarily through the twin enemies of murder and lying, which Luther finds first in his paraphrase of John 14:30; 16:11 and his citation of John 8:44.[131] Satan performs his murders repeatedly through deception; Luther attributes virtually every sudden or unnatural death to Satan ('such murders and misfortunes'). Since he is 'a prince of this world,' we must realize we are, in Luther's analogy, guests at Satan's inn, over which hangs the

---

erhöre],' just as he heard Abel's blood cry out from the ground (Gen. 4:10), a biblical metaphor Luther used in reference to the burning of Henry and John in 1523; Luther compares Winkler's blood to a divine 'seed' that will be sown on earth by Satan but will sprout forth a hundred other true preachers and do a 'thousand times more' damage to Satan, just like he could not 'listen [*hören*]' to many more; as the pope did not want Huss to 'whisper [*mucken*]' in one little corner, now he won't be able to prevent 'shouting [*schreien*]' to the four corners of the earth; the 'outcry [*Auffhören*]' has not stopped yet (*WA* 23:403.14–32).

[129] Dr. Phill McGraw, Columbia Broadcasting System.

[130] One particularly striking phrase occurs when Luther says that Satan inflames princes and kings against one another until there is such bloodshed that it seems as though men were 'born for nothing but killing [*zu Morden geboren*].' Satan's greatest delight (*am Liebsten*) is in murdering those who proclaim Christ's word, for to do that is to expose Satan's rule and identity as murderer and liar (*Morder und Lügener*), lying being what he next explores (*LW* 43:146 wrongly translates *Euch aber und uns* [*WA* 23:403.3] as 'But you and I').

[131] *LW* 43:146 omits chapter 8 in Luther's citation.

sign, 'Death and Untruth.' He elaborates on Satan's domain by enumerating instances of violent deaths and through an accumulation of
violent phrases, in which he uses 'murder' seven times in 11 lines.[132]
Following such an emphasis on Satan's *murderous* agenda, Luther next
explains the Devil's *deceptive* tactics. Given that his comforting strategy
is to expose Satan to his readers, so that they recognize his schemes
and understand his ways, 'In the same way' Satan unwittingly reveals
his lies in the deceptions of heresy, disbelief, and factionalism.[133] In
wrapping up the first goal Luther again loudly accuses *Das Capitel zu
Mentz* of consenting to the murder, if not ordering it directly, by their
lack of vigorous investigation and prosecution, especially since they have
more legal power than the bishop. This strong accusation against the
alleged perpetrators also helps to build a case for George's innocence:
what *they* did (seven third person plural pronouns, in addition to all the
nouns, in 12 lines) was illegal and unjust, and readers can take comfort
in that (*WA* 23:409.12–24).

Goal (B) of the *petitio* is to exonerate Winkler of any charge of insub-
ordination—against clerical and divine authority. This short section (17
lines) makes a strong argument that George's loyalty both to God and
the bishop was above reproach, and Luther does some interesting things
with scriptural evidence in making this argument. First, he claims that,
in the face of danger to his life, George obeyed 'his true Lord Jesus
Christ.' In making this obvious point, Luther uses the word 'obedient

---

[132] *WA* 23:405.1–26. *LW* 43:146 wrongly reads 'liar and a murderer'; Luther stays
with the order of John 8:44.

[133] Observe Luther's blend of repetition (anaphora) and epithet as he lists some of
Satan's subtleties, and notice how Luther moves from third person, to first person, to
second person, as he brings this exposition on Satan back to the case at hand, Winkler's
murder: All of this is sheer deviltry, intended to seduce souls and to lead them back
to damnation, to say nothing of hidden temptations by which the devil attacks each
person, particularly a person's faith, *with doubt, with false intuitions, with false comforts, with
false fears*, etc., for he is the very father, master, and juggler of lies, so leading us in
thought and imagination that were God not with us in strength and mercy, he would
lead astray, if possible, even the elect [Matt. 24:24]. He dealt with you in this same
manner in Halle [Welchs auch alles sind eitel teuffels werck, die seelen zu verfuren
und verdammen, on was seines heimlichen anfechtens ist, damit er einen iglichen
ynn sonderheit ynn seinem glauben ansicht mit zweifel, mit falschem eingeben, mit
falschem trost, mit falschem schrecken etc.: wie er denn ein vater das ist ein meister
und tausantkunstler ist auff lugen zur dencken und furzubilden, das wo Gott nicht
starck und gnediglich uber uns hellt, auch die ausserweleten ynn yrthum fallen . Eben
also thut er mit euch auch itzt zu Halle:] (*WA* 23:405.30–407.5). *LW* 43:147 fails to
retain the repetition of preposition with [*mit*] in Luther's tripled 'false', omitting the
first 'with' [doubt] altogether.

[*gehorsam*]' four times, the crucial time in the close paraphrase of Phil. 2:8. Second, he reasons that because George's actions were obedient to Paul's words in Rom. 13:1, he was obedient to the word of God and, therefore, died in the Lord.[134] Third, Luther argues that Winkler's previous record of loyalty to the bishop speaks loudly that he 'loved his superior' and was ignominiously 'rewarded' for that.[135]

Goal (C) of the *petitio* is that Luther expose further the details of what happened to George. Therefore, he proceeds to narrate a brief account (18 lines) of the capture and murder.[136] His report emphasizes the plotting and deviousness of the villains, over against the vulnerability and innocence of George. Speaking entirely in third person, Luther brackets the story by his interpretation of motive ("had to defend themselves so that no further inroads would be made")[137] and outcome ("earning for themselves a crown in hell, in so far as they do not repent, and they and their masters will be crowned in hell by the devil himself").[138] Far different from his detailed account of the burning of Henry at Dithmarschen two years earlier, Luther's account here has little direct evidence of witnesses to rely on, so he does not give names but rather attributes blame to four categories of participant in the planned capture and killing (Satan, Bishops, unknown attackers and accomplices, a traveling companion).[139] At the end of the narrative

---

[134] Luther's use of *singen* harks back to the hymn commemorating the burnings of Henry and John (1523), and he has here changed the plural of Rev. 14:13 ('blessed are they...') to a singular, to apply directly to George.

[135] Luther's irony turns to bitter sarcasm: "People like him are supposed to be murdered by the church officials, but whores and knaves ought rather to be honored by them" [Solche leute sollen von geistlichen stifften ermordet werden, Aber huren und buben sollen dafur geehret werden] (*WA* 23:411.8–9).

[136] *WA* 23:411.15–413.2).

[137] "...das nicht weiter einriffe" (*WA* 23:411.14).

[138] "...Und haben die hellischen kron, wo sie nicht bussen, verdienet, welche yhn auch werden wird sampt yhren herren und dem teuffel ynn der helle" (*WA* 23:411.32–413.1). He uses several descriptive terms to accentuate the stealth of the deed: 'secretly and treacherously [*heimlich und verretherlich*],' Winkler was summoned into 'another diocese, Mainz [*ein anders, als Mentz ist*],' where he was tricked into 'ambush [*Anschlag*],' detained 'alone [*allein*],' and directed into the 'trap of the concealed murderers [*bestelleten Strauchmördern*].'

[139] The first evidence Luther uses that George is better off (as people say today), is a blend of reasoning and authority. As he prepares for his textual support, Luther uses balanced, parallel clauses (with anaphora), preceded and followed by rhetorical questions: "For what is certain in this life? Today we stand; tomorrow we fall. Today one has the true faith; tomorrow he falls into error. Today one hopes; tomorrow he despairs. How many good people fall into the error of the enthusiasts? How many will fall in the future through such sectarian errors?" (*LW* 43:160). Three remarks of Luther

Luther climaxes the account of the capture with a precise, sobering, and ironic statement: "And so, about two miles from Aschaffenburg, these great heroes and papal knights set upon this good man and stabbed him to death..." (*WA* 23:411.31f.).[140]

IV. *Apologia*: Prior to completing the last two goals of the *Petitio*, next is Luther's defense for the orthodoxy of communion in both kinds, a case that I shall omit.

V. *Petitio*, continued: As Luther ends his discourse on communion in both kinds and returns to his *petitio*, he picks up the point he had left—goal (C)—which, we recall, started out to establish the cause for which George was killed, an essential point for the legitimacy of his martyrdom. As with previous transitions, Luther reminds his readers that his purpose is to provide comfort; he has already given five such reminders.[141] Now comes the sixth, which reconnects to the earlier argument that George's obedience to the Word equals dying *in the Lord*: "Let us return to ourselves and to pastor George, comforting ourselves all the more and rejoicing that Christ has found him worthy to die for his word and his truth" (*WA* 23:423.6–8).

(Goal D) Yet Luther goes much farther in this point than merely arguing that George's killing equals authentic martyrdom. His point is that George would not *want* to live again, that his death results in a valued good for him, especially when considered against the fragility and tragic nature of life on earth. This is very consistent with Luther's earlier point about Satan's domain as a prince of this world. Luther even uses hypothetical dialogue from Winkler himself to argue that "If you loved me you would certainly rejoice that I was permitted to go from death to eternal life in this way" (*WA* 23:423.13–17), an argument commonly still used nowadays to bolster the spirits of grieving rela-

---

make clear that he was being cautious with his evidence: "It has been reported to me that...[*Denn also bin ich bericht*]"; "he is supposed to have said...[*er gesagt sol haben*]"; "That is as much as I have learned about the matter [*So viel hab ich dauon erfaren*]" (*WA* 23:411.17 413.2).

[140] "Also haben sie bey zwo meilen von Asschenburg auff den guten man gerannt und yhn erstochen."

[141] "[I]t has long been my intention to write to you to admonish and comfort [*Vermanung und Trost*] you" (*LW* 43:145); "But you and we, dear friends, may take comfort and satisfaction [*trosten und zu friden*]" (*LW* 43:146); "Let this be the first fact of our comfort [*Trostes*]" (*LW* 43:147); "A second comforting fact [*trostet*] in this murder is" (*LW* 43:149); "I am compelled, to discuss the matter...for our own strengthening and comfort [*zu Stercke und Trost*]" (*LW* 43:151).

tives.[142] The authority and wisdom of both St. Cyprian and the Psalter are invoked, as Luther even alludes to the language of 1 Peter 5:8 in warning readers of the dangers awaiting believers today.[143] Speaking in first person—both singular and plural—Luther models the desired attitude by: (1) giving thanks; and (2) singing the "beautiful and comforting words from Sapi [entia] 4 [:10–15, 17–18]" (*LW* 43:161f.).[144] So, again, Luther has reminded his readers of his goal—comfort—and he has tried to demonstrate its origin (the Word of God) and model its activity (he sings).[145]

Goal (E) for Luther is to argue that such murders are a 'sure indication' that God is preparing a great catastrophe for unbelievers. In both His acceptance of the death of the one who pleased him (Wisdom of Solomon) and with His permitting disaster to fall, God is in control. Luther argues that God removes his own for their own protection, and he invokes the stories of Lot being taken from Sodom (Gen. 19), Noah and his family surviving in the ark (Gen. 8), and King Josiah being buried peacefully before the Chaldeans overthrew Jerusalem (2 Chron. 35). Luther summarizes the principle at work in these examples: "In this way he has at all times first saved his own from among the godless, and then let loose his anger mightily upon the unbelieving" (*WA* 23:427.11–13).[146] As he then finishes the *petitio*, Luther moves toward his concluding *exhortatio*. The purpose is to urge readers to mourn and pray for the tyrants who did this, a response both difficult to do and

---

[142] "Denn was ist yn diesem leben sichers, heute stehet einer, morgen ligt er, heute gleubt einer recht, morgen fellet er ynn yrthum, heute hofft einer, morgen verzweifelt einer. Wie gar viel seiner leute fallen itzt teglich ynn der Schwermer yrthum, Wie viel wird yhr noch fallen durch dieselbigen und andere kunsstige rotten."

[143] *LW* 43:160 fails to record Luther's citation (*wie der Psalter klagt*) at *WA* 23:423.21 and does not catch the language of 1 Peter 5:8 ('roaring lions' [*die grimmigen Lewen*]) as the Weimarer Ausgabe editors do.

[144] Luther's own words, prior to the quotation, are poetic: *und singe von hertzen den schonen tröstlichen spruch* (*WA* 23:425.19–20).

[145] The quotation from Sapientia (Wisdom of Solomon) is lengthy and speaks obliquely of 'one who pleased God' through his innocence, God having removing him from an evil environment, leaving others to misunderstand what has happened. The quotation seems to provide an allegory that interprets Winkler's blessed fate and survivors' confused feelings as expected and normal for a legitimate martyr. The final line of the quote (*WA* 23:425.30) nicely effects the apparent paradox, through inclusio (syntactically arranging the opposing terms at the beginning and ending of the sentence), clear only in German and literal translation: *Sie sehen und achten sein nicht, Aber der Herr spottet yhr* ("*They* see and understand him not, but the Lord mocks *them*").

[146] "Und so fort an hatt er allewege die seinen zuvor aus dem Gottlosen hauffen geriffen und darnach lassen gegen seinen zorn uber die Gottlosen mit aller macht."

perfectly consistent with the previous arguments, especially with the
line we just quoted above.[147] Forthrightly insisting, in first person plural,
that 'we must do the same,' Luther quotes Matt. 6:12 in the Lord's
Prayer. His language in this part (18 lines) contains seventeen uses of
the first person plural pronoun; only six of them are found in Bible
quotations. He concludes the *petitio* with a rhetorical question that he
answers with a series of doublets.[148] This appeal to exceed the forgiving and *quid pro quo* behavior of sinners is without question something
Luther got from Luke 6:32–34, where 'sinners' is used four times in
3 verses, as Jesus makes three comparisons of sinners' and believers'
behavior ('love...do good...lend to...').

VI. *Exhortatio* (*LW* 43:164–165): Luther concludes the letter of comfort with 35 lines that appeal to readers, in second person, to guard
their attitudes and to work toward the repentance of their persecutors.
In the previous 66 lines, while he spoke of the events being a sign of
impending calamity for unbelievers, Luther did not utter the words
murder or *assassin*. Now, with his fifth endearment of the document
(*lieben Herrn und Freunde*), he implores his struggling readers to follow
his scriptural admonitions. His opening line is very similar in meaning
and style to Paul in Rom. 12:1.[149] Luther's recommendation is two-fold:

---

[147] In a volley of doublets, Luther outlines the response he wants: they should 'praise
and thank God [*Gotte loben und dancken*]' since he has called martyrs away in such a
'wonderful and merciful fashion [*wunderbarlich und barmhertziglich holet*]'; they ought not
become 'angry and impatient [*zurnen und ungedültig*]' with the 'tyrants and mercenaries
[*Tyrannen und Wueterichen*]' but rather 'pray and weep [*bitten und uns yhr jamern*]' (*WA*
23:429.9–12). Luther's proof texts not only provide authority and precedent for such
behavior, but they contain doublet language as well: immediately after 'pray and weep,'
Luther follows with 'as Christ teaches us in Matt. 6' (*LW* 43:163). Both *LW* 43:163 (in
the text) and *WA* 23:429.11 (in the margin) cite Matt. 5:44, while in the text Luther
plainly cites Matt. 6. I believe both editors are incorrect and that Luther cited the
wrong text. The text I think Luther really had in mind is Luke 6, for his quote is a
conflation of Luke 6:27 and 6:35. These two verses, when put together, allow Luther to
juxtapose the striking responses he advocates alongside—actually to precede—the bad
behavior done by the enemy: pray for...those who wrong and persecute; bless...those
who curse; do well...to those who hate.
[148] He urges readers to exceed the forgiveness of 'heathens and sinners [*Heiden und
sunder*],' even 'murderers and criminals [*Morder und allerley Buben*],' by forgiving more
than just 'friends and decent people [*Freunden und guten gesellen*].' They are to forgive
their enemies' debts (*Feinden Schuld vergeben*), pray for them and do good to them (*fur sie
bitten und dazu wolthun*), for this is the 'true Christian virtue [*eine rechte Christliche Tugent*]'
(*WA* 23:429.17–23).
[149] In fact, it is stronger: 'Accordingly, I beg and exhort you...' [*Dem nach bitte auch
ich und vermane euch*] (*WA* 23:429.25). In acknowledging their suffering ("this disturbing
matter, which rightly pains and grieves you so [*diese verdriesliche sache, darynn euch billich*]

pursue a righteous cause and take consolation from Matt. 5:10, which he paraphrases, "'Blessed are those who are persecuted for righteousness' sake.'" Luther's closing paragraph of the *exhortatio*, as with the first, uses a form of the word 'exhortation [*Vermanung*],' and he appeals for his readers' acceptance of his advice, based on his invoking of Christ's suffering on the cross: because He suffered, we should not escape suffering; God gets to decide who suffers, when, and how. Luther's ending invokes the same 'Christ our Lord and Savior' as did the *salutatio*.

IX. *To Leonhard Kaiser (20 May 1527)*

A native of Raab, in Upper Austria,[150] Leonhard Kaiser (also Kaeser, Käser, Keyser; ca. 1480–1527) was a Lutheran pastor who was jailed and eventually burned for his beliefs.[151] In late 1524, while a vicar at Waizenkirchen,[152] Kaiser was forced by authorities of the Passau diocese to abandon his evangelical preaching. So he moved to Wittenberg and began to study at the University, from which he spread Luther's message back to his homeland via books and letters he sent to acquaintances. When he received news in early 1527 that his father was gravely ill, Kaiser returned home to Raab, helped bury his father, and remained with his mother for five more weeks. During this time he was openly preaching about his convictions and was arrested in March. After imprisonment and interrogation by an imperial commission that included Luther's opponent at the Leipzig debate in 1519, Johann Eck of Ingolstadt (1486–1543), Kaiser was charged. When word reached Wittenberg, Luther requested that Saxon Elector John the Steadfast and Margrave Casimir of Brandenburg intervene; however, not even they could prevail. Luther wrote a letter of consolation on 20 May, and on 16 August Leonard Kaiser was executed in Schärding.[153] After the execution, Kaiser's death was the subject of exchanges from both

---

wehe und leid]"), he advises them—through double authority—to leave vengeance to the one who judges justly (*da recht richtet*), "as Saint Peter teaches [1 Pet. 2:23], which Christ has done [*wie S. Petrus leret, das Christus gethan hat*]" and steer a middle course between wrong extremes (*WA* 23:429.26f.).

[150] About 25 kilometers southeast of Schärding.

[151] *WABr* 4:204. At the time, this area was part of Bavaria.

[152] Innviertel; another 25 kilometers further east, toward Linz.

[153] Tappert, 213f.; Martin Brecht, *Martin Luther*, 2:349f.; *OER*, s. v. "Kaiser, Leonhard," by Robert Kolb.

sides, including those from Eck and Luther.[154] Luther's is an expanded edition of a description of Kaiser's death, which saw nine editions in six cities by the end of 1527.[155]

What we examine here is Luther's short letter (28 lines)—filled with scriptural language, especially Paul's—intended to encourage Kaiser. Luther blames no one but Satan for this imprisonment, and he says nothing about praying for the captors (Tappert, 214f.; *WABr* 4:205). Since there was still hope for Kaiser's release, it makes sense to have made no accusations. Given that the letter focuses exclusively on the imprisoned reader's state of mind, it would seem that Luther believed that death was probably imminent for Kaiser: three times he mentions being 'free' (lines 9 [twice], 23), and none of them speaks plausibly of tangible release. Moreover, four times referring to it specifically (lines 4, 8 [twice], 23), Luther most assuredly placed Kaiser's fate—whatever it be—in the *will* of God.

The *salutatio* (lines 1–3) is noteworthy for three reasons: (1) Luther omits his name until the end of the letter, thus consistent with his pattern of having abandoned classical form in the early part of the decade; (2) abundant epithets surrounding Kaiser's full name (*D. Leonhardo Keyser*) identify not only the reader's roles, but also the respect and affection with which Luther holds him;[156] and (3) the typical Pauline greeting ('grace and peace') is bolstered with an expression that proves significant for the body of the letter: 'grace, strength [*fortitudinem*], and peace in Christ.' Although Luther does not remind his reader here that his name literally means 'lion-hearted,' the notion of *strength* is a dominant feature of the *petitio/exhortatio*.[157] As with "To Lambert Thorn" (1524), the endearing greeting in the vocative—'my Leonhard'—is not part of the *salutatio* but is embedded in the first sentence of the *narratio*.

The *narratio* (lines 3–7) in this letter to a prisoner awaiting execution is not a reiteration of the facts of the case—particularly of the reader's situation—but rather is an interpretation of what the facts mean. Avoiding any mention of details of Kaiser's arrest and imprisonment, Luther

---

[154] Kolb, ibid.

[155] *Von Er Lenhard Keiser ynn Beyern, umb des Euangelii willen verbrandt, Eine selige geschicht* (*WA* 23:452–476; Benzing, Nr. 2444–2452).

[156] '[V]enerable brother in Christ [*Venerabili in Christo fratri*],' 'his faithful servant and beloved prisoner of Christ [*vincto Christi et servo eius fideli et charo*],' 'his in the Lord [*suo in Domino*].''

[157] Later Luther does this, when writing about the death of Kaiser; cf. *WABr* 4:270.1–17, cited by Martin Brecht, *Martin Luther*, 2:350.

tries to encourage his reader by offering a prophetic prediction of the outcome of the case. He does so by stringing together expressions in Pauline language.[158] That Kaiser's body is imprisoned is in accord with the will and calling of Christ, and Luther says this has happened so that Kaiser might be redeemed and become Christ's 'brother and joint heir of eternal life,' language of Paul's from Rom. 8:17.[159]

The *petitio/exhortatio* (lines 7–21)—the bulk of the letter—argues that Luther and his colleagues are grieved because of Kaiser's plight and are working and praying for his release. But the greater cause is not for Kaiser's sake alone but for others and for God's glory. This larger purpose obviously means that Kaiser might not be released, something Luther puts in God's hands.[160] He reminds Kaiser that he should be free in spirit, even if not released. However, he must remain strong, and for help in reaching that goal, Luther gives Kaiser promises from Scripture and assurances in the language of 'strength.'[161] Luther assures Kaiser that Christ is with him in the cell and will remain with him in all his 'afflictions [*tribulatione*].' Presumably, he means that Kaiser must be bold in his prayers, for especially there Satan would hinder him. For the matter of Satan's capabilities, Luther assures Kaiser that the devil not only cannot harm him but virtually loses power the more he threatens. Luther's assurance ('in the certainty that') is expressed by a single term (*certus*), set off by commas and placed in the very center of his sentence: fourteen words precede *certus*, and thirteen words follow it. Then, for clinching proof, Luther quickly strings together a series of three Scriptures, for only one of which he cites Paul, making this the only explicit scriptural attribution in the letter. The three Scriptures together offer a tidy inclusio—matching beginning with ending, forming a pair of 'book-ends': [A] a rhetorical question (RQ) that

---

[158] "That your old man [*homo tuus vetus*] should be a prisoner" borrows Paul's 'old self' phrase (there speaking of *all* Christians) from Rom. 6:6. "[F]or you and your sins [Christ] also offered up his new man [*novum suum hominem*]" uses Paul's expression from Eph. 4:24.

[159] In Rom. 8:15–17 Paul speaks of being 'children of God,' 'heirs,' and 'fellow heirs with Christ'; thus, Luther's doublet ('brother and joint heir of eternal life') is not only faithful to the context but also consistent stylistically with Paul's diction in v. 17.

[160] The idea of the earlier doublet (the 'will and calling of Christ') now comes up again, this time as 'if it be his will [*si ipse voluerit*]' and 'if it be the will of heaven [*voluntas est in coelo*].'

[161] He must be 'constantly overcoming the weakness of the flesh [*constanter infirmitatem carnis vincas*]' and should 'patiently endure with the strength of Christ [*toleres saltem per virtutem Christi*].'

would be all too real for Kaiser and which 'tests' whether Luther is right about Satan's lack of power; [B] a 'syllogism' (Syl) that proves the answer to the rhetorical question; and finally [A₁] a prolepsis (Pr), another 'test'—complete with refutation—put to the argument applied to Kaiser's situation:

> [A] (RQ): If God is for us, who can be against us? Answer: The devil? [No, because...]
>
> [B] (Syl): Maj. Prem: God has put all [created] things under Jesus' feet (Ps. 8:6).
> Min. Prem: [Satan is a created thing] (Implied).
> Conclusion: God has put Satan under Jesus' feet.
>
> [A₁] (Pr): Does Jesus' ability (*potest*) to succor (*auxilio esse*) extend to those (like Kaiser) who might succumb to the temptation to doubt his power? Yes, for even Jesus experienced, and defeated, such a temptation (perhaps in Gethsemane?).

The context of Heb. 2 supports the argument that Luther implicitly is making.

Luther's final appeals in the *petitio/exhortatio* are injunctions from Paul to 'my dearest brother [*mi charissime frater*],' a superlative endearment that sweetly elevates the intimacy of the earlier *venerabili in Christo fratri* (the more formal epithet of the heading) and *mi Leonharde*, the more personal, endearing apostrophe of the *salutatio*.[162] Luther then embellishes this quotation with his own variation on Paul's text.[163] The Benediction—along with the Place, Date, and Signature—has in fact already begun with the final appeal of the previous section, which ends with 'according to his riches in grace and glory. Amen': 'In him fare well, and pray for us, too.' The signature is the simple *Martinus Luther*, the place is *Wittembergae*, and the date is 20 May 1527.

---

[162] Luther's first injunction comes from Eph. 6:10, to which Luther attaches results that Kaiser should desire. Luther's quotation uses all the same key terms as the Pauline text in the Vulgate: 'be strong [*confortare*]' in the Lord, 'and be robust [*et esto robustus*]'—which Luther adds—'in the power of his might [*in potentia virtutis eius*].'

[163] Instead of elaborating on the 'armor of God [*arma Dei*],' as Paul does in Eph. 6:11ff., Luther drops all mention of the enemy (indeed, his last use of *Sathana* was in line 16), and he finishes the exhortation with a rich array of positive terms: "so that, whether or not you are set free, you may acknowledge, bear, love, and praise the Fatherly will of God with a good heart [*sive libereris sive minus, paternam Dei voluntatem in te agnoscas, toleres, ames ac laudes bono corde*]." Note that, despite the fact that translation requires that 'Satan' still be mentioned after line 16, Luther does so only through relative pronouns.

X. *Conclusion*

Just a few short years ago, what Brad Gregory had argued eloquently that same year, Heiko Oberman affirmed: "The modern interpreter of the martyr's baffling willingness to die is bound to hit the brick wall of total incomprehension unless he is willing to respect certain alien modes of seeing the world."[164] In this richly heterogeneous 'genre' Luther's consolation strives mostly to embolden receivers' faith, so they can endure persecution they may face (or doubts about their own faith or the rightness of their cause). He offers less 'sympathy' (if by that term we understand acknowledgement of feelings) than we will see in the consolatory letters, whose recipients do not necessarily face imminent death. Two principal ways to embolden readers are to offer eulogistic narratives of the heroic deeds of the martyred and to use Scripture to remind readers of the promises they have in Christ. In the martyrological literature Luther uses the letter, the song, the narrative, and the exposition of Scripture to comfort his readers and celebrate Christ's victory.

---

[164] Heiko A. Oberman, "Varieties of Protest," 41; Gregory, *Salvation at Stake*, 1–29.

CHAPTER FOUR

"TO WHOM SHALL WE GO? YOU HAVE THE WORDS OF ETERNAL LIFE": LUTHER'S 1532 FUNERAL SERMONS

The life spans of people in industrialized countries have witnessed the contemporary transformation—particularly in English-speaking countries—of the sacred funeral into a secular memorial.[1] Even within the walls of some Protestant churches, many services are now dominated by eulogies and testimonials of friends and family, where the focus is not on the human role in the divine plan, but rather on the personal significance of the decedent—her or his virtues, relationships, and accomplishments.[2] This transformation parallels the rise of the modern therapeutic culture, whereby death is a phenomenon rarely experienced by many adults who, unlike their ancestors, seldom plead, "Protect us, oh Lord, from plague, famine, and war!"[3] For the most part, caring for the dying is the domain of the medical profession alone, which has confined its efforts—almost exclusively devoted to extending life—primarily to the hospital. The mental health professions have claimed as their domain the study of death and dying, grief and bereavement processes, which focus on the normalcy of death and grief, and the clergy have studied at their feet. Through acknowledging the magnitude of the loss, establishing the significance of the decedent, recognizing the stages of grief along paths toward 'recovery,' laypersons are assisted in their grief 'journey' by professionals and support groups, who valiantly try to

---

[1] Tony Walter, "Secularization," in *Death and Bereavement Across Cultures*, ed. Colin Murray Parkes, Pittu Laungani and Bill Young (London, 1997), 166–190.

[2] "Even if using religious language, the funeral should be what the Australians call *life centred* [Tony Walter, *Funerals*, 20]. Without necessarily going to the extreme of the deceased participating through tape or video recorded messages, he or she should be present to the extent that mourners go away saying 'Jill would have approved of that service' or 'Jack would have enjoyed that.' Increasingly, people want to do the funeral in a way that honours the deceased as a unique individual, not the undertakers' way, or the crematorium's way, or the religious way"; Tony Walter, *The Revival of Death*, 33; Kathleen Garces-Foley and Justin S. Holcomb, "Contemporary American Funerals: Personalizing Tradition," in *Death and Religion in a Changing World*, ed. Kathleen Garces-Foley (Armonk, N.Y., 2006), 207–277.

[3] Arthur E. Imhof, *Lost Worlds: How Our European Ancestors Coped with Everyday Life and Why Life is So Hard Today*, trans. Thomas Robisheau (Charlottesville, Va., 1996), 162.

offset the loss of family and community systems that have succumbed
to pressures that value 'getting over it' and 'moving on.'

Among scholars of early modern Europe there is a resurgence of
interest in death rituals, including the funeral sermon.[4] Throughout
Christian history the funeral sermon has played a key role in the rituals of burying the dead, and it derives from the traditions of both
the *laudatio* (eulogy) and *consolatio* (speech of comfort).[5] Much recent
research has been done on the traditions of the Lutheran funeral sermon
(1550–1750), but little is known about funerals and their sermons during
the early years of the German Reformation.[6] While the traditions of
the *Leichenpredigten* are said to stem from Luther's own funeral messages,
it has yet to be shown how, or in what ways, that influence occurred.
For whatever reasons, we have only four extant funeral messages from
Luther, and they derive from two funerals, both of them for heads of
state—Frederick the Wise (1525) and John the Steadfast (1532).[7]

We need to know much more about these messages, for Luther also
addressed a 'paganizing' influence that would minimize the power and
legitimacy of grief.[8] At the same time, however, he was not shy about

---

[4] Donald L. Deffner, "Proclaiming Life in Death: The Funeral Sermon," *CTQ* 58
(1994): 5–24, especially 6, 16; John P. Ferre, "Last Words: Death and Public Self-
Expression," in *Quoting God: How Media Shape Ideas about Religion and Culture*, ed. Claire
H. Badaracco (Waco, Tex., 2005), 129–142.

[5] Siegfried Bräuer, "The Genesis and Transmission of the Texts," in *"Vom Christlichen
abschied aus diesem tödlichen leben des Ehrwirdigen Herrn D. Martini Lutheri": Drei zeitgenössische
Texte zum Tode D. Martin Luthers* (Stuttgart, 1996), 116. For background see John M.
McManamon, "The Ideal Renaissance Pope: Funeral Oratory from the Papal Court."
Archivum Historiae Pontificiae 14 (1976): 9–70.

[6] Rudolf Lenz, *De mortuis nil nisi bene? Leichenpredigten als multidisziplinäre Quelle unter
besonderer Berücksichtigung der Historischen Familienforschung, der Bildungsgeschichte und der
Literaturgeschichte.* Marburger Personalschriften-Forschungen 10 (Sigmaringen, 1990);
Studien zur deutschsprachigen Leichenpredigt der frühen Neuzeit. Marburger Personalschriften-
Forschungen 4 (Marburg, 1981); *Leichenpredigten as Quellen historischer Wissenschaften*
(Cologne, 1975); "Leichenpredigten: Eine bislang vernachlässigte Quellengattung."
Archiv für Kulturgeschichte 56 (1974): 296–312. Cornelia Niekus Moore, *Patterned Lives:
The Lutheran Funeral Biography in Early Modern Germany.* Wolfenbütteler Forschungen 111
(Wiesbaden, 2006).

[7] *LW* 51:231–255; The 1525 sermon is found in *WA* 17¹:196–227. Marius, *Martin
Luther*, comments on the 1525 sermon on pages 428–430.

[8] Eileen T. Dugan, "The Funeral Sermon as a Key to Familial Values in Early
Modern Nördlingen," *SCJ* 20 (1989): 634, considers the text to be only verses 13–14
and argues that Luther used the deceased "as an example of a model Christian in
life and death." Robert Kolb, "Burying the Brethren: Lutheran Funeral Sermons as
Life-Writing," in *The Rhetorics of Life-Writing in Early Modern Europe: Forms of Biography
from Cassandra Fedele to Louis XIV*, ed. Thomas F. Mayer and D. R. Woolf (Ann Arbor,
1995), 99, maintains that the sermons "presented a model of sober textual exposition,
with little mention of the deceased at all."

urging Christians to moderate their grief. For Luther, the comforting resources of Christ and the immeasurable hope of resurrection outweighed any amount or severity of grief here on earth. As scholars studying the social and theological dimensions of death practices, we must constantly reexamine what threats and fears persist at time of death. In what follows I examine Luther's 1532 funeral sermons, to show how he takes a medieval concern for the decedent's soul and directs it toward the faith of survivors.[9] In order to do that he must get his listeners to think about living as a dying—to sin and with Christ. For Luther, the recent death of a Christian is a concrete instantiation of the prospect of every man's death, something that is a subject of every gospel sermon. As Sin's apparent victory over the gospel, a Christian's death is really the soul's sleep as it awaits the resurrection call. Rather than representing a genre of sermons (or the promulgation of a genre) designed solely for responding to the threat that death brings to family or community, these sermons reveal characteristics more consistent with Luther's textual sermons in general. Later Lutheran funeral sermons that respond to a need to establish the significance of the decedent by praising personal virtues derive that feature from other antecedent traditions (or contemporary influences) more than from Luther's own burial messages.

I. *Context and Scope of the Sermons*

The backdrop of the sermons can be appreciated by applying Bitzer's concept of rhetorical situation—a natural context of persons, events, objects, relations, and an exigence that strongly invites utterance.[10] If we examine the situation surrounding these funeral sermons according its three constituents—exigence, audience, and constraints—we see discourse 'invited' by a rhetorical situation. Exigence is an imperfection marked by urgency, some flaw we want fixed; a rhetorical exigence is one that can be completely or partially modified by discourse. When Elector John died unexpectedly on 15 August 1532, Saxony lost a champion of

---

[9] For an outline of the medieval funeral, see Joachim Whaley, "Symbolism for the Survivors: The Disposal of the Dead in Hamburg in the Late Seventeenth and Eighteenth Centuries," *Mirrors of Mortality: Studies in the Social History of Death*, ed. Joachim Whaley (New York, 1981), 80–105, here at 82f.

[10] Lloyd F. Bitzer, "The Rhetorical Situation," *Philosophy and Rhetoric* 1 (1968): 1–14.

the Reformation.[11] The woodcut illustration on the cover of one edition
of these sermons shows the head of John the Baptist being delivered on
a platter.[12] Indicating the degree of loss felt by the people, the woodcut
is also revealing in how it symbolizes Elector John as a hero of the
faith. Additionally, any concerns for the status of John's soul and its
progress through purification would probably have been absent in the
Wittenberg of 1532. Held in the *Schloßkirche*, the funeral would be—we
might expect—a kind of state funeral that tried to reassure the people
that their government will continue.[13] The funeral message would then
address the issues of the loss of the head of state and protector of the
Reformation. We also expect that the message responded to listeners'
concerns about their own mortality; the new Elector John Frederick
had requested of Luther that he preach not only on Sunday, 18 August
(Twelfth Sunday After Trinity), but also the following Thursday, 22
August, using the same text (1 Thessalonians 4:13–18), a text he had
used only in his funeral messages.[14] If the speaker's discourse somehow
ignored these needs or failed to offer relevant words to help listeners
adapt to the loss, the exigence would remain.[15]

---

[11] Three Tabletalk entries by John Schlaginhaufen (*LW* 54:164f.) bear the date of
18 August 1532, the date of Elector John's funeral: No. 1738 has Luther saying, "How
forsaken this great prince was when he died! Neither a son, nor a cousin, nor any relative
was there. Physicians say that he died of a heart seizure." In no. 1747 Schlaginhaufen,
after the burial on 18 August, writes that the Elector died in Schweinitz (at his hunting
lodge, according to the *LW* editors), on 15 August of an apoplectic spasm. In no. 1751
Luther is recorded to have said to Katy, after the burial service, that he also wanted to
die in the same way as the Elector. When she protested, Luther answered, "Ah, dear
Katy, it happens to a person quickly, as we've seen in the case of our prince."

[12] *Zwo Predigt vber der* || *Leiche des Kurfur=* || *sten Herzog IO=* || *HANS zu Sachs-
sen.* || D. Mart. Luthers || Wittemberg, || M D XXXII. [Schlußschr.:] Gedruckt
zu Wittemberg / durch || Nickel Schirlentz / im jar MD XXXII. 24. Bl., dav.das
letzte leer. 8^0 (4^0) UB Marburg XIX d B 1034^d, XIII, 10; cited by Uwe Bredehorn
and Rudolf Lenz, p. 498. According to Benzing, p. 355, there were 5 editions of the
sermons printed in 1532–1533. The above edition seems to be Benzing, no. 3028,
designated as 'A1' by *WA*.

[13] Donovan Ochs, *Consolatory Rhetoric: Grief, Symbol, and Ritual in the Greco-Roman Era*
(Columbia, S.C., 1993); Heinz Zahrnt, "Luthers Predigt am Grabe: Dargestellt an seiner
Leichenpredigt für Kurfürst Johann von Sachsen 1532," *Luther* 29 (1958): 106–114.

[14] Apparently in November 1544, the 25th Sunday after Trinity, Luther preached
on 1 Thess. 4:13–18, found in Cruciger's *Sommerpostille*, Po. 302.

[15] Craig M. Koslofsky, *The Reformation of the Dead: Death and Ritual in Early Modern
Germany, 1450–1700* (New York, 2000), 109: "The gradual spread of the funeral sermon
was promoted by church ordinances which required pastors to preach at funerals when
asked to do so. The authors of these ordinances recognized the emotional force of the
funeral sermon: the church ordinance for Halle (1573) noted that although it was not
possible to provide a sermon at all funerals, pastors should not refuse to give funeral

Audience members are the 'change agents' that hear, weigh, and act upon discourse that responds to the exigence facing audience and speaker. With his discourse, the speaker assists the audience in understanding the exigence and responding to it. Constraints are those beliefs, attitudes, documents, facts, traditions, images, and motives that are part of the situation because they have the power to constrain decision and action needed to modify the exigence. When the speaker and his speech enter the situation, his character, his proofs, and his style become additional constraints.[16]

From the way Luther began the sermon, what he and his audience believed and wanted to practice about death rituals emerges to reveal elements of exigence and constraints:

> My dear friends, since this misfortune has happened to our beloved sovereign prince, and the habit and custom of holding masses for the dead and funeral processions when they are buried has ceased, we nevertheless do not wish to allow this service of worship to be omitted, in order that we may preach God's Word to the praise of God and the betterment of the people. For we must deal with the subject and also do what is right on this occasion, since the Lord our God has again taken unto himself and graciously summoned our beloved head (*WA* 36:237.14–21).[17]

Thus Luther recognized a need to preach a sermon, for that task constitutes the heart of corporate worship—indeed, not only the "greatest divine service, but also the best we can have in every situation" (*WA* 36:237.30f.).[18] He wanted to address grief and uncertainty, occasioned again (*abermal*), just seven years after burying John's brother Frederick the Wise, who had reigned for forty-one years. These elements of exigence and constraints reside not just in participants' minds but also

---

sermons, 'because they are indeed powerful and effective sermons: when God strikes us down they go to the heart more than others.'" The ordinance from which the quote comes is found in Emil Sehling, ed., *Die evangelischen Kirchenordnungen des XVI. Jahrhunderts* (Leipzig, 1902–), 2:442. Such ordinances were not in effect in 1532, however.

[16] Bitzer, op. cit., 8, cf. Neil R. Leroux, "The Rhetor's Perceived Situation: Luther's Invocavit Sermons," *RSQ* 28 (winter 1998): 49–80.

[17] "MEin lieben freunde, weil sich der fall jtzt also mit unserm lieben Landsfürsten zugetragen, und die gewonheit und weise mit den Seelmessen und Begengnissen, wenn man sie zur erden bestetiget hat, abgangen ist, Wollen wir dennoch diesen Gottes dienst nicht lassen nach bleiben, das wir Gottes wort predigen, Dar jnn Gott gepreiset und die leute gebessert werden, Denn wir müssen, da von handeln und der zeit auch jr recht thun, Weil unser Herr Gott abermal unser liebes haubt zu sich genomen und mit gnaden gefoddert hat."

[18] "…grösseste Gottes dienst, sondern auch unser bestes, das wir haben können jnn allen fellen.

derive from the scriptural text, for Luther took his proofs not only from human experience but also chiefly from divine authority. He found among the Thessalonians those "who held that it was a manly virtue *not* to grieve or weep when a good and loved friend died," as well as those contemporaries who "try to make sticks and stones of us by alleging that one must eliminate the creature altogether and not accept anything that is natural" (*WA* 36:238.15–19, emphasis added).[19]

As the Reformation matured, church visitation ordinances, visitation instructions, and visitation reports addressed the matter of how clergy and parishioners should *act* in response to death—their own manner of dying, mourning, and funeral and burial procedures. Through argument and exhortation, Luther's funeral sermons present what people should *think* and *feel* about death. Since vigils, masses for the dead, and other forms of intercession had apparently fallen away, what can be done about death—as a discursive response to a rhetorical situation—pertains not to the deceased but to the living. Instead of a mass that performs a work intended to provoke God to act on behalf of the dead—thus rectifying the exigence of an endangered soul—Luther's funeral sermons comfort and encourage listeners to adjust their thinking about death and life, in order to grieve properly and live victoriously. If the discourse 'works' for the audience, the exigence consisting in a threat to the truth of the gospel's message, the efficacy of one's faith and the stability of the realm is favorably modified. Amy Nelson Burnett summarizes the important differences of a funeral sermon from other preaching occasions:

> To begin with, it was not limited to the preacher's regular parishioners. The funeral of a prominent individual could attract a large audience from outside the parish boundaries. Moreover, the pastor needed to offer consolation and comfort specifically tailored to the circumstances of death and the emotional state of the bereaved. Last but certainly not least, the finality of a funeral service presented the pastor with a unique opportunity to instruct his hearers in the Christian response to existential questions of suffering and death.[20]

---

[19] "...die es da für hielten, es solt ein manliche tugend sein, sich gar nicht bekümmern noch weynen, wenn einem ein gutter und lieber freund stürbe....wolten eitel stein und klötzer au suns machen, gaben für, man müste die Creatur gar aus ziehen und sich der nature gar nichts annehmen."

[20] Amy Nelson Burnett, "'To Oblige My Brethren': The Reformed Funeral Sermons of Johann Brandmüller," *SCJ* 36 (2005): 37–54, here at 38.

Let us entitle the sermons, "A Good Death: Fitting Grief for the New Man." They follow a two-step progression, whereby the first message (*LW* 51:231–243; *WA* 36:237–254) expounds 1 Thess. 4:13–14, acknowledging audience grief over the Elector's death as proper and godly and directs that focus onto Christ's death. The second message (*LW* 51:243–255; *WA* 36:255–270) develops verses 15–18, taking the focus on Christ's death and discussing the 'new man.' Luther shows how God cares about the dead, explicating the Christian hope in the return of Christ. Through several comparisons, both sermons emphasize the power of words, especially God's Word, to overcome not only fear of death but death itself. To help his listeners succeed at that, Luther tries to show that people must dwell on how faithful God is, rather than how good they think they are. Thus, in using a text whose context is human fears about their dead, Luther's preaching shows the text to emphasize the trustworthiness and power of God's Word ('by the word of the Lord [1 Thess. 4:15]') and to be based on the already accomplished fact of Christ's death and resurrection, leaving no room for the efficacy of *post mortem* human efforts to aid the dead. Undercutting any preoccupation with the *state* of the dead, Luther establishes their *jurisdiction*—that the dead in Christ are in God's hands and that God is faithful to deliver them instantaneously—and he admonishes his audience to comfort one another. Therefore, these messages stress horizontal relationships among, and responsibilities to, the living.[21]

The first sermon's introduction (*LW* 51:231–233; *WA* 36:236–239) is uncharacteristically lengthy, for it not only states the reason for the occasion and the sermon and shares the Scripture text (1 Thess. 4:13–14); in addition, immediately drawing upon v. 13, Paul argues that grief is godly and proper behavior for the Christian. The conclusion (*LW* 51:242f.; *WA* 36:254) concurs that survivors should outwardly grieve the Elector, for they do not know the Lord's reason for taking him but must be ready for death by believing in, confessing, and dying with Christ. Binding these ends together is a three-part argument, wherein only the second part dwells on the Elector. First, Paul helps focus on Christ's death, which, compared to ours (= only sleep), is real and has power to cover ours (*LW* 51:233–236; *WA* 36:240–244). Luther shows

---

[21] For discussion of Luther's writings on dying, see Jared Wicks, "Applied Theology at the Deathbed: Luther and the Late-Medieval Tradition of the *Ars moriendi*," *Gregorianum* 79 (1998): 345–368.

the superiority of Christ's death over ours, amplifying his argument through comparisons derived from 1 Corinthians 15, on which he had preached the previous Sunday.[22] Second, Luther thanks God for the Elector's being 'in Christ' (*LW* 51:236–239; *WA* 36:244–249). Here, his 'virtue' is that he was a devout, forgiven sinner; his failings in government should be considered in light of our own shortcomings. Having died in Christ, which covers sins, he is therefore among those who sleep in Jesus Christ. Third, we too want this death and its resurrection (*LW* 51:239–242; *WA* 36:249–254). Luther makes a glorious comparison of our righteousness with our death, making the Christian death something different when seen with Christian, scriptural eyes. Included in this section is prolepsis, as he considers objections to the argument (*LW* 51:240f.; *WA* 36:250f.), responding to the devil's onslaught against our confidence. When we depend on our own righteousness, the devil always tops it, making deadly the reliance on one's goodness. Luther's dialogue with the devil celebrates victory when one refuses to compare personal righteousness but relies on Christ's righteousness.

The second sermon begins with an extended introduction (*LW* 51:243–245; *WA* 36:255–257) that quickly recaps the previous message and immediately proceeds to a new theme: our grief is different because the Christian is a new man. Neither death nor suffering is the worst ordeal for a Christian since, for him, death has lost its power. Luther then exhorts his audience to believe that in 1 Thess. 4:13 Paul meant that Christians are different. Luther develops his argument in four parts. First, he shows that the Old Testament testifies of those who hoped in Christ and manifested proper grief (*LW* 51:245–248; *WA* 36:257–262). Using the example of Abel's death (plus selected Psalms), Luther argues in strong language that many people suffered harsh deaths but that God cares more for dead saints than he does for the living! By identifying who are God's saints and the promise to raise them up again, Luther assures his listeners that the Elector is among those saints. Second, Luther argues that the text teaches that our new grief is held in hope (*LW* 51:248–250; *WA* 36:262–264). He claims that we must act like heavenly men, drawing strength from God's word, even though still stuck in the old Adam and having to withstand the devil's attacks. Third, Luther moves into the remaining verses of the text (14–18) to expound

---

[22] On 11 August Luther preached on 1 Cor. 15:1–7; the series continues for seventeen sermons (to 27 April 1533); see *WA* 36:478–696.

on Paul's declaration that God will raise us up (*LW* 51:250–252; *WA* 36:264–267). We must trust God's word, not our senses, and believe that He will raise us up in an instant, just as Christ was raised. Paul's text assures that the dead in Christ will be raised with us, their bodies restored, in a glorious resurrection like unto Jesus' own. Fourth, Luther discusses verses 16–18 on *how* the Lord will come (*LW* 51:253–255; *WA* 36:267–269). God will orchestrate a simultaneous resurrection of both living and dead saints, who together respond to the power and beauty of the Lord's voice, which is greater than sickness and death. Our joy at witnessing such a coming will be as great as that of the first advent shepherds, and this joy brings a comfort that we must now share with one another. Comfort comes from confidence in God, whose Word and Presence are much better than what this life holds. A conclusion (*LW* 51:254f.; *WA* 36:269f.) holds that our hope for the Elector is precisely and confidently expressed in today's text.

II. *Analysis of Sermon One*

A. *Introduction (LW 51:231–233; WA 36:237–239)*

Luther states the reason for the occasion and the sermon, shares the Scripture text (1 Thess. 4:13–14), and argues that grief is godly and proper behavior for the Christian.[23] Accordingly, for the beginning of the introduction, Luther employs the same kind of solidarity with his audience as Paul, using an abundance of first person plural pronouns (9 pronouns in 8 German lines). While Paul balances the 'we' and 'you,' Luther uses a much higher proportion of 'we,' for he stands along with his audience in their grief. Paul, on the other hand, stands with the other Apostles in affirming the certainty of Christ's return to troubled Thessalonian readers.[24]

A second prominent feature of the introduction's opening paragraph reveals another strong tendency in both funeral sermons: (1) a frequent reference to the scriptural text with a rather full citation formula, and (2)

---

[23] As is typical for how he begins a sermon, Luther opens with an endearment ('My dear friends [*MEin lieben Freunde*]') that is faithful to his text, for Paul also uses apostrophe (ἀδελφοί), although in middle position in v. 13. Yet in his 1522 New Testament Luther himself has Paul say "lieben Bruder."

[24] It should be noted, however, that several of Luther's first person plural pronouns are not inclusive but rather editorial.

the prolific use of doublets—some are simple and others are extended. As it happens, Luther's use of doublets in these sermons—although completely characteristic of his style—corresponds with Paul's doublet in the text, 'that Jesus died and rose again [*das Jhesus gestorben und aufferstanden ist*],' which becomes a crucial and oft-repeated declaration in these sermons, especially the first. As he initially identifies our beloved sovereign prince, whom God has 'taken unto himself and graciously summoned,' Luther explains that the 'habit and custom' of holding 'masses for the dead and funeral processions [*Seelmessen und Begengnissen*]' has ended. Still, God's word must be preached to the 'praise of God and the betterment of the people.'[25]

Following the reading of his text (1 Thess. 4:13–14), Luther's next move (*WA* 36:237.28–238.27) is to begin to explicate v. 13 by arguing that his listeners have every right to grieve, for this is one of those solemn occasions of sorrow for which the greatest divine service—*grossest Gottes dienst* (used twice in successive lines)—is preaching. Yet he wants to limit the first sermon to vv. 13–14, so as not to overburden (*uberlade*) 'myself and you.' Luther's case for grief's legitimacy is based on his argument that God made us so: only pagans and heathens of Paul's time and sectarians of Luther's time hold that it is a manly virtue not to 'grieve or weep' when a 'good and loved' friend dies. Such is an 'artificial virtue and a fabricated strength' that would make 'sticks und stones' of God's creatures, eliminating what is natural. To proceed with 'dry eyes and a serene heart [*trocken Augen und stillem Hertzen*]' in the face of even such losses as that of 'father, mother, son, daughter' shows no virtue but rather that one has a hard heart, that one never did have a 'real liking or love' for the deceased, and that God is not pleased. Thus Luther has added longer series and dialogue to his stylistic weapons of exposition.

Having essentially expounded upon 'those who have no hope,' the remainder of Luther's introduction argues for the legitimacy and naturalness of Christian grief. The first step (*WA* 36:238.28–239.16) is to bolster his previous assertions with evidence from Scripture. He builds his case around his quotation of v. 18: 'Therefore, comfort one another,'

---

[25] Luther introduces the text with: "Therefore we shall take as our text what St. Paul says to the Thessalonians in the fourth chapter" (*LW* 51:231) [Darumb wollen wir den text Sanct Paulus für uns nehmen, da er also sagt zun Thessalonichern am Vierden Capittel:] (*WA* 36:237.21f.).

omitting 'with these words.'[26] He brackets the quotation with doublets and triplets, blasting the opposing view—this 'fabricated sectarian and heathen [*rottengeisterische und ertichte heidnissche*]' virtue we 'condemn and say that it is not right.' Using what we might call a progressive antithesis, Luther claims that examples from not only (*nicht allein*) the holy fathers but also (*sondern auch*) the word of God in the Scriptures declares how 'right and fitting, even godly' it is to mourn (*betrüben*) a good friend.[27] Rather than disapprove of this grief, Paul—so Luther asserts—urges that it be 'Christian and in moderation.'

In what is still the same paragraph in *WA* 36:239 (lines 16–31), Luther then uses two more Scriptures, reasoning from the human condition of personal relationships to argue that grief is good.[28] His texts are Phil. 2:27 and John 11:33. Both texts stress the emotional needs of human beings: Paul's heart was grieved (*Leid*) over the grave illness (= anticipated loss) of his servant Epaphroditus, so God had mercy (*erbarmet*) on both men, restoring Epaphroditus's health, so that Paul would not have sorrow upon sorrow (*ein Trawrikeit uber die ander*). Even Jesus was deeply moved (*erbrimmet*) at the death of his friend Lazarus. Luther closes this introduction with a return to inclusive first person plural pronouns: "These and similar examples are to us far more sure and better than this unprofitable chatter which would make stones and sticks[29] [*Stein und Holtz*] of us and forbid us to weep or sorrow [*weynen noch betrüben*] over the deceased."

B. *Part One (WA 36:240–244)*

Paul helps focus on Christ's death, which, compared to ours (only sleep), is real and has power to cover ours. Luther shows the superiority of Christ's death over ours, amplifying his argument through comparisons derived from 1 Corinthians 15, on which he had preached the previous

---

[26] Luther prefaces his quote with another full citation formula, "as Paul himself indicates [*anzeigt*] at the end of this chapter."

[27] Luther reasons from his quoted text (v. 18) that comfort implies 'sorrow, grief and mourning [*trawen, kümmernis und klagen*]' on the part of Paul's Thessalonian readers, people who were—we can safely assume—"Christian people, who were pleasing to God and possessed of the Holy Spirit [*Christen leut gewesen, die Gott gefallen haben und den heiligen Geist gehabt*]."

[28] For whatever reason, Luther makes no reference to the fact that in v. 18 Paul uses an imperative (παρακαλεῖτε), which Luther here renders *Tröst euch*, omitting *So* (*Thus, Therefore*).

[29] *LW* 51:233 wrongly reverses the doublet.

Sunday. In this part of the sermon Luther expounds both v. 13 and v. 14. Here he is not contradicting his earlier justification of grief, but rather trying to put into proper perspective—to make it 'Christian.'

A. Exposition of v. 13: Luther begins by providing a transition from his previous remarks, which he calls a 'preface and introduction [*Vorrede und Eingang*].' As he moves to exposition, Luther provides another very full citation formula: "Now let us listen to the text as he comforts us. This is what the beloved Paul says" (*WA* 36:240.12f.).[30] Luther then quotes v. 13 again, the same way as before, using 'dear brethren.' Following the quote, he then uses dialogue to expound upon Paul's words in v. 13. First he names, acknowledges, and praises his readers for their grief; then he discriminates—employing antithesis and chiasmus—between [A] Christian and [B] heathen death. Luther employs concrete epithets to heighten his exposition, claiming that Paul puts in some good sugar, mixing the bitterness with the sweetness. The dialogue speaks directly to the listener:

> You are sorrowful and grieving over those who have died. It is true that it hurts to lose a good friend. I do not reproach you for this; I praise it, for it is a sign that these are good hearts that are thus concerned about the deceased. But you must discriminate [*unterschiet*] between [A] your death and [B] the death of the heathen, between [A$_1$] your sorrow and [B$_1$] that of the heathen. They have [B$_2$] no hope after this life, but you know [A$_2$] that you do not die but only fall asleep (*WA* 36:240.18–25).[31]

In the next paragraph (*WA* 36:240.29–241.20) Luther adds no additional texts but rather keeps using dialogue and doublets, especially antithetical doublets, to amplify Christ's death—and its power—over against human death—and its being merely a sleep. Luther begins with another formula, though not a citation formula but rather a meta-communication—that which calls attention to the process of communication. He calls attention to the text by pointing out what Paul does not say—namely, that Christ fell asleep (*entschlaffen ist*). Luther declares that Paul says (1) of us, that 'we do not die, but only fall asleep,' that he

---

[30] "Nu wollen wir den text hören, wie er uns tröstet, Also sagt der liebe Paulus."

[31] "Jr seid trawrig und bekümmert euch uber den verstorbenen, Es ist war, es thut wehe einen guten freund so verlieren, Jch straffe es nicht, sondern lobe es, denn es ist ein zeichen, das es gute hertzen sind, die sich der verstorbenen so annehmen, Aber macht gleich wol ein unterschiet zwisschen ewrem sterben und der Heiden sterben, zwisschen ewer trawrikeit und der Heiden, Jhene haben nach diesem leben keine hoffnung, jr aber wisset, das jr nicht sterbet, sondern nur entschlaffet."

calls our death 'not a death, but a sleep' and (2) of Christ, that His death has such exceeding power that we should consider our death a sleep. Realizing that this consideration takes effort on our part, Luther nevertheless claims this is the right way to give comfort, by taking our death as far as possible from our eyes, at least according to the spirit, and looking straight at the death of Christ. Because Paul speaks more sternly of Christ's death, Luther uses *Christus Tod* or *Tod Christi* 5 times (in 18 lines) and says twice more that Christ died (*gestorben*). Moreover, three more times he calls Christ's death real (*recht*), while ours is far less by comparison (*WA* 36:240.38–241.20).[32]

As Luther continues to contrast our death to Christ's, he retreats somewhat from calling ours a sleep, and he continues to use doublets—particularly, extended ones—to amplify the magnitude of Christ's death. Using some more dialogue, he argues that our 'sorrow and grief' over the loss of good friends should prompt us to look to Christ and 'mingle, yea, cover' with the death of Christ all other human deaths; we should so magnify His death so that other deaths are only sleep in comparison.

In the next paragraph (*WA* 36:242.10–23), as Luther continues to champion the death of Christ, he calls attention to Paul's goal, "to turn us around and draw us into the death of Christ," so we can see how immeasurably great it is. Using anaphora to pose two rhetorical

---

[32] Using an abundance of first plural pronouns (7 in 10 lines), Luther sharply discriminates between 'our' death and Christ's. This distinction is Paul's, for he is the one who calls (*heisset*) Christ's death real, who attributes (*gibt*) such power to it that we should consider ours, by comparison (*da gegen*), a sleep. Luther is using a metaphorical, not metaphysical, argument, one which the Passion evokes, for there Christ died "as no one else dies or ever will die [*als nimmer mehr keiner so stirbt noch sterben wird*]." Luther's dialogue reveals the comparison, where he has Paul say: "Why do you think so much about your death? Look at him who is really dead, compared with whom all the other dead are as nothing. They did not die, but he died. Therefore, if we are going to grieve, we should also grieve over Christ's death. That was a real death, not only in itself, because it was so bitter, ignominious, and grandiose [*bitter, schmehlich und gros*], but also because it is so potent [*krefftig*] that it has baptized all the other dead, so that now they are called [*heissen*] not dead, but sleepers [*nicht Todten, sondern Schlefer*]" (*WA* 36:240.38–241.20). [Was denckt jr viel an ewren tod? Sehet hie den an, der ist recht tod, gegen welchem alle andere todten nichts sind, die sind nicht gestorben, sondern er ist gestorben, Darumb wolten wir uns bekümmern, solten wir uns ja auch umb Christus tod bekümmern, das hat ein rechter tod geheissen, nicht allein jnn sich selbs, das er so bitter, schmehlich und gros gewesen ist, sondern auch des halben, das er so krefftig ist, das er alle andere todten getaufft hat, das sie sollen nicht todten, sondern schleffer heissen].

questions that invite affirmation, Luther says that when we indeed grieve over a good friend, we should use the following soliloquy:

> Here you are grieving [bekümmerst] so much over our friend, who would surely have to die some day anyhow; why don't you also grieve over this death? Why aren't you also weeping and lamenting [weynest und klagest] over your Lord Christ, whose death was so much greater and more horrible than that of all other men?[33]

It is clear that Luther's strategy for putting normal grief into perspective is not to deny grief's legitimacy, for he thoroughly dispatched that pagan position earlier; rather, one is to magnify the importance and power of Christ's death. Indeed, turning to comparatives and superlatives, Luther goes on to indicate that the beloved apostles experienced the passing (abscheiden) of Christ, thinking he would remain dead, which is what, according to the senses, we would also think. But when we contemplate this death of Christ, and see how 'mighty and glorious' it now is, and that it devours all other deaths, becoming the 'most grievous and cruel of all [schwereste und grewlichste],' we receive no better comfort.

B. Exposition of v. 14 (WA 36:232.24–244.26): Although Luther has already introduced this verse and has developed the truth, significance, and magnitude of Christ's death, he has not yet fully shown how this information can produce comfort. He has begun such a process, particularly through dialogue that strengthens the teaching of Paul and introduces the process of one's allowing Christ's death to put all other deaths into perspective. Now Luther moves the comforting process closer to home, especially relating it to the death of Elector John, whose lifeless body—though in full view for now—will soon be returned to the earth from which it came. For comfort must always move beyond theory to practice, must take the principle of comfort in loss to the nexus of the loss one is now experiencing; comfort is not very satisfying as merely an abstract concept.

In the first paragraph of this section (WA 36:242.24–243.19) Luther quotes v. 14, turns again to dialogue put into Paul's mouth, to show how the text can encourage. There is no easy way for us today to know where the dialogue ends, where Paul stops and Luther resumes speak-

---

[33] "Ey bekümmerst du dich denn so hoch umb deinen freund, der doch zuletzt ein mal hat sterben müssen, Warumb bekümmerst du dich nich auch umb diesen tod? Warumb weynest und klagest du nicht auch uber deinen HERREN Christum? Welchs tod so viel grosser und elender gewesen ist denn aller andern menschen?" (WA 36:242.13–17). LW 51:234 reverses the doublet deinen HERREN Christum.

ing. This is a feature of Luther's sermons that is not unusual, and here it seems that his understanding of God's comfort inheres in listening carefully to the biblical author. The comfort comes, not by minimizing our loss, but rather by realizing fully its scope. He makes absolutely no attempt to distinguish among listeners as to who has greater or lesser sorrow (e.g., family and close friends). Rather, the political and social uncertainty of losing a head of state is something Luther suggests all share in, though he does acknowledge that some are not as concerned as others. He has Paul saying (through more rhyming doublets) that this means a new 'ruler and government [*Regent und Regiment*]' will take over, and the uncertainty may well make us 'afraid and distressed.' Even calloused audience members need to know that shifts in power were not an easy matter; 'changing and improving [*endern und bessern*]' are not the same. The matter of improving is entirely God's doing (*stehet allein bey Gott*, in final position).

In his next paragraph (*WA* 36:243.20–31) Luther continues to argue that Paul's text shows that one's devastation over the loss of the Elector, and the concomitant fear of one's own impending death, can be overcome by concentrating on the death of Christ, thus receiving the best consolation.[34] In overcoming what 'our reason and five senses' tell us when a corpse lies in front of us, Luther admonishes one to say with St. Paul, "Beloved, look not at this dead body; you have something higher and better to contemplate, namely, the death and resurrection of Jesus Christ." Using anaphora and extended doublets, Luther argues that such contemplation will enable one to see 'where you will go and where those will go' that remain alive when Christ returns. God will bring 'you and all others' who are 'baptized and have fallen asleep in Christ,' because he has "wrapped them in Christ's death and included them in his resurrection."

In the next paragraph (*WA* 36:24332–244.37) Luther continues to argue that we must allow our faith to overcome what our senses report. He uses a new quote—a condensed paraphrase of 1 Cor. 15:42–50—that acknowledges explicitly the contrast, even paradox, between all the negatives that the corpse suggests and all the positives that faith embraces. In contrast to today's tendency in funeral messages

---

[34] Luther uses more dialogue, this time intended as soliloquy, that his listeners can summon and use to bolster their own faith. Notice how Luther's dialogue treats the listener ever so gently, employs visual verbs, and uses the second person singular.

to ignore the obvious—viz., to avoid talking about the corpse—Luther uses metaphors and then blunt, concrete language for what horrifies the senses as well as what delights our faith. He says the Holy Spirit mingles the sour vinegar of death with the 'honey and sugar' of comfort, so that our faith may 'soar up to God and learn to see the dead,' not in the 'grave and coffin' but (*sondern*) in Christ: though the carcass (*Ass*) be 'foul and stinking,' it matters not; turn the 'eyes and nose and all five senses' away and remember (*gedencke*) what St. Paul says in 1 Cor. 15, Luther says.[35] His closing explanation sums up nicely what he has been saying is God's project and Paul's strategy: to have us turn from the senses to the mind (heart), from the deceased to Christ:

> Thus he is constantly turning our hearts, because he cannot turn our eyes, away from that which the eyes see to that which God is saying and to Christ, so that we may have no doubt that he will bring us with Christ. So anyone who can believe this will have good comfort in his own death and the death of other people (*WA* 36:244.33–37).[36]

C. *Part Two (WA 36:244–249)*

Luther thanks God for the Elector's being 'in Christ.' Here, his 'virtue' is that he was a devout, forgiven sinner; his failings in government should be considered in light of our own shortcomings. His 'real' death occurred at the Augsburg diet two years previous and was better than his present 'baby' death—a mere going to sleep—because it swallows up death. Thus, having died in Christ—which covers sins—the Elector is therefore among those who sleep in Jesus Christ. Let us examine this part in what seem to be four sequential components. The first two are similarly brief; the latter two are twice as long as the first two.

A. Luther begins his praise of the deceased, something that is standard fare in later Lutheran *Leichenpredigten* and especially prominent in

---

[35] "Wie Sanct Paulus jnn der Ersten zun Corinthern am funfftzehenden Capitel sagt" (*WA* 36:244.17f.). In his paraphrase, Luther essentially follows the four paradoxical progressions of the body (*corper*) in vv. 42–50: (1) buried in all dishonor (*aller unehre*), yet will rise again (*widder auffstehen*) in all glory (*aller Herrligkeit*); (2) 'buried and sown [*begraben und gesteet*]' as perishable (*verweslich*), rising as imperishable (*unverweslich*); (3) sown (*gesteet*) in weakness (*Schwacheit*), rising in power (*Krafft*); and (4) sown a natural body (*naturlicher Leib*), rising a spiritual body (*geistlicher Leib*).

[36] "Also füret er jmmer unser hertz (weil er die augen nicht kan so füren) von dem, das die augen sehen, jnn das, das Gott redet, und jnn Christum, das keinen zweivel dar an sollen haben, er werde uns mit Christo füren, Wer nur das also gleuben könde, der hette einen guten trost jnn seinem eigen sterben und ander leute sterben."

the classical Latin *laudatio*. Yet Luther's 'praise' is constrained by the premise already established—namely, that only the death of Christ bears any transformative comfort in death. Thus, Luther's praise of John is 'Christianized': (1) Our beloved elector, thanks to God's grace, has been "included in the death of Christ and embraced in his resurrection." Luther's evidence is John's participation in the Augsburg Diet (1530); (2) he was a sinner, like us all, but holding fast to the forgiveness of sins. Luther prefaces this step with reprehension, wherein his departure from classical tradition is characterized by his unwillingness to praise the deceased for his great virtues; (3) again calling John 'our beloved lord,' Luther continues his remarks on virtues with more reprehension, wherein he then proceeds to use descriptors in a series of triplets—three positive, three negative, three positive traits—that forms an inclusio.[37]

B. A second move relates to John's public deeds, rather than personal character—certainly fitting the exigence of a state funeral. The arguments appeal more to experience than to Scripture. Luther's dealings in this step are brief and laudatory of John's actions; it is clear that the perspective Luther offers is that of John as lonely leader. His use of inclusive first plural pronouns allows Luther to include himself among an audience of those who were quick to criticize and slow to understand. This move, therefore, opens with an appeal to shame; it closes with rebuttal, making the entire step a prolepsis. Obtaining agreement from his audience in the *Schloßkirche*—no doubt consisting of many city and territorial officials—on John's faith and virtue, Luther may elicit sympathy for the plight of a harried prince. As to his occasional failings in governing, Luther asks, what can be said? Notice all the 'we' pronouns in Luther's summarizing remark as he transitions back to Scripture, with a paraphrase that refers back to today's text:

> So nobody can do right as far as we are concerned, and if we look at ourselves we have never yet been right. All this we shall pass over now and we shall stick to praising him, as St. Paul praises his Christians, saying that God will bring with him those who are in Christ, and we shall not look upon him according to his temporal death [*zeitlichem Sterben*],

---

[37] While not altogether pure (*gar rein*), John was a 'very devout, kindly man, free of all guile [*seer fromer, freundlicher man gewesen ist*],' completely lacking—in his own lifetime, Luther declares—'pride, anger, or envy [*Stoltz, Zorn noch Neid*]' and able to "bear and forgive... and was more than mild [*tragen und vergeben... mehr denn zu viel mild*]." With a third reprehension, Luther declares that he is now finished with discussing virtues (*LW* 51:236; *WA* 36:244.27–245.20).

but according to Christ's death and his spiritual death [*geistlichen Sterben*], which he died in accord with Christ (*WA* 36:245.26–32).[38]

Thus, Luther has defended his praise of John by first identifying him as a Christian; hence he serves as exemplary of all who would die as Christians (*WA* 36:245.21–32).

C. The longer third step of two full paragraphs (*WA* 36:24611–247.21) is one of developing what was involved in John's 'spiritual death' in Augsburg. Luther explains and celebrates the significance of what the Elector did for his people and the faith, and he does so using several comparisons and ending with yet another Scripture from 1 Cor. 15. He characterizes what occurred at Augsburg: Our beloved elector, Christ's death and resurrection, before the whole world 'openly confessed and stuck to it.' With a pair of rhyming doublets that progress from professional to personal, Luther claims John staked his 'land and people [*land und leut*],' indeed, his own 'body and life [*leib und leben*]' upon his confession. He continues to amplify the significance for this death (*Dis sterben*, in first position) and this confession, arguing that they merit praise (*rhumen*, used twice in four lines), overshadowing any lack there might be in John's character. "Such insignificant sins in such a great person [*solche geringe sunde jnn so grosser Person*]" pale in comparison to his confessing 'Christ's death and resurrection,' by which Christ swallowed up 'death and hell' with all sins. John's confession, to which he remained steadfast, 'covers and swallows up' many sins as a great ocean swallows a spark of fire (*Füncklin Fewers*). Luther concludes the first paragraph thus: "Therefore all other sins are as nothing compared with this one thing, that Christ's death and resurrection be not denied, but openly confessed" (*WA* 36:246.26f.).

In the second paragraph of this move Luther makes his case for how the knowledge of John's confession at Augsburg should bring comfort (*trösten*). He does so by characterizing John's 'two deaths' as so different from one another that the easier death is obviously preferable. We should be comforted, Luther argues, by two facts: (1) that Christ died and our beloved prince is 'caught up and fallen asleep' in Christ's death, and (2) that John suffered a far more bitter death (*viel einen*

---

[38] "Das uns also niemand kan recht thun, und wenn wir uns selber ansehen, sind wir selbst noch nie recht worden, Dis alles lassen wir jtzt faren und wollen da bey bleiben, das wir jn loben, wie Sanct Paulus seine Christen lobet, das jn Gott mit Christo füren wird, und wollen jn nicht ansehen nach seinem zeitlichem sterben, sondern nach Christus sterben und seinem geistlichen sterben welches er Christo nach gethan hat."

herbern Tod) at Augsburg than now. That Luther is speaking of comfort not only for the loss of their prince but also for contemplating their own mortality is clear from how he then connects John's confession at Augsburg to what all listeners must do. Luther argues that the bitter death is one that we must suffer 'daily and incessantly' from the 'tyrants and sectarians.' Indeed (*Ja auch wol*), Luther interjects as correction, our own 'conscience and the devil' inflict this real death, whereas the other—physical death—is but a passing away in bed, only 'a childish death and an animal death [*ein kinder Sterben und ein vihe Sterben*].' He will return to the metaphors of the lesser death (childish, animal) in a few sentences, but now Luther wants quickly to turn to the real death, the bitter death, which he then names twice in four lines as 'real, manly' death, 'manly and real' death. What typifies this greater death is that (1) it still faces us, and (2) it is one where we would rather risk our neck than deny Christ. Luther then quotes 1 Cor. 15:31, "By our pride in you, which I have in Christ Jesus, I die daily."[39] This is the heroic dying motif, but it is not the battle of fleshly military, for Luther concludes his paragraph of comparisons thus:

> The other death is only when the reason and the five senses die, the eyes no longer see, the ears do not hear, the hands no longer feel, etc. So a cow also dies; it is only an outward dying away of the body and a poor bag of worms; it is only a childish death compared with the other death (*WA* 36:247.17–21).[40]

D. In the fourth and final move of this second part of sermon one, Luther continues to discuss 'our beloved prince' (used twice), and yet his goal is to have his hearers find comfort about their own future deaths, as they are reassured about John's. He has now passed away, and we can feel that his was only a childish death, "for our Lord God had so caught him up in His death." What Luther then assures his listeners is what he himself cannot have known empirically about John's death, for he was not there. But what Luther believed was the blessing of every Christian, if one only claims it, is that for John there was no buffeting

---

[39] *LW* 51:238, perhaps following Paul too closely, wrongly translates Luther's quote, in which he uses 'our' pride, not 'my' pride; Luther is consistent here with his translation in *SeptBib* and in his sermon of 1532.

[40] "Der ander to dist nür, wenn die vernunfft und funff synn sterben, das die augen nicht mehr sehen, die oren hören nicht, die hende fülen nicht 2c. So stirbet ein kue auch, Jst nur ein eusserlichs absterben des leibes und armen sacks, es ist ein kinder sterben gegen ihenem."

(*Püff keine gelitten*), no disputing with the devil, no despair (*Verzweivelung*) at the end. Luther employs doublets and a quadruplet with anaphora to claim that John avoided what others often suffer: the grievous thought of "sin, the last judgment, hell, and the like," as well as "cold sweat breaks out and they are almost paralyzed." As readers today, we naturally have noticed Luther's inconsistency with the expression 'real death.' For he has used it first of John's confession at Augsburg—and also of the daily courage one must have—and now he uses 'real death' to speak of one's death struggle with temptation, regret, and despair. He is grasping for metaphors in order to distinguish between the difficult and the easy, and he wants to call the death of the body easy—when one belongs to Christ and has been swallowed up already by His death. Luther's own explanation here, with yet another pair of metaphors, helps clarify his point:

> But when it happens, as it did with our beloved prince, that the body merely lies upon the bed and there is no fright and trembling, because he was called into Christ's kingdom through baptism and afterwards openly confessed Christ and listened with all diligence, with the whole heart to God's Word, and thus only the five senses died away—then this is the least of death and only half of death, when a man struggles only with physical death, even though we untempted folk think it the greatest (*WA* 36:247.29–248.15).[41]

In a second paragraph of the fourth move, Luther completes his assessment of John's Christian death and how it is one in which listeners can take comfort, chiefly because it foreshadows their own death. Luther ends his move, before summarizing the entire argument of part two, with dialogue that he says God speaks: (1) as soliloquy to Himself, regarding His plans for John. These remarks bolster by echoing what Luther has already said; (2) as direct communication to every believer. Acting in tandem with what was already verified about John, these remarks testify as a second witness to the comfort believers derive from this argument about death in Christ as only a sleep in Christ. Luther concludes that the kind of death John met was comforting (*tröstlicher*)

---

[41] "Wenn es aber so zu geht, wie es mit unserm lieben Fürsten hat gangen, da nur der leichnam auff dem bette bleibet, on alles schrecken und zittern, darum das er zum reich Christi durch die tauff gefoddert und darnach Christum frey bekennet hat und Gottes wort mit allem vleis, von gantzem herten gern gehöret, Das also nur die funff synn dahin sterben, Das ist das geringst sterben und nur die hülfen vom tod, da man allein mit dem leiblichen tod ringet, Wie wol es uns unversüchte leute das grösseste düncket."

and gentle (*sanfft*), his five senses simply dying away. Notice the terms of contemplation—which express themselves in commands to *see*—as Luther argues that this comfort can be found when one looks upon his own death rightly, for when he passes on so wrapped in our Lord Christ's suffering, our Lord God says *to him* (8 second person singular pronouns in 5 lines):

> I will allow the devil to destroy you only physically; therefore do not look so steadily at your death, but look at the fact that my Son died for you and the fact that you have already been spiritually killed. So now I will send death to you only in the sense that you will die as far as your five senses are concerned, as in a sleep (*WA* 36:248.27–31).[42]

As he summarizes this second part of the sermon, we recall that the focus is not on the legitimacy of grief—as in Part One—but rather on the status of the deceased, Elector John. While Luther has praised him for his confession of faith, he has frequently acknowledged frailty in his prince. In this summary Luther works in all of the key expressions thus far as he distinguishes <u>personal righteousness</u>, which he will not make the focus of our judgment of John, from <u>group membership</u>, as it were—viz., all that Christ has done. He begins with John's strengths: We shall, Luther concludes, reckon our beloved sovereign among those who sleep in Jesus Christ, since he did not depart from his confession of the death and resurrection of Christ, suffering much 'injury and affront [*Schaden und Schmach*]' for it. Moving to the other side of the ledger, Luther acknowledges that we will not make John a living saint and that any sin having crept in can be dismissed, allowing him to be human. He finishes with a rhetorical question that invites the audience to agree with the implied answer (Nothing!): "For what can the devil bring up against his personal righteousness, since Christ is standing there alongside him and for him with His death and resurrection, which is more than the sin of the whole world? (*WA* 36:249.15–18).[43]

---

[42] "Jch wil dich den teuffel allein leiblich lassen würgen, Darumb sihe du nicht so hart auff deinen tod, Sihe dis an, das mein Son für dich gestorben ist, und du vor hin auch geistlich gewürget bist, So wil ich dir nu den tod so zuschicken, das du allein sterbest jnn deinen funff synnen, wie jnn einem schlaff."

[43] "Denn was wil der teuffel auff bringen widder seine personalem iusticiam, weil Christus neben und fur jn da stehet mit seinem tod und aufferstehen, welchs mehr ist denn der gantzen welt sunde?"

D. *Part Three (WA 36:249–254)*

Luther argues that we too want this death and its resurrection. He makes a glorious comparison of our righteousness with our death, making the Christian death something different when seen with Christian, scriptural eyes. Included in this section is prolepsis, as he considers objections to the argument, responding to the devil's onslaught against our confidence. When we depend on our own righteousness, the devil always tops it, making deadly the reliance on one's goodness. Luther's dialogue with the devil celebrates victory when one refuses to compare personal righteousness but instead relies on Christ's righteousness. Luther makes his argument in three moves, each successively much longer than the one before it. In the first move he uses a series of images—both metaphor and simile—to set forth the goal for every listener: to experience the same kind of death as John—one that transforms shame into glory. In the second move Luther urges his listeners—with several commands—to take up a new attitude toward Christian death, one that follows the lead of John and derives great comfort from the words of Christ. In the third move Luther engages in prolepsis, a lengthy series of dialogues with the devil, intended to expose every kind of temptation he puts before us that would make us fear death, mistrust our faith in Christ, and cause one to despair.

A. Luther's first move (*WA* 36:249.18–30) is brief and filled with inclusive first plural pronouns (12 in 12 lines), for death is one foe before which every person stands in need of encouragement. Luther uses no Scripture, only three doublets, and yet he works in two key expressions and several important images, some of which we have heard him use already. His hope is that we too die as John did, bringing with us to heaven a poor sinner—meaning one's self, for Luther frequently called himself a poor *Drecksack*; his final written words (1546) were the bilingual *Wir sind Pettler, hoc est verum* ("We are beggars, this is true").[44]

B. In a second move (*WA* 36:249.31–250.30) Luther turns to imperatives as he begins to exhort his listeners to adopt a new image of Christian death and to draw comfort from the Scriptures. He begins by staying with similes—humorous ones—that can disarm an audience's fears and help them relax. Using antitheses, Luther urges that one look at Christian death with different eyes, but not as a cow staring at a new

---

[44] Recall that Luther referred to the body as a poor bag (*armen Sacks*) at *LW* 51:238 (*WA* 36:247.21).

gate. With a different nose we must smell [Christian death], but not as a cow sniffs grass. We must learn 'to speak and think' of it as the Scriptures do; we must no longer consider (*rechne*) deceased Christians as 'dead and buried' people. 'With these words' (first position in the sentence), Luther commands his hearers:

> Learn to comfort [*trösten*] yourselves…and instill [*bildets*] in your hearts the fact that it is far more certain that Duke John of Saxony will come out of the grave and be far more splendid than the sun is now,[45] than that he is lying here before our eyes. This is not so certain as the fact that he will live again and go forth with Christ. The reason? Because God cannot lie (*WA* 36:250.19–23).[46]

C. Luther's third and final move (*WA* 36:250.31–254.20) in this third part of the sermon is where he engages any doubters. Here he may have in mind conservative believers holding to the Catholic faith, or he may be interested mostly in bolstering the faith of Reformation believers who still need encouragement at such a time as the death of their prince. No matter who, they all can profitably ponder Luther's argument. Moreover, the predominant strategy here is prolepsis, the rebuttal of objections. Their voice is gentle in the ear of a troubled listener: "My dear, who knows whether God will consider you to be good?" (*WA* 36:250.31f.).[47] Luther interrupts immediately with a blunt report. Moviegoers who saw *Luther* (Till, 2003) will recall similar scenes:

> [H]e often tries it on me. He asks me how good and how evil I am and can make his masterful use of the Scriptures and the law. 'You must do this and that [*Das und das*]. You must be good and keep the law. But you have not kept it? How are you going to get out of that?' (*WA* 36:251.20–24).[48]

Luther knows very well how skillfully the devil argues, for he has created—in the devil's mouth—a conundrum, wherein if one accepts

---

[45] Recall that Luther was preaching at 7 AM in August, so the sun could very well have been shining brightly when he uttered this remark.

[46] "Mit solchen worten lernet euch sein trösten und bildets euch wol ein, Das es viel gewisser ist, das Hertzog Hans von Sachssen wird widder erfür komen aus dem loch und viel schooner denn die Sonn jtzt ist, denn das er hie für unsern augen ligt, Das ist nicht so gewis als jhenes, das er widder leben wird und mit Christo da her faren, Ursach: Gott kan nicht liegen."

[47] "Lieber, wer weis, ob dich Gott auch für from halten wil?"

[48] "…er an mir auch offt versucht, Fraget mich, wie from und wie bös ich sey und kan sein meisterlich die Schrifft und das Gesetz da zu brauchen: Das und das solt du thun, Solt from sein und das Gesetz halten, Aber du hast es nicht gehalten, Wo aus?"

the premise of having to keep the law, one is ultimately caught in the conclusion that she or he is in violation of the law, for the devil has reminded her or him of particular sins. Then Luther rushes to the rescue, with a precise and concrete declaration: "I make haste and seize hold [*lauff ich denn und ergreiff*] of the article of the forgiveness of sins through Jesus Christ, who died and rose again for my sins."[49] He is, of course, speaking of Article IV of the Augsburg Confession, to which Luther has taken the occasion of this funeral message to offer a commendatory tribute.[50] Turning the corner—from amplifying the objections to rebutting them—Luther strongly exhorts his listeners to resist the devil (and any person unwittingly assisting him). Indeed, late medieval artwork and literature was rife with images of demons and angels lurking under and hovering over the deathbed. Accordingly, Luther gives listeners some of their own dialogue to shout back to the devil:

> But by all means take care not to let anybody persuade you of this on your deathbed; for then the devil is not far away; he can throw in your face a little sin which reduces all such fine virtues to nothing, so that you come to such a pass that you say: 'Devil, rage as much as you please, I do not boast of my good works and virtues before our Lord God at all, nor shall I despair on account of my sins, but I comfort myself with the fact that Jesus Christ died and rose again, as the text here says' (*WA* 36:251.32–252.13).[51]

---

[49] "Da lauff ich denn und ergreiff den artikel der vergebung der sunde durch Jhesum Christum, der für meine sunde gestorben und widder aufferstanden ist" (*WA* 36:251.26–28).

[50] "Also they teach that men cannot be justified before God by their own strength, merits, or works, but are freely justified for Christ's sake, through faith, when they believe that they are received into favor, and that their sins are forgiven for Christ's sake, who, by His death, has made satisfaction for our sins. This faith God imputes for righteousness in His sight. Rom. 3 and 4"; *Concordia or Book of Concord: The Symbols of the Evangelical Lutheran Church* (St. Louis, 1952), 12–13; "IV. DE IUSTIFICATIONE. Item docent, quod hominess non possint iustificari coram Deo propriis viribus, meritis aut operibus, sed gratis iustificentur propter Christum per fidem, quum credunt se in gratiam recipi, et peccata remitti propter Christum, qui sua morte pro nostris peccatis satisfecit. Hanc fidem imputat Deus pro iustitia coram ipso. Rom. iii et iv." in *Documents Illustrative of the Continental Reformation*, ed. B. J. Kidd (Oxford, 1911), 263.

[51] "Aber bey leib hute dich da für, das man dirs am tod bett nicht ein bilde, Denn der teuffel ist nicht weit da von, der kan dir ein kleine sunde für rücken, die solche schöne tugent alle zu nicht macht, das man doch endlich da hin komen uns sagen mus: Teuffel, sey so zornig du jmmer wilt, Jch rhüme mein gute werck und tugent gar nichts für unserm Herr Gott, wil auch meiner sunder halben nicht verzweiveln, Sondern tröste mich dam it, das Jhesus Christus gestorben und widderstanden ist, wie der text hie sagt." In a second full paragraph (*WA* 36:252.14–253.15) of this third part of the

With another reference to the text of the sermon (1 Thess. 4:13–18), Luther claims once again that the purpose of Paul's text is to bring comfort, and that a step in deriving comfort is learning to 'defend myself from the devil and say. . . .' Note the simplicity, the frequent <u>negatives</u>, the sarcasm, and even the rhyme:

> Even though I have sinned, it does <u>not</u> matter; I will <u>not</u> argue with you about what evil or good I have done. There is <u>no</u> time to talk of that now; go away and do it some other time when I am being a bad boy [*böser Bube bin*], or go to the impenitent and scare them all you please. But with me, who have already been through the anguish and throes of death, you'll find <u>no</u> place now (*WA* 36:252.20–25).[52]

In the third and final paragraph (*WA* 36:253.16–254.20) of this last part of the sermon Luther continues to hammer away at the devil, for his attempt to trick Christians into looking away from Christ's death and resurrection, the key expression of the sermon—found in 1 Thess. 4:14 and one which he has repeated now about 15 times, and he will use it three more times yet, two of which are shouted back at the devil. Notice how personal is this discourse, as it appropriates (*I*, *my*, *for me*, etc.) Christ's comfort:

> Devil, you're coming at the wrong time. No devil is going to argue *with me* now, but rather *I* shall talk with *my* Lord Jesus Christ, that *I* may learn

---

sermon, Luther resumes more dialogue with the devil. It is probably inaccurate to call what he wants his listeners to tell the devil 'dialogue,' for that term implies a reciprocal communication process, and Luther's goal is to shout the devil down. This paragraph makes it clear that Luther is now on a very significant point for him: that at the root of anxiety and despair lies sin, and that, for the Christian, sin has been taken care of by Christ. However, in order to experience victory over temptation to doubt, one must in one's heart believe in the "death of Christ and the power he has wrought [*Tod Christi und seine Krafft, die er gewircket hat*]." When I do that I have the greatest treasure (*höchste Schatz*) and hence will concern myself less with what I have done (*ich gethan habe*) and more on Christ's death. Luther's discourse to the devil is framed in first person singular, for he wants every listener to employ such bold invective: "Therefore, devil, be gone with both my righteousness and sin [*meiner Gerechtigkeit und Sunde*]. If I have committed some sin, you go eat the dung; it's yours. I'm not worrying myself about it, for Jesus Christ has died" [Darumb Teuffel, fare hin, beide mit meiner gerechtigkeit und sunde, Habe ich etwas gesundiget, so fris du den mist da von, der sey dein, Jch bekümmere mich nichts darumb, denn Jhesus Christus ist gestorben] (*WA* 36:252.16–19).

[52] "Ob ich schon gesündiget habe, das schadet mir nicht, Jch wil nicht mit dir da von disputiren, was ich böses odder gutes gethan habe, Es hat jtzt nicht zeit davon zu handeln, Gehe hin und thu es zur andern zeit, wenn ich ein böser bube bin. Odder gehe zu den verstockten, da schrecke, wie du wilt, Aber bey mir, de rich vor jnn engsten und todtes nöten bin, findest du jtzt keinen platz."

that he suffered *for me* and died and rose again *for my* sins, and that God
will bring *me with him* on the last day (*WA* 36:253.24–28).[53]

E. *Conclusion to Sermon One (WA 36:254.21–35)*

Luther provides a brief summary of what the text 'is,' and he prefaces
the content of his summary with the endearment 'dear friends,' similar
to his introductory 'my dear friends.' The summary is not pure exhortation, for there is only a single imperative. In his summary Luther
brings together an understanding of what has happened to Elector
John, then moves on to an appeal to the mortality of all listeners, then
to the promise that is possible in Christ. Three declarations, then: (1)
that sorrow (*Bekümmern*) over our beloved ruler is right, according to the
outward man; (2) that all listeners should soberly consider their own
mortality;[54] and (3) that all use their ruler's example at Augsburg.

Clearly Luther has kept the audience remembering whose funeral it
is, for he has referred specifically to the deceased 16 times, with nearly
as many different epithets.[55] Yet he has taken great pains not to praise
the deceased for his virtues, for the real topic of the sermon is the death
and resurrection of Jesus, stipulated explicitly as a phrase 21 times, and
mentioned in other ways at least double that. That makes this funeral
sermon much like any sermon of Luther's, as Gerhard Sauter concludes
about Luther's weekly Sunday afternoon sermons on 1 Cor. 15, begun
a week before this first funeral message:

---

[53] "Teuffel, du kompst zu unrechter zeit, Es sol jtzt kein teuffel mit mir disputiren,
sondern mein HERR Jhesus Christus, das ich lerne, wie er für mich gelidden und für
meine sunde gestorben sey und widder aufferstanden, wie mich Gott mit jm füren
wird am jüngsten tage."

[54] Here Luther uses three doublets to amplify the implication—initiated by the
rhetorical question—that everyone ought to regard seriously her or his guilt before
God. He tells his audience that we are all 'wicked, ungrateful villains [*böse, undanckbare
Buben*],' that 'both young and old [*beide Jung und Allt*]' are utterly wanton (*gar mutwillig*)
and lacking 'discipline or fear [*Zucht noch Schew*].' With a striking word play, he warns
listeners that God's manifesting (*erzeiget*) himself in removing the head (*heubt*), not even
sparing a prince, surely means every 'head' (*Kopff*) is vulnerable. These statements
prompt Luther to call upon every listener to 'humble yourself and better your life
[*demütige dich und besser dein Leben*],' in order to be able to celebrate (*feiest*) among those
who 'suffer and die [*leiden und sterben*]' with Christ.

[55] *[O]ur beloved sovereign prince; our beloved head; our head, the beloved sovereign; our sovereign
prince, our beloved lord and father; our beloved elector (2x); our beloved lord/our beloved ruler; our
beloved prince (3x); the good prince; our beloved sovereign; Duke John of Saxony; our beloved lord
and prince; my ruler.*

Arguments and counterarguments characterize every evangelical sermon, not only a sermon on the resurrection. The proclamation of the resurrection of the dead as the promise of life with God is the heart of every sermon; it is not one theme among others, which may be brought forth when the need arises. The evangelical sermon is not meant to teach a more successful way of life, or better management of one's life, or a mastery of responsibilities for others. These things reasonable people can find of their own accord; for such things no preaching is needed. Preaching is needed because it leads us out of the 'vale of tears' into the future life.[56]

III. *Analysis of Sermon Two*

The second sermon, preached four days after the first, uses the same text (1 Thess. 4:13–18) and eventually develops vv. 15–18. However, that exposition does not begin until well past the midpoint of the sermon. Prior to that, Luther moves in the direction of a new theme, yet one he derives from v. 13: our grief is different because the Christian is a new man. Thus Luther fits the previous message about grief—that it is normal, God-given, and finds consolation in the Gospel—with its complement: that grief should be moderated and appropriate. He begins with an introduction (*LW* 51:243–245; *WA* 36:255–257) that quickly recaps the previous message and proceeds immediately to the new theme. Neither death nor suffering is the worst ordeal for a Christian since, for him, death has lost its power. Luther then exhorts his audience to believe that in 1 Thess. 4:13 Paul meant that Christians are different. He develops his argument in four parts.

First, he shows that the Old Testament testifies of those who hoped in Christ and manifested proper grief (*LW* 51:245–248; *WA* 36:257–262). Using the example of Abel's death (plus selected Psalms), Luther argues in strong language that many people suffered harsh deaths but that God's care for them is made plain in Scripture. By identifying who are God's saints and the promise to raise them up again, Luther assures

---

[56] Gerhard Sauter, "Luther on the Resurrection," in *Harvesting's Martin Luther's Reflections on Theology, Ethics, and the Church*, ed. Timothy J. Wengert (Grand Rapids, 2004), 99–118, here at 99f. Sauter's essay was originally published as "Die Verkündigung des Auferstandenen als Zusage des Lebens bei Gott," in *Relationen-Studien zum Übergang vom Spätmittelalter zur Reformation: Festschrift zu Ehren von Prof. Dr. Karl-Heinz zur Mühlen*, ed. Athina Lexutt and Wolfgang Matz (Münster, 2000), 383–398, and in its English Translation (by Austra Reinis) in *LQ* 15 (2001): 195–216.

his listeners that the Elector is among those saints. Second, Luther argues that the text teaches that our new grief is held in hope (*LW* 51:248–250; *WA* 36:262–264). He claims that we must act like heavenly men, drawing strength from God's word, even though still stuck in the old Adam and having to withstand the devil's attacks. Third, Luther moves into the remaining verses of the text (14–18) to expound on Paul's declaration that God will raise us up (*LW* 51:250–252; *WA* 36:264–267). We must trust God's word, not our senses, and believe that He will raise us up in an instant, just as Christ was raised. Paul's text assures that the dead in Christ will be raised with us, their bodies restored in a glorious resurrection like unto Jesus' own. Fourth, Luther discusses verses 16–18 on *how* the Lord will come (*LW* 51:253–255; *WA* 36:267–269). God will orchestrate a simultaneous resurrection of both living and dead saints, who together respond to the power and beauty of the Lord's voice, which is greater than sickness and death. Our joy at witnessing such a coming will be as great as that of the first advent shepherds, and this joy brings a comfort that we must now share with one another. Comfort comes from confidence in God, whose Word and Presence are much better than what this life holds. A conclusion (*LW* 51:254f.; *WA* 36:269f.) holds that our hope for the Elector is precisely and confidently expressed in today's text.

A. *Introduction (WA 36:255.15–257.35)*

Using the inclusive first plural (3 pronouns in 4 lines), Luther opens with a statement of status and intent, indicating that it is still the week of mourning and that we have already begun to comfort ourselves. The source of comfort is God's word from St. Paul's Epistle; the goal is to "speak on and the chosen text fully expound [*redden und den fürgenomen text vollend aus füren*]" (literal translation).

In a second paragraph (*WA* 36:255.19–256.17) Luther begins his thesis about the New Man, starting with how Christians differ from others in their grief and view of death. With abundant doublets and some triplets, Luther asserts half of his distinction (the world)—identifying Christians as 'new' four times (and three more times in the succeeding paragraph). In the third paragraph (*WA* 36:256.18–29) of the introduction, he gives the contrary category—the Christian. Employing correction, Luther asserts that as a new person, one is made to have 'far different, yes even completely opposite' thoughts. Luther finds grounds for this claim in Rom. 5,[57] arguing that one can then 'boast and be happy or rejoice' at hardship. The new, living man begins now at death. Using some form of 'new' a total of 10 times in the last two paragraphs, here is how Luther summarizes:

> In short, he must gain a completely new heart and courage and thereby make all things on earth new, and thus begin here a prelude [*Vorspiel*] to the life to come, when all things will become as new, manifestly and visibly, as he now imagines and conceives [*erscheffpt und erdenckt*] them by faith according to his new nature (*WA* 36:256.26–29).[58]

In the fourth paragraph (*WA* 36:256.30–257.22) of the introduction, Luther turns up the emotional level, as he argues that the newness he is describing is not in us but in Christ. Luther insists that He alone, meaning Christ, has made all things new already in this 'manifest and visible' life. The Christian will never die again, for death has no 'power or dominion' over him; all death's capabilities—even physical—are removed, so it can no longer 'bind nor imprison nor torment' him with 'hunger, thirst, and wounds.' Hearing Luther's precise *Summa*—as he draws in his audience with first plural pronouns—is worthwhile:

> In short, it [= death] has all its venom, cords, spear, and sword, and whatever evil it possesses lost to Christ. In this Man we too should allow ourselves to think even now that all things have become new and accustom ourselves to the strong thoughts of faith, keeping ever before the eyes the beloved image of the dead and risen Christ and carrying it with us against the old nature, which still assails and confronts us and tries to frighten us with misery and distress, misfortune, poverty, death, and whatever else there may be (*WA* 36:257.15–22).[59]

---

[57] "(wie Sanct Paulus zun Romern am funfften saget)" [*WA* 36:256.19f.]. *LW* 51:244 cites Rom. 5:3, looking ahead to Paul's 'rejoice' (καυχώμεθα)—*rhumen* for Luther. *WA* cites v. 2 in the margin of line 30, referring to the ground for rejoicing, which is better found in v. 2.

[58] "Und Summa, das er eitel newe hertz und mut gewinne und alle ding auff erden mit jm new mache und also hie ein vorspiel ansahe des zukünfftigen wesens, da es alles am tage und für augen so new werden wird, wie ers jtzt erschepfft und erdenckt durch den glauben nach seinem newen wesen."

[59] "Summa: Er hat alle seine gifft, strick, spies und schwert und was er böses hat, an Christo verloren, Jnn dem selbigen man sollen wir uns auch bereit an lassen düncken, das es alles new worden sey, und uns gewehnen jnn die starcken gedancken des glaubens und das liebe bild des gestorbenen und aufferstanden Christi stets jnn die augen fassen und mit uns tragen widder das allte wesen, so uns noch ansichtet und unter augen stösst und uns schrecken wil mit jamer und not, unglück, armut, tod und was es sein mag."

In the final paragraph (*WA* 36:257.23–35) of the introduction, Luther brings his argument about the new man back to the text of 1 Thess. 4:13, from which he claims to derive the theme. Using dialogue for the first time in this sermon, he puts discourse into Paul's mouth to stress repeatedly the notion of difference (*anders*). Whereas the distinction he made in the introduction of sermon one was regarding the legitimacy of grief—our citizenship in humanity—here he emphasizes our citizenship in Christ's kingdom. We notice the doublets and other series, and that throughout his paragraph Luther—then Paul—uses the second person plural (9 pronouns in 13 lines), gently engaging his listeners directly. He will end, though, in first plural, appropriating the benefits of his case for all—including him—in boldness. All this because Christ's resurrection ensures that He will take (*fetzete*) us with him, away from death and into 'life and eternal glory.'

B. *Part One (WA 36.257.36–262.17)*

Luther shows that the Old Testament testifies of those who hoped in Christ and manifested proper grief. Using the example of Abel's death (plus selected Psalms), Luther argues in strong language that many people suffered harsh deaths but that God will not allow them to remain in death. By identifying who are God's saints and the promise to raise them up again, Luther assures his listeners that the Elector is among those saints. Thus, in this part Luther prepares his listeners for a return to the text of 1 Thess. 4, in Part II.

In laying out his thesis about the dear patriarchs, Luther's goal is to make his readers feel modestly ashamed—though proud of the patriarchs for their faith—yet self-consciously wanting more of that for themselves. Luther asserts that the patriarchs had not yet seen what his listeners have now heard so much about. They saw the resurrection through a 'blue, dark cloud,'[60] whereas we have the 'clear, bright sun' shining in the eyes.[61] Turning to parallel spatial metaphors, Luther depicts their dependence (*hengen*) on Christ from afar as having required them to soar up to the comforting thought (*jnn die tröstlich Gedancken erschwingen*) that in the resurrection they would 'rise up from death and live with him.' Luther then quotes three Psalms in succession, identifying

---

[60] *LW* 51:245 wrongly translates the doublet *eine blawe dunckel Wolcken* as 'dark blue clouds.'

[61] *LW* 51:245 does not translate *jnn die Augen scheinet*, where Luther may be alluding to 1 Cor. 13:12.

the latter two, but quoting the first (the uncited one) in both Latin and then German; it becomes the thematic text of his argument, for he quotes it again near the end of Part I: "Precious in the sight of the Lord is the death of his saints" (Ps. 116:15).[62] The next two Psalms (72:14 and 9:12)—'Precious is their blood in his sight' and 'He who avenges blood is mindful of them'—together form an inclusio: *Jr Blut...Jrem Blut* (*LW* 51:245; *WA* 36:257.36–258.21). Both Ps.116:15 and Ps. 72:14, which begin with 'precious,' are examples of hyperbaton—where special emphasis is given to a predicate by placing it first in the sentence—as in "Great is Artemis of the Ephesians" (Acts 19:28, 34).[63]

Luther then turns to dialogue to develop a rich vocabulary that describes the power and function of the claims of the three quoted Psalms.

> Beloved, you may well think otherwise and to your eyes it looks as if the death of the saints is pure defeat and destruction and it appears as if they now were utterly forgotten and silenced, as if they had no God to befriend them, because he did not befriend them while they were living and allowed them to perish so miserably as those who are torn, devoured, burned, and pulverized [*zu rissen, zu fressen, verbrand und zu pulvert sind*]. So no rational mind can say anything else but that their death was a pitiful, miserable, shameful [*jemmerlich, elend, schendlich*] thing. But before God (say the patriarchs) you must take it as sure truth that when a saint (which means every Christian) dies, then there is offered to him excellent, precious, costly sacrifice, the loveliest and sweetest odor of incense and the best, highest worship that can ever be given to him (*WA* 36:258.26–36).[64]

---

[62] "'Preciosa in conspectu Dominj mors sanctorum erus,' 'Wie theur und werd ist für Gott der tod seiner heiligen'" (*WA* 36:258.17f.). Ps. 115 Vulgate reads *Gloriosa*, not *Preciosa*.

[63] For discussion of that sentence in Acts, see R. H. Carpenter, "Essential Schemes of Syntax: An Analysis of Rhetorical Theory's Recommendations for Uncommon Word Orders," *Quarterly Journal of Speech* 55 (1969): 161–168, here at 164.

[64] "Lieber, es düncket dich wol anders und ist für deinen augen an zu sehen, das der Heiligen tod sey ein lauter untergang und verderben, Und scheinet, als sey jr nu gar vergessen und geschwiegen und haben keinen Gott, der sich jr anneme, weil er sich jr bey jrem leben nicht hat angenomen und so elendiglich da hin sterben lassen, als die zu risen, zu fressen, verbrand und zu pulvert sind, Das keine vernunfft kan anders sagen, denn es sey ein jemmerlich elend, schendlich ding umb jren tod, Aber für Gott (sagen die lieben Veter) solt jrs gewislich da für halten, wenn ein Heiliger (das ist: ein iglicher Christen) stirbt, das jm geschehe ein trefflich theur köstlich opffer, der lieblichst und sussest geruch von wieb rauch und der beste höheste Gottes dienst, so jm widderfaren mag." Observe the elevated style of Luther's dialogue, with its doublets, triplets, and concrete language—all in the third person narrative of the patriarchs' 'arguments'—about what is apparent and what is real—yet spoken lovingly (as Luther would) to the listener.

Moreover, what Luther means by the highest worship offered to a saint who dies—the preaching of the Gospel of Christ—we have already learned in Sermon One.

At the midpoint of his argument about how the Christian is a new man, as seen through dead saints, Luther makes a startling and provocative statement. He asserts that God does not care so much for the living saints as he does for the dead. The remark seems to contradict somewhat his previous emphasis on the preaching to the living. However, Luther is being provocative here, playing up the paradox of how God can have so much good awaiting those whose physical presence suggests loss and shame. Now, such a bold assertion as Luther has just made, must be supported, for one cannot assume—at a funeral, especially one of a prince—that it is self evident that God is still in control and that the deceased (and ultimately everyone in attendance) is still in His care. Luther supports his claims in a series of four moves.

First, he provides a concrete example (*WA* 36:259.23–260.21) of God's care for His dead saints—the story of Cain and Abel (Gen. 4). Luther extends this example, through the use of quotes from the Genesis text—which includes, of course, those haunting rhetorical questions of the LORD to Cain—and through his own vivid commentary on the story and how it exemplifies the principle of the three aforementioned Psalms (116, 72, 9). Luther finds the principle in the blood of Abel, made even more precious through murder by his brother.

Second, Luther argues (*WA* 36:260.21–34) that the dear patriarchs took the example of God's concern for Abel's blood and derived their teachings (*Spruch*) about the precious nature of dead saints in God's sight. Both key terms (*dead, saints*) must be explicated in the argumentation. His argument contrasts the dire existence of saints while alive with a more glorious one after death. Yet Luther's argument also upholds the value of what God's saints already have—before death—to whatever sin and the world offer, and which they have forsaken.

Third (*WA* 36:260.35–261.19), Luther addresses more explicitly the second key term (*saints*), which he has just uttered in the assonant phrase—'called God's saints [*heissen Gottes Heiligen*]'—and which he has previously defined as 'every Christian,'[65] and here specified with the modifiers *Baptism, Faith, Word*. His explication is not an argument per se, in that he offers no quoted scriptural evidence, nor does he appeal to

---

[65] *LW* 51:246; *WA* 36:258.33.

life experience as analogy. Rather, he reminds his listeners of what—he presumes—they already know from the Bible, yet he does so using the rhetorical device of *expeditio*, wherein he successively removes competing definitions and then—turning via antithesis—celebrates his own surviving definition. Scripture teaches that saints are not: (1) those in heaven above, as the pope makes saints, "whom one should invoke, their days one should observe with fasting, and whom one should choose as mediators"; (2) Nor those who sanctify themselves and try to be holy in their deeds—namely, the "Carthusians, the barefooted friary, and other monks or pilgrims and such like devils." Rather (*Sondern*), to be saints means:

> Those whom God has sanctified, without any of their works and cooperation, by reason of the fact that they are baptized in Christ's name, sprinkled and washed clean with his blood, and with his dear Word and gifts of the Holy Spirit endowed and adorned. All of which we have not engendered and cannot engender, but [*sondern*] must receive from him by pure grace. But he who does not have this and seeks some other holiness is a stench and abomination to the Lord, because he denies that this bath of the blood of the innocent Lamb does not make one holy and clean (*WA* 36:261.12–19).[66]

Fourth, Luther returns (*WA* 36:261.20–31) to the theme of 'the dead,' and what specific promise of Scripture—viz., Ps. 11:15, which he quotes—dead saints have from God. The promise, moreover, is nestled within a series of threats Luther poses. In other words, no matter what manner of death one experiences, God will emerge victorious.

Following the four moves, Luther returns to his main theme—we are not like those 'who have no hope' because we are *new men*. He then summarizes all that God will do for him—specifically, Elector John, whose funeral this is.

---

[66] "Sondern die Gott geheiligt hat on alle jre werck und zuthun, da durch, das sie jnn Christus namen getaufft sind, <u>mit</u> seinem blut besprenget und rein gewasschen und <u>mit</u> seinem lieben wort und gaben des Heiligen geists begabt und gezieret, Welchs alles wir nicht erzeuget haben noch erzeugen können, sondern aus lauter gnaden von jm empfahen müssen. Wer aber solchs nicht hat und andere heiligkeit süchet, der ist eitel stanck und grewel für Gott, als der da leugket, das solch bad des unschuldigen Lemblins blut nicht heilig und rein mache." I have underlined the repeated prepositions to show Luther's use of anaphora. Whereas *LW* 51:248 translates "without any of their words or cooperation *whatsoever*" (my emphasis), there is no justification for 'whatsoever' in Luther's sentence.

Though we have lost him according to the body and the old nature, he is not lost and not forgotten [*unverloren und unvergessen*] before God in Christ, who has received him and brought him to rest, so that now he is safe from the devil and all enemies, and on the last day will bring him and all the saints with him before our eyes and the eyes of the whole world (*WA* 36:261.35—262.16).[67]

C. *Part Two (WA 36:262.17–264.11)*

Luther argues that the text of 1 Thess. 4:13–18 teaches that our new grief is held in hope. He claims that we must act like heavenly men, drawing strength from God's word, even though still stuck in the old Adam and having to withstand the devil's attacks. Luther thus returns to the text of the two funeral sermons, not to expound them but to use them as a basis for encouraging his listeners, for he argues that that is precisely what Paul's intention is with his readers. Luther's citation formula shows this: "Behold, this is what St. Paul is trying to do with this text." To bring about this comfort, he will make three moves, only the last one of which cites any additional Scripture (or quotes any Scripture at all). Moreover, he returns to the inclusive first plural pronoun for exhortation.

Prior to the three moves, he lays out his thesis (*WA* 36:262.17–21), which he draws from Paul: that the Thessalonians are to comfort one another, and with that same text we are to comfort ourselves as they comforted themselves.[68] Further, Luther admonishes his listeners to thank God when the body of a believer is carried off, for that person is in the knowledge of his Word, despite the fact that the outward man still has 'grief and sorrow.'

In his brief, first move (*WA* 36:262.21–27) Luther amplifies his noncontroversial claim about inward / outward, now / not yet, and he does it all in first plural, resorting again to graphic language: We are still stuck in the 'muck and mire' of our old Adam, who still (*noch*) 'befouls himself, hawks and snuffles.'

Second (*WA* 36:262.27–263.19), Luther takes more time to amplify what is not so obvious–that beyond and above the grief should be faith

---

[67] "…ob wir jn wol leiblich und nach dem alten wesen verloren haben, Aber für Gott jnn Christo unverloren und unvergessen ist, der sich seiner angenomen und jn zu ruge bracht, das er für dem Teuffel und allen feinden sicher ist und jn am jüngsten tag emit allen Heiligen für unsern und aller welt augen mit sich füren."

[68] "…wie sie sich getrösten haben" (*WA* 36:262.18f.). Luther is using periphrasis, while *LW* 51:249 abbreviates: "as they did."

that Christ 'died and rose again.' Turning to visual tactics, he uses anaphora to contrast what the world and its reason sees (grief) with what God sees—new hearts and new thoughts. The visual metaphors and similes are also bolstered by the Word, which, Luther contends, we do not see but rather hear spoken.[69] He asserts that Christ's death and resurrection was for the sake of Christians; that their death is a 'noble, precious treasure.' Faith will help us distinguish (*unterscheiden*) "between the world's eyes and God's eyes, between reason…and faith." Reason tells us the old man stays buried.

Luther's third (*WA* 36:263.20–264.12) and final move of Part Two is to reassure his listeners that what 1 Thess. 4:14ff. teaches remains true, reliable, and applicable to them. He makes no mention of Elector John. Luther's strategy is to rally his listeners around Christ's promise by helping them unite against the common foe. He cites the author of Hebrews (2:14) for proof of his case against the devil as the 'master and author' of death. In addition to doublets, Luther uses triplets and longer series—the longest yet of these two sermons—to generate emotional response in favor of Christ and against the devil. Then Luther uses epithets to make the ultimate accusation:

> [H]e employs all kinds of plagues, war, sword, fire, water, pestilence, syphilis, apoplexy, dysentery, etc., which as the Scripture says, are all his weapons, arrows, armor, and equipment, by which he accomplishes nothing less than to kill the Christians. For he is the master and author of death, who first introduced death, says the Epistle to the Hebrews [Heb. 2:14], and the chief hangman to destroy the believers. And he also honestly pursues his craft throughout the whole world and kills us all in the end, as he also killed Christ, so that every Christian owes his death to him (*WA* 36:263.31–264.12).[70]

---

[69] "…das wir nicht sehen, sondern allein da von hören sagen jnn dem Wort" (*WA* 36:262.35)

[70] "…schleicht jn tag und nacht nach und hat nicht ruge, bis er sie mordet und weg reumet, Und brauchet da zu allerley plage, krieg, schwerd, fewer, wasser, pestilentz, frantzosen, tropff, rote rhur 2c. welchs sind all zumal, wie die Schrifft saget, seine woffen, pfeil, harnisch und rustung, da mit er nichts mehr aus richtet denn die Christen zu tödten, Denn er ist des tods meister und ursacher, der den tod erstlich eingefuret hat, spricht die Epistel zun Ebreern, und der oberst hencker, die fromen zu würgen, drumb treibt er auch sein handwerck redlich durch die gantze wellt und todtet uns doch alle, wie er auch Christum getödtet hat, das jm doch ein jglicher Christ einen Marterer schuldig ist."

D. *Part Three (WA 36:264.13–267.17)*

Luther turns to the remaining verses of the text (14–18) to expound on Paul's declaration that God will raise us up (*WA* 36:264–267). We must trust God's word, not our senses, and believe that He will raise us up in an instant, just as Christ was raised. Paul's text assures that the dead in Christ will be raised with us, their bodies restored in a glorious resurrection like unto Jesus' own. Luther's argument, which he bolsters with evidence from 1 Cor. 15 and a return to the use of dialogue, can be seen as a series of five moves.

First (*WA* 36:264.13–27), he turns back—from his recent focus on the devil—to Christ, and to the promise of 1 Thess. 4:15, on the *manner* of Christ's return for His own, having spent all of the previous sermon and the first half of this one on the *fact* of Christ's return. The more detail one can give to a promise, the more probable and tangible it seems. Listen to Luther's depiction, both of what happened to Christ and what will happen to believers:

> Just as Christ also, though he lay in the grave, yet in a moment he was both dead and alive and rose again like a lightning flash from heaven. So he will raise us too in an instant, in the twinkling of an eye, out of the grave, the dust, the water, and we shall stand in full view, utterly pure and clean as the bright sun (*WA* 36:264.17–21).[71]

Second (*WA* 36:264.28–265.12), Luther begins to comment upon the text of v. 15, which will occupy him for all of the rest of Part Three. His first task—which takes him through the second, third, and fourth moves—is to vouch for the veracity and authority of the Word of God. He begins, in this second move, by calling attention to the opening clause of v. 15, what he calls a preface (*Vorrhede*). Paul—the dear Apostle—is concerned (*Sorge*), lest his message (*Predigt*) "be considered too slightly and not be taken as the Word of God." Luther supports his claim that Paul was not an impressive figure in person with Paul's own testimony in 2 Cor. 10:10.[72] The accusation posits a distinction between Paul's credibility in writing versus face-to-face speech. Luther magnifies the

---

[71] "Wie auch Christus, ob er wol im grab lag, doch war er jnn einem augenblick tod und lebendig und fur widder eraus wie ein blitz am himel, So wird e runs auch jnn einem nu eraus rucken, ehe wir uns umb sehen, aus dem sark, pulver, wasser, das wir da für augen gantz lauter und rein stehen wie die helle Sonne."

[72] *LW* 51:251 cites vv. 7–12 (the broader context), whereas *WA* 36:264.35 cites only v. 10 (Paul's actual statement about the accusations of the Corinthians).

difference between writer and speaker by exaggerating both forms of credibility, explicitly attributing them to Paul:

> He himself says that the Corinthians were saying of him that he preached and wrote as if he were a god and yet was such a small, insignificant person, with a thin and dried-up [*durres und magers*] body, which was the reason why the false apostles proudly despised and belittled him (*WA* 36:264.35–265.12).[73]

Luther has misconstrued what 2 Cor. 10:10 says, for there the accusation was that both Paul's physical presence and oral speech were weak. Whether he found it incredible that Paul's oral address be found wanting, nevertheless his point here is that the messenger, especially one some find weak, can complicate people's perception of a message's authority. So Luther takes more time in the next move to develop his argument that Paul has taken great pains in 1 Thess. 4:15 to attribute his authority to the Word of the Lord.

In the third move (*WA* 36:265.12–266.21), then, Luther's commentary on Paul's *Vorrhede* (1 Thess. 4:15a)—"For this we declare to you by the word of the Lord"—employs nearly every stylistic and reasoning tool he has used thus far: dialogue (for the first time in this sermon), analogy, simile, doublets, triplets, and a frequent repetition of the expression *Gottes wort*.[74] Paul, Luther implies, is taking no chances on God's word, which derives from all the Apostles, being mistakenly seen as 'one man's opinion':

> So he says, 'I know very well that I am speaking of things so high that the world and reason is offended. Therefore I beg and admonish [*bitte und vermane*] you not to look upon us, nor to accept as our word what we are saying to you, but rather to forget our person and listen to it as the word of the divine majesty spoken from heaven (*WA* 36:265.12–16).[75]

---

[73] "Er predigte und schriebe da her, als were er ein Gott, und were doch so ein kleine geringe person, durres und magers leibs, Daher jn die falschen Apostel stoltziglich verachteten und verkleineten."

[74] Luther explicates that term to mean the speaking power that inaugurated creation and still sustains it ever anew. His first instance of dialogue is to create a speech for Paul to use in explaining *why* he insists that his word is from God. Filled with doublets, the speech is almost entirely in first person; there are only two 'you's, and it culminates with a pregnant periphrasis for 'the word of the Lord.'

[75] "Darumb spricht er: Jch weis wol, das ich so hoch ding rede, das sich die wellt und vernunfft dran ergert, Darumb bitte und vermane ich, jr wolt nicht uns ansehen noch als unser wort annemen, was wir euch sagen, sondern unser person vergessen und so zuhören als der Göttlichen maiestet wort von himel gesprochen."

Luther's fourth move (*WA* 36:266.22–35) takes up the remaining part of 1 Thess. 4:15, or that which Paul, by the word of the Lord, says:

> We shall all go thither together at the same time, both those who have died previously and those who have lived until Christ's coming and that thus all will soar up together in an instant and see one another again...[W]e shall be drawn upward with open eyes and still be living in the body, whereas the others have long since decayed and, to our minds, become nothing and even though it would seem that we, who are still living, would be the first and would see the Lord much sooner than the dead. But he would have it that the dead would all rise with us in the same moment and have eyes as pure and fine as ours to see as well as we do. (Reason calls this ridiculous, but he [= Paul] tells me that he is speaking the Word of God.) (*WA* 36:266.25–35).[76]

Luther's fifth and final move (*WA* 36:266.36–267.17) of this Part Three completes the exposition of v. 15, moving beyond the timing—which he has just done—to the beauty of Christ's coming. In so doing he pulls images from 1 Cor. 15. What binds this exposition together is Christ as prototype and agent; thus, it would seem that Luther is exegeting the concept of 'Lord' from v. 15, while at the same time anticipating the drama of vv. 16–18, which he addresses explicitly in Part Four. As he ends this Part Three, Luther takes up Paul's voice: "He who will not believe this cannot believe us either. It's one and the same thing" (*WA* 36:267.16f.).[77]

E. *Part Four (WA 36:267.17–269.27)*

Luther discusses verses 16–18 on *how* the Lord will come. God will orchestrate a simultaneous resurrection of both living and dead saints, who together respond to the power and beauty of the Lord's voice, which is greater than sickness and death. Our joy at witnessing such a coming will be as great as that of the first advent shepherds, and

---

[76] "Wir werden alle zu gleich mit einander daher faren, beide, die zuvor gestorben und bis zu Christus zukunfft gelebt haben und also jnn einem augen blick alle semptlich da her schweben und uns zu gleich widder sehen...ob wol wir mit offenen augen da hin gezückt und noch bey lebendigem leibe sein werden, jene aber lang verweset und unserm düncken nach nichts mehr sein werden, Das es scheinet, das wir, die noch bey leben sind, solten die ersten sein und viel ehe den HERRn sehen denn die todten, Aber er wils so machen, das die todten alle jnn dem augen blick mit uns erfür komen und so rein und schön augen haben und sehen sollen als wir." The final line (Ratio ridet. Dixi me dei verbum dicere) is from Rörer's text, line 9.

[77] "Wer dan nicht wil glewben, der darff auch uns nicht gleuben. Das ist eines."

this joy brings a comfort that we must now share with one another. Comfort comes from confidence in God, whose Word and Presence are much better than what this life holds. In this part Luther uses a few additional Scriptures as examples of God's power of command over the natural world—including death—demonstrated at other times. He uses only one brief instance of dialogue, in the second of three moves, wherein the middle one is the longest.[78] However, his argumentation is not discretely divided, as the distributio suggests; rather, it flows almost seamlessly.

First (*WA* 36:267.28–37), Luther says everything will happen at once (*zu gleich*), that one should not think that we who are living will 'arrive and see Christ sooner [*ehe komen und Christum sehen*].' Rather (*Sondern*), we will be caught up together with him, all in one moment, and we shall be changed (*verwandelt*) and they made alive again from the 'grave and dust' in the self-same moment. And thus together, wherever we may be found, we shall fly straightway into the air, most beautifully clothed.[79]

Second, Luther uses his longest move (two paragraphs) to expand on the means of Christ's return, by discussing the cry of command, archangel's call, and trumpet of God. Since all three mechanisms are vocal and auditory, Luther's listeners hear a variety of terms for sound. Paul used, Luther avers, language normally reserved for describing a

---

[78] Note that there is both triplet and doublet, strung together syntactically, in Paul's own words: "For the Lord himself—with a cry of command and the archangel's call and with the sound of the trumpet of God [*mit einem Feld geschrey und Stimme des Ertzengels und mit der Posaunen Gottes*]—will descend from heaven. And the dead in Christ will rise first; then we—we who are alive and are left [*die wir leben und uberbleiben*]—shall be caught up together with them in the clouds, the Lord to meet in the air; and so we shall be with the Lord always. Therefore comfort ye now, with these words, one another" (*LW* 51:253) ['Denn er selbs der HERR wird mit einem feld geschrey und stimme des Ertzengels und mit der Posaunen Gottes ernider komen von himel, Und die todten jnn Christo werden aufferstehen zu erst, darn ach wir, die wir leben und uberbleiben, wrden zu gleich mit den selben hin gezuckt werden jnn den wolcken, dem HERREN entgegen jnn der lufft, Und werden also bey dem HERREN sein alle zeit. So tröstet euch num it diesen worten unter einander'] (*WA* 36:267.20–27).

[79] Closing this move with two polysyndetic triplets—the second one parallel to the triplet structure of 1 Thess. 4:16—Luther declares (in third person) how 'he, the Lord himself [*er, der HERr selbs*]' will come in his own person, as a Lord in his majesty. No longer sending "apostle or preacher or John the Baptist [*Apostel odder Prediger odder Johann den Tauffer*]," he will come with a great "shout of command and the voice and trumpet [*Feldgeschrey und Stimme und Posaune*]" of the archangel. Since Luther ends that statement with 'etc' (*2c.*), he clearly refers to the whole context of vv. 16–18. Moreover, by invoking three human mediators—and through the use of antithesis (*sondern*)—he unmistakably implies the finality and superiority of this visitation over all previous ones. That superiority he explicates next.

'grand, magnificent march of an army [*herlichen prechtigen Herr Zug*],' the kind used in a royal parade of triumph, with 'lifegards, banners, trumpets, and canisters,' in order that all may hear the arrival. This is Luther's example for Christ's coming, accompanied with shout of command (*Feldgeschrey*) and the sounding of the trumpet, called the trumpet of God (*Gottes Posaune*). Listen to the rest of Luther's auditory depiction:

> This will be done by the archangel with his innumerable host of angels, who will be his vanguard or forerunners and set up such a tumult that heaven and earth will be burned in an instant and lie in a heap and transformed, and the dead will be brought together from everywhere. That will be quite a different trumpet, and it will sound quite different from our trumpets and canisters on earth. But it will be his own voice or language, perhaps Hebrew, but even if it is not a particular language, it will be such a voice that will awaken all the dead (*WA* 36:268.17–25).[80]

Luther then develops another paragraph in this second move, employing a brief bit of dialogue that accompanies one of four quoted texts from the Gospels. His explanation closes with an analogy:

> Just as here on earth the preacher's voice which proclaims God's Word is not called man's word but God's Word, so here the voice of the archangel and yet the voice of the Lord Christ, as being spoken by his command and power [*Befelh und Krafft*] (*WA* 36:269.14–17).[81]

Third, Luther ends his exposition of 1 Thess. 4:16–18—although he still deals mainly with v. 16—by returning to the theme of comfort; hence, he uses several first plural pronouns. He argues that Paul portrayed the coming of Jesus and the rising of the dead in grand terms, so that we be 'confident and bold' and not so frightened about our loved ones, which would include—although Luther does not say so—Elector John.

---

[80] "…das wird thun der Ertzengel mit einem unzelichen hauffen Engel, die seine vordraber odder fürgenger sein werden und solch geschrey ansahen, da von himel und erde auff einen augenblick verbrand, auff einem hauffen ligen und verendert und die todten aus allen orten sollen zusamen bracht werden. Das wird eine ander Posaune sein und viel anders schallen dennunser drometen und büchssen auff erden, Es wird aber sein eine stimme odder sprache, villeicht auff Ebreisch, Odder ob es nicht ein sonderliche sprach were, so sol es doch eine solche stimme sein, davon alle todten erwachen mussen."

[81] "Gleich wie jtzt auff erden des predigers stimme, der Gottes wort predigt, heisst nicht des menschen, sondern Gottes wort, So ist auch die stim des Ertzengels und doch des HERRN Christi stim, als aus seinem befelh und krafft." Note the chiasmus in "stimme des Ertzengels und doch des HERRN Christi stim."

His final depiction invokes the beautiful image of the first advent, which was initially frightening but later joyous:

> That the archangel will come first with his trumpets and thousands of angels (like the angel in Luke 2 [:13] who appeared to the shepherds at Christ's birth with the multitude of the heavenly host) and strike up the cry of command, with Christ suddenly striding forth, and afterwards, when we have been raised and caught up into heaven [*erweckt und gen Himel gerückt sind*], sing everlastingly: *Gloria in excelsis Deo*, 'Glory to God in the highest' [Luke 2:14] (*WA* 36:269.21–27).[82]

F. *Conclusion (WA 36:269.28–270.18)*

Luther's conclusion comes in two steps (and two paragraphs): first, he applies the hope of Paul's exhortation in 1 Thess. 4:16–18 to all his hearers (4 first plural pronouns in the first 5 lines); second, he returns to the immediate cause in the funeral sermons—Elector John's death—assuring his listeners of John's being taken mercifully by God and exhorting them to hope in the return of Christ. In both paragraphs, moreover, Luther's words exude confidence in God and—for the immediate audience—find present comfort in the words of Paul.

The first paragraph (*WA* 36:269.28–270.9) invokes Paul's teaching in 1 Cor. 15:43, as Luther uses many doublets to bring comfort. He begins by paraphrasing Paul's concluding words from 1 Thess. 4:18 ('comfort one another with these words'), deviating from the syntax of GNT, Vulgate, *SeptBib* (and in 1534)—all of which emphasize the command ('comfort ye') by placing the verb in first position. However, we soon see that Luther's tactic is not to use mostly positive images, for he launches a barrage of doublets that are both positive and negative. The net effect is not one of mere balance, however; for, strung together, the doublets—inspired by Paul's own—often rhyme, and they paint a strongly positive picture (*schöne Bilde*) of seasonal metaphors:

> [W]hen out of this present winter in which everything is dead and buried he will make a beautiful, eternal summer and bring forth the flesh, which lies buried and decayed [*verscharret und verweset*], far more beautiful and glorious than it ever was before, as St. Paul says in 1 Cor. 15 [:43]:

---

[82] "Also das der Ertzengel mit seiner Posaunen wird vorher zihen mit viel tausent Engeln (wie der Engel Luce im andern Capitel, der den Hirten erschein bey werden ansahen), und Christus flugs mit da her faren, Und darn ach, wenn wir erweckt und gen himel gerückt sind, ewig singen: 'Gloria in excelsis Deo', 'Ehre sey Gott jnn der hohe.'"

'It is sown in dishonor and is raised in glory. It is sown in weakness and is raised in power.' For dishonor and weakness means that miserable, shameful [*jemerlich, schendlich*] form of man, than which there is no more shameful, insufferable [*schendlicher, unleidlicher*] carcass on earth, which is a great dishonor and shame to this noble creature. But this does not matter, for it will be raised in honor and a glorious form [*ehren und her-rlicher Gestalt*], just as a seed which is cast into the ground must decay and become nothing, but when summer comes it comes forth again with beautiful blades and ears of corn (*WA* 36:269.34–270.9).[83]

The second paragraph (*WA* 36:270.10–18) consists in two sentences: (1) a brief benediction—"To this end help us, God the Father, Son, and Holy Spirit. Amen," preceded by; (2) a lengthy exhortative sentence that reminds listeners of Elector John's Christian 'virtue' and uses that to invite hope for all in that same promise. "[H]e will, when the trumpet of the archangel is sounded, joyfully rise in an instant from this crypt and go to meet Christ, shining more brightly than the sun and all the stars, with us and all Christians (*WA* 36:270.14–17).[84] Thus, together, the two sermons begin and end with Luther's focus on his listeners: 'My dear friends...with us and all Christians.'

IV. *Prominent Themes and Strategies in the Sermons*

While he reflects on the contemporary religious funeral attended by a decidedly nonreligious audience,[85] Tony Walter's remarks are still worth

---

[83] "...aus dem jtzigen winter, dar jnn alles erstorben und verscharret ist, einen schönen ewigen Somer machen wird und das fleisch, das da ligt verscharret und ver-weset, viel schooner und herrlicher erfur bringen, denn es jhe gewest ist, Wie Sanct Paul jnn der Ersten zun Corinthern am funfzehenden Capitel da von redet: 'Es wird geseet jnn unehre und wird aufferstehen jnn herrligkeit, Es wird geseet jnn schwacheit und wird aufferstehen jnn krafft'. Denn unehre und schwacheit heisst die jemerlich, schendlich gestalt, das kein schendlicher, unleidlicher ass auff erden ist denn des men-schen, welchs eine grosse unehre und schande ist der edlen creatur, Aber das sol nicht schaden, denn es sol widder auff stehen jnn ehren und herrlicher gestalt, Gleich wie das körnlin, jnn die erden geworffen, mus gar verfaulen und zu nicht werden, aber wenn der Somer kömpt, so gehets widder erfur mit einem schönen halm und ehern."

[84] "...er werde, wenn die Posaune des Ertzengels gehen wird, gar frölich jnn einem augenblick aus diesem loch faren Christo entgegen und heller denn die Sonn und alle sterne leuchten mit uns und allen Christen."

[85] Related to the question of the modern funeral attendant, Tony Walter reviews many studies—mostly in the U.K.—in his "Why Are Most Churchgoers Women?: A Literature Review," *Vox Evangelica* 20 (1990): 73–90. Studies that have attempted to survey religious beliefs in the USA and how they might serve their holders are Daniel J. Klenow and Robert C. Bolin, "Belief in An Afterlife: A National Survey," *Omega*

hearing, for he has captured the significance of the funeral sermon especially, and its occasion. His remarks also help us contrast a preacher less experienced with death than Luther:

> In the religious funeral the celebrant can articulate the faith that the mourners doubt they have, but would like to have. Even believers need to have that done for them at this time of all times when faith is assailed. Many clergy have told me what an unexpected privilege it was when they conducted their first funeral. They always use that word 'privilege.' I am sure what they are referring to is the privilege of affirming for others in their time of need what they so desperately want to affirm, but in either their grief or their unbelief, cannot.[86]

One unmistakable feature of Luther's 1532 funeral sermons is their treatment of grief. In the first sermon Luther's initial argument is that human grief over the loss of a loved one is natural, God-given, and laudable. Since it comes within the exposition of the text, the argument is surprising, for a natural expectation is that in 1 Thess. 4:13 Paul meant that the Thessalonians, in their worries that their faithful dead would miss the resurrection, were *overdoing* their grief. Luther does address that issue, but not until the second sermon. In the first, he gives verse 13 the opposite meaning—that Paul intended to commend proper grief by the hopeful, especially since some people want to avoid it or hide it, either instance of which, says Luther, is evidence of unnaturalness or hypocrisy. His terms challenge what he says is an artificial and fabricated concept of virtue (*Tugend*), which heathens were trying to re-establish, but which he condemns as not created by nor pleasing to God. His evidence for his claim invokes and upholds the authority of Scripture: (1) 'Comfort one another' (verse 18) implies that there was sorrow and grief; (2) the Thessalonians were Christians; (3) Paul is not disapproving of their grief; and (4) we also have exemplary tales of Paul's grieving at the prospect of losing his friend Epaphroditus

---

20 (1989–1990): 63–74; Peggy C. Smith, Lillian M. Range, and Ann Ulmer, "Belief in Afterlife as A Buffer in Suicidal and Other Bereavement," *Omega* 24 (1991–1992): 217–225. For a superb and broader study centered outside the USA see Tony Walter, *The Eclipse of Eternity*. A recent USA poll is summarized in Thomas Hargrove and Guido H. Stempel III, "Truth or Fiction? Poll: Most Don't Believe in Resurrection," Scripps Howard News Service, 15 April 2006, http://www.newspolls.org/story.php?story_id=54 (accessed 21 April 2006); cf. C. Kirk Hadaway and Penny Long Marler, "How Many Americans Attend Worship Each Week? An Alternative Approach to Measurement," *Journal of the American Academy of Religion* 44 (2005): 307–322.

[86] Tony Walter, *Funerals*, 128.

(Phil. 2:27) and Christ's grief at the death of Lazarus (John 11:33). In addition to this sanction of grief, Luther adds his own stipulation that Paul meant for grief to be 'Christian and in moderation [*guter massen thun*]' and be done 'properly [*billich*]' (*WA* 36:239.15f.). In the second sermon he begins his recap of the first sermon by again sanctioning grief, but this time from the opposite angle. On that earlier occasion he had begun by affirming the feelings and concerns of his listeners. Now he starts with a presumption that those listeners have been sufficiently 'admonished and comforted' by the text, especially in the Christian hope that should inform their grief. Hence, in order to show the difference between pagans and those in Christ, he reminds them that proper grief will not be marked by weeping and wailing over the deceased. Their sorrowful feelings indicate a God-given and divinely supported humanity; at the same time, however, their behavior should characterize those who understand their new nature, brought about by the death and resurrection of Jesus. Thus, in his treatment of grief Luther displays aspects of a sermon that seems uniquely suited for comforting newly bereaved, yet its message contains some of the characteristic admonitions of any gospel sermon. Ultimate grief and gratitude are to be directed toward God and the gift of His Son.

A second feature of these sermons that clearly marks them as uniquely designed for the funeral occasion is Luther's frequent, endearing mention of the deceased. However, in this regard, there are distinct differences between the first and second sermon. In the first sermon—excluding general references to him as *a good friend, a prince*, etc.—Luther uses 14 different, specific epithets, 11 of which begin with the personal pronoun *our* (and one with *my*). Moreover, for all but 2 of the epithets, he attaches the adjective *beloved*.[87] The second sermon, however, contains only 2 such epithets of any kind—general or specific. Still, this sec-

---

[87] In order of occurrence in *LW* 51:231–255: *Our beloved sovereign prince* (231); *our beloved head* (twice: 231, 248); *our head, the beloved sovereign* (232); *our sovereign prince, our beloved lord and father* (235); *our beloved elector* (twice: 236, 237); *our beloved lord* (236); *our beloved ruler* (243); *our beloved prince* (thrice: 237, 238, 238); *the good prince* (238); *our beloved sovereign* (239); *Duke John of Saxony* (240); *our beloved lord and prince* (242); *my ruler* (243); *our beloved, deceased elector* (255). In *WA* 36:237–270: *unserm lieben Landsfürsten* (237.15); *unser liebes Haubt* (237.21); *unsers lieben Heubts* (261.35); *unser Haubt, die liebe Lands Fürste* (239.17); *unser Landesfürst, unser lieben Herr und Vater* (242.31); *unsern lieben Kürfürsten* (244.28); *unser lieber Kurfürst* (246.16); *unser lieben Herrn* (245.17); *unsern lieben Herren* (254.21); *unser lieber Fürst* (246.28; 247.22); *unserm lieber Fürsten* (247.29); *der fromme Fürst* (248.20); *unser lieben Landsfürsten* (248.32); *Hertzog Hans von Sachssen* (250.21); *unser lieber Herr und Fürst* (252.32); *mein Herr* (254.30); *unsern liben Kurfürsten (seligen)* (270.11).

ond sermon is distinctly oriented around death as exigence, and the initial and concluding remarks make it clear that the occasion is the Elector's death. Why then would Luther barely mention the Elector in the second sermon?

First, the initial message is the principal occasion for acknowledging the deceased, the grief of mourners, and the scriptural support for taking comfort in light of those facts (1 Thess. 4:13–14). The second message is driven chiefly by the imperative in v. 18—'comfort one another with these words'—and the glorious promise of Christ's return for his own, in vv. 15–17. Further, excluding 1 Thess. 4:13–18, Luther used many more Scriptures in the second message (14) than in the first (4), even though he spent equal time quoting Scripture in each message.[88] He did so in order to support his claims about the 'new man' and about God's care for the saints, especially the dead in Christ. In the first sermon Luther used nearly three times as much dialogue as in the second, for he often used such discourse to battle the natural (and demonic) tendencies toward fear and doubt at time of death, especially of a popular head of state.[89] In both sermons Luther identifies inclusively with his audience, for there is a much greater use of the first person plural (and far less use of the second person plural) than in nonfuneral preaching.[90]

In addition, his extended remarks about the deceased, Elector John, are instructive. While there is no mention whatsoever of his deathbed behavior, nor any comment on John's course of life, or about his family, Luther does develop important arguments centering on John's professional function and personal faith. We might expect these of the head of state who supported the Reformation, and Luther blends these functions to fashion John's 'virtues' of faithfulness as exemplary. He does not argue that John was perfect but that he was a "very devout, kindly man, free of all guile, in whom never in my lifetime have I seen the slightest pride, anger, or envy, who was able to bear and forgive

---

[88] By rough count of lines of English text in *LW* (Sermon I, 26 lines; Sermon II, 25 lines).

[89] By rough count of lines of English text in *LW* (Sermon I, 81 lines; Sermon II, 33 lines).

[90] Somewhat surprisingly, the rate of first plural pronoun usage is higher in the first sermon (1 pronoun per 3.05 lines of *WA* text) than in the second sermon (1 pronoun per 5.02 lines). In other words, the length of each sermon is virtually identical (Sermon I, 375 lines; Sermon II, 372 lines), but Sermon I has many more first plural pronouns (123, compared to 74, respectively).

all things readily and was more than mild" (*WA* 36:245.16–19).[91] But beyond his character, Luther says more about John's efforts to lead the nation: he sometimes failed, but few could have done better. Luther builds a strong case for appreciating the deceased as a person under the authority of God, and as a Christian leader who, not surprisingly, was subject to stronger onslaughts of the devil than the average person. In this argument Luther elevates the discussion beyond a consideration of personal merit and onto cosmic proportions. It is *God*'s strength that sees the faithful through demonic temptation. Critical in this argument is Luther's comparison between 'real,' 'manly' death and 'childish,' 'baby' death. The former occurs when the Christian dies to sin, dies with Christ; the latter is only the cessation of bodily functions. No matter how menacing the latter, we have nothing to fear when our senses stop and our body decays. Luther dwells on the signs, evidence, and validity of John's 'real' death, locating them in his baptism and his faithful, public confession of Christ's death and resurrection at the Augsburg Diet. While comprising less than one-sixth of the two sermons, these arguments about Elector John characterize this first sermon as a distinctive, funeral message.

Yet these sermons share many important features with *all* of Luther's preaching. For example, Cranach's painting above the *Reformationsaltar* in the *Schloßkirche* depicts Luther preaching the crucified Christ from the *Kanzel*, with the flesh and blood crucifix standing on the church floor, between himself and his audience. The scene represents Luther's understanding and practice of preaching, and these sermons preach Christ—his death, resurrection, and coming again—much more than they preach the faith or virtue of Elector John. It is John's identity *as a Christian*, not his own virtue or success, that ensures his status as 'among those who sleep in Jesus Christ' (*WA* 36:248.32f.).[92] It is 'such exceeding power' that *Christ*'s death has that makes, by comparison, our death a sleep.[93] It is the certainty and authority of *God's Word* that alone raises the dead and which alone can be trusted to enable us to withstand the devil's efforts to get us to try to measure up on our own.

---

[91] "…seer fromer, freundlicher man gewesen ist, on alles falsch, jnn dem ich noch nie mein lebtag einigen stoltz, zorn noch neid gespüret hab, der alles leichtiglich tragen und vergeben kunde, und mehr denn zu viel mild gewesen ist."

[92] "…unter die rechen, die jnn Jhesu Christo schlaffen."

[93] "…solche treffliche macht" (*WA* 36:240.34).

In commenting on Luther's preaching on 1 Cor. 15, beginning on 11 August 1532, Gerhard Sauter observes:

> Preaching is needed because it leads us out of the 'vale of tears' into the future life.[94] If this does not happen, then preaching is wasted time and a useless or even damaging enterprise....What is true of faith—that it comes from preaching (Rom. 10:17)—is equally true of hope. Preaching is the indispensable ground of hope because hope comes from God and cannot be invented by human beings. Preaching declares to us what we could never tell ourselves. How else are we able to speak of resurrection, of which we cannot discover even a trace within ourselves?[95]

The methods of preaching Christ on this occasion are characteristic of most of Luther's preaching: (1) he makes more than 20 explicit citations of Scripture, several more allusions, and altogether calls attention to the words of Christ, Paul, or the text more than 60 times. In these references and the arguments they anchor Luther unashamedly admonishes his listeners to focus on Jesus and God's love far more than on their loss; (2) he compares the glory and power of the good and eternal to the futility or even disgust of what is evil and temporary. With a vividness that today would make us wince, Luther plainly employs sensual imagery in speaking about death and decay (quoted earlier): "When you see him there [in Christ], then the dead body is no longer in the coffin. Even though the carcass be foul and stinking it makes no difference; turn your eyes and nose and all five senses away and remember what St. Paul says in the fifteenth chapter of 1 Corinthians" (*WA* 36:244.16–18). Luther uses 'carcass' twice more, in just as graphic ways (earlier in this chapter). Often this earthy, concrete imagery comes in doublets: 'fright and trembling' (*LW* 51:238), 'abominable and horrible,' 'weak and sick,' 'shame and ignominy,' 'bind or imprison' (*LW* 51:244).[96] Some of the vivid language comes in longer lists, speaking about the lofty as well as the lowly: God cared for the dead, even though some were 'torn and devoured and burned and pulverized' (*WA* 36:258.31). This style of speaking builds emotional power, even when using so-called abstractions: the old nature "tries to frighten us with misery, distress,

---

[94] "Sed si baptisatus, ut incipiam aliam vitam, et ista praedicatio ist nicht gericht ad praesentem vitam, sed quodmodo ex isto jamertal in futuram" (*WA* 36:534.17–19); LW 28:100; "Sed hoc discite, ut cor vestrum zu richten auff ein ander leben und wesen" (*WA* 36:544.12–13); LW 28:108.

[95] Gerhard Sauter, "Luther on the Resurrection," 195, 197.

[96] Neil R. Leroux, "Luther's Use of Doublets," *RSQ* 30 (summer 2000): 35–54.

misfortune, poverty, death" (*WA* 36:257.21); the patriarchs saw the resurrection from afar, through "dark blue clouds, whereas for us the clear, bright sun is shining" (*WA* 36:257.37–39).

In other words, Luther's rhetorical repertoire was not subdued for a somber occasion. Like any other pulpit opportunity, these sermons try to unleash the meaning in the text, using imagery and affect that renders the proclamation of the gospel potent.

CHAPTER FIVE

"FAITHFUL ARE THE WOUNDS OF A FRIEND": LUTHER'S CONSOLATORY LETTERS

When the close relative of a friend or acquaintance dies, many people stay away, offering the excuse to others (or themselves) that "I wouldn't know what to say." Sensing social obligation and linguistic barriers, we want to avoid the chapel visitation, the funeral service, and even the 'sympathy card.'[1] Sometimes we alter our routines in order to make a face-to-face encounter with the bereaved less likely. It is easier to order flowers or sign off on a group card (even beg a secretary or spouse to handle this) than it is to talk—or write to—a bereaved person.[2] 'What do I say?' captures the frustration a writer of the consolatory letter feels, and only part of that frustration can be blamed on a lack of practice writing personal letters, a condition much older than e-mail. Authoring a consolatory letter forces us to speak about the unspeakable, to face severe unhappiness, to address an insoluble problem. Just what that problem is, and how it is a rhetorical problem, is the broad subject of this chapter. More specifically, I investigate how Martin Luther—in whose career as a healer of souls (*Seelsorger*) we are interested—handled the rhetorical problem of the consolatory letter.[3]

---

[1] "Comfort is a lost art, except for choosing a greeting card. (Our ambivalent feelings about death are reflected here, even: the manufacturers have not yet produced personalized sympathy cards for a favorite nephew, a sister-in-law, or a dear aunt)"; Joseph Bayly, *The Last Thing We Talk About*, 20. On American attitudes and behaviors toward emotion, see Peter N. Stearns, *American Cool: Constructing a Twentieth-Century Emotional Style* (New York, 1994).

[2] The literature on grief and mourning offers differing accounts for this phenomenon. Geoffrey Gorer, *Death, Grief, and Contemporary Mourning in Britain* (London, 1965), 64, claims there are no longer rules of mourning, "so neither the bereaved nor their friends and neighbours know how to relate to each other. Mutual avoidance is the solution adopted by one or both sides." Jane Littlewood, *Aspects of Grief* (London, 1992), suggests that individuals have strong personal norms about the proper way to grieve, but these are not necessarily shared by their intimates. As Walter, who suggested these sources, claims: "it may be that there are too many norms, specific to family of origin, and not well enough understood by outsiders—including those marrying in"; *The Revival of Death*, 18f.

[3] Rudolf Keller, "Luther als Seelsorger," *Lutherische Kirche in der Welt* 44 (1997): 101–118; Gerhard Ebeling, *Luthers Seelsorge*; idem, "Trostbriefe Luthers an Leidtragende,"

After discussing briefly what kind of rhetorical problem a consolatory
letter addresses, I outline some of what the rhetorical and epistolary
traditions in the sixteenth century had to say about consolation, and
what connections Luther might have had with them. Then I present
an analysis of 20 letters Luther wrote to bereaved parents, spouses,
and siblings—all of them of the Evangelical faith. Finally, I offer some
tentative conclusions.

I. *Consolatory Letter as Rhetorical Response*

Proverbs 25:11 reads, "A word *fitly spoken* is like apples of gold in a
setting of silver" (emphasis mine). Bitzer's notion of 'fitting response'
requires that the rhetor address the appropriate audience, operate within
given constraints and—most important—properly assess the exigence.[4]
Of the constraints facing consoler and bereaved, the former has values,
beliefs, and opinions on what the bereaved needs in order to find comfort. Without personal bereavement experience, the consoler may think
the exigence is one of severe sadness, even depression, which requires
'cheering up.'[5] Depending on the consoler's (and the culture's) value
system and experiences, bereavement may be perceived as a radical
anomaly in an otherwise stable, happy life.[6] Accordingly, the exigence
then would be seen as: threat to the well being of the bereaved and to

---

in *Kirche in der Schule Luthers: Festschrift für D. Joachim Heubach*, ed. Bengt Hägglung and
Gerhard Müller (Erlangen, 1995), 37–48; Herbert Anderson, "Whatever Happened to
Seelsorge?" *WW* 21 (winter 2001): 32–41 (The entire issue of was devoted to pastoral
care).

[4] Lloyd Bitzer, "The Rhetorical Situation"; cf. "Functional Communication: A Situational Perspective, in *Rhetoric in Transition: Studies in the Nature and Uses of Rhetoric*, ed.
E. E. White (University Park, Pa., 1980), 21–38.

[5] "[S]ympathetic assessment of another's suffering, not to mention the offer of
effective relief, is more likely to come from those who have suffered than from those
who have not"; D. A. Carson, *How Long, O Lord? Reflections on Suffering and Evil* (Grand
Rapids, 1990), 122.

[6] Such a perception is consistent with Aristotle's view of the pleasant (*Rhetoric* 1.11,
1370a–1372a)—that Pleasure is a "movement, a movement by which the soul as a whole
is consciously brought into its normal state of being; and that Pain is the opposite.
If this is what pleasure is, it is clear that the pleasant is what tends to produce this
condition, while that which tends to destroy it, or to cause the soul to be brought into
the opposite state is painful. It must therefore be pleasant as a rule to move towards a
natural state of being, particularly when a natural process has achieved the complete
recovery of that natural state"; Aristotle, *Rhetoric*, trans. W. Rhys Roberts (New York,
1954), 67.

the stability of the family and, ultimately, the surrounding community.[7] However, as unavoidable and common as death is—as universal[s], 'independent of culture' as the 'phases of personal bereavement' seem to be—not all historic periods and cultures handle consolation alike.[8] If we perceive a death as a danger to the economic and psychic equilibrium of the social system, our understanding of the exigence may be somewhat at odds with how the bereaved construes it. Consequently, the consoler may then see bereavement as an unnatural episode, a glitch in the system—a problem to be *remedied*. The consoler may then offer, as remedy, well intentioned but ill-timed efforts that are not 'fitting' because they are not in harmony with the bereaved's perceptions and feelings. For example, the consoler may try too hard to cheer up, may listen too little, offer advice too soon, or act surprised or dismayed at the lack of 'progress' the bereaved is making. In other words, the consoler's perception suggests that modification of the exigence requires 'fixing' the bereaved's sadness; while the bereaved's perception of the exigence is that it cannot be modified, that there is no 'fix.'[9] Possible outcomes here, when consolation does not work and grief becomes seen (by others) as pathological, are despair or 'mummification,' where the bereaved continues not only to treasure the deceased's memory but also to care for a loved one's belongings, room, etc.[10] What I am suggesting is that the 'rhetorical situation' of consoling a bereaved person,

---

[7] Donovan J. Ochs, *Consolatory Rhetoric*, 20–25. Ochs's book deals with funeral ritual and discourse, and treats consolatory literature very little.

[8] Ibid., 16; cf. Peter N. Stearns and Mark Knapp, "Historical Perspectives on Grief," in *The Emotions: Social, Cultural and Biological Dimensions*, ed. Rom Harré and W. Gerrod Parrott (London, 1996), chapter 6. The 'phases' or stage-theory of grief has now come under scholarly question; see Charles W. Brice, "Paradoxes of Maternal Mourning," *Psychiatry* 54 (1991): 1–12; Margaret Stroebe, et al., "Broken Hearts or Broken Bonds: Love and Death in Historical Perspective," *American Psychologist* 47 (October 1992): 1205–1212; C. B. Wortman and R. C. Silver, "The Myths of Coping with Loss," *Journal of Consulting and Clinical Psychology* 57 (1989): 349–357.

[9] Although—consistent with Aristotle's view of the pleasant, the normal, and the habitual—the bereaved may indeed view her grief as compulsory (i.e., forced upon her) and therefore unnatural, grief soon can become habitual. And what is habitual—happening often, according to Aristotle—is strangely pleasant, feeling normal. In early periods of profound grief it is common for the bereaved to feel guilty at an occasional pleasant memory or unexpected smile. Therefore, attempts by others to help the bereaved feel 'better' may be rejected as unnatural and even insulting, implying—as perceived by the bereaved—that the bereaved's deceased loved one has been forgotten or is not worthy of sadness.

[10] Paul C. Rosenblatt, *Bitter, Bitter Tears*, 36f.; cf. idem., *Parent Grief: Narratives of Loss and Relationship* (Philadelphia, 2000).

particularly through a single letter, is a complicated and delicate matter. Even for experienced consolers, who could probably be more effective in face-to-face interaction, the problem of 'what to write' is daunting. So much so, that too often people simply put off the matter entirely. And it is an absence of people—isolation—that the bereaved too often have to endure.

Kenneth Burke speaks of a Symbol working—i.e., having appeal—in several ways: (1) as the interpretation of a situation; (2) by favoring the acceptance of a situation; (3) as the corrective of a situation.[11] He further argues that a work of literature should 'fit' one sort of situation rather than another, that 'fit' may mean corrective to the situation, or it may fit "simply because the situation enables it to be well received. The two ways are not necessarily opposed, but are often opposed."[12] For letters of consolation, I believe Burke has it right: how to avoid opposing viewpoints about *post mortem* survival! A crucial match of perceived exigence by consoler and bereaved is necessary—first to interpret the situation properly, then to find acceptance. Only when both have occurred will any 'corrective' result. Accordingly, the Vulgate's reading of 'fitly spoken' (Prov. 25:11) suggests that timing is crucial: "qui loquitur verbum in tempore suo." In addition, the writer's credibility with the bereaved is essential. Therefore, I try to trace Luther's relationship with the bereaved (and the deceased), as well as note Luther's increasing experiences with death in his own family.

II. *Consolatory Genre in Rhetorical and Epistolary Traditions*

The classical tradition has examples of consolation as one of the standard formal speeches—written for public funerals of war dead, private individuals, etc.—but they were oral speeches or written records of what

---

[11] Kenneth Burke, *Counter-Statement*, 2nd ed. (Berkeley, 1953; reprint ed., 1968), 154f.

[12] Ibid., 184, n. 1. Bitzer, "Functional Communication," 36f., quotes Burke here and argues that the 'corrective' is essential. For example, one of the perplexing issues for consolers is the paradoxical world in which the bereaved now lives: "individuals experiencing different degrees of disorientation, uncertainty, and insecurity.... contradictory and incompatible urges on the one hand to 'push the dead away,' and, on the other, to 'keep the dead alive'"; Donovan Ochs, *Consolatory Rhetoric* 27, quoting Robert Blauner, "Death and Social Structure," *Psychiatry* 29 (1966): 387. The most astonishingly astute article I have ever read, for articulating *and* analyzing the feelings of contemporary bereaved parents, is Brice, "Paradoxes of Maternal Mourning."

might have been said by the consoler. Hardly any genuine examples exist of private epistolary consolations in Greek, but we do have examples in Latin.[13] The themes of consolatory writers, whose task is to reconcile the bereaved to the inevitable, are of two categories: (1) to convince the mourner that she or he has no cause to grieve because nothing bad has happened or is happening to the dead; (2) to advocate moderation in grief. In the latter category, reason is said to ease or completely remove grief; for example, that others have had worse to bear. Other themes are a laudatory description of the deceased, the participation of the consoler in the sense of bereavement, and the suggestion that the mourner apply to himself the good advice with which he has comforted others.[14] While some of these themes show up in Luther's letters, the Christian tradition offered correctives to the subject of consolation: (1) there is a need for reassurance about the deceased's prospects in the afterlife; (2) there is the matter of how God's hand is at work in the death; and (3) there is the possibility of God, Christ, the Holy Spirit, and the Word being comforters of the bereaved.

In her work on the Renaissance letter, Judith Rice Henderson has helped us understand the complexity of the *ars dictaminis* of the Medieval and Renaissance humanists.[15] Letter writing was a far more serious business then than now. The distinctions we make between private and public letter writing—and between the familiar and the official letter—were more blurred for the humanists. They sometimes composed letters that were not original, and they always paid strict attention to the protocol of social rank—of both writer and recipient. We also know that the humanists saw and taught letter writing as an exercise in rhetoric. So, like the classical oration, the letter usually contained five parts: *salutatio, exordium, narratio, petitio,* and *conclusio.* Moreover, the humanists had views about what style to use for each type of letter.[16]

---

[13] Hubert Martin, Jr. and Jane E. Phillips, *"Consolatio ad Uxorem (Moralia 608A–612B),"* in *Plutarch's Ethical Writings and Early Christian Literature,* ed. Hans Dieter Betz (Leiden, 1978), 399–401.

[14] Ibid., 402f.

[15] Judith Rice Henderson, "Defining the Genre of the Letter: Juan Luis Vives' *De Conscribendis Epistolis,*" *Renaissance and Reformation* 7 (1983): 89–105; idem, "On Reading the Rhetoric of the Renaissance Letter," in *Renaissance Rhetoric,* ed. Heinrich F. Plett (Berlin, 1993), 143–162.

[16] Henderson, "On Reading the Rhetoric," 143–150.

Because he recognized the letter as a persuasive exercise, Erasmus (1466/69–1536), in his *de conscribendis epistolis* (1522), classified letters under the traditional genera of the classical oration: deliberative, demonstrative, and judicial. He also discussed familiar letters, under which comes the letter of consolation, which is deliberative, since it attempts to persuade the correspondent not to grieve. Most importantly, Erasmus judged that a letter should be flexible, adapting itself to the argument, place, time, and person; that its style should likewise be flexible. He advised that "in consoling [,] it should be soothing and friendly."[17] Erasmus maintained that a letter is 'a conversation between absent friends.'[18] He offers direction for the letter of consolation, by first acknowledging its importance:

> …no obligation arises more often than that of comforting our friends with consoling words. Timely and friendly consolation is no ordinary act of kindness; for in times of distress, when it is not possible to remedy the anguish of those whom we love through deeds, it at least enables us to ease their sufferings by words. Yet we must perform this duty skillfully.…[19]

The skill needed will involve determining the state of mind of the bereaved, whether that person is able to receive reasonable arguments, or whether a more indirect approach is needed. By today's standards, much of Erasmus's advice is wise, especially for strategically winning the confidence of the recipient by identifying with the pain of grief *before* offering any 'medicine' to help ease it. In addition, Erasmus includes what "piety and the Christian faith should demand of us."[20] This arsenal of arguments—about how much more blessed is 'immortality' than the misery of life here—adds to the persuasive repertoire.

Whether Luther had read Erasmus's *de conscribendis epistolis*, or other Renaissance humanists on letter writing, is still uncertain (my sample of Luther's letters begins in 1524).[21] Despite their literary debate of 1524,[22] we know from letters of early 1519 that by then Luther had

---

[17] Henderson, "Defining the Genre," 98, quoting *de conscribendis epistolis*, I.ii.222–3.

[18] Desiderius Erasmus, *On the Writing of Letters*, trans. Charles Fantazzi, in *Collected Works of Erasmus*, vol. 25, ed. J. K. Sowards (Toronto, 1985), 50.

[19] Ibid., 148.

[20] Ibid., 162–164.

[21] Timothy P. Dost's survey runs only through 1522; see his *Renaissance Humanism in Support of the Gospel in Luther's Early Correspondence: Taking All Things Captive* (Aldershot, 2001).

[22] Desiderius Erasmus, "Dialogue on Free Will" (September 1524) and Martin Luther, "Bondage of the Will" (December 1524 [*LW* 33:3–295]). Both works are available in

not only read most of Erasmus's works but also that he had a great affection for his work.[23] We also know that by 1536 many of Erasmus's works were available at the University of Wittenberg library.[24] Moreover, although I have examined only a tiny sample (1%) of Luther's letters,[25] we can see many of the humanist elements in his consolatory letters, both in form and themes. Yet we see many differences, not the least of which are: (1) that Luther often restrains his language when speaking to officials; (2) he often uses self-deprecating remarks; and (3) he always speaks in far greater detail about the theological resources of Christianity than merely about 'immortality.' His manner of speaking fondly of the deceased, of gently affirming the loss which the bereaved has experienced, of arguing that since the deceased was a Christian God has both taken and protected her or him, and that God has not only caused the grief but will also heal it, shows resources of Christianity far beyond that which Erasmus offered. Yet Luther still urges moderation in grieving, sometimes to the point of seeming harsh; he is especially so to bereaved parents. His letters try to operate within an ethos that advocates and models the fact that pain and comfort are not evils to be avoided but are resources that especially allow us to be close to God.

III. *Luther's Letters*

The twenty letters I have selected were written during roughly the last two decades of Luther's life (1524–1545), because for nearly all of this period Luther was a 'family man.'[26] He married on 13 June 1525 and, over the next nine years, became the father of six children (four of

---

Luther and Erasmus: Free Will and Salvation, ed. E. Gordon Rupp and Philip S. Watson (Philadelphia, 1969).

[23] See Luther's 28 March 1519 letter to Erasmus, and Erasmus's 30 May 1519 letter to Luther in Lisa Jardine, "Before Clarissa: Erasmus, 'Letters of Obscure Men,' and Epistolary Fictions," in *Self Presentation and Social Identification: The Rhetoric and Pragmatics of Letter Writing in Early Modern Times*, ed. Toon Van Houdt, Jan Papy, Gilbert Tournoy, and Constance Matheeussen. Supplementa Humanistica Lovaniensia 18 (Leuven, 2002), 385–403, here at 396–399.

[24] Ernest G. Schwiebert, "Remnants of A Reformation Library," *Library Quarterly* 10 (1940): 494–531, here at 528.

[25] Approximately 2,580 of Luther's letters are extant; cf. Gottfried G. Krodel, "Introduction to Luther's Letters," *LW* 48:xiii.

[26] Nearly all the letters come from Tappert, Chapter II, "Consolation for the Bereaved," 53–81. A few letters were found in *LW*. I have also consulted the texts of these letters in *WABr*; other volumes cited include *WATr*.

whom survived him). He also buried both of his parents (father Hans
and mother Margaret both died in May 1530 and 1531, respectively).
With two exceptions these letters are written to: (a) bereaved widows
(three) or widowers (eight) who had recently lost their spouses; and (b)
bereaved parents (seven) who had recently buried sons.[27] The remaining letters (c) were addressed to Elector John (1525), four days after the
funeral of his brother, Frederick the Wise, and to Luther's firstborn son
Johannes, who was grieving the loss of his sister Magdalena, who died
on 20 September 1542, at age thirteen.

From the contents and strategies of the letters it becomes evident that
Luther is preoccupied with two, equally strong, forces: (1) the witness
the death of a Christian has for the world, testifying about the truth
and power of the Gospel over sin and death. This witness speaks not
only through the words and ritual of the funeral, but also through the
behavior of the bereaved; (2) the existential reality of life in Christ for
believers, who must adjust to life without their deceased loved ones.
The life of faith means living each day in the simultaneous grips of
death and life so that, as humans, we experience death in all its worldly
pain and horror. That is why we sometimes face death bravely yet still
mourn the loss of a loved one.

Unlike many contemporary societies, which find the deaths of adolescent and adult children to be the most difficult from which to recover
successfully, Luther's letters show no such tendency. He is more likely
to address the suddenness or severity of death (e.g., accident or suicide)
as meriting greater consolation than he is to indicate that a bereaved
parent needs more comfort than a bereaved spouse. Several consistent
themes emerge: that God, who knows better than we, is the one who
has taken the loved one; that God created us as feeling, loving creatures,
who naturally will grieve the loss of loved ones; that God, Christ, and
the Word are greater consolers than any human; that a faithful death
is better than a miserable life, through suffering or sinning; and that
there is, however, a need for moderation in grief. Moreover, as he ages,
Luther's efforts to identify with the grieving through empathy and self-
disclosure continue to intensify as his own personal experiences with
grief accumulate. A brief survey of the letters bears evidence of this

---

[27] Two widowers, Ambrose Berndt (1532) and Andreas Osiander (1545), had also
lost a child during childbirth.

dual tendency: to affirm survivors in their grief experiences and to admonish them to moderate their grief.

A. *Letters to Bereaved Parents*

Twice in Scripture we read that mourning 'for an only son' (Jer. 6:26; Amos 8:10) is implied to be the worst of all forms of grief. Luther not only wrote several letters to bereaved parents but also became one himself. Since all the following letters were written after 1528, when Elizabeth died at 8 months, we can only speculate about how Luther would have spoken to bereaved parents prior to becoming one as well.[28] In a 1530 letter to Conrad Cordatus (1480–1546) (Tappert, 60f.),[29] pastor at Zwickau and father of a three-month old son who had died, Luther begins the body of the letter (*petitio*) by skipping any *exordium* or *narratio* (with which he would normally begin, especially when he is the one conveying the news of death, or when he reveals who asked him to write the letter). He uses doublets to intensify his points: "May Christ comfort you in this sorrow and affliction [*humilitate et afflictione*] of yours. Who else can soothe such a grief? I can easily believe what you write, for I too have had experience of such a calamity, which comes to a father's heart sharper than a two-edged sword, piercing even to the marrow, etc.?" (*WABr* 5:273.1–5).[30] This is two years after Elizabeth had died, and Cordatus knew that, since he and his wife had then lived with the Luthers in Wittenberg. Cordatus is a close friend, one who had picked Luther to sponsor the child at his baptism. Luther wanted, however, to remind him that others have felt—and still feel—such grief; that, according to his allusion to Heb. 4:12, death wields a power that rivals that of the Word of God. His rhetorical question ("Who else can soothe such a grief?") affirms the intensity of Cordatus's plight, yet at the same time offers hope in Christ alone. Luther does not tell him *how* to find comfort in Christ, but he assures him that through this experience that he will learn the "power of the Word and of faith

---

[28] Luther's sister Margaret Kaufman died in 1529, leaving four children, whom Martin and Katy then raised to adulthood.

[29] *WABr* 5:273f. [Nr. 1544].

[30] "Christo, qui consoletur te in ista humilitate et afflictione tua, mi Cordate. Quis enim alius hunc dolorem possit mitigare? Nam facile credo, quae scribis, omnia, utpote expertus huiusmodi casum, qui patris viscera visitat, penetrabilior omni gladio ancipiti, pertingensque usque ad medullas etc."

which is proved in these agonies" (*WABr* 5:273.12f.).[31] He also reminds Cordatus that God is "more truly and properly [*verior et proprior*] a father than you were" and that He preferred 'for his own glory' that the son should be with him "rather than with you, for he is safer there than here" (*WABr* 5:273.6f.).[32] Luther's personal friendship with Cordatus and his own experience with bereavement help establish the ethos in this letter that can help console him by perhaps convincing him of these things, so that he can turn to Christ for comfort. Yet now—two years after burying his own infant daughter, and just weeks before his own father will die—Luther acknowledges how difficult it is to hear these things when newly bereaved. Employing a euphemism ('a story that falls on deaf ears'),[33] Luther tells the humanist and theologian Cordatus that since his grief is so new, he will "therefore yield to your sorrow. Greater and better men than we are have given way to grief and are not blamed for it" (*WABr* 5:273.9f.).[34] But still Luther claims it is a good thing for Cordatus to have had this kind of trial, for he can then find his faith tested. It seems to us, then, that grief is a natural experience, while at the same time an instrument of God for establishing one in the faith and testifying to him, and others who observe him, of God's power to console and to sustain. Finally, we note an important feature of consolation, at the end of the *petitio* and continued as *conclusio*: that grief is somehow easier to bear when significant others not simply notice but care. As with most of the letters to close friends, Luther advises Cordatus to stay busy (to 'labor with the Zwickauers'); he tells him to "Greet the companion of your sorrow"; and he assures him that "My Katie and our whole household send you greeting."[35] So, not until the letter's end does the bereaved mother receive any attention! It is not so unusual, however, given Luther's personal friendship with Conrad, that he would speak to him alone.

---

[31] "...auae sit vis verbi et fidei, quae in his agonibus probata sit."

[32] "...qui verior et propior pater est, quam tu fueris, pro zelo suo maluerit filium tuum, imo suum, apud se quam apud te essu."

[33] "...surdo fabula" (*WABr* 5:273.8). Luther may be alluding to Terence, *Heauton-timorumenos*, 2.1.10 or Erasmus, *Adagia* 1.4.87. Cordatus will later become one of the recorders of Luther's *Tischreden*. See *OER*, 1:430.

[34] "...auia luxerunt huiusmodi luctum maiores et meliores, quam nos sumus, nec tamen reprehenduntur."

[35] "Poteris autem advolare tempore congruo....Saluta sociam doloris tui....Salutat te mea Ketha et domus tota" (*WABr* 5:273.21–25).

By midyear 1531 Luther has suffered the deaths of both of his parents—his father Hans in April 1530 and his mother Margaret in May 1531. In a 21 October 1531 letter to Mr. and Mrs. Matthias Knudsen (Tappert, 61f.)[36] Luther explains in his *exordium / narratio* that the preceptor had asked him to write. As is characteristic in all the letters where he is writing to people he hardly knows, and especially when the death—as here—was that of a Wittenberg University student, Luther uses the doublet in his first mention of the deceased, with warm, endearing, familial epithets ('your dear son of blessed memory').[37] Speaking throughout the letter to both parents, he acknowledges their right to grieve ("it is quite inconceivable that you should not be mourning"), Luther quotes Jesus Sirach, "Weep for the dead, for light hath failed him; but do not mourn much, for he hath found rest (Ecclus. 22:11)."[38] This gives him the transition he needs to suggest in his *petitio* that the parents not only can find solace in the Scriptures, but that they need to grieve 'moderately.'[39] He discloses no experiences of his own grief but rather argues that moderation in mourning is justified by 'such a good end' their son had and that he has joined Jesus in 'the eternal rest of Christ.'[40] This is a common argument that Luther makes to parents he is consoling, as he tells them about their sons' deaths and also—from his recent vantage point as their academic and spiritual mentor—about their lives. Such reassurance for the Knudsens includes what all bereaved parents desperately what to know: *how* their son died (he went 'to sleep in Christ so peacefully').[41] In addition, Luther adds evidence in affirming that this good death was noted by observers ("everyone marveled that he continued steadfast to the end in his prayers and in his confession of Christ").[42] He exhorts the parents to take solace in the fact that they

---

[36] *WABr* 6:212f. (Nr. 1877).

[37] "Eurs lieben Sohns seliger Gedächtnis" (*WABr* 6:212.2).

[38] "Und ist wahr, dasz Euch nicht leid sollt daran geschehen sein" (*WABr* 6:212.6); "Du sollt trauren uber den Toten, denn sien Licht ist verloschen; doch sollt du nicht zu sehr trauren; denn er ist zur Ruge kommen" (*WABr* 6:213.9–11).

[39] "…mit Masze" (*WABr* 6:213.12).

[40] "…der ewigen Ruge Christi" (*WABr* 6:213.15f.).

[41] "Susziglich und sanft schlafen" (*WABr* 6:213.16).

[42] "Denn jedermann sich verwundert hat uber der groszen Gnade, dasz er mit Beten und Bekenntnis Christi bis an sien Ende beständig blieben ist" (*WABr* 6:213.17–19). The 'good death' is a subject too vast to be explored here. See Frederick S. Paxton, *Christianizing Death: The Creation of a Ritual Process in Early Medieval Europe* (Ithaca, 1990); Jane Littlewood, *Aspects of Grief: Bereavement in Adult Life* (London, 1992), Chapter 1, "The Way We Die"; Sister Mary Catharine O'Connor, *The Art of Dying Well.*

had a major part in raising a fine son who met such an enviable end; they had sent him to the right school and invested their love and means well. Further, they (and all of us) should 'by God's grace have such a death.'[43] Luther's argument that their son died not only peacefully but also victoriously assists the parents in appreciating their son's wishes and perspective (he is now better off, for he is 'sleeping sweetly and softly [*süsziglich und sanst schlafen*]') as well as in focusing their adjustment to life without him. This argument is climaxed in the *conclusio* with a powerful benediction-doxology, one that includes an appeal that touches all survivors (they will meet again):

> The Lord and supreme Comforter Jesus Christ, who loved your son even more than you did and who, having first called him through his Word, afterward summoned him to himself and took him from you, comfort and strengthen you with his grace until the day when you will see your son again in eternal joy. Amen (*WABr* 6:213.30–34).[44]

It is an affirmation of hope that Luther himself can cling to, for he looks forward to a reunion with daughter Elizabeth and with both of his parents.[45] Once again, Luther has used the doublet to make a potent point, whether speaking of the intensity of grief, the manner of dying, or the power of God's love.

Luther wrote a very similar letter a year later (1532) to Thomas Zink, the father of John Zink, who had been a student at the University for two years and had died two days earlier in Wittenberg (Tappert, 64f.).[46] Although the letter is addressed to the father, Luther speaks from the beginning in second person plural, to both parents. The letter conveys details of how their son died; the writer uses doublet and triplet to express himself: In the *exordium / narratio* Luther reassures the parents that nothing was spared in the way of 'care, attention, and medicine' in efforts to save him but that "the disease got the upper hand and he was carried off to heaven, to our Lord Jesus Christ."[47] From the writer's perspective, Luther tells them how much John was loved, particularly

---

[43] *Solchen Abscheid durch Gottes Gnad haben möchten* (*WABr* 6:213.25f.).

[44] "Der Herr und höchter Tröster, Jesus Christus, der Euren Sohn lieber denn Jhr selbs gehabt und zu sich selbs erstlich durch sein Wort beruffen und hernach zu sich gefoddert und von Euch genommen, der tröste und stärk Euch mit Gnaden bis auf den Tag, da Jhr Euren Sohn wieder sehen werdet in ewigen Freuden, Amen."

[45] Martin Brecht, *Martin Luther*, 2:377f.

[46] *WABr* 6:300–302 (Nr. 1930).

[47] "...so ist doch die Krankheit zu mächtig worden und hat ihn weggenommen und zu unserm Herrn Jesu Christo gebracht in den Himmel" (*WABr* 6:301.6–8).

by Luther himself, who often had the young man sing at mealtimes in his home; as a student, the boy was 'quiet, well-behaved, and diligent' in his studies. He tells the father that all the University community feels distress at this death; that they would have preferred to 'save him and keep' him, but that God loved him and desired him more. In the *petitio*—invoking the parents' perspective—Luther tells them what they already know but should also thank God for: that John was such a 'good, pious' son; that God deems them worthy of the 'pains and money' and that they must "Grieve in such a way, therefore, as to console yourselves."[48] They have not lost their son but have only "sent him on ahead of you," after which Luther paraphrases 1 Thess. 4:13, the text he had used at the 1525 funeral sermons for Elector Frederick and which, about four months from the writing of this letter (1532), he will use again for Elector John's funeral sermons.[49] To assist them in that, he asks the preceptor to send "some of the beautiful words your son uttered before his death. They will please and comfort you."[50] Luther seems confident that he knows what will comfort them, for he continually assures the parents not only that theirs was a good son but that his death was a testimony to all that the Reformation stands for, particularly about death:

> But let this be your best comfort, as it is ours, that he fell asleep (rather than departed) decently and softly with such a fine testimony of his faith on his lips that we all marveled. There can be as little doubt that he is with God, his true Father, in eternal blessedness, as there can be no doubt that the Christian faith is true. Such a beautiful Christian end as his cannot fail to lead heavenward. In addition, you should also consider how grateful you ought to be that, unlike many others, he did not have a perilous and pitiful death. Even if he had lived a long time, you could not, with your means, have helped him to anything higher than some sort of office or service. And now he is in a place that he would not exchange for all the world, even for a moment (*WABr* 6:301.19—302.30).[51]

---

[48] "Darumb betrubt Euch also, dasz Jhr Euch viel mehr auch trostet" (*WABr* 6:302.30f.).

[49] *WA* 17¹:196–227 (1525); *LW* 51:231–255 [=*WA* 36:237–270] (1532).

[50] "...werde Euch etlich seiner schonen Wort, fur seinem Ende geredt, zuschreiben, die Euch gefallen und Euch trosten werden" (*WABr* 6:302.34–36).

[51] "Aber das soll Euch (wie es auch uns tut) auf hohest trosten, dasz er so säuberlich und sanft entschlaffen ist (mehr dann verschieden) mit solchem seinen glauben, Vernunft, Bekenntnis, dasz uns alle Wunder hat und kein Zweifel sein kann, so wenig der christlich Glaub falsch sein kann, er sei bei Gott seinem rechten Vatter ewiglich selig; den nein solch schon christlich Ende kann des Himmelreichs nit feilen. Wollet auch daneben bedenken, wie viel Euch zu danken und zu trosten sein will, dasz er nicht

In June 1533 Luther comforted the Wittenberg jurist and *Bürgermeister*, Benedict Pauli, whose only son had died in a bird hunting accident.[52] Not a letter in the strict sense, but oral remarks (thus lacking *salutatio, exordium / narratio,* and *conclusio*), this address—delivered to Pauli personally, in his home, in the company of others—is roughly twice as long as most of the consolatory letters (Tappert, 67–69).[53] It takes a much firmer, even harsh stance towards its recipient, which is Pauli alone. However, since others are present, these remarks take on many characteristics of a funeral sermon, except that there is no Scripture text. Luther talks about the accidental death as an evil (*malum*) and discusses this death in a fashion that shows God at work, not directly in the taking of life but in the consolation process. He begins by acknowledging the rightness of grief, supplying scriptural examples of godly fathers who grieved; there are many examples, he says, of godly 'patriarchs and kings' who mournfully wailed (*gravissime luxerunt*) their sons' deaths. But Luther argues forcefully for 'a certain moderation in our grief.'[54] Making no disclosure of his own parental grief of five years earlier, Luther implies that Pauli is now overdoing it. He argues that Job saw that there is consolation in recognizing that the good we receive from God far outweighs the bad, for even though he lost his 'goods and his children,' he measured both the 'good and the evil' and learned what Pauli must also learn: that 'more and much greater [*multo maiora et plura*]' good comes from God. Indeed, Luther uses more superlatives and doublets to show Pauli that his present grief has blinded him from remembering God's "great and most excellent goods and gifts [*maximorum et praestantissimorum bonorum ac donorum*]." Moreover, several patriarchs suffered more: (1) While not even having buried his son, Abraham had 'more and greater [*longiorem et acerbiorem*]' grief than Pauli, by having been ordered to slay his own son; (2) likewise, for Jacob, by having believed his son suffered a terrible death; and (3) David, by having a rebellious son. 'These and similar' examples should help Pauli compare the 'misfortune and grief' of these others with his

---

(wie vielen andern geschicht) färlich oder jämmerlich umbkommen ist. Und wenn er schon lang gelebt hätte, wurdet Ihr doch mit Eur Kost ihm nit hoher haben helfen mugen, denn etwa zu einem Ampt oder Dienst. Nu aber ist er an dem Ort da er gar ungern mi taller Welt mechslen wollte, auch nicht auf ein Augenblick."

[52] Pauli had served with Luther on the four-man Saxon Visitation of 1528; Martin Brecht, *Martin Luther,* 2:270.

[53] *WATr* 1:474–480 (Nr. 949).

[54] "Sed tamen debet quidam modus esse lugendi" (*WATr* 1:475.1f.).

own, and thus be greatly 'relieved and lightened.' Knowing full well
that every grief is personal, Luther uses prolepsis to anticipate how
Pauli's grief is unique for him—in that he lost his only son, through a
tragic accident—thereby invoking typical features of grief's measures:
the significance of the child and the manner of death—as measures
of parental grief, both must be perceived by them and not assessed by
others. So Luther tells Pauli he may receive more sons from God.[55]
Realizing that he cannot guarantee that, Luther boldly uses his typical topos of consolation—God's great love. Luther assures Pauli that,
should he remain childless and even lose 'your wife, your fortune, and
all that you have,' he still has Christ's favor, God's graciousness to him,
and spiritual gifts that remain 'safe and everlasting' long after even
death. However, he does acknowledge and affirm Pauli's feelings, seen
especially in the following concessions: "But at the present time your
eyes are fixed only on the evil...."; "We concede, of course, that the
evil that has befallen you is a very grave one."[56] Through paraphrase,
Luther also anticipates Pauli's concerns, thus acknowledging them,
and then gently rebutting them with arguments: "'But,' you will say,
'he died such a horrible death!'"; "Are you afraid, then, that the Lord
took your son in wrath?"; "although human nature cries out against
this and imagines that God is angry."[57] The persuasive purpose in this
message is to blend refutation of any thoughts that God's wrath is at
work in sudden or accidental death (compare the legal term 'acts of
God') with the consolatory message that God is at work in the midst
of, and in spite of, tragedy, ready to comfort. Small wonder, then, that
early printed versions of this document circulated, for the message has
an enduring rhetorical appeal.[58] What we may still wonder, though, is
whether Luther will be so firm once he has himself experienced the
pain of losing his favorite child.

In 1538 Luther learned of the death in Freiberg of his old and
trusted friend Nicholas Hausmann (1478/79–1538) who, according

---

[55] Luther's second son Paul was born in January 1533. Bereaved parents today are
enraged when told they 'can always have more children.' Such is less likely to happen
today than in the sixteenth century. Indeed, Pauli later had more children.

[56] "Sed isto tempore in hoc tantum malum defixi sunt oculi tui (*WATr* 1:476.3f.); Sed
concedimus sane malum quod accidit tibi, esse gravissimum (*WATr* 1:476.13).

[57] "At horribili genere mortis periit, inquies" (*WATr* 1:478.6); "Et times, ne succensens
tibi Dominus filium eripuerit?" (*WATr* 1:478.11); "...quamlibet reclamet natura humana
et Deum fingat iratum" (*WATr* 1:478.13f.).

[58] See editor's remarks at Tappert, 67.

to Harry Haile, was 'his chief comforter in distress,' particularly in letters.[59] At first, news of his friend's death was kept from Luther. Yet even in a 1539 letter to Catherine Metzler of Breslau (Tappert, 72f.) he urges moderation in grieving.[60] Like the letter to Zink, this one reminds us of Luther's affection and concern for his students.[61] Mrs. Metzler's husband had died nine months earlier, and now, seven months after her son Kilian has died, Luther "could not refrain from writing."[62] Focusing only on the loss of the son—while seldom using the deceased's first name—Luther here continues his practice of familial language through endearing epithets and personal pronouns ('your beloved son'; 'our dear Father'). He uses the doublet abundantly, even in his endearing epithets; often these doublets are asyndetic, as seen first in his *salutatio*: "To the honorable, virtuous Mrs. Catherine Metzler, citizen in Breslau, my gracious, good friend."[63] Using more doublets, Luther acknowledges her grief ('sorely oppresses and hurts you') and argues that it is right and natural to grieve, especially one's own 'blood and flesh,'[64] that God created us this way; we are not 'stones and sticks' but should 'mourn and bewail' our dead.[65] Yet he suggests to her that "our grief should be moderate, for our dear Father is testing us here to see whether we can love and fear both in joy and in sorrow [*Lieb und Leydt*] and whether we can give back to him what he has given us in view of his intention to give us something more and better" (*WABr* 8:485.11–15).[66] The appeal is to duty to God—whose will is 'gracious,

---

[59] H. G. Haile, *Luther: An Experiment in Biography* (Garden City, N.Y., 1980), 76. Susan Karant-Nunn also reminds us of Luther's correspondence with Hausmann, concerning the death of Elizabeth in 1528 (*WABr* 4:511, Nr. 1303); see her "'Fast ware mir ein weibliches Gemüt verblieben': Martin Luthers Männlichkeit," in *Luther zwischen den Kulturen*, ed. Hans Medick and Peer Schmidt (Göttingen, 2004), 49–65, here at 49, 60f.

[60] An English translation of this letter is also now found in *Luther on Women: A Sourcebook*, ed. and trans. Susan C. Karant-Nunn and Merry Wiesner-Hanks (Cambridge, 2003), 214f.

[61] *WABr* 8:484f. (Nr. 3354). On Luther's concern for his students see Lewis Spitz, "Luther's Social Concern for Students," in *The Social History of the Reformation*, ed. Lawrence P. Buck and Jonathan W. Zophy (Columbus, Ohio, 1972), 249–270.

[62] "Habe nicht können wegern Euch zw schreyben" (*WABr* 8:485.4).

[63] *WABr* 8:485.1f.; Tappert, 72 inserts conjunctions in both these doublets.

[64] Tappert, 72 reverses the doublet. When she rereads the letter, Mrs. Metzler may notice that Luther uses the same terms to describe her, her son, and God the Father.

[65] "Hertiglich drucken wirdt vnd schmertzen" (*WABr* 8:485.6–10). This is precisely the warrant for grief that Luther used in the 1532 funeral sermons of Elector John the Steadfast.

[66] Tappert, 72 reverses the first two doublets: "Sonderlich zu den vnsern, Doch das es eine masse habe, Denn der liebe vater vns dadurch versucht, ob wir auch ihn konnen

good [*gnedigen guthen*]'[67] but also to a motivation out of love and the prospect of a better future. He closes the appeal by reminding her that God bore a harder cross 'for you and for all of us,' making our crosses 'nothing or small.'[68] As with previous letters of consolation, there is also reassurance of: (1) her son's faithful death, though it is treated sparsely, for Luther is not conveying news but rather recalling what his recipient already accepts but needs to be put into a context of contrast: his 'Christian and blessed'[69] departure from wretched world; (2) his dutiful life, as a 'well behaved, godly' boy;[70] (3) and of God's desire to 'protect and save' from the world's harm, given the 'perilous, evil' times. Luther uses a biblical argument to invite Mrs. Metzler to consider her suffering in comparison to a biblical character who suffered worse (David and his rebellious son, Absalom). In this same appeal, Luther helps his reader align her grief with others in Scripture (Elijah and Jonah), the latter of whom said, "It is better for me to die than to live" (1 Kings 19:4; Jonah 4:3). This appeal to count her blessings is completed with Luther's assertion that even 'emperors and kings' have lower stations than her son now occupies. He also tells her, as he did the Knudsens, that one can be of good cheer when comparing the benefits of the good death to the misery of the shameful death. The concluding benediction incorporates the words of 2 Cor. 1:3, which, surprisingly, Luther has used only once thus far in these letters: "God, the Father of all comfort, abundantly strengthen your faith with his spirit. Amen."[71] Luther must believe that this is indeed possible, many months and even years *post mortem*.

In December 1544, two years after his beloved daughter Magdalena died at home at age thirteen,[72] Luther had the task of bearing bad news to Georg Hoesel, the father of another of his young students, Jerome (Tappert, 78f.).[73] As he writes to Hoesel, a mine clerk in Marienberg, Luther reports that he is 'reluctant' but that "necessity requires that

---

lieben vnd furchten beyde jn lieb vnd leydt, auch ob wir jhm konnen wieder geben, was er vns gegeben hat, auff das er vrsach habe, mehr vnd bessers zugeben."

[67] Tappert, 73 adds a conjunction.

[68] Tappert, 73 reverses the doublet.

[69] *WABr* 8:485.20.

[70] Tappert, 73 inserts a conjunction in the doublet.

[71] "Gott, der vater alles trostes, stercke ewern glauben mit seynem geist reichlich, Amen" (*WABr* 8:485.29f.).

[72] Luther's niece Lene Kaufman Berndt, whom Martin and Katy had raised, lost her husband in 1541.

[73] *WABr* 10:698f. [Nr. 4049].

this be done," that he tell him "your dear son Jerome departed this life
in accordance with God's will" (in his first semester at University).[74] In
mentioning his own experience as a bereaved father, Luther uses his own
credibility gently to urge his reader to moderate his grief, based upon
the fact that Christ is savior (three times 'Jesus' or 'Christ' is paired with
'saviour') and that the young man was *in Christ*: Using two quotations
from Matthew 18, Luther makes the following argument:

> Inasmuch as Christ here clearly asserts [Matt. 18:14] that this young
> man, who had a knowledge of God and was in the Church, is acceptable
> to God and is not to perish, and inasmuch as Christ indicates… [Matt.
> 18:10], you must have no doubt that your son is rejoicing with our Sav-
> iour, Christ, and with all the saints (*WABr* 10:699.9–13).[75]

In the 8 lines of personal exhortation (nearly one-third of the letter),
Luther uses 9 first person pronouns, and only two of them are singular. In other words, having stipulated his own experience (*I/my*), he
proceeds to identify with his reader (*we/us/our*). Luther first reassures
him that Christ's words prove it is not God's will that any 'little ones
should perish' (Matt. 18:14), that the young man was faithful, and
now better off. Moreover, he argues that the pain must be resisted and
comfort taken in the knowledge of eternal salvation: "But our sorrow
should be temperate and not too severe."[76] The contemporary notion
of 'grief *work*' has nothing on Luther, for his recommendations imply
an active strategy of countering (or complementing) the memories of
pain with the comfort of Christ's consolation.[77] His concluding infor-

---

[74] "Wiewohl ich euch nicht gerne diese traurige Botschaft zu erkennen gebe, dasz
euer lieber Sohn Hieronymus aus dieser Welt in Gottes Willen verschieden ist, so
fordert es doch die Nothdurst" (*WABr* 10:699.3–6).

[75] "Dieweil dann Christus klar spricht, dasz diese Jugend, so in Gottes Erkennt-
nisz und Kirchen ist, sey Gott gefällig und sole nicht verloren seyn, sagt dabey ein
Zeichen…sollet ihr nicht zweifeln, er sey bey unserm Heiland Christo und bey allen
Seligen in Freuden."

[76] "…doch soll die Traurigkeit mäszig und nich zu heftig seyn" (*WABr* 10:699.
18f.).

[77] Paul C. Rosenblatt, *Bitter, Bitter Tears*, 32–40. I recommend reading this chapter
on "The Theory of Grief Work" for anyone whose knowledge of contemporary grief
theory and therapy consists only in Elizabeth Kübler-Ross's 'stages' of grief (1969).
Rosenblatt shows how the theory of grief work has its beginnings in Freud's "Mourning
and Melancholy" (originally published in 1917), whose foundation was subsequently
built upon by Lindemann's work (1944) with survivors and relatives of the Cocoanut
Grove night club fire, and by Gorer's (1967) work on pathologies of the grief work
process. Of stage theories of grief Jane Littlewood concludes: "Grief simply does
not follow any kind of ordered linear progression. If anything [,] the experiences of

mation in the *petitio* provides details about the fever that caused not only Jerome's death but also that of others Luther discusses. He offers the perspective of shared suffering to bring some solace. However, the few simple doublets offered speak exclusively of Christ's resources—the *salutatio*'s "grace and comfort of God through his only-begotten Son, Jesus Christ our Saviour"; the *conclusio*'s invocation to God to 'comfort and strengthen.'

Our final letter to a bereaved father comes in 1545 to Caspar Heydenreich, a former table companion of Luther and now chaplain at court in Freiberg, of Duchess Catherine of Saxony (Tappert, 79f.).[78] The letter is brief, the *exordium / narratio* reporting having heard that a little son was born and died and that "you are deeply distressed by this because you did not even get to see the fruit of your flesh."[79] This natural desire to see the corpse and find closure is acknowledged by Luther, but in rather terse way: "Lay aside your sorrowing. Rejoice, rather, because he was reborn in Christ[80] and because you will see him in glory whom you have not seen here in this wretched world."[81] Quoting the Wisdom of Solomon (4:11, 13), Luther reminds Heydenreich that he also knows and teaches these things. Whether or not that strategy works, at least it acknowledges to the bereaved that he has a profession to maintain, and work that needs him. Luther then reaffirms tenderly the right to grieve, assuring him there is no disgrace in being moved "somewhat by the natural, carnal affection of a father. The term 'father' is in itself one of sweet affection. For we are not stones, nor ought we to be."[82] However, included in the recognition that God made us

---

grief are better characterized in terms of wave after wave of violently contradictory emotional impulses. Paradoxically, the stage/phase presentation may only ever make sense to people who have not had the experience, i.e., in all probability most young to middle-aged health care professionals"; "Aspects of Grief," quoted in Walter, *Revival of Death*, 69. See also Paul C. Rosenblatt, Patricia R. Walsh, and Douglas A. Jackson, *Grief and Mourning in Cross-Cultural Perspective* (n. c., 1976). For a very recent and trenchant discussion of concepts of bereavement and grief, see Philip Bachelor, *Sorrow & Solace*, 23–37.

[78] *WABr* 11:75f. (Nr. 4094); cf. John T. Pless, "Baptism as Consolation in Luther's Pastoral Care," *CTQ* 67 (2003): 19–32, here at 26.

[79] "…id quod te aegerrime ferre dicunt, quod scilicet fructum carnis tuae non videris" (*WABr* 11:76.3f.).

[80] Late Medieval Christians were often prohibited from burying their unbaptized dead children in the church cemetery.

[81] "Sed desine contristari, gaude potius, eum esse in Christo renatum, quem visurus sis in gloria, quem hic non videris in ista miseria" (*WABr* 11:76.4f.).

[82] "Si carnali et naturali affectu patris, quod nomen est dulcissimum, ex parte moveris. Non enim saxa sumus nec esse debemus" (*WABr* 11:76.9–11).

feeling creatures is the obligation to maintain balance: "But moderation is necessary in these things."[83] It seems that Luther's bereaved recipient is not so immobilized but rather capable of responding to appeals not only to scriptural comfort and personal empathy, but also to the eloquence of wisdom and reason.

In all these letters to bereaved parents, then, Luther affirms the right to grieve, while in all but two (Cordatus and Zink) he admonishes parents to grieve moderately. In every case he tells them they have much to be thankful for, even though they may not be able to understand or appreciate it now. Luther's words about the deceased are tender, and he assures each parent of God's faithfulness in taking each child unto Himself. With language that is mostly affectionate, he reminds all parents that God understands their loss, and in several cases Luther briefly recounts his own losses (including the loss of two daughters), for he believes that knowing one is not alone and not misunderstood is some consolation. Luther speaks constantly in familial language, and he calls God a loving Father; indeed, more than once Luther argues that God is a greater father than the parent he now addresses. He characterizes eternal life with Christ as far better than anything this life offers, sometimes adding the thought that the deceased child would not want to return. Included in what one thanks God for is the Reformation faith, which marks believers as considerably better off than the papists, and having less sorrow than some biblical characters.

B. *Letters to Surviving Spouses*

Among the eleven letters there is one from 1524 (Tappert, 53–55), thus predating Luther's marriage.[84] This letter stands apart from the others in that, like the 1533 letter to Pauli, it was printed in leaflet form the same year, with the preface (in an unknown hand) stating its intention "as a comfort for those who are mourning for loved ones who have fallen asleep or died" (Tappert, 55).[85] Appreciated by others as an exemplary

---

[83] "...sed modus est in rebus"; the quote comes from Horace, *Satires* 1.1.106: "There is measure in all things. There are, in short, fixed bounds, beyond and short of which right can find no place [est modus in rebus, sunt certi denique fines, quos ultra citraque nequit consistere rectum]"; H. Rushton Fairclough, trans., *Horace: Satires, Epistles and Ars Poetica* (London, 1961), 13.

[84] *WA* 18:1–7; the text of the letter is on pp. 5–7.

[85] "...ain trost deren so sich beschmertzen vmb die verstorbenen oder schlaffenden" (*WA* 18:2).

consolation, Luther's message focuses more on the proper Christian position with respect to the living and the dead; it says nothing about controlling grief, save for the exhortation to 'cheerfully give God what is his.'[86] In fact, of all this group of letters, only one (to Ambrose Berndt in 1528) exhorts *directly* its recipient to moderation. Since Luther's 1532 (first) funeral sermon for Elector John the Steadfast stated at the outset that "the habit and custom of holding masses for the dead and funeral processions when they are buried has ceased" (*LW* 51:231), scholars have speculated about precisely how and when such Catholic practices came to be abandoned by Luther and his followers in the early years of the Reformation.[87] Luther's 1 September 1524 letter to Bartholomew von Staremberg sheds a small ray of light on this historical question, for in two of the *petitio*'s three paragraphs it admonishes the Austrian nobleman to discontinue his 'masses, vigils, and daily prayers' for his wife's soul. 'Once or twice' is enough, he says, quoting John 14:12–14, for repeated asking for the same thing is a sign of unbelief, which will anger (*ertzürnen*) God. Masses and vigils are unchristian and greatly anger God; they lack earnestness and faith and are a useless mummery (*unnutz Gemürmel*), a mockery (*spot*) of God, a 'shameful and terrible' thing. Piling on the accusations—at clergy, priests, and monks—Luther offers the antitheses that God instituted the mass as "sacrament for the living and not an offering for the dead" and that men changed a "sacrifice for the living into a good work and sacrifice for the dead" (*WA* 18:7.6–10).[88] "Do not participate in this horrible error."[89] The strategy and power of this three-paragraph *petitio* is its trajectory of climax, building upon a gentle start towards a strong finish, without any personal accusation. Indeed, in his *exordium* and *narratio* Luther clarified how he came to write to this virtual stranger with Reformation sympathies. He acknowledges gently the character of the deceased wife and how deserving she is of her husband's good works. By demonstrating his sincerity and appreciation for his receiver's needs, Luther can then begin his *petitio* by first arguing—through the use of a series of balancing doublets—that von Staremberg should accept God's 'just exchange and strange barter'

---

[86] "Darumb gebe Got das seine fro(e)lich" (*WA* 18:6.15).

[87] Craig Koslofsky, *The Reformation of the Dead*, 81–115.

[88] "…die messz nicht für die todten sonder zu(o)m sacrament für die lebendigen; …machen ausz disem und andern gotes einsetzungen ein werck und opfer für die todten ausz dem sacramentt der lebendigen."

[89] "…sich nit tailhafftig machen dises greülichen jrtumbs" (*WA* 18:7.10f.).

whereby a 'dear, faithful [*trewen lieben*]' God has first given, and now taken away, a 'dear, faithful [*theüren Truwen*]' wife.[90] In her death von Staremberg has lost a 'dear, tender [*zartes liebs*]' wife and has gained a 'dear, tender [*zarten lieben*]' will of God, which must be apprehended by faith, and it must be cheerfully acknowledged. The *conclusio* assures von Staremberg of the support and best wishes of their mutual friend, Vincent Wernsdorfer, who asked Luther to write and who supports the aforementioned position on prayers, masses, and vigils; it is others who would lead him astray. The benediction models the attitude Luther tries to maintain in this letter, and it summarizes his priority for the message: "Christ enlighten and strengthen you in true faith and in love of your neighbor. Amen" (Tappert, 55).[91]

During summer and fall of 1527 Luther had severe health problems, and then plague broke out in Wittenberg. The University was temporarily moved to Jena, while Luther and Johannes Bugenhagen (1485–1558) remained in the city to care for the sick. Greatly shaken by the deaths of Hanna, wife of deacon Georg Rörer (1492–1557), and of Bugenhagen's sister—as well as little Hans's illness and Katy's pregnancy—Luther wrote *Whether One May Flee From a Deadly Plague*, in response to a request from Johan Hess (1490–1547) of Breslau.[92] Three months after Elizabeth died he wrote to a widow Margaret in December 1528 (Tappert, 58f.). He focuses primarily on comforting the woman by addressing her specific concern: whether her husband, who had committed suicide, died in the Lord.[93] Having learned of the matter through her son, Luther reassures her that her husband was engaged in a hard struggle—a battle between Christ and the devil—and that Christ both 'engaged and won' the victory. Using more of this battle language—that he uses in no other letter of consolation—Luther likens

---

[90] Tappert, 55 includes conjunctions in the latter two doublets.

[91] "Christus erleücht und sterck in rechttem glawben und lieb gegen dem nechsten. Amen" (*WA* 18:7.19f.).

[92] *LW* 43:113–138.

[93] *WABr* 4:624f. (Nr. 1366). Suicides were often prohibited from churchyard burial. See R. C. Finucane, "Sacred Corpse, Profane Carrion: Social Ideals and Death Rituals in the Later Middle Ages," *Mirrors of Mortality: Studies in the Social History of Death*, ed. Joachim Whaley (New York, 1981), 40–60, here at 56; Craig M. Koslofsky, "Controlling the Body of the Suicide in Saxony." *From Sin to Insanity*, ed. J. R. Watt (Ithaca, 2004), 48–63. The 2003 film *Luther* (Directed by Eric Till), includes a fictional account of Father Martin taking it upon himself to bury a young man who hung himself. Luther assures the horrified gravedigger, and the onlookers, that the devil provokes suicide and that such victims are not outside the grace of God.

the husband's struggle to how Christ struggled in the garden and won. While the self-infliction is a sign of the devil's power over the body's members—the devil can break 'arms, legs, backs, and all members'—the Christian confidence that the husband had when he died is a sign of his coming to himself and turning to Christ's victory. Luther quotes several Scriptures to assure the woman that those who die in the Lord are blessed (Rev. 14:13; John 11:25) and that there must be mourning if there is to be comfort (Matt. 5:4; Ps. 44:22 [= 43:22 Vulgate]). Throughout this letter Luther provides mostly assurance, scarcely any exhortation to moderate her grief, and credits God for it all.

Luther's letter in early 1532 to a former student, Ambrose Berndt, comforts the man after the deaths of his wife and newborn son in childbirth, addressing almost entirely a husband's loss (Tappert, 62f.).[94] Since Berndt had studied in Wittenberg and was a friend (six years later he would marry Luther's niece, Lene Kaufmann), Luther's letter, in Latin, skips the *exordium* and *narratio* and immediately begins a four-paragraph *petitio*.[95] The first paragraph focuses on acknowledging the grief by stating—as Luther has frequently done—that Berndt is a man. However, Luther's very first words are that he "is not so inhuman that [he] cannot appreciate how deeply the death of Margaret distresses you" (Tappert, 62).[96] He also acknowledges that a husband's bond to his wife is strong; therefore, the commensurate sorrow is not displeasing to God. Since He has implanted these feelings for a wife, it is consistent with being both man and husband to grieve. One cannot 'at once throw off' one's grief.[97] However, the *petitio* then develops an argument for moderation—to keep within God's will, 'to put a limit to one's sorrow and grief' (Tappert, 62).[98] Luther's rationale for this argument begins with a moving description of why Berndt should miss his wife, listing her gifts and abilities and how they beautifully matched her husband's needs. Note how Luther employs doublet and <u>anaphora</u>:

---

[94] *WABr* 6:279–281 (Nr. 1915). Berndt received the master's degree in 1528 (Tappert, 62).

[95] Martin Brecht, *Martin Luther*, 3:238.

[96] "Non sum adeo inhumanus, mi Ambrosi, ut nesciam, quantopere te exerceat mors Margarethae" (*WABr* 6:280.1f.). Note that Tappert's *salutatio* ('My dear Ambrose,' 62) is actually apostrophe in the middle of Luther's opening sentence. A second apostrophe ("mi Ambrosi") is found in the opening sentence of the petitio (*WABr* 6:280.7).

[97] "...poerorem eiicere posses" (*WABr* 6:280.8).

[98] "...eatenus tibi permitto moerorem illum, quatenus non est contra voluntatem Dei. Necesse est enim, tandem tristitiae, et sollicitudinum quendam fieri modum" (*WABr* 6:280.7–9).

Wherefore you ought to reflect in this manner: You are at first wretched in this world because your wife and son have been taken away. No hurt so painful as this can befall a man in his domestic life. It is especially so in your case because you had a wife <u>who was</u> furnished with such uncommon gifts, <u>who was</u> so accommodating to you in all respects, <u>who was</u> so modest and adorned with the best manners, and, what is most important, <u>who was</u> able in an unusual degree to delight your heart and move your soul with pleasant and Christian conversation. And I know for certain that nothing makes you more wretched than the realization that she was a gentle spirit who was well suited to your temperament (*WABr* 6:280.9–16).[99]

The rationale continues to suggest how Berndt can orchestrate his thoughts, stimulating him to recall that his wife died in the "performance of her God-given duty and in the exercise of her proper calling" of giving birth. Moreover, she faced her death with 'resolute spirit and a firm faith' in Christ. Luther's argument thus presents Berndt with a model of how he should now think, feel, and act—by recounting for him how the deceased died and by reciting some of the beloved's wishes. While there is no evidence that either Luther or Berndt worried about the medieval proscriptions against churchyard burial of unbaptized infants,[100] God's goodness is championed, for He allowed the baby John not only to be born, but also 'baptized and then buried together with his mother.'[101] Hence, how can he remain sad or despondent, for Luther reminds Berndt that he has the capacity to allow his spiritual gifts and thoughts to overcome the physical loss. In attempting to exhort Berndt to manage his grief, Luther has blended tender talk with tough reasoning:

You should give careful thought to these two things....Occupy yourself with these thoughts unceasingly and control your grief [*exerce et minue*] as much as you can. Comfort yourself with the Word of God, the preeminent consolation. Learn too to thank God for the spiritual gifts that he gave your wife, Margaret. At the same time pray that our common

---

[99] "Quare ita tecum cogitabis: primum te esse miserum in hoc mundo, cum ablata sit uxor cum filio; qua re in privatis rebus nihil potest homini acerbius accidere, maxime cum talem habueris uxorem, quae praedita fuit non vulgaribus donis, quae tibi fuit morigera in rebus omnibus, item pudica et optimis ornata moribus, tum etiam, quod maximum est, quae iucundo et christiano colloquio animum tuum oblectare et afficere non vulgariter potuit."

[100] Finucane, "Sacred Corpse, Profane Carrion," 54–60.

[101] *WABr* 6:280.24.

Father may allow you and all of us to die in faith in Jesus Christ (*WABr* 6:280.24–31).[102]

These sensitive and practical remarks offer some concrete help for a grieving survivor.

Later that same year, on 3 November 1532 (less than three months after preaching the funeral of Elector John the Steadfast), Luther responded to the letter of a friend, Lawrence Zoch, chancellor to the archbishop of Magdeburg (Tappert, 65–67).[103] In his letter Luther delivers a personal sermon for his friend, outlining God's action in death. The *benevolentia* of the *salutatio* itself departs from his typical, this time using two doublets:[104] "God's grace and peace in Christ be your comfort and strength. Amen" (Tappert, 66).[105] The *salutatio* is particularly touching—and revealing of what is to come: 'My dear Doctor and special Friend.' In the *exordium / narratio* Luther reports his heartfelt sorrow at learning the great 'misfortune and grief' that has befallen Zoch. While he does not elaborate with details, Luther clearly finds God at work in the matter: "God has taken your dear wife in such a way as to make it very hard to bear."[106] The *petitio* develops a coherent portrayal of God's action in death, seen in five ways: (1) God's son endured plenty, too—quoting key doublets from Isa. 53:4 ('smitten of God, and afflicted') and Psalm 22:6 ('I am a worm, and no man'), and what is hard is that God himself seems to be smiting us. This paradox ('What must distress us most…') is that God both smites and comforts us. Meanwhile, the godless seem loved and exalted by God and the world; using both doublet and antithesis, Luther concludes that "they can doubly boast, and we must doubly sorrow";[107] (2) Using the *qal*

---

[102] "Haec duo diligenter tecum considerabis, et conferes inter se bona corporalia et spiritualia, omnino ita statueris, quod maiora sint dona spiritualia, quam illa corporalia. In his assidue te exerce et minue luctum, quantum potes. Consolare te verbo Dei, praestantissima consolatione. Tantum discito etiam in dies magnas agere Deo gratias pro spiritualibus donis tuae uxori Margarethae concessis, simul orans communem patrem, ut te nosque omnes in fide Iesu Christi faciat mori."

[103] *WABr* 6:382f. (Nr. 1971).

[104] Luther's most common *salutatio* is 'grace and peace in Christ.'

[105] "Gottes Gnad und Fried in Christo sei Euer Trost und Stärke, Amen" (*WABr* 6:382.1).

[106] "…dass Euch Gott Euer liebes Weib genommen hat hit solcher Weise…welches sonderlich hoch beschweren musz" (*WABr* 6:382.3–5).

[107] "…dasz die letzte Betrübnis musz den Namen gewinnen" (*WABr* 6:383.9f.); "…auf dasz sie zwiefältig sich rühmen und wir zwiefältig trauren sollen" (*WABr* 6:383.13f.).

wachomer syntax of 'not only...but also,'[108] Luther amplifies the paradox by asserting that "it appears as if God himself has now attacked you," while enemies boast.[109] His doublets now become progressive: "This is more than suffering and dying; it is being buried and descending into hell." Thus Luther characterizes the grief experience as participating in the biblical world of Christ's suffering; (3) Luther admonishes 'my dear sir doctor' to be steadfast, for Christ had this experience and God did not forsake him; he was raised and so will we be.[110] This likens grief to dishonor and holds out hope for honor, one day; (4) Part of the comfort for Zoch now comes from remembering his wife's faithful death; but even greater comfort is in knowing he is a type of Christ, and is being 'punished and confounded,' as He was, by the devil and God, who 'is and wishes to be' his comfort; and (5) The paradox is completed by recognizing that, although one's flesh now 'murmurs and cries out,' one's spirit should be 'ready and willing' to cry out to God as 'Abba, dear Father,' just as Jesus cried out in his weakness. Luther tries to help Zoch identify with Jesus, to find comfort in His sufferings, not simply as companionship in pain, nor even only as model sufferer, but as Source of Consolation. That this is Luther's argument is clear in his concluding benediction: "Our dear Lord and Saviour, who is also the model of all our sufferings, comfort you and stamp himself upon your heart that you may offer him this sacrifice of a broken spirit and give him your Isaac willingly. Amen" (*WABr* 6:383.33–36).[111] Luther finds the bereavement experience to be a test of our faithfulness to God, one coordinated (if not ordered) by Him, requiring that we give up our right of possession of our beloved dead. In shifting the imagery from the suffering Christ to the obedient servant Abraham, Luther urges Zoch to identify himself in Scripture and also to relish his place in the family of God, the father and comforter—not to turn away from God, but rather toward Him.

---

[108] There are two instances of "nicht allein...sondern auch" and a third of "nicht allein...sondern" in this letter.

[109] "Also hat Euch Gott nun selbs auch angegriffen, als es scheinet" (*WABr* 6:383.15).

[110] Upon release from prison for his faith, Zoch entered the service of the elector of Saxony and became professor of law in Wittenberg; Tappert, 66.

[111] "Unser lieber Herr und Heiland, ja auch unser liebes Furbild alles unsers Liedens, tröste und drücke sich selbs in Euer Herz, auf dasz Jhr dies Opfer dieses betrübten Geistes vollbringen und ihm Euren Isaac mit willigem Geist übergeben möget, Amen."

John Reineck, superintendent of a foundry in Mansfeld, had been Luther's boyhood schoolmate there. Having himself been the one in 1530 to convey the news to Luther about the death of his father, Hans Luther, Reineck's wife died in April 1536. In his written response (Tappert, 69f.; *WABr* 7:399f.) Luther's *exordium / narratio* displays the affection he has for his old friend ('Honored Sir and good Friend'), and it reveals the endearing, familial epithets we have come to expect him to use when referring to his recipient, the Lord, and the deceased ('your dear wife'; 'our dear Lord and Father').[112] Nevertheless, God is responsible for the affliction, having taken her 'unto himself.'[113] Therefore, it is only natural to 'grieve sorely,' and Luther says he is 'heartily sorry' for this man for whom he has such 'good, friendly' will.[114] The *petitio* begins with a classic question: "How should we conduct ourselves in such a situation?"[115] The question nicely summarizes our topic, and Luther's inclusive language maintains an affectionate relationship with his receiver. Luther's argument, in response to the question, is to explain what God is doing. Through a prolific use of doublets, he explains that God has so 'ordered and limited [*geordnet und gemäsziget*]' our life here that we may 'learn and exercise' our knowledge of his will, so that we may 'test and discover' whether we 'love and esteem' Him more than things he has given us to 'have and to love' on earth.[116] The inscrutable goodness (*unmäszige Güte*) of the divine will is so 'great and profound' that man finds no pleasure in it, only 'grief and lamentation [*Trauren und Klagen*]'; nevertheless, we have his 'holy, sure' Word.[117] Luther even quotes James 1:2 ("we should count it all joy when we fall into divers tribulations"), followed by Rom. 5:3–4 ("for tribulation works patience, and patience, experience"), in Latin, in hoping that the Word, which Reineck has, will help him find more pleasure in 'God's grace and fatherly will' than in the pain of his loss.[118] Luther has written an encouraging, empathizing letter to his friend. Without any real self-disclosure of his own grief experiences, he affirms his friend's pain

---

[112] "Ehrbar, Fürsichtiger, guter Fruend!...liebe Gott Vater...Euer liebe Hausfrauen" (*WABr* 7:399.1–3).

[113] "...zu sich" (*WABr* 7:399.3).

[114] "...wehe tun musz...herzlich leid" (*WABr* 7:399.4f.).

[115] Tappert, 69 reverses the doublet and adds a conjunction. "Aber wie sollen wir tun?" (*WABr* 7:399.7).

[116] *WABr* 7:399.7–11.

[117] *WABr* 7:399.12–15.

[118] *WABr* 7:399.18–23.

through inclusive language ('we'; 'us'; 'ourselves');[119] in a paragraph of six and one-half lines Luther uses 6 first plural pronouns (no first singular), arguing that we can learn from Job and allow our spirit—not our flesh—to praise God's 'will and activity' in our 'sorrow and suffering [*Leiden und Jammer*].' Using alliteration, Luther argues that when we put aside our 'carnal, rotten flesh [*fleischliche faule Fleisch*],' our sinful carcasses, God will help us proceed to our 'home and fatherland.' He provides honest and accurate assessment that, over time, the pain diminishes; healing occurs as, eventually, joy supplants the pain and as memories continue to allow joy to be appreciated. Pain *teaches* spiritual sensitivity.[120] Moreover, Luther does not omit the reassurances a bereaved seeks: reminders of his wife's admirable characteristics, of her faithfulness to Christ, of her good death. He tells Reineck that he cares about him and that God does too:

> I have wished to write this hasty note to you because you are one of my best friends, and I hope that our dear Lord Christ will be with you in his Holy Spirit and comfort you better than I can. For he has begun a good work in you [Phil. 1:6] and called you to his Word. From you He will his blessing not withdraw nor will He forsake you" (*WABr* 7:400.31–35).[121]

Three years later we find another letter to a friend—Luther's 10 January 1539 letter to John von Taubenheim who, according to Tappert, (70), was the chamberlain of Prussia.[122] However, Martin Brecht gives us more information about Taubenheim: (1) he had served with Luther on the four-man team that conducted the Saxon Visitation of 1528, and Luther had a deep respect for the man, both for his faith and his fiscal responsibilities;[123] (2) in addition, Taubenheim was *Landrentmeister* of Wittenberg, not Prussia, and later in 1539 Katy Luther was able to convince him to allow her purchase of a small farm near Wittenberg.[124]

---

[119] One paragraph of the petitio contains six first person plural pronouns (*WABr* 7:400.24–30).

[120] Twice in his letter to Elector John (Tappert, 55f. (*WABr* 3:496f.) Luther refers to the grief experience as a "school in which God chastens us and teaches us to trust in him [die schule, darynnen vns Gott zuchtiget vnd leret auff yhn trawen]" (*WABr* 3:497.26f.).

[121] "Solchs habe ich mit Euch in der Eile, als mit meiner besten Freunde einem, wöllen reden, und hoffe, unser lieber Herr Christus werde mit seinem heiligen Geist Euer Herz gegenwärtig selbs wohl besser trösten. Den er hat angefangen und Euch zu seinem Wort berufen; er wird die Hand nicht abziehen noch ablasseen."

[122] *WABr* 8:352–54 (Nr. 3289).

[123] Martin Brecht, *Martin Luther*, 2:270; 3:241.

[124] Ibid., 3:241. Katy's greetings to Taubenheim are conveyed by Luther in the final paragraph.

Luther's is a very gracious letter, filled with empathy and tenderness, offering no commands to moderate grief. The *salutatio* itself is effusive: "To the gracious, esteemed John von Taubenheim, collector of revenues, my gracious and kind, dear sir and friend: grace and peace in Christ," which he then repeats (Tappert, 70f.).[125] In the *exordium / narratio* Luther says he is truly, heartily sorry (*warlich von hertzen leid*) for Taubenheim's 'loss and grief.' In the *petitio* Luther compliments and affirms Taubenheim for his love of Christ and the word, finding him one who loved his wife and disliked vice. In contrasting him to loose fellows (*losen Leuten*) who don't mind losing their wives, Luther takes great care to acknowledge Taubenheim's weighty duties, tactfully comparing his recipient's character with his own. The rhetoric is unique among these consolatory letters, distinguishing it as both moving and more polite than the others:

> I think that I know you very well to be one who is not hostile to Christ, who loves his Word and Kingdom, and who dislikes all vice and dishonor [*Untugent und Unehr*], as I have had occasion to experience. In short, I esteem you a godly man about whom I am not mistaken, even as you consider me a godly man, and God grant that you are not mistaken. My situation is different from that of a man who deals with important matters in the world, and consequently I should sin more gravely if God were to withhold his help. Since I know that you are not God's enemy, he cannot be your enemy, for he has first enabled you not to be his enemy, and he has loved you before you have loved him, which is the case with all of us" (*WABr* 8:353.9–16).[126]

Luther reminds Taubenheim to allow God's 'rod' to 'smart,' in order to find greater comfort from His 'gracious, Fatherly' will.[127] God's peace can be found in the struggle with grief, even when the flesh 'gags and grumbles [*schlucket und mucket*],' for it is not a matter of the "five senses or of the understanding but (*sondern*) goes beyond these and is a matter

---

[125] *WABr* 8:352.1f.

[126] "…das ich euch wol kenne, als der ja Christo nicht feind ist, sondern sein wort und Reich liebet, auch aller untugent und unehr von hertzen gram ist, wie ich wol erfaren. Jn summa, ich halt euch für einen fromen Man, daran ich nicht feile, wie jr widerumb auch mich für from haltet, Gott gebe, das jr nicht feilet. Denn mit mir ists ein anders, als, der in grossen Sachen stecket, und derhalb, wo Gott hand abzüge, fehrlicher (wid dieses Standes unfall ist) sündigen müste."

[127] "DArumb lasset euch das Rütlein des lieben Vaters also smertzen, das jr euch seines gnedigen veterlichen willens gegen euch viel höher tröstet" (*WABr* 8:353.21f. God's 'rod' (*Ruten*) is used earlier, at 352.5).

of faith."[128] In a sincere gesture of availability, Luther commends himself to his reader:

> God knows, and I hope that you have no doubt, that I am kindly disposed toward you and love you with all my heart. To be sure, I am nothing and am not worth anything at all now, yet Christ must have such a poor, rusty instrument and suffer me to occupy a corner of his Kingdom. God grant that I may be and remain such an instrument (*WABr* 8:353.28–33).[129]

In two different paragraphs Luther tries to model the kind of submission he advocates, ending each section with a blessing: "Our dear Lord Jesus Christ be with you"; "God grant that I may be and remain such an instrument."[130] Even in turning briefly to matters of business, Luther works to sustain the bereaved in his need to keep functioning in his work: the tax collector in Wittenberg needed Taubenheim's 'favor and help,' and the prefect was an enemy,[131] in the service of the 'envy and hate' that 'offend God and crucify' His son. Thus, in this message Luther gently but firmly urges his reader to work at his grieving, to submit willingly and actively to his heavenly Father's chastisement, for in so doing his comfort will be commensurately bestowed. In closing, Luther sends Katy's 'cordial greetings,' allowing her to urge the same kind of support: she 'bitterly laments his misfortune' and says God must love him much or he would not allow such a loss.[132] In the sixteenth

---

[128] "...sondern weit darüber in glauben schweben sol" (*WABr* 8:353.27).

[129] "Denn ich bin euch ja, das weis Gott, hoffe, auch, das jr daran nicht zweiuelt, günstig und habe euch mit Ernst lieb, ob ich wol nichts bin, und auch nu schier nirgend zu taug, So musz doch Christus ein solch arm rüstrig Werckzeug haben und mich in seinem Reich dulden hinder der thür, und helffe Gott, das ichs werd sey und bleybe." Luther, of course, loved to refer to himself as 'poor,' a concept (and term?) he may have picked up from the Hebraist Johannes Reuchlin (1455–1522). In a letter to Staupitz (30 May 1518), we find Luther saying: "Besides this, I have no other answer to my threatening friends than the word of Reuchlin, '*He who is poor has nothing to fear; he has nothing to lose.*' I have no property, and desire none. If I possessed any prestige and honor—well, he who loses them now will simply continue to lose them. There is only one thing left: my poor worn body, which is exhausted by constant hardships. If they take this away by force or guile (in order to serve God), then they will deprive me of perhaps only one or two hours of life. It is enough for me to have the dear Savior and Redeemer, my Lord Jesus Christ" (*LW* 48:64–70 [Nr. 21], here at 69f., my emphasis; cf. *WA* 1:525–527]).

[130] "Unser lieber Herr Jhesus Christus sey mit euch" (*WABr* 8:353.28), where the editors place the benediction at the beginning of the next paragraph); "vnd helffe Gott, das ichs werd sey vnd bleybe" (*WABr* 8:353.32f.).

[131] See Tappert, 71, notes 54–56. On the prefect Hans von Metzsch, see also Brecht, *Martin Luther,* 3:257–259.

[132] "...hertzlich grussen...bitterlich vber ewerm vnfal" (*WABr* 8:353.44f.).

century, unlike today, accepting that characterization of God as a loving and chastising father was quite plausible.[133]

In a brief letter of 8 May 1542 to Mrs. John Cellarius (Tappert, 74) Luther includes many of the appeals used before. Moreover, he employs many doublets and one series. In the *exordium / narratio* he conveys his own sorrowful feelings about the death, twice claiming (through parenthesis) that the death affects him ('us,' probably including Katy). God is applying his rod (*Ruten*), but John is now enjoying a better life—a 'good, blessed' rest.[134] The *petitio* argues that her sufferings are much less than many others who 'suffer and endure' much more, and that 'all our sufferings on earth' heaped together are nothing compared to what the innocent Son, our 'Lord and Saviour' Christ[135] suffered 'for us and for our salvation.'[136] The comfort Luther offers to this woman can be seen in the close of his *petitio*, with its inclusive language, its ubiquitous doublets, its series, and its being one of Luther's favorite verses (Rom. 14:8):

> Be therefore comforted in the Lord, who died for you and for us all, and who is worth more than we, our husbands, wives, children, and all that we possess. For we are the Lord's, whether we live or die, are rich or poor, or whatever our condition may be. And if we are his, then he is ours, with all that he is and has. Amen (*WABr* 10:63.13–17).[137]

Having recently made out his own Last Will, elaborating this time on the disposition of property (as well as about his own statement of faith), Luther was at this time keenly aware of the sobering, yet comforting, truth of Romans 14:8.[138] In just four months he and Katy—who also sends her prayers for comfort—would be sorely tested, when Magdalena dies on 20 September.

The first consolatory letter to follow Magdalena's death, which Luther wrote on 26 December 1542, was to one of his closest friends,

---

[133] See Steven Ozment, *When Fathers Ruled: Family Life in Reformation Europe* (Cambridge, Mass., 1985); idem, *Flesh and Spirit: Private Life in Early Modern Germany* (New York, 1999).

[134] Tappert, 74 inserts a conjunction in the doublet at *WABr* 10:63.5.

[135] Tappert, 74 reads 'Jesus Christ.'

[136] "...aller leiden auff Erden" (*WABr* 10:63.8 [Nr. 3751]).

[137] "Also tröstet euch in dem Herrn, der für euch vnd vns alle gestorben, vns viel mal besser ist, denn wir, vnsere Menner, weiber, kinder vnd alles ist. Den wir sind doch sein, wir sterben oder leben, darben oder haben, vnd wie es gehet. Sind wir aber sein, so ist Er auch vnser mit allem, was er ist vnd hat, Amen."

[138] Martin Brecht, *Martin Luther*, 3:243f.

Justas Jonas (Tappert, 75f.).[139] Born Jodocus Koch (1493–1555), Jonas was a humanist and theologian with many ties to Luther: educated at Erfurt, he served long on the theological faculty at Wittenberg (dean from 1523–1533), accompanied him to the Diet at Worms (1521), and since 1541 preached at Halle.[140] The family connections also ran deep, for Jonas had sponsored the Luthers' son Paul at his baptism in 1533, and their wives were close friends.[141] Catherine Jonas had died four days earlier while giving birth to her thirteenth child. One of the sons had drowned three months earlier, but Luther does not refer to this. In this letter Luther finds superlatives entirely appropriate. The *salutatio* is revealing for, following the customary greeting ('distinguished and excellent' gentleman) and recognition of Jonas's official titles, Luther adds: "my venerable brother in Christ: grace and peace in Christ, *who is our consolation and salvation.* Beloved Jonas."[142] This theme of Luther's own grieving for the deceased becomes even more present in the *exordium / narratio*: "I have been so completely prostrated by the unexpected calamity which has befallen you that I do not know what to write."[143] He continues along this line, describing how much he loved Jonas's wife; how she shared all 'our joys and sorrows' as her own; how he now grieves for her, and he elaborates on her gifts: (1) the 'chief and best' comforter; (2) her "sweet spirit, quiet manner, faithful heart [*suavissimi ingenii, placidissimorum morum, fidelissimi cordis*]"; and (3) her 'piety and nobility, modesty and friendliness.' Only fleetingly in this paragraph does Luther refer to Jonas's own loss ('calamity that has befallen you'; 'the dearest companion of your life [*Suavissimam vitae sociam*]'). However, this is precisely what newly bereaved survivors treasure most: to have loved ones talk and act out how *they* valued, and miss, the deceased.

---

[139] *WABr* 10:226–228 (Nr. 3829).

[140] *OER*, "Jonas, Justus," by Robert Rosin.

[141] Martin Brecht, *Martin Luther*, 3:20. Writing of the personal relationship between Jonas and Luther, Jerome Weller addressed the senate of Halle eleven years after Jonas's death: "Luther took more delight in his intimacy with Jonas than with his other friends. As often as Luther was sadder than usual, his wife, being a wise woman, immediately summoned Jonas in secret for a meal so that he might gladden her husband with his very pleasant conversation. For no one could revive the languishing spirit better by conversation than he"; M. E. Lehmann, "Justas Jonas—A Collaborator With Luther," *LQ* 2 (1950): 198.

[142] "...suo in Domino maiori venerabili. Gratiam et pacem in Christo, qui est salus et solatium nostrum, optime Iona!" (*WABr* 10:227.2–4. italics mine).

[143] "Quid scribam, prorsus nescio, ita me subitus iste casus tuus prostravit" (*WABr* 10:227.4f.).

In this fellowship of the hurting there is less pain, less isolation; the loss seems more bearable when shared. But in his *petitio* Luther also can honestly and consciously affirm his friend's pain ("How you feel I can easily imagine from the effect...on me"; "you have good cause to mourn").[144] He then describes where consolation can be found—in the spirit, that she's now better off away from the 'misery and wickedness [*miseria et malitia*]' of this world—not in the flesh. Luther even provides a measure of instruction for finding comfort: to remember 'our common Christian lot,' which includes bitter parting but also the promise of sweet communion—'reunited and gathered [*copulatos et congregatos*]'—with Him in eternal life, secured by Christ's own 'blood and death.' He incorporates the teaching of 2 Tim. 2:11 and recalls that unbelievers are worse off. Ticking off a list of opponents more typical of his polemical writings—'Turks, Jews, and (what is worse) the papists, cardinals, Heinz and Mainz'—who not only have weeping hereafter, but they lack the 'goodness and mercy [*meliorem misericordiam*]' of God and do not have the joy unspeakable (1 Pet. 1:6, 8) of reunion with loved ones to anticipate. This reunion was a theme Luther often used with bereaved parents but has seldom yet included it for spouses. Perhaps the freshness of his own loss of a beloved daughter triggered this, for Luther blends the mention of Jonas's wife ('your Cathy') and his own daughter ('my Magdalene').[145] He turns the reunion theme into a conscious musing of how world-weary and heaven-conscious newly bereaved tend to be. The world is a hell of evils where our 'souls and eyes' are constantly tormented 'day and night.' Luther uses the language of Eph. 4:30 and Rom. 8:22, 26 to help Jonas (and himself) identify with the common task and experience they share with the Holy Spirit's aid in helping them live in, but not of, the world (John 17:9–18):

> [T]hey grieve the Holy Spirit so that he is displeased with the whole creation which, together with us, groans for its and our redemption with

---

[144] "Quid tibi pariat, facile possum exemplo meo aestimare....Interim tu sic...doleas (nam causa subest)" (*WABr* 10:227.13–18).

[145] See Luther's letter of 23 September to Jonas (*LW* 50:236–238 [Nr. 299]; *WABr* 10:149f. [Nr. 3794]), where he reports the overwhelming grief he feels at the death of Magdalena. He acknowledges a duty to give thanks joyfully for her good death, but the difficulty in doing so: "even the death of Christ...is totally unable to take away all this as it should [ut nec Christi mors...penitus excutere possit, sicut oporteret]." He asks Jonas to thank God "in our stead [Tu ergo gratias age Deo vice nostra!]" (*WABr* 10:150.27–29). Here we see the supportive role of a human consoler.

groanings which cannot be uttered. He who knows and understands our groanings will shortly hear them. Amen (*WABr* 10:227.33–36).[146]

Luther does not exhort or admonish Jonas to moderate his grief, for he finds it entirely appropriate for now. The *conclusio* continues to affirm Jonas in his grief, reminding him of his wife's good deeds and good death—this 'good and pious' woman, with her 'many godly and blessed expressions of faith'—reassuring him that Katy is grieving too ("My Katy was beside herself [when she heard the news], for she and your wife were as intimately united as if they were one soul").[147] God alone is comfort at this time, and Luther again discloses that it is his knowledge of Magdalena's faithful death that is 'my great and only consolation.'[148] And the *conclusio* offers a fitting benediction, one that matches the *salutatio*: "May the Lord, who has suffered you to be humbled, comfort you again now and forever. Amen" (Tappert, 76).[149]

Less than nine months later, while Jonas is visiting in Wittenberg, he and Luther learn that one of the thousands who have died from the plague raging in Jonas's own city of Halle is Eva Heinze, wife of organist Wolf Heinze. Luther writes a letter of consolation to Heinze (Tappert, 77).[150] The *exordium / narratio* reveals that Luther learned of the death within the hour, and his affectionate epithets show—for the deceased—how the Christian's death means reunion with the heavenly family: "your beloved Eva has gone to God, her Father."[151] However, for the surviving husband, her gain means his loss. Consequently, Luther first conveys his sincere feelings of understanding, and he does it without explicit mention of his own recent loss:

> I can well imagine how painful this parting is to you, and I assure you that I am deeply grieved for your sake. You know how faithfully and truly I love you. I know too that God loves you. And because you love his Son, Jesus, your loss moves me deeply" (*WABr* 10:394.5–8).[152]

---

[146] "…contristant Spiritum sanctum, usque ad poenitentiam creaturae totius, quae nobiscum una gemit inenarribilibus gemitibus pro redemptione et sui et nostrum, quam propediem exaudiet ille, qui gemitus istos scit et intelligit, Amen."

[147] "Mea Ketha exanimata fuit. Namque illius et sua fuit una anima unitissima" (*WABr* 10:227.38f.).

[148] "…magno et unico meo solatio" (*WABr* 10:227.44).

[149] "Dominus, qui te passus est humiliari, soletur te rursum, hic et in aeternum, Amen" (*WABr* 10:227.44f.).

[150] *WABr* 10:394f. (Nr. 3912).

[151] "…ewer liebe Heua zu Gott jrem Vater gefahren" (*WABr* 10:394.3f.).

[152] "…kan ich wol sülen, wie euch solch scheiden zu hertzen gehet, vnd ist mir warlich

Once the personal relationship is clarified, Luther uses inclusive language (7 first plural pronouns in 7 lines) to argue what God is up to—showing us how much we have been saved from—and that Christ will comfort. The customary assurance that she is better off, and that 'all of us' desire such a 'blessed end' closes the *petitio*. Just a week short of the one-year anniversary of Magdalena's death, Luther writes a brief but tender letter.

In October 1544 Luther wrote an even shorter letter to Eva Schulz, whose husband Georg had been a student at Wittenberg and had lived there for many years, before moving to Freiberg, Saxony, in 1535, where he died (Tappert, 77f.).[153] As he did with Heinze, Luther says he is 'deeply grieved' at her misfortune, and that he "can well believe that such parting is painful to you."[154] Surprisingly, he does not refer to the deceased with any endearing epithet! However, he assures Eva that grief is a sign of a warm love, that he finds Georg's 'Christian and blessed' departure, and that she knows that the parting is God's will for her. Shifting into first person plural, Luther argues that since God gave his son for us, it is only fitting that we should sacrifice our own will to his. Not only is this our duty, but also 'great and eternal' blessing (*Frucht*) and comfort (*Trost*) will then result. Luther thanks the widow for sending him some mining shares. The brevity of the letter permits little concrete detail about how Christ will comfort; through a pronouncing benediction, it only tries to convey such reassurance to her. Luther does not offer 'God's will' as a terse, grief-deflecting platitude; rather, he generally offers amplification about what God has already done (sent his Son) and plans to do (reunite us with him and loved ones) for us.

The final letter (Tappert, 80f.) to bereaved spouses is Luther's 3 June 1545 letter to Andreas Osiander (1498–1552).[155] An important Lutheran theologian at Nürnberg, Osiander had frequently disagreed with Luther: over baptism, over confession, even about Copernicus's new book on the heliocentric universe (1543), for which Osiander had

ewer hertzlich hertzleid leid, Denn jr wisset, das ich euch mit ernst vnd trewen lieb hab, weis auch, das euch Gott lieb hat, denn jr seinen Son Jhesum lieb habt, darumb mich ewer Leid recht wol rüret." Tappert, 77 reverses the doublet 'ernst vnd trewen.'

[153] *WABr* 10:663f. (Nr. 4034).

[154] "Es ist mir ewr vnfall fast leid, kans wol gleuben, das solch scheiden euch wehe thun mus" (*WABr* 10:664.4f.).

[155] *WABr* 11:113f. (Nr. 4122).

written a preface.[156] When Luther had written him back in 1538, he
found Osiander's independent attitude on theological matters trouble-
some; he recognized his theological giftedness, but he perceived danger
in a self-possessed, pedantically arrogant, and contentious attitude.[157]
Yet Luther valued Osiander's reforming work in Nürnberg, and he did
not let their differences prevent him from extending Christian charity
when it was so obviously appropriate. When Osiander's first wife died
in 1537, Luther sent condolences. Now, eight years later, the second
wife and a daughter died about the same time. Luther's *salutatio* is the
most elaborate of any from our sample: following the titles, plus the
normal 'grace and peace in Christ,' comes this: "who is our consolation
and is altogether ours, even as we are altogether his, for, as St. Paul
says, 'Whether we live or die, we are the Lord's' [Rom. 14:8]. Excellent
and beloved Osiander" (Tappert, 80).[158] In the *exordium / narratio* Luther
tells of having heard about the death 'of your wife and of your dearly
loved daughter,' which represents a cross, 'indeed, a twofold cross.'[159]
Luther's twin objectives in the *petitio* identify with Osiander's grief
through self-disclosure and reconcile it in view of the cross of Christ:
First, he discloses that he 'knows from the death of my own dearest
child' (Magdalena, nearly three years earlier) how great Osiander's grief
must be.[160] Then, additional deep disclosure:

> It may appear strange, but I am still mourning the death of my dear
> Magdalene, and I am not able to forget her. Yet I know surely that she is
> in heaven, that she has eternal life there, and that God has thereby given
> me a true token [*magnum signum*] of his love in having, even while I live,
> taken my flesh and blood to his Fatherly heart (*WABr* 11:114.9–12).[161]

---

[156] They essentially agreed on the Lord's Supper, however; cf. Martin Brecht, *Martin
Luther*, 2:327–334; 3:118.

[157] Martin Brecht, *Martin Luther*, 3:312.

[158] "...qui nostrum solatium est, imo totus noster est et nos toti sumus eius, sicut
Paulus ait: 'Sive vivimus, sive morimur, Domini sumus'...optime et charissime Osiander" (*WABr* 11:113.3–6). The ellipsis represents the beginning of the next sentence,
which precedes 'optime et charissime Osiander.'

[159] "...tesse denuo mortificatum et simul duplici mortificatione, nempe morte uxoris
et filiae suavissimae" (*WABr* 11:114.6f.).

[160] "Et ego exemplo filiae mihi charissimae valde et valdissime credo" (*WABr*
11:114.7f.).

[161] "Mirum est, quantum torqueat me mors Magdalenae meae, quam nec adhuc
oblivisci possum. Sed scio certissime esse in loco refrigerii et vitae aeternae, dederitque
mihi Deus in hac ipsa magnum signum amoris sui, qui carnem meam in sinum suum
me vivente recipit."

Using an abundance of doublets, Luther then argues that the love they (he and Osiander) have for their deceased is natural love, something 'good and human' but which must be crucified so that the 'good and acceptable and perfect will of God' (Rom. 12:2) can be done.[162] Luther asserts, using language from 1 John 1:3, that "God's Son, through whom and by whom all things were made, gave his very life although this was neither deserved nor required of him."[163] Claiming that this disclosure amounts to a testimony, Luther tells his recipient he is sure they share the belief that "we are partakers together in your sufferings,"[164] that God has made Osiander a 'true and faithful [*syncerum et fidelem*] participant in our faith and doctrine.' He closes with a biblical exhortation, saying that Osiander must:

> yield up your dear Isaac as a burnt offering and for a sweet-smelling savor to God—not your daughter or your wife, for these live and are blessed in the Lord, but that natural and strong affection which asserts itself too powerfully in us. While for the Lord this burnt offering is necessary, for us it is a consolation. But why should I try to explain these things to you when you understand them far better than I? (*WABr* 11:114.19–22).[165]

Luther seems to have concluded that even our most profound human relationships (with spouses and children) must be subject to our devotion to God. This is the third time he has used the Isaac image (cf. 'To Pauli,' 'To Zoch'). He offers an explanation to his grieving friend that he hopes makes sense, but he realizes that making sense takes time and effort. It cannot be done alone; other sufferers can console. Ultimately, however, Christ alone is the source of all comfort.

C. *Letters to Surviving Siblings*

Two of Luther's letters were written to brothers who had recently seen their siblings buried, and the letters are hardly similar. One comes from Luther's unmarried years (1525); he wrote the other three months after Magdalena's death (1542). The letter to Elector John the Steadfast (Tappert, 55f.), brother to the recently deceased Elector Frederick the

---

[162] "...bona, beneplacens et perfecta voluntas Dei" (*WABr* 11:114.14f.).

[163] "Quandoquidem et ipse filius, per quem et propter quem omnia perire et mori voluit, cum non oporteret nec deberet" (*WABr* 11:114.15f.).

[164] "...nos esse participes harum tentationum" (*WABr* 11:114.17f.).

[165] "Mactabis enim hunc tuum Isaac dilectissimum in holocaustum, in odorem suavitatis Domino, non filiam neque uxorem, quae vivunt et salvae sunt, in Domino, sed affectum illum naturae validum et amarissimum, qui in nobis nimis vivax est."

Wise, is a message understandably more formal than the others, with nine instances of the epithet 'Your Grace' found in the letter's body, not counting the heading, salutation, and signature. Accordingly, Luther's letter is perceptively attentive to the challenging political situation facing his new Prince. Yet the letter is also filled with many of Luther's consoling appeals—particularly to quotations of Scripture, especially the Psalter; of course, it lacks any self-disclosure of his own grief.[166] The *exordium / narratio* acknowledges the gravity of his recipient's being suddenly thrust into power in these 'perilous, terrible'[167] times—near the end of the Peasants' War   and it expresses the conflict felt when needing to write a consolation, though words are inadequate. Luther thus identifies with John's plight, and he defines it by putting the words of Psalm 40:12 (39:13 Vulgate) into the voice of the Elector. The *petitio* makes an argument about God's faithfulness, by linking His wrath with His mercy, which is available for those who trust him. They will receive 'courage and strength' to bear and, ultimately, 'ways and means [*Wege vnd Weysze*]' to escape.[168] Luther cites and quotes several Scriptures in rapid succession—Ps. 118:18 [117:18 Vulgate]; Ps. 34:19 [33:20 Vulgate]; Prov. 3:12, 11; John 16:33—following those teachings, as cited by two of their authors (Solomon and Christ), with the following argument:

> This is the school in which God chastens us and teaches us to trust in him so that our faith may not always stay in our ears and hover on our lips but may have its true dwelling place in the depth of our hearts. In this school Your Grace is even now enrolled. And without doubt God has taken away our leader in order that He may himself take the deceased man's place and draw nearer to Your Grace to give up and surrender your comforting and tender [*trostliche und liebliche*] reliance upon that man and draw strength and comfort [*Starck und Getrost*] only from the goodness and power of Him who is far more comforting and tender (Tappert, 56).

For a prince so committed to the Reformation faith as John will become, Luther invokes the 'Psalter and the Holy Scriptures' as acceptable evidence and source, not only of comfort and strength but also of authority—even over a sovereign prince.

Luther's letter of 27 December 1542 (*LW* 50:240f.) to his son Johannes (or John or Hans, age 16) is a very brief note, one quite

---

[166] Nr. 867.
[167] Tappert, 55 inserts a conjunction in the doublet (*WABr* 3:496.10).
[168] *WABr* 3:496.16f.

incongruent—in many ways—with the other letters, and perhaps not really a letter of consolation at all.[169] One day after the tender and emotional letter he wrote to Jonas—and 67 days after Magdalena's death—Luther writes an almost terse note to his own grieving son. As the Luthers' firstborn, Hans had been extremely fond of Magdalena, and in September his father brought him back hastily from school in Torgau so Hans could be at his sister's side before she died.[170] Now, with the boy back at school, father Martin's first sentence is a succinct report on how things are going at home since Hans left: "I and your Mother [*Ego et mater tua*], along with the whole house, are fine."[171] What immediately follows are direct, concise orders from father, and indirect, more elaborated reports of mother's wishes that are said to be in harmony with father's: to 'overcome those tears like a man,' so he won't worry his mother;[172] to stay there and be educated, to come home only if sick. "In addition, she wishes you to put aside this mourning so that you may study in a happy and peaceful frame of mind."[173] One must consider today that this letter stands apart from all the others in that: (1) the writer (and his wife) are in an obviously authoritative position over the recipient, as parents to son; (2) the grieving experiences surrounding Magdalena's death had been shared for several days already; (3) the writer's signature ('Your father, Martin Luther') differs drastically from the previous letter to Elector John and considerably from all the others. For all others include only name, or name and title (doctor), or 'servant' / 'willing servant' and name; and (4) the letter's style is more 'plain' than most, with only two doublets and the crisp pair of imperatives: 'You see to it that...' and 'You be obedient to God...'[174] However, additional evidence for the harsh tone and firm hand that Luther took with his son can also be seen in his instructions, written the previous day, to the boy's teacher in Torgau, Marcus Crodel: "I readily believe, my Marcus, that my son has turned soft through the words of his mother, in addition to mourning over his sister's death. Talk seriously with him.... Order him, therefore, to curb that womanish feeling, to get

---

[169] Nr. 301 (*WABr* 10:229 [Nr. 3831]).

[170] *LW* 50:234f. (Nr. 298); *WABr* 10:147. Tappert, does not include it in his collection.

[171] "Ego et mater tua cum tota domo salui sumus" (*WABr* 10:229.2f.).

[172] "Tu vide, ut istas lachrymas viriliter superes" (*WABr* 10:229.3).

[173] "Caeterum istum moerorem vult deponi, ut laetus et quietus studeas" (*WABr* 10:229.9f.).

[174] "Tu vide,.... Tu obedias Deo..." (*WABr* 10.229.3–6).

accustomed to enduring evil, and not to indulge in that childlike weakness" (*LW* 50:239).[175] Obviously, Luther felt a weighty responsibility to his children—especially sons—to tutor them to become strong adults, and he took a sterner tack with them than with others he consoled.[176] His message to Johannes bore a father's ethos, a father who had both toughness to admonish and tenderness to gather his children to wait, together with Magdalena, for God to take her.[177] In both letters—to Elector John and to son John—the sober responsibilities of survival in, and service to, a brutal world looms large.

IV. *Conclusion*

Luther's consolatory letters only slightly adhere to the formal dispositional requirements of Erasmus. There is even little thematic difference between the Latin and the vernacular letters. While I have discussed the letters according to each part (*salutatio*, etc.), Luther often omits the *exordium* or *narratio*, using them only when conveying the news of a death or for clarifying why he was writing. His *salutatio* differs markedly from the Renaissance genre, which demanded that the names of both sender and recipient appear.[178] Luther uses consistently his Christian greeting ('grace and peace in Christ') rather than the classical *salutem*.[179] He does, however, make productive use of epithets, and his richest ones not only characterize the recipient (or the deceased) but also God himself. Moreover, Luther has made even less use of the thematic resources of the consolation genre. Unmistakably, he urges moderation in grieving, either directly or implicitly, by arguing in detail about the richness of

---

[175] *WABr* 10:229.

[176] In *Flesh and Spirit* (268), Steven Ozment summarizes perhaps just this kind of parental concern: "The fear has been that the young would not be properly equipped to tackle life's less glamorous but more essential tasks, or to fulfill society's more modest yet realistic dreams, both of which are vital to individual souls and the body politic."

[177] Speaking of Magdalena's death, the conclusion of Steven Ozment, writing in 1983, is nevertheless overstated: "Despite the lessons of his own heart, Luther...continued to look upon grief as an unchristian tribute to death"; Steven Ozment, "The Family in Reformation Germany: The Bearing and Rearing of Children," *Journal of Family History* 8 (summer 1983): 159–176, here at 172.

[178] Desiderius Erasmus, *On the Writing of Letters* 50–62.

[179] Timothy J. Wengert, "Apostolic Self-Awareness," 77, says Paul 'coined the phrase.' However, while Paul's epistles use it far more often than others, 1 Peter, 2 Peter, 2 John, and Jude also use it. By 'Paul's epistles,' of course, I mean those acknowledged thus by Luther, not by contemporary academic New Testament scholars.

God's comforting resources, the blessedness of the Christian death, and the misery that the earthly life offers. Yet we have seen him time and again speak warmly and tenderly about the deceased and about his own affection for them. In this respect, Luther's attitudes and behavior fly in the face of much criticism leveled against 'the new Lutheran family' as the prototype of 'the unconditionally patriarchal and authoritarian household.'[180] What is particularly noteworthy is Luther's own tendency to disclose, on occasion, his own grief experiences, especially after 1542. While he acknowledges the difficulty for a bereaved person (especially, newly bereaved) to appreciate adequately what he is telling them, still Luther expounds upon the comforting resources of God who, he boldly tells bereaved parents, is more of a father to their child than they are. He argues that God not only knows their pain but that such pain can make them truly alive unto Him.

Such 'advice' differs dramatically from our contemporary grief therapies, which, based in secular psychological grief theories, have written God out of their prescriptions. Accordingly, much contemporary pastoral counseling, which is derived from secular grief theories, has eschewed the kind of counsel Luther offered, since the contemporary *Weltanschauung* focuses exclusively on coping with grief, having to do so without the resources of family, faith, church, and God. It encourages bereaved to seek support groups of strangers for help. Consequently, Luther's talk about restraint and self-effacement seems disturbingly out of fashion; wisdom about God's chastisement seems revolting.[181] Viewed from the contemporary perspective, much of Luther's consolation rings

---

[180] Steven Ozment, *Ancestors: The Loving Family in Old Europe* (Cambridge, Mass., 2001), 31. Countering the more received view that the concept of the modern family is a post-Enlightenment phenomenon, Ozment argues that the "modern sentimental family exists as far back in time and as widely in space as there are proper sources to document it" (109). He further argues that such a concept is not to be lamented but rather: "For a modern age faced with a family crisis, there is good news from the recovered history of the family: this smallest and seemingly most fragile of institutions is proving itself to be humankind's bedrock as well as its fault line. Its strength lies in the cohesion and loyalty of the parent-child unit around which the larger worlds of household and kin, community and nation, and the global village necessarily revolve" (111f.); cf. also, Linda A. Pollock, *Forgotten Children: Parent-Child Relations from 1500–1900* (Cambridge, 1983).

[181] Steven Ozment, *Flesh and Spirit* 261; cf. Susan C. Karant-Nunn, "'Christians' Mourning and Lament Should not Be Like the Heathens': The Suppression of Religious Emotion in the Reformation," *Confessionalization in Europe 1555–1700: Essays in Honor and Memory of Bodo Nischan*, ed. John M. Headley, Hans J. Hillerbrand, and Anthony J. Papalas (Aldershot, 2004), 107–129.

hollow. Yet, from that same vantage point, one has to be impressed with his efforts to acknowledge the immensity of loss and to recognize the reality of grief. Indeed, bereaved parents have probably always found themselves having to cope with both the power of their own grief and their concerns for their surviving children.[182] As one heals, one can later appreciate how important and necessary was advice to 'keep going' despite how futile, insensitive, and unwanted such counsel seemed at the time.[183] From what we have learned about Luther's characterizations of family members and their uniqueness, we realize that family love is indeed precious, for it schools us in the task of loving a God who first loved us. When we grieve, Luther would have our attitudes mirror that of the distraught father in Mark 9:24, who, *with tears*, said to Jesus, "Lord, I believe; help thou mine unbelief" (KJV).[184]

---

[182] Jeannie Labno, "Child Monuments in Renaissance Poland," *SCJ* 37 (2006): 351–374.

[183] "Even if grief is an inner psychological process, it is manifested in behaviour which others have to live with: grief therefore is also inevitably an interpersonal negotiation"; Tony Walter, *The Revival of Death*, 160.

[184] "…ich glewb lieb er herr / hilff meynem vnglawben"; *Luther's "September Bible" In Facsimile*, ed. Kenneth A. Strand (Ann Arbor, 1972), XXXIII.

CHAPTER SIX

"AM I MY BROTHER'S KEEPER?": LUTHER'S "ON WHETHER ONE MAY FLEE FROM A DEADLY PLAGUE" (1527)

'Fight or Flight' is a dilemma all creatures share. For us humans, how-ever, the anguish from advance notice of danger heightens the difficulty. People have always feared pestilence, yet today our fears are exacerbated by rapid communication; they are complicated by expectations that the government 'do something.' Recent fears are of communicable disease throughout the world—particularly, the H5N1 'bird-flu virus,' which has been compared to the influenza epidemic of 1918—and terrorism using biological agents.[1] Previous generations, however, faced pandem-ics much more frequent and probably as virulent—at least as deadly, when factoring in the state of medical knowledge.[2]

---

[1] Tim Appenzeller, "Tracking the Next Killer Flu," *National Geographic* (October 2005): 2–31. The Center for Disease Control and Prevention (CDC) is calling the threat 'Avian Influenza (Bird Flu).' <http://www.cdc.gov/flu/avian/>. (accessed 6 October 2005). Michael T. Osterholm, director of the Center for Infectious Disease Research and Policy, School of Public Health, University of Minnesota, has continued through all of 2005 to sound an ominous warning of impending catastrophe: "This is a critical point in history. Time is running out to prepare for the next pandemic. We must act now with decisiveness and purpose. Someday, after the next pandemic has come and gone, a commission much like the 9/11 Commission will be charged with determin-ing how well government, business, and public health leaders prepared the world for the catastrophe when they had clear warning. What will be the verdict?" ("Preparing for the Next Pandemic," *Foreign Affairs* 84, no. 4 [July–August 2005], <http://www.foreignaffairs.org/20050701faessay84402/michael-t-osterholm/preparing-for-the-next-pandemic.html>, (accessed online 6 December 2005); idem, "Preparing for the Next Pandemic," *NEJM* 352 (5 May 2005): 1839–1842; "A Weapon the World Needs," *Nature* 435 (26 May 2005): 417–418. Osterholm is quoted frequently in Jerry Adler, "The Fight Against the Flu," *Newsweek*, 31 October 2005, 38–45 [cover story]; cf. Shane Harris, "The Bug Bloggers," *Bulletin of the Atomic Scientists* 62 (2006): 38–43; John J. Treanor et al, "Safety and Immunogenenicity of an Inactivated Subvirion Influenza A (H5N1) Vaccine," *NEJM* 354 (30 March 2006): 1343–1351; Gregory A. Poland, "Vaccines against Avian Influence—A Race against Time," *NEJM* 354 (30 March 30 2006): 1411–1413; Katherine Hobson, "Are We Ready?" *U. S. News and World Report*, 1 May 2006, 57–62.

[2] While not yet able to be transmitted from human to human, those infected by the H5N1 virus—through contact with infected poultry blood or manure—have died at a rate of approximately 50 per cent.

In the late summer of 1527 plague struck northern Germany, arriving in Wittenberg around the end of July.[3] The situation so concerned Elector John of Saxony that on 10 August he ordered Luther and his family to leave the city, for he had arranged to move the university from Wittenberg to Jena; it would remain housed there until the following April.[4] Luther, however, refused to leave! He and Johannes Bugenhagen (1484–1558), pastor of the city church (and Luther's longtime confessor), and chaplains Georg Rörer and Johannes Mantel stayed to minister to the sick and dying. Luther continued to lecture—on 1 John and then Titus—to a small group of students who also did not leave. Among Luther's acquaintances, the plague claimed its first victims within days after its arrival.[5] On 19 August he wrote to Spalatin that the wife of Bürgermeister Tilo Dene had that very day died virtually in his arms.[6]

Fear of plague began to spread in the city. By mid-September, additional deaths to plague began to take their toll on the populace. In response to reports that drunken gravediggers had been rude to grieving family members, Luther spoke out in the pulpit, admonishing listeners to show love for their neighbors. He also rebuked those who left their wives because of the plague.[7] In early November things got worse for the tightly-knit circle of Wittenberg reformers: on 2 November the Luthers were shaken by the deaths of their good friend Georg Rörer's wife and her newborn child.[8] Bugenhagen and his family—in whose home the Rörer deaths had occurred—moved in with the Luthers, providing companionship as well as preserving resources and confining

---

[3] *WABr* 4:227.14f. (Nr. 1126), Luther to Melanchthon (2 August 1527): "Pestem hic esse persuasi sumus." By 15 August Melanchthon reported to Joachim Camerarius (1500–1574) in Jena that Wittenberg was definitely infested ("Urbs Witteberga infesta est pestilitate"); cf. *WABr* 4:227, note 9.

[4] *WABr* 4:227f. (Nr. 1127), Elector Johann to Luther (10 August 1527).

[5] Martin Brecht, *Martin Luther*, 2:207.

[6] *WABr* 4:232.16f. (Nr. 1130); Luther to Spalatin (19 August 1527): "Hodie Tilonis Deni vxorem sepeliuimus, que fere inter brachia mea expirauit heri, atque hoc primum funus in media vrbe."

[7] Brecht, *Martin Luther*, 2:207. The record of these events comes from a letter of Urban Balduyn to Stephan Roth (15 September 1527), in Georg Buchwald, *Zur Wittenberger Stadt- und Universitäts-Geschichte in der Reformationszeit: Briefe aus Wittenberg an M. Stephan Roth in Zwickau* (Leipzig, 1893), 5–7.

[8] *LW* 49:174, note 25; cf. *WABr* 4:276 (Nr. 1165), Luther to Justus Jonas (4 November 1527).

the disease.[9] Also staying there (and seriously ill) was Margaret von Mochau, sister-in-law to Karlstadt. The Luthers' year-old son Hans was gravely ill, and Katy Luther was pregnant with Elizabeth. Luther called his home 'a hospital.'[10]

Moreover, from his former student Johann Hess (1490–1547)—leader of the Reformation in Breslau (Wroclaw), capital of Silesia—came a letter, written on behalf of the evangelical pastors in Breslau, asking for advice on whether the clergy there should stay or flee the plague in their city.[11] Plague had arrived there on 10 August, a little over a week later than in Wittenberg.[12] Having written Luther about the same problem in 1525, Hess would not get a written response for nearly two years, due to Luther's own health problems.[13] Luther's answer finally came in the form of an open letter to Hess and his fellow servants (*Dienern*).

Johann Hess was a native of Nuremberg, who was sent to school in Zwickau, Saxony. He became a well-educated pastor, having earned the bachelor of arts (1507) at Leipzig, the master of arts (1511) at Wittenberg, and a doctorate in theology (1519) at Ferrara. Upon his return from Italy to Silesia, Hess visited in Wittenberg; hence, a lifelong correspondence with both Luther and Melanchthon ensued.[14] Always appreciating the arts, Hess had been mentored by Johannes Turzo (1464–1520), the humanist bishop of Breslau, who had sent him back to Wittenberg for further study, only to send him first to Italy, where

---

[9] Luther told a friend that Bugenhagen (Pomeranus) moved in "not so much for his sake as for mine..., so he could be a companion in my isolation" (Salutat te Pomeranus quam officiosissime, apud me habitans, non tam sui quam mei causa..., scilicet vt sotius solitudinis mea sit); *WABr* 4:277.14–16 (Nr. 1166), Luther to Nikolaus Hausmann (7 November 1527), translation by Heinrich Bornkamm, in *Luther in Mid-Career, 1521–1530*, ed. Karin Bornkamm, trans. E. Theodore Bachmann (Philadelphia, 1983), 562.

[10] *WABr* 4:274f. (Nr. 1164), Luther to Amsdorf (1 November 1527): "In domo mea coepit esse hospitale."

[11] Heinrich Bornkamm, *Luther in Mid-Career*, 562.

[12] *LW* 43:115f.

[13] "Die Pest" was first reported in Breslau during 10 August to 19 November 1525. On 22 April 1526 Luther wrote to Hess that he had his request but would be unable to answer at that time (*WA* 23:323).

[14] There are about twenty extant letters from Luther and thirty from Melanchthon; cf. *OER*, s.v. "Hess, Johann," by Manfred P. Fleischer. There are no biographical works on Hess in English; cf. Carl Adolph Julius Kolde, *Dr. Johann Heß, der schlesische Reformator* (Breslau, 1846).

Hess studied both theology and law.[15] In 1523 Hess was appointed by the Breslau city council as preacher of St. Mary Magdalene's church. This bold move in support of reformation teaching led to a public disputation in 1524, which culminated in the council's ordering of evangelical teaching by all pastors in the city—despite pressure from the cathedral chapter, Pope Adrian VI, and the king of Hungary-Bohemia, to which Silesia belonged.[16] In 1525 Hess pressured the city council of Breslau until they provided an All Saints' hospital for the care of the sick and the homeless.[17] On 8 September 1525 (three months after Luther's marriage), Hess married Sara Jopner (d. 1531), the daughter of a Breslau city council member; in 1533 he married Hedwig Wahle. These marriages produced six surviving children.[18]

I. *Structure of Luther's Book*

Ob man fur dem sterben fliehen muge was a popular pamphlet of fourteen quarto pages.[19] Luther's response to the question about behavior in

---

[15] According to Manfred P. Fleischer, "Humanism and Reformation in Silesia: Imprints of Italy—Celtis, Erasmus, Luther, and Melanchthon," in *The Harvest of Humanism in Central Europe: Essays in Honor of Lewis W. Spitz*, ed. Manfred P. Fleischer (St. Louis, 1992), 27–107, here at 44, "Historians agree that Turzo was the only Renaissance prince Silesia ever had." Fleischer (63) points out Gustav Bauch's argument that Hess always remained under the influence of the Renaissance and followed his humanist inclinations throughout his life, being even closer to Melanchthon in friendship than he was to Luther; cf. Gustav Bauch, "Beiträge zur Litteraturgeschichte des schlesischen Humanismus," *ZVGS* 26 (1892): 213–225; idem, "Johann Thurzo und Johann Heß," *ZVGS* 36 (1901): 193–224; idem, "Zur Breslauer Reformationsgeschichte," *ZVGS* 41 (1907): 336–352; Julius Köstlin, "Johann Heß, der Breslauer Reformator," *ZVGS* 6 (1864–1865): 97–131; 181–265.

[16] Werner Laug, "Johannes Heß und die Disputation in Breslau von 1524," *Jahrbuch für schlesische Kirchengeschichte* 37 (1958): 23–34. The disputation *Protokoll* can be found in Kolde, *Dr. Johann Heß*, 110–121. For a Catholic view on the Lutheran takeover of Breslau, see Fleischer's discussion ("Humanism and Reformation," 50ff.) of Kurt Engelbert's account; cf. also Fleischer's "Silesiographia: The Rise of a Regional Historiography," *ARG* 69 (1978): 219–247, especially 232f. on the disputation of 20–23 April 1524; cf. D. Erdmann, "Luther und seine Beziehungen zu Schlesien, insbesondere zu Breslau," *Schriften des Vereins für Reformationsgeschichte* 5 (1887): 1–75 (Schrift 19).

[17] Fleischer, "Hess," in *OER*.

[18] Fleischer, "Humanism and Reformation," 69.

[19] Benzing, Nr. 2424–2433; *WA* 23:325–327 lists the ten German editions as: A^x, A^y, B^x, B^y, C-H. Printed in Wittenberg in four different editions in 1527 by Hans Lufft, the work was also published the same year in Augsburg, Nuremberg, Marburg, Magdeburg (in both High- and Low German), Zwickau, and Hagenau. Beginning with a Danish edition in 1534, there were also eleven later German editions published in the next several decades (1552–1631); Benzing, Nr. 2434–2435. *WA* 23:327–329 lists

the face of a deadly epidemic provides a glimpse of several important ethical issues of the day.[20] By the time he has added to it for printing, Luther's document contained three parts, including the Preliminaries: (I) discussion on the question (*LW* 43:120–134; *WA* 23:339–371) of whether one should flee from death due to plague; this section constitutes about 80 per cent of the document; (II) discussion (*LW* 43:134f.; *WA* 23:371–373) on how one should prepare his soul for death; this section constitutes about 10 per cent of the document and was also added for printing; (III) discussion on burial practices (*LW* 43:135–138; *WA* 23:373–379); this section constitutes about 10 per cent of the document and was added for printing.

The simple organizational macrostructure of part I is: 26 lines of preliminaries, followed by the heart of the case: A. Title, Signature, and *salutatio*: five lines (*LW* 43:119: *WA* 23:339.1–4); B. *Narratio*: twenty-one lines (*LW* 43:119f.; *WA* 23:339.5–25); C. Substance of the Case (*LW* 43:120–134; *WA* 23:339.26—371.4). In my analysis of the heart of the pamphlet I shall lay out the microstructure.

II. *Analysis of Luther's Book*

A. *Preliminaries*

The *salutatio* is the familiar Pauline formula that Luther often uses, "Grace and peace from God our Father and our Lord Jesus Christ" (*WA* 23:339.4f.).[21] In the two-paragraph *narratio* Luther uses the first paragraph to state the question (*Frage*)[22] that Hess sent to him and to explain his reasons for the delay in answering. In the second paragraph

---

the eleven later editions as: 'a'–'l'. I have not attempted to investigate to what extent plague activity coincided with the publication dates after 1527.

[20] The modern edition of the document Luther wrote is found in *WA* 23, and in *LW* 43. *WA* 23:339–379; *LW* 43:119–138, translation by Carl J. Schindler. The reader should bear in mind that the text of *WA* 23 that I cite will not be of sequential pagination; rather, the text is found on p. 339, 341, 343, etc. The text is found in two separate versions, printed on alternating pages; one version derives from Luther's manuscript and the other from the earliest print. I shall follow the print version, since it is more complete, by which I mean that it contains a second section that Luther later added to his original writing. The original section addresses the questions pertaining to plague, about which Hess had written; the later section discusses matters of Christian burial. This latter section was not included in the translation contained in Tappert.

[21] "Gnad und fride von Gott unserm vater und dem HERRN Jhesu Christo."

[22] Tappert, 230; *LW* 43:119 translates *Frage* as 'letter.'

he supplies a rationale for why he is now writing, giving permission also for the letter to be published.

In his first paragraph, the syntax of the opening sentence allows the explanation for the delay to register as fittingly sincere. Yet Luther is not merely apologizing, for he then supplies two reasons, each set forth through doublets, why he had not responded sooner: First, God had 'disciplined and scourged [*zucht und staupe*]' him so that he was unable to do much 'reading or writing [*lesens noch schreibens*]' (*WA* 23:339.10f.).[23] Second, Luther appears to flatter his reader, Hess, by delineating his gifts: he has been richly endowed with 'wisdom and truth [*Verstand und Warheit*]' in Christ and is well qualified to 'decide and anwer [*entscheiden und richten*]'[24] this matter in Christ's 'Spirit and grace [*Geist und Gnade*]' without assistance. Yet more substantively, it is "God, the merciful Father, [who] has endowed you so richly." The locution *der vater aller barmhertzickeit* is better rendered 'father of all mercy' (cf. 2 Cor. 1:3) and becomes a key phrase in this document.[25]

In the second paragraph Luther relents, acknowledging that Hess has humbled himself by seeking Luther's view. Luther then reciprocates, agreeing humbly to submit his own opinion for Hess and all devout Christians who 'desire or use [*begeren und brauchen*]' his instructions.[26] As a meaningful conveyance, the doublet is a natural stylistic tool, since Luther's scriptural proof text for agreeing to supply an answer is a two-fold expression gleaned from Paul that is itself an extended doublet: "we may always agree with one another and be of the same mind."[27] Indeed, the exigence is urgent, for the rumor of death is, or

---

[23] Intermittent bouts of fainting, dizziness, and ringing in his ears are well documented and discussed by Brecht. Luther believed that he was also under severe spiritual *Anfechtungen* during the summer of 1527, and Brecht agrees: "The combination of the psychological and the physical is unmistakable in this illness; Brecht, *Martin Luther*, 2:205. The period 1527–1529 was so marked by Luther's poor health that Brecht discusses the open letter to Hess within the context of his section on Luther's 'Illness' (205–210).

[24] '[D]ecide and answer' is Tappert's translation (230); *LW* 43:119 ignores the doublet and renders it 'decide.'

[25] Luther acknowledges that his opinion is subject to what God grants (*verleyhet*)—namely, that he might 'understand and perceive [*begreiffen mügen zuerkennen*]'—and is submitted for his readers' own 'decision and conclusion [*urteilen und richten*].' Tappert (230) ignores *Barmhertzickeit*, rendering only 'God the Father.'

[26] Fleischer, "Humanism and Reformation in Silesia," (55), calls attention to Luther's 'forthrightness' with Hess, especially in their correspondence.

[27] 1 Cor. 1:10; 13:11; Phil. 2:2. Tappert (230) translates *urteilen und richten* as doublet verbs ('weighed and judged').

will be, heard in 'these and many other' parts (*WA* 23:339.16–25). As it happens, Luther is not claiming sole credit for the ideas he is writing about: in paragraph one he uses the first person singular pronoun (*I, me*), but in the second he uses the plural (*we, our*). He wants Hess and other readers to take these ideas as representative of the Wittenberg teaching.[28]

One final comment on the preliminaries is in order. In stating the question of Hess, and hence the issue he is addressing, Luther does not use the word 'plague.' As with the title of the document, the expression is 'to flee death.' Only later in the document does Luther use the explicit term *Pestilenz*.[29] So 'rumor of death,' the feared outcome rather than the precise cause, is certainly an accurate way to construe the situation people fear.

B. *The Substance of the Case*

Luther's argument, in a nutshell, is that neither fleeing nor remaining is right or wrong per se; both positions have their problems. He shows the fallacy of fleeing to be that of violating one's duties or one's responsibilities to his 'neighbor.' He points out the error of remaining, if done so as to be thereby 'tempting God.' Luther's strategy is to delay this latter argument until later in the piece, and when he gets there he grounds his position on Psalm 91:11–13. This is text used by the devil—the 'middle temptation' against Jesus in the Wilderness (Matt. 4:5–7 // Luke 4:5–8).

Luther essentially divides the question into two parts: (i) if one flees, is it right or wrong? and (ii) how should one decide whether to flee? I say essentially, because he makes no tidy distinction between the two parts; indeed, they intertwine throughout the piece. Yet he begins with the matter of (i) if one flees, by stating the two positions already being

---

[28] It is in the first sentence of paragraph two that Luther switches from singular to plural, leading his readers directly to the Pauline text: 'writing to me...requesting our view.' '[M]e' is only assumed (correctly, I believe, from the prior context) by the *LW* translator, for it is not explicit in this sentence. Tappert, 230 does not use a singular pronoun, but he is definitely seeing not only the prior context as singular, but indeed also the rest of the paragraph. For he proceeds to translate all the personal pronouns (*unser / uns / wir / wir / uns / wirs / unser*) as singulars, perhaps taking Luther to be using plural pronouns editorially.

[29] Marius, *Martin Luther*, 9 points this out.

offered by some people, and then others. Thus, *WA* 23:339.26–341.2
(6 lines) is a *narratio* that lays out (a) the firm opinion—that one 'need
not and should not' flee; and (b) the flexible opinion—that one, particularly if not holding public office, may properly flee. But Luther does
not explicate these two positions with equal space.

Luther then renders a judgment about (a) the firm position (*WA*
23:341.3–10), for he does not censure but rather commends these folks
for their excellent decision to uphold a good cause—namely, a strong
faith; indeed, their 'strong, firm faith [*starcken festen Glauben*]' is one which
they want all Christians to have. However, Luther characterizes this
faith as rare, for most of the saints 'have been and still are in dread' of
death. He contrasts this strong faith with an opposing neologism—the
'milk faith' most have. Yet he makes no criticism of this position; rather,
he praises it highly, describing its firmness with respect to fleeing, and
its disregard for death, with the same term (*Achten*). He also clearly
sees this position as one of faith *toward God*,[30] for he also considers the
plague to be sent from God, and thus one's response toward it is also a
response toward God. However, this strong faith is not only exemplary
but also rare.

From *WA* 23:341.12–347.12 on, Luther pursues his own set of arguments, not abandoning the initial two positions but altering them to
fit the contingent situation, with respect to people's faith, as he sees it.
He arranges his arguments about who must remain—and who might
be excepted—into two categories: (1) those with obligations to ministry—first, sacred and second, secular—to subordinates, i.e., subjects
they serve; and (2) those who have reciprocal social responsibilities to
superiors above them or to subordinates below them. Luther provides
evidence of strong and weak faith, and how each requires a commensurate treatment; he brings two examples from Scripture and elaborates
upon them with lessons from experience.[31] In these explanations, not
only has Luther found the two texts to interpret each other; he has
also used the conjunction *aber* three times to enact the contrast between

---

[30] *LW* 43:120 translates *starcken Glauben* as 'strong faith in God,' while Tappert, 231
does not.

[31] A person of strong faith (*Ein Starckgleubiger*) suffers no ill effects from drinking poison (Mark 16:18), while one of weak faith (*Ein Schwachgleubiger*) would, however (*aber*),
drink to his death. Peter walked upon water, when his faith was strong (*da er starck yn
Glauben war*), but (*aber*) when he started to doubt and his faith weakened (*und schwach
in Glauben ward*), he almost drowned (Matt. 14:30).

strong and weak. To add scriptural authority to the logic of these biblical examples, Luther then concludes (*Nu*)[32] a principle from them, to
which he also cites—without any quotation from—two Pauline texts
(Rom. 15:1; 1 Cor. 12:22ff.): "Christ does not want his weak ones to
be abandoned" (*WA* 23:341.12–21).[33]

Having thus argued that one cannot simply assert that all fleeing is
wrong and having also established that Scripture recognizes that persons
differ in their faith and that situations seem to affect that, Luther next
shifts back toward a broader principle. He claims that there are two
types of situation for which flight is wrong:[34] the first way is wrongful
flight from death in disobedience to God's 'word and command.' His
example goes far beyond the ethically murky waters of plague, to the
clear and uncontroversial case of renouncing the faith, where one is
imprisoned precisely for the sake of God's word. Here one 'denies or
repudiates'[35] God's word in order to escape death. There is Christ's
plain 'mandate and command' not to flee but rather (*sondern*) to suffer

---

[32] Neither Tappert, 231 nor *LW* 43:120 includes the concluding particle in their
translation.

[33] Richard T. Rada, "Luther, Ethics and the Plague in Wittenberg: The Reformer's
Faith Approaches Disease and Suffering," in *Let Christ Be Christ: Theology, Ethics and World
Religions in the Two Kingdoms. Essays in Honor of the Sixty-Fifth Birthday of Charles L. Manske*,
ed. Daniel N. Harmelink (Huntington Beach, Cal., 1999), 251–260 [here at 257–259],
discusses Luther's ethics in "Whether One May Flee" along three lines: teleological
('What is the goal?'), deontological ('What is the law?'), and relationalist ('What is happening?'). He argues that Luther's consideration of strong and weak faith inheres ("shines
brightly,' 258) on the relationalist side, based "not on some law...but is completely
grounded in the notion of personal responsibility in relationship with one's neighbor"
and that this consideration was intended by Luther for the 'reassurance and comfort'
of his readers. While Rada's conclusion is accurate, it is by no means complete. For,
as already seen above, Luther grounds all his arguments in Scripture, and he strives
to show how scripturally based arguments also resonate with lived experience. Rada,
an M.D., has written the only scholarly article devoted solely to discussing Luther's
"Whether One May Flee" that I have found.

[34] When he claims to put it 'briefly and concisely [*kurtz und eigentlich*]' that there are
two ways (*zwereley*) that 'dying and fleeing death [*Sterben und Tod fliehen*]' may happen
(so Tappert, 231), Luther appears to suggest a tidy and clear structure to follow, but
that is not the case. He gives the first instance immediately and transparently, but the
second is by no means readily discernible. What he could mean is what he handles
as exceptions to the responsibilities spiritual leaders have, or what he might mean by
the second way is the secular office holders (*Amt*) that others had in mind earlier (*LW*
43:120; *WA* 23:341.2) and which he discusses after the spiritual leaders.

[35] For *odder LW* 43:120 uses 'and' instead of 'or'; Tappert's 'denies or recants' is
apt (231), for my modern German dictionary prefers *widerrufen* for recanting religious
belief.

death.[36] Then he offers a paraphrase of Matt. 10:33, 28a, putting Christ's words before his readers: "Whoever denies [*verleucket*] me before men, I will also deny [*verleucken*] before my Father who is in heaven" and "Do not fear those who kill the body but cannot kill the soul, etc." (*WA* 23:341.22–30).[37] So Luther has established the most serious violation of flight—avoiding death by denying Christ—and he has done so quite concisely.[38] Next he turns to those sacred responsibilities that share similar scriptural admonition.

Likewise, those engaged in spiritual ministry—e.g., 'preachers and pastors [*Prediger und Seelsorger*]'—must 'stay and remain'[39] steadfast before the peril of 'dying and death.'[40] The argument for this group's responsibilities is obviously a contrast to the prior example (negative—the worst case, about what not to do), for this one is positive. What is similar, though, is the authority, which again comes from a plain command of Christ. The scriptural quotation is a combination of John 10:11a and 12b. As another antithesis, it provides first the positive, exemplary action, followed by the negative, which corresponds to Luther's prior category: "A good shepherd lays down his life for his[41] sheep, but the hireling sees the wolf coming and flees." Not only has Luther here supplied scriptural command and human need; he has in addition offered

---

[36] Tappert, 231, reads 'rather to die'; a literal reading is 'to prefer dying.' We cannot miss three things here about this example: (1) Luther has used doublets to stress the severity of the offense and the authority of the rule being violated; (2) he has three times repeated *gotts wort* to hammer home the origin of the rule; (3) he has asserted that the rule is Christ's.

[37] In *SeptBib* it reads *bekennet*, but in 1534 Luther uses *verleugnet*. The first text clearly conveys threat against denial of Christ, which Luther obviously wants to establish as the most serious offense. The second text, in the form of an antithetical imperative, also maintains mild threat but in addition contains wisdom and promise, especially considering that Luther's 'etc' is invoking the broader context of Matt. 10, which is about God's provision and care.

[38] He could have used the scriptural example of Peter's denial of Jesus (Matt. 26:75 // Mark 14:30 // Luke 22:61), but that text may have been counterproductive for his readers. Luther's objective here is not to argue that flight from plague is the worst possible offense, but rather that it needs to be measured and weighed according to Scripture's teachings about duties and responsibilities—and about God's comfort.

[39] Tappert, 231; *LW* 43:121 misses the doublet.

[40] Both Tappert, 231 and *LW* 43:121 fail to translate the doublet. While the first doublet is complementary, designating different offices, the latter two are progressive; Luther will soon provide another complementary doublet.

[41] *SeptBib*; both Tappert, 232 and *LW* 43:121 miss the second *seine*. In 1534 Luther will go with 'the sheep.'

promised reward to caregivers—not escape or success in this life but that which a Christian should value even more highly.

Next (*WA* 23:343.6–16) Luther discusses exceptions to the command that spiritual leaders must stay.[42] The resource exception can be granted when sufficient numbers of preachers are available and agreement is reached that some may leave in order to avoid danger. Luther does not consider such leaving sinful because spiritual services are provided[43] and because all are 'willing and ready'[44] to stay if necessary. He then supplies one example from church history and two from the life of Paul, both of which are given scriptural attribution. First, is the example (*Gleich*) of Athanasius (296–373), who fled his church in order to save his life because many others were there to administer his office.[45] Next (*Item*), Paul was lowered over the city wall of Damascus in a basket so he could escape (Acts 9:25). Finally, Paul let the disciples keep him from risking danger in the marketplace (Acts 19:30), because it was not essential for him to do so. These examples, without commentary, are intended by Luther to show how key spiritual leaders were convinced to permit their lives to be spared, so they could live to serve another day and because sufficient spiritual resources were already in place. These exceptions uncover fundamental values (such as the will to live and to protect)—values that Luther will address later on in this document.

In *WA* 23:343.16–28 Luther moves to a second dimension of persons obligated to remain. Here he identifies the offices, duties, and dangers that scriptural principles—exclusively from Paul—indicate are relevant in the case of plague. Those in public office must stay because God's word 'institutes and commands' secular authority so that 'town

---

[42] In his synopsis of "Whether One May Flee," Rada, "Luther, Ethics and the Plague" (255–257), mentions Luther's discussion of these exceptions. He could have perhaps discussed these under his rubric of teleological ethics, for Luther seems to ground these exceptions in what will provide the desired outcome, 'other things being equal.'

[43] Tappert, 232 translates this clause as 'an adequate ministry is provided.'

[44] Both Tappert, 232 and *LW* 43:121 reverse the doublet.

[45] The most likely incident—one of several in the career of this Bishop of Alexandria, all of it during the Arian controversy—Luther has in mind occurred on 8 February 356 (described by Athanasius in *Apol. de fuga* 24), when he escaped arrest at the Church of St. Thomas. He spent the next six years in exile in Upper Egypt, returning to his bishopric in 361. From this exiled period come some of his most important writings. See Cornelius Clifford, "St. Athanasius," *Catholic Encyclopedia on CD-ROM*, <http://www.newadvent.org/cathen/02035a.htm>, (Accessed 22 August 2006).

and country' be 'ruled, protected, and preserved.' Paul teaches this in Rom. 13.[46] The appeal to experience (fear) employs the asyndetic quadruplet—'fires, murder, riots, and every imaginable disaster'—as dangers to an entire community that one has been called to govern. Not only would such abandonment—leaving the *Gemeinde* without 'official or government'—be a great sin (*grosse Sunde*; in first position in the sentence);[47] it is just what the devil seeks (appeal to shame) when order is lacking.[48]

In *WA* 23:343.29–347.12 Luther discusses social obligations of a reciprocal nature. Four categories are included: (1) servants-master and maids-mistress; (2) father-children and children to parents; (3) common public servants; and (4) orphaned children-guardians or friends. Not every category has the same level of reciprocity, however; Luther seems more interested in demonstrating a 'neighbor-principle' inductively than in being rigorously systematic. He begins with the principle: persons who stand in a relationship of 'service or duty' toward one another have the same responsibilities as the two offices already discussed—sacred and secular.[49]

Luther's final category in this section (*WA* 23:345.14–23) begins with the somewhat precise 'children who are orphaned' but essentially broadens out to address any situation involving sick friends and the

---

[46] Luther's quotation is a conflated paraphrase from Rom. 13:3–6 (*WA* 23:343.16–25; *LW* 43:121). In *SeptBib* (and later), Luther uses *Dienerin*, but he does not use *Obrigkeit* until 1534; in *SeptBib* Luther uses *geweltigen*. The '*etc*' makes clear that Luther has more than just v. 4 in mind, as *LW* 43:121 cites. *WA* 23:343 and Tappert, 232 both cite only Rom. 13:6.

[47] So Tappert, 232.

[48] Tappert, 232 reads 'no order there'; *LW* 43:121 uses the euphemistic doublet 'law and order.'

[49] In the following, I have underlined the key signal of an exception: A servant (*Knecht*) should not leave the master, nor a maid (*Magd*) her mistress, <u>without</u> 'knowledge and permission [*Wissen und Urlaub*]' of 'master or mistress [*Herrn odder Frawen*].' Accordingly, master must not desert servant—or lady her maid—<u>unless</u> suitable provision (*Versorgen gnugsamlich*) for care is made. These cases—'servants and maids [*Knecht und Megde*],' 'masters and ladies [*Herrn und Frawen*]'—are all mandated (*Gotts Gebot*): obedience (*Gehorsam*) by subordinates and care (*Versorgen*) by superiors. Parents also—'fathers and mothers [*Vater und Mutter*]'—are divinely bound (*Gotts Gebot*) to 'serve and help [*zu dienen und zu helffen etc*]' their children, and children, in turn, their 'fathers and mothers [*Vater und Mutter*].' Likewise (*Item*) those who are hired for 'wages or duty [*Sold und Lohn*]'—such as "city physicians, city clerks, constables, or whatever their titles [*Stad artzt, Stad diener, Söldener, und wie die mögen genennet werden*]" should not flee without 'proficient and able [*tüchtige und gnugsame*]' substitutes their employer will accept. There is no reciprocal responsibility mentioned here, because these are officials to whom no member of the populace owes any allegiance.

neighbor. Those who are 'guardians or close friends' of these folk are obligated to remain or to arrange for nursing care. Using a verbal doublet, Luther then repeats his principle: no one should dare leave his neighbor unless there are others who will take his place in 'waiting upon and nursing' the sick.[50]

In *WA* 23:345.24–347.6 Luther summarizes his principles for the nonemergency and sufficient resources situations.[51] He describes both the situations and the intentions of patient and caregiver: (1) where sufficient people are available 'for nursing and attending [*warten und versorgen*]' the sick, they can make provision for care services, and may leave; (2) those 'bold and strong' in faith can stay in God's name, for it is no sin. Both decisions—to flee or to remain—are equally sound, when the conditions are met.

C. *Self-Preservation is Biblical*

Luther next moves to support the tendency for self-preservation (*WA* 23:347.6–349.8). Paul says this in Eph. 4 (*sic*), "No man ever hates his own flesh but nourishes and cherishes" it (Eph. 5:29). Luther then cites Paul at 1 Cor. 12:21–26, arguing that all people should 'body and life[52] preserve and not neglect.'[53] Luther next strengthens his argument about the biblical support of self-preservation and how that should inform

---

[50] So Tappert, 233. He uses a second doublet to wrap up this point, that no one may forsake (*lassen*) the other in his distress (*Nöten*) but is obliged (*schüldig*) to 'assist and help [*beyzustehen und helffen*]' him as he himself would like to be helped. In between these two doublets is Luther's scriptural prooftext; he argues that we must respect (*zufurchten*) Christ's word (*Spruch*), "I was sick and you did not visit me, etc," Luther's paraphrase of Matt. 25:43. Both Tappert, 233 and *WA* 23:345.19 cite Matt. 25:43, which reads 'sick and in prison'; *LW* 43:122 cites vv. 41–46, clearly in recognition of Luther's 'etc' that invokes the entire passage, for *LW*—in an uncharacteristic move—inserts an ellipsis after 'me.'

[51] Doublets and a triplet help him itemize those cases for which caregivers have an equal choice either 'to flee or to remain [*zu fliehen und zu bleiben*]'; the choice made is commensurate with the faith of the caregiver. Note that in this case Luther prefaces his doublet with 'both' (*beyde*) and uses the coordinate connector *und* rather than the disjunctive connector *odder*.

[52] One wonders if *Leib und Leben* is not the German counterpart to 'life and limb' in English.

[53] My syntactically literal translation. As is his habit thus far, Luther uses abundant doublets—synonymous, antithetical, complementary, and progressive—and two Pauline texts to argue this point; the first is a nominal doublet within an extended verbal doublet: 'to flee from dying and death and to save one's life [*sterben und Tod zu fliehen und das Leben zurretten*]' is *naturlich*, 'implanted by God and not forbidden [*von Gott eingepfantzt und nicht verboten*]'—unless against 'God and neighbor [*Gott und den Nehesten*].'

ethical decisions in the face of plague—for both how to act and how
to respond to others' actions.

The argument (*WA* 23:347.13–349.8) responds particularly to the
'firm opinion' above—that one must not and need not flee. Luther's
argument is a combination of reasoning from scriptural truths, bolstered
by citation, and a series of examples from heroic persons in the Bible
who protected themselves from harm, without censure.[54] Therefore, it
is not 'forbidden but rather much more[55] commanded' to work to seek
'food, clothing, and all we need' to avoid 'destruction and disaster,'
provided we do not neglect our 'love and duty' to our neighbor. In
fact, it is more appropriate to seek to 'preserve life and avoid death,'
if we can avoid harm to the neighbor.[56]

Luther's second paragraph (*WA* 23:347.24–349.8) provides the
exemplary illustrations from Bible history, while citing just one text. He
begins by stating that to flee from death is not wrong in itself: Abraham
was a great saint who 'feared death and escaped it [*furcht er den Tod und
floch yhn*],' through pretending Sarah was his sister; Isaac did likewise.
His conclusion: All of them fled death when it was possible, but they
did so without depriving their neighbors and while first meeting their
obligations toward them.

D. *Prolepsis: But Should One Try to Avoid Death* from Plague?

WA 23:349.9–351.10 is an extended rebuttal, in two stages, of the
'firm opinion': (1) it begins with the stated objection that the preceding
examples only apply to avoiding death from persecution and do not
speak to death from pestilence—this is the first occurrence of *Pestilentz*
in the document; (2) it ends with a form of *reductio ad absurdum* that

---

[54] Luther uses several doublets, two triplets, and longer series, even incorporating
anaphora. His first paragraph (*WA* 23.347.13–23) invokes Christ's statement (*sagt*) in
Matt. 5 (*sic*) that 'body and life [*Leib und Leben*]' are more than 'food and clothing [*Speyse
und Kleider*]' (Matt. 6:25); so Tappert, 234. *LW* 43:123, probably following Matt. 6:25,
simply reads the doublet as 'life.'

[55] Neither Tappert, 233 or *LW* 43:123 translate *viel mehr*.

[56] Contrarily, the one strong in faith who can willingly suffer 'nakedness, hunger,
and want [*Blosse, Hunger und Not*]' "without tempting God and not trying to escape [*on
Gotts versuchen, und sich nich wil eraus erbeiten*]" should forego flight and remain, but he
must not condemn (*verdamme*) those who "will not or cannot do the same [*solchs nicht
thun odder nicht thun können*]."

engages the "one [who] must remain in the face of death or else one would be resisting God's will" position, what Luther had earlier referred to as tempting God (*WA* 23:339.10).[57]

The rebuttal consists in Luther's own reasoning from Scripture—namely, that death is death, no matter what form it takes. His immediate support is to remind his readers that in the Scriptures God sent four 'plagues or punishments.'[58] Using a rhetorical question that implies an affirmative answer, Luther reasons analogically that flight 'with God and with clear conscience'[59] from one form of dying should mean that flight from all four is permissible, and he proceeds to deal directly with three of the four—the fourth being pestilence itself.[60] However, Luther is not finished with his rebuttal of the firm position, for in *WA* 23:349.23–351.10) he engages in *reductio ad absurdum* against the firm opinion. Six times Luther will use 'God's punishment' sarcastically to show how one cannot easily find the limits of such a concept. He momentarily ridicules his hypothetical interlocutor, then keeps up this line of ridicule, using rhetorical question, continuing to employ 'God's punishment' strategically, and resorting to more frequent doublets to pile on the descriptions of perils and responses.[61] Finally, Luther turns

---

[57] As he generally does, Luther signals his prolepsis with "'Yes,' you may reply [*Ja sprichtstu*]," followed by the stated objection mentioned above. He does not develop the objection, but immediately moves to reply (*Antwort*).

[58] So Tappert, 234; *LW* 43:124 renders the doublet as 'scourges.'

[59] Tappert, 234, reverses the doublet ('with good conscience and with God's permission'), while *LW* 43:124 omits God ('in clear conscience').

[60] He reminds readers that they have already learned in his previous examples that (1) the holy fathers (*lieben heiligen Veter*) escaped the sword; and that (2) the three patriarchs—Abraham, Isaac, and Jacob—fled the other scourge (*andere Plage*; Tappert, 234 reads the 'second plague'), namely, 'hunger and death [*Hunger odder Theurunge*]' when fleeing to Egypt, as Gen. 40–47 tells (*lesen*). Again using rhetorical question, Luther then argues that, by extension, people should escape wild beasts. Then, using invented dialogue for the first time, he inserts the objection—pertaining to sword—that if 'war or the Turks [*Krieg odder der Turck*]' come, one should not flee from 'village or town [*Dorffe odder Stedlin*]' but remain for God's punishment (*Straffe Gotts*), a phrase he will later use several times. Luther rebuts this objection on two grounds, although only using one—namely, by recalling his previous conclusion that such a firm opinion should pertain only to one who has a strong faith (*Wer so starck ist ym Glauben*). Those who flee should not be condemned (*verdamme*).

[61] 'Freezing weather and winter [*Frost und Winter*]' are also *Gottes Straffe* and can cause death. Why try to get 'to a fire or into the house [*zum Fewr odder ynn die Stuben?*]' (Tappert, 235; *LW* 43:124 reverses the doublet). 'Be strong and stay outside [*Sey starck und bleibe yn frost*]' until it warms up! With a clear signal that he is mocking the opponent's view—'According to this opinion [*Mit der Weise*]' (Tappert, 235; *WA* 23:352.2; *LW* 43:124 omits this phrase)—Luther continues to extend his line of reasoning. He offers the

to hypothetical blasphemy, reasoning *with* his reader.[62] He then supplies his reasoning for the final claim, arguing that every kind of evil is also *Gotts Straffe*, so we would naturally want to stop seeking deliverance and even escape from it. He ends with the contemplative rhetorical question, "Where would all this end?"

E. *Positive Instructions for One's Actions Toward Self and Others*

From his previous arguments Luther now advances guidance (*Unterricht*), for both strong and weak in faith, about how to think and act in one's own regard. Following that, he takes up one's obligations to others. While he makes no explicit distinction between strong and weak, Luther first speaks to everybody and then allows for exceptions.[63] One must also note that the instructions here (*WA* 23:351.11–27) are spoken inclusively, for the personal pronouns are mostly first plural; only when using personal dialogue, which is extensive here, does Luther shift to first singular. As usual, the doublets are ubiquitous; not so usual is that there are no Scriptures cited. There are, however, two biblical allusions from the Gospels.

The first doublet is extended: we should pray against all evil and, to our best ability, guard against it, so we do not behave contrary to God—the 'Do Not Tempt God' argument previously advanced.[64] Luther's invented dialogue is the prayer of Matt. 6:10b, taking the apostrophic 'Lord,...' and four times making emphatic (first position) use of the second person singular, intimate pronoun, breaking in but once with a variation. To preserve the parallelism I present here a

---

absurdity first—through polysyndetic triplet—and the reason last (= epistrophe): we then need no 'apothecaries or drugs or physicians [*Apoteke noch Ertzeney noch Ertzte*]' because (*Denn*) all illness is *Gottes Straffe*. Luther's line of reasoning now becomes outlandish (= *reductio ad absurdum*): 'Hunger and thirst [*Hunger und Durst*]' are now 'punishments and torture [*Straffe und Marter*]'; therefore, why 'eat and drink [*issestu und trinckestu*]' rather than submit to *Straffen* until they [i.e., hunger and thirst] abate themselves?

[62] "[T]he Lord's Prayer abbreviate and no longer pray [*abtheten und betten nicht mehr*], 'deliver us from evil, Amen" (literal translation). Here Luther quotes Matt. 6:13b (*WA* 23:351.7 and Tappert, 235 cite Luke 11:4).

[63] In fact, he indicates otherwise ("Everybody [*ein iglicher*] must take this to heart"). The exceptions: one free (*los*)—of commitments, presumably—and weak in faith.

[64] Accordingly, all statements of this section retain explicit orientation to God. If His will is that evil 'come upon us and destroy us [*drynnen haben und wurgen*],' nothing can be done anyway. What one must resolve is to feel bound to stay and face death to serve one's neighbor. The wherewithal to do this will only happen when one will 'commend himself to God and say... [*so befehl er sich Gott und spreche*].'

syntactically literal translation: "Lord, in thy hands am I; thou hast me here kept; thy will be done; for I am thy lowly creature. Thou canst kill me or preserve me in this pestilence in the same way as if I were in fire, water, drought, or any other danger" (*WA* 23:351.16–20).[65] Having his argument culminate in a prayer of such scriptural language and style should certainly make it more compelling. Luther does precisely the same thing for the weak in faith.[66] He ends with an allusion to John 8:44:

> Lord God, I am weak and fearful. Therefore I am running away from evil and am doing what I can to protect myself against it. I am nevertheless in thy hands in this and any other danger that might overtake me. Thy will be done. My flight alone will not succeed of itself because calamity and harm [*Ubel und Unsal*] are everywhere. Moreover, the devil never takes a holiday[67] and sleeps not. He is a murderer from the beginning [John 8:44] and tries everywhere to instigate murder and misfortune (*WA* 23:351.21–27).[68]

Luther's argument about how to regard and treat others (*WA* 23:351.28–353.12) invokes the same principle that informs the previous argument. By that I do not mean some 'live and let live' motto of insularity that our era might insinuate from what Luther has just said. On the contrary, when he says, 'In the same way we must and we are obliged' to our neighbor to accord him the same treatment, Luther means that other 'troubles and perils' must find us acting to aid our neighbor with the same attitude and energy with which we

---

[65] "Herre, ynn deiner hand bin ich, du hast mich hie angebunden, Dein wille geschehe, Denn ich bin dein arme Creatur. Du kanst mich hieryn todten und erhalten so wol, als wenn ich etwa ym fewr, wasser, durst odder andere ferlickeit angebunden were." In *SeptBib* Luther included 'Thy will be done [*Dein Wille geschehe*]' in Luke 11:2.

[66] He states that if one is, however (*Jst er aber*), 'free and can escape [*los und kan fliehen*],' let him 'commend himself and say [*befehl er sich abermal und spreche:*].' Although, given that the dialogue is continuing what he already began—with its multiple deferential acknowledgements of deity—it continues to be centered around Matt. 6:10b but is more openly reflective.

[67] Tappert, 236 reverses the doublet and reads 'does not sleep or take a holiday'; *LW* 43:125 misses the doublet and reads 'never sleeps.'

[68] "Herr Gott ich bin schwach und furchtam. Drumb fliehe ich das ubel und thun so viel dazu als ich kan, das ich mich dafur huete. Abe rich bin gleichwol ynn deiner hand ynn diesem und allerley ubel, so mir begegen mugen, Dein wil geschehe, Denn mein flucht wirds nicht thun, Sintemal eitel ubel und unsal allenthalben ist. Denn der teuffel feyret und schleff nicht, welcher ist ein morder von anfang und sucht allenthalben eitel mord und ungluck an zurichten."

protected ourselves.[69] In summarizing the argument I call attention to the syntax.[70]

First, if a neighbor's house catches fire, love compels me 'to run and to help him [*zu lauffen und helffen*]'; if sufficient people are already there to help, I may 'go home or remain' to help. Second, should the neighbor fall into 'water or a pit,' I dare not turn away but (*sondern*) must rush to help, as I am able; if others are present to help, I am released. Third, when encountering one 'hungry or thirsty,' I cannot ignore him but (*sondern*) must offer 'food and drink,' whatever the personal cost.[71] A man who does not 'help or support [*helffen und beystehen*]' another unless both 'his goods and his body'[72] are preserved will never help his neighbor. He will always, as today we might say, be 'looking out for number one.' As immediate rebuttal, Luther then asserts that no neighbor can avoid risk to his own 'safety, property, wife, or child.'[73] He must run the risk that 'fire or some other accident' will 'come and destroy' him "bodily, or his goods, wife and child, and everything" (*WA* 23:353.6–13).

F. *Warnings to Those Who Forsake Their Neighbor*

Luther next returns to Scripture, using three biblical texts to anchor an argument of warning—essentially an appeal to shame—against those who violate the neighborly-responsibility principle, which is akin to the Golden Rule he has just stated and which he had concluded earlier: "According to this passage [Matt. 25:41–46], we are bound

---

[69] Then he supplies the examples of these perils, which he has earlier considered by way of what lack of responses would be ludicrous for one's self. Now he revisits these perils and models proper responses, using the first person singular. By doing so he puts himself in the forefront of what must be done, something that will make the speaker much more credible than if he used the confrontational '*you* must.'

[70] Notice also the modals Luther uses—imperative or subjunctive—and the ubiquitous doublets—some synonymous or complementary, others progressive or even antithetical—for describing the range of activity or situation. Finally, notice the antithetical sentences that depict the wrong, then (using *sondern*) the right, action to take.

[71] Luther uses another doublet to say this, literally: 'whether I become poor or puny [*ob ich arm odder geringer*]' (*WA* 23:353.5). Neither *LW* 43:125 or Tappert, 236 translates this as a doublet. At the half-way point in this argument Luther shifts into third person singular, for he is preparing to shift the discussion, in the next paragraph, to a somber warning about shirking these duties. As he prepares for this Luther employs longer, progressive series, in addition to the doublet.

[72] Tappert, 236 reverses this doublet, as does *LW* 43:126.

[73] Luther uses the very epithet Jesus used in the Good Samaritan story (Luke 10:36, "Which of these three…*proved neighbor?*").

to each other...that no one may forsake the other in his distress but is obliged...as he himself would like to be helped" (*LW* 43:122).[74] Luther's third and final text in his warning here is a return to Matt. 25. He begins with 1 John, the very book he was lecturing on during the fall of 1527 (19 August to 7 November):[75] "Whoever does not love his brother is a murderer."[76] Luther then turns to the Old Testament, finding in his cited quotation of Ezek. 16:49 the horrific accusation of sin like Sodom (who is made Israel's sibling!) "Behold, this was the sin of your sister Sodom: idleness, abundance and sufficiency, and [her] hand did not aid the poor" (*WA* 23:353.20f.).[77] Luther then completes his scriptural evidence with a quotation of the final compound clause of Matt. 25:43, "I was sick[78] and you visited me not" (literal translation), which he asserts is precisely what Christ will say in condemnation on the last day to those murderers (*Mörder*, final position) of whom Ezekiel speaks. In a *qal wachomer* argument (*WA* 23:353.14–29) that is rife with progressive doublets, Luther uses rhetorical question to conclude some dire implications for those who neglect victims of plague and pestilence, neither of which term he has used for the last 75 lines.[79]

---

[74] *LW* 43:122 in fact cites Matt. 7:12.

[75] Heinrich Bornkamm, *Luther in Mid-Career*, 567. In his lectures on the epistle, Luther had said, "Of all the Epistles, this is the one most richly comforting since it buoys up afflicted hearts"; cf. *LW* 30:219 (*WA* 20:600.1f.).

[76] 1 John 3:15a. He quickly adds v. 17, which itself is built around a progressive doublet; I translate literally: "If anyone this world's goods has and sees [*dieser welt Güter hat und sihet*] his neighbor in need, how abides God's love in him [*wie bleibt die Liebe Gottes ynn yhm*]?" Here (v. 17) Luther has substituted neighbor (*Nehesten*) for brother (*Bruder*), which seems fair to the biblical context; in fact, both English translations of Luther read 'brother' here. But earlier (v. 15a) Luther changed the biblical text, which reads 'hates his brother,' toning down the language—although making the simple equation of 'not love equals murder'—and fitting the wording of v. 15a more closely to v. 17.

[77] "Sihe das war die sunde deiner schwester Sodoma: Mussiggang, fulle und gnuge und reichten den armen die hand nicht." Both Tappert, 236 and *LW* 43:126 fail to retain the first position of the triplet that follows 'Sodom,' and both make a doublet 'poor and needy' of *den Armen*. Both translators essentially have followed the biblical text rather than Luther. *LW* uses the RSV wording for the triplet.

[78] Luther drops 'and in prison' from the first clause of Matt. 25:43. In his subsequent application of the text, however, he says 'poor and sick [*den Armen und Krancken*]' (Tappert, 236).

[79] He reasons that if such judgment as those who failed the 'poor and sick [*den Armen und Krancken*]' when they did not 'go...and help offer [*gehen und Hülffe anbieten*],' what will become of those who 'abandoned them and let them lie there [*lauffen und lassen sie liegen*]' like 'dogs and pigs [*die Hunde und Sewe*]?' As readers contemplate that question, a second immediately follows. This one raises the stakes, beginning with Luther's 'Yes,...': how will they fare who "rob the poor...and plague them in all kinds of ways [*nemen was sie*

G. *Caring for the Sick*

Having virtually completed part I—whether fleeing death, from all
perils, is right or wrong—Luther now shifts to part II: how to decide
whether to flee or stay; he argues for staying, and he offers many
appeals to convince readers. Before he begins specific recommendations for handling an epidemic, Luther discusses, in a single paragraph (*WA* 23:353.30–355.8), two types of support system needed to
care for plague victims. Both will require great personal sacrifice and
commitment from all Christians: (1) the first, and ideal, system is for
secular government (*Regiment*) in the 'cities and states' to operate 'munici-
pal homes and hospitals' where sick patients could be sent to be cared
for;[80] (2) since so few institutions exist, however, personal attention is
needed. Luther argues that all must 'for one another give hospital care
and be nurses' (literal translation)—in any need—or else risk loss of
'salvation and the grace of God.' Luther's harsh stance here—which
must be taken in the context of all he has said before about the flexibility
due to adequate resources and weakness of faith—is then bolstered by
the only Scriptures of this paragraph. Both come from Matthew and
are set up by Luther's rich citation formula, "Thus it is written [*stehet*]
in God's word and command."[81] With those strong texts Luther ends
this part of the discussion and is ready for specific instructions and
encouragement for staying to help care for the sick.

   Luther's instructions for caring for victims of plague (*WA* 23:355.9–
24) begins, as did the document itself, by referring to dying—specifically

---

haben und legen yhn alle Plage an]?" The way Luther ends this section betrays a suspicion
that he has overdeveloped this point and even digressed: "That is what the tyrants do
to the poor who accept the gospel. But let that be; they have their condemnation [*Aber
las gehen, sie haben yhre Urteil*]" (*WA* 23:353.27–29; *LW* 43:126).

   [80] Luther claims that such was the 'intent and purpose [*gesucht und gemeinet*]' of those
predecessors (*Vorfaren*) who planned for 'foundations, hospitals, and infirmaries [*Stifften,
Spitalen und Sieckheusern*]' (Tappert, 237), so every citizen would not have to provide a
hospital at home. However, such a 'fine, commendable, and Christian [*wol sein, löblich
und Christlich*]' plan would take the 'contributions and generous help [*mildiglich zu geben
und helffen solte*]' (both *LW* 43:126 and Tappert, 237 reverse the doublet) of everyone,
especially the government (*Öberkeit*).

   [81] "Was yhr wollet, das euch die leute thun sollen, das thut auch yhr den selbigen"
(*WA* 23:355.7f.). His first text, "Love your neighbor as yourself [*Liebe deinen Nehisten
dich selbs*]" is from Matt. 22:39, where Luther has dropped the initial 'You shall' and
has placed the imperative verb in first position; thus, his quote matches that of Matt
19:19b. The second quote is Matt. 7:12a: "So whatever you wish that men would do
to you, do so to them."

here, as when dying begins. He ends the first paragraph (15 lines) with a Scripture quotation, and he does not use another until 44 lines later. Accordingly, Luther presses on—not digressing along medical lines—to reassert that the plague, and its insidious origins and pervasive means, is 'God's decree and punishment,' and we must patiently submit, serving our neighbor and risking our lives, as John 'teaches, saying':[82] "If Christ his life for us laid down, so ought we also, for the brethren, our lives lay down" (1 John 3:16, literal translation).[83]

Now that he has framed the matter of instructions for caring for the dying as one of faith toward God and love of neighbor, Luther offers some extended counsel and encouragement for those of us—he continues in the inclusive first person plural—who will find such a self-sacrificial task difficult, particularly with regard to the unseemly symptoms plague victims manifest, and the risks they present to others. In other words, this section operates as prolepsis. The first paragraph (*WA* 23:355.24–357.10) uses no Scriptures but consists in Luther's ubiquitous doublets and triplets as he juxtaposes two opposing forces: God and the devil. He will next offer his first answer to the devil (*WA* 23:357.11–359.2) in the form of extended dialogue.

H. *What One Should Tell the Devil*

Luther's speech to the devil, which employs the first of two points (*zwey Stuck*) of attack against him, is 24 lines long and encourages the timid reader in two ways: (1) it heaps scorn on the opponent, the devil; (2) it multiplies praise to God and benefits to self. Showing the devil's terrors to be *falschen*, the speech culminates in two final, parallel sentences. Moreover, the speech is almost perfectly bracketed (= inclusio) with apostrophe at beginning and end. Luther does not take on the devil alone; he keeps invoking Christ as at his side. Further, the language is confrontational: Luther speaks in first person singular, and even Christ is 'my' Christ; he addresses the devil directly in second person singular[84]

---

[82] Another doublet neither Tappert, 237 nor *LW* 43:127 translates.

[83] "Hat Christus sein leben fur uns gegeben, so sollen wir auch fur die brüder unser leben lassen." Luther has paraphrased 3:16a (which says 'he laid down') but quoted 3:16b verbatim.

[84] He begins with apostrophe ("Get away, you devil, with your terrors [*Schrecken*]") and continues with an onslaught of promises to be on the attack against the devil—by helping his neighbor. These promises then invite a bevy of doublets, nearly all of which are in praise of God and his resources: Because you hate it (*dichs verdreust*), I'll spite

("If you can terrorize, so can my[85] Christ strengthen;[86] if you can kill, so can Christ give life. If you have poison in your fangs, Christ has far greater medicine") [*WA* 23:357.27–29]. Luther then climaxes his speech with more parallelism, apostrophe, and more opposing epithets: "Should not my dear Christ, with his precepts, with his kindness and all that encouragement (*Trost*) be greater in my spirit than you, roguish devil, with your false terrors in my weak flesh?" Luther's speech ends decisively—with two concise clauses to begin, one to close, and an emphatic, extended statement in the middle: "God forbid! Get thee behind me, Satan.[87] Here is Christ and I am his servant in this work. He shall prevail. Amen" (*WA* 23:357.32–359.2).[88]

I. *God's Mighty Promises for Ministers of the Needy*

In the next 60 lines (*WA* 23:359.3–361.20) Luther returns to Scripture in order to encourage Hess and other readers about the rewards for those who serve the sick. This he calls 'the second' point of attack against the devil,[89] the first being the invented speech he just gave to readers to use. He identifies his weapon with another rich expression,

---

you by helping my sick neighbor more quickly (*nur deste*); I'll pay you no heed (*dich nicht ansehen*). I have two weapons to use, beginning with the certainty (*war weis*) that helping my neighbor is well-pleasing (*wolgefellet*) to 'God and all the angels [*Gotte allen Engeln*]'; by helping my neighbor I do God's will and render true 'service and obedience [*Dienst und Gehorsam*].' The more you hate and oppose this, the more I know it is particularly acceptable (*freylich gefallen*) to God. I would do this 'readily and gladly [*willig und frölich*]' to please just one angel. But I know it pleases my 'Lord Jesus Christ and the whole heavenly host [*Herrn Jhesu Christo und dem gantzem hymlischen Heere*]' because it is the 'will and command [*Willen und Gepot*]' of 'God, my Father [*Gotts meins Vaters*].' So how could fearing you spoil 'such joy in heaven, such delight for my Lord [*solche Freude ym Hymel und Lust meins Herrn*]?' How could I flatter you and give 'you and your devils in hell [*dir mit deinen Teuffeln ynn der Helle*]' cause (*anrichten*) to 'mock and laugh [*gelechter und gespöt*]?' No, your word will not be final. Since Christ shed (*vergossen*) his blood and died for me, how could some small dangers (*eine kleine Fahr*) for his sake keep me from facing the effects of a powerless pestilence (*amechtige Pestilentz*)?

[85] *LW* 43:128 misses 'my.'

[86] Note the rhyme in the matching, oppositional verbs: *schrecken, stercken.*

[87] "…das volt Gott nymer mehr. Heb dich teuffel hinder mich" (*WA* 23:357.32). Tappert, 238 cites Matt. 16:23 in the footnotes.

[88] "Hie ist Christus und ich sein diener ynn diesem werck, der sols walten. AMEN."

[89] *LW* 43:128. Luther says only *Das ander*, for this is his oral style, where a speaker often abbreviates, expecting his audience to supply the referents. Tappert, 238 reads, "The other point on which to attack the devil."

'God's mighty promise,' later saying 'glorious, mighty[90] promises of God,' still later 'these comforting promises' and 'such promises and rewards of God.' In addition to the doublet and triplet, Luther expounds on his topic by quoting Psalm 41 and 1 Tim. 4.

The first text, Psalm 41:1–3 (41:2–4 in the German Bible), is a nearly verbatim quote that captures two doublets (the second one is extended) in vv. 1–2—they essentially form a polysyndetic, apparently random series—yet, taken together with v. 3, the six actions prove climactic.[91] As he moves to his second text, Luther uses two rhetorical questions to bridge the texts together, interpreting his quotation of Ps. 41 and preparing for 1 Tim. 4.[92] His use of the passive voice in that sentence places the object of promise at the end of the sentence; God is the subject, the minister is the object. It is the minister, not the needy, who receives the blessing. Then Luther quotes Paul, "Godliness is of value in every way, and it holds promise both for the present life and for the life to come" (1 Tim. 4:8bc).[93] The connections between texts—the terms, and their concepts of service and reward—require Luther now to justify the principal term of 1 Tim 4:8, 'Godliness' (used 6 times by Paul in 1 Tim.).[94] Then he appeals to experience (*Erfarunge*) and a repetition of Ps. 41:3 to argue that service to neighbor—now, specifically,

---

[90] Luther's doublet is asyndetic, while both *LW* 43:128 and Tappert, 239 ('great and glorious') insert a conjunction.

[91] "Blessed [*Wol dem*] is he that considereth the poor [*Dürfftigen*]: the Lord will deliver him in time of trouble. The Lord will preserve him, and keep him alive [*yhn bewaren und beym leben erhalten*]; and he shall be blessed upon the earth: and thou wilt not deliver him [*yhm lassen wol gehen*] unto the will of his enemies. The Lord will strengthen [*erquicken*] him upon the bed of languishing: thou wilt transform [*wandelstu*] his whole bed in his sickness."

[92] He asks, expecting an affirmation, if these declarations (of David) are not the 'glorious and mighty promises of God' heaped up upon (*mit hauffen eraus geschut auff*) those who minister to the needy? (Ps. 41:0: 'To the choirmaster. A Psalm of David' [Ps. 41:0, RSV]; *Ein Psalm Davids, vorsusingen* [Ps. 41:1, *LB*]).

[93] The quote is verbatim from *SeptBib*, but in later editions Luther used *Frömmigkeit* in place of *Gottselickeit*.

[94] He does so using a concise sorites, his premises established earlier in his quotation from 1 John 3:15, 17 (*WA* 23:353.17) and his strong connection between faith (acting toward God) and love (acting toward neighbor), which was grounded in his quotation of 1 John 3:16 (*WA* 23:355.13–23); the proof takes on chiastic form, hence becoming a progressive chiasmus: Godliness [a] is nothing else (*nicht anders*) but service to God (*Gotts dienst* [b]). Service to God (*Gotts dienst* [b] is indeed (*freylich*) service to neighbor (*man dem Nehesten dienet* [a₁]. *Gottesdienst* is the modern German word for the Protestant worship service.

the sick ('nurse the sick')—in fact does produce tangible reward.[95] However, only authentic service is positively rewarded; disingenuous service is commensurately punished.

J. *God's Attention and Healing Dwarf the Risks of Serving Plague Victims*

Luther next turns to a lengthy discussion of the fears people have of caring for plague victims. This section runs all the way to *WA* 23:363.31, and in it the writer employs all of the argumentative and stylistic strategies and tactics we have already seen, and some more besides. However, this section begins with Luther continuing to discuss the gracious promise (*tröstlich Verheissung*) for those engaging in authentic care. This short section (5 lines) alludes to one Scripture only, and the point of that text is peripheral to the main point of this brief part and the extended discussion that follows. Whereas the day laborer (*Taglöhner*), according to Jesus, is worthy of his hire (*Lohns*),[96] the dominant reward is the great assurance that one will himself be cared for: this person's 'attendant and physician' will be God himself![97] Luther's subsequent persuasion (*WA* 23:361.1–17) juxtaposes the mighty resources of God against the physical risks and fears that caring for plague victims poses. His argument is that no risk of harm can withstand the enormous and sure resources of God; the argument ends with a proof text from Psalm 91, the second of three texts that Satan used against Jesus in the wilderness (Matt 4:1–10). Stylistically, Luther begins in third person singular,

---

[95] Luther uses doublets and triplets to show (*beweiset*) this process: those serving with 'love, devotion, and sincerity [*Lieb, Andacht und Ernst*]' are generally protected (*gemeyniglich behütet*); although poisoned, they are unharmed, as the Psalm says (he quotes a conflation of 41:3a and 4b). Luther then explains the verse, claiming that the 'sickbed and recovery room [*Siechbette und Krancklager*]' are changed (*macht*) into a health room (*gesund lager*). Conversely, Luther immediately asserts that one serving in 'greed and expectation of inheritance [*Geitzs und Erbteil*]' should anticipate becoming eventually 'infected, disfigured, or even dying [*letzt vergifft werde und beschmeist . . . sterbe*]' before realizing (*besitze*) the 'estate or inheritance [*das Gut odder Erbe*]' (*WA* 23:359.3–25).

[96] An allusion to Luke 10:7 (also quoted by Paul in 1 Tim. 5:8). Additional concession: although the servant of the sick can accept suitable reward (*zymlichen Lohn*) to which he is entitled (*wol bedarff*).

[97] This prompts Luther to use anaphoric exclamatio (Tappert, 239 omits the interjection of exclamatio ('O'). Since the statements also have the same ending (*ist das* [= epistrophe]), the precise figure is symploce, the combination of anaphora and epistrophe: "O what an attendant [*Warter*] is he! O what a physician [*Artzt*] is he."

and then he turns directly to the reader, in second person singular, for a sustained confrontation. The first half of the section is filled with doublets; both halves contain numerous rhetorical questions.[98]

---

[98] In a rhetorical question inviting an affirmative answer, Luther suggests that one should be encouraged (*einen mut machen*) to 'go and serve [*zu gehen und yhn dienen*]' without regard for the patient's 'buboes and boils [*Druse und Pestilentz*],' though they be as numerous as body hair (*Hare am gantzen Leibe*) and though the caregiver lift many bodies (*hundert Pestilentz*) and be bent double (*feym halfe eraus tragen*). The doublet is translated by *LW* 43:129 as 'contagious boils' and by Tappert, 239 as 'pestilential boils.' *Drüs* is the Early New High German word for *Beulen*, translated as *Pest.* in Alfred Götze, *Frühneuhochdeutsches Glossar*, 7th ed (Berlin, 1967), 57. In modern German *Beulen* means 'dent' or 'boil,' and *Beulenpest* means 'bubonic plague.' 'Bubo,' from the Greek word βουβων ('groin'), referring to an inflammatory swelling in the lymph gland, especially in the groin, is the nodule for which Bubonic plague got its name. In using this term I am, of course, engaging in conjecture. The epidemiology of bubonic plague has only recently been researched exhaustively by modern scholars. During the 1894 outbreak in Hong Kong the French scientist—and pupil of Louis Pasteur—Alexandre Yersin discovered the bacillus responsible for the disease. His discovery was that rats (*R. rattus*) carry the disease and that rat fleas (*X. cheopis*) then contracted the bacillus, which subsequently came to be called *Yersinia Pestis* (*Y. pestis*). Modern research has also identified three clinical manifestations of plague: bubonic, septicemic, and pneumonic; the first two are generally lethal, and all three forms are thought to have appeared during outbreaks. However, the literature—both historical and medical—on plague is massive, particularly on the fourteenth-century outbreak, and fraught with controversy. A strong consensus—up until the last twenty years—held that the Black Death of fourteenth-century Europe and England, and an earlier outbreak in the sixth to eighth centuries, were two pandemics of plague and were probably bubonic plague. It gets more complicated, however, for the historical sources up to the nineteenth century—including Luther's document—are virtually silent on the presence of rats or dead rats. Whether that is an indication that rats were simply not thought noteworthy at the time, or whether some plague outbreaks were for other diseases, is difficult to know; there is even question as to rat survival in colder European climates. It is characteristic of bubonic plague to occur in warm weather—and this coincides with the 1520s German plagues, whereas the pneumonic form usually develops in winter. The latter disease affects the lungs and spreads through airborne droplets when the victim coughs, sneezes, or even talks; its characteristic symptom is not the appearance of painful boils or buboes but the coughing or spitting of bloody sputum. 'Droplet Infection,' as the principal means of disease transmission, is one of several arguments of some recent scholars for their contention that the Black Plague of the fourteenth century, and intermittent plagues up through the mid-seventeenth century was not Bubonic Plague. Susan Scott and Christopher Duncan, *Return of the Black Death: The World's Greatest Serial Killer* (Chichester, U.K., 2004), argue that the aforementioned plagues were all spread from person to person via droplet infection, and that virtually everyone of those eras knew that. Scott and Duncan argue that Bubonic Plague is an Asian disease. The European plagues, they claim, were caused by viral agents, not by bacteria, and they label these plagues haemorrhagic plague, because extensive haemorrhaging is an important symptom (167). In their *Biology of Plagues: Evidence from Historical Populations* (Cambridge, 2001), 330, Scott and Duncan list eight outbreaks of plague to strike Wittenberg during 1500–1549. On p. 55 of *Return of the Black Death* they show the major trade routes in Europe during the Middle Ages, along which came infected

> Shame and more shame on you, you out-and-out unbeliever, that you are
> despising such great comfort and letting yourself become more frightened
> of a small boil or uncertain danger than emboldened by such Godly, sure,
> faithful promises (*WA* 23:361.5–8).

The series of rhetorical questions directs the reader to choose God
above all else, and the last question suggests strongly that with God it
is a 'win-win' outcome. Luther uses a final rhetorical question to lead
into his quote from Psalm 91. Having prepared for and quoted Psalm
91:11–13, which is a fundamental text for this entire document, Luther
expounds the consequences of failing to remain to care for plague victims—what he is thinking of as the 'sin on the left hand' (on the 'worse
side'). Following this, he will argue what he labels explicitly the 'sin on
the right hand' (on the 'better side'). Luther asks rhetorically, "If God
withdraws his hand and forsakes" us, what can happen except "sheer
devilment and every kind of evil?" He then answers his own question
(= anthypophora), adding the stipulation that identifies precisely what
is wrongful flight: that the result is obviously as he has just said, when

---

travelers bringing the plague to the important centers of commerce. Thus, accord-
ing to their theory, the plague would have moved inland (i.e., southward), arriving in
Silesia before Saxony. Some representative sources on the fourteenth-century Black
Death are the Introduction to the *Decameron* of Giovanni Boccaccio (1313–1375), in a
critical edition by Mark Musa and Peter E. Bondanella (New York, 1977); cf. Shona
Kelly Wray, "Boccaccio and the Doctors: Medicine and Compassion in the Face of
Plague," *Journal of Medieval History* 30 (2004): 301–322; Philip Ziegler, *The Black Death*
(New York, 1969); Robert S. Gottfried, *The Black Death: Natural and Human Disaster in
Medieval Europe* (New York, 1983); Ann G. Carmichael, *Plague and the Poor in Renaissance
Florence* (Cambridge, 1986); John Henderson, "The Black Death in Florence," in *Death
in Towns: Urban Responses to the Dying and the Dead, 100–1600*, ed. Steven Bassett (London,
1992), 136–150. Literature on plague in the sixteenth century is more difficult to find,
but see Paul Slack, "Mortality Crises and Epidemic Disease in England 1485–1610,"
in *Health, Medicine and Mortality in the Sixteenth Century*, ed. Charles Webster (Cambridge,
1979), 9–59; A. Lynn Martin, *Plague? Jesuit Accounts of Epidemic Disease in the 16th Century*.
SCES 28 (Kirksville, Mo., 1996). For sources that have called into question bubonic
plague as primary cause of the Black Death, see Graham Twigg, *The Black Death: A
Biological Reappraisal* (New York, 1985), who argues that the Plague of 1346–1350 may
have been anthrax (*Bacillus anthracis*), as does Chris Holmes, *Spores, Plagues and History: The
Story of Anthrax* (Dallas, Tex., 2003); David Herlihy, *The Black Death and the Transformation
of the West*, ed. Samuel K. Cohn, Jr. (Cambridge, Mass., 1997); idem, *The Black Death
Transformed: Disease and Culture in Early Renaissance Europe*. London, 2002, reviewed by Jon
Arrizabalaga in *Speculum* 79 (2004): 1053–1055. A recent, more popular treatment—by
which I mean only that the work lacks documentation—is by the eminent medieval
historian, Norman F. Cantor, *In the Wake of the Plague: The Black Death and the World That
It Made* (New York, 2001). There are also economic studies that focus on population
dynamics and what role plague might have played in them; e.g., John Hatcher, *Plague,
Population and the English Economy 1348–1530* (London, 1977).

one abandons his neighbor against 'God's word and command'—in emphatic final position (*WA* 23:363.4–8).[99]

As he brings this section on wrongful flight to a close, Luther shifts to a different appeal—back to honor and shame. Among readers who would wrongfully flee, or who might remain to serve under false motives, Luther tries to create feelings of shame. Implicit in this appeal is another one to honor, for he tries to evoke in readers the desire to serve with proper motives, based upon their valuing the commands of Christ. In this appeal he uses ubiquitous doublets, two Scriptures from Matthew, and the confrontational second person singular again. Prior to the first quotation, however, Luther uses the third person to make his appeal to shame.

The signal with which Luther begins his appeal is the disjunctive[100] (*aber*), accompanied by his observation, 'This I well know' and then his hypothetical condition: if 'Christ himself[101] or his mother' were sick. The hypothetical outcomes Luther projects consist in four—three positive and one negative. He then stays in the intimate, personal—even con-frontational—second person singular.[102] He comments (= *interpretatio*) on the commands of Christ, taking them in reverse order (Matt. 22:39; 25:40). His tone begins gently and becomes more stern:

> There you hear that the command to love the neighbor is equal to the first commandment to love God: and that what you do or fail to do for your neighbor means doing the same to God. If you wish to serve Christ himself[103] and to wait on him, very well, you have your sick neighbor close at hand. Go to him and serve him, and you will surely find Christ in him, not outwardly but in his word. If you are unwilling to serve your neighbor, you can be sure that if Christ himself[104] lay there instead, you would do the same thing—run away and let him lie there.[105] Those are nothing but illusions on your part, which leave you in unprofitable ignorance,[106] namely, that you would really serve Christ if he were there in person. Those are nothing but lies; whoever wants to serve Christ in person [*leiblich*] would surely serve his neighbor as well (*WA* 23:363.15–26).[107]

---

[99] So Tappert, 240; *LW* 43:130 misses the doublet as well as the emphatic syntax.

[100] Neither Tappert, 240 or *LW* 43:130 translates *aber*.

[101] So Tappert, 240; *LW* 43:130 appears to ignore *selbs*.

[102] Not counting those implied in the imperative verbs, I count 11 second person singular pronouns in 10 lines (*WA* 23:363.16–25).

[103] Again, both Tappert, 241 and *LW* 43:130 fail to translate *selber*.

[104] So Tappert, 241; *LW* 43:130 fails to translate *selbs*.

[105] So Tappert, 241.

[106] So Tappert, 241.

[107] "Da hörestu, das der liebe gebot zum nehesten gleich sey dem ersten gebot der

The theme of serving Christ through serving one's neighbor is prominent in Luther's "Fourteen Consolations" (1519).[108]

K. *Tempting God*

Luther now engages the opposite mistake—that of taking unnecessary health risks in ministering to plague victims. In this section (*WA* 23:363.30–365.22) he will open the subject of medical care and what should be a person's responsible attitude toward it before God. This will then lead to advice he gives plague victims themselves, in the next section. As argumentative strategies Luther again uses *reductio ad absurdum*, one bit of dialogue, and no Scripture at all. For stylistic tactics, the doublet and the third person pronoun are the weapons of choice; keeping the discussion centered on 'others' allows the speaker to prosecute without humiliating the reader. The key expression in this section is, again, 'God's punishment,' the term this position's advocates presumably use as *apologia*.

Those who sin on the right hand are too 'rash and reckless,' 'tempting God and disregarding' all that might counteract 'death and the plague.'[109] They forego medicine; they do not avoid 'places and persons' that are 'infected and overcome'[110] by the plague; they 'trifle and play with it' to prove their independence. They call it God's punishment, which he will protect 'without medicines or our carefulness' (*WA* 23:365.4–8).

The remainder of this section is Luther's plainest arguments yet against what he has just twice called 'tempting God.' His argument parallels his *reductio ad absurdum* argument earlier (*WA* 23:349–51) in regards to natural emergencies, but here he extends the argument, applying it directly to medical care. He uses no Scripture; only analogies

---

liebe zu Gott: Und was du deinem nehisten thust odder lessest, sol heissen so viel als Gott selber gethan und gelassen. Wiltu nu Christo selber dienen und sein warten, Wolan so hastu da fur dir deinen krancken nehisten, gehe hin zu yhm und diene yhm, so findestu gewislich Christum an yhm, nicht nach der person, sondern ynn seinem wort. Wiltu aber und magst deinem nehisten nicht dienen, so gleube fur war, wenn Christus selbs da were, du thettest eben auch also und liessest yhn liegen. Und ist nichts bey dir denn eitel falsche gedancken, die dir einen unnutzen dunckel machen, wie du Christo woltest dienen, wenn er da were. Es sind eitel lugen: denn wer Christo leiblich dienen wurd, der dienete seinem nehisten auch wol."

[108] *LW* 42:121–166; *WA* 6:104–134. See Chapter One in this book.

[109] Tappert, 241 reverses the doublet.

[110] *LW* 43:131 misses the doublet; Tappert, 241 extends it into two clauses.

are employed. The style is all in the third person, and the doublets are still present. Luther completes the section with more dialogue from the opposition. The first argument (*WA* 23:365.8–14) is that refusing medicine—already labeled as tempting God—is tantamount to suicide (*selbs Mörder*), a term he uses twice. The second argument (*WA* 23:365.14–22) worsens the culpability, for now there are pragmatic results harmful to others: it is even more shameful to neglect one's own body by failing to protect himself from plague (*die Pestilentz*) and then 'infect and poison [*beschmeissen und vergifften*]' others who might have stayed alive if he had taken care of himself. Luther then concludes the outcome of such negligence: that one is responsible for his neighbor's death and is a murderer. He uses the house fire analogy, which he had previously used, to caricature the offense in the most ridiculous possible light: these people are acting like people who allow a burning house to go up in flames, doing nothing to stop it or to protect other homes. They allow the flames to grow into a citywide conflagration, their rationale being, "if it's God's will, he can preserve the city without water and without quenching the flames."[111]

L. *Instructions for Caregivers*

Luther turns his discussion of tempting God into prescriptions for counteracting it (*WA* 23:365.23–367.9). He addresses caregivers, about whom he has been speaking, who must develop a new attitude toward the disease and those who contract it—toward self and toward God. Still using no Scripture passages,[112] Luther first gives crisp, pithy instructions; then he follows them with dialogue that models what one ought to think in order to carry out such orders. Stylistically, Luther returns to the intimate second person singular pronoun, but he places his dialogue in the first person singular; it is meant for the community, though.

Notice how Luther uses triplet, doublet, compact and parallel phrasing, even rhetorical question, to redress the errors of mistaken readers:

> Use medicine; take potions which can help you; fumigate house, yard, and street; shun persons and places wherever your neighbor does not need your presence or has recovered, and act like a man who wants to

---

[111] So Tappert, 242.
[112] The gap between uses of Scripture is 63 lines.

help put out the burning city. What else is the epidemic but a fire that, instead of consuming wood and straw, devours body and life[113] [*Leib und Leben*]? (*WA* 23:365.23–28).[114]

Since the rhetorical question invites an affirmative response, Luther then provides a progression of actions—in the form of soliloquy—to think (*dencke*); nearly all the successive actions are spoken with verbs in their normal, final position.

> Very well, by God's decree the enemy has sent us poison and deadly offal. Therefore I shall ask God mercifully to be gracious and preserve[115] us. Then I shall fumigate, help purify the air, administer medicine and take it.[116] I shall avoid places and persons where my presence is not needed in order not to become contaminated and thus perchance infect and pollute [*vergifften und anzunden*] others, and so cause their death as a result of my negligence. If God should wish to take me, he will surely find me, and I have done what he has expected of me and so I am not responsible for either my own death or the death of others. If my neighbor needs me, however, I shall not avoid place or person but will feel free to visit and help[117] him (*WA* 23:365.29–367.8).[118]

---

[113] Tappert, 242; *LW* 43:132 reverses the doublet.

[114] "…sondern brauche der ertzney, nym zu dir was dich helffen kan, reuchere haus, hoff und gassen, meyde auch person und stet, da dein nehester dein nichts bedarff odder auffkomen ist, und stele dich als einer, de rein gemein feur gerne wolt helffen dempffen. Denn was ist die Pestilentz anders den nein feur, das nicht holtz und stro, sondern leib und leben auffrisset." In his letter to Jonas (10 November 1527) one can find Luther himself practicing these recommendations. He mentions a surgical procedure performed on Margaret von Mochau, draining pus from an abcess ("Margarithae Mochinnae apostema heri incisum est, et pure pestilente emisso incipit melius habere"); he discusses quarantine procedures that confined her—and little Johannes Luther ['*Henschen*']—to a different room than others who are still healthy ("inclusi eam hybernaculo nostro usitato, nos in anteriore magna aula versamur…in meo hypocausto"); and he stipulates that the sick wife of a local physician (Augustine Schurf, teacher of medicine in Wittenberg since 1521) is staying with them ("Augustini uxor in suo"). Undoubtedly these strategies and precautions were taken in consultation with the physicians; cf. *WABr* 4:280.29–33; *LW* 49:174 (Nr. 1168).

[115] So Tappert, 242.

[116] Tappert, 242 translates the doublet; *LW* 43:132 does not.

[117] So Tappert, 242; *LW* 43:132 does not translate the doublet.

[118] "Wolan der feind hat uns durch gotts verhengnis gifft und tödliche geschmeis herein geschickt, so wil ich bitten zu Gott, das e runs gnedig sey und were. Darnach wil ich auch reuchern, die lufft helffen fegen, ertzney geben und nemen, meiden stet und person, Da man mein nichts darff, auff das ich mich selbs nicht verwarlose und dazu durch mich villeicht viel andere vergifften und anzunden möchte und yhn also durch meine hinlessickeit ursach des todes sein. Wil mich mein Gott daruber haben, so wird er mich wol finden: so hab ich doch gethan das er mir zu thun gegeben hat, und bin wider an meinem eigen nach ander leute tode schuldig. Wo aber mein nehester mein darff, wil ich wider stet noch person meiden, sondern frey zu yhm gehen und helffen."

Luther finishes this section with what he calls a God-fearing faith (*Gottfürchtiger Glaube*), a key expression that is meant to counter—and conquer—the misguided 'God's punishment.'

M. *Instructions to Plague Victims and Potential Disease Carriers*

Luther now stays in the third person, addressing his readers about what victims, potential victims, and particularly survivors should do to protect and provide for their own health and that of others. Some of what he says here will remind readers today of another infectious disease—the AIDS epidemic—and the situations, and responsibilities, of persons who are HIV-positive. This section is more discussion about tempting God in one's care-giving, yet is not as vitriolic and is more concretely about plague. Luther seems to be responding to people's customs and to rumors he has heard about behavior in the face of an epidemic. He gives what he believes is sound advice, informed by analogical reason and the biblical example of leprosy. The style continues to be filled with doublets and <u>qualifying phrases</u>.

Luther argues that he who 'contracted the disease and recovered' should 'keep away from others and not admit them' into his presence, <u>unless necessary</u> (*on Not*). One should not risk others' lives by exposing them <u>unnecessarily</u> (*on Not*) to danger; Luther then paraphrases Ecclus. 3:26b as his proof text. Everyone should help ward off contagion <u>as best he can</u> (*kündte*), for then the death toll would be moderate (*gnedigs*). As he continues this section (*WA* 23:367.27–371.2) his argumentation gets more negative in tone. He now moves on to examples of repulsive behavior that is probably no longer hypothetical. Since he is writing to pastors with administrative responsibilities in their congregations, which would include secular rulers having oversight over others, Luther appears to find that the dire situation warrants such stern language. Eventually he will recommend the death penalty for the worst offenders, and his reference to the case of leprosy in the Old Testament is meant as a more practical and effective—since preventive—measure. Stylistically, doublets are the chief weapons, and Luther uses several key expressions—all of which are negative.

He reports having heard of some who are so incredibly vicious that they go about 'among the people and into homes'[119] because they regret that *Pestilentz* has not yet arrived and wish to bring it. Luther

---

[119] Tappert, 243.

characterizes this horrendous behavior with two analogies designed to render the plague-spreading behavior more reprehensible by virtue of its dissimilarity with the analogies: they operate as though this behavior is a prank (*Schertz*), along the lines of—out of malice (*zur Schalckeit*)—'putting lice into fur garments or flies into someone's living room' (*WA* 369.1–8). Yet Luther then admits that such persons are a minority but still the work of the devil, who is never idle. He suggests that the judge should take any such people by the hair[120] (*Kopffe*) and turn them over to the hangman, as 'real, malicious murderers and scoundrels[121] [*die rechten mutwilligen Mörder und Bösewichter*].' Then Luther projects out some shared details that the analogy reveals. Because the analogy leads to more epithets, I quote him at length:

> Here and there an assassin will jab a knife through someone and no one can find the culprit. So these folk infect [*schmeissen*] here a child, there a woman and can never be caught. They go on laughing as though they had accomplished something. Where this is the case, it would be better to live among wild beasts than with such murderers. Such killers I do not know how to preach to. They heed not. I appeal to the authorities to take charge and turn them over to the help and advice [*Hulff und Rad*], not of physicians but of the hangman [*nicht der Ertzte, sondern Meister Hansen*] (*WA* 23:369.14–20).

Luther's concluding remarks (*WA* 23:369.29–371.4) about whether to flee a deadly plague bring an assessment of the current situation in Wittenberg, and then succinctly Luther closes this portion of the document with a postscript. He claims that *unser Pestilentz hie zu Wittemberg* has been caused by nothing else but such contagion.[122] He thanks God that the Wittenberg air is still 'clean and pure'; he charges that because of 'foolhardiness and neglect'[123] that some few have been infected; he concludes that the devil enjoys himself at the 'terror and flight' he has caused among us. He closes with a malediction, "May God thwart him! Amen."[124]

---

[120] Tappert, 243.
[121] Tappert, 243.
[122] Tappert, 244.
[123] Tappert, 244.
[124] "Gott wolt yhm weren. AMEN." Tappert, 244 reads, "May God hold him in check. Amen." Luther's postscript is a terse summary and a benediction: This is what 'we think and conclude [*unser Verstand und Meynung*]' on the subject of fleeing from death. "If you are of a different opinion, may God reveal it to you. Amen."

N. *Brief Instructions on Preparation for Death*

In both the manuscript and the printed editions, Luther's document—what he calls this letter (*brief*)—continues without any major break, other than a new paragraph. Yet it is clear that Luther added this section later,[125] for he signals his intentions with a two-sentence (5 lines) *narratio* (*WA* 23:371.5–10).[126] He then explains in such a way as to suggest that preparing for death from plague is not essentially different from preparing for other kinds of death.[127] For he says, "This, orally from the pulpit, we have done and daily still do in fulfillment of our[128] ministry [*Seel sorgern*] to which we have been called as pastors" (*WA* 23:371.8–10).[129] Based on what Luther says in his summary at the end of this discussion, it becomes more evident that he intended these remarks first for the people of Wittenberg and Saxony. Here was an opportunity to make some concentrated remarks against those who put off concern for their souls, or those of loved ones, until their eleventh hour on their deathbeds.

The major discussion of preparation for death is organized into three enumerated parts. The first two fill a paragraph each; the third uses two paragraphs. Logically they proceed deductively—from general to particular, from all to some, from more time before death to less, from routine readiness through daily living to special preparation as death approaches. In other words, Luther argues that in order to know how to die one must know how to live. This is consistent with his "Sermon on Preparing to Die" (1519).[130]

First: Always Attend to God's Word: Luther argues that all must stay close to God through attention to the word—which is available primarily in church. The urgency and seriousness with which Luther holds this claim is demonstrated immediately in his first part (*WA*

---

[125] Tappert ends his translation without including this section or the last one.

[126] He uses the first person singular in the first sentence, the plural in the second. He states that since the letter will be printed for 'our' (*LW* 43:134 omits the pronoun) people to read, he thought it useful to include brief instructions on how to 'care and provide for [*schicken und halten… leufften*]' the soul in time of death. With *ynn solchen* we understand Luther to have in mind death from plague.

[127] Rada, "Luther, Ethics and the Plague in Wittenberg," does not discuss this section in his synopsis (255–257).

[128] *LW* 43:134 omits the pronoun.

[129] "…wie wir denn die selbigen auch mündlich auff der Kantzel gethan und teglich thun, damit wir auch unserm ampt gnug thun, die wir zu seel sorgern beruffen sind."

[130] *LW* 42:99–115; *WA* 2:685–697. See Chapter Two of this book.

23:371.10–22). The argument operates as a mandate from Scripture ('Do this, or I will…'). Such a strategy downplays the crisis nature of 'how to die,' putting it into a larger context of 'how to live.' For argumentative evidence Luther uses one Scripture passage. Stylistically he uses many doublets and one instance of anaphora. His stance uses the third person to speak of the people, and the first person plural to include other pastors—his target audience. Thus Luther speaks about parishioners while addressing their pastors.

People must be admonished, Luther maintains, 'to attend church and listen to the sermon' so they learn from the word 'how to live and how to die.' That is the goal; everything else Luther says on this subject pertains to failure to reach the goal, and what pastors should do about it.[131] Then the writer resumes his criticism of the wicked, arguing that one living like 'a heathen or dog' and not repenting publicly should not expect we would "administer the sacrament nor have [us] count him a Christian" (*WA* 23:371.17f.). Let him die as he lived and see that "we shall not throw pearls before swine nor give to dogs what is holy" (Matt. 7:6).[132] The many doublets contribute to a coherent argument; aided by parallel syntax—that, particularly in the example of how *not* to live and die—dying and living are inseparably fused.

<u>Second: Constantly Prepare Through Obedience</u>: As time may grow shorter before one contracts the disease, one should use the opportunity to 'prepare in time and get ready for death' by 'confessing and taking the sacrament' 'weekly or biweekly' (*WA* 23:371.23–25). With those three doublets Luther lays out a lifelong program of obedience. However, as he proceeds, the urgency becomes ever more apparent: not only can one not predict when she or he may become sick, but there

---

[131] Those so 'uncouth and wicked [*rohe und rauchlos*]' as to despise the word while in good health—by this Luther undoubtedly means, at the least, people who frequently miss church—should be ignored (*lassen liegen*) when they become sick. Before continuing to lambaste the derelict, however, Luther mentions the exception to what he has just declared: when they show 'remorse and repentance [*Rew und Busse*]'—'with great earnestness, with tears, and lamentation [*mit grosse Ernst, mit Weinen und Klagen*]'; with the series in final position, the signs become as important as the actions they accompany.

[132] "Denn wir sollen den sewen nicht perlen fur werffen noch den hunden das heiligthum" (Luther has quoted the verse backwards). Luther closes with a sad (*leider*) observation—that there are many 'churlish, hardened [*grobs verstocks*]' ruffians (*Pösels*) who care nothing for their souls 'when they live or when they die [*ym leben noch sterben*]'; these simply 'lie down and die like hulks' that have 'neither sense nor thought [*Synn noch Gedancken*]' (*WA* 23:371.18–22).

are only so many pastors to go around. In addition to confession and sacrament, there are the matters of reconciliation (*versune*) with one's neighbor and the making of a will (*Testament*).[133] Then Luther provides the reason why the three-fold action on the parishioner's part—and the continuing routine of confessing and partaking of sacrament—is necessary: with many dying and 'only two or three' pastors (*Seelsorger*) on duty, they cannot get to everyone 'to give instruction and to teach' what one must know in the anguish of death.[134]

Thus far, Luther's instructions are highly consistent with what he recommended in "Sermon on Preparing to Die" (1519). There he set forth instructions in 20 sections, the first five of which are parallel to what he has said here, particularly in his second part, containing four instructions (confession, sacraments, reconciliation, last will).[135] The order varies between these two documents because the situations are slightly different. "Sermon on Preparing to Die" was written by request for readers who are presumably already ill and dying; "Whether to Flee" was written to those facing the possibility of becoming ill.

<u>Third: Clergy Must Be Called While Patients Are Still Alert</u>: Luther addresses the situation here of *when* the pastor should be called to the bedside of the dying. His argument makes a definite distinction between Lutheran and Catholic practices at the deathbed. This part is twice as long as either of the previous two, for he addresses specific problems in trying to minister to people who are already comatose or incoherent; there is exasperation in the writer's language. As with the previous part, no Scripture is used, doublets abound, and a couple of longer series are found. In addition, Luther uses some dialogue and utters one strong expression that characterizes the attitude of the negligent—an

---

[133] The reason for these is that if "the Lord knocks and he should depart [*der Herr anklopffet und er ubereilet würde*]" before the 'pastor or chaplain [*Pfarher odder Caplan*]' arrives, the sick person will have: "his soul provided for, nothing undone left, but rather to God himself committed]" (*WA* 23:371.27f.).

[134] Luther's instruction culminates in more sad declarations for those who fail to heed: the 'careless and negligent [*lessig und seumig*]' must account for themselves; it is their own fault. A 'private pulpit and altar [*sonderlichen Predigstuel und Altar*]' cannot be set up just because they have despised the 'public pulpit and altar [*gemeinen Predigstuel und Altar*]' to which God 'has summoned and called [*beruffen und gefoddert hat*]' them (*WA* 23:371.32–373.2).

[135] The differences from "Sermon on Preparing to Die": (1) there his very first section dealt with the surrender of possessions (*LW* 42:99)—what he listed here in fourth position; (2) there his second instruction was to forgive and seek forgiveness (*LW* 42:99), while here it was third in order; (3) there, in section four (*LW* 42:100), he instructed his reader to confess and receive sacrament while here he listed them first and second.

issue pervading all four paragraphs of this topic. In paragraph one he continues to use the third person; in the final paragraph he switches to first person plural, as he had begun with in the *narratio*.

Luther explains the importance of notifying the 'chaplain or pastor' soon enough, before the illness overwhelms the patient and one still has 'sense and reason'[136] (*WA* 23:373.3–5). Luther's purpose for asserting this is the negligent practice of those who 'make no request or[137] send no message' until the patient is on the last breath[138] and is no longer 'able to speak or be rational.'[139] Worse, Luther says, the family then begs.[140] With a rhetorical question exhibiting exasperation, he depicts in harsh terms the behavior of families like the one described:

> What should a diligent pastor do with such people who neglect both body and soul? They live and die like beasts. Such folks at the last minute want the Gospel taught and the sacrament administered as when they lived under the papacy, when nobody asked whether they believed or understood the Gospel but just stuffed the sacrament down their throats as if into a bread bag (*WA* 23:373.11–17).

Luther's second paragraph comments further on this behavior that he considers so wrongheaded and contrary to Reformation teaching. In addition to the improper behavior already described, he now offers first an account of what positive signs in the patient must be seen by a pastor.[141] Luther continues to assert that pastors are commanded not to give the holy sacrament 'to unbelievers but rather to believers' who can 'state and explain' their faith.[142] In closing, he stays in

---

[136] *LW* 43:135 misses the doublet.

[137] *LW* 43:135 translates *odder* as 'and.'

[138] *LW* 43:135 reads literally, "the soul is perched for flight on the tip of their tongues [*die Seel auff der Zungen sitzet*]" (*WA* 23:373.7), noting (n. 17) that popular belief held that the soul left the body at death through the mouth.

[139] *LW* 43:135 reverses the doublet.

[140] "'Dear Sir, say the very best you can for him,' etc." Such behavior from the family might be understandable (and excusable), were it not for what Luther then says the same family did: "But earlier," he reminds his readers, "when the illness first began [*ansehet*], they wanted no visit but would say, 'Oh, there's no need. I hope it will get better.'"

[141] If someone cannot 'talk or indicate by signs [*redden odder zeichen geben*]'—particularly if he has willfully neglected it—that he 'believes, understands, and desires [*glaube, versehe und begere*]' the sacrament, "we will not give it to him just anytime he asks."

[142] He further urges that the others (*andern*)—i.e., those unbelievers—be left alone (*faren*), to continue believing as they do. "We are guiltless (*entschüldigt*)," he declares, "for we have not neglected (*feylet*) preaching, teaching, exhortation, consolation, visitation, nor anything else [*predigen, leren, vermanen, trosten, besuchen noch an yrgent*] that pertains to our office or ministry [*unsern ampt odder dienst*]" (*WA* 23:373.18–25; [*LW* 43:135 reverses

the first person plural, in which he has already begun ('We are guilt-less'), addressing his readers in Breslau once again, using for the first time the second person plural to address them. He clarifies what he has briefly written as 'our instruction, what we practice here.' Luther then offers a disclaimer—that what he has written in this section was not intended for folks in Breslau (but presumably for people closer to Wittenberg). His reason is that Christ is with them and that, without aid of Wittenberg He will amply instruct them and supply their needs with His own ointment (*Salbe*). "To him be praise and honor together with God the Father and the Holy Spirit, world without end. Amen" (*WA* 23:373.25–29).

O. *Advice about Burial Practices*

In what Craig Koslofsky calls "apparently the first discussion of the subject in the context of the Reformation," Luther's second subject of the additions to the document—and the third topic overall—is burial practices (*Begrebnis*).[143] More specifically, his concern is not with the funeral, burial preparation or rites, prayers for the dead, or the state of the dead; his concern is strictly with the burial site. Thus, Luther participates in a growing movement in the early sixteenth century toward extramural burial, where the rationale driving efforts to relocate cemeteries outside of city walls was not necessarily an effort to expunge Catholic beliefs in the merit of *ad sanctos* burial, but rather was nearly always health reasons, particularly plague.[144] As it happens, Luther also advocates extramural burial for health reasons, but he does not stop there. He divides the topic in two: (I) location of the cemetery (*Kirchhoff*);[145] (II) behavior within the cemetery. Following discussion of these two topics, Luther concludes the entire document. He does not

---

the last doublet). That series of six pastoral functions takes roughly the same order as Luther has followed in this discussion on care and provision for the soul for death.

[143] Craig M. Koslofsky, *The Reformation of the Dead*, 47. He stipulates that Luther was the first theologian to argue that the place of the dead should be determined by medical rather than religious considerations. Rada, "Luther, Ethics and the Plague in Wittenberg," does not discuss this section in his synopsis (255–257).

[144] See Koslofsky, "The Rise of Extramural Burial in Sixteenth-century Germany," 41–46, in *The Reformation of the Dead*, where he discusses documented extramural burial initiatives occurring in the first two decades of the sixteenth century. Koslofsky mentions five cities, starting with Freiburg/Breisgau (1514) and ending with Zwickau (1521). Munich is a case where the initiative came in 1480.

[145] In this document Luther does not use *Friedhof*, the more common term for cemetery.

summarize, in particular, any of the three parts, however. Instead, he uses plague terminology metaphorically to ask for prayer support in battling Satan's attack on the sacrament.

Location of Cemeteries: Luther organizes his remarks about cemetery location into three steps: (A) possible health risks of intramural cemeteries (*WA* 23:373.31–375.10)—to whose authoritative word he defers to medical experts; (B) precedents in antiquity (e.g., biblical times) for burial (*WA* 23:375.11–23), which Luther argues are clearly supportive of extramural cemeteries; and (C) brief concluding recommendation (*WA* 23:375.24–27). Taken altogether, these three steps constitute an argument for changing burial policies. As he begins to address the health issue, we must note that in this final topic of burial Luther uses only two short quotes from Scripture. Yet, as already noted, he draws upon biblical material for evidence.

Luther claims to submit to doctors of medicine and others with greater experience on the issue of possible danger of cemeteries that are intramural—within the city limits (*ynn Stedten Kirchhofe*). Accordingly, he twice stipulates his lack of knowledge in this area: 'I do not know and do not claim to understand,' he avers, whether 'vapors or[146] mists' emanate from graves and pollute the air. Yet, on the chance that this danger is likely, Luther concludes that his previously stated warnings are sufficient grounds to move the cemeteries outside the city. He says all people are responsible to ward off the poison, to our best ability, because of God's commandment to us to care for our bodies, that we 'protect and nurse' them so we are not needlessly exposed. However, emergencies require that we be bold enough to risk our health, if necessary. Preparing to quote Scripture, Luther concludes that we must be ready 'to live and to die [*zu leben und zu sterben*],' according to His will.[147]

Now that he has drawn upon Scripture quotation, Luther turns to ancient burial practices to lay a foundation for concluding ultimately that extramural burial should be used. He uses three examples—two from the life of Christ and one from the Old Testament. Using anaphoric doublets, he begins with a general assertion that it was the custom of the ancients, "both among Jews and pagans, both among saints and

---

[146] *LW* 43:136 translates *odder* as 'and.'

[147] Altering Rom. 14:7, Luther employs anaphora in quoting Paul in Rom. 15 (*sic*): "No one lives to himself, no one dies to himself" (*WA* 23:375.9f.). Luther has substituted *niemand* for *unser keiner* ('none of us'). *LW* 43:136 follows the biblical text in its translation. The wording of Luther's quote downplays 'us' in deference to the other.

sinners," to bury their dead outside the city. Luther then asserts that the reason for such practice was prudence (*Klug*), suggesting that we should be equally wise. Such a strong suggestion becomes the strategy for this argument—a stategy informed by exegesis. He then moves to the biblical examples, each of which he draws upon by calling attention to the notion that people put distance between their dwellings and their buried dead: First, in Luke it thus shows that Christ raised the widow's son from the dead, 'at the gates of Nain.' Having put that phrase of location (*ym Stadthor zu Naim*) in emphatic (final) position, Luther then quotes Luke 7:12, "He was being carried out of the city to the grave, and a large crowd from the city was going with her" (*WA* 23:375.15f.).[148] Luther's second, brief example is very similar to what he has just said about the first: he links it to the preceding example by a connector (*Also*), implies special significance to Christ's tomb itself, and finishes with the location being prepared outside the city (*aussen fur den Stad bereit war*).[149] The third example is one that Luther will use to base philological significance upon—a point that would not be lost on Hess and his humanist colleagues.[150]

The example is Abraham's burial, signaled as similar to Christ's, but explained so simply, with clues about (a) remoteness of location (in the field of Ephron near the double cave);[151] (b) broader approval—a cave where all the Patriarchs later wished to be buried. Yet somehow the example seems incomplete, leaving the reader hanging—ready for further development.[152] Luther compiles—from all three examples, I believe—two claims: (1) that the Hebrews not only carried the dead

---

[148] "Man trug hyn zur stad hinaus zum grabe and gieng viel volcks mit yhr." With one final statement about location—thus, three times he has said it—Luther then comments on the Lucan text, saying that it was to bury the dead outside the town (*ausser den Stedten die Begrebnis zu haben*, in final position) that was the custom in that country.

[149] *WA* 23:375.18 cites John 19:41 in the margin.

[150] Fleischer, "Humanism and Reformation in Silesia" (80), reminds us of Hess's strong relationship with Melanchthon, who had high regard for the humanist Hess. Melanchthon accompanied the career of Hess from 'cradle to grave' with his epigrams. He bid him farewell as Hess left Wittenberg for Breslau (1520) with a Latin *Propemtikon* (in Greek letters), "assuring him of God's guidance and their 'sweet' friendship. . . . Finally, the twelve Greek lines by Melanchthon on Hess's epitaph on a pillar of the church summed up his life and work as a biblical scholar and ecclesiastical reformer."

[151] ". . . auff dem acker Ephron bey der zwisachen hüle" (*WA* 23:375.19f.). Gen.23:9 is cited by *LW* 43:136 and *WA* 23:375.19.

[152] Indeed, Luther then extracts from the Vulgate text the clues about remote location, as he explains that the Latin language employs the term *Efferri*, which means 'to carry out [*hinaus tragen*]' and that Germans would similarly say 'to carry to the grave [*zum grabe tragen*].'

out (*sie trugen . . . hinaus*) but also burned the corpses to powder; (2) they did so in order to keep the air as pure as possible. Thus, putting those twin claims both in final position, Luther has summarized the common features of all three examples: they took the dead outside of town. He has also used the final example's historical details (a double cave for repeated burials, plus his unsupported assertion that cremation was the practice) to try to anchor the examples to the previous suggestion that health concerns warrant extramural burial (*WA* 23:375.19–23). His conclusion is clearly signaled (*Darumb*), duly constrained as advice (*mein Rat*), and succinct: follow these examples and bury the dead outside the town.[153] Then he labels the rationale for following his conclusion: necessity should induce us to provide a public burial ground outside the town. Yet necessity is only one rationale; he mentions two others also—'piety and decency.' It is those needs to which he next turns (*WA* 23:375.24–27).

<u>Behavior Within Cemeteries</u>: Luther's discussion follows a problem-solution format, in three steps: (a) the ideal; (b) the sorry status quo; and (c) the remedy. He uses doublets abundantly—plus a couple of triplets—to argue that the Wittenberg churchyard (*Kirchhoff*) is far from what the ideal cemetery (*Begrebnis*) ought to be. His remedy is no specific plan but rather several complaints that attempt to show how far from the ideal Wittenberg has fallen, how far she has to go.

The ideal cemetery should rightfully be a 'fine, quiet place' that is separated from other places. Its purpose is to provide for the living: to be a place one 'can go and can reverently meditate' upon 'death, the Last Judgment, and the resurrection, and pray.' Such a place should properly be 'a decent—yes, almost hallowed place," one entered with 'trepidation and much reverence [*Furcht und allen Ehren*]' because, without doubt, there are saints resting there. One might even arrange to have religious 'pictures and portraits [*Bilder und Gemelde*]' painted on the walls (*WA* 23:375.28–34).

I point out that Luther's ideal cemetery says nothing about dead saints who need the prayers of the living; conversely, neither does he mention the prayers of the saints being needed by the living. Thus, his argument flies directly in the face of traditions that highly valued access to graves, which for centuries had deliberately been placed

---

[153] "...solchen exempeln nach das begregnis hinaus fur die stad machen (*WA* 23:375.24f.).

on the south side of the church, the original purpose that of being near the saints (*ad sanctos*).[154] Instead, Luther focuses entirely upon the cemetery's function as a reminder of the ineluctability of death, and of the certainty of what comes after death. Further, since he offers no evidence, Luther makes no real argument here. Rather, he may have assumed that the previous biblical examples—and perhaps especially that Rom. 14:7—imply piety and decency in cemeteries. This may be a large presumption, given what he says next.

The status quo in Wittenberg, according to Luther, is anything but pious and decent,[155] and for Susan Karant-Nunn, Luther's description is quite plausible for many cities at that time.[156] However, his chacterization of the Wittenberg cemetery is mostly done in the third person. Later there are signs that the speaker is not unwilling to be associated with the place and what goes on there. He begins with rhetorical question, inviting readers to ponder and see if they do not agree with him:

> But our cemetery, what is it like? Four or five alleys and two or three marketplaces, with the result that no place in the whole town is busier or noisier [*gemeiner odder unstiller*] than the cemetery. Both people and cattle roam over it at any time—yes, day and night.[157] Everyone has a door and pathway to it from his house, and all sorts of things take place there, probably even some that are not fit to be mentioned (*WA* 23:377.1–6).

---

[154] For a discussion of traditional medieval burial see Susan C. Karant-Nunn, *The Reformation of Ritual*, 170–178.

[155] Beginning both a new sentence and a new paragraph with *Aber*, he describes both place and behavior as anything but ideal, in his judgment. We should note that in the following description of 'our cemetery [*unser Kirchhoff*]' Luther is, for only the second time in the document, speaking negatively about his own city. The overwhelming majority of the document is the opposite—a model for how other German cities and towns should take example from Wittenberg.

[156] Karant-Nunn, *The Reformation of Ritual*, 176. Her description is strikingly similar to Luther's, and she supplies the many vested interests people, including clergy, had in wanting to keep burial intramural. When Luther says things happen in the cemetery that should not be mentioned, perhaps he had in mind such problems as people using it for a latrine. Karant-Nunn says, "It is likely that the people themselves ducked into the cemetery when they needed to relieve themselves, so frequent in the Protestant visitation registers are the pastors' and civic leaders' complaints about the noisome smells emerging from the cemeteries, and their enjoinders to the sextons to remove filth. Decaying corpses laid too close to the surface were not the only source of the stench, and they did not produce new filth" (176). The first Lutheran visitation was in the summer of 1527.

[157] *LW* 43:137 omits 'both' and reverses the doublet *Tag und Nacht*.

The proposition that current cemetery conditions are cause for shame and not satisfaction is what Luther must then pursue. So he follows his brief description with an explanation invoking an appeal to honor and shame. He interweaves statements of status quo and ideal, showing how the former undermines the latter. He asserts that what he has described violates the purpose of the cemetery.[158] The cemetery totally destroys 'respect and reverence [*Andacht und Ehre*]' for the graves, and people tramp around as if it contained executed criminals. Not even the Turk would dishonor the place 'as we do.' Yet a cemetery should inspire such devout thoughts and the contemplation of 'death and resurrection' and respect for saints lying there.

Now it is more clear to us how Luther's policy is consistent with Reformation teaching and distinct from traditional Catholicism: piety is to be directed toward God, death, and resurrection. Decency is one's proper attitude toward the memory of those buried there. As Luther attempts to reconcile status quo and ideal, he employs anthypophora—rhetorical question with answer. The question is not an easy one, for solving a vexing problem—where real and ideal are far apart—never is. Question: how can the ideal (quiet contemplation) be reached in a public place that has such unregulated access?[159] Answer: I would rather be put to rest 'in the Elbe or in the forest,' if a cemetery is to have some dignity.[160] While that retort seems not to have much interest in a practical, political solution for the *Gemeinde*, Luther may be simply using hyperbole to make his point—that the lack of privacy and quiet has prevailed for too long. Furthermore, he has earlier suggested that a wall with limited access would help.[161] He ends with concise, forthright

---

[158] We should note that all descriptions were general assertions in plural, and no specific incidents were offered.

[159] "Everyone thinks he must walk there and everyone has direct access" (*da yderman mus uberlauffen und fur ydermans thür auffstehet*).

[160] A similar sentiment had been expressed at the Homberg synod of 1526 in Hesse, by theologians who said it made no difference if one was buried in a churchyard or in an open field: "Es ist ungehörig, zu glauben, das Begräbnis (nämlich an geweihter Stätte) trage etwas zum Heile bei. Denn es ist ganz einerlei, ob jemand auf freiem Felde oder auf einem Kirchhof bestattet wird." Herbert Derwein, *Geschichte des Christlichen Friedhofs in Deutschland* (Frankfurt, 1931), 80. I thank Craig Koslofsky for steering me to this source.

[161] Using *Aber* to begin, Luther makes a final, sincere appeal for a change of course—at least, of attitude among cemetery goers, if no change in cemetery design and administration takes place. His suggestion reverts to the oft-repeated phrase from the biblical examples: to locate the cemetery in a 'remote, quiet spot [*abgesondert stillen Spot*]' (*LW* 43:137 reverses the doublet) that would preclude ready access from townspeople

comments that indicate that these are not instructions (*Unterricht*), as the previous two parts of the document are.[162] Using anaphora, he indicates that the preceding is his advice (*mein Rat*); whoever wishes may follow. If anyone can improve on it, he should do so (*WA* 377:1–16).

III. *Conclusion*

In broadening the issue, Luther transforms a medical plague into spiritual pestilence, while still clinging to the rational aspects of health care, when necessary (*WA* 23.377.20–379.6). In a document responding to ethical questions about plague, he takes this occasion to place into context the entire Reformation effort at the time. Luther uses plague terminology to describe the satanic forces at work to oppose him, particularly with regard to controversy over the Sacrament. In addition to metaphor, the tactics Luther uses are doublets and an inclusive first person plural, which is communal for sympathetic readers and divisive for any readers from the opposition. The more one talks about others (in third person), the more effective can be one's use of first person plural to talk to friends.

Luther urges: we (*wir*) 'admonish and plead [*vermanen und bitten*]' with you (*euch*, plural) in Christ's name, that you help us (*uns*) with your prayers to God, so we may battle with teaching against 'the real, spiritual[163] pestilence' of Satan in his wickedness now used as he 'poisons and defiles' the world. Luther directs prayers to support the teaching against those blasphemers of the sacrament, though there are other sectarians.[164] Satan is 'infuriated and feels' that the day of Christ is

---

would make a 'spiritual, proper and holy sight [*geistlich, ehrlich und heilig anzusehen*]' and could be administered so as to inspire devotion (*Andacht*) among visitors.

[162] More of Luther's 'forthrightness' with Hess.

[163] *LW* 43:137 inserts a conjunction in this doublet.

[164] One of the 'sacrament blasphemers' Luther has in mind is Zwingli, whom he mentions as 'raging, foaming and threatening' and having a 'haughty spirit' in his letter to Luther that accompanied his "Friendly Exegesis of Christ's Words" to Luther (1 April 1527); cf. Preserved Smith and Charles M. Jacobs, *Luther's Correspondence and Other Contemporary Letters*, Vol. 2: *1521–1530* (Philadelphia, 1918), 398 (Letter 757, "Luther to Wenzel Link at Nuremberg," ca. 4 May 1527). Another was Karlstadt, and a third was Johannes Oecolampadius (1482–1531); cf. Luther's, "That These Words of Christ, 'This is my body,' etc., Still Stand Firm Against the Fanatics" (1527 [*LW* 37:13–150, esp. 13–25; *WA* 23:64–283]). On the fanatical view of the sacrament that "rages like a plague and grows stronger and stronger" (*LW* 37:5), see *WABr* 4:123.6f. ("in hanc pestilentem et sacrilegam haeresina") and *WABr* 4:125.7f. ("Pestis sacramentaria sevit").

close, so he raves fiercely to take away 'the Savior, Jesus Christ' from us, through his enthusiasm (*geisterey*, final position) (*WA* 23:377.20–26).

Having now moved from blaming Satan to identifying the enthusiasts as the agents, Luther explains the nature of the problem. According to him, orthodoxy has swung from one extreme to the other in its mistaken view of Satan's power and how it works: under the papacy people were so confused that they feared Satan no more than mere flesh, compared to their misguided perceptions as to what is sacred—they took a monk's cap as holy. Now many of these same people have swung so far the other way as to find the devil sheer spirit, and Christ's 'flesh and word' no longer mean anything. In other words, the view of sacrament has for some people completely shifted—from overly mystical to devalued completely, from transubstantiated body and blood of Christ to merely symbolic bread and wine. As Luther continues to discuss his opponents—in third person plural—he contrasts them and their responses to himself and his writings—in first person singular:

> They made me an answer to my treatise long ago, but I am surprised it has not yet reached Wittenberg. I shall, God willing, only once more answer them and then let the matter drop. I can see that they will only become worse. They are like a bedbug which itself has a foul smell, but the harder one rubs the more it stinks. I hope to have written enough in my pamphlet for those who can be saved so that, praise God, many may thereby be snatched from their jaws and many more may be in the truth strengthened and confirmed. May our Lord and Savior preserve you all in pure faith and fervent love [*reinem Glawben und brünstiger Liebe*] unspotted and pure [*unbefleckt und unstrefflich*] until his day. Amen. Pray for me, a poor sinner (*WA* 23:377.28–379.6).[165]

The Wittenberg cemetery was not relocated any time soon. In 1539 Luther would write to Hieronymous Krapp, the Burgermeister, complaining that the churchyard's condition was no better—in fact, was worse. He called for an end to the abuse of the churchyard, referring

---

[165] "Sie haben mir auff mein büchlin longest geantwortet, Mich wundert aber, das bis auff diesen tag nicht her gen Wittemberg komen ist. Jch wil, so Got verleyhet, noch ein mal drauff antworten und darnach sie lassen faren. Jch sehe doch, das sie nur erger davon werden, und sind wie eine wantzke, wilche von yhr selbs ubel stinckt, Aber yhe mehr man sie zu reibt, yhe erger sie stinckt. Und hoffe, wer zuerhalten ist, dem sey furch mein buchlin gnug geschrieben, wie Denn Gottlob viel dadurch aus yhrem rachen geriffen und noch viel mehr ynn der warheit gesterckt und bestetiget sind. Christus unser Herr und Heiland behalte euch alle ynn reinem glawben und brünstiger liebe unbefleckt und unstrefflich auff seinen tag sampt uns allen. AMEN. Bittet fur mich armen sunder."

specifically to a carpenter working there. The appeal was, again, for respect. Luther argued that if the dead, who "await the resurrection in the churchyard...are not given a bit more respect and peace...it will seem that we think nothing of the dead or the resurrection of the dead" (*WABr* 8:364.2–16).[166] If Koslofsky is correct in arguing that population growth in the fifteenth and sixteenth centuries was more responsible than health concerns for increasing the acceptance of extramural burial, perhaps Luther's arguments fell mostly on deaf ears, until Wittenberg's cemetery at the *Stadtkirche* grew sufficiently overcrowded.[167] As it happens, despite some cities adopting it early in the century, there was strong resistance against extramural burial. Koslofsky presents a thorough analysis of the 1536 controversy surrounding burial in Leipzig, particularly the arguments of Georg Witzel (1501–1573), who answered Luther's arguments with his own lengthy tract, "On the Dead and their Burial [*Von den Todten und yhrem Begrebnus*]."[168] Koslofsky calls Luther's 1527 tract "the only known Protestant defence of extramural burial published prior to Witzel's work."[169] Eventually, Duke George of Saxony ordered extramural burial for Leipzig in 1536.

---

[166] "... und auff dem kirchhofe der ausserstehung gewarten....ein wenig grosser eher vnd ruge vergonnet werde....als halten wir nichts von den Todten noch ausserstehung der Todten," translation by Koslofsky, *The Reformation of the Dead*, 178, note 38.

[167] Koslofsky, *The Reformation of the Dead*, 44–46. On cemetery relocation see Fritz Schnelbögl, "Friedhofverlegungen im 16. Jahrhundert," *Jahrbuch für frankische Landesforschung* 34/35 (1974–1975): 109–120; Katharina Peiter, *Der evangelische Friedhof von der Reformation bis zur Romantik* (Ph.D. Diss., Berlin, 1969), reviewed in *Theologische Literaturzeitung* 95 (1970): 951–952.

[168] *Ware trostung, grund und ursach auß Götlichem wort*...(2nd. ed., Freiburg/Breslau, 1536); cf. Georg Richter, *Die Schriften Georg Witzels* (Niewkoop, 1963); Koslofsky, *The Reformation of the Dead*, 44–77.

[169] Koslofsky, *The Reformation of the Dead*, 51.

CONCLUSION

The dying today want to know that their lives 'mattered.' Those surviving the death of a loved one want to 'make sense of it.' In what follows I make some observations on how Luther offers much more than acknowledging the loss experienced in death, something that today both dying and survivors need, according to Walter:

> Grief is manifestly interpersonally negotiated, but because it is widely believed now to be a natural process that must run its course within each individual, there are no rules by which to negotiate. The result is anomie and yet further pain. Now that social mourning is a thing of the past, we are not left with a psychological process playing out its natural course within the grieving individual; nor are we left with a postmodern choice for each individual to grieve as he or she will. What we are left with is the potential for confusion and conflict. The need for a more sociological understanding of grief is, in some families, desperate.[1]

What Luther offers is distinctly theological, because he puts one's loss into a perspective that recognizes that death is not the end for the believer in Christ. For today's generations that may know only the *Sinatra Syndrome* ('I did it *my* way') for how to die or grieve,[2] Luther's remarks about Christ's victory over death and God's sovereignty in all things can be healing balm.

I. *Acknowledging Loss*

In the 1532 funeral sermons and the consolatory letters (see Chapter Four and Chapter Five of this book) Luther affirmed his audience's present sorrow and offered reasons why God's people have grounds for

---

[1] Tony Walter, *The Revival of Death*, 161.
[2] Ibid., 33. Walter pays special attention to how funerals are increasingly humanist and centered around the significance of the deceased and a celebration of one's earthly life as 'all there is.' At the same time, however, there is a significant increase in fascination with the near-death experience. See Carol Zaleski, *Otherworld Journeys: Accounts of Near-Death Experience in Medieval and Modern Times* (New York, 1987); Glenn Roberts and John Owen, "The Near-Death Experience," *British Journal of Psychiatry* 153 (1988): 607–617; Allan Kellehear, *Experiences Near Death: Beyond Medicine and Religion* (New York, 1996).

feeling sad, despite their hope. In the first sermon especially Luther interprets 1 Thess. 4:13 as legitimating, rather than challenging, a Christian's need to grieve. Luther's summary of this argument shows that: (1) Paul's imperative, "Comfort one another" (1 Thess. 4:18), implies that there was sorrow and grief; (2) the Thessalonians were Christians; (3) Paul is not disapproving of their grief; and (4) we also have exemplary tales of Paul's grieving at the prospect of losing his friend Epaphroditus (Phil. 2:27) and Christ's grief at the death of Lazarus (John 11:33). In addition, Luther shows that the Old Testament testifies of those who hoped in Christ and manifested proper grief. Moreover, in the 1532 funeral sermons Luther did not shy away from endearing remarks about the deceased (Elector John). The same is true in the consolatory letters, where we have seen him often speak warmly and tenderly about the deceased and about his own affection for them—in these situations, speaking directly to surviving relatives. As Jane Strohl affirms, Luther "does not underestimate the sorrow such losses cause, but he does put them in perspective."[3]

II. *Putting Loss into Perspective*

In the consolatory letters Luther unmistakably urges moderation in grieving, either directly or implicitly, by arguing in detail about the richness of God's comforting resources, the blessedness of the Christian death, and the misery that the earthly life offers. He usually concentrates on Christ, "on the Word incarnate...as the guarantor of everlasting life. Luther frequently consoles survivors with the assurance that their loved one died confessing Christ and thus successfully withstood temptation in the most critical last hour."[4] In the 1532 funeral sermons he builds a strong case for appreciating the deceased as a person under the authority of God, and as a Christian leader who, not surprisingly, was subject to stronger onslaughts from the devil than was the average person. In this argument Luther elevates the discussion beyond a

---

[3] Jane E. Strohl, "Luther and the Word of Consolation," 27f.

[4] Ibid., 27. In his *Galatians* (1519), Luther writes: "Therefore I like the practice that nothing but the crucified Christ is impressed on those who are about to die, and that they are exhorted to faith and to hope. Here at least—no matter to what extent the deceivers of souls may have deluded our whole life—free will collapses, good works collapse, the righteousness of the Law collapses. Only faith and the invoking of God's completely free mercy remain, so that there are either more or better Christians in death than in life" (*LW* 27:328f.).

consideration of personal merit and onto cosmic proportions. It is *God's* strength that sees the faithful through demonic temptation. Critical in this argument is Luther's comparison between 'real,' 'manly' death and 'childish,' 'baby' death. The former occurs when the Christian dies to sin, dies with Christ; the latter is only the cessation of bodily functions. No matter how menacing the latter, we have nothing to fear when our senses stop and our bodies decay. Luther reminds listeners that their baptism marks their real death and that what the grave holds is merely a sleep.[5] With these understandings, a person can begin to submit to the counsel of Ps. 90:12: "So teach us to number our days, that we may apply our hearts unto wisdom."[6] Such a theological perspective is not an escapist fantasy; quite the contrary. As D. A. Carson argues, we "quickly turn to God for comfort when, metaphorically, we skin our knee: This is not a sign of immaturity; it is a sign of belonging."[7] To widen one's perspective to include the One who has conquered Death is a healthy strategy and reveals a discipline of faith.

III. *Emphasizing Resurrection Victory*

Luther's 1532 funeral sermons, particularly the second, celebrate the certainty of Christ's resurrection and ours. We must trust God's word, not our senses, and believe that He will raise us up in an instant, just as Christ was raised. Paul's text assures that the dead in Christ will be raised with us, their bodies restored in a glorious resurrection like unto Jesus' own. As Ninna Jørgensen says it, Luther tells his audience "to cultivate the art of looking at Christ's death whenever anxiety for deceased friends or for themselves should befall them. This is the best consolation which can be found."[8] Jørgensen argues that Luther uses in his preaching a "deliberate rehearsal of the well-known formulas"[9]

---

[5] Dorothea Wendebourg, "Luther on Monasticism," *LQ* 19 (2005): 125–152, here at 131f.

[6] Psalm 90 is attributed to Moses, of whom D. A. Carson avers: "He would have utterly scorned the modern mood that wants to live life as if death were not waiting for us at the end"; D. A. Carson, *How Long O Lord? Reflections on Suffering and Evil* (Grand Rapids, 1990), 118.

[7] Ibid., 127.

[8] Ninna Jørgensen, "'*Sed manet articulus*': Preaching and Catechetical Training in Selected Sermons by the Later Luther," *Studia Theologica* 59 (2005): 38–54, here at 43.

[9] Ibid., 52.

people would recognize, in order to help them remember principles of
the Gospel. Speaking of the first 1532 funeral sermon, she says:

> In this way, Luther links the two verses [1 Thess. 4:13–14] in Paul's text
> together by pointing to the exact words of the Creed as the basis from
> which Christians may learn the consolation of the Holy Ghost—or the
> art of 'looking beyond' the senses. Here again, it may be observed how
> he concentrates on the article of the Creed that says Christ has died and
> is risen. It should be added that in this he is a pupil of Paul, who made
> the same point clear in his letter to the Thessalonians.[10]

For the 1532 funeral sermons, particularly the first one, the real topic of
the sermon is the death and resurrection of Jesus, stipulated explicitly
as a phrase—Jesus 'died and rose again'—21 times, and mentioned in
other ways at least double that. While my study here has not pursued
deliberately the 'memorizable formulas of faith' that Gerhard Ebeling
addresses, this expression comes the closest.[11]

In "Fourteen Consolations" (see Chapter One of this book) Luther
constructed his consolatory meditation around seven evils and seven
blessings; he offered comfort to the dying by turning each potential dis-
appointment to victory. He employed the resources of Latin to develop a
variety of rhetorical figures. With ample use of these devices, including
a strong reliance on doublets, comparatives, superlatives, and anthypophora, Luther follows a 'how much more' (*qal wachomer*) argumentative
strategy. Using abundant scriptural quotations and constructed dialogue,
he creates a strong presence for each image (*spectrum*), both of evil and
blessing. He argues that the blessings one has in Christ's resurrection
will be won at Christ's return, despite the brief sleep of death. Yea,
even now the blessings are ours through the communion of the saints.
Much of what Luther does in this document invites the reader to focus
on visual images depicted.

In "Sermon on Preparing to Die" (see Chapter Two of this book)
Luther employed strong linguistic images evoking vision, by using verbal
depiction rather than the illustrations found in the *ars moriendi*. Using a
language of conquest, Luther employs strong terms for characterizing
Christ's (and the Christian's) victory at death: *uberwunden*—all but once
used as verb. This conquest language is not as ubiquitous as the vision

---

[10] Ibid., 43.
[11] "...memorierbare Glaubenssätze"; Gerhard Ebeling, *Luthers Seelsorge*, cited by
Jørgensen, "Sed manet articulus," 40.

talk, but for the most part it occurs in the same places: The conquest language begins at Article 8, while the vision talk is heard only sparingly in the earlier articles. In his 26 uses of *uberwunden* (and its variants), Luther makes victory seem certain.

IV. *Exhorting Christians to Suffer Willingly*

In "On Whether to Flee A Deadly Plague" (see Chapter Six of this book) Luther made clear an expectation that Christians have a duty to their fellows, subordinates, and superiors that transcends personal desires or even the survival instinct. Just as he spoke out against fear and cowardice in the face of plague, Luther today would be horrified (but not shocked) to hear about hoarding the flu vaccine oseltamivir (Tamiflu)[12] or putting human corpses into preserved states for art galleries.[13] In the martyrological literature (see Chapter Three of this book) he wrote that Christians should expect suffering and persecution; that God's word is at work in death, and hence is the subject, rather than death itself; and that martyrdom is a gift from God.[14] Characterizing this expectation as 'apocalyptic Luther' may be helpful in seeing his sense of God's imminent ending brought into history.[15] However, Luther also perceives suffering and death as man's lot in a fallen world over which God is still sovereign, regardless of the timetable. God has already dealt death a lethal blow, and *soon* He will come to claim His

---

[12] Allan S. Brett and Abigail Zuger, "The Run on Tamiflu—Should Physicians Prescribe on Demand?" *NEJM* 353 (22 December 2005): 2636–2637.

[13] Gene Edward Veith, "Corpse Art," *World*, 8 October 2005, 30. The article features a discussion of the plastination technique of Gunther von Hagens of Heidelberg. See "Body Worlds: The Anatomical Exhibition of Real Human Bodies," <http://www.bodyworlds.com/index.html>, (Accessed 1 September 2006). The exhibit ran from 5 May to 3 December 2006 at the Science Museum of Minnesota. It is also scheduled for Boston and Houston.

[14] Robert Kolb, "God's Gift of Martyrdom: The Early Reformation Understanding of Dying for the Faith," *Church History* 64 (1995): 399–411; Gene Edward Veith, "Praying for Persecution," *World*, 1 October 2005, 24, cites a leader of the Chinese house-church movement, who says American Christians should "stop praying for persecution in China to end."

[15] Michael Parsons, "The Apocalyptic Luther: His Noahic Self-Understanding," *JETS* 44 (2001): 627–645. Parsons argues that apocalypticism persisted in Luther's career, and he cites the "Letter of Consolation to all who Suffer Persecution" (1522)—which I examined in Chapter Three—as well as his understanding of Noah as martyr (Gen. 6–9), in the "Genesis Commentary" (1542), found in *LW* 2; *WA* 42. Ken Sundet Jones, "The Apocalyptic Luther," *WW* 25 (2005): 308–316, finds apocalypticism in Luther's hymn, "A Mighty Fortress" (1528).

own and put an end to all suffering and death (Rev. 22:20). As John Donne puts it: "One short sleep past, we wake eternally, And Death shall be no more; Death, Thou shalt die."[16]

In his "Letter to a Soldier about Death," Helmut Thielicke sums up much of what we have seen in Luther's comforting literature that I have examined in this book:

> I do not want to close this long letter, dear comrade and brother, without opening to you yet one last perspective. Luther says in similar situations that only he who inflicts the wounds and permits them is able also to heal them. No one else. Illusions about death cannot do this; neither can hushed silence on the subject. Even the atheistic method of easy dying effects no healing; it only teaches how to bleed to death without looking. It proclaims the demise of an impersonal collective entity, not the end of a human being who is wrenched from just such anonymity when he is called by his name to be God's possession. No, God alone can heal the wound because he is the one who inflicted it. Only he can heal it whose love reveals to us—so painfully and yet with such joy and promise—'the infinite value of the human soul.' For now we know for certain that what dies in me is not an 'it' but an 'I,' an 'I' for which there is no substitute among all the comrades who march over my grave. In death I am really and irretrievably and in actual fact at my end. But at the same time I am one whose history with God cannot stop, since I am called by my name and I am the friend of Jesus. The Resurrected One is victorious and I stand within his sphere of power. Once more it is his 'alien' life with which I am in fellowship and which brings me through everything and receives me on the other side of the gloomy grave. It is not the intrinsic quality of my soul nor something supposedly immortal within me that brings me through. No, it is this Wanderer who marches at my side as Lord and Brother and who can no more abandon me on the other side than he could let me out of his hand here on this side of the grave.[17]

Joseph Bayly comments on the biblical Job, who was "in the dark the whole time of his agony." Like Thielicke, Bayly concludes that, "we accept life's mysteries and suffering unexplained because they are known to God, and we know Him." As a bereaved father of three sons, Bayly argued that one must focus more on Christ than on death or loss: "We believe that in this world of evil, God's primary work, for our children

---

[16] John Donne, *Holy Sonnets*, X; cf. *Sonnets* I, IV, VI, VII, and XIII; <http://www.luminarium.org/sevenlit/donne/sonnet10.htm>. (Accessed 20 October 2005).

[17] Helmut Thielicke, *Death and Life*, trans. Edward H. Schroeder (Philadelphia, 1970), xxv–xxvi.

and for us, is not to shield us from suffering, but to conform us to the image of Jesus Christ."[18]

If we must 'make sense' out of tragic death, particularly catastrophes involving multiple deaths, we need faith.[19] We need to acknowledge God and be learning not only his acts but also his ways. Bayly insisted that many people are like the Israelites after the Exodus—interested only in God's acts (especially today—his healing!). "But the ones who want an answer to the problem of suffering must get behind and beyond the acts of God, as Moses did, and discern His ways."[20] Bayly contended that Moses' prayer in Exod. 33:13, "Show me now thy ways, that I may know thee and find favor in thy sight," was answered, as preserved in Psalm 103:7 ("He made known his ways to Moses, his acts to the people of Israel"). We who are so averse to pain need to recall that Luther called grief a 'rod' (*Ruten, Rütlein*)[21] and a 'school (*Schule*),[22] neither of which is pleasant; both, however, are beneficial and necessary. Those who are first to agree are athletes and soldiers, and Paul the Apostle invoked both exemplars in exhortations to persevere.[23] We who can be so impatient with God should be grateful that Luther did, in fact, not only practice pastoral care but also wrote about it.[24] He wrote in such a way as to "testify to the two sides of the intended spiritual balance between fear and hope."[25]

In his *Martin Luther* (1999), Richard Marius set out to show that Luther's "greatest terror, one that came on him periodically as a horror of darkness, was the fear of death—death in itself" (xxiii). In what has been presented in these chapters, I trust that my readers will now want to review Marius's book under new light. One should no longer allow an author to speak so boldly about the inner thoughts of one so far removed from us, unless we permit that one to 'speak.' Indeed, an attempt to display the inner thoughts of a man who lived five centuries ago, no matter how high a 'mountain of his literary output,' is an

---

[18] Joseph Bayly, *The Last Thing We Talk About*, 104–106.
[19] Bayly reminds us: "Mass death produces monumental problems for survivors, but it does not change the nature of death for those who die"; ibid., 23.
[20] Ibid., 104.
[21] *WABr* 8:353.21; 352.5; 10:63.5.
[22] *WABr* 8:497.26; 3:497.26f.
[23] 1 Cor. 9:25; 2 Tim. 2:5 (*athlete*); 1 Cor. 9:7; Phil. 2:25; 2 Tim. 2:3–4; Philem. 1:2 (*soldier*).
[24] Herbert W. Stroup, Jr., "Pastoral Theology: Reformation or Regression?" (48).
[25] Heiko A. Oberman, "Varieties of Protest," 43.

ambitious endeavor, and in my estimation Marius's conclusions extend beyond the selective evidence he produced. My goal in this book is far less lofty and, hopefully, more successful. I have tried to show the extent to which Luther, regardless of his own doubts or foes or illnesses, provided comfort to many whom death threatened to devour. That Luther did so—with creativity and eloquence, through many of the same language strategies and style that pervade all of his preaching and writings—is, I believe, amply demonstrated. Rather than speak for him, I tried to let Luther himself speak.

Did Luther find death to be a formidable threat to his own family and himself? Undoubtedly, the answer is yes; we have seen so from his disclosures of personal grief in his consolatory letters.[26] Moreover, there is much more disclosure in other letters—most of them pertaining to Magdalena's death—and many scholars have commented on them.[27] However, to the extent that literary sources can capture a person's thoughts, the sources stemming from actual witnesses are agreed that—when it comes to his behavior—Luther faced his own death with faith in Christ.[28] Jane Strohl compares profitably the differences between Luther's characterization of death and that of Friedrich Schleiermacher (1768–1834), for both men buried beloved children:

> This 19th century theologian construes death neither as a judgment against sin nor as the painful but certain gateway to the sure joys of redemption for the believer. The imperishable and eternal do not lie beyond this world but in its midst for Schleiermacher. The experience of bereavement chastens him but not in such a way that he discerns in it the hand of God refining his faith so that he may stand firm in his own final hour.... For Luther, on the other hand, death, originally inflicted as a punishment, becomes a blessing for the believer. His grief over his lost child is obviously no less crushing than Schleiermacher's, but he can

---

[26] For additional material on Luther's comments on death, see Ewald M. Plass, *What Luther Says: A Practical In-Home Anthology for the Active Christian* (St. Louis, 1959), "Death," no. 1065–1138 (pp. 363–388).

[27] Literature that comments on Luther's remarks about Magdalena's death is abundant; for two important authorities, see Steven Ozment, "The Family in Reformation Germany: The Bearing and Rearing of Children," *Journal of Family History* 8 (summer 1983): 159–176, esp. 172f.; idem, "Luther and the Family," 48–53; idem, *Protestants: The Birth of A Revolution* (New York, 1991), 164–168; Jane E. Strohl, "The Child in Luther's Theology: 'For What Purpose Do We Older Folks Exist, Other Than to Care for.... the Young?'" in *The Child in Christian Thought*, ed. Marcia J. Bunge (Grand Rapids, 2001), 134–159, esp. 157f.

[28] Marius, *Martin Luther*, 481f.; Brecht, *Martin Luther*, 3:375–377; Oberman, *Luther: Man between God and the Devil*, trans. Eileen Walliser-Schwarzbart (New York, 1992), 3–8.

find real comfort in the thought that she is out of this dangerous world sooner rather than later. This reflects Luther's view of the undiminished virulence of sin in the creation. Sin's punishment shall prove to be its cure. It is only on our deathbed that our daily prayer, 'Lead us not into temptation, but deliver us from evil,' is finally answered.[29]

Whether today's generations are any more 'prepared' for death than our predecessors is an open question. It is a matter for our societies to ponder soberly. Our contemporary understandings of grief as psychological process and of mourning as 'adjustment,' are commendable; our efforts to restore personal, familial, and social involvement in the 'dying process' are laudable. Our children and grandchildren are not as insulated from death as we were: few in the Western world can escape the ubiquitous coverage of disaster and death on cable television. When it happens too 'close to home' to ignore, turning to professional crisis counselors is a common response to these tragedies. Listening politely to a eulogy and speaking emotionally about a deceased loved one are well-known, though not frequent, experiences. However, Luther would have us prepare for death in more ways than these familiar, now mostly secularized, situations. Moreover, he would urge us to ponder much earlier and more often than securing a diversified investment portfolio, locating adequate medical insurance, creating a living will or health care directive, and purchasing a prepaid funeral. No matter what our present chronological age, he would grimace at the contemporary turn to 'spirituality'[30] and instead direct our attention, right now, to Christ: back to our baptism, onto the cross, and toward heaven. He would have us be students of the Word and serve one another in love. Persistently he has already pushed us in those directions.[31]

---

[29] Jane E. Strohl, "Luther and the Word of Consolation," 32f.; cf. idem, "Suffering as Redemptive: A Comparison of Christian Experience in the Sixteenth and Twentieth Centuries," in *Revisioning the Past: Prospects in Historical Theology*, ed. Mary Potter Engel and Walter E. Wyman (Minneapolis, 1992), 95–111. Strohl analyzes Schleiermacher's funeral eulogy for his son, and contrasts it to evidence from Luther's letters.

[30] Helen Walterhouse and Tony Walter, "Reincarnation Belief and the Christian Churches," *Theology* 106 (2003): 20–28; Dennis Klass, "Grief, Religion, and Spirituality," in *Death and Religion in a Changing World*, ed. Kathleen Garces-Foley (London, 2006), 283–304; Glenn Lucke, Richard B. Gilbert, and Ronald K. Barrett, "Protestant Approaches to Death: Overcoming Death's Sting," in ibid., 122–146; Lizette Larson-Miller, "Roman Catholic, Anglican, and Eastern Orthodox Approaches to Death," in ibid., 93–121.

[31] As I have shown in Luther's Invocavit Sermons (Leroux, *Luther's Rhetoric*), Luther's style in preaching displays an eloquence that often resorts to dialogue, pronoun manipulation, and frequent doubling of words and phrases. In the comforting

Therefore, Luther's writings on death take it out of the realm of the dreary and depressing and onto something of infinite promise, because, for the dying believer, death provides the best opportunity to redeem the benefits of Christ's death and resurrection. In his lecture on Psalm 90 Luther said: "The law says: 'In the midst of life we are surrounded by death,' but the gospel reverses this sentence: 'In the midst of death we are surrounded by life because we have the forgiveness of sins.'"[32] For survivors, death is not sweet, but it can be filled with healing and hope, for death provides the greatest opportunity to proclaim—to others and ourselves—Christ's death and resurrection.

---

literature here examined, those features also emerge. Christine Helmer has tracked much of the literature in German that has investigated Luther's rhetorical style; cf. her *The Trinity and Martin Luther: A Study on the Relationship between Genre, Language and the Trinity in Luther's Works (1523–1546)*. Veröffentlichungen des Instituts für Europäische Geschichte Mainz 174 (Mainz, 1999), 197–249. She notes (194) that Luther himself argues that preaching contains nothing less than the divine word of power to raise the dead ("Sermon On Keeping Children in School" [1530] in *LW* 46:207–258; *WA* 30[II]:517–588, first examined fruitfully by Birgit Stolt, "Docere, delectare und movere bei Luther. Analysiert anhand der 'Predigt, daß man Kinder zur Schulen halten solle,'" *Deutsche Vierteljahrsschrift für Literaturwissenschaft und Geistesgeschichte* 44 (1970): 433–474 and reprinted in Stolt, *Wortkampf: Frühneuhochdeutsche Beispiele zur rhetorischen Praxis* (Frankfurt, 1974), 31–77. Helmer also relies on the research of Karl-Heinrich Bieritz, "Verbum facit fidem: Homiletische Anmerkungen zu einer Lutherpredigt," *Theologische Literaturzeitung* 109 (1984): 481–494; Hans Thimme, "Martin Luther als Prediger," in *Luther und der Pietismus: An alle, die mit Ernst Christen sein wollen*, ed. Kurt Heimbucher (Giessen, 1983), 23–56; Eberhard Winkler, *Impulse Luthers für die heutige Gemeindepraxis*. Arbeiten zur Theologie 67 (Stuttgart, 1983); Winkler, "Luther als Seelsorger und Prediger," in *Leben und Werk Martin Luthers von 1526 bis 1546*, vol. 1, ed. Helmar Junghans (Göttingen, 1983), 225–240; and Manfred Haustein, "Luther als Prediger," *Standpunkt* 11 (April 1983): 93–95. Helmer (223) notes the dialogical style that Bieritz (483) finds in Luther's use of pronouns and the 'feigned speech' (*fingierte Reden*) found in Luther by Ruppert Mayr, "'Einfeldig zu predigen, ist eine große kunst.' Zu Luthers Sprache in seinen Predigten," in *Reformations gedenken. Beiträge zum Lutherjahr 1983 aus der Evangelischen Kirche im Rheinland*, ed. Joachim Mehlhausen (Cologne, 1985), 83–100, here at 97).

[32] "Das ist vox legis: Mitten: Vox Euangelii: Media etc., quia remissionem peccatorum habeamus" (*WA* 40[III]:96.4f.); translation by Carter Lindberg, "Eschatology and Fanaticism in the Reformation Era: Luther and the Anabaptists," *CTQ* 64 (2000): 259–278, here at 268.

GLOSSARY OF RHETORICAL TERMS

Definitions of rhetorical, literary, and epistolary terms are derived from M. H. Abrams, *A Glossary of Literary Terms*, 3rd ed. (New York, 1971); Thomas M. Conley, *Rhetoric in the European Tradition* (New York, 1990); Heinrich Lausberg, *Handbook of Literary Rhetoric*, ed. D. E. Orton and R. Dean Anderson (Leiden, 1998); Laurent Pernot, *Rhetoric in Antiquity*, trans. W. E. Higgins (Washington, D.C., 2005); and "Silva Rhetoricae" (rhetoric.byu.edu).

Anaphora: Repetition of the same word or phrase at the beginning of successive clauses, sentences, or lines.

Anthypophora: A figure of reasoning in which one asks and then immediately answers one's own questions (or raises and then settles imaginary objections). Reasoning aloud.

Antithesis: Juxtaposition of contrasting words or ideas (often, although not always, in parallel structure).

Apostrophe: Turning one's speech from one audience to another. Most often, apostrophe occurs when one addresses oneself to an abstraction, to an inanimate object, or to the absent.

Asyndeton: The omission of conjunctions between clauses, often resulting in a hurried rhythm or vehement effect.

Benevolentiae captatio: Second part of a Medieval letter (following the salutation), where the writer offers a statement of wishing well to the recipient.

Causa: Speech bearing on a concrete subject and referring to 'circumstances.'

Chiasmus: Repetition of grammatical structures in inverted order. Sometimes called antimetabole, when identical or nearly identical words are repeated and inverted.

Conclusio: The last part of a letter, similar to the peroration of an oration.

Contrarium: Offering a counter-example in argumentation.

Data: Term sometimes used in argumentation to refer to the supporting evidence or appeal.

Distributio: Dividing a whole into its parts.

Doublet: Two words of the same grammatical form (e.g., noun, verb, etc.), which may or may not be linked by a conjunction, offered for elaboration of a point. The relationship between terms can be synonymous, antithetical (contrasting), progressive, regressive, or complementary.

Enthymeme: The informal method of reasoning typical of rhetorical discourse. It is sometimes called a 'truncated syllogism' since one premise is left implicit. The enthymeme typically occurs as a conclusion coupled with a reason.

Epistrophe: Ending a series of lines, phrases, clauses, or sentences with the same word or words.

Epithet: An adjective or adjectival phrase used to define the special quality of a person or thing.

Exhortatio: Portion of a discourse that pleads with, warns, urges, or makes appeals to the reader or listener.

Exigence: A situational need or problem facing both orator and audience.

Exordium: Introduction of an oration, or the second part of a Rennaisance letter, where it would follow the salutatio.

Expeditio: After enumerating all possibilities by which something could have occurred, the speaker eliminates all but one.

Hyperbaton: An inversion of normal word order.

Inclusio: The placing of similar material (words or phrases) at the beginning and end of a section.

Interpretatio: Offering an explanation or account of a term or saying.

Inventio: That part of rhetoric concerned with the discovery of arguments, of things to say about a given subject.

Meiosis: Understatement; reference to something with a name disproportionately lesser than its nature.

Narratio: The second part of an oration or the third part of a letter. The speaker provides a narrative account of what has happened and generally explains the nature of the case.

Periphrasis: Use of several words instead of just one.

Petitio: Fourth part of a letter, in which the writer makes a request.

Polysyndeton: Employing many conjunctions—between words, phrases, or clauses, often slowing the tempo or rhythm.

Prolepsis: To foresee an objection and answer in advance.

Qal Wachomer: Rabbinic argument that reasons from minor to major; that is, "how much more" is the admittedly stronger item, granted the significance already attributed to the weaker.

Ratiocinatio: Reasoning (typically with oneself) by asking questions; sometimes equivalent to anthypophora.

Rhetorical Question: To affirm or deny a point strongly by asking it as a question. It can include an emotional dimension such as expressing wonder, indignation, sarcasm, etc.

Salutatio: First part of a letter, where the writer identifies and greets the recipient.

Sententia: One of several terms describing short, pithy sayings. Others include adage, apothegm, gnome, maxim, paroemia, and proverb.

Soliloquy: The act of talking to oneself.

Sorites: Concatenated enthymemes; that is, a chain of claims and reasons which build upon one another.

Topos: Basic category of relationships among ideas, which can serve as a template or heuristic for discovering things to say about a subject; a line of argument, also called locus.

Warrant: Reasoning principle justifying a proper link between an argument's conclusion (or claim) and the evidence supporting it; equivalent to major premise in formal argument.

BIBLIOGRAPHY

Aden, LeRoy. *In Life and Death: The Shaping of Faith*. Minneapolis, Minn., 2005.

Adler, Jerry. "The Fight Against the Flu." *Newsweek*, 31 October 2005, 38–45.

———. "Freud in Our Midst." *Newsweek*, 27 March 2006, 43–49.

Akerboom, Dick. "'Only the Image of Christ in Us': Continuity and Discontinuity between the Late Medieval ars moriendi and Luther's Sermon von der Bereitung zum Sterben." In *Spirituality Renewed: Studies on Significant Representatives of the Modern Devotion*, edited by Hein Blommestijn, Charles Caspers, and Rijcklof Hofman, 209–272. Leuven, 2003.

———. "'Ein neues lied wir heben an': Over de eerste martelaren van de Reformatie en het ontstaan van het eerste lied van Martin Luther." *Luther-Bulletin* 14 (2005): 27–43.

Albers, Robert H. "The Faith Factor in Wholistic Care: A Multidisciplinary Conversation." *WW* 21 (2001): 51–60.

Amundsen, Darrel W. "The Physician's Obligation to Prolong Life: A Medical Duty without Classical Roots." *The Hastings Center Report* 8 (August 1978): 23–30.

———. "Medicine and Faith in Early Christianity." *BHM* 56 (1982): 326–350.

Anderson, H. George; J. Francis Stafford; and Joseph A. Burgess, eds. *The One Mediator, The Saints, and Mary*. Lutherans and Catholics in Dialogue 8. Minneapolis, 1992.

Anderson, Herbert. "Whatever Happened to *Seelsorge*?" *WW* 21 (2001): 32–41.

Appel, Helmut. *Anfechtung und Trost im Spätmittelalter und bei Luther*. Leipzig, 1938.

Appenzeller, Tim. "Tracking the Next Killer Flu." *National Geographic*, October 2005, 2–31.

Arbusow, Leonid Jr. *Die Einführung der Reformation in Liv-, Est- und Kurland*. Quellen und Forschungen zur Reformationsgeschichte 3. Aalen, 1964.

Ariès, Philippe. *Western Attitudes Toward Death: From the Middle Ages to the Present*. Translated by Patricia M. Ranum. Baltimore, 1974.

———. *The Hour of Our Death*. Translated by Helen Weaver. New York, 1981.

Aristotle. *Rhetoric*. Translated by W. Rhys Roberts. New York, 1954.

Arrizabalaga, Jon. "Review of Cohn Jr., *The Black Death Transformed*." *Speculum* 79 (2004): 1053–1055.

Asimakoupoulos, Gregory E. "The Contribution of Martin Luther to Congregational Singing." *Covenant Quarterly* 56 (1998): 23–33.

Attig, Thomas. *How We Grieve: Relearning the World*. New York, 1996.

Bachelor, Philip. *Sorrow & Solace: The Social World of the Cemetery*. Amityville, N.Y., 2004.

Bainton, Roland H. "Luther: Pastor, Consoler, Preacher." In *Encounters with Luther*. Vol. 1, *Lectures, Discussions and Sermons at the Martin Luther Colloquia 1970–74*, edited by Eric W. Gritsch, 167–180. Gettysburg, 1980.

Bailley, Steven E.; Michael J. Kral; and Katherine Dunham. "Survivors of Suicide Do Grieve Differently: Empirical Support for a Common Sense Proposition." *Suicide and Life-Threatening Behavior* 29 (1999): 256–271.

Balk, David E. "The Self-Concepts of Bereaved Adolescents: Sibling Death and Its Aftermath." *Journal of Adolescent Research* 5 (1990): 112–132.

———. "Sibling Death, Adolescent Bereavement, and Religion." *DS* 15 (1991): 1–20.

Ballard, Richard G. "The Pastoral Care of the Sick and Dying and of the Bereaved." *LuthFor* 34 (spring 2000): 37–41.

Barth, Hans-Martin. "'Pecca fortiter, sed fortius fide...': Martin Luther als Seelsorger." *Evangelische Theologie* 44 (1984): 12–25.

———. "Leben und Sterben können: Brechungen der spätmittelalterlichen 'ars moriendi' in der Theologie Martin Luthers." In *Ars Moriendi: Erwägungen zur Kunst des Sterbens*, edited by Harald Wagner, 45–66. Freiburg, 1989.

Battin, Margaret Pabst. *Ending Life: Ethics and the Way We Die*. Oxford, 2005.

Bauch, Gustav. "Beiträge zur Litteraturgeschichte des schlesischen Humanismus." *Zeitschrift des Vereins für Geschichte Schlesiens* 26 (1892): 213–225.

———. "Johann Thurzo und Johann Heß." *Zeitschrift des Vereins für Geschichte Schlesiens* 36 (1901): 193–224.

———. "Zur Breslauer Reformationsgeschichte." *Zeitschrift des Vereins für Geschichte Schlesiens* 41 (1907): 336–352.

Baumeister, R. F. *Meanings of Life*. New York, 1991.

Bayly, Joseph. *The View from A Hearse*. Elgin, Ill., 1969.

———. *The Last Thing We Talk About*. Colorado Springs, Col., 1972.

Beaty, Nancy Lee. *The Craft of Dying: A Study in the Literary Tradition of the Ars Moriendi in England*. New Haven, 1970.

Beck, Gordon A. "Questions About Current Lutheran Music Practices." *LuthFor* 37 (spring 2003): 52–55.

Becker, Arthur E. "Luther as Seelsorger." In *Interpreting Luther's Legacy: Essays in Honor of Edward C. Fendt*, edited by Fred W. Meuser and Stanley D. Schneider, 136–150. Minneapolis, 1969.

Becker, Howard. "The Sorrow of Bereavement." *Journal of Abnormal and Social Psychology* 27 (1933): 391–410.

Beecher, Henry Ward. "Relations of Music to Worship." *Yale Lectures on Preaching 2*, 114–145. Boston, 1902.

Bell, Catherine. "Ritual Tensions: Tribal and Catholic." *Studia Liturgica* 32 (2002): 15–28.

Benedek, Therese. "Parenthood as A Developmental Phase: A Contribution to the Libido Theory." *Journal of the American Psychoanalytic Association* 7 (1959): 389–419.

Benne, Robert, "Review of Marius, *Martin Luther: The Christian between God and Death*." *Review of Politics* 62 (2000): 188–191.

Berry, Wendell. *Another Turn of the Crank*. Washington, D.C., 1995.

Benzing, Josef. *Lutherbibliographie: Verzeichnis der Gedruckten Schriften Martin Luthers bis zu dessen Tod*. Bibliotheca Bibliographica Aureliana 10. Baden-Baden, 1965.

Bieritz, Karl-Heinrich. "Verbum facit fidem: Homiletische Anmerkungen zu einer Lutherpredigt." *Theologische Literaturzeitung* 109 (1984): 481–494.

Bibliotheca Reformatoria Neerlandica. Geschriften uit den tijd der hervorming in de Nederlanden. Edited by S. Cramer and F. Pijper. The Hague, 1903–1914.

Bitzer, Lloyd F. "The Rhetorical Situation." *Philosophy and Rhetoric* 1 (1968): 1–14.

———. "Functional Communication: A Situational Perspective." In *Rhetoric in Transition: Studies in the Nature and Uses of Rhetoric*, edited by E. E. White, 21–38. University Park, Penn., 1980.

Blank, Robert H. and Janna C. Merrick, ed. *End-of-Life Decision Making: A Cross-National Study*. Cambridge, Mass., 2005.

Blankenburg, Walter. "Luther und die Musik." In *Kirche und Musik: Gesammelte Aufsätze zur Geschichte der Gottesdienstlichen Musik*, edited by Walter Blankenburg, 17–30. Göttingen, 1979.

Blauner, Robert. "Death and Social Structure." *Psychiatry* 29 (1966): 378–394.

Bloch-Smith, Elizabeth M. "The Cult of the Dead in Judah: Interpreting the Material Remains." *JBL* 111 (1992): 213–224.

Blum, Elisabeth. "Tod und Begräbnis in evangelischen Kirchenliedern aus dem 16. Jahrhundert." In *Studien zur Thematik des Todes im 16. Jahrhundert*, edited by Paul Richard Blum, 97–110. Wolfenbütteler Forschungen 22. Wolfenbüttel, 1983.

Boccaccio, Giovanni. *The Decameron: A New Translation*. Edited by Mark Musa and Peter E. Bondanella. New York, 1977.

Boettcher, Susan R. "The Rhetoric of 'Seelsorge' for Miners in the Sermons of Cyriakus Spangenberg." In *Frömmigkeit—Theologie—Frömmigkeitstheologie: Contributions to European Church History. Festschrift für Berndt Hamm zum 60. Geburtstag*, edited by Gudrun Litz, Heidrun Munzert, and Roland Liebenberg, 453–466. SHCT 124. Leiden, 2005.

Böhmer, Wolfgang. "Martin Luther und das Wittenberger Medizinalwesen zu seiner Zeit." *Die Zeichen der Zeit* 37 (1983): 107–116.

Boutcher, Warren. "Literature, Thought or Fact? Past and Present Directions in the Study of the Early Modern Letter." In *Self-Presentation and Social Identification: The Rhetoric and Pragmatics of Letter Writing in Early Modern Times*, edited by Toon Van Houdt et al., 137–163. Supplementa Humanistica Lovaniensia 18. Leuven, 2002.

Bouwsma, William J. "Conclusion: Retrospect and Prospect." In *Facing Death: Where Culture, Religion, and Medicine Meet*, edited by Howard M. Spiro, Mary G. McCrea Curnen, and Lee Palmer Wandel, 189–198. New Haven, 1996.

Bowlby, John. "Processes of Mourning." *International Journal of Psycho-Analysis* 42 (1961): 317–340.

Branson, Roy. "Is Acceptance a Denial of Death? Another Look at Kübler-Ross." *ChrCent* 92 (1975): 464–468.

Bräuer, Siegfried. "The Genesis and Transmission of the Texts." In *"Vom Christlichen abschied aus diesem tödlichen Leben des Ehrwirdigen Herrn D. Martini Lutheri": Drei zeitgenössische Texte zum Tode D. Martin Luthers*. Stuttgart, 1996.

Brecht, Martin. "Zum Verständnis von Luthers Lied, 'Ein feste Burg.'" *ARG* 70 (1979): 106–121.

———. *Martin Luther*. 3 vols. Translated by James L. Schaaf. Minneapolis, 1985–1993.

———. "Review of Marius, *Martin Luther: The Christian between God and Death*." *Church History* 69 (2000): 143–147.

———. "Luthers reformatorische Sermone." In *Fides et Pietas. Festschrift Martin Brecht zum 70. Geburtstag*, edited by Christian Peters and Jürgen Kampmann, 15–32. Historia profana et ecclesiastica 8. Münster, 2003.

Brednick, Rolf Wilhelm. *Die Liedpublizistik im Flugblatt des 15. Bis 17. Jahrhunderts*. Vol. 1, *Abhandlung*. Baden-Baden, 1974.

Bregman, Lucy. *Beyond Silence and Denial: Death and Dying Reconsidered*. Louisville, Ky., 1999.

———. *Death and Dying, Spirituality and Religions: A Study of the Death Awareness Movement*. American University Studies in Theology and Religion 228. New York, 2003.

Brett, Allan S. and Abigail Zuger. "The Run on Tamiflu—Should Physicians Prescribe on Demand?" *NEMJ* 353 (2005): 2636–2637.

Brice, Charles W. "Paradoxes of Maternal Mourning." *Psychiatry* 54 (1991): 1–12.

Brodde, Otto. "'Ein neues Lied wir heben an'! Martin Luther als 'Phonascus.'" *Luther* 34 (1963): 72–82.

Brody, Jane E. "Facing Up to the Inevitable: In Search of a Good Death." *New York Times*, 30 December 2003, F5.

———. "Doctors Should Keep Bonds to Dying Patients." *Minneapolis Star-Tribune*, 12 August 2004, E10.

Bornkamm, Heinrich. *Luther in Mid-Career, 1521–1530*. Edited by Karin Bornkamm. Translated by E. Theodore Bachmann. Philadelphia, 1983.

Broeck, John. "Music of the Fears." *Film Comment* 12 (1976): 56–60.

Brooks, Peter Newman. "A Lily Ungilded? Martin Luther, the Virgin Mary and the Saints." *Journal of Religious History* 13 (1984): 136–149.

Brown, Christopher Boyd. *Singing the Gospel: Lutheran Hymns and the Success of the Reformation*. Cambridge, Mass., 2005.

Brown, Peter. *The Cult of the Saints: Its Rise and Function in Latin Christianity*. Haskell Lectures on the History of Religions 2. Chicago, 1981.

Bryant, Clifton D., ed. *Handbook of Death and Dying*. 2 vols. Thousand Oaks, Calif., 2003.

Bryant, Martel C. "Commentary: Fathers Grieve, Too." *Journal of Perinatology* 9 (1989): 437–441.

Bubenheimer, Ulrich. "Andreas Rudolff Bodenstein von Karlstadt: Sein Leben, seine Herkunft und seine inner Entwicklung." In *Andreas Bodenstein von Karlstadt, 500—Jahr-Feier: Festschrift der Stadt Karlstadt zum Jubiläumsjahr 1980*, edited by Wolfgang Merklein, 19–28. Karlstadt, 1980.

Buchwald, Georg. *Zur Wittenberger Stadt- und Universitäts-Geschichte in der Reformationszeit: Briefe aus Wittenberg an M. Stephan Roth in Zwickau.* Leipzig, 1893.

Burke, Kenneth. *Counter-Statement.* 2nd ed. Berkeley, 1953. Reprint, 1968.

Burnett, Amy Nelson. "'To Oblige My Brethren': The Reformed Funeral Sermons of Johann Brandmüller." *SCJ* 36 (2005): 37–54.

Burschel, Peter. *Sterben und Unsterblichkeit: Zur Kultur des Martyriums in der frühen Neuzeit.* Ancien Régime Aufklärung und Revolution 35. Münich, 2004.

Buszin, Walter E. "Theology and Church Music as Bearers and Interpreters of the *Verbum Dei.*" *CTM* 32 (1961): 15–27.

Callahan, Daniel. "Death and the Research Imperative." *NEMJ* 432 (2 March 2000): 546–556.

Cameron, Jackie. "Palliative Care: Suffering and Healing at the End of Life." In *Aging, Death, and the Quest for Immortality*, edited by C. Ben Mitchell, Robert D. Orr, and Susan A. Salladay. 134–149. Grand Rapids, 2004.

Cantor, Norman F. *In the Wake of the Plague: The Black Death and the World That It Made.* New York, 2001.

Carmichael, Ann G. *Plague and the Poor in Renaissance Florence.* Cambridge, 1986.

Carpenter, Ronald H. "Essential Schemes of Syntax: An Analysis of Rhetorical Theory's Recommendations for Uncommon Word Orders." *Quarterly Journal of Speech* 55 (1969): 161–168.

Carson, D. A. *How Long, O Lord? Reflections on Suffering and Evil.* Grand Rapids, 1990.

———. "On Distorting the Love of God." *BSac* 156 (1993): 3–12.

Casey, Paul F. "'Start Spreading the News': Martin Luther's First Published Song." In *In Laudem Caroli: Renaissance and Reformation Studies for Charles G. Nauert*, edited by James V. Mehl, 75–94. SCES 49. Kirksville, Mo., 1998.

Cheshire, William P., Jr. "In Search of the Philosopher's Clone: Immortality through Replication." In *Aging, Death, and the Quest for Immortality*, edited by C. Ben Mitchell, Robert D. Orr, and Susan A. Salladay, 175–192. Grand Rapids, 2004.

Childe, Gordon V. "Directional Changes in Funerary Practices During 50,000 Years." *Man* 45 (January–February 1945): 13–19.

Clark, John C. "Luther's View of Cross-Bearing." *BSac* 163 (2006): 335–347.

Clemen, Otto. "Die ersten Märtyrer des evangelischen Glaubens." *Beiträge zur Reformationsgeschichte aus Büchern und Handschriften der zwickauer Ratsschulbibliothek* 1 (1900–1903): 40–52.

———. "Zum St. Annenkultus im ausgehenden Mittelalter." *ARG* 21 (1924): 251–253.

Clifford, Cornelius. "St. Athanasius." *Catholic Encyclopedia on CD-ROM.* <http://www.newadvent.org/cathen/02035a.htm>. Accessed 22 August 2006.

Cohn, Samuel K., Jr. *The Black Death Transformed: Disease and Culture in Early Renaissance Europe.* London, 2002.

Collopy, Bartholomew J. "Theology and the Darkness of Death." *Theological Studies* 39 (1978): 22–54.

Coontz, S. *The Way We Never Were: American Families and the Nostalgia Trap.* New York, 1992.

Cornette, James C., Jr. *Proverbs and Proverbial Expressions in the German Works of Martin Luther.* Edited by Wolfgang Mieder and Dorothee Racette. Sprichwörterforschung 19. Bern, 1997.

Cornick, David. "The Reformation Crisis in Pastoral Care." In *A History of Pastoral Care*, edited by G. R. Evans, 223–234. London, 2000.

Corpus documentorum inquisitionis haereticae pravitatis neerlandicae. Edited by Paul Dredericq. Ghent, 1889–1902.

Corr, Charles A.; Clyde M. Nabe; and Donna M. Corr. *Death and Dying, Life and Living.* 4th ed. Belmont, Calif., 2003.

Crawford, O. C. "Laudatio Funebris." *Classical Journal* 37 (1941): 17–27.

Cutler, David M., Allison B. Rosen, and Sandeep Vijan. "The Value of Medical Spending in the United States, 1960–2000." *NEMJ* 355 (2006): 920–927.

D. Martin Luthers Werke: Kritische Gesamtausgabe. 67 vols. Weimar, 1883–1997.

D. Martin Luthers Werke: Kritische Gesamtausgabe, Briefwechsel. 15 vols. Weimar, 1930–1978.

D. Martin Luthers Werke: Kritische Gesamtausgabe, Tischreden. 6 vols. Weimar, 1912–1921.

Dabney, Lyle D. "Review of Marius, *Martin Luther: The Christian between God and Death.*" *Theological Studies* 61 (2000): 156–158.

Dalferth, Ingolf U. "'I Determine What God Is!': Theology in the Age of 'Cafeteria Religion.'" *Theology Today* 57 (2000): 5–23.

Davis, Marion et al. "Incorporating Palliative Care into Critical Care Education: Principles, Challenges, and Opportunities." *Critical Care Medicine* 27 (1999): 2005–2013.

Davis, Natalie Zemon. "Some Tasks and Themes in the Study of Popular Religion." In *The Pursuit of Holiness in Late Medieval and Renaissance Religion: Papers From the University of Michigan Conference on Late Medieval and Renaissance Religion,* edited by Charles Trinkaus and Heiko A. Oberman, 307–336. SMRT 10. Leiden, 1974.

D'Avray, David. "The Comparative Study of Memorial Preaching." *Transactions of the Royal Historical Society* 40 (1990): 25–42.

Deffner, Donald L. "Proclaiming Life in Death: The Funeral Sermon." *CTQ* 58 (1994): 5–24.

Delehaye, Père H. *The Legends of the Saints: An Introduction to Hagiography.* Translated by V. M. Crawford. Notre Dame, 1961.

Delumeau, Jean. *Sin and Fear: The Emergence of a Western Guilt Culture, 13th–18th Centuries.* Translated by Eric Nicholson. New York, 1990.

der Veer, E. van. "Ars Moriendi bij Luther." *Gereformeerd theologisch tijdschrift* 96 (1996): 20–30.

Derwein, Herbert. *Geschichte des Christlichen Friedhofs in Deutschland.* Frankfurt, 1931.

Dipko, Thomas E. "The Paradox of the Funeral Order." *CW* 38, no. 3 (2004–2005): 15–20.

Donaldson, Peter J. "Denying Death: A Note Regarding Some Ambiguities in the Current Discussion." *Omega* 3 (1972): 285–290.

Donne, John. *Holy Sonnets.* <http://www.luminarium.org/sevenlit/donne/sonnet10.htm>. Accessed 20 October 2005.

Dörfler-Dierken, Angelika. "Luther und die heilige Anna." *LuJ* 64 (1997): 19–46.

Dornmeier, Heinrich. "Religiös motiviertes Verhalten von Laien und Klerikern in Grenz- und Krisensituationen: die Pest als 'Testfall wahrer Frömmigkeit.'" In *Laienfrömmigkeit im späten Mittelalter: Formen, Funktionen, politisch-soziale Zusammenhänge.* Edited by Klaus Schreiner, 331–397. Schriften des Historischen Kollegs, Kolloquien 20. Munich, 1992.

Dost, Timothy P. *Renaissance Humanism in Support of the Gospel in Luther's Early Correspondence: Taking All Things Captive.* Aldershot, 2001.

Downey, Michael, ed. *The New Dictionary of Catholic Spirituality.* Collegeville, Minn., 1993, s.v., "Saints, Communion of."

Duffy, Eamon. "An Apology for Grief, Fear and Anger." *Priests & People* 5 (1991): 397–401.

——. "Review of Marius, *Martin Luther: The Christian between God and Death.*" *Commonweal,* 10 September 1999.

Dugan, Eileen T. "The Funeral Sermon as a Key to Familial Values in Early Modern Nördlingen." *SCJ* 20 (1989): 631–644.

Dumont, Richard G. and Dennis C. Foss. *The American View of Death: Acceptance or Denial?* Cambridge, Mass., 1972.

Durgnat, Raymond. "Rock, Rhythm and Dance." *British Journal of Aesthetics* 11 (1971): 28–47.

Durlak, Joseph A. and Lee Ann Riesenberg. "The Impact of Death Education." *DS* 15 (1991): 39–58.

Dyregrov, Atle and Stig Berge Matthiesen. "Similarities and Differences in Mothers' and Fathers' Grief Following the Death of an Infant." *Scandinavian Journal of Psychology* 28 (1987): 1–15.

Ebeling, Gerhard. "Des Todes Tod: Luthers Theologie der Konfrontation mit dem Tode." *Zeitschrift für Theologie und Kirche* 84 (1987): 162–194.

——. "Der theologische Grundzug der Seelsorge Luthers." In *Luther als Seelsorger*, edited by Joachim Heubach, 21–48. Veröffentlichungen der Luther-Akademie e. V. Ratzeburg 18. Erlangen, 1991.

——. "Luthers Gebrauch der Wortfamilie 'Seelsorge.'" *LuJ* 61 (1994): 7–44.

——. "Trostbriefe Luthers an Leidtragende." In *Kirche in der Schule Luthers; Festschrift für D. Joachim Heubach*, edited by Bengt Hägglung and Gerhard Müller, 37–48. Erlangen, 1995.

——. *Luthers Seelsorge: Theologie in der Vielfalt der Lebenssituationen an seinen Briefen dargestellt.* Tübingen, 1997.

Edwards, Mark U. "Review of Marius, *Martin Luther: The Christian between God and Death*." *ChrCent*, 17 November 1999.

Eire, Carlos M. N. *War Against the Idols: The Reformation of Worship from Erasmus to Calvin.* Cambridge, 1986.

Ellison, Christopher G. and Jeffrey S. Levin. "The Religion-Health Connection: Evidence, Theory, and Future Directions." *Health Education & Behavior* 25 (1998): 700–720.

Elze, Martin. "Spätmittelalterliche Predigt im Angesicht des Todes." In *Leben angesichts des Todes: Beiträge zum theologischen Problem des Todes: Helmut Theilicke zum 60. Geburtstag*, edited by Bernhard Lohse and H. P. Schmidt, 89–99. Tübingen, 1968.

Endriß, Albrecht. "Nachfolgung des willigen Sterbens Christi." In *Kontinuität und Umbruch: Theologie und Frömmigkeit in Flugschriften und Kleinliteratur an der Wende vom 15. Zum 16. Jahrhundert*, edited by Josef Nolte, Hella Tompert, and Christof Windhorst, 93–141. Beiträge zum Tübinger Kolloquium des Sonder-forschungsbereichs 8. Stuttgart, 1978.

Engel, George L. "Is Grief a Disease?" *Psychosomatic Medicine* 23 (1961): 19–22.

Erasmus, Desiderius. *On the Writing of Letters.* Translated by Charles Fantazzi. In *Collected Works of Erasmus.* Vol. 25. Edited by J. K. Sowards. Toronto, 1985.

Erdmann, D. "Luther und seine Beziehungen zu Schlesien, insbesondere zu Breslau." *Schriften des Vereins für Reformationsgeschichte* 5 (1887): 1–75.

Erwin, Guy R. "Flesh Made Words: Luther's Reform of Piety." Paper presented at the North American Luther Forum, Luther Seminary, St. Paul, Minn., 28–30 April 2006.

Eybl, F. M. "Leichenpredigt und Leichenrede." In *Historisches Wörterbuch der Rhetorik*, edited by Gert Ueding et al., 5:124–151. Tübingen, 2001.

Fairclough, H. Rushton, trans. *Horace: Satires, Epistles and Ars Poetica.* London, 1961.

Falck, Robert. "Parody and Contrafactum: A Terminological Clarification." *The Musical Quarterly* 65 (1979): 1–2.

Farrell, James J. *Inventing the American Way of Death, 1830–1920.* Philadelphia, 1980.

Fern, Sister Mary Edmond. *The Latin Consolatio as A Literary Type.* St. Meinrad, Ind., 1941.

Ferngren, Gary B. "Early Christianity as A Religion of Healing." *BHM* 66 (1992): 1–15.

Ferre, John P. "Last Words: Death and Public Self-Expression." In *Quoting God: How*

Media Shape Ideas about Religion and Culture, edited by Claire H. Badaracco, 129–142. Waco, Tex., 2005.

Fields, Rona M. *Martyrdom: The Psychology, Theology, and Politics of Self-Sacrifice*. Westport, Conn., 2004.

Finucane, R. C. "Sacred Corpse, Profane Carrion: Social Ideals and Death Rituals in the Later Middle Ages." In *Mirrors of Mortality: Studies in the Social History of Death*, edited by Joachim Whaley, 40–60. New York, 1981.

Fischer, Mary A. "Thrills That Kill" *Reader's Digest*, February 2006, 116–122.

Fleischer, Manfred P. "Silesiographia: The Rise of a Regional Historiography." *ARG* 69 (1978): 219–247.

———. "Humanism and Reformation in Silesia: Imprints of Italy—Celtis, Erasmus, Luther, and Melanchthon." In *The Harvest of Humanism in Central Europe: Essays in Honor of Lewis W. Spitz*, edited by Manfred P. Fleischer, 27–107. St. Louis, 1992.

Foley, Edward. "Martin Luther: A Model Pastoral Musician." *Currents in Theology & Mission* 14 (1987): 405–418.

Freud, Sigmund. "On Mourning and Melancholia." London, 1917. Reprint, *The Standard Edition of the Complete Psychological Works of Sigmund Freud*, 14:237–258. London, 1959.

Friedländer, Max J. and Jakob Rosenberg. *The Paintings of Lucas Cranach*. Rev. ed. Ithaca, 1978.

Frith, Simon. *Performing Rites: On the Value of Popular Music*. Cambridge, Mass., 1996.

Fudge, Thomas A. "'The Shouting Hus': Heresy Appropriated as Propaganda in the Sixteenth Century." *Communio Viatorum* 38 (1996): 197–231.

Fulton, Robert L. "The Clergyman and the Funeral Director: A Study in Role Conflict." *Social Forces* 39 (1961): 317–323.

Gaines, Robert. "Detachment and Continuity: The Two Tasks of Mourning." *Contemporary Psychoanalysis* 33 (1997): 549–571.

Garces-Foley, Kathleen and Justin S. Holcomb. "Contemporary American Funerals: Personalizing Tradition." In *Death and Religion in a Changing World*, edited by Kathleen Garces-Foley, 207–277. Armonk, N.Y., 2006.

Geary, Patrick J. "The Saint and the Shrine: The Pilgrims' Goal in the Middle Ages." In *Walfahrt kennt keine Grenzen*, edited by Lenz Kriss-Rettenbeck and Gerda Möhler, 265–274. Munich, 1984.

———. *Living With the Dead in the Middle Ages*. Ithaca, 1994.

Gerke, Friedrich. "Die satanische Anfechtung in der ars moriendi und bei Martin Luther." *Theologische Blätter* 11 (1932): 321–332.

———. "Anfechtung und Sakrament in Martin Luthers Sermon von Sterben." *Theologische Blätter* 13 (1934): 193–204.

Gerson, Gary S. "The Psychology of Grief and Mourning in Judaism." *Journal of Religion and Health* 16 (1977): 260–274.

Gill, Philip. "Death in The Christian Community: Theology, Funeral Ritual and Pastoral Care From the Perspective of Victor Turner's Ritual Process Model." *Modern Believing* 35, no. 2 (1994): 17–24.

Goez, Werner. "Luthers 'Ein Sermon von der Bereitung zum Sterben' und die spätmittelalterliche ars moriendi." *LuJ* 48 (1981): 97–114.

Gorer, Geoffrey. "The Pornography of Death." *Encounter* 5 (October 1955): 49–52.

———. *Death, Grief, and Mourning*. Garden City, N.Y., 1965.

———. *Death, Grief, and Contemporary Mourning in Britain*. London, 1965.

Goss, Robert E. and Dennis Klass. *Dead but Not Lost: Grief Narratives in Religious Traditions*. Walnut Creek, Calif., 2005.

Götze, Alfred. *Frühneuhochdeutsches Glossar*. 7th ed. Berlin, 1967.

Gray, Francine Du Plessix. "At Large and At Small: The Work of Mourning," *The American Scholar* 69 (summer 2000): 7–13.

Gray, Madeline. *The Protestant Reformation: Belief, Practice and Tradition*. Brighton, 2003.

Gregory, Brad S. "Prescribing and Describing Martyrdom: Menno's *Troestelijke Vermaninge* and *Het Offer des Heeren*." *MQR* 71 (1997): 603–613.

——. *Salvation at Stake: Christian Martyrdom in Early Modern Europe*. Harvard Historical Studies 134. Cambridge, Mass., 1999.

——. "Late Medieval Religiosity and the Renaissance of Christian Martyrdom in the Reformation Era." In *Continuity and Change: The Harvest of Late Medieval and Reformation History. Essays Presented to Heiko A. Oberman on his 70th Birthday*, edited by Robert J. Bast and Andrew C. Gow, 379–399. Leiden, 2000.

——. "Martyrs and Saints," *A Companion to the Reformation World*. Edited by R. Po-chia Hsia, 455–470. Malden, Maine, 2004.

Grindal, Gracia. "The Rhetoric of Martin Luther's Hymns: Hymnody Then and Now." *WW* 26 (2006): 178–187.

Gruman, Gerard J. "Ethics of Death and Dying: Historical Perspective." *Omega* 9 (1978–1979): 203–237.

Grün, Hugo. "Die Leichenrede im Rahmen der kirchlichen Beerdigung im 16. Jahrhundert." *Theologische Studien und Kritiken: Beiträge für Theologie und Religionswissenschaft* 95/96 (1929): 289–312.

——. "Das kirchliche Begräbniswesen im ausgehenden Mittelalter." *Theologische Studien und Kritiken* 102 (1930): 341–381.

Gubbins, James P. "Grief's Lesson in Moral Epistemology: A Phenomenological Investigation." *The Annual of the Society of Christian Ethics* 17 (1997): 145–165.

Gutierrez, David. *The Augustinians from the Protestant Reformation to the Peace of Westphalia 1518–1648*. History of the Order of St. Augustine 2. Villanova, 1979.

Haas, Alois M. "Didaktik des Sterbens: Zur Botschaft der spätmittelalterlichen Sterbebüchlein." In *Gewißheit angesichts des Sterbens*, edited by Reinhard Schwarz, 13–31. Veröffentlichungen der Luther-Akademie e. V. Ratzeburg 28. Erlangen, 1998.

Hadaway, C. Kirk and Penny Long Marler. "How Many Americans Attend Worship Each Week? An Alternative Approach to Measurement." *Journal for the Scientific Study of Religion* 44 (2005): 307–322.

Hagens, Gunther von. "Body Worlds: The Anatomical Exhibition of Real Human Bodies." <http://www.bodyworlds.com/index.html>. Accessed 1 September 2006.

Hagman, George. "Death of a Selfobject: Toward a Self Psychology of the Mourning Process." *Progress in Self-Psychology* 11 (1995): 189–205.

——. "Mourning: A Review and Reconsideration." *International Journal of Psycho-Analysis* 76 (1995): 909–925.

——. "Bereavement and Neurosis." *Journal of the American Academy of Psychoanalysis* 23 (1995): 635–653.

——. "The Role of the Other in Mourning." *Psychoanalytic Quarterly* 65 (1996): 327–352.

——. "Beyond Decathexis: Toward A New Psychoanalytic Understanding and Treatment of Mourning." In *Meaning Reconstruction and the Experience of Loss*, edited by Robert A. Neimeyer, 13–31. Washington, D.C., 2001.

Hahn, Gerhard. *Evangelium als literarische Anweisung: Zu Luthers Stellung in der Geschichte des deutschen kirchlichen Liedes*. Munich, 1981.

——. "Zur Dimension des Neuen an Luthers Kirchenliedern." *Jahrbuch für Liturgik und Hymnologie* 26 (1982): 96–103.

——. ed. *Martin Luther. Die geistlichen Lieder*. Tübingen, 1967.

Haile, H. G. "Luther and Literacy." *Publications of the Modern Language Association* 91 (1976): 816–828.

——. "Luther as Renaissance Writer." in *The Renaissance and Reformation Germany: An Introduction*, edited by Gerhart Hoffmeister, 141–156. New York, 1977.

——. *Luther: An Experiment in Biography*. Garden City, N.Y., 1980.

Hanson, Mark J. "Defining Health and Health-Related Concepts: Conceptual and Theological Considerations." *WW* 21 (2001): 23–31.

Harding, Vanessa. "Burial Choice and Burial Location in Later Medieval London." In

Death in Towns: Urban Responses to the Dying and the Dead, 100–1600, edited by Steven Bassett, 119–135. London, 1992.

Hargrove, Thomas and Guido H. Stempel III. "Truth or Fiction? Poll: Most Don't Believe in Resurrection." Scripps Howard News Service, 15 April 2006, <http://www.newspolls.org/story.php?story_id=54>. Accessed 21 April 2006.

Harris, Shane. "The Bug Bloggers." *Bulletin of the Atomic Scientists* 62 (2006): 38–43.

Hauerwas, Stanley. "Reflections on Suffering, Death, and Medicine." In *Suffering Presence*, 23–38. Notre Dame, Ind., 1986.

Haustein, Manfred. "Luther als Prediger." *Standpunkt* 11 (April 1983): 93–95.

Hatcher, John. *Plague, Population and the English Economy 1348–1530*. London, 1977.

Hawkins, Anne Hunsaker. "Constructing Death: Three Pathographies about Dying." *Omega* 22 (1990–1991): 301–317.

Hayward, Paul Antony. "Demystifying the Role of Sanctity in Western Christendom." In *The Cult of Saints in Late Antiquity and the Middle Ages: Essays on the Contribution of Peter Brown*, edited by James Howard-Johnston and Paul Antony Hayward, 115–142. Oxford, 1999.

Hebenstreit-Wilfert, Hildegard. "Märtyrerflugschriften der Reformationszeit." In *Flugschriften als Massenmedium der Reformationszeit: Beiträge zum Tübinger Symposion 1980*, edited by Hans-Joachim Köhler, 397–446. Stuttgart, 1981.

Helm, Jürgen. "Wittenberger Medizin im 16. Jahrhundert," *Martin Luther und seiner Universität: Vorträge analßlich des 450. Todestages des Reformators, in Auftrag der Stiftung Leucorea an der Martin-Luther-Universität-Halle-Wittenberg*, edited by Heiner Lück, 95–115. Cologne, 1998.

Helmer, Christine. *The Trinity and Martin Luther: A Study on the Relationship between Genre, Language and the Trinity in Luther's Works (1523–1546)*. Veröffentlichungen des Instituts für Europäische Geschichte Mainz, Abteilung abendländische Religionsgeschichte 174. Mainz, 1999.

Heming, Carol Piper. *Protestants and the Cult of the Saints in German-Speaking Europe, 1517–1531*. SCES. Kirksville, Mo., 2003.

Henderson, John. "The Black Death in Florence." In *Death in Towns: Urban Responses to the Dying and the Dead, 100–1600*, edited by Steven Bassett, 136–150. London, 1992.

Henderson, Judith Rice. "Defining the Genre of the Letter: Juan Luis Vives' *De Conscribendis Epistolis*," *Renaissance and Reformation* 7 (1983): 89–105.

——. "On Reading the Rhetoric of the Renaissance Letter" In *Renaissance Rhetoric*, edited by Heinrich F. Plett, 143–162. Berlin, 1993.

——. "Humanist Letter Writing: Private Conversation or Public Forum?" In *Self-Presentation and Social Identification*, edited by Toon Van Houdt et al., 17–38. Supplementa Humanistica Lovaniensia 18. Leuven, 2002.

Hendrix, Scott. "Review of Marius, *Martin Luther: The Christian between God and Death*." *Theology Today* 56 (October 1999).

——. "Angelic Piety in the Reformation: The Good and Bad Angels of Urbanus Rhegius." In *Frömmigkeit—Theologie—Frömmigkeitstheologie: Contributions to European Church History. Festschrift für Berndt Hamm zum 60. Geburtstag*, edited by Gudrun Litz, Heidrun Munzert, and Roland Liebenberg, 385–94. SHCT 124. Leiden, 2005.

Herl, Joseph. *Worship Wars in Early Lutheranism: Choir, Congregation, and Three Centuries of Conflict*. Oxford, 2005.

Herlihy, David. *The Black Death and the Transformation of the West*. Edited by Samuel K. Cohn Jr. Cambridge, Mass., 1997.

Hinton, John. "Whom Do Dying Patients Tell?" *British Medical Journal* 281 (1980): 1328–1330.

Hitt, Jack. "The American Way of Death Becomes America's Way of Life." *New York Times*, 18 August 2002, Week in Review 1, 6.

Hobson, Katherine. "Are We Ready?" *U.S. News and World Report*, 1 May 2006, 57–62.

Hogg, Charles R., Jr. "The Ever-Virgin Mary: Athanasius to Gerhard." *LuthFor*, winter 2004, 18–23.

———. "The Ever-Virgin Mary: Gerhard to the Present." *LuthFor*, spring 2005, 36–39.

Holifield, E. Brooks. *A History of Pastoral Care in America: From Salvation to Self-Realization.* Nashville, 1983.

Holloway, Paul A. "*Bona Cogitare*: An Epicurean Consolation in Phil. 4:8–9." *HTR* 91 (1998): 89–96.

Holmes, Chris. *Spores, Plagues and History: The Story of Anthrax.* Dallas, 2003.

Howes, Frank. "A Critique of Folk, Popular and 'Art' Music." *British Journal of Aesthetics* 2 (1962): 239–248.

Hoyert, D. L. et al., "Deaths: Final Data for 1999." *National Vital Statistics Reports* 49, no. 8. Hyattsville, Md., 2001.

Hughes, Robert G. *A Trumpet in Darkness: Preaching to Mourners.* Philadelphia, 1985.

Hull, Robert F., Jr. "The Myth of Luther's Barroom Music and A Plea for a Theology of Church Music." *Christian Standard*, 4 May 2003, 4–5.

Huntington, Richard and Peter Metcalf. *Celebrations of Death: The Anthropology of Mortuary Ritual.* Cambridge, 1979.

Ihlenfeld, Kurt. "Die himmlische Kunst Musica: Ein Blick in Luthers Briefe." *Luther* 34 (1963): 83–90.

Imhof, Arthur E. "From the Old Mortality Pattern to the New: Implications of A Radical Change From the Sixteenth to the Twentieth Century." *BHM* 59 (1985): 1–29.

———. "An *Ars Moriendi* for Our Time: To Live a Fulfilled Life; to Die a Peaceful Death." In Spiro, Curnen, and Wandel, eds., *Facing Death*, 114–120.

———. *Lost Worlds: How Our European Ancestors Coped with Everyday Life and Why Life is So Hard Today.* Translated by Thomas Robisheau. Charlottesville, Va., 1996.

International Theological Commission. "Some Current Questions in Eschatology." *Irish Theological Quarterly* 48 (1992): 209–243.

Irish, Donald P. "Diversity in Universality: Dying, Death and Grief." In *The Unknown Country: Death in Australia, Britain and the USA*, edited by Kathy Charmaz, Glennys Howarth, and Allan Kellehear, 242–256. Houndmills, U.K., 1997.

Irwin, Joyce. "Shifting Alliances: The Struggle for a Lutheran Theology of Music." *Journal of the American Academy of Religion Thematic Studies* 50, no. 1 (1983): 55–69.

Ishida, Yoshiro. "Luther the Pastor." In *Piety, Politics, and Ethics: Reformation Studies in Honor of George Wolfgang Forell*, edited by Carter Lindberg, 27–37. SCES 3. Kirksville, Mo., 1984.

James, John W. and Frank Cherry. *The Grief Recovery Handbook.* New York, 1988.

James, Nicky and David Field. "The Routinization of Hospice: Charisma and Bureaucratization." *SSM* 34 (1992): 1363–1375.

Jardine, Lisa. "Before Clarissa: Erasmus, 'Letters of Obscure Men,' and Epistolary Fictions." In Van Houdt, et al., ed. *Self Presentation and Social Identification.* 385–403.

Jenny, Markus. "The Hymns of Zwingli and Luther: A Comparison." In *Cantors at the Crossroads: Essays on Church Music in Honor of Walter E. Buszin*, edited by Johannes Riedel, 45–63. St. Louis, 1967.

———. "Der Märtyrertod zweier Gesinnungsgenossen in Brüssel ließ Luther zum Lied als dem besten Medium der Propaganda für den neuen Glauben greifen." *Martin Luther und die Reformation in Deutschland*, 296–297. Frankfurt, 1983.

———. *Luther—Zwingli—Calvin in ihren Liedern.* Zürich, 1983.

———. *Luthers Geistliche Lieder und Kirchengesänge: Vollständige Neuedition in Ergänzung zu Band 35 der Weimarer Ausgabe.* Cologne, 1985, s. v., "Ein neues Lied wir heben an," 75–76.

Johann von Staupitzens Sämmtliche Werke. Edited by J. F. K. Knaake. Vol. 1, *Deutsche Schriften.* Potsdam, 1867.

Jones, Ken Sundet. "The Apocalyptic Luther." *WW* 25 (2005): 308–316.

Jordahn, Ottfried. "Sterbebegleitung und Begräbnis bei Martin Luther." In *Liturgie im Angesicht des Todes: Reformatorische und katholische Traditionen der Neuzeit*, edited by Hansjakob Becker and Michael Fischer, 1–22.Tübingen, 2004.

Jørgensen, Ninna. "'*Sed manet articulus*': Preaching and Catechetical Training in Selected Sermons by the Later Luther." *Studia Theologica* 59 (2005): 38–54.

Jörns, Klaus-Peter. "Luther als Seelsorger." *Wege zum Menschen* 37 (1985): 489–498.

Jüngel, Eberhard. *Death: The Riddle and the Mystery*. Translated by Iain and Ute Nicoll. Philadelphia, 1975.

Karant-Nunn, Susan C. *The Reformation of Ritual: An Interpretation of Early Modern Germany*. London, 1997.

———. "'Not Like the Unreasoning Beasts': Rhetorical Efforts to Separate Humans and Animals in Early Modern Germany." In *Cultures of Communication from Reformation to Enlightenment: Constructing Publics in the Early Modern German Lands*, edited by James Van Horn Melton, 225–238. Aldershot, 2002.

———. "'Fast ware mir ein weibliches Gemüt verblieben': Martin Luthers Männlichkeit." In *Luther zwischen den Kulturen*, edited by Hans Medick and Peer Schmidt, 49–65. Göttingen, 2004.

———. "'Christians' Mourning and Lament Should not Be Like the Heathens': The Suppression of Religious Emotion in the Reformation." *Confessionalization in Europe 1555–1700: Essays in Honor and Memory of Bodo Nischan*, edited by John M. Headley, Hans J. Hillerbrand, and Anthony J. Papalas, 107–129. Aldershot, 2004.

Karant-Nunn, Susan C. and Merry Wiesner-Hanks, eds. *Luther on Women: A Sourcebook*. Cambridge, 2003.

Kastenbaum, Robert. *Death, Society, & Human Experience*. St. Louis, 1977.

———. "Ars Moriendi." In *Encyclopedia of Death*. Edited by Robert and Beatrice Kastenbaum, 17–19. Phoenix, Ariz., 1989).

Kauffman, Jeffrey. "Dissociative Functions in the Normal Mourning Process." *Omega* 28 (1993–1994): 31–38.

Kawerau, G., ed. *Vierzehn Trostmittel für Mühlselige und Beladene*. In *Luthers Werke für das christliche haus*. Edited by G. Buchwald et al. Vol. 7. *Erbauliche Schriften*, 5–60. Braunschweig, 1891.

Kellehear, Allan. "Are We A 'Death-Denying' Society? A Sociological Review." *SSM* 18 (1984): 713–723.

———. *Experiences Near Death*. New York, 1996.

Keller, Rudolf. "Luther als Seelsorger und theologischer Berater der zerstreuten Gemeinden." *Kirche in der Schule Luthers: Festschrift für D. Joachim Heubach*, edited by Bengt Hägglund and Gerhard Müller, 58–78. Erlangen, 1995.

———. "Luther als Seelsorger." *Lutherische Kirche in der Welt* 44 (1997): 101–118.

Kieckhefer, Richard. *Unquiet Souls: Fourteenth-Century Saints and Their Religious Milieu*. Chicago, 1984.

Kidd, B. J., ed. *Documents Illustrative of the Continental Reformation*. Oxford, 1911.

Klass, Dennis. "Elisabeth Kubler-Ross and the Tradition of the Private Sphere: An Analysis of Symbols." *Omega* 12 (1981–1982): 241–267.

———. "Self-help Groups for the Bereaved: Theory, Theology, and Practice." *Journal of Religion and Health* 21 (1982): 307–324.

———. "The Deceased Child in the Psychic and Social Worlds of Bereaved Parents During the Resolution of Grief." In *Continuing Bonds: New Understandings of Grief*, edited by Dennis Klass, Phyllis R. Silverman, and Steven L. Nickman, 199–215. Washington, D.C., 1996.

———. *The Spiritual Lives of Bereaved Parents*. Philadelphia, 1999.

———. "Grief, Religion, and Spirituality." In *Death and Religion in a Changing World*, edited by Kathleen Garces-Foley, 283–403. London, 2006.

Klass, Dennis and Richard A. Hutch. "Elisabeth Kubler-Ross as a Religious Leader." *Omega* 16 (1985–1986): 89–109.

Kleckley, Russell C. "Review of Marius, *Martin Luther: The Christian between God and Death.*" *Journal of Religion* 81 (2001): 643–644.

Klenow, Daniel J. and Robert C. Bolin. "Belief in An Afterlife: A National Survey." *Omega* 20 (1989–1990): 63–74.

Koenig, Harold G. and David B. Larson. "Use of Hospital Services, Religious Attendance, and Religious Affiliation." *Southern Medical Journal* 91 (1998): 925–932.

Koenig, Harold G.; Michael E. McCullough; and David B. Larson. *Handbook of Religion and Health.* Oxford, 2001.

Kohut, Heinz. "Observations on the Psychological Functions of Music." *Journal of the American Psychoanalytic Association* 5 (1957): 389–407.

Kolb, Robert. *For All The Saints: Changing Perceptions of Martyrdom and Sainthood in the Lutheran Reformation.* Macon, Ga., 1987.

———. "'Saint John Hus' and 'Jerome Savonarola, Confessor of God': The Lutheran 'Canonization' of Late Medieval Martyrs." *Concordia Journal* 17 (1991): 404–418.

———. "Burying the Brethren: Lutheran Funeral Sermons as Life-Writing." In *The Rhetorics of Life-Writing in Early Modern Europe: Forms of Biography from Cassandra Fedele to Louis XIV*, edited by Thomas F. Mayer and D. R. Woolf, 92–114. Ann Arbor, 1995.

———. "God's Gift of Martyrdom: The Early Reformation Understanding of Dying for the Faith." *Church History* 64 (1995): 399–411.

Kolde, Carl Adolph Julius. *Dr. Johann Heß, der schlesische Reformator.* Breslau, 1846.

Kopelman, Loretta M. "Normal Grief: Good or Bad? Health or Disease?" *Philosophy, Psychiatry, & Psychology* 1 (1994): 209–220.

Koslofsky, Craig M. "Death and Ritual in Reformation Germany." Ph.D. diss., University of Michigan, 1994.

———. "Die Trennung der Lebenden von den Toten: Friedhofverlegungen und die Reformation in Leipzig, 1536." In *Memoria als Kultur*, edited by Otto Gerhard Oexle, 335–385. Veröffentlichungen des Max-Planck-Instituts für Geschichte 121. Göttingen, 1995.

———. *The Reformation of the Dead: Death and Ritual in Early Modern Germany, 1450–1700.* London, 2000.

———. "Controlling the Body of the Suicide in Saxony." In *From Sin to Insanity: Suicide in Early Modern Europe*, edited by Jeffrey R. Watt, 48–63. Ithaca, 2004.

Krause, Gerhard. "Luthers Stellung zum Selbstmord: Ein Kapitel seiner Lehre und Praxis der Seelsorge." *Luther* 36 (1965): 50–71.

———. "Luther the *Seelsorger.*" *CTQ* 48 (1984): 153–163.

Kreeft, Peter. *Love Is Stronger Than Death.* San Francisco, 1992.

Kreitzer, Beth. "Luther Regarding the Virgin Mary." *LQ* 17 (2003): 249–266.

Krispin, Gerald. "The Consolation of the Resurrection in Luther." *Lutheran Theological Review* 2 (fall-winter 1989–1990): 38–51.

Krodel, Gottfried G. "Luther's Work on the Catechism in the Context of Late Medieval Catechetical Literature." *Concordia Journal* 25 (1999): 364–404.

Kroker, Ernst. *Katharina von Bora, Martin Luthers Frau: Ein Lebens- und Charakterbild.* Biographien bedeutender Frauen 6. Leipzig, 1906.

Krupp, George R. and Bernard Kligfeld. "The Bereavement Reaction: A Cross-Cultural Evaluation." *Journal of Religion and Health* 1 (1962): 222–246.

Kübler-Ross, Elisabeth. *On Death and Dying.* New York, 1969.

Laager, Jacques, ed. *Ars Moriendi: die Kunst, gut zu leben und gut zu sterben: Texte von Cicero bis Luther.* Zürich, 1996.

Labno, Jeannie. "Child Monuments in Renaissance Poland." *SCJ* 37 (2006): 351–374.

Lackmann, Max. "Thesaurus Sanctorum: Ein vergessener Beitrag Luthers zur Hagiologie." in *Festgabe Joseph Lortz.* Vol. 1, *Reformation, Schicksal und Auftrag*, edited by Erwin Iserloh and Peter Manns, 135–171. Baden-Baden, 1958.

———. *Verehrung der Heiligen: Versuch einer lutherischen Lehre von den Heiligen.* Stuttgart, 1958.

Laderman, Gary. *The Sacred Remains: American Attitudes Toward Death, 1799–1883*. New Haven, 1996.

Larson-Miller, Lizette. "Roman Catholic, Anglican, and Eastern Orthodox Approaches to Death." In Garces-Foley, ed. *Death and Religion in a Changing World*. 93–121.

Laug, Werner. "Johannes Heß und die Disputation in Breslau von 1524." *Jahrbuch für schlesische Kirchengeschichte* 37 (1958): 23–34.

Lawton, M. Powell; Miriam Moss; and Allen Glicksman. "The Quality of the Last Year of Life of Older Persons." *The Milbank Quarterly* 68 (1990): 1–28.

Leaver, Robin A. "The Lutheran Reformation." *The Renaissance: From the 1470s to the End of the Sixteenth Century*, edited by I. Fenelon, 263–285. Englewood Cliffs, N.J., 1989.

Lehmann, Martin. *Justus Jonas, Loyal Reformer*. Minneapolis, 1963.

Lenz, Rudolf. "Leichenpredigten: Eine bislang vernachlässigte Quellengattung." *Archiv für Kulturgeschichte* 56 (1974): 296–312.

———. *Leichenpredigten as Quellen historischer Wissenschaften*. Cologne, 1975.

———. *Studien zur deutschsprachigen Leichenpredigt der frühen Neuzeit*. Marburger Personalschriften-Forschungen 4. Marburg, 1981.

———. "Zur Funktion des Lebenslaufes in Leichenpredigten." In *Wer schreibt meine Lebensgeschichte? Biographie, Autobiographie, Hagiographie und ihre Entstehungszusammenhänge*, edited by Walter Sparn, 93–104. Gütersloh, 1990.

———. *De mortuis nil nisi bene? Leichenpredigten als multidisziplinäre Quelle unter besonderer Berücksichtigung der Historischen Familienforschung, der Bildungsgeschichte und der Literaturgeschichte*. Marburger Personalschriften-Forschungen 10. Sigmaringen, 1990.

Leroux, Neil R. "Perceiving Rhetorical Style: Toward A Framework for Criticism." *RSQ* 22 (fall 1992): 29–44.

———. "The Rhetor's Perceived Situation: Luther's Invocavit Sermons." *RSQ* 28 (winter 1998): 49–80.

———. "Luther's Use of Doublets." *RSQ* 30 (summer 2000): 35–54.

———. *Luther's Rhetoric: Strategies and Style in the Invocavit Sermons*. St. Louis, 2002.

Levin, Jeffrey S. "Religion and Health: Is There an Association, Is It Valid, and Is It Causal?" *SSM* 38 (1994): 1475–1482.

———. "How Religion Influences Morbidity and Health: Reflections on Natural History, Salutogenesis and Host Resistance." *SSM* 43 (1996): 849–864.

Levine, Robert. *Persuasion: How We're Bought and Sold*. Hoboken, N.J., 2003.

Lifton, Robert Jay. "On Death and the Continuity of Life: A 'New' Paradigm." *History of Childhood Quarterly* 1 (1974): 681–696.

Lifton, Robert Jay and Eric Olson. *Living and Dying*. New York, 1974.

Lindberg, Carter. *The European Reformations*. Oxford, 1996.

———. "Review of Marius, *Martin Luther: The Christian between God and Death*." *LQ* 13 (1999): 359–362.

———. "Eschatology and Fanaticism in the Reformation Era: Luther and the Anabaptists." *CTQ* 64 (2000): 259–278.

Lindemann, Eric. "Symptomatology and Management of Acute Grief." *American Journal of Psychiatry* 101 (1944): 141–148.

Littlewood, Jane L. *Aspects of Grief: Bereavement in Adult Life*. London, 1992.

——— et al. "Gender Differences in Parental Coping Following Their Child's Death." *British Journal of Guidance & Counselling* 19 (1991): 139–147.

Lofland, Lyn H. "The Social Shaping of Emotion: The Case of Grief." *Symbolic Interaction* 8 (1985): 171–190.

Long, Thomas G. "The Unbearable Lightness of Memorial Services." *CW* 38, no. 3 (2004–2005): 3–8.

Longenecker, Richard N. *Biblical Exegesis in the Apostolic Period*. Grand Rapids, 1975.

Lucke, Glenn; Richard B. Gilbert; and Ronald K. Barrett. "Protestant Approaches to Death: Overcoming Death's Sting." In Garces-Foley, ed. *Death and Religion in a Changing World*. 122–146.

Luther's Correspondence and Other Contemporary Letters. Vol. 1, *1507–1521.* Edited by Preserved Smith. Philadelphia, 1913.

Luther's Correspondence and Other Contemporary Letters. Vol. 2, *1521–1530.* Edited by Preserved Smith and Charles M. Jacobs. Philadelphia, 1918.

Luther's "September Bible" In Facsimile. Edited by Kenneth A. Strand. Ann Arbor, 1972.

Luther's Works: American Edition. 55 vols. Edited by Jaroslav Pelikan and Helmut T. Lehman. St. Louis and Philadelphia, 1955–1986.

Luther's Works. 6 vols. Philadelphia, 1916–1943.

Lynch, Thomas. "HBO's 'Six Feet Under': Grave Affairs." *ChrCent,* 2 November 2004, 18–23.

Macek, Ellen. "The Emergence of a Feminine Spirituality in *The Book of Martyrs.*" *SCJ* 19 (1988): 63–80.

MacIntyre, Alasdair. "Patients as Agents." In *Philosophical Medical Ethics: Its Nature and Significance,* edited by S. F. Spicker and H. T. Engelhardt, 197–212. Dordrecht, 1977.

———. "Medicine Aimed at the Care of Persons Rather Than What...?" In *Changing Values in Medicine,* edited by Eric J. Cassell and Mark Siegler, 83–96. Frederick, Md., 1979.

Mager, Inge. "Lied und Reformation: Beobachtungen zur reformatorischen Singbewegung in norddeutschen Städten." In *Das Protestantische Kirchenlied im 16. und 17. Jahrhundert,* edited by Alfred Dürr and Walther Killy, 25–38. Wolfenbütteler Forschungen 31. Wiesbaden, 1986.

Magness, Jodi. "Ossuaries and the Burials of Jesus and James." *JBL* 124 (2005): 121–154.

Marius, Richard. *Luther, A Biography.* Philadelphia, 1974.

———. *Martin Luther: The Christian Between God and Death.* Cambridge, Mass., 1999.

———. "Author's Response [to Martin Brecht's Review]." *Church History* 69 (2000): 147–149.

Marshall, Peter. *Beliefs and the Dead in Reformation England.* Oxford, 2002.

Martin, A. Lynn. *Plague? Jesuit Accounts of Epidemic Disease in the 16th Century.* Sixteenth Century Studies 28. Kirksville, Mo., 1996.

Martin, Hubert Jr. and Jane E. Phillips. "*Consolatio ad Uxorem (Moralia 608A–612B).*" In *Plutarch's Ethical Writings and Early Christian Literature,* edited by Hans Dieter Betz, 399–401. Leiden, 1978.

Marzolf, Dennis. "Luther in the Pew: Song and Worship." *Reformation & Revival* 8 (1999): 105–120.

———. "Luther and Music Education." *Lutheran Synod Quarterly* 46 (2006): 68–105.

Matulis, Janis. "Die ersten Schritte der Reformation in Riga." In *Luther und Luthertum in Osteuropa: Selbstdarstellungen aus der Diaspora und Beiträge zur theologischen Diskussion,* edited by Gerhard Bassarak and Günter Wirth, 354–363. Berlin, 1983.

Mayr, Ruppert. "'Einfeldig zu predigen, ist eine große kunst.' Zu Luthers Sprache in seinen Predigten." In *Reformations gedenken. Beiträge zum Lutherjahr 1983 aus der Evangelischen Kirche im Rheinland,* edited by Joachim Mehlhausen, 83–100. Cologne, 1985.

McCue, Jack D. "The Naturalness of Dying." *Journal of the American Medical Association* 273 (5 April 1995): 1039–1043.

McCulloh, John M. "The Cult of Relics in the Letters and 'Dialogues' of Pope Gregory the Great: A Lexicographical Study." *Traditio* 32 (1976): 145–184.

McGuire, Brian Patrick. *Jean Gerson and the Last Medieval Reformation.* University Park, Penn., 2005.

McGuire, Martin R. P. "The Christian Funeral Oration." In *Funeral Orations by Saint Gregory Nazianzen and Saint Ambrose.* Translated by Leo P. McCauley et al., vii–xxiii. Fathers of the Church 22. New York, 1953.

McManamon, John M. "The Ideal Renaissance Pope: Funeral Oratory from the Papal Court." *Archivum Historiae Pontificiae* 14 (1976): 9–70.

——. *Funeral Oratory and the Cultural Ideals of Italian Humanism*. Chapel Hill, 1989.

McNeill, John T. *A History of the Cure of Souls*. New York, 1951.

Meador, Keith G. and Shaun C. Henson. "Growing Old in A Therapeutic Culture." *Theology Today* 57 (2000): 185–202.

Meilaender, Gilbert. "Mortality: The Measure of Our Days." *First Things* (February 1991): 14–21.

——. "'Love's Casuistry': Paul Ramsey on Caring For the Terminally Ill." *Journal of Religious Ethics* 12 (fall 1991): 133–156.

Mellor, Philip A. and Chris Shilling. "Modernity, Self-Identity and the Sequestration of Death." *Sociology* 27 (1993): 411–431.

Mennecke-Haustein, Ute. *Luthers Trostbriefe*. Quellen und Forschungen zur Reformationsgeschichte 56. Gütersloh, 1989.

——. "Luther als Seelsorger." In *Martin Luther ungewohnt*, edited by Evangelische Akademie Baden, 55–78. Karlsruhe, 1996.

Menninger, Karl A. *Whatever Became of Sin?* New York, 1973.

Mermann, Alan C. "Learning to Care for the Dying." In Spiro, Curnen, and Wandel, eds., *Facing Death*, 52–59.

Miller, Scott. "Reclaiming the Role of Lament in the Funeral Rite." *CW* 38, no. 3 (2004–2005): 34–48.

Mills, Mina; Huw T. O. Davies; and William A. Macrae. "Care of Dying Patients in Hospital." *British Medical Journal* 309 (3 September 1994): 583–586.

Milton, Michael A. "'So What are You Doing Here?' The Role of the Minister of the Gospel in Hospital Visitation, or A Theological Cure for the Crisis in Evangelical Pastoral Care." *JETS* 46 (2003): 449–463.

Mitchell, C. Ben. "The Quest for Immortality." In Mitchell, Orr, and Salladay, eds., *Aging, Death, and the Quest for Immortality*, 153–162.

Mitchell, Jane F. "Consolatory Letters in Basil and Gregory Nazianzen." *Hermes* 96 (1968): 299–318.

Mitford, Jessica. *The American Way of Death*. New York, 1963.

——. *The American Way of Death Revisited*. New York, 1998.

Moeller, Bernd. "Piety in Germany Around 1500." In *The Reformation in Medieval Perspective*, edited by Steven E. Ozment, 50–75. Chicago, 1971.

——. "Religious Life in Germany on the Eve of the Reformation." In *Religion and Society in Early Modern Europe 1500–1800*, edited by Kaspar von Greyerz, 13–42. London, 1984.

——. "Inquisition und Martyrium in Flugschriften der frühen Reformation in Deutschland." In *Ketzerverfolgung im 16. und frühen 17. Jahrhundert*, edited by Silvana Seidel Menchi, 45–71. Wolfenbütteler Forschung 51. Wiesbaden, 1992.

Möller, Christian. "Luthers Seelsorge und die neueren Seelsorgekonzepte." In Heubach, ed., *Luther als Seelsorger*, 109–128.

——. "Martin Luther." In *Geschichte der Seelsorge in Einzelporträts*. Vol. 2, edited by Christian Möller, 25–44. Göttingen, 1992.

——. "'Ein neues Lied wir heben an': Überlegungen zum 'neuen' geistlichen Lied." In *Der heilsame Riss: Impulse reformatorischer Spiritualität*, edited by Christian Möller, 257–273. Stuttgart, 2003.

Moller, David W. *Confronting Death: Values, Institutions, and Human Mortality*. New York, 1996.

Monter, William. "Heresy Executions in Reformation Europe, 1520–1565. In *Tolerance and Intolerance in the European Reformation*, edited by Ole Peter Grell and Bob Scribner, 48–64. Cambridge, 1996.

Moore, Cornelia Niekus. "Das erzählte Leben in der lutherischen Leichenpredigt: Anfang und Entwicklung im 16. Jahrhundert." *Wolfenbütteler Barock-nachrichten* 29 (2002): 3–22.

——. *Patterned Lives: The Lutheran Funeral Biography in Early Modern Germany*. Wolfenbütteler Forschungen 111. Wiesbaden, 2006.

Moore, Virginia. *Ho for Heaven! Man's Changing Attitude Toward Dying.* New York, 1946.

Müller, Gerhard Ludwig. "Communio Sanctorum: Das Kirchenverständnis Martin Luthers." *Edith-Stein-Jahrbuch* 4 (1998): 215–223.

Music, David W. *Hymnology: A Collection of Source Readings.* Studies in Liturgical Musicology 4. Lanham, Md., 1996.

Musurillo, Herbert, ed. and trans. *The Acts of the Christian Martyrs.* Oxford, 1972.

Myers, Eric T. "The Burial Rites of John Calvin?" *CW* 38, no. 3 (2004–2005): 28–33.

Nebe, August. *Luther as Spiritual Adviser.* Translated by Charles A. Hay and Charles E. Hay. Philadelphia, 1894.

New Catholic Encyclopedia. 2nd ed. s.v. "Fourteen Holy Helpers." By J. Dünninger.

Nixon, Virginia. *Mary's Mother: Saint Anne in Late Medieval Europe.* University Park, Penn., 2004.

Noy, Pinchas. "The Psychodynamic Meaning of Music, Part I: A Critical Review of the Psychoanalytic and Related Literature." *Journal of Music Therapy* 3 (1966): 126–134.

——. "The Psychodynamic Meaning of Music, Parts II–V." *Journal of Music Therapy* 4 (1967): 7–23, 45–51, 81–94, 128–131.

Nuland, Sherwin B. *How We Die: Reflections on Life's Final Chapter.* New York, 1994.

——. "Do You Want to Live Forever?" *Technology Review* 108 (February 2005): 36–45.

Oberman, Heiko A. "The Virgin Mary in Evangelical Perspective." *Journal of Ecumenical Studies* 1 (1964): 271–298.

——. "Luther and the Devil." *LTSB* 69 (1989): 4–15.

——. *Luther: Man between God and the Devil.* Translated by Eileen Walliser-Schwarzbart. New York, 1992.

——. "Varieties of Protest," *New Republic*, 16 August 1999, 40–45.

——. Review of Marius, *Martin Luther: The Christian between God and Death.*" *The Historian* 62 (2000): 926–927.

Ochs, Donovan. *Consolatory Rhetoric: Grief, Symbol, and Ritual in the Greco-Roman Era* (Columbia, S.C., 1993).

Oden, Thomas C. *Care of Souls in the Classic Tradition.* Philadelphia, 1984.

O'Connor, Sister Mary Catherine. *The Art of Dying Well: The Development of the Ars moriendi.* New York, 1942.

Oettinger, Rebecca Wagner. *Music as Propaganda in the German Reformation.* Aldershot, 2001.

Osterholm, Michael T. "Preparing for the Next Pandemic." *Foreign Affairs* 84 (July–August 2005). < http://www.foreignaffairs.org/20050701faessay84402/michael-t-osterholm/preparing-for-the-next-pandemic.html>. Accessed 6 December 2005.

——. "Preparing for the Next Pandemic." *NEMJ* 352 (2005): 1839–1842.

——. "A Weapon the World Needs." *Nature* 435 (2005): 417–418.

Oxford Dictionary of Saints. 4th ed. Edited by David Hugh Farmer. Oxford, 1997. s.v. "Fourteen Holy Helpers."

Oxford Encyclopedia of the Reformation. 4 vols. Edited by Hans J. Hillerbrand. New York, 1996. s. v. "Books of Martyrs," by Jean-François Gilmont; s.v. "Frederick III of Saxony," by Ingetraut Ludolphy; s. v. "Hess, Johann," by Manfred P. Fleischer; s. v. "Hutten, Ulrich von," by Eckhard Bernstein; s. v., "Jonas, Justus," by Robert Rosin; s. v. "Kaiser, Leonhard," by Robert Kolb; s. v. "Saints: Sainthood," by Franz Courth; s. v. "Sickingen, Franz von," by Ulman Weiß.

Ozment, Steven. "The Family in Reformation Germany: The Bearing and Rearing of Children." *Journal of Family History* 8 (1983): 159–176.

——. "Luther and the Family." *Harvard Library Bulletin* 32 (1984): 36–55.

——. *When Fathers Ruled: Family Life in Reformation Europe.* Cambridge, Mass., 1985.

——. *Protestants: The Birth of A Revolution.* New York, 1991.

——. *Flesh and Spirit: Private Life in Early Modern Germany.* New York, 1999.

———. *Ancestors: The Loving Family in Old Europe*. Cambridge, Mass., 2001.

Pabel, Hilmar M. "Humanism and Early Modern Catholicism: Erasmus of Rotterdam's *Ars Moriendi*." In *Early Modern Catholicism: Essays in Honour of John W. O'Malley, S. J.*, edited by Kathleen M. Comerford and Hilmar M. Pabel, 26–45. Toronto, 2001.

Palisca, Claude V. "Music and Rhetoric." In *Music and Ideas in the Sixteenth and Seventeenth Centuries*. Studies in the History of Music Theory and Literature 1. Urbana, Ill., 2006.

Pankratz, Herbert R. "Luther's Utilization of Music in School and Town in the Early Reformation." *Andrews University Seminary Studies* 22 (1984): 99–112.

Paradis, L. and S. Cummings. "The Evolution of Hospice in America Toward Organisational Homogeneity." *Journal of Health and Social Behaviour* 27 (1986): 370–386.

Parkes, Colin Murray. "Bereavement as a Psychosocial Transition: Processes of Adaptation to Change." *Journal of Social Issues* 44, no. 3 (1988): 53–65. Reprint in Stroebe, Margaret S.; Wolfgang Stroebe; and Robert O. Hansson, eds. *Handbook of Bereavement: Theory, Research, and Intervention*, 91–101. Cambridge, 1993.

Parsons, Michael. "The Apocalyptic Luther: His Noahic Self-Understanding," *JETS* 44 (2001): 627–645.

Paxton, Frederick S. *Christianizing Death: The Creation of a Ritual Process in Early Medieval Europe*. Ithaca, 1990.

Perelman, Chaim and L. Olbrichts-Tyteca. *The New Rhetoric: A Treatise on Argumentation*. Translated John Wilkinson and Purcell Weaver. Notre Dame, 1969.

Piepkorn, Arthur Carl. "Mary's Place Within the People of God According to Non-Roman-Catholics." *Marian Studies* 18 (1967): 46–83.

Pietsch, Helen. "On Luther's Understanding of Music." *Lutheran Theological Journal* 26 (1992): 160–168.

———. "Luther's Attitude to Music in Worship and Implications for Today." In *Perspectives on Martin Luther*, edited by M. W. Worthing, 141–154. North Adelaide, So. Australia, 1996.

Pinomaa, Lennart. "Die Heiligen in Luthers Frühtheologie." *Studia Theologica* 13 (1959): 1–50.

Plass, Ewald M. *What Luther Says: A Practical In-Home Anthology for the Active Christian*. St. Louis, 1959.

Pless, John T. "Baptism as Consolation in Luther's Pastoral Care." *CTQ* 67 (2003): 19–32.

Poland, Gregory A. "Vaccines against Avian Influence—A Race against Time." *NEMJ* 354 (2006): 1411–1413.

Pollock, Linda A. *Forgotten Children: Parent-Child Relations from 1500–1900*. Cambridge, 1983.

Posset, Franz. "St. Bernard's Influence on Two Reformers: John von Staupitz and Martin Luther." *Cistercian Studies Quarterly* 25 (1990): 175–187.

———. "*Divus Bernhardus*: Saint Bernard as Spiritual and Theological Mentor of the Reformer Martin Luther." In *Bernardus Magister: Papers Presented at the Nonacentenary Celebration of the Birth of Saint Bernard of Clairvaux, Kalamazoo, Michigan*, edited by John R. Sommerfeldt, 517–532. Kalamazoo, Mich., 1992.

———. *Pater Bernhardus: Martin Luther and Bernard of Clairvaux*. Cistercian Studies 168. Kalamazoo, Mich., 1999.

———. "Lehrer der Seelsorge: Das ökumenische Potential der Seelsorge-Konzeption des alten Luther." *Luther* 72 (2001): 3–17.

Powell, Susan and Alan J. Fletcher. "'In die sepulture seu trigintali': The Late Medieval Funeral and Memorial Sermon." *Leeds Studies in English* 12 (1981): 195–228.

Preul, Rainer. "Der Tod des ganzen Menschen: Luthers Sermon von der Bereitung zum Sterben." In *Der 'ganze Mensch': Perspektiven lebengeschichtlicher Individualität. Festschrift für Dietrich Rössler zum siebzigsten Geburtstag*, edited by Volker Drehsen et al., 111–130. Arbeiten zur Praktischen Theologie 10. Berlin, 1997.

Prior, Lindsay and Mick Bloor. "Why People Die: Social Representations of Death and Its Causes." *Science as Culture* 3 (1992): 346–374.

Rada, Richard T. "Luther, Ethics and the Plague in Wittenberg: The Reformer's Faith Approaches Disease and Suffering." In *Let Christ Be Christ: Theology, Ethics and World Religions in the Two Kingdoms. Essays in Honor of the Sixty-Fifth Birthday of Charles L. Manske*, edited by Daniel N. Harmelink, 251–260. Huntington Beach, Cal., 1999.

Rahmelow, Jan M. "Das Volkslied als publizistisches Medium und historische Quelle." *Jahrbuch für Volksliedforschung* 14 (1969): 11–26.

Rahner, Karl. "Dimensions of Martyrdom: A Plea for the Broadening of a Classical Concept." *Concilium* 163, no. 3 (1983): 9–11.

Ramsey, Paul. "The Indignity of 'Death with Dignity.'" *Hastings Center Studies* 2 (May 1974): 50–62.

Reames, Sherry L. *The* Legenda aurea*: A Reexamination of Its Paradoxical History*. Madison, 1985.

Reed, Luther D. *Luther and Congregational Song*. Papers of the Hymn Society 12 (New York, 1947.

Reinis, Austra. "Evangelische Anleitung zur Seelsorge am Sterbebett 1519–1528." *Luther* 73 (2002): 31–45.

——. *Reforming the Art of Dying: The Ars Moriendi in the German Reformation (1519–1528)*. St. Andrews Studies in Reformation History. Aldershot, U.K., 2007.

——. "How Protestants Face Death: Johann Gerhard's Funeral Sermon for Kunigund Gotsmännin, Widow of Hans Dietrich von Haßlach zu Stockheim (d. 1616)." *Theological Review* 25 (2004): 24–45.

Renner, H. P. V. "A Christian Rite of Burial: An Instrument of Pastoral Care." *Lutheran Theological Journal* 26 (1992): 72–77.

Retsinas, Joan. "A Theoretical Reassessment of the Applicability of Kübler-Ross's Stages of Dying." *DS* 12 (1988): 207–216.

Riches, Gordon and Pamela Dawson. "'An Intimate Loneliness': Evaluating the Impact of A Child's Death on Parental Self-Identity and Marital Relationships." *Journal of Family Therapy* 16 (1996): 1–22.

——. "Communities of Feeling: The Culture of Bereaved Parents." *Mortality* 1 (1996): 143–161.

Richter, Georg. *Die Schriften Georg Witzels*. Niewkoop, 1963.

Riedel, Johannes. *The Lutheran Chorale: Its Basic Traditions*. Minneapolis, 1967.

Riemann, Hugo. *Dictionary of Music*. 2 vols. Translated by J. S. Shedlock. New York, 1970. s.v. "Lied."

Rittgers, Ronald. "The Reformation of Suffering." *Crux* 38 (December 2002): 15–21.

Roberts, Glenn and John Owen. "The Near-Death Experience." *British Journal of Psychiatry* 153 (1988): 607–617.

Roberts, Robert C. "Psychotherapy and Christian Ministry." *WW* 21 (2001): 42–50.

Robinson-Hammerstein, Helga. "The Lutheran Reformation and its Music." In *The Transmission of Ideas in the Lutheran Reformation*, edited by Helga Robinson-Hammerstein, 141–171. Dublin, 1989.

Rodgers, Beth L. and Kathleen V. Cowles. "The Concept of Grief: An Analysis of Classical and Contemporary Thought." *DS* 15 (1991): 443–458.

Roper, Lyndal. "Luther: Sex, Marriage and Motherhood." *History Today* 33 (Dec. 1983): 33–38.

Rosenblatt, Paul C. *Bitter, Bitter Tears: Nineteenth-Century Diarists and Twentieth-Century Grief Theories*. Minneapolis, 1983.

——. "Grief That Does Not End." In Klass, Silverman, and Nickman, eds. *Continuing Bonds*, 45–58.

——. "Grief: The Social Context of Private Feelings" in Stroebe, Stroebe, and Hansson, eds. *Handbook*, 102–111.

——. *Parent Grief: Narratives of Loss and Relationship*. Philadelphia, 2000.

Rosenblatt, Paul C.; Douglas A. Jackson; and Rose P. Walsh. "Coping with Anger and Aggression in Mourning." *Omega* 3 (1972): 271–284.

Rosenblatt, Paul C.; Patricia R. Walsh; and Douglas A. Jackson. *Grief and Mourning in Cross-Cultural Perspective*. n. c., 1976.

Rössler, Martin. "Ein neues Lied wir heben an: Ein Protestsong Martin Luthers." In *Reformation und praktische Theologie: Festschrift für Werner Jetter zum siebzigsten Geburtstag*, edited by Hans-Martin Müller and D. Rössler, 216–232. Göttingen, 1983.

Rowell, Geoffrey. *The Liturgy of Christian Burial: An Introductory Survey of the Historical Development of Christian Burial Rites*. London, 1977.

Royse, David. "The Near-Death Experience: A Survey of Clergy's Attitudes and Knowledge." *JPC* 39 (March 1985): 331–342.

Rubin, Simon Shimshon. "The Death of A Child is Forever: The Life Course Impact of Child Loss." In Stroebe, Stroebe, and Hansson, eds. *Handbook*, 285–299.

Rudolf, Rainer. *Ars Moriendi: Von der Kunst des Heilsamen Lebens und Sterbens*. Forschung zur Volkskunde 39. Cologne, 1957.

——. "Ars Moriendi I: Mittelalter." In *TRE* 4: 143–149.

——. "Ars Moriendi II: 16.–18. Jahrhundert." In *TRE* 4: 149–154.

Rupp, E. Gordon and Philip S. Watson, eds. *Luther and Erasmus: Free Will and Salvation*. Philadelphia, 1969.

Rush, Alfred C. *Death and Burial in Christian Antiquity*. Washington, D.C., 1941.

Rutherford, H. Richard. "Luther's 'Honest Funeral' Today: An Ecumenical Comparison." *Dialog* 32 (summer 1993): 178–184.

Rynearson, E. K. "Psychotherapy of Pathologic Grief: Revisions and Limitations." *Psychiatric Clinics of North America* 10 (1987): 487–499.

Saak, Eric L. *High Way to Heaven: The Augustinian Platform between Reform and Reformation, 1292–1524*. SMRT 89. Leiden, 2002.

Sanders, Catherine M. "A Comparison of Adult Bereavement in the Death of A Spouse, Child, and Parent." *Omega* 10 (1979–1980): 303–322.

Saulnier, Verdun L. "L'Oraison Funèbre au XVIᵉ Siècle." *Bibliothèque d'humanisme et Renaissance* 10 (1948): 124–157.

Saunders, Cicely. "The Last Stages of Life." *American Journal of Nursing* 65 (March 1965): 70–75.

Sauter, Gerhard. "Die Verkündigung des Auferstandenen als Zusage des Lebens bei Gott." In *Relationen-Studien zum Übergang vom Spätmittelalter zur Reformation: Festschrift zu Ehren von Prof. Dr. Karl-Heinz zu Mühlen*, edited by Athina Lexutt and Wolfgang Matz, 383–398. Münster, 2000.

——. "Luther on the Resurrection: The Proclamation of the Risen One as the Promise of Our Everlasting Life with Go." *LQ* 15 (2001): 195–216.

——. "Luther on the Resurrection." In *Harvesting's Martin Luther's Reflections on Theology, Ethics, and the Church*, edited by Timothy J. Wengert, 99–118. Grand Rapids, 2004.

——. "How Do 'I' Encounter My Own Death?" *Theology Today* 60 (2004): 497–507.

Schade, Werner. *Cranach: A Family of Master Painters*. Translated by Helen Serba. New York, 1980.

Schalk, Carl F. *Luther on Music: Paradigms of Praise*. St. Louis, 1988.

Schiappa, Edward; Peter B. Gregg; and Dean E. Hewes. "Can A Television Series Change Attitudes About Death? A Study of College Students and *Six Feet Under*." *DS* 28 (2004): 459–474.

Schild, Maurice E. "Luther as Comforter." In *Perspectives on Martin Luther: Papers from the Luther Symposium held at Luther Seminary Adelaide, South Australia, 22–23 March, 1996, Commemorating the 450th Anniversary of the Reformer's Death*, edited by M. W. Worthing, 9–20. North Adelaide, So. Australia, 1996.

Schnelbögl, Fritz. "Friedhofverlegungen im 16. Jahrhundert." *Jahrbuch für frankische Landesforschung* 34/35 (1974–1975): 109–120.

Schöffel, Johann Simon. "Luther als Seelsorger." *Luther* 23 (1941): 1–10.

Schreiber, Georg. *Die Vierzehn Nothelfer in Volksfrömmigkeit und Sakraldultur: Symbolkraft und Herrschaftsbereich der Wallfahrtskapelle, vorab in Franken und Tirol.* Schlern-Schriften Veröffentlichungen zur Landeskunde von Südtirol 168. Innsbruck, 1959.

Schreiner, Susan. "Unmasking the Angel of Light: The Problem of Deception in Martin Luther and Teresa of Avila." In *Mystics, Presence, and Aporia*, edited by Michael Kessler and Christian Sheppard, 118–137. Chicago, 2003.

Schultz, Ned W. and Lisa M. Huet. "Sensational! Violent! Popular! Death in American Movies." *Omega* 42 (2000–2001): 137–149.

Schulz, Richard. *The Psychology of Death, Dying, and Bereavement.* Reading, Mass., 1978.

Schulz, Richard and David Aderman. "Clinical Research and the Stages of Dying." *Omega* 5 (1974): 137–143.

Schwab, Reiko. "Effects of A Child's Death on the Marital Relationship: A Preliminary Study," *DS* 16 (1992): 141–154.

Schwarz, Reinhard. "Das Bild des Todes im Bild Lebens überwinden: Eine Interpretation von Luthers Sermon von der Bereitung zum Sterben." In Schwarz, ed. *Gewißheit angesichts des Sterbens*, 32–64.

Schwiebert, Ernst. "Remnants of A Reformation Library." *Library Quarterly* 10 (1940): 494–531.

——. *Luther and His Times: The Reformation from a New Perspective.* St. Louis, 1950.

Scott, Susan and Christopher Duncan. *Biology of Plagues: Evidence from Historical Populations.* Cambridge, 2001.

——. *Return of the Black Death: The World's Greatest Serial Killer.* Chichester, 2004.

Scott, Tom. "Review of Marius, *Martin Luther: The Christian between God and Death*." *English Historical Review* 114 (1999): 1301–1302.

Scribner, R. W. "Ritual and Popular Religion in Catholic Germany at the Time of the Reformation." *Journal of Ecclesiastical History* 35 (1984): 47–77.

Seale, Clive F. "What Happens in Hospices: A Review of Research Evidence." *SSM* 28 (1989): 551–559.

Secker, Philip J. "Martin Luther's Views on the State of the Dead." *CTM* 38 (1967): 422–435.

Sehling, Emil, ed. *Die evangelischen Kirchenordnungen des XVI. Jahrhunderts.* Leipzig, 1902.

Sessions, Kyle C. "Luther In Music and Verse." in *Pietas et Societas: New Trends in Reformation Social History. Essays in Memory of Harold J. Grimm*, edited by Kyle C. Sessions and Phillip N. Bebb, 123–139. SCES 4. Kirksville, Mo., 1985.

Sevensky, Robert L. "Religion and Illness: An Outline of Their Relationship." *Southern Medical Journal* 74 (1981): 745–750.

——. "The Religious Foundations of Health Care: A Conceptual Approach." *Journal of Medical Ethics* 9 (1983): 165–169.

Shapiro, Ester R. "Grief in Freud's Life: Reconceptualizing Bereavement in Psychoanalytic Theory." *Psychoanalytic Psychology* 13 (1996): 547–566.

Sheppy, Paul P. J. *Death Liturgy and Ritual.* Vol. 1, *A Pastoral and Liturgical Theology.* Aldershot, U.K., 2003.

Shuman, Joel. "Desperately Seeking Perfection: Christian Discipleship and Medical Genetics." *Christian Bioethics* 5 (1999): 139–153.

Shuman, Joel and Keith G. Meador. *Heal Thyself: Spirituality, Medicine, and the Distortion of Christianity.* Oxford, 2003.

Siggins, Ian D. K. "Luther's Mother Margarete." *HTR* 71 (1978): 125–150.

Simmonds, Anne L. "Pastoral Perspectives in Intensive Care: Experiences of Doctors and Nurses with Dying Patients." *JPC* 51 (1997): 271–281.

Slack, Paul. "Mortality Crises and Epidemic Disease in England 1485–1610." In *Health, Medicine and Mortality in the Sixteenth Century*, edited by Charles Webster, 9–59. Cambridge, 1979.

Slenczka, Reinhard. "Luther's Care of Souls for Our Times." *CTQ* 67 (2003): 33–63.

Smith, Archie, Jr. "'Look and See If There Is Any Sorrow Like My Sorrow?': Systemic Metaphors for Pastoral Theology and Care." *WW* 21 (2001): 5–15.

Smith, Warren J. "Martyrdom: Self-Denial or Self-Exaltation? Motives for Self-Sacrifice from Homer to Polycarp, A Theological Reflection." *Modern Theology* 22 (2006): 169–196.

Smith, Lacey Baldwin. *Fools, Martyrs, Traitors: The Story of Martyrdom in the Western World.* New York, 1997.

Smith, Peggy C.; Lillian M. Range; and Ann Ulmer. "Belief in Afterlife as A Buffer in Suicidal and Other Bereavement." *Omega* 24 (1991–1992): 217–225.

Snyder, C. R. "Unique Invulnerability: A Classroom Demonstration in Estimating Personal Mortality." *Teaching of Psychology* 24 (1997): 197–199.

Söhngen, Oskar. "Fundamental Considerations for a Theology of Music." In *The Musical Heritage of the Church.* Vol. 6, edited by Theodore Hoelty-Nickel, 7–16. St. Louis, 1963.

——. "Music and Theology: A Systematic Approach." *Journal of the American Academy of Religion Thematic Studies* 50, no. 1 (1983): 1–19.

Sommer, Ernst. "Die Metrik in Luthers Liedern." In *Jahrbuch für Liturgik und Hymnologie.* Vol. 9, edited by Konrad Ameln, Christhard Mahrenholz, and Karl Ferdinand Müller, 29–81. Kassel, 1965.

Spiegel, Gabrielle M. "The Cult of St. Denis and Capetian Kingship." In *Saints and their Cults: Studies in Religious Sociology, Folklore and History*, edited by Stephen Wilson, 141–168. Cambridge, 1983.

Spinks, Bryan D. "Adiaphora: Marriage and Funeral Liturgies." *CTQ* 62 (1998): 7–23.

Spitz, Lewis W. "Luther's Social Concern for Students." In *The Social History of the Reformation*, edited by Lawrence P. Buck and Jonathan W. Zophy, 249–270. Columbus, Ohio, 1972.

——."Psychohistory and History: The Case of Young Man Luther." *Soundings* 56 (1973): 182–209.

Sprunger, Keith L. "Dutch Anabaptists and the Telling of the Martyr Stories." *MQR* 80 (2006): 149–182.

St-Onge, Charles P. "Music, Worship, and Martin Luther." *Logia* 13, no. 2 (2004): 37–42.

Stadlen, Peter. "The Aesthetics of Popular Music." *British Journal of Aesthetics* 2 (1962): 351–361.

Stearns, Peter N. *American Cool: Constructing a Twentieth-Century Emotional Style.* New York, 1994.

Stearns, Peter N. and Mark Knapp, "Historical Perspectives on Grief." In *The Emotions: Social, Cultural and Biological Dimensions*, edited by Rom Harré and W. Gerrod Parrott, 134–148. London, 1996.

Steinmetz, David C. *Luther and Staupitz: An Essay in the Intellectual Origins of the Protestant Reformation.* Duke Monographs in Medieval and Renaissance Studies 4. Durham. N.C., 1980.

Stelten, Leo F. *Dictionary of Ecclesiastical Latin.* Peabody, Mass., 1995.

Stevenson, Robert M. *Patterns of Protestant Church Music.* Durham, N.C., 1953.

Stoddard, Sandol. "Hospice in the United States: An Overview." *Journal of Palliative Care* 5, no. 3 (1989): 10–19.

Stolt, Birgit. "Docere, delectare und movere bei Luther. Analysiert anhand der 'Predigt, daß man Kinder zur Schulen halten sole.'" *Deutsche Vierteljahrsschrift für Literaturwissenschaft und Geistesgeschichte* 44 (1970): 433–474.

——. *Wortkampf: Frühneuhochdeutsche Beispiele zur rhetorischen Praxis.* Frankfurt, 1974.

Strauss, Gerald. "Review of Marius, *Martin Luther: The Christian between God and Death.*" *History* 28 (2000): 27–28.

Stroebe, Margaret. "Coping With Bereavement: A Review of the Grief Work Hypothesis." *Omega* 26 (1992–1993): 19–42.

Stroebe, Margaret and Henk Schut. "Culture and Grief." *Bereavement Care* 17 (1998): 7–10.

———. "The Dual Process Model of Coping with Bereavement: Rationale and Description." *DS* 23 (1999): 197–224.

Stroebe, Margaret and Wolfgang Stroebe. "Does 'Grief Work' Work?" *Journal of Consulting and Clinical Psychology* 59 (1991): 479–482.

Stroebe, Margaret S.; Wolfgang Stroebe; and Robert O. Hansson. "Bereavement Research: An Historical Introduction." *Journal of Social Issues* 44. no. 3 (1988): 1–18.

Stroebe, Margaret et al. "Broken Hearts or Broken Bonds: Love and Death in Historical Perspective." *American Psychologist* 47 (1992): 1205–1212.

Strohl, Jane E. "Luther and the Word of Consolation." *LTSB* 67 (winter 1987): 23–34.

———. "Suffering as Redemptive: A Comparison of Christian Experience in the Sixteenth and Twentieth Centuries." In *Revisioning the Past: Prospects in Historical Theology*, edited by Mary Potter Engel and Walter E. Wyman, 95–111. Minneapolis, 1992.

———. "The Child in Luther's Theology: 'For What Purpose Do We Older Folks Exist, Other Than to Care for...the Young?'" In *The Child in Christian Thought*, edited by Marcia J. Bunge, 134–159. Grand Rapids, 2001.

Stroup, Herbert W., Jr. "Pastoral Theology: Reformation or Regression?" *LTSB* 67 (winter 1987): 39–53.

Studer, Gerald C. "A History of the *Martyrs' Mirror*." *MQR* 22 (1948): 163–179.

Swartzentruber, A. Orley. "The Piety and Theology of the Anabaptist Martyrs in Van Braght's *Martyrs' Mirror* I." *MQR* 28 (1954): 5–26.

———. "The Piety and Theology of the Anabaptist Martyrs in Van Braght's *Martyrs' Mirror* II: The Earliest Testimonies—1539–46." *MQR* 28 (1954): 128–142.

Tappert, Theodore G., ed. *Luther: Letters of Spiritual Counsel*. Library of Christian Classics 18. Philadelphia, 1955.

Tarry, Joe E. "Music in the Educational Philosophy of Martin Luther." *Journal of Research in Music Education* 21 (1973): 355–365.

Tavard, George. "Luther's Teaching on Prayer." *LTSB* 67 (winter 1987): 3–22.

Taylor, Charles. "Philosophical Reflections on Caring Practices." In *The Crisis of Care: Affirming and Restoring Caring Practices in the Helping Professions*, edited by Susan S. Phillips and Patricia Benner, 174–187. Washington, D.C., 1994.

Thielicke, Helmut. *Death and Life*. Translated by Edward H. Schroeder. Philadelphia, 1970.

Thimme, Hans. "Martin Luther als Prediger." In *Luther und der Pietismus: An alle, die mit ernst Christen sein wollen*, edited by Kurt Heimbucher, 23–56. Giessen, 1983.

Thompson, Craig R., trans. "The Funeral." In *The Colloquies of Erasmus*, 359–373. Chicago, 1965.

Tomlin, Graham. "Review of Marius, *Martin Luther: The Christian between God and Death*." *Journal of Ecclesiastical History* 51 (2000): 409.

Tracy, James D. "Review of Marius, *Martin Luther: The Christian between God and Death*." *Catholic Historical Review* 86 (2000): 324–326.

Treanor, John J. et al. "Safety and Immunogenenicity of an Inactivated Subvirion Influenza A (H5N1) Vaccine." *NEMJ* 354 (2006): 1343–1351.

Treu, Martin. "Trost bei Luther: Ein Anstoß für heutige Seelsorge." *Pastoraltheologie* 73 (March 1984): 91–106.

———. "Die Bedeutung der consolatio für Luthers Seelsorge bis 1525." *LuJ* 53 (1986): 7–25.

———. "Zwischen Psychotherapie und Dämonenaustreibung: Beobachtungen und Überlegungen zu Luthers Seelsorge für die Gegenwart." *Luther* 58 (1987): 32–45.

Tromly, Frederic B. "'Accordinge to sounde religion': The Elizabethan Controversy Over the Funeral Sermon." *Journal of Medieval and Renaissance Studies* 13 (1983): 293–312.

Truvillion, Jesse Garfield. "Faith and Integrity At Graveside." *CW* 38, no. 3 (2004–2005): 21–27.

Twigg, Graham. *The Black Death: A Biological Reappraisal*. New York, 1985.

Uhlenberg, P. "Death and the Family." *Journal of Family History* 5 (1980): 313–320.

Videka-Sherman, Lynn. "Coping with the Death of A Child: A Study Over Time." *American Journal of Orthopsychiatry* 52 (1982): 688–698.

Veith, Gene Edward. "Praying for Persecution." *World*, 1 October 2005, 24.

———. "Corpse Art." *World*, 8 October 2005, 30.

Volkart, Edmund H. "Bereavement and Mental Health." In *Explorations in Social Psychiatry*, edited by Alexander H. Leighton, John A. Clausen, and Robert N. Wilson, 281–307. New York, 1957.

Voragine, Jacobi a. *Legenda Aurea: Vulgo Historia Lombardica Dicta*. 3rd ed. Edited by Th. Graesse. Leipzig, 1890. Reprint, Melle, 2003.

———. *The Golden Legend: Readings on the Saints*. 2 vols. Translated by William Granger Ryan. Princeton, 1993.

Wagner, Harold. "Catholic Theology's Main Thoughts on Death." In Spiro, Curnen, and Wandel, eds., *Facing Death*, 137–141.

Walter, Tony. *Funerals And How to Improve Them*. London, 1990.

———. "Why Are Most Churchgoers Women? A Literature Review." *Vox Evangelica* 20 (1990): 73–90.

———. "Modern Death: Taboo or Not Taboo?" *Sociology* 25 (1991): 293–310.

———. "Death in the New Age," *Religion* 23 (1993): 127–145.

———. "Dust Not Ashes: The American Preference for Burial." *Landscape* 32, no. 1 (1993): 42–48.

———. *The Revival of Death*. London, 1994.

———. "Natural Death and the Noble Savage." *Omega* 30 (1994–1995): 237–248.

———. "A New Model of Grief: Bereavement and Biography." *Mortality* 1 (1996): 7–25.

———. *The Eclipse of Eternity: A Sociology of the Afterlife*. Houndmills, U.K., 1996.

———. "Developments in Spiritual Care of the Dying." *Religion* 26 (1996): 353–363.

———. "The Ideology and Organization of Spiritual Care: Three Approaches." *Palliative Medicine* 11 (1997): 1–10.

———. "Letting Go and Keeping Hold: A Reply to Stroebe," *Mortality* 2 (1997): 263–266.

———. "Secularization." In *Death and Bereavement Across Cultures*, edited by Colin Murray Parkes, Pittu Laungani and Bill Young, 166–190. London, 1997.

———. *On Bereavement: The Culture of Grief*. Buckingham, 1999.

———. "Emotional Reserve and the English Way of Grief." In Charmaz, Howarth, and Kellehear, eds., *The Unknown Country*, 127–140.

———. "Grief Narratives: The Role of Medicine in the Policing of Grief." *Anthropology and Medicine* 7 (2000): 97–114.

———. "Spirituality in Palliative Care: Opportunity or Burden?" *Palliative Medicine* 16 (2002): 133–139.

———. "Hospices and Rituals after Death: A Survey of British Hospice Chaplains." *International Journal of Palliative Nursing* 9, no. 2 (2003): 80–85.

———. "Disaster, Modernity, and the Media." In *Death and Religion in a Changing World*, edited by Kathleen Garces-Foley, 265–282. London, 2006.

Walter, Tony; Jane Littlewood; and Michael Pickering. "Death in the News: The Public Invigilation of Private Emotion." *Sociology* 29 (1995): 579–596.

Walterhouse, Helen and Tony Walter. "Reincarnation Belief and the Christian Churches." *Theology* 106 (2003): 20–28.

Wambach, Julie Ann. "The Grief Process as A Social Construct." *Omega* 16 (1985–1986): 201–211.

Warren, Raymond. "Music and Spirituality: A Musician's Viewpoint." *Theology* 109 (2006): 83–92.

Waybright, Gregory. "Local Church Ministry to and through Older Adults." In Mitchell, Orr, and Salladay, eds., *Aging, Death, and the Quest for Immortality*, 107–120.

Webb, Diana. "Eloquence and Education: A Humanist Approach to Hagiography." *Journal of Ecclesiastical History* 31 (1980): 19–39.

Weinrich, William C. "Death and Martyrdom: An Important Aspect of Early Christian Eschatology." *CTQ* 66 (2002): 327–338.

Weiss, James Michael. "Hagiography by German Humanists, 1483–1516." *Journal of Medieval and Renaissance Studies* 15 (1985): 299–316.

Weiss, Robert S. "Loss and Recovery." *Journal of Social Issues* 44.3 (1988): 37–52.

Wendebourg, Dorothea. "Luther on Monasticism." *LQ* 19 (2005): 125–152.

Wengert, Timothy J. "Martin Luther's Movement toward an Apostolic Self-Awareness As Reflected in His Early Letters." *LuJ* 61 (1994): 71–92.

———. "'Peace, Peace…Cross, Cross': Reflections on How Martin Luther Relates the Theology of the Cross to Suffering." *Theology Today* 59 (2002): 190–205.

Whaley, Joachim. "Symbolism for the Survivors: The Disposal of the Dead in Hamburg in the Late Seventeenth and Eighteenth Centuries." In *Mirrors of Mortality: Studies in the Social History of Death*, edited by Joachim Whaley, 80–105. New York, 1981.

Wicks, Jared. "Applied Theology at the Deathbed: Luther and the Late-Medieval Tradition of the *Ars Moriendi*." *Gregorianum* 79 (1998): 345–368.

———. "Facts and Fears in and around Martin Luther." *Moreana* 37/141 (2000): 5–32.

Wikan, U. *Managing Turbulent Hearts*. Chicago, 1990.

Wilkinson, John. "The Medical History of Martin Luther." *Proceedings of the Royal College of Physicians of Edinburgh* 26 (1996): 115–134.

Wilkinson, Stephen. "Is 'Normal Grief' A Mental Disorder?" *Philosophical Quarterly* 50 (2000): 289–304.

Winkler, Eberhard. *Die Leichenpredigt im deutschen Luthertum bis Spener*. Forschungen zur Geschichte und Lehre des Protestantismus 34. Munich, 1967.

———. "Luther als Seelsorger und Prediger." In *Leben und Werk Martin Luthers von 1526 bis 1546: Festgabe seinem 500. Geburtstag*. edited by Helmar Junghans, vol. 1, 225–240. Göttingen, 1983.

———. *Impulse Luthers für die heutige Gemeindepraxis*. Arbeiten zur Theologie 67. Stuttgart, 1983.

Witten, Marsha. *All Is Forgiven: The Secular Message in American Protestantism*. Princeton, 1993.

Wortman, C. B. and R. C. Silver. "The Myths of Coping with Loss." *Journal of Consulting and Clinical Psychology* 57 (1989): 349–357.

Wray, Shona Kelly. "Boccaccio and the Doctors: Medicine and Compassion in the Face of Plague." *Journal of Medieval History* 30 (2004): 301–322.

Wriedt, Markus. "Johann von Staupitz." In *Geschichte der Seelsorge in Einzelporträts*. Vol. 2, edited by Christian Möller, 45–64. Göttingen, 1992.

Wright, David F. "Mary in the Reformers." In *Chosen By God: Mary in Evangelical Perspective*, edited by David F. Wright, 161–183. London, 1989.

———. "The Testimony of Blood: The Charisma of Martyrdom." *BSac* 160 (2003): 387–397.

Young, Bill and Danai Papadatou. "Childhood Death and Bereavement across Cultures." in *Death and Bereavement Across Cultures*, edited by Colin Murray Parkes, Pittu Laungani and Bill Young, 191–205. London, 1997.

Zager, Daniel. "Popular Music and Music for the Church." *LuthFor* 36 (fall 2002): 20–27.

Zahrnt, Heinz. "Luthers Predigt am Grabe: Dargestellt an seiner Leichenpredigt für Kurfürst Johann von Sachsen 1532." *Luther* 29 (1958): 106–114.

Zaleski, Carol. *Otherworld Journeys: Accounts of Near-Death Experience in Medieval and Modern Times*. New York, 1987.

Ziegler, Philip. *The Black Death*. New York, 1969.

INDEX OF SCRIPTURES

Apocrypha

New Testament

INDEX OF PERSONS AND PLACES

INDEX OF SUBJECTS

Studies in the History of Christian Traditions

(formerly Studies in the History of Christian Thought)

Edited by Robert J. Bast

49. Martin, D. D. *Fifteenth-Century Carthusian Reform*. The World of Nicholas Kempf. 1992
50. Hoenen, M. J. F. M. *Marsilius of Inghen*. Divine Knowledge in Late Medieval Thought. 1993
51. O'Malley, J. W., Izbicki, T. M. and Christianson, G. (eds.). *Humanity and Divinity in Renaissance and Reformation*. Essays in Honor of Charles Trinkaus. 1993
52. Reeve, A. (ed.) and Screech, M. A. (introd.). *Erasmus' Annotations on the New Testament*. Galatians to the Apocalypse. 1993
53. Stump, Ph. H. *The Reforms of the Council of Constance (1414-1418)*. 1994
54. Giakalis, A. *Images of the Divine*. The Theology of Icons at the Seventh Ecumenical Council. With a Foreword by Henry Chadwick. 1994
55. Nellen, H. J. M. and Rabbie, E. (eds.). *Hugo Grotius – Theologian*. Essays in Honour of G. H. M. Posthumus Meyjes. 1994
56. Trigg, J. D. *Baptism in the Theology of Martin Luther*. 1994
57. Janse, W. *Albert Hardenberg als Theologe*. Profil eines Bucer-Schülers. 1994
59. Schoor, R. J. M. van de. *The Irenical Theology of Théophile Brachet de La Milletière (1588-1665)*. 1995
60. Strehle, S. *The Catholic Roots of the Protestant Gospel*. Encounter between the Middle Ages and the Reformation. 1995
61. Brown, M. L. *Donne and the Politics of Conscience in Early Modern England*. 1995
62. Screech, M. A. (ed.). *Richard Mocket, Warden of All Souls College, Oxford, Doctrina et Politia Ecclesiae Anglicanae*. An Anglican Summa. Facsimile with Variants of the Text of 1617. Edited with an Introduction. 1995
63. Snoek, G. J. C. *Medieval Piety from Relics to the Eucharist*. A Process of Mutual Interaction. 1995
64. Pixton, P. B. *The German Episcopacy and the Implementation of the Decrees of the Fourth Lateran Council, 1216-1245*. Watchmen on the Tower. 1995
65. Dolnikowski, E. W. *Thomas Bradwardine: A View of Time and a Vision of Eternity in Fourteenth-Century Thought*. 1995
66. Rabbie, E. (ed.). *Hugo Grotius, Ordinum Hollandiae ac Westfrisiae Pietas (1613)*. Critical Edition with Translation and Commentary. 1995
67. Hirsh, J. C. *The Boundaries of Faith*. The Development and Transmission of Medieval Spirituality. 1996
68. Burnett, S. G. *From Christian Hebraism to Jewish Studies*. Johannes Buxtorf (1564-1629) and Hebrew Learning in the Seventeenth Century. 1996
69. Boland O.P., V. *Ideas in God according to Saint Thomas Aquinas*. Sources and Synthesis. 1996
70. Lange, M.E. *Telling Tears in the English Renaissance*. 1996
71. Christianson, G. and Izbicki, T.M. (eds.). *Nicholas of Cusa on Christ and the Church*. Essays in Memory of Chandler McCuskey Brooks for the American Cusanus Society. 1996
72. Mali, A. *Mystic in the New World*. Marie de l'Incarnation (1599-1672). 1996
73. Visser, D. *Apocalypse as Utopian Expectation (800-1500)*. The Apocalypse Commentary of Berengaudus of Ferrières and the Relationship between Exegesis, Liturgy and Iconography. 1996
74. O'Rourke Boyle, M. *Divine Domesticity*. Augustine of Thagaste to Teresa of Avila. 1997
75. Pfizenmaier, T. C. *The Trinitarian Theology of Dr. Samuel Clarke (1675-1729)*. Context, Sources, and Controversy. 1997
76. Berkvens-Stevelinck, C., Israel, J. and Posthumus Meyjes, G. H. M. (eds.). *The Emergence of Tolerance in the Dutch Republic*. 1997
77. Haykin, M. A. G. (ed.). *The Life and Thought of John Gill (1697-1771)*. A Tercentennial Appreciation. 1997
78. Kaiser, C. B. *Creational Theology and the History of Physical Science*. The Creationist Tradition from Basil to Bohr. 1997
79. Lees, J. T. *Anselm of Havelberg*. Deeds into Words in the Twelfth Century. 1997
80. Winter, J. M. van. *Sources Concerning the Hospitallers of St John in the Netherlands, 14th-18th Centuries*. 1998
81. Tierney, B. *Foundations of the Conciliar Theory*. The Contribution of the Medieval Canonists from Gratian to the Great Schism. Enlarged New Edition. 1998
82. Miernowski, J. *Le Dieu Néant*. Théologies négatives à l'aube des temps modernes. 1998
83. Halverson, J. L. *Peter Aureol on Predestination*. A Challenge to Late Medieval Thought. 1998.
84. Houliston, V. (ed.). *Robert Persons, S.J.: The Christian Directory (1582)*. The First Booke of the Christian Exercise, appertayning to Resolution. 1998

85. Grell, O. P. (ed.). *Paracelsus.* The Man and His Reputation, His Ideas and Their Transformation. 1998
86. Mazzola, E. *The Pathology of the English Renaissance.* Sacred Remains and Holy Ghosts. 1998.
87. 88. Marsilius von Inghen. *Quaestiones super quattuor libros sententiarum.* Super Primum. Bearbeitet von M. Santos Noya. 2 Bände. I. Quaestiones 1-7. II. Quaestiones 8-21. 2000
89. Faupel-Drevs, K. *Vom rechten Gebrauch der Bilder im liturgischen Raum.* Mittelalterliche Funktions-bestimmungen bildender Kunst im *Rationale divinorum officiorum* des Durandus von Mende (1230/1-1296). 1999
90. Krey, P. D. W. and Smith, L. (eds.). *Nicholas of Lyra.* the Senses of Scripture. 2000
92. Oakley, F. *Politics and Eternity.* Studies in the History of Medieval and Early-Modern Political Thought. 1999
93. Pryds, D. *The Politics of Preaching.* Robert of Naples (1309-1343) and his Sermons. 2000
94. Posthumus Meyjes, G. H. M. *Jean Gerson – Apostle of Unity.* His Church Politics and Ecclesiology. Translated by J. C. Grayson. 1999
95. Berg, J. van den. *Religious Currents and Cross-Currents.* Essays on Early Modern Protestantism and the Protestant Enlightenment. Edited by J. de Bruijn, P. Holtrop, and E. van der Wall. 1999
96. Izbicki, T. M. and Bellitto, C. M. (eds.). *Reform and Renewal in the Middle Ages and the Renaissance.* Studies in Honor of Louis Pascoe, S. J. 2000
97. Kelly, D. *The Conspiracy of Allusion.* Description, Rewriting, and Authorship from Macrobius to Medieval Romance. 1999
98. Marrone, S. P. *The Light of Thy Countenance.* Science and Knowledge of God in the Thirteenth Century. 2 volumes. 1. A Doctrine of Divine Illumination. 2. God at the Core of Cognition. 2001
99. Howson, B. H. *Erroneous and Schismatical Opinions.* The Question of Orthodoxy regarding the Theology of Hanserd Knollys (c. 1599-169)). 2001
100. Asselt, W. J. van. *The Federal Theology of Johannes Cocceius (1603-1669).* 2001
101. Celenza, C.S. *Piety and Pythagoras in Renaissance Florence* the Symbolum Nesianum. 2001
102. Dam, H.- J. van (ed.), *Hugo Grotius, De imperio summarum potestatum circa sacra.* Critical Edition with Introduction, English translation and Commentary. 2 volumes. 2001
103. Bagge, S. *Kings, Politics, and the Right Order of the World in German Historiography c. 950-1150.* 2002
104. Steiger, J. A. *Fünf Zentralthemen der Theologie Luthers und seiner Erben.* Communicatio – Imago – Figura – Maria – Exempla. Mit Edition zweier christologischer Frühschriften Johann Gerhards. 2002
105. Izbicki, T. M. and Bellitto, C. M. (eds.). *Nicholas of Cusa and his Age: Intellect and Spirituality.* Essays Dedicated to the Memory of F. Edward Cranz, Thomas P. McTighe and Charles Trinkaus. 2002
106. Hascher-Burger, U. *Gesungene Innigkeit.* Studien zu einer Musikhandschrift der Devotio moderna (Utrecht, Universiteitsbibliotheek, MS 16 H 94, olim B 113). Mit einer Edition der Gesänge. 2002
107. Bolliger, D. *Infiniti Contemplatio.* Grundzüge der Scotus- und Scotismusrezeption im Werk Huldrych Zwinglis. 2003
108. Clark, F. *The 'Gregorian' Dialogues and the Origins of Benedictine Monasticism.* 2002
109. Elm, E. *Die Macht der Weisheit.* Das Bild des Bischofs in der *Vita Augustini* des Possidius und andere spätantiken und frühmittelalterlichen Bischofsviten. 2003
110. Bast, R. J. (ed.). *The Reformation of Faith in the Context of Late Medieval Theology and Piety.* Essays by Berndt Hamm. 2004.
111. Heering, J. P. *Hugo Grotius as Apologist for the Christian Religion.* A Study of his Work *De Veritate Religionis Christianae* (1640). Translated by J.C. Grayson. 2004.
112. Lim, P. C.- H. *In Pursuit of Purity, Unity, and Liberty.* Richard Baxter's Puritan Ecclesiology in its Seventeenth-Century Context. 2004.
113. Connors, R. and Gow, A. C. (eds.). *Anglo-American Millennialism, from Milton to the Millerites.* 2004.
114. Zinguer, I. and Yardeni, M. (eds.). *Les Deux Réformes Chrétiennes.* Propagation et Diffusion. 2004.
115. James, F. A. III (ed.). *Peter Martyr Vermigli and the European Reformations*: Semper Reformanda. 2004.
116. Stroll, M. *Calixtus II (1119-1124).* A Pope Born to Rule. 2004.
117. Roest, B. *Franciscan Literature of Religious Instruction before the Council of Trent.* 2004.
118. Wannenmacher, J. E. *Hermeneutik der Heilsgeschichte.* De septem sigillis und die sieben Siegel im Werk Joachims von Fiore. 2004.
119. Thompson, N. *Eucharistic Sacrifice and Patristic Tradition in the Theology of Martin Bucer, 1534-1546.* 2005.
120. Van der Kool, C. *As in a Mirror.* John Calvin and Karl Barth on Knowing God. A Diptych. 2005.
121. Steiger, J. A. *Medizinische Theologie.* Christus medicus und theologia medicinalis bei Martin Luther und im Luthertum der Barockzeit. 2005.

122. Giakalis, A. *Images of the Divine*. The Theology of Icons at the Seventh Ecumenical Council – Revised Edition. With a Foreword by Henry Chadwick. 2005.
123. Heffernan, T. J. and Burman, T. E. (eds.). *Scripture and Pluralism*. Reading the Bible in the Religiously Plural Worlds of the Middle Ages and Renaissance. Papers Presented at the First Annual Symposium of the Marco Institute for Medieval and Renaissance Studies at the University of Tennessee, Knoxville, February 21-22, 2002. 2005.
124. Litz, G., Munzert, H. and Liebenberg, R. (eds.). *Frömmigkeit – Theologie – Frömmigkeitstheologie – Contributions to European Church History*.
125. Ferreiro, A. *Simon Magus in Patristic, Medieval and Early Modern Traditions*. 2005.
126. Goodwin, D. L. *"Take Hold of the Robe of a Jew"*. Herbert of Bosham's Christian Hebraism. 2006.
127. Holder, R. W. *John Calvin and the Grounding of Interpretation*. Calvin's First Commentaries. 2006.
128. Reilly, D. J. *The Art of Reform in Eleventh-Century Flanders*. Gerard of Cambrai, Richard of Saint-Vanne and the Saint-Vaast Bible. 2006.
129. Frassetto, M. (ed.). *Heresy and the Persecuting Society in the Middle Ages*. Essays on the Work of R.I. Moore. 2006.
130. Walters Adams, G. *Visions in Late Medieval England*. Lay Spirituality and Sacred Glimpses of the Hidden Worlds of Faith. 2007.
131. Kirby, T. *The Zurich Connection and Tudor Political Theology*. 2007.
132. Mackay, C.S. *Narrative of the Anabaptist Madness*. The Overthrow of Münster, the Famous Metropolis of Westphalia (2 vols.). 2007.
133. Leroux, N.R. *Martin Luther as Comforter*. Writings on Death. 2007.
134. Tavuzzi, M. *Renaissance Inquisitors*. Dominican Inquisitors and Inquisitorial Districts in Northern Italy, 1474-1527. 2007.
135. Baschera, L. and C. Moser (eds.). *Girolamo Zanchi*, De religione christiana fides – Confession of Christian Religion (2 vols.). 2007.

Prospectus available on request

BRILL — P.O.B. 9000 — 2300 PA LEIDEN — THE NETHERLANDS